Robert Frank

15 Aug 92

IN THE

HANDS OF

PROVIDENCE

The
University
of North
Carolina
Press
Chapel Hill
and
London

In the Hands of

In the Hands of Providence

JOSHUA L. CHAMBERLAIN

AND THE AMERICAN CIVIL WAR

BY ALICE RAINS TRULOCK

Manufactured in the United States of America

The paper in this book meets the guidelines for permanence and durability of the Committee on Production Guidelines for Book Longevity of the Council on Library Resources.

96 95 94 93 92
5 4 3 2 1

Library of Congress Cataloging-in-Publication Data
Trulock, Alice Rains.
In the hands of Providence : Joshua L. Chamberlain and the American Civil War / by Alice Rains Trulock.
p. cm.
Includes bibliographical references (p.) and index.
ISBN 0-8078-2020-2 (cloth : alk. paper)
1. Chamberlain, Joshua Lawrence, 1828–1914.
2. Generals—United States—Biography. 3. United States. Army. Maine Infantry Regiment, 20th (1862–1865) 4. United States—History—Civil War, 1861–1865—Campaigns. 5. United States. Army—Biography.
I. Title.
E467.1.C45T78 1992
973.7'44'092—dc20 91-50791
[B] CIP

For my dear children,

Ruth Wise Shaull,

William Dale Wise, and

David Curtis Wise,

and in loving memory

of their brother,

Charles Torin Wise,

our long lost,

green-eyed Chuck

CONTENTS

MAPS

ILLUSTRATIONS

FOREWORD

This is a superb book. It is, on the one hand, a biography. But because the writer has firmly placed her protagonist in the social, political, and military history of his times, it is also an exceptional narrative history. Three essential elements seem to me to account for the excellence of the book: the historical milieu of the life of Joshua L. Chamberlain, the facts of his remarkable life, and the author's skill in research and in the telling of Chamberlain's life.

Robert Penn Warren has written: "The Civil War is, for the American imagination, the great single event of our history. Without too much wrenching, it may, in fact, be said to *be* American history." At first blush, Warren's statement may strike one as an exaggeration, but the fact is that it is difficult to overstate the significance of the Civil War in our history. Translated into an equal proportion of today's population, Civil War fatalities from combat and disease would account for five million American deaths. It is estimated that three soldiers were wounded for each soldier killed in combat, another staggering loss. In spite of our efforts to rationalize, even to romanticize it, the Civil War is the American holocaust, standing like a giant and grotesque statue in the midst of our generally optimistic national experience. The consequences of the war were surely profound. The American nation was saved and redefined. Slavery was abolished. In the latter regard, let us once and for all acknowledge that the South seceded to protect slavery and that, however flawed and inept the trial, freedom was at stake.

The presence of the issue of freedom sets up the startling contradiction of the war: it was at the same time tragic and redemptive. Denis W. Brogan has captured this contradiction. The war, he writes, "put the American people, decisively, once and for all, among the peoples who have lived in interesting times and who have paid an extravagantly high price for this experience." Brogan says further, "I do not for a moment suggest that the American Civil War was a good thing—merely that it was and is felt by the unregenerate (a majority of the Western races now and for as long as we can inspect the past) to be the most moving, interesting, dignified thing that has ever occurred in America." The war and the period of the war are the milieu of this book. That is the first element of its excellence.

By any standard, Joshua Chamberlain is a fascinating human being, an ordinary man of his times who, in the context of the war and its aftermath, was somehow *extraordinary*. An academic at Bowdoin College, a seminarian with no significant military background or education, he had a natural gift for soldiering and for military leadership. Essential to this gift in the kind of personal war in which he became involved, Chamberlain had exceptional physical courage and the capacity, whatever it is called, to withstand the searing pain of wounds and the primitive discomforts of Civil War soldiering.

Chamberlain started his Civil War career as the lieutenant colonel of the Twentieth Maine Volunteers. He progressed to the rank of brigadier general, not by brevet but by commission. He commanded a regiment, a brigade, and a division. Along the way he was wounded six times, grievously at Petersburg. Perhaps his best-known wartime exploit occurred at Gettysburg. Great events like Gettysburg are made up of a number of "little events," particular incidents that were unusually dramatic. A few of these particular, dramatic little events were also decisive in terms of the outcome of the battle. In the case of Gettysburg, the defense by the Twentieth Maine of the Federal left at Little Round Top on the second day of the battle was clearly decisive. Chamberlain commanded the Twentieth in this fight.

Although Chamberlain returned to academia after the war, his distinction during the war inevitably drew him into politics, in which his career was also remarkable. He was four times elected governor of Maine before becoming the president of Bowdoin College. His fascination with the war caused him to be one of the most studious and prolific postwar writers and lecturers about his own experiences and the larger aspects of the war. This is the citizen-soldier about whom Alice Rains Trulock writes. His significance, his many-faceted character, and his rich experiences are the second element in the strength of this book.

To the promising milieu and fascinating protagonist, Ms. Trulock brings exceptional skills. First there is her research. She has found a wide range of hitherto unknown primary sources, including Chamberlain's personal and family papers and other manuscript materials in obscure repositories and in private hands. She has studied the substantial body of Chamberlain's own writings, published and in manuscript. She has mastered the *Official Records* and the vast secondary literature of the war.

Research alone, however well done, does not make a book. Ms. Trulock also writes exceptionally well, but she does more. Biography can be, but sometimes is not, an excellent vehicle for describing "the times" of its subject. Ms. Trulock tells us of the context of Chamberlain's life without losing the focus on the man. In addition, without compromising the historian's detachment, she *understands* Chamberlain. I particularly admire her technique of letting him speak for himself about the great events of his life. Ms. Trulock's skills in research and in the telling of Joshua Chamberlain's tale and his times is the third element that distinguishes this book.

This, then, is the life of Joshua L. Chamberlain and his times, what is customarily called the definitive biography. It is an important book.

Alan T. Nolan
Indianapolis, Indiana
April 1, 1991

PREFACE

Joshua L. Chamberlain was a great American hero and a genuinely good man. He was also intelligent, creative, handsome, and well educated—the embodiment of the nineteenth-century ideal of manhood. Such a man is also an ideal subject for a biographer, at least this one, who spent years immersed in his century and his life. But he was not perfect. In some ways, his life paralleled the course of his beloved country: he rallied to save the Union, became a part of ending the slavery he abhorred, was nearly mortally wounded in the fight, and championed the equality of the freedmen. Then, sharing the moral blindness of other good men, he and they failed the former slaves utterly and allowed evil to fall upon them and prevail.

His leadership and bravery in our country's great Civil War, along with his dramatic action at the surrender ceremony at Appomattox, made Chamberlain's deeds legendary in his own era; the filmy veil of time, however, has somewhat obscured his fame. As I thought about these things and his other impressive attributes, I wondered what conditions and what kind of people produced a man capable of them. What influences shaped his character? What motivated him to leave everything he loved to fight for the Union? What was his true personality?

Many of the answers to these questions lay in the correspondence in the various manuscript repositories and in private hands. Chamberlain's own letters and those of others who wrote to and about him revealed an honorable and thoughtful human being who tried to live up to the high values and behavior inculcated by his parents, church, and community. Possessing an extraordinary facility with words, he expressed his strong ethical and political beliefs in his writings and speeches. On matters of great importance to him, Chamberlain could speak for himself without equal; therefore, he does so throughout this book.

The Civil War years fill most of this volume. As it did for so many who served in the armies on both sides of the conflict, the war would prove to be the most significant event in Chamberlain's life. It would always influence him, and not only because of the pain he endured over the years from his terrible wound. I have tried to present him as the nineteenth-century man that he was, add dimension to his family, friends, and comrades, and tell the story of the "boys in blue" in our country's most rending war. The years of research and writing about Joshua Lawrence Chamberlain have been a challenge and a joy. I am sorry that they are over.

* * *

My obligation and debt of gratitude is immense to the following generous people who contributed to the writing of this book:

My husband, James A. Trulock. This volume could not have been written without his enthusiastic support for the project and his assistance, especially on battlefield trips and in assembling research materials. His criticism and suggestions added much to my thinking.

Alan T. Nolan, my mentor and friend, without whose encouragement, advice, and help over the years this book would hardly have been fairly started, let alone finished. It was from his classic Civil War history, *The Iron Brigade*, that I learned to write military history; its literary excellence is still an inspiration.

Rosamond Allen, General Chamberlain's granddaughter, made available family photographs, letters, and other materials and gave generously of her hospitality, time, and memories of her grandfather. At her direction, I was able to find other valuable Chamberlain information.

Elizabeth D. Copeland, who is now my close friend, took a stranger under her wing and made it possible for me to locate and obtain much original research. Bette and her husband, Paul R. Copeland, Jr., led the Pejepscot Historical Society to buy the Chamberlain house at Brunswick and renovate it into the Joshua L. Chamberlain Civil War Museum and opened their home to me whenever I visited there.

My thanks also to my daughter, Ruth Wise Shaull, Cincinnati, Ohio, who read every chapter as it was written, gave excellent comments, and exhibited an unwavering faith in my writing. I am also grateful to Alan Gaff and Maureen Gaff, Fort Wayne, Indiana; Wilda Skidmore and Richard Skidmore, Greencastle, Indiana; and Carol Colombo of Indianapolis, who read the manuscript upon its completion and gave valuable advice. Maureen Gaff also proofread the manuscript. Gary W. Gallagher, head of the history department at Pennsylvania State University, gave his excellent counsel and encouragement, and Harry W. Pfanz, former historian at Gettysburg National Military Park, made very helpful suggestions.

Abbott Spear of Warren, Maine, grandson of Bvt. Brig. Gen. Ellis Spear, Twentieth Maine, generously made available to me copies of his grandfather's Civil War diaries and the *cartes de visite* of several members of the regiment. He also provided me with his grandfather's view of the battle of Fredericksburg and other material. Theodore S. Johnson of Falmouth, Maine, grandson of Maj. Holman S. Melcher, Twentieth Maine, made identifications and allowed me to use the Twentieth Maine Gettysburg reunion photograph from his collection. A. A. Warlam of Saddle River, New Jersey, first permitted me access to the Chamberlain Letterbook and other related material, which he subsequently donated to the Pejepscot Historical Society, Brunswick, Maine.

My distinguished predecessors in recounting the life of General Chamberlain, John J. Pullen, author of *The Twentieth Maine*, Willard M. Wallace, who wrote *Soul of the Lion*, and Robert M. Cross, writer of "Joshua Lawrence Chamberlain," 1945 senior essay, Bowdoin College, have generously extended their hospitality, goodwill, and advice.

Special thanks are due Bowdoin College president emeritus A. LeRoy Greason, Bowdoin librarian Arthur Monke, and the Honorable Rodney Quinn, Maine secretary of state, for many courtesies they extended. I am also indebted to my friends the Pejepscot Historical Society Board of Trustees for reserving the contents of the Chamberlain Letterbook and the daguerreotype of Mrs. Chamberlain for my use. John P. Mullooly, M.D., and William H. Annesley, Jr., M.D., both of Milwaukee, Wisconsin, gave me expert professional opinions about General Chamberlain's wound at Petersburg. Jon H. Winemiller of Cheyenne, Wyoming, consulted on the maps.

In my research in person and by mail, the expertise of the staffs of many institutions was indispensable. All were courteous and helpful; my expressed appreciation to them cannot be considered enough:

Sylvia Sherman, director, Archives Services, Maine State Archives; Paul Rivard, director, Jane Radcliffe, assistant, Maine State Museum; Constance Holling, head librarian, Brewer Public Library; Susan Wight, head of adult services, Bangor Public Library; Sally A. Kaubris, assistant librarian, Bangor Theological Seminary Library; Janice L. Haas, reference librarian, Rutherford B. Hayes Presidential Center.

The Reverend William Imes and his staff, First Parish Church, Brunswick, Maine; William Toner and Elizabeth J. Miller, directors, Thomas Gaffney, curator, Lisa Fink and Gregory Kendall-Curtis, assistant curators, and Margo McCain, librarian, Maine Historical Society, Portland, Maine; Eric C. Jorgenson, director, Pejepscot Historical Society, David Bray and Peter Bals, curators, Joshua L. Chamberlain Civil War Museum, Brunswick, Maine; Russ A. Pritchard, director, War Library and Museum, Military Order of the Loyal Legion of the United States, Philadelphia; Louise T. Jones, manuscript and archives librarian, Historical Society of Pennsylvania, Philadelphia; Dorothy Allen, director, Lackawanna Historical Society, Scranton, Pennsylvania; John R. Claridge, executive director, and Helen R. Andrews, librarian, Erie County Historical Society, Erie, Pennsylvania.

Eric S. Flower, head, Special Collections Department, and Janet Tebrake, graduate assistant, Raymond H. Fogler Library, University of Maine, Orono, Maine; Eva Moseley, curator of manuscripts, and Anne Engerhart, assistant curator of manuscripts, Schlesinger Library, Radcliffe College; Sister M. Lawrence Franklin, RSM, archivist, Mercyhurst College Library. In addition, Dianne Gutscher and Susan Ravdin, Special Collections Room curators at Hawthorne-Longfellow Library, Bowdoin College, gave unstintingly of their time and expertise over several years.

Kathleen Georg Harrison, chief historian, Thomas Harrison, former chief historian, and John Heiser, Gettysburg National Military Park; Ms. Harrison made certain that I saw all the relevant material, old and new, in the park files and library. John Davis and Christopher M. Calkins, park historians, Petersburg National Battlefield; Mr. Calkins was particularly helpful in recommending sources and consulting on maps, especially that of Five Forks, Virginia.

Richard Sommers, archivist/historian, and Michael J. Winey, curator, U.S. Army Military History Institute, Carlisle Barracks, Pennsylvania; James H. Hutson, chief, and David Wigdor, assistant chief, Library of Congress; Leroy Bellamy, Photograph Division, and Michael Musick, Army-Navy Branch, National Archives.

I am also very grateful to the following individuals for various contributions:

Howard F. Kenney, Brewer, Maine; L. M. Sturtevant, North Belgrade, Maine; John Haskins, Warren Randall, Emery Booker, and Philip S. Wilder, Brunswick, Maine; Sally W. Rand, Freeport, Maine; Jane Nolan, Steven F. Belcher, Rudolph K. Haerle, Peter Carmichael, George Siskind, Ellie Siskind, Robert E. Currie, D.D.S., Thomas Plimpton, Marilyn Hoffman, John Hoffman, Fayez Tushan, M.D., James S. Brown, M.D., William D. Wise, and David C. Wise, all of Indianapolis, Indiana; James R. Wright and Myra E. Wright of Columbiana, Ohio; Vickie Heilig, Germantown, Maryland; Charlene Stull and Gladys Alcorn, Waterford, Pennsylvania; Christine Alling, Richmond, Virginia; F. Harmon Furney, Chillicothe, Ohio, formerly of Gettysburg.

I am indebted for permission to publish illustrations and quotations from books, manuscripts, and collections from these individuals and institutions: John J. Pullen, Theodore S. Johnson, and Abbott Spear; Brewer Public Library, Brewer, Maine; Bangor Public Library, Bangor, Maine; First Parish Church, Brunswick, Maine; Hawthorne-Longfellow Library, Bowdoin College; Sterling Memorial Library, Yale University; Raymond H. Fogler Library, University of Maine; Schlesinger Library, Radcliffe College; Maine State Archives; Maine State Museum; Pejepscot Historical Society; Maine Historical Society.

My former teachers, Miss Rebecca S. Grubb, Logan Demonstration School, Philadelphia, Pennsylvania, in 1945, and Miss Ella C. Sengenberger, director of journalism at Arsenal Technical Schools, Indianapolis, Indiana, in 1950–51, stimulated me to the sustaining belief that I could write, for which I am forever grateful.

It has been a pleasure to work with Matthew Hodgson, director of the University of North Carolina Press, and his staff. Besides approving the inclusion of a large number of photographs and maps, they have evinced a great deal of commitment to this book. Ron Maner, the assistant managing editor and my project editor, and Mary Reid, copyeditor, have worked expertly with courtesy, tact, and patience, while making excellent suggestions. I thank them all for their help through the unfamiliar publishing process.

Finally, I would be remiss if I did not acknowledge that Morris Schaff, Union Civil War officer, suggested a part of my dedicatory phrasing in his book, *The Sunset of the Confederacy*.

Alice Rains Trulock
Indianapolis, Indiana
July 1991

PROLOGUE : 1913

"I went—it is not long ago—to stand again upon that crest whose one day's crown of fire has passed into the blazoned coronet of fame; to look again upon the rocks whereon were laid as on the altar the lives of Vincent and O'Rorke."

The old man in a black suit stood remembering on the low hill a short distance below the small crossroads town in southeastern Pennsylvania. Although his back was still ramrod straight, a cane steadied his slight limp, one consequence of an old and terrible wound. His mustache and the hair that touched his collar in back were ivory white now, but they had just begun to gray the first time he saw this rock-strewn height nearly fifty years before.

Then, the fate of the United States had hung in the balance on a stifling hot day in July. Now, the names of Gettysburg and Little Round Top had long passed into the nation's storied history; they were as familiar to its children as those of Bunker Hill and Lexington were to him as a schoolboy. The dead colonels Vincent and O'Rorke were still on the hill, but now transfigured in bronze sculpture, O'Rorke on the spot where he had lain still and white in death, and Vincent, whose general's promotion came too late for his knowing, looking forever toward the direction of the oncoming Confederates.

Beyond, eyes gazing in the same direction, field glasses in hand, the courageous Gen. Gouverneur K. Warren stood too in heroic statuary, the green patina of age and weather softening the hard metal image. In the distance the low mountains purpled in the sunset light, a notch in the horizon marking the passage through which Robert E. Lee's retreating wagons carried suffering, wounded Confederate soldiers after the great battle.

Guarding the left flank of the whole Union line as the high keening sounds of the Rebel yell echoed above the roar of battle, the regiment the old man had commanded, enlisted from his wildly beautiful native Maine, had stood stalwart farther back on the spur of the hill, its men fighting and dying with valorous abandon. The old man had been in the early summer of his life then, and silver eagles had shone from the shoulder straps of his army-blue officer's coat. His mind, still bright in the twilight of his life, was that of a warrior-poet:

"And farther on where my own young heroes mounted to fall no more—Billings, the valor of whose onward-looking eyes not death itself could quench; Kendall, almost maiden-sweet and fair, yet heeding not the bolts that dashed his life-blood on the rocks; Estes and Steele, and Noyes and Buck, lifted high above self . . . and far up the rugged sides of Great Round Top, swept in darkness . . . where the impetuous Linscott halted at last before the morning star."[1]

CHAPTER

One

THE UNION FOREVER, HURRAH BOYS, HURRAH!

It was a wonderful gift. Standing splendidly on the camp parade ground in its full trappings, a beautiful stone-gray stallion, dappled white, with a heavy white mane and tail, and well known in the area as "the Staples horse," awaited its new owner. Two men, one a civilian and the other an army officer, stood for the presentation ceremony about to begin at Camp Mason, near Portland, Maine. Around them the officers and men of Maine's newest volunteer infantry regiment, the twentieth to be sworn into Federal service from the state since the beginning of the war, were drawn up in a "hollow square" formation, colorful in their new blue uniforms.[1]

Although used to appearing and speaking in public, Lt. Col. Joshua

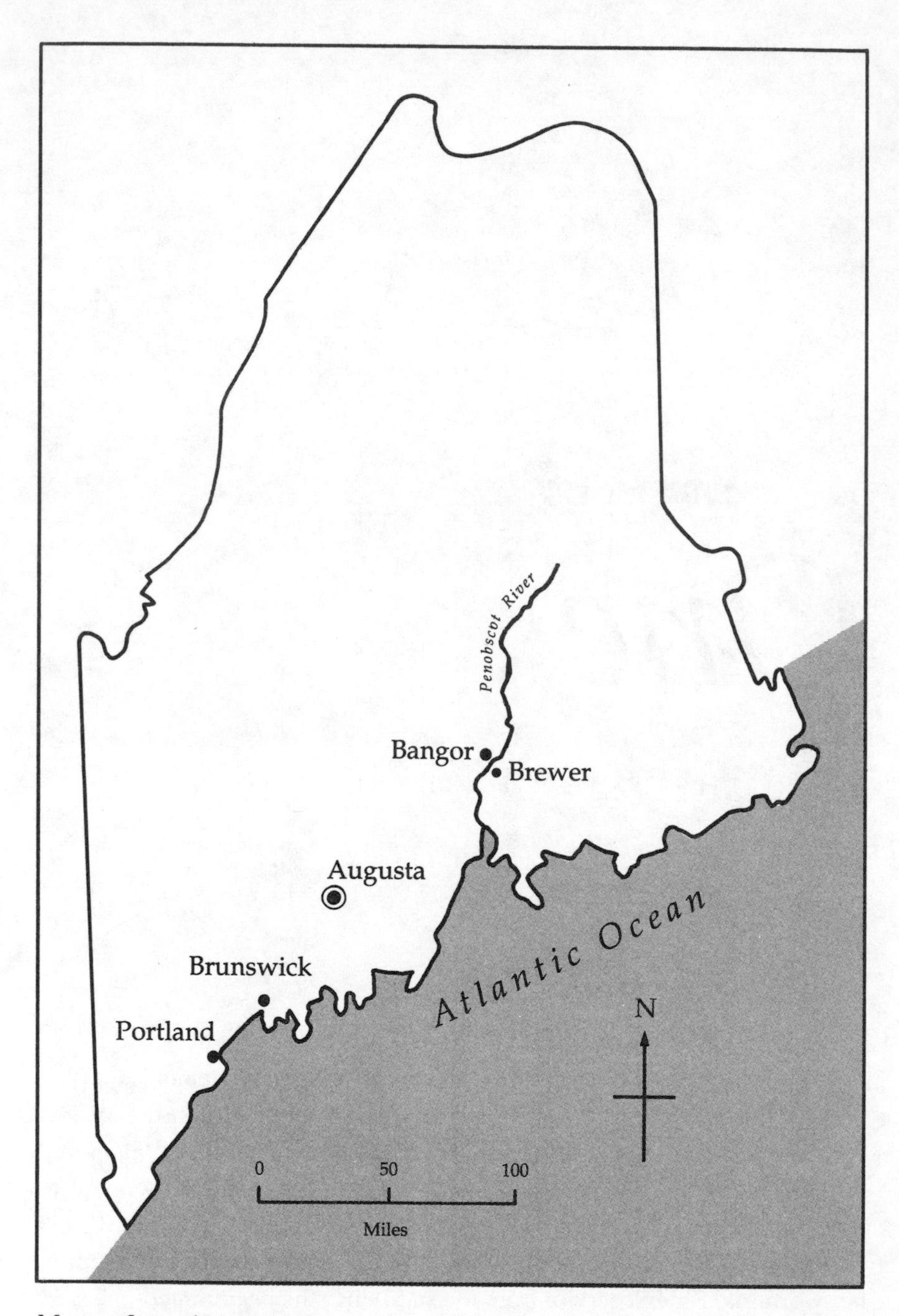

MAP 1. *State of Maine*

Lawrence Chamberlain was a little uncomfortable hearing the phrases of the flattering speech made to him by his friend William Field, who spoke for other friends and townspeople from the college town of Brunswick. "We beg you to accept this gift . . . appreciating the sacrifice you have made . . . that you may be borne on it only to victory . . . till the spirit of rebellion is crushed and you return, laden with honors"; Field's words came to him in flowery praise, finally invoking God's blessing and protection on him during his impending absence.[2]

Chamberlain thanked Field with feeling. His strong, resonant voice carried in a rhythmic, almost musical fashion to the officers and men—nearly a thousand in all—who were looking on:

"Sir:—A soldier never should be taken by surprise, and it would be doubly inexcusable in me were I to deem anything surprising in the way of generosity on the part of those whose sentiments and deeds of kindness I have known so long.

"I thank you, sir, and through you, my fellow citizens, for this noble gift, and for the touching manner in which you are pleased to confer it. Nothing, surely, which I have done, renders me deserving of so costly and beautiful a memorial. No sacrifice or service of mine merits any other reward than that which conscience gives to every man who does his duty. But I know at least how to value a kindness and a compliment like this. I accept it, as a bond to be faithful to my oath of service, and to your expectations of me. I accept it, if I may so speak, not to regard it as fairly my own, until I have earned a title to it by conduct equal to your generosity.

"Let me bid you . . . farewell, commending these brave men who surround you, to your remembrance and care; and all of us to the keeping of a merciful God on high."[3]

Even though he was taller than the average Maine soldier, and Maine men were taller than most in the Federal armies, Chamberlain's slim, muscular frame lacked an inch and one-half of reaching six feet. He had an erect way of carrying himself, however, which gave the impression of more stature; his presence was so remarkable and gave such an effect that, in the words of one private, he was "a brave, brilliant, dashing officer . . . who, when once seen, was always remembered."[4]

Chamberlain's narrow face had tended toward roundness in his young manhood, but in this week before his thirty-fourth birthday, it was thinner and looked longer, the high cheekbones prominent. Almost hidden by a small, triangular tuft of beard worn below the full lower lip of his mouth, a slight dimple indented his wide chin; above his high, broad forehead the dark hair, which was parted on the left side and worn short, was streaked

Lt. Col. Joshua L. Chamberlain, 1862
(Alice Rains Trulock and James A. Trulock)

prematurely with silvery gray. His light, gray-blue eyes were arresting, especially when he looked up, and they often commanded attention with their flashing vitality. The handsome, classic nose, shaped like a hawk's beak, gave him a fine profile, and the long, full mustache below it, romantic and faintly swashbuckling, swept to his jaw on each side.[5]

As the ceremony ended on that first day of September in 1862, Chamberlain undoubtedly appeared as handsomely dressed as when he had his photograph taken the month before at Pierce's in Brunswick, the silver oak leaves denoting his rank gleaming from the gold-edged, light blue shoulder straps of his new uniform. Two rows of seven brass buttons each shone gold against the dark army blue of his double-breasted frock coat, while a leather belt, with fittings that held his officer's sword and scabbard, wound around his narrow waist and was fastened by a gilt and silver buckle.[6]

A crimson sash usually worn for dress occasions looped around the belt and knotted at his left side, its tasseled ends hanging beneath his scabbard. Completing his dress were blue wool trousers and a cap called a kepi, the latter having the circular horn or bugle of the infantry embroidered in gold on its front, just above the unused black leather chin strap buckled over the visor. In the center of the bugle was a small silver "20," the identifying numeral of his regiment.[7]

* * *

Just seven weeks before, on July 14, 1862, Chamberlain had made up his mind and knew the time had come to act. Casting caution to the winds of the Civil War that threatened his country's existence, the young Bowdoin College professor on that day began to mesh his own destiny with that of his native land. "To His Excellency Governor Washburn," he began, writing carefully, formally, on heavy white paper, his usual hurried scrawl tamed at first to a sedate script, "In pursuance of the offer of reinforcements for the war, I ask if your Excellency desires and will accept my service."[8]

Earlier that month President Abraham Lincoln had called for 300,000 more men for three years service in the Federal armies from the governors of the Northern states of the Union. By that summer, Maine had already sent fifteen infantry regiments, plus artillery and cavalry units, to the war. Governor Israel Washburn's blazing rhetoric had characterized the conflict as a contest between "the Army of the Union and the Band of Rebellious

Traitors." Impetuous men, most of them young, flocked to their country's defense against those who would dare destroy it by disunion. With the sounds of impassioned speeches, martial tunes, and marching feet reverberating all over the state, regiments were raised and sent off to war with battle flags and patriotic cheers and tears. But now, over a year after the war began, the new call meant more regiments were needed to fulfill Maine's Federal quota. With the help of bounties paid by the state, cities, and towns, Governor Washburn relied on leading men of the state to raise the companies needed to fill the new regiments and appealed to the citizenry again to heed their country's call.[9]

Chamberlain came from a long line of citizen soldiers, with forebears on both sides of his family fighting in the American Revolution. Governor Washburn knew Chamberlain's grandfather and father, both also named Joshua; the former had been a colonel of militia in the war with the British in 1812, and the latter a lieutenant colonel of the militia in the bloodless Aroostook War. He also knew something of the latest Chamberlain in the succession, so it was with some hope of acceptance that the college teacher offered his help.[10]

Although able men were harder to come by than they were the year before in the Pine Tree State, Chamberlain was confident he could quickly raise the "thousand strong" needed for an entire regiment. Nearly a hundred of his former pupils had gone to the army as officers since that April day in 1861 when the war began, but he thought he could call on many more in all parts of the state who would respond enthusiastically. He was not particularly concerned about matters beyond that, telling the governor, "I have always been interested in military matters, and what I do not know in that line, I *know how to learn*."[11]

"But, I fear, this war, so costly of blood and treasure, will not cease until the men of the North are willing to leave good positions, and sacrifice the dearest personal interests, to rescue our Country from desolation, and defend the National existence against treachery at home and jealousy abroad. This war must be ended, with a swift and strong hand; and every man ought to come forward and ask to be placed at his proper post."[12]

Deferring to the obligations to his family and the college long enough, Chamberlain was determined now to let nothing stand in the way of his duty. His stern, wintry-eyed father, who had wanted him to go to West Point and become a career soldier, would declare the raging conflict "not our war." His wife was opposed to his going—she liked the life of a college professor's wife, and then, too, he was risking not only his life but the entire support of her and their two young children. It was clear now that the conflict was not "a short madness," for the papers were full of the Union's reverses in the summer campaign in the East, which filled him with renewed determination. His father notwithstanding, Chamberlain thought it was his war indeed; he had thought of going almost since its beginning fifteen months before. Perhaps one reason he had stayed his hand until this short vacation when the college closed before commencement in August was that he doubted he could get military leave from the conservative elements of the boards that ran the small but excellent liberal arts college.[13]

Bowdoin's Boards of Trustees and Overseers were usually conservative groups of men, and it was said that the college president, Leonard Woods, would have let the Southern brethren depart in peace if it were left to him. At commencement four years before, the boards had conferred a doctor of laws degree on the visiting United States senator Jefferson Davis, whose views on secession and slavery were well known. At the same time they had given a like honor to their own antislavery senator, William Pitt Fessenden, but there was some embarrassment over the affair now that Davis was president of the Confederacy.[14]

There was, however, a legitimate way to leave the college that no one suspected Chamberlain would use, one which entailed such a great personal sacrifice that few men would do it, but it would be a responsible means of solving his dilemma. After three or four years of pressure and persuasion, he had the previous year finally agreed to take the chair of professor of modern languages of Europe and was given lifetime tenure, although he had not wanted to leave his former position as professor of rhetoric.[15]

Chamberlain had felt pride in his innovative teaching methods in rhetoric and had developed entirely new ways of instruction, which were very valuable to his students. Combining teaching in composition, speech, and great literature with individual attention and encouragement of good mental discipline, thought processes, and habits, Chamberlain spent long hours, with his whole heart and mind, at this work. He enjoyed it, counting none of it as drudgery as his students responded and attended voluntary classes he organized. But he met no encouragement from his superiors, only coldness and insistence that he continue some old methods of teaching. This opposition must have worn down his resolve to "allow myself neither to be seduced nor driven from my place," because he finally gave up his teaching of rhetoric—but apparently not without disappointment and some resentment.[16]

When Chamberlain was finally persuaded to take the new department, a great inducement for him to accept was the privilege of a two-year leave of absence to travel in Europe whenever he chose, expenses and salary paid by the college, with a $500 bonus. Although he was already teaching French and German in addition to his other duties, the leave was intended to further fit him for the position, and he apparently intended to avail himself of it the next autumn. But the war came, and he thought he would put off the trip until it was over. Now, he still had the leave from the trustee and overseer boards of the college, and he could use it in another, better cause. If Governor Washburn had a place for him to serve the war effort, he would be free of his obligations in Brunswick early in August at the end of the college term. However, he would have to give up the treasured trip, probably entirely, and certainly the salary and expenses.[17]

Within two days Chamberlain had a favorable answer from Governor Washburn and an invitation to see him immediately. Nothing definite was promised, but there was enough in the governor's note to buoy his hopes that his services not only would be welcome but could be used in the field, rather than as a staff aide in Augusta. Several of Chamberlain's former students had come to him on their own, declaring they would go with him as privates or in any way, and his instant reply to the governor showed he could barely suppress his desire to oblige them.[18]

So the next day he went to Augusta to see the governor, and there was talk about the uncertainty of everything; it had not been decided if another new regiment would be needed. The field officers of the four new regiments then organizing already had been appointed, but Chamberlain was asked if he wanted to be the colonel of a new outfit in the event one was formed. Pleased at the offer, Chamberlain was hesitant to start that high. His military experience was limited to a short time at a military school near his hometown of Brewer when he was fourteen years old, and he would rather take a lesser place that would give him some time to learn about soldiering.[19]

Two days later Brig. Gen. Oliver O. Howard, a Bowdoin man who graduated two years ahead of Chamberlain and had gone on to West Point, spoke to a large crowd at the Brunswick train depot. His jacket sleeve empty from the amputation of his right arm after the battle of Fair Oaks the month before, Howard, whose devoutness would cause him to be called by some the "Christian General," was spending the last part of his convalescence raising volunteers in his home state. Chamberlain had maintained a "discrete silence" about the outcome of his trip to Augusta, and it placed him in a difficult position, but he too attended the meeting and spoke. He privately asked General Howard's advice on how to handle his situation, with the result that he told those pressing to go into the army with him to enlist in the first regiment they could find.[20]

To his embarrassment, an article appeared in the newspaper the following week reporting that Chamberlain had accepted the colonelcy of the Twentieth Maine Regiment. Although it was complimentary to him, he was afraid the story might damage his relations with the governor, should the chief executive think it came from him. In addition to that, the faculty at the college were alerted that he had something other than Europe in mind for his leave, and an uproar ensued. In the internal politics of Bowdoin there was a continuing religious power struggle for control of the college, and Chamberlain found himself in the middle of it. If his position became vacant, the much sought after position would most likely be filled with a man not of strict orthodox Congregationalist persuasion, a situation his friends on the faculty wanted to avoid above all other considerations. They tried to talk him out of going to war, apparently believing he might not come back at all, which would create the feared vacancy. One professor, in spite of having been a leading antislavery man for over thirty years, warned him that he might come home "shattered" and "good for nothing."[21]

Failing to convince him, they sent a representative to the governor, telling him that their junior colleague was "no fighter, but only a mild-mannered common student." An important state official, writing from Portland, warned the governor about Chamberlain, saying "his old classmates &c here say that you have been deceived: that C. is *nothing* at all." However, Chamberlain had other friends who knew the governor. The town's highly respected physician of some political influence, Dr. John D. Lincoln, wrote the governor that Chamberlain not only was a man of "energy and sense," but was "as capable of commanding a Reg't as any man out of . . . West Point." After telling Governor Washburn that many young men "would rally around his standard as they would around a hero," Dr. Lincoln concluded pointedly, "I trust, and I speak for all your friends here, that you feel induced to appoint him to some honorable position."[22]

On August 8, 1862, after declaring the day before that still another infantry regiment would be organized from the state, the governor assigned Chamberlain as lieutenant colonel and Adelbert Ames, a Regular Army officer and a Mainer from Rockland, as colonel of Maine's Twentieth Infantry Regiment. Chamberlain was extremely pleased; he preferred the commission as lieutenant colonel above any other and immediately accepted. Although the Bowdoin faculty had previously passed a vote disapproving the use of his leave for the purpose of entering the military, when Chamberlain made his required appearance before them, he had his commission in hand. He insisted that while he regretted going against their wishes, he was taking his leave regardless. Undoubtedly, his friends on the faculty otherwise were very fond of the serious young professor and had true concern for his welfare; when they finally realized they had no other choice, the matter was settled, and his colleagues reluctantly acquiesced to his departure.[23]

The next three weeks were busy ones for Chamberlain. A regiment had to be organized, with rallies, speeches, signing up of men from all over the state, and getting them to the rendezvous near Portland, nearly thirty miles south of Chamberlain's home at Brunswick. Things were helped along considerably by the governor's order that those companies already enlisted, but not specifically comprised for the other four regiments formed since President Lincoln's call for troops on July 2, report for service at the Twentieth Maine's designated camp near Portland. An early August announcement of a draft of several regiments of militia for nine-month terms of Federal service encouraged men to volunteer for three-year regiments like the Twentieth, because bounty was not to be paid to volunteers or draftees for the shorter-term militia regiments.[24]

Whole companies were recruited by energetic and ambitious men like Chamberlain's former student Ellis Spear, who hoped for appointments as officers. Other extensive recruiting was done in rousing war meetings around Brunswick by an 1861 Bowdoin graduate, William W. Morrell, assisted by the dashing James H. Nichols. Matters were helped considerably when Brunswick called a town meeting and voted a bonus of $100 for each man enlisting by the twenty-sixth of August. With the added state bounty and Federal advance totaling $185, the result was "a good sum for a poor man to leave behind," in the opinion of one townsman. Cities and towns that did not meet their quotas for the three-year regiments would have to draft for them, and Chamberlain at one point thought it might come to that at Brunswick. Variations of these scenes and activities were repeated in other towns and cities all over Maine and the nation in that late summer of 1862, as the people of the United States came to realize more and more the price they would pay in lives and wealth to keep the American Union.[25]

Chamberlain reported in Portland on August 18 because troops were arriving at Camp Mason and Col. Adelbert Ames was not expected until near the end of the month. Meanwhile, it must have been difficult for him: in spite of his concerns about recruiting, signed-up men were arriving constantly and had to be housed, fed, and somehow kept busy. An unsoldierly appearing lot, they were mostly independent and proud Maine men—farmers, clerks, lumbermen, storekeepers, lawyers, fishermen, builders, and sailors, some of whom had even been around Cape Horn. Others, from upstate counties like Aroostook and Piscataquis, must have never been so far from their homes as Portland. They were of all ages from eighteen to forty-five, with a few older and younger but eager enough to pass for the required age. Married and single, tall and short, fat and thin, they were healthy enough to pass a physical examination by a not-too-particular doctor. Somehow this unwieldy mass of inexperienced men, raised by "hook or crook," who resembled more a town meeting than a regiment, would have to be turned into soldiers, and in a very short time.[26]

Only two men were in uniform, one who had served briefly in another regiment the year before and the major, Charles D. Gilmore, who had served with the Seventh Maine and received his commission on the same day as Ames and Chamberlain. Gilmore, who had some idea of how to proceed, organized a guard and armed them with stove wood. The first officer of the day was uniformed in a brown cutaway coat, striped trousers, and a silk hat and instead of a sword, brandished a ramrod as his insignia of office. The line officers' commissions from the governor had yet to reach the camp, so those who expected to be named because of their recruiting efforts acted as the officers. Instead of giving orders, the "officers" would have a conference with the men, and then they would agree on what was to be done. The new companies trying to drill sometimes presented a ludicrous sight, but their members manfully blundered on, determined to do their part so that they could go fight the Rebels. Chamberlain, as head of the enterprise, undoubtedly attended to all of the details.[27]

Into this earnest but inept organization one evening arrived a tall, thin, dark-haired, mustachioed young man, twenty-six years old and a graduate of West Point. When he approached the headquarters tent, the man in civilian garb acting as guard, half slouching by the entrance, did not salute but, seeing the silver eagles adorning the shoulder straps of the straight-backed officer's uniform, cheerfully said, "How do you do, Colonel." Col. Adelbert Ames, who had been wounded seriously at the 1861 battle of Bull Run and whose gallantry there would earn him the Medal of Honor from Congress, cast a baleful eye on the genial sentinel. His military experience did not include commanding green volunteer citizen soldiers; since graduating from the military academy he had mostly served as a lieutenant in the artillery. There the relatively small groups of men serving the big guns were drilled until they performed their duty in precision teams like parts of well-oiled machines. After looking around in growing astonishment at the camp of his decidedly unmilitary new command, barking incomprehensible questions to the bewildered citizen designated officer of the day, the disgusted Ames pronounced the whole lot "a hell of a regiment."[28]

Those who had enlisted men for the ten companies of the new regiment at their own expense and sometimes at their peril—one irate mother drove off the would-be recruiter with a pitchfork—expected to be appointed officers by the governor. One man who became a captain by a stroke of Governor Washburn's pen humorously characterized the process: "The Governor, when he saw the enlistment rolls, and heard that the men had been placed in camp at the rendezvous, said to himself and his counsellors: 'These fellows who have recruited so many men and have actually landed them in camp must have military qualifications,' and straightway he commissioned them all."[29]

Eventually the commissions came from Augusta. Since they had to pay for their own clothing, the new line officers procured their uniforms from overworked tailors, but the men were issued their government uniforms and accoutrements. The regiment was thus gloriously arrayed in new blue woolen suits and caps with shiny gold buttons and brass belt plates and equipped with some of the necessities of army life—among them were tin mess articles, woolen and rubber blankets, haversacks, and canteens. Most wore their uniforms proudly, even those who had drawn a poor fit, but

Col. Adelbert Ames (National Archives)

with varying degrees of modesty. A few new lieutenants, one private observed, wore their crimson sashes, which were usually reserved only for dress occasions, at full width: "These had a peculiar way of looking sidewise at their shoulder straps. . . . They had a strut in their walk and the swords . . . would trail along at quite a respectable distance in the rear.

One glance would be sufficient to convince the most careless observer that each felt as if the destiny of the country depended largely upon their individual efforts."[30]

Ames knew he probably had little time to turn this virtual mob of patriotic civilians into an effective fighting force, and besides, his pride must have driven him to whip this outfit into some kind of shape. He would be judged by his superiors on the performance of his regiment. The men started to learn about the fundamentals of drill taught by officers who surely pored over readily available infantry tactics books into the night. In those days, before the advent of other deadly engines of war, mobile firepower was massed and brought to bear on the enemy by cannon pulled by teams of horses and infantrymen equipped with small arms, trained to move together in almost any direction. So it was of primary importance that the men learn the increasingly complex and confusing movements of the infantry, marching from battle line into column and in and out of intricate formations in the precise order that would ultimately bring deadly fire on the enemy and not, by mistake, into their own troops.[31]

Ames was an impatient man, and it became apparent to everyone in camp when he arrived that an apt expression to use was the old shipbuilding term, "There was the devil to pay and no pitch hot." After the recruits had achieved a rudimentary knowledge of their left foot from right and had scarcely mastered the first basic movements in and out of a line of battle, the colonel called for a dress parade. With much fussing and straightening, everyone finally got lined up in the correct places, the field officers Chamberlain and Gilmore in theirs, line officers with their companies, and Ames looking increasingly disgusted and indignant. Suddenly, the regimental fife and drum corps, each man drumming and fifing independently and discordantly, each out of step with the other, careened down the field in front of the line![32]

Ames roared at the captain nearest the point of confusion, "Captain Bangs, stop that damned drumming!" Captain Bangs could hear nothing over the loud din and cacophony, and Ames, anger turning to rage, lost his temper completely and charged the unfortunate offenders brandishing his sword! After the band had beaten a hasty retreat around the flank of the line to the rear, not to be seen again that day, the colonel proceeded to give a lengthy instruction to individuals in particular and the regiment in general. His choice of method was bellowing, yelling at, and dressing down unlucky fellows singled out wherever his outraged eye happened to fall on

Frances Caroline Adams Chamberlain, ca. 1862
(courtesy Pejepscot Historical Society, Brunswick, Maine)

hapless offenders of military form. It was the time-honored way of the professional soldier, and Ames, well trained, coupled it with his own temperament, which was short-fused to explode when provoked.[33]

Finally, on the twenty-ninth day of August, an officer of the Regular Army appeared and mustered the 979 officers and men of the Twentieth

Grace Dupee Chamberlain, left, *and Harold Wyllys Chamberlain, ca. 1862 (Alice Rains Trulock and James A. Trulock)*

Maine into the United States Army. Pledging their allegiance to the United States, to serve them "honestly and faithfully" against their enemies and obey the orders of the president and officers appointed, "according to the rules and articles for the government of the armies of the United States," they were really in the army now, and officially soldiers. On September 1 they were scheduled to leave the state and that morning managed to form a hollow square formation to witness Lieutenant Colonel Chamberlain receive the beautiful gray war-horse from his admirers, but then there was a long delay, and night found them still at Camp Mason.[34]

Chamberlain bade his two children farewell at his home in Brunswick; his wife, the former Frances Caroline Adams, affectionately known as Fannie, came to Portland to see him off accompanied only by her father, the Reverend George E. Adams. It must have been especially hard for him to leave his little daughter Grace, called Daisy, who was nearly six years old. With her light brown hair and hazel eyes, she looked much like her father and was a constant source of pleasure to him. His dark-haired son, who was two years younger than his sister and had bright brown eyes, more closely resembled Fannie. When the boy appeared with his hair in curls and clothed in the dresses that were the style of the day for small boys, the similarity between Harold Wyllys Chamberlain and his mother was striking.[35]

As the wind howled and the rain pelted against the officer's tent that sheltered them that night, Chamberlain, Fannie, and Dr. Adams huddled against the wet and cold. The storm was one of the tempests that could blow up in Maine in early September—a real southeaster—and the Reverend Dr. Adams hardly slept an hour through the dark night while the lightning flashed and the sound of rolling thunder filled the air. It would not be like him to complain or even show any displeasure, but Chamberlain undoubtedly regretted the presence of his father-in-law during those last few hours before he had to say farewell to his dear wife. He had loved her for more than ten years, and his passion for her had diminished little over the nearly seven years of their marriage.[36]

On the damp morning of September 2, 1862, reveille blew at three o'clock, and after the three hours it took the men of the regiment to make final preparations, they marched from camp to the Portland train station. Fannie Chamberlain rode in a coach to say good-bye, but the hardy Dr. Adams walked the distance, his old legs the preferred means of locomo-

Dr. George E. Adams
(courtesy First Parish Church, Brunswick, Maine)

tion. As the last regiment raised in Maine that summer, the Twentieth had received all the leftover men from the other new regiments. Because of this, and perhaps due to the fact that Chamberlain's former students had recruited near their homes throughout the state, the volunteers for Maine's twentieth regiment came from ten counties. It may have been for these reasons that its regimental historian declared, "It was not, as Chamberlain later noted, one of the state's favorites; no county claimed it; no city gave it a flag; and there was no send-off at the station." But it was this same regiment—disciplined, hardened, and winnowed down to fighting trim—that Chamberlain would lead to imperishable glory exactly ten months later at Gettysburg, and its name, "The Twentieth Maine," would blazon across time and down through history.[37]

CHAPTER *Two*

WHAT MANNER OF MEN WE WILL BE

As the train carrying the new soldiers chugged toward Boston, the regiment's first destination after leaving Maine, it had to leave behind the lieutenant colonel's youngest brother, Thomas Davee Chamberlain, because of a temporary incapacitating illness. At twenty-one, Tom was nearly thirteen years younger than his brother and stood one inch shorter. A handsome young man, with blue eyes and very dark hair, he cut a slight figure at 120 pounds. Tom had nearly five years experience as a store clerk but had been anxious to leave his mundane job with its hard work and low pay. When he had tried to join the army a few months earlier, his mother refused to entertain the thought of his going to war, but after he read in the newspaper of his brother's appointment, Tom renewed his appeal and

Thomas Davee Chamberlain, 1865 (courtesy Abbott Spear)

finally convinced both parents that he should be allowed to go with Lawrence.[1]

Although he signed up as a private, when the regiment was completely organized and mustered, with officers and noncommissioned officers chosen, Tom was a sergeant in Company I. In a letter to Lawrence about Tom, their father gave his advice so bluntly that it read much like military orders: Tom should be given easy work, until he was "seasoned to the trenches." There was no one like Tom on an observation post, or he could do work on military stores, the older man was sure, and he should be promoted to an officer if he did not receive an appointment as one! Seeming to struggle with his pride in his oldest son and his apparent disapproval of the war, the elder Chamberlain rather glumly observed that the lieutenant colonel was "in for good so distinguish yourself and be out of it." Relenting, he concluded, "Come home with honor, as I know you will if that lucky star of yours will serve you in *this war*." Speaking for their mother also, he added, "We hope to be spared as tis not *our war*. Take care of Tom. . . . Good Luck to you."[2]

* * *

Joshua Chamberlain, the father of the two brothers, had been born in 1800 at Orrington, in the Massachusetts district of Maine, twenty years before it became a state. His father, the first Joshua Chamberlain, the son of one and brother of two other Revolutionary War soldiers, had moved there from Cambridge a year before the second Joshua's birth. By that time, this branch of the Chamberlain family had been mostly in Massachusetts for five generations, since William Chamberlain had arrived from England in 1648. The mother of the first generation of Chamberlains born in the New World had even been charged with witchcraft, a "preposterous charge," and jailed in Cambridge, where she died in 1692.[3]

When pioneers settled the land east of the Penobscot River in the last half of the eighteenth century, the region around the town of Orrington was little more than a wilderness. In the forbidding climate of northern New England it took rugged men and women to scratch a living from the uncleared land and rushing waters. But game and fish were abundant, and the river deep and navigable from the falls and rocks just above Bangor, a large town on its west bank, down to the sea. Villages formed as more settlers came, and the forest provided the lumber for, among other things, houses, barns, and shipbuilding.[4]

During the War of 1812 the British sailed up the Penobscot, destroying property and firing cannon into towns to terrorize the populace. They destroyed two ships in the prosperous shipyard owned by the first Joshua Chamberlain, one still on the stocks and the other lying at the dock—a grievous financial loss from which he did not easily recover. But tough and resilient, in 1817 he moved six miles upriver to what became the town of Brewer and bought a large farm there. Building a house near the river, he and his wife, Ann, raised a large family; later he engaged in some shipbuilding again and served as a colonel in the militia. He named several of his sons for famous men he admired, but the second he named for himself. That son became known as Joshua, Jr., to differentiate the two.[5]

In 1827 Joshua Chamberlain, Jr., married Sarah Dupee Brastow, sometimes known as Sally, whose family had settled in the area even before the Chamberlains. She was a granddaughter of Capt. Thomas Brastow, Jr., a private in the French and Indian War and a Revolutionary War officer, and the daughter of Billings Brastow from Wrentham, Massachusetts. On her mother's side she was descended from the Huguenot Jean Dupuis, who fled France and religious persecution there, arriving in Boston in 1685. The spelling of the name of her grandfather, Charles Dupuis, was changed to Dupee on the military rolls when he served as a Revolutionary War soldier.[6]

On September 8, 1828, in a cottage on the river near the old family homestead, the first son was born into this family with such proud military traditions. The new father's experiences with the British in the War of 1812 when he was a lad must have made a deep impression; the child's name, Lawrence Joshua Chamberlain, was recorded in the heavy family Bible with the notation "named for Commodore Lawrence of the American Navy" written underneath. With words that stirred generations of American schoolchildren—"Don't give up the ship!"—the dying young hero James Lawrence, captain of the American warship *Chesapeake* in 1813, had urged his men on in his losing fight with a British frigate. Chamberlain was called Lawrence throughout his life by his family and boyhood friends, but as he grew into full manhood, he tried out variations of the names and their initials. Joshua was the name of his father and grandfather, and the Bible stories about King David's chief general by that name could not have

Joshua Chamberlain, Jr. (Alice Rains Trulock and James A. Trulock)

escaped his notice. As an adult, he finally chose the sequence Joshua Lawrence, and his formal signature became "Joshua L. Chamberlain."[7]

Chamberlain's childhood in Brewer was a busy and happy one. Playing in the forest, meadows, and streams with his friends and cousins, the little boy grew up strong and secure. When he was six, the family welcomed another boy, Horace Beriah, in the two-story frame house their father had

Sarah Dupee Brastow Chamberlain
(courtesy Brewer Public Library, Brewer, Maine)

built in Brewer on the road leading to their farm. Two years later a girl, named Sarah Brastow for their mother, joined the growing family. In 1838 his father again named a new son for a famous man—John Calhoun, South Carolina's powerful champion of slavery and states' rights. Nearly three years later the last child, Thomas Davee, was born.[8]

Sarah Chamberlain's calm, loving voice encouraged her children, and her grace and liveliness filled the home with warmth and gaiety. The center

Horace Beriah Chamberlain
(courtesy Bowdoin College, Archives class photograph albums, Hawthorne-Longfellow Library)

Sarah Brastow Chamberlain
(Alice Rains Trulock and James A. Trulock)

of the home, she carried herself with remarkable beauty; when she was a child, a light board had been fastened to her shoulders in order that she acquire a perfectly straight posture. In her old-fashioned way, she habitually wore some kind of a cap, plain muslin for every day and something more elaborate for dress occasions, and three curls fell below it on each side in front of her ears. Both parents contributed in bringing up the children to be moral and upright, with integrity and honor in the forefront,

John Calhoun Chamberlain
(courtesy Bowdoin College, Archives class photograph albums, Hawthorne-Longfellow Library)

but willingness, manners, and cheerfulness were also required in the Chamberlain household.[9]

Industry was a prized value taught early and continuously in New England homes, and the Chamberlains' was no exception. As the boy grew, school lessons and farm chores took up most of the long hours of the passing days. Clearing fields, plowing, mowing hay, chopping wood, hoeing, weeding—the work on the hundred-acre farm seemed endless. When he was fourteen, Lawrence attended a nearby military school for a while where French was a compulsory subject; it began a study of languages that would have him master nine besides English in only a few years. Because of temporary family financial difficulties, he worked at one time in a brickyard and a rope-walk to bring in some scarce dollars. Hard manual labor produced in him a muscular, fit body, and school helped feed Lawrence's keen mind, but his life was not all seriousness and work.[10]

Riding a favorite mare at breakneck speed over rough back fields and through the forest could not help but make Lawrence an excellent horseman, and swimming, old-fashioned roundball, and other games occupied more of the boy's free time. Bangor, the city rising on hills immediately across the river from Brewer, was a busy port from which ships cruised the world. In the spring, when the ice had left the river and there was a fast wind, the vessels crowded up the river, their sails spread in the freshening breeze. Shipbuilding was a big business in the area, and it was young Lawrence's special feat to hang his hat on the main truck of every ship launched on the Brewer side of the Penobscot.[11]

Lawrence learned to love sailing; with haying done, a happy vacation time found the whole family on a trip down the bay on the sloop *Lapwing*. The small boat was crewed by home-grown "hands" who fancied it a man-of-war, with Lawrence as the oldest naturally ordering his next two younger brothers, Horace and John, about. Joining in the annual Fourth of July celebrations, he had his share of burnt fingers and singed eyebrows from firecrackers to show for it. And there was good sweet gingerbread to eat after the annual militia muster, where his father, who reached the rank of lieutenant colonel, was an officer.[12]

Serving as county commissioner and holding other civil offices, Joshua Chamberlain, Jr., was a leading citizen in Brewer and possessed great strength of character. A taciturn man, he was not demonstrative or playful with his children, and when he told them to do something, he meant it, even if the task at hand seemed impossible to accomplish. When Lawrence and his brothers told their father they could not move a particularly heavy rock from a field they were clearing, his only reply was "Move it!" They did just that, no doubt after figuring out that a fence post or rail used as a lever could make part of the task a lot easier.[13]

At one haying time, Lawrence was pitching hay and driving the wagon, his father gathering and raking behind, in a natural meadow made by long-ago beavers and surrounded by forest. One of the front wheels got wedged between two large stumps when the wagon crossed a brook, and the back wheels sank into the sand under the load. "Clear that wheel!" the older man ordered from across the stream. "How am I going to do it?" the boy called, thinking his father could not see the entire situation. Only a combined effort could solve this problem, Lawrence thought, his distress increased by knowing that he should have avoided the treacherous stumps. "Do it, that's how!" was the stern rejoinder.[14]

Angry now, instead of maneuvering the team of oxen to back out the wheel and then straddle the stump, Lawrence jumped down and seized the hub. With a prodigious effort, he lifted the wheel clear of the stump. The force of the sudden action caused the wagon tongue to strike the nose of the "off-ox," and thus prodded, the team suddenly lunged forward and freed everything from the creek—cart, oxen, hay, and all. After a moment's shocked astonishment, not a word was said between the two hayers. The young man had obeyed his father's command to the letter, and it was not the elder Chamberlain's custom to engage in unnecessary talk.[15]

Recalling the value of his father's teaching later, Chamberlain said, "'Do it, that's how!' . . . was a maxim whose value far exceeded the occasion." It was, he continued, "an order for life" that was "worth infinitely more" than years of book learning and dilatory irresolution—action, not words! The same admonishment repeated over the years undoubtedly forced Chamberlain's growing mind to seek creative solutions to problems, besides stimulating his quick intellect to notice everything that could be useful to him. In order that independence of character could be nurtured and not broken by such harsh-sounding dictates, the father's sternness was somewhat offset by his generosity and genuine interest in his children's well-being and happiness. He had "a chivalrous strain of blood in his composition," Chamberlain later said of his progenitor, suggesting for his father the inbred knightly traits of honor, courtesy, and magnanimity toward foes that later were used often by others to describe himself.[16]

Although Lawrence became a good shot and did his share of hunting, he never killed for sport. Some Saturdays, with the week's work done, he walked deep in the woods, taking his gun to forestall annoying questions. As he roamed, he engaged in dreamy reverie, watching the birds and other wild creatures and looking at the bright, delicate flowers by some clear stream. Listening carefully, he noticed that the wind blowing through variously shaped leaves made different sounds, and he learned to identify trees by only their songs overhead.[17]

Other times Lawrence would join the Indians who camped in his father's back lot and still lived in birchbark wigwams. He learned their language and listened to their dark tales of the fearful Mohawks of old and myths of the mighty storm god whose throne was the mountain Katahdin. That peak was the highest in Maine, and although it was about a hundred miles from Brewer, it could be seen from the top of Whiting's hill outside the town. Beyond remembered time the Indians would not go above its timberline; there was, they believed, no return for those who dared. But when he and his father led a party of vacationers on a backpack trip to the fabled mountain, Lawrence climbed to its very top and shinned up the tallest rock, which formed a pillar at its summit.[18]

Religion pervaded the lives of nearly all the descendants of those who settled the northeastern shores of the United States. They called Sunday the Sabbath and enjoyed going to church. Puritan and Huguenot doctrines combined to make the religious requirements considerable in the Chamberlain home. The family worshipped in the First Congregational Church in Brewer, where there was much fellowship and benevolence, but the congregation's rules of conduct were strict. Quarreling with neighbors without remorse or spending time even looking in on a ballroom were reasons enough for errant members to be confronted and chastised. After thoughtfully deciding he needed "saving grace and a loving divine brotherhood," sixteen-year-old Lawrence was accepted as a member when he gave his required public account of personal religious experience. His presentation was more prosaic than that of a great sinner or "sudden saint," but he was formally welcomed into the fellowship of the church and remained a member there until his death.[19]

For years there had been a tacit truce between his parents about the life's work their oldest son should undertake. Joshua Chamberlain, his imagination fired by the ideals and experiences of his youth, thought the army an honorable profession for Lawrence. When the youth attended Whiting's Military and Classical School, his father intended it to fit Lawrence for West

Point. But his mother was a religious woman; the idea of any of her sons going to the army was one that she would always oppose or lament. She thought the army "narrowing and enervating"—dulling to the intellect and a danger to morals. And Sally Dupee Brastow Chamberlain was not to be disputed lightly, especially in matters having to do with her children: although she was usually deferential and persuasive, she also could maneuver adroitly in an argument and spiritedly win her way. She wanted Lawrence to study for the ministry.[20]

Not happy with either choice, but opposed especially to the army in time of peace, Lawrence thought that "both alike offered but little scope and freedom. They bound a man by rules and precedents and petty despotisms, and swamped his personality." Wanting to please his mother, he agreed on the ministry if he could become a missionary to some foreign and exotic land, a lifework then increasingly popular with many of his contemporaries in Brewer. The question remained open, however, held in abeyance until maturer judgment, and perhaps the Providence he always looked to for guidance in his affairs, gave him indication of a final choice. Deciding in 1846 to attend Bowdoin College, downstate in the town of Brunswick, he hoped to enter there with his nineteenth birthday, over a year away. But much must be done first, and there was the land itself, where part of his heart belonged. He would always feel nostalgic for it, and as he worked it in the last summer before preparing for his leave-taking, it was with a growing sense of farewell.[21]

"But the ever remembered glory of that summer's work was the sowing with grain and 'laying down to grass' of a dear old familiar field. The furrows well cross-plowed and harrowed down, leaving the natural slopes like a smooth ground-swell of ocean. It was a remote field, a gentle hill-side stooping toward the west, and over the low banks of the brook commanding a view of the city across the river. . . . One would gladly be alone in such a service, when a field that had been associated with many works of youthful years was to be sealed down under a sod for the long, eventful years to come. . . . Now in the declining day the sower, guiding the faithful, knowing mare, companion of his youthful toils, traverses breadth by breadth the field,—the figures standing out against the shadows luminous in the sunset glow which has touched the mists above the city across the river with wondrous glory,—and thus, all bathed in a golden dream, tenderly pressing that precious earth, for the last time of the dear old times!"[22]

In the winter after his eighteenth birthday, Lawrence spent some time "keeping school" at North Milford, upriver from Brewer, which would add to his slender purse. Teaching the sometimes overgrown students in those upriver communities usually required more qualifications than mere book learning: many masters had been unceremoniously thrown bodily out of the window, bringing education to a halt before it had hardly begun! When challenged in like manner, Lawrence established his authority conclusively by reversing this procedure, gaining the respect of roughneck and more tractable scholars alike.[23]

Boarding with a family whose home was already crowded and quite rowdy, Lawrence suffered from loneliness until some young people of the region convinced him to start a "singing school" to learn new hymns. Singing schools were more social events than schools, popular especially because they provided an opportunity for courting, and Lawrence's drew eager pupils from ten miles around. In order to accompany the singers, he soon obtained from home an instrument he had taught himself to play, his old bass viol, and many a winter's evening was thus brightened for him with music and song.[24]

The youthful Chamberlain had a sense of time beyond his years, inculcated by his mother, who urged her children to realize how short a life had been given to be useful and good to others. "All things are fleeting, we are fleeting. *Time*, how it flies," he observed to a cousin. "We are no longer children." A little wistfully, he added, "I sometimes wish myself a child always, for then it is that sport is the most innocent and joy most unbeclouded." Soon the winter teaching term ended, and it was time to face the future squarely with its grown-up, if unknown, responsibilities. If he were to attend college when he intended, preparations must be made, and there was no more time to be lost. Bowdoin's entrance requirements were stringent, and the prospective student knew no Greek and little Latin.[25]

Fitting out a room for study at one end of the attic of the Chamberlain home, with windows that faced west and north, Chamberlain tacked a daily schedule to its bookcase door. On it he filled in the hours of the day from five in the morning to ten at night. Latin was absorbed from Caesar through Sallust and Cicero, aided by William Hyde, a Bowdoin man who had taught at Whiting's. There were hours of mind-wrenching study and the daily three-hour recitation to his Greek language tutor in Bangor—Kuhner's unabridged Greek grammar had to be memorized and recited verbatim before going on to Homer, Herodotus, and Thucydides! On some cold days he split firewood from logs that had been rejected as tough knots, an exercise that he believed had no equal for putting muscle on a man's frame and strength and suppleness from his shoulders down to his feet. Sometimes a pleasant hour was spent in warmer weather in the open garret, where Chamberlain and his father fenced with broadswords, adding to the youth's physical grace and skill.[26]

The long months went by. September came, his nineteenth birthday came, and the college term opened, but the scholar was not half ready. A new goal took shape. If his continued accelerated studies could make him achieve enough to be on equal terms with his new classmates by the close of the college's long winter vacation, it might be possible then for Chamberlain to enter Bowdoin. The fall term was a short one, and for freshmen it was known to be devoted more to acquiring form than advancing knowledge. More months of "wood-splitting and head-splitting" by the determined student followed, until February of 1848 found him in a one-horse sleigh driven by his Latin tutor, William Hyde, bound for Brunswick and the halls of Bowdoin College.[27]

Taking the coastal route over the winter snow, his trunk containing his possessions lashed behind the runnered conveyance, Chamberlain watched the seaports of Belfast, Rockland, Wiscasset, and Bath be overtaken and then left behind. He arrived at Bowdoin on the second morning after leaving the family home. As the college came into view, he could see the beautiful pale granite chapel, its twin spires rising over a hundred feet toward the sky, sitting well back from the wide main street on the south edge of the town. On either side of the chapel, three- and four-story brick buildings containing student living quarters and classrooms stood stolidly, rows of tall, thin, rectangular chimneys sticking up blackly from their roofs.[28]

Here and there stark, leafless trees promised shade in warmer days, and worn pathways crisscrossed the spacious campus. But tall, stately pines symbolized Bowdoin; they had grown over the sandy college grounds before the first buildings were raised, and their songs usually filled the air. The wind still sighed and whispered through the long stretches of them that began now at the old graveyard behind the college. Sometimes the sound would come up from the nearby shores of Harpswell Neck across the plains and, loud in a rising tempest, whirl around the buildings and fill the cemetery with a roar like the sea.[29]

By special arrangement, a committee of learned professors examined Chamberlain at length in what must have been a harrowing process. Late that night the exhausted young man was told he passed all the entrance

Bowdoin College, ca. 1850
(courtesy Bowdoin College, Archives campus views, Hawthorne-Longfellow Library)

requirements, conditioned only in Sallust's "Jugurtha," an advanced Latin text. Beginning his first class in the dark and foggy cold at six o'clock the next morning, he thought the sleepy students looked like galley slaves as they sat at their benches. But the neophyte collegian was well grounded: he found that he did not have to study as hard at college as he had when preparing for his entrance there. Looking back at those fearful times in the home attic after a few months had passed, he thought the extent of his labors then almost impossible and wondered that he was able to accomplish what he did.[30]

Since he presented a rather mild appearance, only a nominal hazing of the new freshman occurred, but a nod to that hoary tradition took place in the form of a "smoke out" of his room on the fourth floor of Maine Hall. Chamberlain obligingly outlasted the horde of sophomores who sealed his room and filled it so thick with tobacco smoke that the lamp looked "like a red moon in a foggy night." He was a little lonely at first; besides seldom hearing from home, his late start surely put him at a disadvantage in forming initial friendships. But while the schoolwork still kept him very busy, he was happy to meet several kindred souls who took religion as seriously as he. And though he wanted to be liked by his classmates, he established standards for his own behavior, demurring to join class "sprees" and other tempting undergraduate escapades. He found himself alone sometimes, the inevitable penalty for not bowing to these strong social pressures, but he began to be understood and accepted favorably by the other young men as time went on. Final freshman examinations gave him a clean ticket for his sophomore year, and the relieved and happy scholar left for home without regret at vacation time.[31]

Chamberlain's sophomore year found him hard at work and learning good study habits. Assessing his scholastic weaknesses, he resolved to overcome his lack of strength in mathematics, accomplished by sometimes all-night study sessions as he struggled with intricate problems. Under the stimulating instruction of Professor Daniel R. Goodwin, studying French became an adventure. The professor not only inspired, Chamberlain remembered, "he broadened; . . . he integrated knowledge and animated it." Not only was Chamberlain able to see into the nature of languages, a skill that was to enable him to become fluent in several, but his quick intelligence allowed him to generalize beyond the problems of language: to understand how to "think into a thing, as well as think it out."[32]

As an assignment for rhetoric class, Chamberlain finally read a novel—*The House of Seven Gables* by Bowdoin graduate Nathaniel Hawthorne. He had been forbidden such reading because of a notion in his strict home that novels were somehow immoral—even James Fenimore Cooper's *The Deerslayer* had been prohibited. Strangely enough, however, poetry did not seem to come under the ban; before he entered college, the young Lawrence could freely quote Lord Byron, whose verses, if the more romantic ones had been read by the domestic authority, would have surely suffered the same fate as the dreaded novels.[33]

His classmates and others began to call him Jack that year, a nickname that pleased Chamberlain, since he considered it an indication that they really liked him. Choices about his personal behavior were sometimes difficult; he almost constantly had to weigh and think through his own values as new experiences and questions arose. His home training did not exclude the enjoyment of an occasional glass of cider, but he decided not to drink at all at Bowdoin, fearing complications and perhaps endless explanations if he drank with one friend and not another due to different circumstances. As he thought the matter over, it seemed better for him to abstain from alcoholic beverages altogether, but "without putting on superior airs," the latter course of conduct probably a good-sized factor in his growing popularity.[34]

Such decisions were no protection from the consequences of cider drinking, however. One day Chamberlain and some classmates, with a hayrick and a two-horse team, set out in search of a customary "class tree" to plant on the border of the college grounds. The perfect tree could only be finally found ten miles from Brunswick, of course, and many in the party liberally helped themselves on the way to some private stores of "refreshments." With the wagon recklessly careening around corners in every town on the way back, colliding with boys, carts, and dogs, the carousers gave hilarious and impudent answers to sober citizens' protests. Outraged complaints about the conduct promptly came to the college faculty, those learned gentlemen who also acted as college policemen against undergraduate deviltry.[35]

The next day, after interviewing several miscreants about the scandalous episode to no avail, Bowdoin's president Leonard Woods sent for Chamberlain, who left a solemn group of students in his room, at least those who had recovered enough to be there. Even though he had discouraged the wild behavior as much as he could, his classmates knew that their Jack would neither lie about the affair nor betray them. Chamberlain readily admitted to his own presence on the hay-wagon, and when President Woods said he could not believe that the youth had anything to do with the "disgraceful occurences," Chamberlain agreed that he had not. However, when asked who the guilty parties were, Chamberlain said he had conscientious scruples against revealing them, whereupon, saying such scruples came from a "false sense of honor," President Woods declared Chamberlain suspended from the college.[36]

Accepting the punishment, Chamberlain yet protested that for him to do otherwise, he would have to be "an informant—a betrayer of confidence, which is much like a traitor." Even if his stand was from a mistaken, not false, sense of honor, it should still be respected, he argued, since "confidence between man and man is one of the lessons which the College should inculcate." Suspension was usually regarded as a disgrace, and the transgressors met with parental wrath, but Chamberlain disabused President Woods of any idea that he would meet this fate. "I know well my father will be proud to see me coming home for this," he said and then added, standing up for himself, "more so than I shall be to return here again." With that he was dismissed and returned to his waiting comrades. When he declared to them that he was "going home, boys; there's no help for it," they decided that Jack should not suffer for them, and they would "own up to the cider," at least. Apparently moved by Chamberlain's arguments and mollified by the tardy confession of the others, the lenient Woods let them all off with a reprimand.[37]

Chamberlain had kept secret at Bowdoin a condition that plagued him—his propensity to stammer badly when required to pronounce words beginning with the letters p, b, and t, known in grammar books as "close mutes." The speech impediment had made his life so miserable and constantly on guard for the treacherous consonants that he spoke as little as possible. Often using synonyms and other devices to circumvent dangerous words, he had to stand mute at other times, even in class, while combined feelings of anger and shame welled up in him. The condition not only put him on the defensive, he realized, but added to his normal shyness, and the habits of speech and action required to constantly deal with the disability put him at serious disadvantage in college. It was not to be borne any longer; he was finally forced to take action. Devising ways of solving this enigmatic problem, he may have heard the echo of his father's words "do it," the phrase that often inspired him to find that "obstacles irremovable can be surmounted."[38]

Paying close attention to his written work, he found that if he was forewarned of their presence by scanning a text, he could touch on the perfidious syllables and be off of them on a "wave of breath," which worked up to a point. But he learned, especially in conversation, that he did well if he could convince himself he was "singing" the difficult phrases by speaking in a rhythmic style. He practiced so that the method was not detectable by his listeners—if it were obvious, it would not only detract from the content of his discourse but make him appear ridiculous. In time he learned to use his system so skillfully that he became a public speaker of great eloquence and power, the melodic quality of his voice no doubt contributing to the great popularity of his speeches. Looking back later, Chamberlain knew that the experience of having the speech impediment and overcoming it affected his "habits and perhaps character, and the indirect effects of which may have reached into the whole of life."[39]

Toward the end of the year, because of his high rank in the department of modern language, Chamberlain became one of Professor Goodwin's library assistants, a post that gave him the privilege of a social relationship with the professor and his family. His close friendship with the son of Professor Alpheus Packard gave him another family whose invitations brightened the long weeks of study, religious meetings, and duties when he missed the familiarity and love of his own family and friends. The summer of his second year he enjoyed teaching a Sunday school on Sabbath afternoons, walking two miles out on the Bath Road to a little yellow schoolhouse, until the last of August brought the end of the college year with a three-week vacation and the return of the scholar to Brewer.[40]

Then ill fortune struck. Chamberlain's twenty-first birthday, a milestone he had looked forward to celebrating, found him delirious with fever, and the illness continued so long and so severely that the family physician gave up hope for his recovery. Discharging the doctor, his distraught mother brought in a homeopathic physician on the case, and the patient began to improve. Through the disability and pain came the realization that there would be no school for him that year, but with constant nursing by his mother and his now teenaged sister Sarah, usually known as Sae or Sadie, he began to get better. With the long months of convalescence lightened by high-spirited repartee with his nurses, he enjoyed what he termed the "old Huguenot hilarity" and then reviewed his studies in the pleasant summer among the fields and forests of home.[41]

Returning to Bowdoin, Chamberlain found his old classmates exalted seniors, and although there was no help for it, he found it hard to see them every day and no longer be a part of their class. But his new classmates knew him well, and he was especially glad he had not been a part of hazing them when they were first-year men. He settled down to work: besides mathematics, Latin, and beginning German, he studied Hebrew literature in the class of the new professor of natural and revealed religion, Calvin Stowe, who had recently moved to Brunswick with his wife and several children. After considerable study of his rhetoric textbook and laborious practice at construction of essays and themes, he found to his surprise and pleasure that he had won the college prizes in both composition and oratory at the end of the year. Finding still more time in his busy days, he began to play tunes on the organ in the college chapel; he progressed so quickly and well that he soon became organist of the society that had charge of the Sunday music.[42]

Although generally overburdened with the running of a large household with too little money, Professor Stowe's wife, Harriet Beecher Stowe, held "Saturday Evenings" for a group of friends, mostly young and including Chamberlain, in her home on Federal Street. The highlight of these evenings was the hostess reading the newest installment of her latest work before it was sent to *The National Era*, an abolitionist paper that had been publishing it in serial form since June 1851. She called it *Uncle Tom's Cabin*, *or Life among the Lowly*, and its publication as a book in March 1852, before the serialization was complete, immediately caused a great sensation across the country. Its depiction of slavery, written in the dramatic and emotional style popular in mid-nineteenth-century America, helped exacerbate the high feelings above and below Mason and Dixon's line that led to the Civil War nearly ten years later.[43]

Mrs. Stowe had had the inspirational vision that caused her to write *Uncle Tom's Cabin* as she sat in her pew in the First Parish Church on Communion Sunday in March 1851. Compulsory student attendance there on Sundays was monitored by the college, and though his own devout feelings did not need the impetus of that policy, it was likely that Chamberlain was present at this service. About that time he became the choir conductor in the huge, beautiful, wooden Gothic church built five years before on a rise of ground near the college. The choir was invited to give concerts at nearby towns, giving more chances for meeting young people. Frequenting the social activities, and often playing the church organ for the choir, was the pretty, dark-haired daughter of the revered pastor of First Parish Church. Frances Caroline Adams was her name, and Chamberlain fell passionately in love with her.[44]

Fannie Adams, as she was known, was the adopted daughter of the Reverend George E. Adams and his wife, the former Sarah Ann Folsom. She had been born to Ashur and Amelia Wyllys Adams in Boston on August 12, 1825, when her distant cousin, John Quincy Adams, was president of the United States. Ashur Adams was old enough to be Fannie's grandfather, and for reasons that seemed best to him and Fannie's mother, his third wife, he allowed the little girl to come to live "at a very early age" in the home of his childless nephew in Brunswick. She called her new parents mother and father, even though she was old enough to remember her original family well; when she learned enough in school to write letters, she made contact with them again. Later, visits were sometimes exchanged, and Fannie became part of a large extended family where art and music were highly valued, and talent in both encouraged.[45]

Fannie was dearly loved and even indulged by her new parents, who provided her with an excellent education and were proud of her accomplishments in music and art, but the fact that she had been given away must have made a deep impression on the child. The Adams home was strictly religious, befitting that of the settled pastor of the town's oldest and most prosperous church with its straitlaced Puritan traditions. As Fannie grew, the household also contained her adopted mother's younger maiden sister, Deborah G. Folsom, whom Fannie called Cousin D, and the granddaughter of a member of the Bowdoin medical faculty, Anna D. Davis, whom the Adamses also adopted. Fannie was happy in her new home. When she was unkindly teased on a visit to Boston that another sister would take her place permanently in Brunswick, little Fannie wrote home about it but then added, a little doubtfully, "If all the people in Boston should tell me so, I should not believe it."[46]

Growing up as George E. Adams's daughter must have been difficult for Fannie. The Yale and seminary-educated clergyman was not only wholly committed to God's service, he was also on the prestigious Board of Overseers at Bowdoin and an upstanding community leader. He was a genial man with a good sense of humor but tended to worry and fret. He could be inquisitive and meddlesome at times, and his advice to his daughter occasionally took the form of exasperated scolding. Expecting Fannie to measure up to a high standard of behavior, he wanted her to possess what he thought were correct attitudes befitting the daughter of a clergyman. Fannie steadfastly refused, however, to become a full member of the church, an omission that could have only been painful to her father.[47]

There undoubtedly was the usual community interest and gossip about the family of such a prominent man, and the willful Fannie, well dressed with fur trimmings on her winter coat and other fine materials and ornaments that she loved, surely received more than a small amount of attention. Her mother, a former schoolteacher from New Hampshire and several years older than her husband, was wise but mild in manner, a great helpmeet to her husband and tireless in church service. In February of 1850, after a long illness, Sarah Folsom Adams died, leaving a large empty place in the family circle in the parsonage.[48]

Although she had some reputation for not thinking much of men, it was in the time of greatly changing circumstances of her life that Fannie's large brown eyes must have sparkled encouragement to the shy, serious Chamberlain. As he worked hard at his studies in his junior year in 1851, his blossoming romance with the dark-haired, teasing Fannie would have been a considerable distraction. The Reverend Dr. Adams attended a convention in Chicago much of that summer; his long absence surely gave the young couple a little more freedom than they would have ordinarily enjoyed. The long summer days provided opportunities for outings in the countryside and along the beautiful shores of the ocean, the warm summer nights then kindling romantic interludes with the minister's daughter. With his extended social calendar in the first part of his senior year including events attended by Fannie, and further enjoying snatches of time alone arranged by her, Chamberlain fell deeply in love, and it would not have taken long for him to press for her promise to marry him.[49]

During his Chicago trip Dr. Adams had met and seen much of a young woman, Helen M. Root, who was a sister of Professor George F. Root, the noted musician. The two-story, wooden, Federal-style parsonage across from the town mall on Maine Street became the scene of a flurry of activity that autumn. It was painted, papered, and carpeted in anticipation of an important event that would bring even more change to Fannie Adams's life. On the last day of 1851 Dr. Adams brought home his new bride, who was only six months older than Fannie. It proved a delicate and awkward situation for everyone in the household, especially for the women. Fannie traveled away from home almost immediately, considering her own future very seriously, especially the prospect of marrying Chamberlain. She wrote to a trusted friend, Stephen Merrill Allen, seeking his advice in the matter, and he penned a frank and thoughtful response that casts some light on Fannie's own feelings at the time.[50]

"You say you love him—yet cannot feel that sort of love for him of which you have for years dreamed so wildly. . . . Yet I fear that your ideas of love are still too highly colored with your early pictures of romance," Allen wrote. After cautioning her not to allow unrealistic fancies to cloud her judgment, he added that it was unfortunate that Chamberlain was not several years older than she and further along in his studies or profession. Then he took up other concerns: "From the hints you gave me of his character I should suppose he might be of a rather jealous, sanguine, and ardent temperament. . . . One who possesses your hand should have the utmost confidence in you or you could not be happy with him." More correspondence with Allen followed as Fannie left Brunswick to continue her musical education in New York with Professor Root, finishing in July.[51]

During Fannie's absence Chamberlain worked hard at his senior year subjects at Bowdoin. He learned Italian and was Professor Parker Cleaveland's special assistant in chemistry and physics, with its accompanying advanced mathematics requirements. He must have given much time to that capstone of the nineteenth-century college education, moral philosophy, reading Professor Thomas Upham's books on *The Intellect*, *The Sensibilities*, and *The Will* and attending lectures given by President Woods. As an outstanding scholar, he was elected to Phi Beta Kappa. Broadening his social life even more, he joined "The Round Table," a circle of young men and women who met every two weeks to present and discuss their various literary offerings. He also belonged to the Peucinian Society, Bowdoin's oldest literary society, and Alpha Delta Phi social fraternity.[52]

These activities did not keep him from missing Fannie, however, and he would fall into dark, despondent moods when her infrequent letters and their lack of reassurance of her love kept him in uncertainty. Barely sustaining him were his memories of their past times together when he had felt that she cared for him and they had exchanged loving kisses; he wrote her long letters that reflected his love and the hope of hers. "Fannie, dear Fannie," he wrote, "only tell me that you do love me as I *do* love you . . . tell me may I be sure of that." But, perhaps referring to her penchant for beautiful clothes and other fine things, he added, "I know I have nothing to offer you—not one of those things to which you most incline."[53]

Then, when home on his spring vacation less than two weeks later, Chamberlain was sent to "the loftiest pinnacle of transports." Deborah Folsom, Fannie's Cousin D, sent to him from Brunswick a letter Fannie had written to her, the younger woman apparently telling of her future plans, her feelings for Chamberlain, his good qualities, and her intention to marry him. Proudly he showed it to his mother, who declared, he reported to Fannie, "It gave the lie to all that had ever been whispered to her by certain ladies about you—& that she knew you were good . . . that it was seldom one saw so beautiful a letter so full of good sense." All his fears and doubts dissolved now: "I *know* in *whom* all my highest hopes & dearest joys are centered I *know* in whom my whole heart can rest—so sweetly and so surely." Sending her a rose, he asked her to write a letter like it to him: "I want to know all those little things that you never tell me."[54]

Fannie must have done just that, because another letter he wrote to her shortly afterward from Brunswick was signed in bold letters, "As ever, truly, your betrothed, Lawrence." He admonished her to let nothing stand in the way of returning home for his commencement near the first of August. Although, Chamberlain added, he was certain she was very dear to her father, and the minister would be very sorry that Fannie could not be happy living in his home, Chamberlain saw more than ever that she was right in her ideas and had chosen the right course. Apparently determined to pursue an independent life away from home, supporting herself by teaching music and repaying a $300 debt to her father, Fannie planned to marry Chamberlain soon after he finished a three-year seminary course. But the waiting time did not trouble him then, because he was aware that he needed more education to pursue any professional career. "Only think, honey-bee," he wrote, referring to the time until their wedding day, "only three years, why its a dream—three years will go like a flash." Playfully, he pretended to kiss her over and over to make her blush and put a sparkle in her eye—"I guess she's a rogue; that's what I guess," he added.[55]

Strain was showing at the Adams house in Brunswick. Deborah Folsom, who had a fondness for Dr. Adams and a financial interest in the parsonage, had no use for Dr. Adams's bride. When calling at the parsonage, Chamberlain formed the opinion that Deborah Folsom would leave her brother-in-law's home after Bowdoin's commencement—a shrewd observation since Dr. Adams suspected Cousin D of making things unpleasant for his new wife. Although Fannie was then nearing her twenty-seventh birthday, her father fumed and fussed at her by mail, exhorting and lecturing her about settling her accounts for her expenses in New York and generally addressing her as a child.[56]

Perhaps as a response to Chamberlain's proprietary attitude, or from lack of faith in Fannie's resoluteness, the good pastor also rebuffed Chamberlain's inquiries for Fannie, acting as if he had no confidence in their new status and the young man's right to know about her. Annoyed, Chamberlain told Fannie, "He has mistaken his man. I am not so easily managed." But he tempered his vexation at his future father-in-law by observing, "There is no knowing how strangely a man will act when he is just married."[57]

Commencement week came, the social event of the year in Brunswick, and was made more elaborate and larger this year by the celebration of the semicentennial anniversary of the college. Although Chamberlain had the honor of the First Class Oration, in the crowded First Parish Church, it was not a success. The excitement, so many distinguished guests, the presence of "certain friends whose love and pride were at utmost tension," and no text from which to read had caused his old speech impediment to threaten. In the middle of the speech he nearly fainted; recovering, he paced the stage speaking extemporaneous phrases, concluding in a straight-out, forced delivery, his face crimson. He "was glad to get out of town" afterward, he said, but his journey home by boat was brightened by the presence of Fannie, who was bound for Bangor to visit friends; she would be presented proudly to his family as his betrothed wife.[58]

Chamberlain considered West Point again but rejected the idea; a peacetime military career still had no attraction for him. Enrolling in Bangor Theological Seminary, he began his usual heavy schedule of studies that October, made harder by his own decision to read his theology in German and Latin, two languages in which he thought he needed practice. Another requirement was the Hebrew language, which fascinated him, especially its structure; the language's "primeval conception of time," expressed in its tenses, opened new ways of thinking for him. "For the past resolved upon becomes the future, and the present but a flash, for while you speak it the future becomes the past," he explained it. With an eye toward possible missionary assignments in what was then considered the Orient, he also mastered "Arabic and Syriac."[59]

During that autumn of 1852, Chamberlain placed an engagement ring on Fannie's finger and they parted, not to see each other for nearly three long years. After being recommended for a position by her music instructor, Professor Root, Fannie traveled south by the steamer *Florida* out of New York, disembarking at Savannah and taking a train to Milledgeville, Georgia. There she taught voice at a school for girls, gave private piano lessons to those who wished them, and played the organ for the Presbyterian church. An old acquaintance of her father, Mrs. Orme, became a kind of sponsor for her and found her a congenial home in which to board. After a period of adjustment to her new situation, Fannie found her life busy and became happy in her new surroundings, but there were drawbacks. While she did not have her father or Cousin D fussing at her in person, she felt a great deal of social pressure from the women of the town to volunteer her time and participate in long and sometimes boring social events.[60]

Bangor Theological Seminary, located on a high hill across the Penobscot River, was over a mile from the Chamberlain home in Brewer; it was reached by the covered wooden bridge that connected the city and the town. Unlike most of his classmates, Chamberlain resolved not to accept financial help there; to finance his expenses, he organized German classes for young ladies in Bangor and played the organ at his own church in Brewer. He was appointed supervisor of schools in Brewer, his teaching experience during vacations, when he had again taught the generally difficult "grown up sailor boys and mill men" in the area, standing him in good stead. During some vacations he accompanied his father, an expert judge of timber, on journeys north into Canada, acting as an interpreter for the elder man among the French. One March and April they walked on snowshoes from the Penobscot to Rimouski on the St. Lawrence River, fished with Indians in their canoes, and then continued their journey by primitive fishing boats.[61]

But there was always his longing for Fannie throughout the long days and nights since he had seen her last. Daydreaming in golden reverie, his vivid imagination drawing on past passionate moments with her, Chamberlain wrote long love letters, pouring out his heart. In the first months of their engagement, Fannie apparently had wanted a platonic marriage only, considering, as he understood it, "that children are the result of a tyrannical cruel abuse and prostitution of woman" and rebelling "at all the Bible said about it." Showing his extreme disappointment at her position and acknowledging his concurrence if she wanted to avoid the danger and pain of childbirth, he chose his words carefully but plainly in a forthright letter. He agreed to drop the subject if she would admit that adhering to her stand in their marriage was a matter that would require as much self-denial on her part as his. "Let me beg of you not to pretend that you have no passionate feelings," he said. "I think you are not so foolish as to suppose either you or I are destitute of a fair degree of humanity." Perhaps he thought she would change her mind in time, because this understanding did not seem to diminish his ardor, and he wrote glowingly of the future when she would at last be his.[62]

Although the young couple often communicated in private, though thinly veiled, phrases, Chamberlain let Fannie know in no uncertain terms how he felt about her and how she affected him. One time he went so far as to warn her, "Be careful how you kiss my lips or you will set me all on fire." Fannie would apparently tease her fiancé with plays on words, causing him once to rejoin with amusement, "I'm afraid you are getting to be a naughty girl aren't you?"[63]

There is no question, however, of the actual moral conduct of the two lovers when they were together. Affectionate and loving, they apparently tantalized each other mischievously sometimes, but Frances Caroline Adams was a woman of virtue and Joshua Lawrence Chamberlain a man of honor, as they would be characterized in their own time. Other than the considerations of religion and self-respect, there was the certain knowledge that to act otherwise would court scandal that would ruin not only Fannie's reputation, but Chamberlain's as well. In their society, especially with his choice of vocation, Chamberlain's whole professional future would be blighted, if not destroyed, by impropriety, and even if marriage ensued, the disgrace would be very hard to live down.[64]

Although Chamberlain had hoped that she would write at least once a week, Fannie wrote him infrequently. By the time she completed her many obligations and attended to her other correspondence, she claimed, she had little time left. In addition, her eyes gave her frequent pain, as they had from the time she could remember; after overuse, they would sometimes be inflamed and swollen nearly shut the next day. As a small child in Boston she had been terrified of becoming blind: in the arms of her Aunt Brewster, who suffered the same malady, she cried for hours with sore eyes, sobbing, "I poor little blind girl."[65]

Attending to the details of her personal appearance took a great deal of her time each day, and Fannie depended on Deborah Folsom to keep her up on the latest fashions. Cousin D, feeling that she and her sister's children had been driven from her brother-in-law's home by the presence of his new wife, had moved to Hoboken, New Jersey. Using funds sent to her by Fannie, Cousin D crossed the Hudson River into New York City to shop for the expensive dresses, silks, ribbons, laces, and furs Fannie loved. She also sewed extensively for her adopted niece, after lamenting that Fannie's lavish tastes and love of such finery were unbecoming a woman expecting to be a minister's wife and disclosed a weak place in her character.[66]

As the months passed slowly, growing into years, the romance between Chamberlain and Fannie had its highs and lows, their communication being incomplete and sometimes misunderstood. A little over a year after her arrival in Georgia, Fannie abandoned her stance that their marriage be a platonic one and, not willing to wait another year and a half to marry, urged Chamberlain to consider employment other than the ministry. Declaring herself unfit by "mind, character and temperament" to be a minister's wife, she asked to struggle with him, helping by teaching if necessary, if he had to take a lesser-paying position. Admitting that she had rather extravagant tastes and loved beautiful things, she stated that she nevertheless was willing to forgo them happily if he started out with a lower salary at some other occupation. In turn, she urged him to sacrifice a little of his "over-fastidious pride."[67]

For his part, Chamberlain's unwillingness to accept an inferior position prematurely seemed to stem from a fear that a poor beginning would blight his professional career to an extent that he could never rise above it. While he said he was willing to be married whenever Fannie felt she was prepared to take the step, Chamberlain made it clear he did not think that either of them were ready to go so far. Declaring his love again, he urged her to come north so they could be nearer each other. During the months that followed, Fannie seemed determined to find him a place teaching in the South, and once Chamberlain almost agreed, but nothing came of the proposals. Moody and downcast at times, Chamberlain took fifteen-mile rambles through the countryside, desperate to see his beloved. He also spent many musical hours playing the airs of German composers like Schubert on his bass viol, with Sae accompanying him on the piano. Joshua Chamberlain, apparently seeing his son's unhappiness, one night surprised him by suddenly declaring that if he were in his son's place, he would take Fannie and go to California and "get up a college or start something," a thought both amusing and attractive to the lovelorn swain.[68]

In the fall of 1854, both Chamberlain and Fannie's natural father, Ashur Adams, insistently urged her to return north as companion to her seriously ill sister Charlotte. She refused, even though things were not going well for her in Georgia. For the self-centered Fannie, life must have seemed to consist mostly of duty and constant seeking to please the important people in it, while striving for some autonomy for herself. The people close to her, including her father, Deborah Folsom, and then Chamberlain, took an attitude that they knew best how to manage her life and generally treated her as a recalcitrant child when she would not do as they wanted. To get her own way, she sometimes acted as if she were a willful, stubborn, thoughtless little girl with pretty charm, the same results playing out in never-ending circuitous cycles all her life.[69]

Seen by some as taking others' kindnesses to her as her due, Fannie apparently thought the demands put upon her by society, church, and her family were mostly unreasonable, but they were typical claims of the times and culture for a woman in her position. She could surely see in the life of Cousin D and other older women that continued spinsterhood was difficult and not usually a desirable status, and her years in Georgia earning her own living were not altogether happy ones. Fannie actually had few choices, and she knew it, but she rebelled at her lot anyway and fought with the wit and weapons she had.[70]

As part of his senior requirements at the seminary, Chamberlain had prepared for criticism and then preached four sermons at different churches, resulting in calls to pastorate from two after he graduated. As a licensed preacher he might earn fees doing occasional preaching to augment his income, but Chamberlain wanted to please Fannie in his choice of occupation if he could and would not permanently accept a "settled" ministry of a church. He knew that sometimes Fannie thought he was somehow deceiving her, suspecting him of "meaning to preach all the time" after they were married, or that he would expect her to live in a place that she would hate. These things troubled him, but he wrote to her that if she could look into his eyes when she doubted him, "she could read there the tenderest love for her, resting on a broad & strong ground—my first & greatest duty to God." And in spite of the fears, doubts, and conflicts that assailed him, he told her of the faith that would guide and sustain him always: "I believe that God is over all things & that he will put me where he wants me and where I ought to be."[71]

The long separation of the young couple was over just before the first day of August in 1855. Fannie returned from Georgia in time to see Chamberlain take his master's degree from Bowdoin and share in his triumph then. Graduating from the theological seminary the week before, he had been invited to represent his class for the second degree at Bowdoin and give the Master's Oration at the Bowdoin commencement. "Law and Liberty" was the subject he chose, and when he stepped out to deliver his speech on the same stage he had left three years before in consternation and failure, his face was flushed with confidence.[72]

Chamberlain posited that "the superabounding life lavished in the universe was proof that the play of infinite freedom was to work out the will of infinite law. The whole universe showed that Freedom was a part of Law." Finishing his performance with the sound of resounding applause in his ears, he found subsequent press notices enthusiastic, and favorable comments about the speech were heard for days. But the best result was that he was offered part of the work in the department of revealed and natural religion at the college.[73]

Chamberlain had to put off his marriage. Much to the vexation of Fannie, who became increasingly mortified as time went on, her family and friends in both Brunswick and Boston kept asking her pointed questions about when the event would take place, their doubts made plain to her. Hoping he would use it to encourage the authorities at Bowdoin to offer him enough salary to be married, she sent him a letter from one of her Southern friends that proposed still another employment scheme for him to keep school in the South. Rejecting it as unsuitable for a man of his education and prospects, Chamberlain nevertheless agreed that an allusion to the offer might help his negotiations with the college. He felt certain that the college authorities had respect for his abilities and admiration for his character and hoped they could offer him enough employment and salary to keep him there.[74]

When the next term opened at Bowdoin, Chamberlain was an instructor in logic and natural theology and, as tutor, was in charge of freshman Greek. The tutorship, preaching, and grading themes would probably help him make a modest living, but it was a beginning, and respectable enough. Two of his younger brothers were enrolled now at Bowdoin: Horace, nicknamed Hod, was beginning his junior year at age twenty, and John, entering as a freshman, had just turned seventeen. The latter's absence from home was particularly felt by their mother, and when she wrote to him in care of her oldest son, she addressed him "Johnny, my good boy, Johnny," as she told him how she missed him and admonished him to "mind Lawrence, be a scholar, be a man, be a Christian."[75]

Chamberlain's mother had advice for her eldest, too, after hearing from him that he was downcast. Apparently disappointed that after all his preparation, his occupation and salary were less than he had hoped, he told her he was seeking guidance and direction from God. She hastened to assure him that "he will find work for you, just where it will be best for you and for his glory . . . therefore be cheerful and not let your heart be troubled." And, answering an important question for him, no doubt, considering his limited finances, Mrs. Chamberlain said warmly that of course he and Fannie could "come home" for the winter months when the college was closed.[76]

Chamberlain finally agreed they should be married at the end of the college term, but Fannie was jealously cross and faultfinding when her foster sister Anna Davis was married in the Adams home early in November. Dr. Adams observed that Fannie and Chamberlain were very unhappy and spoke with his daughter about it, but he thought later he should have taken his wife's advice and said nothing: "It does no good," he wrote. When Chamberlain left for Brewer after the term ended later that month, Dr. Adams made note of it, but if there was anything unusual about his departure at that particular time, it was soon eclipsed by the joy Dr. Adams felt when he noted the birth of his own first natural child, a boy, born soon after.[77]

On December 7, 1855, four months after her return from the South,

Frances Caroline Adams and Joshua Lawrence Chamberlain were married by her father at half-past four in the afternoon on a cold, clear winter's day. They were the first couple to be married in the spacious nine-year-old church building, the wedding undoubtedly not held in the parsonage because of Helen Adams's confinement. Dr. Adams had deep reservations. Although he now regarded his new son-in-law with affection, he wrote his true feelings about the marriage of his dearly loved daughter in his diary: "*I feel sadly about poor Fanny* fearing greatly she will not make herself happy."[78]

But the young couple was happy, and for now, ecstatically. Together at last, after so many years of separation and longing, they spent their wedding night in Fannie's bedchamber. There she had dreamed her own girlish dreams in the years before, and she would always remember the night there, she told him later, "when I first pillowed my head on your bosom, your own beloved wife." Chamberlain remembered that he took her into "the arms that once lifted her up among the leaves and the roses . . . on that wedding night—that sweetest and purest and ever to be honored night." And he loved her then with "a soul and a passion too, as strong as ever a woman could be loved with, almost too much awful desperate power in it, for the peace and safety of a frail sweet honeysuckle girl."[79]

Returning to Brunswick nearly seven weeks later, after a wedding trip and visit with the Chamberlains in Brewer, the young couple settled into the rooms they rented at the Starwood house. When they were apart, Chamberlain had dreamed of the future when they could spend hours together studying and reading, and Fannie could paint and draw; there was time for that now. He had never spoken of her intellectual qualities to her, or how her paintings spoke to him, but he told her now. Spring and summer came and went, and at the next commencement Chamberlain was elected Bowdoin's new professor of rhetoric and oratory. He had come a very long way from his student days when he had stammered so badly he was reticent to speak at all.[80]

And one day in that October, when the harvest was in and the countryside golden with Indian summer, Chamberlain's father came home from Bangor announcing to his delighted wife, "Lawrence and Fannie have a daughter!" Dr. Adams pronounced the new granddaughter "a beautiful child," and the new father, in poetic phrase years later, fancied that an angel of God had visited his house then, leaving "his living smile." For this favor from heaven, the baby was named Grace, and in recognition of her grandmother's Huguenot ancestral line, Dupee.[81]

At the end of the long winter vacation in early 1857, Fannie and the baby, later known as Daisy, stayed in Brewer, where Mrs. Chamberlain and Sae could help with the care of the infant. At age twenty, Sae was eleven years younger than Fannie and a bright, cheerful, and religious young woman who in the years ahead would write much of the hometown and family news to her absent brothers. The two sisters-in-law became good friends. Chamberlain kept their rooms in Brunswick at the Wilde house on Potter Street but lived in his room at the college, which he had fixed up with a new carpet, a stand-up desk, and other touches to give, he noted with satisfaction, a very scholarly look to the place. The young professor was happier than he had ever been, in spite of the absence of his little family, and Fannie was happy in her new life, too, although missing her husband and longing for his presence.[82]

A temporary misunderstanding clouded their bliss for a short time when Chamberlain became angry after reading letters Fannie had written long before to a male friend. By her frantic protestations that he was misunderstanding her words, and repeated reassurances of her love, she was apparently able to convince her new husband of her deep feelings for him. There was nothing in her letters she had not told him of before, and she had avoided showing them to him sooner, she said, because of her fear of inducing one of "those fearful, morbid states of feeling into which you so often fall." Grieving for his hurt and lack of faith in her, Fannie begged him to realize that "if you *knew* the wealth of my soul's love for you, *you would not ask for more.*"[83]

Fannie took a long trip to Boston alone that spring, leaving the baby and Chamberlain in Brunswick, to shop for furniture for their rooms. Wanting to "make your hard-earned money go farthest," she wrote her husband, she decided to buy what she could at auction to get the best prices. At great pains to economize, although she had trusted her husband to buy some things locally without her, she was afraid he was too good-natured and would be taken advantage of when it came to bargaining cost. He must have been so open and guileless that Fannie was afraid the town gossips would know all their business, so she cautioned him against asking others' opinion of his purchases. But her mood was cheerful as she visited her family in Boston, and her letters to her husband were loving and optimistic about their life together.[84]

Chamberlain missed his wife terribly while she was gone, dreaming of her at night and hoping for her return. "Perhaps I am too much a lover for a husband, as the world goes," he reflected. Worried about their finances, he told Fannie she should not have married a "poor boy" like him. But Mrs. Chamberlain offered to act as housekeeper until other help for Fannie could be found, and Mr. Chamberlain was anxious to help his son and daughter-in-law. John Chamberlain came to board with them, his parents paying for him at the prevailing rate, which gave more assistance to the young family's limited finances.[85]

At commencement that year, Chamberlain's brother Horace graduated. He read law and was admitted to the bar, settling afterward at Bangor for a career in law. Chamberlain would miss his brother, who some said was much like him and with whom he had a close relationship. He had enjoyed having him nearby to cheer him and to commiserate with. That November, on the night before Thanksgiving, Fannie gave birth to a son, a child three months premature who was, in the words of Dr. Adams, "the image of Fanny." But the newborn lived only a few hours, and consequently John Chamberlain became the only guest at the saddened holiday dinner table in the Adams home that year. George and Helen Adams could well understand the Chamberlains' grief; their own baby boy had died the previous Christmas.[86]

After being given assistance with some of the work of the department of rhetoric at the college, the earnest Chamberlain, looking dignified with a silk tie under the high collar of his starched white linen shirtfront, taught the modern languages of German and Spanish. But he still worked hard on his new ideas for teaching his rhetoric students the uses and appreciation of their native language while developing their powers of expression by encouragement and stimulation of their undergraduate minds. The year before he had graded and returned over 1,200 themes, and he spent the winter vacation of 1857–58 preparing a series of lectures for his rhetoric classes. Not that the lectures were particularly valuable in themselves, he rather modestly explained to a visiting committee, but they gave refreshment to his own mind, which he thought dulled by the constant work with the themes, and would also serve as teaching devices for his pupils.[87]

Chamberlain moved his family to another house for nearly a year, and when Indian summer came again, another son made his entrance into the world, this child also resembling Fannie. After a few months of anxiety for his young life, in which Mrs. Chamberlain came to help care for him, the boy grew healthily and was named Harold Wyllys Chamberlain, becoming known in the family as Wyllys.[88]

The next spring Chamberlain bought the Wilde house near the college, where he and Fannie had previously lived in rented rooms. A modest but roomy Federal-style, one-and-one-half-story "Cape," it had a large attached ell connected to a barn in the rear and a beautiful garden. It had some drawbacks—Sae thought it "too bad" that Fannie had no front stairs—but it would do for a few years. Chamberlain usually spent every hour he could spare at outside exercise; his garden, where in season he usually began work at five in the morning, gave him additional opportunity to keep fit. The house was attractive to the young couple for another reason: Henry Wadsworth Longfellow, a Bowdoin graduate, former professor at the college, and already renowned as a poet, had brought his bride to this house nearly thirty years before when he rented three rooms of it.[89]

As the months and years passed in Brunswick, Chamberlain became a respected citizen, taking his little family to church, on outings, and on occasional visits to Brewer. He spent what time he could in vigorous outdoor exercise, sometimes fishing in the trout streams and rowing on the bay with his students, forming friendships that would endure for a lifetime. After seeing him working in his garden on early morning drives, a retired sea captain, who was also the town's leading banker, offered to lend the young professor money whenever he wanted. Undoubtedly in recognition of Chamberlain's honesty and integrity, the banker also made him coexecutor of his considerable personal estate in his will.[90]

John Chamberlain graduated from Bowdoin in 1859 and entered the Bangor Theological Seminary, carrying what would be his mother's last hope for a minister in the family. Chamberlain's salary was $1,100 a year in 1860, as much as the older professors were paid and a tribute to the young professor's competence. That spring another Chamberlain daughter made her appearance in the brown cottage on Potter Street. But in September, Dr. Adams had the mournful duty of conducting the funeral of little Emily Stelle Chamberlain, who, her father later remembered, "left but a summer smile and aching hearts, as she departed with the flowers." In addition to the loss of her children, Fannie had seen the deaths of nearly all her Boston family and her foster sister Anna over a period of only a few years.[91]

Tragedy struck the Chamberlains again when Horace Chamberlain died of lung disease in December of 1861. Chamberlain had taken Daisy to Brewer to be with his family during the winter vacation and to spend some time with his dear brother and his young wife during his last days. Fannie

Professor Joshua L. Chamberlain, 1859
(courtesy Bowdoin College, Archives class photograph albums, Hawthorne-Longfellow Library)

remained at home with Wyllys and Cousin D. Deborah Folsom had returned to Brunswick after Anna's death and was staying with the young couple, her former animosity apparently mollified by the kind treatment of George and Helen Adams. Chamberlain was deeply saddened by Horace's death and had a difficult time in the next few months realizing his brother was really gone. Comforted by the fact that Horace had experienced happiness in a pleasant if short life, Chamberlain nevertheless felt that a support had been suddenly removed from him and "one of the greatest sources of pleasure in this world was sealed up."[92]

In a letter to his sister two months later, Chamberlain followed the Christian ideal of the times in hoping that his parents were not only well but "cheerful," apparently bearing up under God's will, and in a passage about Horace, he expressed his beliefs about death:

"So it is not after all for him, *as it is for the thought of the thing, for myself, and for us all, that I feel sad. That he should be cut down at the very opening of his career, and when he had so much reason to anticipate a prosperous course, seems almost against the order of nature. For* him *I have no doubt, the change is not a sad one. I do not think for a moment that it is not infinitely better for him, and that having once passed the great boundary he had no wish to be here again."*[93]

But personal concerns and sorrows were overshadowed by the rapid turn of events in the nation. The institution of slavery had been a source of emotional debate and violence even before its inclusion in the Constitution, and political compromises had kept the nation from splitting apart in the decades following ratification.

"The fathers of the Republic found slavery an existing fact and had to deal with it. Some long recognized property rights were involved in it, and relative wrong would be done by its immediate abolition. There can be no doubt that the sentiment and intent of the whole country was that a system so repugnant to justice and freedom as that of slavery should be limited, not extended,—repress[ed], not encouraged; and that some way should be found to satisfy equitable rights of property, and wipe that blot off from our escutcheon."[94]

The election of Abraham Lincoln as president of the United States the year before had signaled to many Southerners the death knell of their way of life, and one by one, eleven Southern states eventually declared themselves out of the old Union and a part of a new country—the Confederate States of America. Paramount in Chamberlain's political beliefs was that the United States was a Union of one people, that the "fathers did not vote themselves into a people; they recognized and declared that they were a people." That point established, he thought of the people in the singular: "The people was to grow up into a nation." The people living in the states constituted the people of the United States, and all formed the indivisible Union. The country and its land "belonged to us all, and we to it." When secession came, "it was no peaceful separation; it was war upon the Union; and that meant the destruction of the United States,—body, life, and being."

"The slave-holding spirit was not contented with toleration; it demanded mastery of the Country. And it got it. But the people of the free states were unwilling to see slavery established in the territories of the Union, and so made national; it tried their temper to be summoned from their homes to aid in capturing fugitive slaves,—in sending men and women however humble back to be outraged in every sensibility left in their natures. And when this true feeling found expression at last in an election of a President where this was a distinct issue, the slave States threatened secession and resistance. Even at this crisis, humiliating as it was, both Houses of Congress and the President himself declared that they had not the power, the right nor the intentions to meddle with slavery where it was. We would not right the wrong at the cost of Country. Loyalty to freedom was held in abeyance by loyalty to the Union."[95]

On April 12, 1861, the guns of the state of South Carolina opened fire on the United States's Fort Sumter in Charleston harbor, and the country was doomed to civil war as the "old flag," the Stars and Stripes of the United States, was hauled down and the fort surrendered. Thousands of men rallied to the call of President Lincoln for troops to preserve the Union and their country. Over half a million men on both sides would lose their lives in the conflict, but in the beginning it was all excitement, flags, and parades.[96]

"The flag of the Nation had been insulted. The honor and authority of the Union had been defied. The integrity and the existence of the People of the United States had been assailed in open and bitter war."[97]

At Bowdoin, some upperclassmen enlisted immediately; one was in a Confederate prison, wounded, when his class graduated in August. Other students organized drill companies called the Bowdoin Guard and a rival Bowdoin Zouaves, which boasted instructors educated in the Maine militia and a military school—and one who had trained with the famous Elmer Ellsworth's Zouaves. Without uniforms, but armed with guns and ammunition furnished by the government, the students marched and skirmished down Maine Street, the principal thoroughfare in Brunswick, as if bent on capturing the Topsham bridge. An interested onlooker at many of these drills, watching closely the execution of the different commands, was the quiet professor of modern languages, taking it all in.[98]

Bowdoin alumni flocked to the colors: nearly three hundred Bowdoin men would serve the Union cause in the war. And given their patriotic feelings, some of those who remained in school surely longed for adventure and chafed with boredom under the monotonous sameness of everyday life there and in the small, slow town of Brunswick. Chamberlain was probably one of those who thought the war would be a short one, but as time went on and the hostilities heightened, it was not only the students whose minds wandered with unrest. An "irresistable impulse" stirred in their popular young professor to have his hand in the conflict. Chamberlain already had his leave of absence for study in Europe, and when he made his offer of service to Governor Washburn, he was surely hoping to discern the hand of God guiding his future course in whatever response the governor made. As he was always wont to do in making any important decision, he would have been looking for God's will for him on the issue; but his strong convictions, formed early in life, honed by his liberal education, and sharpened by the national debate, must have had a great deal of influence on his actions.[99]

* * *

After a month of animated preparation, when the Twentieth Maine Infantry Regiment left Portland on the train that September morning in 1862 bound for "the seat of war," as the saying went, its lieutenant colonel left behind all who were dear to him to fight the forces that threatened him and them. It seemed ironic to him now that he had once rejected West Point because he thought it would lead to being a soldier in time of peace. A young cousin had once told him that God had chosen him to do a great work, "to be his minister in a higher sense than the word," and would call him when he was needed. He could not know that years later there would be those who thought that she spoke with the words of a prophet—that this quiet professor turned soldier would be a man of destiny. He would go down into the Biblical valley of the shadow of death before this war was over, and he would never know if he followed God's command or if he should seek divine forgiveness. But now an adventuresome unknown stretched in front of him, and the future shimmered tantalizingly, just beyond his vision.[100]

"We know not of the future, and cannot plan for it much. But we can hold our spirits and our bodies so pure and high, we may cherish such thoughts and such ideals, and dream such dreams of lofty purpose, that we can determine and know what manner of men we will be whenever and wherever the hour strikes that calls to noble action. . . . No man becomes suddenly different from his habit and cherished thought."[101]

CHAPTER

Three

THE TWENTIETH MAINE

"Where are you from?" an idling sailor yelled to the new soldiers marching through Boston. Some local residents, who had seen many a green regiment tramp the city's narrow streets on its way to the war, turned to watch. A former Maine lumberman roared back, "From the land of spruce gum and buckwheat cakes!" Everyone laughed; then an old man swung his hat and called for three cheers for the old Pine Tree State, and the following "Hip! Hip! Hip!" and then "Hooray!" rang pleasantly in the ears of Chamberlain and the Twentieth Maine as the citizens' tribute echoed for blocks. Reaching the wharves of the busy Massachusetts port, the regiment then filed aboard the huge United States steamer *Merrimac*, which would take it south.[1]

After making themselves comfortable in their commodious transport, the Maine men heard the sounds of music and cheers heralding the arrival of the Thirty-second Massachusetts Volunteers. The latter was an oversize regiment of 1,200 Union troops, which crowded on and filled the coastal steamer to capacity. As the boat pulled away from the dock, the men nearly packed like sardines, a Massachusetts soldier climbed the rigging and called for three cheers for "Old Abe," then for "the red, white, and blue," and still more until the men were hoarse from cheering. They were going to war, they thought, and just in time too. The papers were full of news of a Union defeat at a second battle of Bull Run in Virginia, not far from Washington, D.C. Old Abe needed all the help he could get. But it took a journey of several days to ply their way through the green Atlantic waters, rolling and placid now before the autumn storms.[2]

Colonel Ames employed much of the time on the voyage teaching the officers tactics, which surely gave him an opportunity to size up his key men. With his quick comprehension and customary study habits, Chamberlain could not have helped impressing him. The vessel was rife with rumors that disaster would befall the ship at any moment, but the only real excitement was engendered by several bunks breaking loose from their moorings, causing a panic that the ship had foundered on the rocks. Arriving safely four days later at Alexandria, Virginia, on the wide Potomac River, the regiment camped on the outskirts of the city. Shortly before, the *Merrimac* had steamed by George Washington's home at Mount Vernon, a place inspiring such reverence that many soldiers took off their caps in respect as they passed.[3]

Before they left for Washington the next day, however, the untried soldiers saw boat after boat with decks filled with wounded from the Bull Run battle, a hard sight for new men. Reaching the arsenal at Washington, they were issued Enfield rifles and forty rounds of ammunition and camped, as Capt. Ellis Spear described it, "on a downy bed of dead cats, bricks and broken bottles." The city of Washington was alive with the military—squadrons of cavalrymen on their hardy mounts, battery horses pulling the big cannon through the streets, wagon trains of supplies, and soldiers everywhere. It was Sunday, and though the church bells would have certainly been ringing for services, the city was a sharp contrast to the quiet Sabbaths the men were used to at home.[4]

By way of Long Bridge across the Potomac, the regiment was marched seven miles without a halt to join its assigned brigade near Fort Craig in Virginia. It was a difficult march, each man burdened with his personal possessions, heavy new musket, and ammunition, and it proved to be a disheartening one. The musicians performed again with nearly the same harmony as at Camp Mason—each kept different time, and each man in the regiment kept a different step. "Old soldiers sneered; the people laughed and cheered; we marched, ran, walked, and galloped, and stood still, in our vain endeavors to keep step," remembered one private. Colonel Ames was so mortified at the ludicrous performance that he bellowed, "If you can't do any better than you have tonight, you better all desert and go home!"[5]

Footsore and tired, the Twentieth stacked arms and made camp near the five other, veteran regiments from New York, Pennsylvania, and Michigan that constituted its new brigade, numbered the Third in the First Division of the Fifth Army Corps, Army of the Potomac. The regiment would stay with this brigade, known as "the Light Brigade" while under the command of Gen. Daniel Butterfield, until after the end of the war, and Chamberlain would never serve with any other division or corps until the great Army of the Potomac was only a memory. Following the harsh Peninsula campaign and the Union debacle at Bull Run, the other battle-scarred regiments were worn and reduced in numbers; the Maine men would be a welcome addition to the brigade's strength. As new members to the outfit, however, they would have to prove themselves adept in drill and courageous in battle before they could be fully accepted by the old soldiers, who had a reputation to uphold.[6]

Confederate Gen. Robert E. Lee and his Army of Northern Virginia had crossed the Potomac into Maryland, threatening Washington, Baltimore, and perhaps Pennsylvania, should they be allowed to proceed unchallenged. Maj. Gen. George B. McClellan, who had been temporarily relieved from the command of the Army of the Potomac after the summer Peninsula campaign, was reinstated after Gen. John Pope had led his Army of Virginia and part of the Army of the Potomac to inglorious defeat at the second battle of Bull Run, or Second Manassas, as it was called by the Confederates. Now, when McClellan learned that Lee was moving north, he moved his army cautiously and disposed his marching columns so that Washington and Baltimore could still be protected.[7]

On September 12, 1862, the First Division of the Fifth Corps moved out of its camps, and the Twentieth Maine began its first long march. The soldiers of the Twentieth looked down from the Arlington Heights to see the blue columns of troops that preceded them crossing the Potomac River, bands playing, sunlight sparkling off the burnished rifle barrels, and artillery, cavalry, and wagons in myriad profusion. Chamberlain was at Ames's

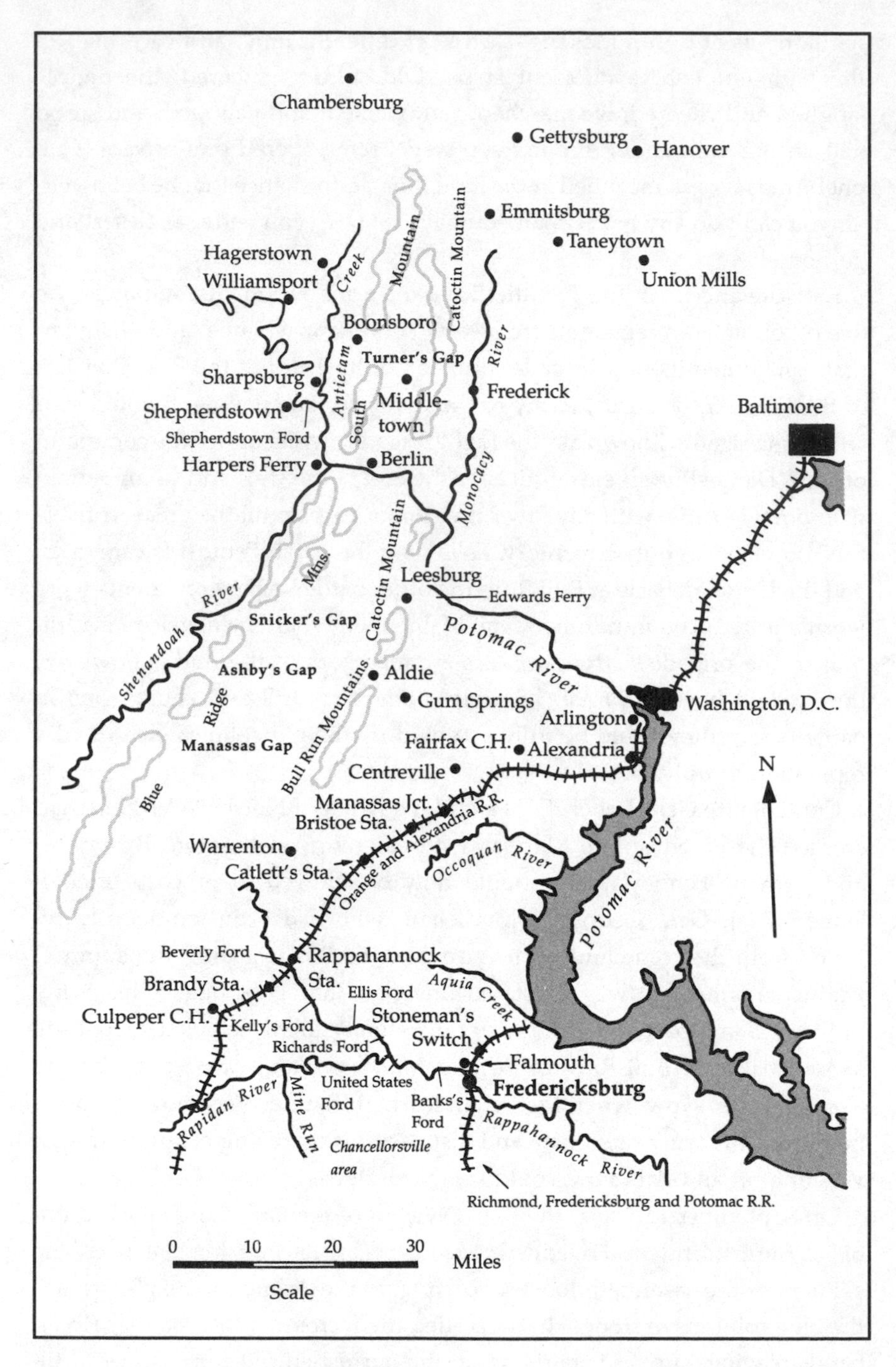

MAP 2. *Chamberlain's Field of War, 1862–1863*

side, the two ranking officers of the regiment making a handsome pair sitting erect upon their horses. Joining the column, the men of the regiment swung into the route step, where march time did not have to be kept, their new uniforms and accoutrements contrasting with the worn and more varied apparel of the veterans. The latter marched with renewed vigor and confidence, their morale restored when they heard that the immensely popular General McClellan was again leading them.[8]

Leaving the city of Washington behind and moving northwest into Maryland toward Frederick the next day, the men in the new regiments began discarding all extra items along the side of the road to lighten their loads. Although some of the winter clothing of the Twentieth Maine's men had been left behind in Washington, like other inexperienced soldiers, they surely were weighted down at first with a great deal of equipment and other items, both official and personal. More experienced veterans rolled many of the bare necessities into a blanket worn across the body and over the shoulder, with canteens and mess articles clinking from their belts. Sweating in their woolen uniforms, with the choking dust rolling up into their mouths, the beginners still struggled to keep up. Strong men, whose will could no longer command their faltering bodies, fell behind under the unaccustomed strain of close order marching for miles in the hot September sun and caught up with their outfits later, some after dark.[9]

One lost private of another new regiment in the same division with the Twentieth came upon Maj. Gen. George W. Morell, the division commander. Undaunted by the officer's superior rank, and innocently thinking that surely the general would be the one to know the answer to his question, the dusty and bedraggled enlisted man touched his cap and asked, "General, can you tell me where the 118th Pennsylvania is?" "Certainly, my man," answered Morell courteously. "Everywhere between here and Washington!"[10]

After a forced march of twenty-four miles on the next day, September 14, the exhausted men of the Twentieth Maine went into bivouac upon arrival at the Monocacy River two miles from Frederick, Maryland. All day they could hear the sounds of distant cannon, as elements of the Union army battled the Confederates for possession of three South Mountain passes. South Mountain was the name for part of a range of low mountains; south of the Potomac River it was called the Blue Ridge. It ran north from the Potomac through Maryland into Pennsylvania, and west of it was most of Lee's army. The next day the division marched through Frederick, welcomed by that city of mostly Union sympathies as enthusiastically as their predecessors had been on previous days, flags and handkerchiefs waving; ladies at their front gates gave out water and loaves of soft bread to the grateful soldiers.[11]

Heading west, the blue columns left the city behind, and the men made camp again in a beautiful, fertile valley near Middletown, after a comparatively short march through Catoctin Mountain. Along the way, the men of the Twentieth saw their first Rebel prisoners being taken to the rear—"tall, lank, slouchy looking fellows clad in dirty gray uniforms," one private described them. After camp was set and darkness fell, everywhere a man could look thousands of fires gleamed and flickered in the night with groups of men around them, and the moon shone blue-white on the pale canvas tops of wagons parked nearby. Beyond South Mountain, which was now in the near distance, the stage was being set for the bloodiest day in the American Civil War.[12]

Very early the next morning, Chamberlain and the Twentieth Maine resumed their march. The signs of war were all around them as they went forward—wounded lay in every house and barn, and fresh mounds of earth showed where others had been buried. In that part of Maryland the mountains do not rise abruptly out of the plain, but the ground gradually rises on either side of them, the country hilly and rolling. Morell's division of three brigades marched on the old National Road, Col. T. W. B. Stockton of the Sixteenth Michigan Regiment commanding the Third Brigade. As it entered Turner's Gap, the main pass through South Mountain, unmistakable signs of battle were seen: debris everywhere at the side of the road, knapsacks, guns, hats, earth torn up, and trees blasted by shells and bullets.[13]

Near a stone wall, where the Confederates had made a desperate stand against the valorous advance of Gen. John Gibbon's "Black Hat" brigade nearly thirty-six hours before, lay the unburied bodies of Rebels killed in the battle. Many of the bodies were bloody and bloated, a terrible sight for the Maine men, who were unused to such scenes. Chamberlain was no exception. He saw the figure of a soldier wearing a Confederate uniform sitting with his back against an old tree, one hand clasping a small Testament, his hat on the ground beside him. Drawing closer, Chamberlain saw that it was a boy "of scarcely sixteen summers," apparently asleep, graceful, fair, even childlike. Startled, it was hard for Chamberlain to realize that "this was my enemy—this boy!" His next thought must have been breathed hurriedly, almost automatically—"Oh, God forgive those who made us so!" He soon saw that the eyes on the young face were soft and dim, and red had stained the shirt; the youth indeed had fallen asleep, perhaps not so soon as his comrades, but he would never awaken here. Sick at heart, Chamberlain would remember that day on South Mountain: "He was dead—the boy, my enemy; but I shall see him forever."[14]

But there was no time to tarry. As the Maine regiment marched down the mountain pass toward the lovely little town of Boonsboro, the booming of cannon could be heard ahead. Lee was fast consolidating his army on a line in front of the small Maryland town of Sharpsburg, positioning his men to give battle. The Confederate line stretched across the rough angle formed by a wide bend in the Potomac River, which snaked a distance behind the town, protecting a vital ford in the river leading to Virginia and the road to Harpers Ferry. Well-concealed Rebel infantry was strengthened with artillery posted on heights of the undulating ground near Sharpsburg. A mile east of the town was a deep stream called Antietam Creek, which ran south into the Potomac, and although Lee's lines effectively controlled the two bridges north of its mouth, high ground behind it on the east gave ample room for the big Union guns placed there. Its upper bridge was in Union hands, and Union infantry was disposed near the heights along the eastern side of the stream. Cannon from both sides sometimes fired at each other across the pastures, woods, and fields of the rolling countryside.[15]

Morell's division with Chamberlain and the Twentieth Maine proceeded on the road from Boonsboro to Keedysville and joined McClellan's massed army near noon on September 16. After many aggravating halts and delays caused by hundreds of wagons, troops, and artillery, they passed through the narrow main street of the picturesque village of Keedysville. It was late afternoon before they camped just beyond it on the south side of the road. Across the way, the slopes were black with men and equipment as far as the eye could see, as preparations for battle proceeded. Musket fire could be heard as Gen. Joseph Hooker's First Corps crossed Antietam Creek to the north and established itself there, ready to attack Lee's left the next morning.[16]

That night it rained, and there was little sleep for anyone. Undoubtedly wondering what part they would have in the battle obviously about to take place, the Maine men could not have had any illusions about their own competence, regardless of their enthusiasm. They could barely march in rudimentary formation, let alone quickly load and fire their cumbersome

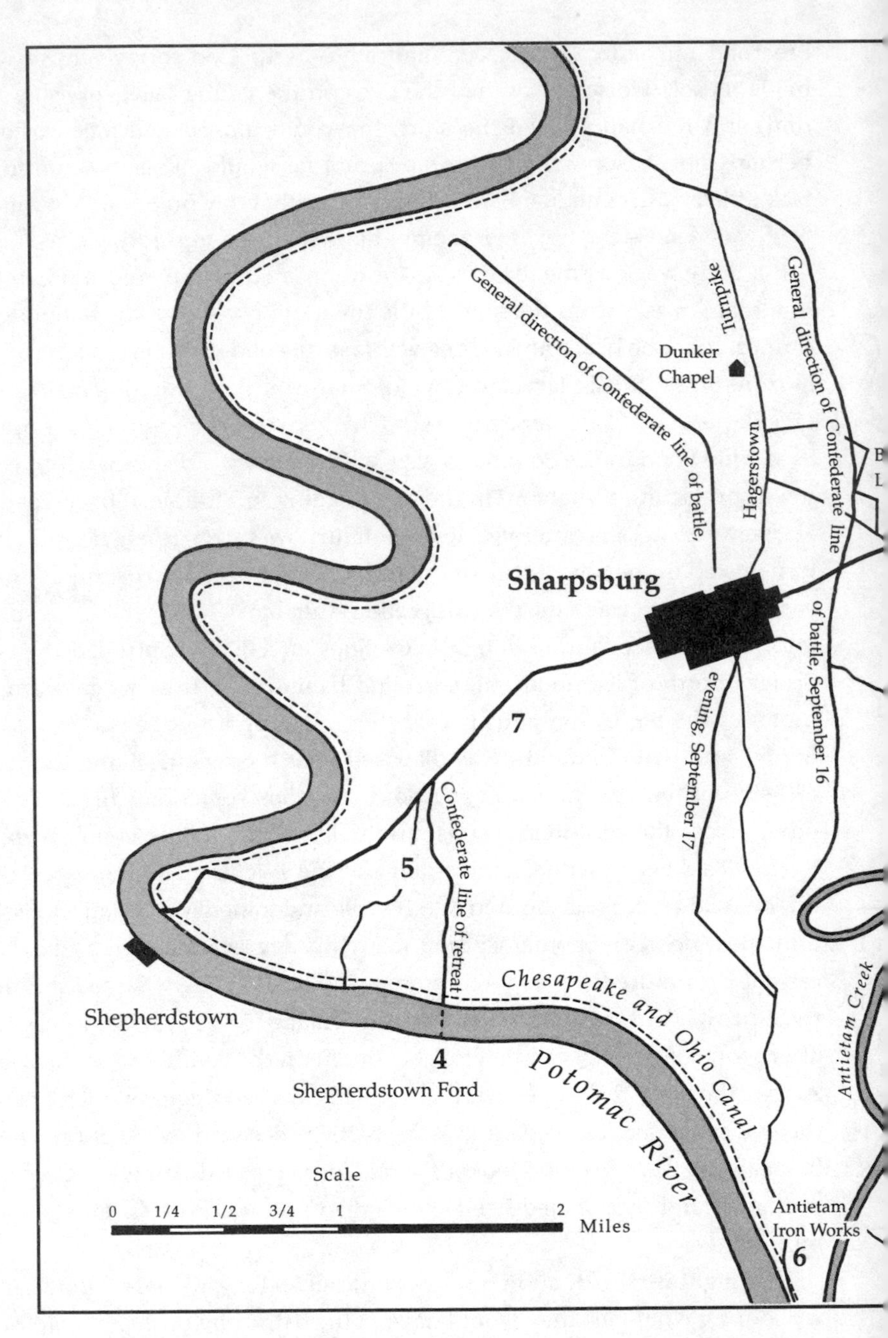

MAP 3. *Battle of Antietam, September 17, 1862*

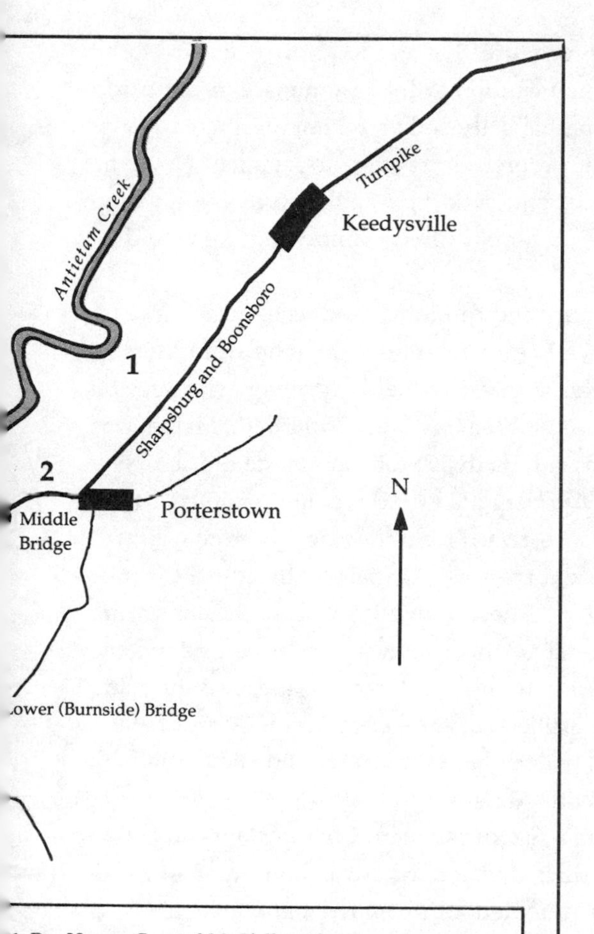
Antietam Creek
Turnpike
Keedysville
Sharpsburg and Boonsboro
1
2
Middle
Bridge
Porterstown
N
ower (Burnside) Bridge
1 Pry House, General McClellan's headquarters during the battle
2 Position of Twentieth Maine during battle
3 Position of Twentieth Maine, September 18
4 Shepherdstown Ford
5 Position of first "training camp" of Twentieth Maine
6 Position of final "training camp" of Twentieth Maine
S. P. Grove House, Fifth Corps headquarters after Confederate retreat

rifle muskets, a complicated procedure that needed much practice to be effective in a fight. All in all, they would hardly be a menace in combat to anyone but themselves and perhaps the other regiments in their own brigade. But if their brigade was ordered into battle, no regiment would be left out due to its inexperience, and who knew what tomorrow would bring? As the sun went down, each man surely wondered if he would be among the living then.[17]

At dawn, the sound of musketry and cannon announced the advance by Hooker's First Corps as it struck Lee's left. Across the road from Morell's division of the Fifth Corps, the slopes and fields teeming with life the evening before were empty. After breakfast, the Twentieth Maine was ordered to "fall in" and moved with its division in column to a place a few yards to the north of the Sharpsburg Pike under a line of hills. Union batteries thundered at intervals westward from the ridge, in front of which a stone bridge crossed the creek at the road. On the south side of the pike was Sykes's division of Regulars. These two Fifth Corps divisions were placed in reserve near the center of the Union position, controlling the bridge from the Union side, ready to move if the call came, and guarding the wagon trains and reserve artillery of the entire army. Occasionally a Confederate shell would burst over them, or a heavy solid shot would fall behind the hill, but there was little danger.[18]

Along with other officers and a few of the men, Chamberlain climbed to the high ground in front of their division where Union batteries were posted. The deadly spectacle unfolded in extended panorama to these observers from afar; the rattle of musketry and boom! boom! boom! of cannon rose with the battle smoke. As the two armies met with a shock and parted, charged and countercharged out of woods and over the fields of corn and meadows, the tiny figures in the distance fell and dotted the ground. High-pitched Rebel yells, the "yi-yihs" sounding in distant scream, were interspersed with ringing cheers from the men in blue; both echoed to the ears of the intensely interested audience on the heights above the Antietam. Trees, battle smoke, and the rolling ground kept much of the far-flung action from sight, but sometimes the lines of battle could be seen, with bright flags marking the different regiments. One private could see "Meagher's Irish Brigade charge on the 'rebs' and wavering once, charge again, with victory as their bloody purchase."[19]

General McClellan rode down from his headquarters at the Pry house, which was to the rear and high above the divisions of the Fifth Corps, and as he came into view, cheers filled the afternoon air. Acknowledging the enthusiastic approval of his men, McClellan smiled, took off his hat, and bowed to them from his horse. The short, sturdy young general had always enjoyed a tremendous popularity with this army, undiminished by the failure of his late "On-To-Richmond" Peninsula campaign. After the debacle at Bull Run, the knowledge that McClellan was again in command of the Army of the Potomac had immediately restored morale, and his soldiers loved the sight of him.[20]

But the bloodshed was not over. Gen. Ambrose E. Burnside, in command of the Union left, was ordered to seize the next lower bridge across the Antietam with his Ninth Corps, move forward, and strike the enemy right. Because of the nature of the terrain, the bridge and its approaches were completely commanded on high ground opposite Burnside, offering any attacking column a deadly flanking fire; it was not until one o'clock that the bridge was finally secured, with gallant bravery and loss by two Union regiments. Burnside did not advance with his whole force toward the town until more costly time had passed. By the time his men attacked, the Confederates had been reinforced by Maj. Gen. A. P. Hill's division, just arrived on the field after a forced march from Harpers Ferry. After a pitched battle, Burnside disengaged his force and withdrew but remained on the west side of the Antietam.[21]

Late in the afternoon, Stockton's brigade with the Twentieth Maine was one of two of Morell's brigades moved a mile or two to the right to support General Franklin's hard-fought men, but they were returned to their original position at sunset by order of General McClellan. It had been a long and terrible day; it would go down in history for generations as the nation's most sanguinary. But the next morning was filled with bright sunshine, with the wounded armies facing each other—wary, waiting, unwilling to renew the fight. Morell's division headed south by the ridge that lined Antietam Creek on the east and, after a long halt, crossed the bullet-marked stone bridge captured by Burnside's men, some relieving the survivors of that corps on the other side. The Union dead lay here in profusion, their silent forms offering grim portent of the future to the Maine soldiers still untried in battle. That night the Army of Northern Virginia disappeared across the Potomac River, its divisions nearly shattered but undestroyed by the reinforced McClellan, who missed his opportunity to crush Lee and his army, the best hope of the Confederacy.[22]

On September 19, Chamberlain and the regiment marched over the contested ground and through the town. Believing that the Union had won a victory over their adversaries, who had abandoned the field to them, the men were in good spirits. The battlefield was a horror. Bodies the burial parties had not yet reached, interspersed with dead horses, overturned caissons, and other debris, were stretched in sickening profusion over the rolling countryside. The stench was overpowering. Any romantic idea of war still lingering in the minds of the inexperienced soldiers must have completely disappeared by the time they entered the shell-damaged town. There the homes, dooryards, and churches overflowed with wounded, as did almost every building around Sharpsburg. The streets were full of wreckage, and staff officers and orderlies rode through them hurriedly as the foot soldiers moved through the mire on the main pike. Turning south off of the roadway beyond the village, the Maine men passed the S. P. Grove house, where the Fifth Corps headquarters would be established, and then bivouacked not far from the Potomac River. The Confederates had come this way the night before, recrossing the Potomac at the ford a mile below the Virginia town of Shepherdstown, where the river was usually shallow enough to allow the passage of men, animals, and supplies.[23]

Early the next morning, there was great excitement in the ranks of the Twentieth Maine as the men prepared for their first confrontation with the Rebels. A reconnaissance in force to ascertain Lee's rear guard was to be made by several Fifth Corps brigades in conjunction with some cavalry. Accordingly, brigades from Morell's and Sykes's divisions crossed the Potomac at the Shepherdstown Ford and climbed the high bluffs across the river to the plateau above. Progress was slow when crossing the stream, as the troops carefully found their footing in the swiftly flowing water. Reaching the Virginia bank, the Twentieth had begun climbing the bluff in their front when rapid firing was heard on their right. Hurrying to the crest, they reformed their line and, as the sound of musketry increased in volume, the men began to hear the zip, zip of bullets whizzing over their heads. A few gray forms were seen in the forest ahead, and some of the boys of the regiment got in a shot, but the order soon came to recross the river as quickly as possible. The Confederates had returned in great force, and Virginia was no place now for only a few Yankee brigades.[24]

Back down the steep incline the regiments scrambled, through the rocks and trees and then across the Potomac, followed by the fire of enemy marksmen whose minié balls splattered and plopped into the water around them like hailstones. One Twentieth Maine private later humorously described his regiment's retreat across the river as making "a most masterly advance on Maryland," but at that moment the men were in their first hot place, and they made for the shore hastily. That day Chamberlain was riding a black horse, lent to him by Major Gilmore in order to spare his own "splendid white horse," which he had named Prince, from exposure to fire. As Chamberlain was calmly steadying men of his own regiment and others through a deep place in the river, the major's steed was wounded in the head near the bridle and became the first of several horses to be shot under the intrepid lieutenant colonel. But the Maine men returned with only a few wounded, and until the other regiments had also crossed back, took their places in the dry Chesapeake and Ohio Canal, which ran parallel to the river and formed a natural breastwork.[25]

The action was not renewed, and the regiment settled down to help guard the river fords for nearly six weeks as the army rested and was refitted. Unfortunately, the officers and men of the Twentieth lived under poor conditions in camps where sanitary measures were not enforced. For a while the stench of the battlefield so permeated the air that the men could hardly bear to breathe it, and the water in the streams was so foul it was unfit to drink. Not completely supplied by the quartermaster department, the men had no tents and were lacking in many comforts that the other regiments had, even after camp was moved to the vicinity of the old Antietam Iron Works near the confluence of the Potomac and Antietam Creek. But grit and determination prevailed, and it was duty, training, and work, from the time the men rolled out of their blankets to fall in for roll call in the morning until they rested on the hard ground at night.[26]

Although he was an officer, whose status usually afforded better conditions, Chamberlain was not exempt from hardships and cheerfully accepted them. He felt lucky to get food to eat, sleep on anything but the ground, or under other than the sky. Apparently Fannie had expressed a wish to join him, a thought he found tantalizing but impractical. "My rubber blanket is not quite big enough to accommodate even so sweet & welcome a guest on the rough hillsides or the drenching valleys that constitute my changing homes," he wrote to her, thinking her "a dear little wife" to suggest it. "I should wonder to see a woman in our camp. Really I think the exposure & hardship would kill her in a week." One of his captains had his wife staying at nearby Boonsboro, he later conceded, but he added, "With my duties I could not get away . . . once in a month." If and when the army went into winter quarters, he said, "I shall let you come some *where near*." Meanwhile, he had arranged that she be sent $100 a month from his salary, and he urged her to do everything she wished and go everywhere she liked.[27]

"If we could get a glimpse of a woman who does not exceed the requirements for *sweepers* in college, we think we are in Paradise," Chamberlain wrote, no doubt trying for a smile from his dear recipient. Fannie would remember the college boys' joke about the primary qualification for sweepers, the hardworking, underpaid women employed to clean the students' rooms and make beds. To avoid potential scandal concerning women in the male dormitory rooms, undoubtedly more imagined than real, care had been taken to remove temptation rather than enforce discipline. A tradition arose that one straitlaced Bowdoin president would first inquire about a nominated applicant, "Is she sufficiently repulsive in her personal appearance?"[28]

Colonel Ames was determined that when his men went into battle the next time, they would be disciplined. The Fifth Corps was a formal outfit with an already proud reputation, its higher commands mostly filled with experienced West Pointers. When Tom Chamberlain came to visit in Chamberlain's tent, for example, as an enlisted man he would not think of sitting down in his older brother's presence unless specifically invited. Ames drilled the men unmercifully, knowing that only their rapid and automatic response to commands would make them effective militarily and save lives in the noise and confusion of battle.[29]

New England independence, curiosity, and tenacity were fine traits—a soldier possessing them had more potential to succeed than others who did not—but something more was needed to make individuals part of a smooth performing unit that could act in unison in a fight. To follow orders from men whom they sometimes considered below them in civilian life was hard for proud Yankees. It was also difficult for them to see why the routines of army life, with its formal schedules and ceremonies, had anything to do with putting down the rebellion in their beloved country.[30]

Drill and discipline, with unquestioned obedience to orders, were the heart and soul of making a recruit into a soldier. Hour by weary hour, four hours a day and more, the commands rang out in the Twentieth's camp. The maneuvers became more intricate as the complexity of the drill progressed, until some of the officers and men developed an intense dislike, even hatred, for their colonel. Tom Chamberlain wrote home that Ames would "take the men out to drill & he would d'n them up hill and down" and that "I tell you we have to do it well, or get a damning."[31]

"It is the discipline which is the soul of armies, as indeed the soul of power in all intelligence. Other things—moral considerations, impulses of sentiment, and even natural excitement—may lead men to great deeds; but taken in the long run, and in all vicissitudes, an army is effective in proportion to its discipline."[32]

In all likelihood most of the recruits from Maine had some knowledge of firearms, but the ability to quickly load and fire the cumbersome army rifle musket under combat conditions was considerably different from hunting in some pleasant forest or field. New soldiers were taught to "load in nine times," a procedure that included the following steps: hold the musket in front of the body, its butt between the feet, tear the paper cartridge with the teeth, pour the gunpowder from it down the barrel of the musket, insert the conical shaped bullet, withdraw the ramrod from under the barrel, tamp down the ball, replace the ramrod, remove the old cap and place a new one, shoulder arms, take aim properly, and fire, a belch of flame and smoke emitting from the rifle.[33]

The Twentieth devoted much practice to loading without firing to save ammunition, because in combat it was vitally important that a soldier reload and fire quickly without thinking of the mechanics. The muskets had a range of a thousand yards and were reasonably accurate at five hundred. In addition, there were stack arms, fix bayonets, bugle calls, and guard mounting instructions—a procedure had to be learned in a short time for almost every move a soldier made. Although he had more to learn, it would tax even Chamberlain to absorb all he needed.[34]

Working hard with Ames as his personal instructor in the tent they came to share, Chamberlain found it "no small labor to master the evolutions of a Battalion or Brigade." Writing to Fannie that "I *study*, I tell you—every military work I can find," he asked that she send his copy of Baron de Jomini's *The Art of War*. Everyone's hard work made the Twentieth so proficient in just a few weeks that Chamberlain was sure no other new regiment could exceed it.[35]

Ames thought later that success in the regiment's discipline was due to having "such hard-hearted men at its head" as the two of them, but the men felt differently about their second-in-command than they did about Ames. One private declared, "Lieutenant Colonel Chamberlain is almost idolized by the whole regiment. He makes a fine appearance, mounted on his rich present, at battalion drill, but he does not ride him in the presence of the enemy." Expanding beyond horses and outward show, the soldier continued: "Of course, I do not have much to do with him, yet, if I wanted any favors, I should apply to him at once, knowing that I should get them if it were in his power to confer them." After the regiment left the environs of Antietam, Ames had his lieutenant colonel conduct the drills.[36]

An affinity and camaraderie grew between Chamberlain and Ames as they worked together, and the jaunty Ames not only came to have a high opinion of Chamberlain but developed a real affection for him. Ames had been born in 1835 into a family of some military tradition. He was a son of a well-to-do sea captain in Rockland, Maine, who also owned his own trading schooner. As a youth, Adelbert went to sea with his father as cabin boy, sailing to many exotic foreign ports in Europe, Africa, and the Pacific islands. Young Ames taught himself through extensive reading when his travels took him from formal school on land, but he also received an excellent education in the public and private schools in Maine. However, Ames was of the opinion that his exposure to the rougher element of sailor and limekiln companions at Rockland was not a good influence on him as a young man; in fact, he thought these associations had somehow done him injury. Entering West Point at age twenty, he attained an excellent record, finishing fifth in his class in 1861. Later proving himself daring but exceedingly calm under fire, he communicated in an invariably polite way to his aides and fellow officers, his orders couched in the form of requests. The profane language of the drill field was gone.[37]

On October 1, 1862, President Lincoln came to talk with General McClellan and visit his army. When Lincoln was a guest at Fifth Corps headquarters, Chamberlain was able to observe a little more of the revered leader of the country than the glimpse of him usually seen at a review. He later remarked upon his "rugged features and deep, sad eyes."

"His figure was striking; stature and bearing uncommon and commanding. The slight stoop of the shoulders, an attitude of habitual in-wrapped thought, not of weakness, of any sort. His features, strong; if homely, then because standing for rugged truth. In his deep, over-shadowed eyes, a look as from the innermost of things. Over all this would come at times a play, or pathos, of expression in which his deeper personality outshone. His voice was rich; its modulations musical."[38]

A grand review of the army was held, an event calculated to enliven the spirits of soldiers and president alike. Lincoln, Chamberlain was to recall later, "wished to see the army together. This had a being, a place, a power, beyond the aggregate of its individual units." As the reviewing cavalcade came in front of the lines, the troops stood side by side, regiment by regiment, mounted officers in front of their commands.

"Slowly he rode along. . . . We could see the deep sadness in his face, and feel the burden on his heart, thinking of his great commission to save this people, and knowing that he could do this no otherwise than as he had been doing,—by and through the manliness of these men,—the valor, the steadfastness, the loyalty, the devotion, the sufferings and thousand deaths, of those into whose eyes his were looking. How he shrunk from the costly sacrifice we could see; and we took him into our hearts with answering sympathy, and gave him our pity in return."[39]

But the president smiled, and it was like an electric shock, moving from elbow to elbow: the men cheered him in response, their voices ringing in the October air. Checking his mount, the president drew McClellan's attention to Chamberlain's beautiful white-dappled horse, Prince, a gesture that the Maine lieutenant colonel would always remember. Then it was all over, and the great divisions dispersed. Chamberlain had thought Lincoln appeared a good horseman and that the review showed him to an advantage, but one unsentimental Twentieth Maine private still wrote home laconically that "old Abe Lincoln was . . . homely as a stump fence."[40]

After only a few weeks in the army, Chamberlain could feel a growing confidence in himself. In his youth, like other boys, he had been taught respect for positions of authority, if not for the person who held the post. He had suffered without comment his hands being blistered with a ferrule by an older boy temporarily in charge of his schoolroom in Brewer, even meting out the same punishment when the tables were turned. When a seminarian, he had made up his mind that he would never "fawn, cringe or supplicate—scarcely *obey*" a certain "stiff, overbearing, unreasonable man" if required to do so to obtain and keep a prospective teaching position.[41]

Now, although he had some cares and irritations when exposed to the military way of doing things, he found himself realizing that "no danger & no hardship ever makes me wish to get back to that college life again. I can't breathe when I think of those last two years. Why I would spend my whole life in campaigning rather than endure that again. One thing though, I won't endure it again. My experience here and the habit of command, will make me less complaisant—will break upon the notion that certain persons are the natural authorities over me."[42]

Chamberlain certainly loved his new life. Every third day he was the brigade field officer of the day and had charge of all the outposts and advanced guards for miles around, spending twelve to fifteen hours a day in the saddle. From the streams and valleys to the rolling countryside, he enjoyed very much his rides in the beautiful Maryland autumn. One day, he wrote, he rode to the summit "of one of these blue hills, whence you can see forty miles into Virginia—see the long lines of rebel fires fifteen or twenty miles away & villages & streams & bright patches of cultivated fields." From the same vantage point he could see "on our own side the great battlefield of Antietam—the hills trodden bare & the fields all veined with the tracks of artillery trains, or movements of army corps."[43]

As time went on, Chamberlain poked fun at himself and the appearance he made as he rode through the country, thinking he cut a ridiculous figure. His face had become bearded and his only uniform ragged, the trousers worn "quite out of the question." In place of his original pants, he wore a sky blue cavalry pair that were much too big for him, and when it was cold, a huge, rough cavalry overcoat. Strapped to his saddle were his talma and shawl, and his saddlebags held some blue beef and hard bread. A large rent appeared in his cap, the result of a picket raid when he led a reconnaissance to one of the passes in South Mountain on the twelfth of October, after the famous Confederate Maj. Gen. James E. B. "Jeb" Stuart was reported to be in the vicinity. Two large pistols in their holsters and a fine three-foot sword at his side completed Chamberlain's outfit. Colonel Ames joked that the Twentieth was recognized everywhere by the sight of its bedraggled lieutenant colonel on his beautiful horse—the latter giving "that peculiar point & quality of incongruity which constitutes the ludicrous," Chamberlain observed. "Rebel prisoners," he added, tongue in cheek, "praise the horse and the sword, but evidently take no fancy to the man."[44]

There were minor inconveniences. Chamberlain and Ames rigged a makeshift fireplace in one end of their tent that smoked so badly they could hardly see; at the same time, it was pouring rain so that they had to "stay inside and be smoked, or outside to be soaked," Chamberlain wrote to Fannie. Regimental officers stopping by for a little sociability crowded in the tent but soon departed, unable to stand the atmosphere. His health was good, however, and he could buy some food at double prices from the sutler to supplement the lesser variety available to officers at that time from the commissary. Officers were given cash allowances to buy their own rations and those of their personal servants, if they had them. Their personal belongings and gear were transported in wagons attached to the regiment, but sometimes the wagons did not keep up on the march, and officers would be as deprived as their men.[45]

Each company's rations were parceled out to the eager men, usually every three days, and were placed in haversacks, tin cups, and cloth bags. A pound or so of meat, a like amount of hard or soft bread, and a few ounces of that absolute necessity of a soldier's life, ground coffee, with a little sugar and salt, made out the daily ration. In addition, a little soap and a few candles were provided. In camp the diet was usually augmented with some beans, split peas, rice, onions, vegetables, and dried fruit. Makeshift company kitchens with men assigned as cooks were organized when possible, but it was usually up to the individual soldier to cook his own food. Some men bought delicacies from the sutler, but the low pay, only $13 a month for a private, did not go far with butter at $1 a pound and condensed milk seventy-five cents a can.[46]

The mainstay of a soldier's diet was bread, but only rarely did he get the soft variety in the field; it usually came in the form of hard bread, universally known as "hardtack." A day's ration of the stuff in the Twentieth Maine was nine crackerlike cakes, each measuring about three by three inches and one-half inch thick. Dry, nearly hard as granite, and sometimes wormy, the stony shingles could be chewed at length by those with good teeth, but resourceful men could find many other ways to make them tastier. One private in Company H was known for chewing hardtack most of the time and nearly drove his captain crazy with the continual grinding of his teeth on drill, dress parade, or review. Unable to stand it any longer, the officer yelled, "Keegan, why on earth are you always crunching hard bread?" "The juice, sir," the man replied with arch innocence. "I am very fond of the juice."[47]

After a severe bout of sickness when his stomach rebelled at the camp food back in Portland, Tom Chamberlain began to put on weight. In the first five months of his army enlistment he packed on thirty pounds, almost in spite of his soldier's diet. Others were not as hardy. The men were without overcoats for several weeks, and when it got cold, they sat shivering around campfires and tried to keep up their spirits. Disease stalked the camp. Unused to the weather, the exposure, the food, and other hardships, many became sick, and others died; the latter were given solemn burials on the hillsides of Maryland, far from their Maine homes. Some had to be sent to makeshift hospitals in nearby houses, desperately ill and without proper food and care; others were transported to hospitals as far away as Baltimore.[48]

But the majority were sturdy enough to thrive. The comradeship, outdoor living, sense of accomplishment, and the simple pleasures of a soldier's life gave these volunteer soldiers experiences that would make friends and fond memories for their lifetimes. When the regiment suddenly moved out with the Fifth Corps on the night of October 30, after several days of being under orders to be ready to march, it was reduced in numbers to about 550. The soldiers who remained, however, were in fine condition and ready for a fight.[49]

* * *

As the Twentieth marched away from its Maryland camp, the men knew that the grounds for the war had changed. No longer was it waged only to preserve the Union and contain slavery to the areas where it existed; now there would be a new dimension to its character. Only a few days after the battle of Antietam, Abraham Lincoln had declared his intention to promulgate on January 1, 1863, what became known as the Emancipation Proclamation, declaring the slaves in states or parts of states where the people were then in rebellion against the United States "thenceforward and forever free." Slave labor was used by the Confederacy in its war effort, and Lincoln had cited the proclamation "as a fit and necessary war measure for repressing said rebellion." Lincoln's bold stroke was fraught with political peril, from conservatives against it to radicals who did not think it went far enough, but he believed in its power and his course and so took the risks.[50]

When the proclamation was officially announced to the army, many of the old school officers disapproved of it and thought it unconstitutional, but Chamberlain reflected that it had "sent thoughts wider and higher than army regulations or text-books of the law." Other officers and enlisted men in the Army of the Potomac had thoughts on the matter too, and their rousing reception of their president at the grand review near the Antietam battlefield soon afterward could be taken as one answer to this manifestation of the greatness of Lincoln's leadership.[51]

"But when slavery was put above the Union,—when the engineries of war were turned against the defences of the country; when the flag was shot down and

trampled on, which stood not only for what had been done under it for man, but what should be done,—then in a miracle of might rose that spirit which slow to wrath, does not stop till its work is done,—does not rest till the cause, which is the evil, is purged from the heart.

"What a century of concession could not do, secession did,—with marvellous demonstration, its own weapons turned to its destruction. It pleased its maddened mood to invoke war; and the very laws of war gave the President power to knell its doom; it proclaimed a Confederacy built on the corner-stone of slavery,—and lo, the corner-stone itself was overturned; it set slavery across the nation's way, and God,—in his wrath, in his justice, in his mercy, in his love, in his far purpose for man and earth,—swept slavery from the path, as the mighty pageant of the free people passed on to its glory."[52]

* * *

Heading south as it left the old camp near the iron works, the regiment stepped out on a beautiful night and marched until after midnight, a bright moon lighting the way. Crossing the Potomac River the next day, the men rested near the village of Harpers Ferry. There old John Brown, the abolitionist insurrectionist, had seized the United States arsenal on a violent night just three years before, barricading himself with his sons and others in the old engine house. The scenery was magnificent, and after traversing the flowing Potomac, the soldiers skirted the base of the Loudoun Heights and proceeded south through the Loudoun Valley. Untouched so far by the war, the valley was one of the most beautiful and fertile in Virginia, and as the Union men marched in long blue columns, they knew that the Confederates were just over the Blue Ridge Mountains on their right. The march was uneventful and almost leisurely, although on the third day out they covered fifteen miles and came within sight of an artillery skirmish.[53]

Chamberlain was in his element as the weather became brisk. He had usually felt strong and well in cold weather, and even as the wagons lagged miles behind with the officers' belongings, he was cheerful and uncomplaining. Lt. John Marshall Brown, the regimental adjutant and recent Bowdoin graduate, could not quite understand how his former professor chose to sleep on the ground under the sky when he had a whole regiment at his command to build him a shelter. "But I hate to see a man always on the spring to get the best of everything for himself," Chamberlain declared with his characteristic unpretentiousness. "I prefer to take things as they come, & I am as well & comfortable as anybody, & no one is the worse for it."[54]

That night as the regiment bivouacked after dark, Chamberlain spread his rubber blanket under a big chestnut tree, taking his saddle for a pillow. Wrapping himself in his shawl, he settled down to sleep. A storm blew up in the Virginia night, with rain and a furious gale. Chamberlain pulled the waterproof around him and over his head, curled up, and proceeded to "*enjoy it hugely!*" Morning found him very cold, especially his feet, but "bright as a squirrel & hearty as a bear." The shawl was undoubtedly left over from his college days, when men's haberdashery included immense blue or gray ones to wear against the cold. When the boys came out into the college yard after chapel prayers, one Bowdoin man remembered, they looked like oversized, long-legged birds as their shawls fluttered and flapped in the freezing wind.[55]

Finally camping near Snicker's Gap, a name that somehow struck Chamberlain and other Yankees as greatly amusing, Chamberlain wrote to Fannie that she could find it on the map he used to look at so longingly. He expected the Confederates to come pouring from the passage through the Blue Ridge at any time. Sounding optimistic and confident, almost wishing for a fight, Chamberlain was sure that a battle was imminent and thought they would "beat the rebels this time." Not long before, he had told her, "Most likely I shall be hit somewhere sometime, but all 'my times are in His hands,' & I can not die without His appointing." Now, he asked her not to worry about him, assuring her no harm could come to him if it were not "wisely & kindly ordered so. I try to be equal to my duty & ready for anything that may come."[56]

Meanwhile, the lovely valley where the Union army camped was rich in livestock, poultry, and harvested vegetables. The local farmers, however, were most unfriendly to the blue-coated soldiers, who helped themselves whenever they could to supplement their meager diets. Although the men of the Twentieth were not yet as adept at foraging as the veterans of other regiments, they soon caught on to that venerable army custom. Even Chamberlain apparently was advised to ignore the ill-concealed evidence of petty thievery, to consider some tolerance better policy. After a woman refused to sell any milk when politely asked, expressing the wish "to kill the whole of us," he suspected that she contributed a few pigs and turkeys to "our good living," courtesy of some "naughty boys." They could not resist these or "other delicate articles of diet, which must be *had* even if they could not be bought or accepted as presents," he added.[57]

Gen. Daniel Butterfield, former Third Brigade commander, was now leading the First Division, replacing General Morell the day the Fifth Corps left Antietam. In the fall of 1861, when Butterfield was in command of the brigade, he had seen the need for a special brigade bugle call to differentiate the commands for his brigade from those of others nearby. Just about all events in army life, from reveille to lights out and many commands during battle, were ordered by bugle calls, which had to be learned by every soldier. Butterfield devised a call that would become dear to the hearts of most of those who served with the brigade from then to Appomattox. It consisted of three long blasts of G, followed by a pair of fast three-note trills running from G to C to E. The men thought the result sounded like "Dan, Dan, Dan, But-ter-field, But-ter-field," and that was how it was characterized from then on. In the summer of 1862 Butterfield had also composed a new tune for "lights out,—time to go to sleep." When it was first played by the Third Brigade bugler, its haunting refrain was heard by others, and it eventually became the official "Taps," played at night and at all military funerals.[58]

* * *

Chamberlain was happy to finally receive two letters from Fannie. He would surely look forward to hearing the "Dan-Dan-Dan Butterfield" followed by "mail call" as eagerly as the other men, but since he seldom heard from her or others, it was disappointing to look through a bushel or more of mail and find a letter for almost everyone but him. The mails were erratic and untrustworthy, and he hoped she was writing more frequently. Because he did not trust the security of his letters, he determined not to write much about the army, battles, victories, or generals. Instead he wrote of commonplace things, keeping up his responsibilities as man of the house. Asking Fannie to have Mr. Booker, a local carpenter and handyman, prepare their home and garden for winter, he provided details about the carpet, the stoves, the windows, the grapevine, the asparagus. Deborah Folsom, "Cousin D" or "Aunty," as the children called her, was living at their home now; she would stay with the little ones when Fannie was away. Chamberlain thought Fannie should buy a set of furs for her.[59]

No doubt remembering that Daisy had not been provided a winter cloak until December the previous year, he cautioned Fannie to get everything for the children to wear. "Wyllys wants a good big overcoat to go with his boots, & a *cap* to keep his ears warm. If you do not have as much money as you want, let me know at once. . . . Don't have them so lacking as they were last winter . . . as for yourself *be happy*—I should be perfectly so if I could see my dear ones under my own little roof." Fannie did not have to ask his permission for her travel plans as she customarily did: Chamberlain told her he did not expect her to stay in Brunswick in the winter but realized that the children and Aunty would. Missing the children, he alternated between feeling sadness and the desire to have a "good frolic" with them. He let her know he loved her and asked her to think about coming to be near him later if it became possible; he even raised the possibility that the army would go to winter quarters in Richmond![60]

Chamberlain kept returning to a subject that seemed to be of some concern to him: his wife's state of mind. With her background and childhood, the later family losses and death of her babies, and her present threatening situation and subsequent actions, Fannie may have been subject to recurring depression. "I want you to be cheerful & occupy your mind with pleasant things so as not to have time to grow melancholy," he wrote. "You mustn't think of me much. . . . Invite the Juniors over to spend the evening with some of the young ladies, as we used to, & keep up your character for hospitality, & your spirits at the same time. I shall write you as often as I can get an opportunity." She would hear immediately if he were injured, he reassured her, and though he expected to get "some sort of a scratch" if they were in a battle, "the chances are it will not be serious." Although optimistic of the army's prospects, and remarking on its confidence in its officers, he was puzzled that "still something seems to strike all the vigor out of our arms just at the point of victory."[61]

* * *

Out of patience with General McClellan's long failure to seek and fight the enemy, on November 5 President Lincoln gave the order to relieve McClellan as commander of the Army of the Potomac and replace him with General Burnside. By the same directive, he ordered McClellan's right-hand man and Fifth Corps commander, Maj. Gen. Fitz John Porter, removed from his position, with Maj. Gen. Joseph Hooker placed in his stead. The next day the Fifth Corps resumed its march, leaving the vicinity of Snicker's Gap and heading southward. After a miserable march through bitter cold, where the water froze hard in the canteens and snow fell to a depth of seven inches, the corps arrived near Warrenton and army headquarters three days later and made camp.[62]

Anger and sadness filled many in McClellan's army after their leader's dismissal; he had organized the Army of the Potomac, and a feeling like magnetic current was said to have run between him and his troops. Chamberlain and the Twentieth Maine arrived in time for the emotional last farewell to the dismissed leader. As cheer after cheer rang from thousands of soldiers lining the sides of the Alexandria and Warrenton Pike, McClellan rode before them for the last time. The Fifth Corps division of army Regulars gave perhaps the most touching tribute: snapping into the highest possible salute, "present arms," these usually unemotional and hardened men stood in stone silence as their former leader passed, tears running down the cheeks of many. Two days later, after General Porter was notified that he too had been relieved, the Fifth Corps held a similar ceremony to honor its popular commander.[63]

McClellan's successor, General Burnside, was not resented by the soldiers; he was well liked, known as a friend of his predecessor, and only reluctantly accepted his appointment. Indeed, he later declared that he had felt himself incompetent to command such a large army, a feeling that would unfortunately prove horribly prophetic. Submitting a plan to his superiors in Washington to change his base and move his whole army to Fredericksburg, after which he proposed to make "a rapid movement . . . direct upon Richmond," he reorganized his army. Changes in command followed as he formed three "Grand Divisions" of two corps each. General Hooker was appointed to command the Center Grand Division, consisting of the Second and Fifth Corps; the other four corps formed the Right and Left Grand Divisions. General Butterfield now commanded the Fifth Corps, and Brig. Gen. Charles Griffin, West Point class of 1847, a man who was to have a great deal of influence on Chamberlain's army career, became the commander of its First Division.[64]

Deviating from a plan finally assented to by General-in-Chief Henry W. Halleck and President Lincoln, Burnside marched his army from Warrenton down the north bank of the Rappahannock to Falmouth, opposite Fredericksburg. He had agreed to cross the river by the fords above Fredericksburg, occupy the heights behind the town, and establish a supply base north of the river. Instead, Burnside determined to cross the river on pontoon bridges directly in front of Fredericksburg. When the army's advance reached the river, Burnside disapproved Maj. Gen. Edwin V. Sumner's proposal that he seize the Fredericksburg heights immediately, a fatefully poor judgment. The pontoons failed to arrive when Burnside expected, and the campaign bogged down, giving Lee an opportunity to occupy the high ground behind Fredericksburg and build a strong defensive position.[65]

Thanksgiving found the Twentieth Maine settling into a cold and muddy camp on a small pine knoll three miles from Fredericksburg, near what would be called Stoneman's Switch on the Aquia Creek Railroad. Shelter tents and new overcoats had been provided the men, giving some protection against the weather. Two of the one-man sections of cotton drilling buttoned together and staked down over a stick ridgepole made a small "dog-tent" big enough for two men. But the line officers had to make do with only a tent "fly" each, augmented with poles and some excavation. The holiday was a cheerless one; rations had not been issued for some time due to the change of supply base, and empty stomachs rumbled on Thanksgiving Day. Shouts of "hard-tack! hard-tack!" were heard from the camp.[66]

* * *

Far away in Maine, Fannie Chamberlain missed her husband terribly and wondered where he was and how he was spending his Thanksgiving. She had sent him a package of clothing and only hoped it would be what he needed. After the holiday church service, George and Helen Adams were hosts to the family Thanksgiving dinner, and their home rang with the happy noise of their own two little girls and the Chamberlain children. When dinner was finished, a small table of "bright red apples, nuts, and candy" was offered the youngsters, "which made four pairs of bright little eyes shine especially when the little hands that go with them had full liberty to help themselves," as Fannie would describe the homey scene. Lawrence wanted to know the small "particulars" of their lives. As she prepared to return through the snow-covered Brunswick streets to the lonely house on Potter Street, she thought of how he ought to be at his own home on this Thanksgiving night, with those who longed to see him.[67]

* * *

On the night of December sixth and seventh, it snowed four inches at Falmouth, Virginia, and two members of the Twentieth Maine froze to death. Three days later, as the regiment returned to camp from picket duty, it was met with orders to prepare to move out the next morning with three days cooked rations. The battle Chamberlain had been expecting for weeks was at hand.[68]

CHAPTER

Four

DEATH-GARDENS, HAUNTED BY GLORIOUS GHOSTS

Shivering in the cold air as dawn lightened the black night into gray morning on December 11, the men of the Twentieth Maine marched over the frosty ground about five miles from camp. They halted near Burnside's headquarters at the Phillips house, which stood well back and above the Rappahannock River opposite the city of Fredericksburg. Massed together, the soldiers of Hooker's Grand Division covered the ground as far as the eye could see, and all had three days rations in their haversacks and were carrying twenty extra rounds of ammunition.[1]

Far below, Union engineers worked in the early morning chill, trying to throw pontoon bridges across the Rappahannock. In spite of heavy mist, Confederate snipers successfully delayed the laying of the pontoon bridges over the river by picking off the Federals as they worked. The sound of the big Union guns shelling buildings that sheltered the Confederate sharpshooters across the river came booming back to the waiting men at the Phillips house. As the morning wore on, Chamberlain and Adj. John M. Brown rode to the Union batteries, which were in line on Stafford Heights. This elevated ground consisted of a crest of hills commanding the city and the countryside around it, lying close to and high above the north bank of the river. A southward bend of the river upstream caused the Union line on the bluffs to face nearly west. The heavy fog that lay on the valley thinned and lifted, enabling the two officers to see the beautiful city of Fredericksburg nestled on the other side of the stream. When the likelihood of a battle became apparent, most of the civilians evacuated, leaving it deserted except for Confederate troops.[2]

The two Maine officers made their way down the gradient to the Lacy house, a stately old residence famous even then, directly opposite the city. From its premises a fantastic scene unfolded before them that surpassed, Chamberlain declared, anything he had ever witnessed. Artillery shells screamed and burst in the bombardment of the city, starting fires that flickered and burned, and thick smoke billowed up in columns. Buildings concealing Rebel sharpshooters were blown to dust in sharp explosions. Musket fire rattled as other gray-uniformed marksmen were seen running, trying to dodge the shells and avoid the bullets of Union marksmen on the opposite bank. With the pontoon bridges but half finished, three regiments of Union infantry eventually had to cross in boats to drive the Rebels away in order to complete the work.[3]

Beyond the city, after the grid of streets containing rows of homes and businesses ended, an undulating plain stretched for a half-mile. This relatively open ground was traversed longitudinally by two main roads and marked by a few well-spaced houses, gardens, and fences as it rose to meet a range of hills. This ridge was not as high as the corresponding Union crests across the river, but Lee had built fortifications and placed many cannon along this natural defensive elevation behind and to the right and left of the city. Immediately in rear of Fredericksburg, the stretch of steeply rising ground called Marye's Heights could be made almost impregnable to infantry assault. From his vantage point Chamberlain could plainly see the Rebel guns, but they rarely replied to the Union barrage. The effect of this entire scene, he thought, exceeded that of Antietam because the action was nearer and sharply in focus, in contrast to the extended sweep of the view at Sharpsburg. After the pontoons were finished, it took until after nightfall and a sharp fight involving a division of General Sumner's men to clear the city of Confederate soldiers.[4]

On the Union side of the river, batteries extended on the ridge of hills to the Federal left. The engineers had met little opposition to their building of two more bridges downriver about a mile and a quarter from the city; elements of Franklin's Left Grand Division crossed the river there in the late afternoon. As the Twentieth Maine men prepared to sleep in a woods behind the Phillips house, the stage was set: Federal guns were commanding the plain over the river on a nearly five mile front, and the Confederates, on the same length of line opposite, were standing solidly in the path of Burnside's Grand Divisions on the "shortest road to Richmond."[5]

But there would be one more day of preparation before the final confrontation; Lee strengthened his lines as the bulk of the Union troops moved across the river on the pontoon bridges and prepared for battle. The Fifth Corps remained on the river's Union side, with Griffin's First Division moving down closer to the city, under arms and not knowing when they would be called on to fight. As they bivouacked in the cold, Twentieth Maine men sat by their campfires until late at night, talking and singing patriotic songs. Soldiers of both armies waited around thousands of such fires, knowing a great battle was drawing near. Chamberlain, drawing on his training as a scholar and apparently determined to keep some sort of record of the most momentous years of his life, wrote in his notebook, "Not ready yet. Moved nearer, however, and waited yet another day."[6]

A fog again enveloped the Rappahannock and the surrounding countryside on the morning of December 13, hiding the opposing armies from each other. Near ten o'clock it began to lift, revealing on the plain across the river below the city a "splendid array" of Franklin's blue-clad Union infantry, their muskets gleaming in the rays of the winter sun, colorful flags waving, in position to attack Lee's right. In the city, however, Sumner's two corps had been deliberately concealed by the buildings and trees, and only a few were visible. As fighting began on the Union left, Confederate corps commander Maj. Gen. Thomas J. "Stonewall" Jackson's guns opened on Franklin's men, and Gen. James Longstreet's cannon began firing from Marye's Heights into the city at any stray Federal, as a diversion to help Jackson.[7]

At the foot of Marye's Heights, toward which Sumner's Union troops would advance, the Telegraph Road to Richmond ran along the base of the high ground as a sunken road, about twenty-five feet wide and lined on the city side with a shoulder-high stone wall. Since the thoroughfare had been cut out of the hill, the ground toward the city was banked to the top of the wall in most places. It was a natural entrenchment and afforded protection for 2,500 riflemen from two of Longstreet's brigades, who were arranged in ranks four deep behind it. The Confederates had placed their artillery on the heights above the infantry, so that the ground in front of the guns would be subjected to a murderous cross fire. Longstreet's artillery chief had assured him that morning, in words exaggerated but ominous, "A chicken could not live on that field when we open on it."[8]

Soon Longstreet's artillery and infantry were firing into brigades of Yankees as they "swarmed out of the city like bees out of a hive" and massed for attack. And there on the plain in front of Longstreet's men began what a Confederate officer called "the most fearful carnage," as line after line of resolute and brave Union soldiers went forward in gallant order. Some leaned into the fearful cross-fire storm of shells and bullets as if advancing against a blizzard wind, and they fell, dead and wounded, in droves.[9]

From across the river Chamberlain watched the panorama behind Fredericksburg in horror and fascination. The whole First Division had moved a little after noon to the heights overlooking the city, and the action over the river was in the plain sight of all the officers and men as the Fifth Corps was held in reserve. Helplessly watching the deadly action and unable to go to the aid of their comrades was a spirit-trying trial for Chamberlain and his fellow soldiers. Sometimes it was better to meet the worst quickly and then be relieved by reinforcements than to be held back until some disaster strikes "and you must recover the lost ground or die trying," he said.[10]

As Chamberlain and the other men of Stockton's brigade watched from across the Rappahannock, the soldiers of the Second and Ninth Corps advanced toward the Confederates in blue lines of battle, colors in front, bayonets shining. The artillery and musket fire that opened upon them as they emerged from the city was frighteningly deadly, but they moved resolutely on, around and over obstacles like a wave, as the stone wall flashed into a ribbon of flame. Then checked by the nature of the ground and the scorching fire, they sank to the earth on the slopes. The living then moved backward, a dark mass receding, as another battle line of men struggled forward over the rolls in the plain, coming even or overreaching their comrades' forward positions, trying to break the enemy line and carry the heights. Chamberlain made another entry in his notebook: "I see tears in the eyes of many a brave man looking on that sorrowful sight, yet all of us are eager to dash to the rescue."[11]

Finally, there was no more time for notebooks. At about three o'clock the Fifth Corps was ordered across the Rappahannock, the First Division crossing on the pontoons at the lower part of the city. General Griffin and his troops had been ordered to the support of Brig. Gen. Samuel D. Sturgis of the Ninth Corps; a silent, wistful, searching look appeared on the face of the tough division commander as he looked at his men, and it spoke to them more than words. The First and Second Brigades left quietly and moved out of sight of the Third, which was still held in reserve. Officers and men waited, saying little, as another hour or so passed. Then the bugle trilled, "Third brigade to the front!" "Fall in," shouted Colonel Ames. When repeated by the company commanders, the order sounded down the line like so many echoes.[12]

The Confederate artillery had the range on the bridge. Solid shot swished just above the soldiers' heads, the compressed wind of its passage causing them to shrink down instinctively as they marched. As the bridge swayed under the tread of the men and shells burst above them, it was hard for the horses as well as the men to keep their balance, but they soon reached a steamboat wharf and solid footing. The enemy cannon was also raking the city, making it perilous for the Union troops as shells exploded in the streets and pieces of debris from damaged buildings flew in the air. One Twentieth Maine officer wanted to set a good example: "I held my breath and set my teeth together, determined not to show fear if I could, by will, keep it down."[13]

Making way through the streets of the war-torn city in a column of fours, the brigade took position along Prince Edward Street in front of the railroad station, its right resting on Charlotte Street and its left extending about one hundred yards south of the depot. There the soldiers waited again, lying down under the partial cover of the slightly rising ground while shells crashed around them and Union guns posted nearby replied with deafening roar. All around them were bodies and parts of bodies, where plunging artillery fire had taken a terrible toll on the brigades of men who had preceded them to this place. In their front an awful scene played itself out, accompanied by a thunderous din. The plain rising before them was now a melee of men and horses, living and dead, wreathed in battle smoke. Wounded soldiers streamed to the rear with the aid of others;

they yelled words of encouragement or caution to Stockton's waiting men. Earlier, while watching his First Brigade pass nearby when he was posting some guns, General Griffin had been heard to say, "There goes one of my brigades to hell, and the other two will soon follow."[14]

Now Griffin's Third Brigade was to follow his other two. At the order "Attention!" the men stood up and the officers dismounted to leave their horses behind, the fences in front presenting obstacles that precluded a mounted advance. After Colonel Ames gave the order, the men loaded their muskets, fixed bayonets, and again waited. The Seventeenth New York was on the right of the brigade's line of battle, and then, in order to the left, the Twelfth New York, Twentieth Maine, Forty-fourth New York, Eighty-third Pennsylvania, and Sixteenth Michigan.[15]

Chamberlain was standing with Ames in front of the regimental colors when they heard the brigade bugler sound the familiar "Dan, Dan, Dan, Butterfield, Butterfield" and then the "Advance." Ames glanced up at the enemy batteries and addressed his lieutenant colonel: "God help us now! Take care of the right wing!" Yelling then to be heard over the din, Ames ordered, "Forward the Twentieth!" As the colors in front of each regiment began to move forward, so did the brigade's long blue lines. But the two New York regiments on the right failed to hear the orders and did not march, leaving the Twentieth on the right of the brigade and exposed to flank fire during the whole advance.[16]

The Mainers waded through two feet of icy water in a ditch or millrace twenty feet wide that ran the width of the city; then a high board fence around which minié balls whistled confronted the right wing, separating it from the rest of the regiment. Ordered to take the fence down, the men hesitated, apprehensive in the midst of their first battle. Ignoring the bullets buzzing near him like angry bees, Chamberlain immediately sprang forward and began to pull the barrier apart, calling, "Do you want me to do it?" to his hesitant men. Following their lieutenant colonel's example, the men suddenly rushed the fence, and it disappeared quickly from the work of many willing hands.[17]

Because the obstacles and the millrace had caused the line of battle to be ragged and unconnected, the regiments were halted. On the left, the Eighty-third Pennsylvania had its line broken by an unfinished railroad cut, and its colonel brought his two left companies out of it and into line again. Then, in an old brick-kiln grounds on the open plain about eight hundred yards in front of the sunken road filled with thousands of Con-

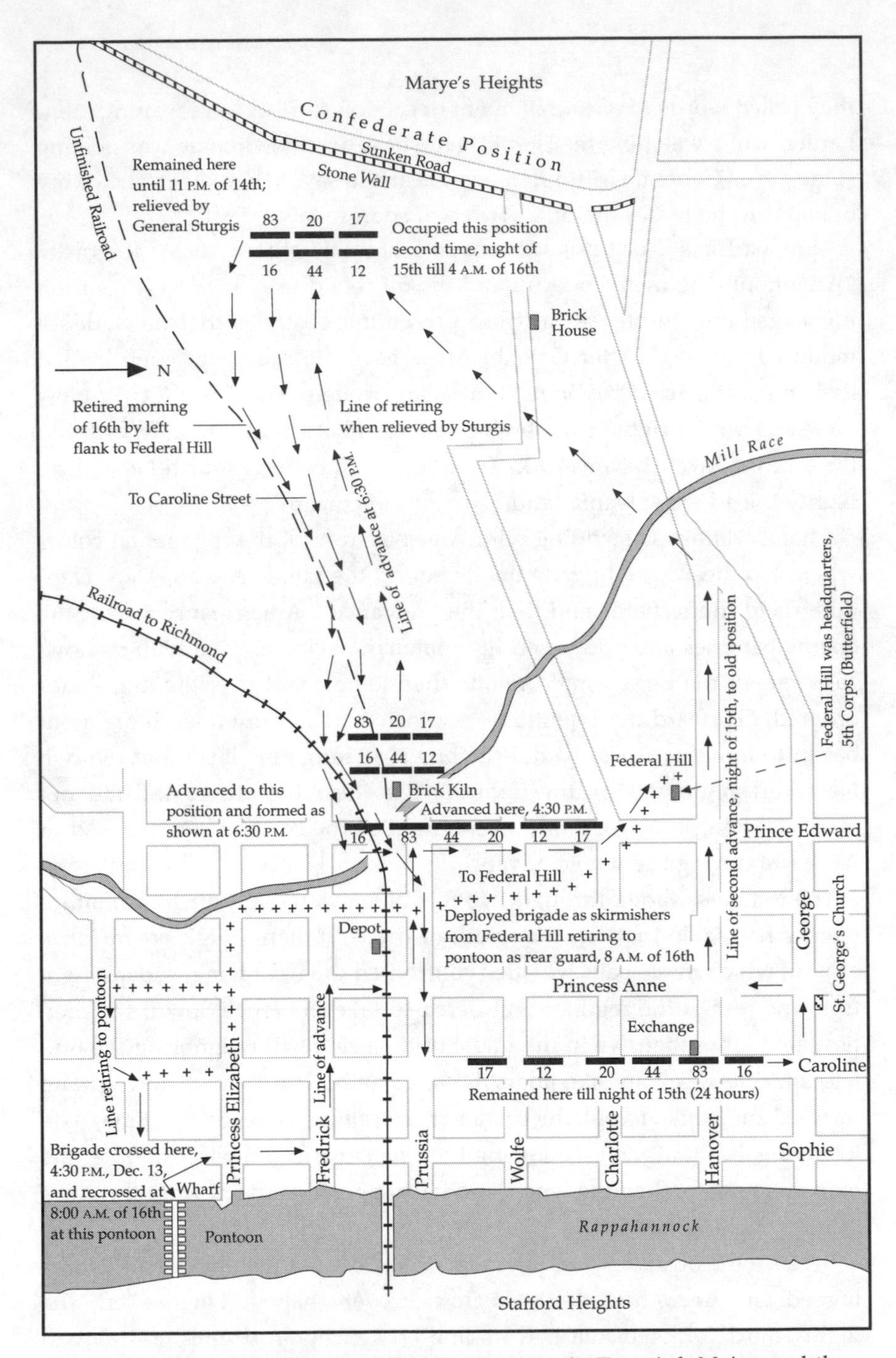

MAP 4. *Routes and Positions Taken by Chamberlain, the Twentieth Maine, and the Other Regiments of Their Brigade, December 13–16, 1862, during the Battle of Fredericksburg (adapted from Hill, "Last Charge at Fredericksburg")*

federate riflemen, the left and left center of Stockton's brigade aligned for the charge. As the cannon placed in the heights above the stone wall continued a deadly cross fire, the regiment double-quicked almost a quarter of a mile. One Twentieth Maine officer just two days later had only the disjointed recollection of the sun setting and "running up and down the line urging the men on."[18]

A private in the division's First Brigade, who had been in the first charge of Griffin's men, was lying in the mud hugging the ground not far from the Confederate fortifications. Looking over his shoulder, he saw "a grand sight"—the Twentieth Maine, easily recognizable to him by their new state colors—"coming across the field in line of battle as upon parade." Chamberlain later said that the regiment charged "over fences and through hedges, over bodies of dead men and living ones, past *four lines* that were lying on the ground." The regiment may have been green, but the discipline and hours at drill were paying off, and the men who followed Ames and Chamberlain into the storm of battle before the stone wall at Fredericksburg did not falter.[19]

Twilight at that season of the year is short, and it was during that time that Colonel Stockton asked Ames if he would relieve a regiment lying even farther to the front. Readily assenting to the order, Ames directed the Twentieth forward in advance of its brigade, the soldiers sweeping over and beyond the prone figures of the men they were replacing, allowing the latter to fall back. The Twentieth exchanged volleys with the Rebels "until the muzzle-flame deepened the sunset red, and all was dark." After night fell, the firing on the lines slackened but did not cease. The men lay in the mud, and as it grew later and colder, they shivered in their damp clothes. General Griffin came up to look at the position of his division and give instructions to his brigade commanders, telling them that they must hold their positions; the Ninth Corps would attack in the morning. The entire Third Brigade was now ordered up; it had been selected with two brigades of Regulars from Sykes's division to take an advanced position within close range of the deadly stone wall.[20]

Chamberlain could not sleep. Since the officers had left their blankets behind with their horses, and Chamberlain also had not taken his overcoat, he was cold in the wintry night. A whole "cacophony" of sound began to be heard over the battlefield, moans and calls from the wounded rising and falling, "of which," he remembered, "you could not locate the source . . . a wail so far and deep and wide, as if a thousand discords were flowing together into a key-note weird, unearthly, terrible to hear and bear." Bodies lay all over the field, and it was difficult to tell which were living and which were not. Trying to shield himself from the biting wind, Chamberlain found room to make his bed between two dark motionless forms, with a third near his head. He used the slight shelter the dead men provided out of necessity; "the living and the dead were alike to me," he later recalled of that strange night in front of the wall.[21]

Finally, near midnight, Chamberlain and Adjutant Brown took bearings on their location and went out on the battlefield to the right and rear of their position. They tended to the severely wounded, giving sips of water, binding up wounds, and soothing fevered, delirious sufferers. As they moved farther away from their position, more and more calls for help came out to them, with some men even asking to be put out of their misery. Shadowy figures wandered about, some looking for lost comrades by leaning close and quick-striking matches near still faces, others seeking blankets and overcoats from the dead. Finding the errand of mercy a never-ending task, Chamberlain felt relieved when ambulances arrived and the hospital stewards began their work.[22]

Chamberlain went back to his macabre resting place, folding the overcoat skirt of the soldier at his head over his face, and slept uneasily. He was startled awake when a hand pulled back the coat skirt and a dark head moved close to peer spookily, "half vampire-like," into his face. At a word from Chamberlain, the figure jerked back, frightened as if the dead had spoken. A small New Testament fell from the coat of the still form at his head, which Chamberlain picked up with the thought of returning it to the man's family. The icy winds blew, and as the night grew longer, he heard the flapping of a loose window blind in a brick house to his right. It seemed to say, "*Never—forever; Forever—never!*" in a mournful, clocklike rhythm that he was to remember all his life.[23]

A beautiful morning dawned on that Sabbath day of December 14, 1862, and as the mists rose and it became a little lighter, an officer at a post nearest the Confederates at the stone wall could see the men in gray talking as they made coffee, took their breakfasts, cleaned muskets, and went about their everyday chores only about eighty yards from him. It seemed strange that here, "absurdly near," he thought, was Lee's Army of Northern Virginia. No fires were allowed the Union men, so their Spartan fare had been hardtack washed down with water. Suddenly shots rang out, and the men in blue dropped to the ground and stayed there.[24]

The Twentieth Maine was in a depression in the ground in rear of the last crest before the stone wall, but if a man lifted his head the length of his forearm, he would draw a shot. The rest of the brigade was in a similar fix, with the uneven ground allowing some men more movement than others. On the brigade left, the Eighty-third Pennsylvania had the comparatively good cover of a crest in their front. When later referring to Stockton's brigade and the two brigades of Sykes's Regulars nearest the stone wall, the Fifth Corps commander, General Butterfield, approvingly remarked that "a more severe test of the discipline and efficiency of these commands could not have been made."[25]

Word was passed along the lines not to reply to the enemy fire except to hold the position. A little later it appeared that the Confederates were going to try to shell out the brigade, and Colonel Stockton could never really understand why they did not. Cannon boomed out three times, and one shell burst over the brigade with a flash, the fragments wounding a few men, but the other balls skimmed off over their heads and did no damage. The men lay in suspense of what would happen next: whether they would be ordered forward again, or the enemy would move against them.[26]

Late in the day, enemy skirmishers moved around on the left flank of the brigade under cover of some woods and began firing, threatening the position. Slight shelters against the gunfire—boards from a fence torn down the previous day, earth dug with bayonets, and piled up bodies where bullets hit with a "dismal 'thud'"—were painstakingly built to ward off the bullets. Sharpshooters from the Sixteenth Michigan, Twentieth Maine, and the Eighty-third Pennsylvania, under cover of these barriers and other features of the terrain, finally drove those Rebels off, but other Confederates posted in front kept Yankee heads down. "We had to take things as they came, and do without the rest," Chamberlain said, a lesson life had taught him before and would again.[27]

Even under such trying circumstances, the soldiers found something to make them laugh and break the tension. The men of the Eighty-third Pennsylvania were used to being shot at. These veterans had stood up to heavy fire at Gaines's Mill, where their regiment had been decimated, and at Malvern Hill and Second Bull Run, too. When they discovered a little hollow that led to the railroad cut, some of them were able to go and come through it unmolested for awhile. Soon, however, they were spotted by Confederate sharpshooters stationed in the upper story of a nearby house, who could just see their heads as they passed. "Our men," boasted one captain with obvious relish, "dreaded running this gauntlet but little more than school boys dread to run the gauntlet of as many snowballs. But the ludicrous operation of passing the fiery ordeal never failed to be accompanied by an uproar of laughter from the rest of the regiment."[28]

Darkness fell on the heights and plain behind Fredericksburg as the day slowly ended. The men could stretch and move a little now, drink some water, and get something to eat from their haversacks. Later more Union men would come to take the places of Griffin's Third Brigade, and they could hurry back to the city with their wounded, glad to leave that place. But now there was a sorrowful duty to perform—the regiments must bury their dead. The Twentieth Maine soldiers carved rude headboards for each man from some debris, shadowed matches in cupped hands for light, and scratched shallow graves in the muddy soil. They planned a burial for their fallen comrades lighted only by the stars, but nature, in a rare display for those latitudes, cooperated to make, as it had for Viking warriors, "a more sublime illumination."[29]

"As we bore them, the forms of our fallen heroes, on fragments of boards torn from the fences by shot and shell, to their honored graves, their own loved North lifted her glorious lights, and sent her triumphal procession along the arch that spanned her heavens. An Aurora Borealis, marvelous in beauty. Fiery lances and banners of blood, and flame, columns of pearly light, garlands and wreaths of gold—all pointing and beckoning upward. Befitting scene! Who would die a nobler death, or dream of more glorious burial? Dead for their country's honor, and lighted to burial by the meteor splendors of their Northern home!"[30]

Back in the city, the brigade's soldiers had little rest for what was left of the night. They were routed from their makeshift beds by false alarms twice before morning when the pickets at the front started firing at some imagined enemy advance. A roll call then revealed that most of the regiment was alive and well, a fact looked upon by the inexperienced men as a kind of proof that each led a "charmed life." When the usually irascible Colonel Ames walked among the men, praising them for their gallant conduct, they surely thought the charm was again at work. They had done their duty in spite of their fear. Although shells burst into the house where Chamberlain and Ames made their headquarters the next day, everyone got hot food and coffee again as the men made flapjacks over fires along the sidewalks.[31]

The city of Fredericksburg, one Maine man wrote in the midst of the uproar the next day, "was a sight worthy of the French Revolution. Bivouacks in the street, artillery moving up and down, and all the noise and confusion of an army." The city was a ruin. Orders were posted against pillage, but looting had started on Friday, when Sumner's men entered the city in great numbers, and it had continued more or less since. Some officers and the provost guard tried to stop or contain the vandalism, and stolen goods were taken from the soldiers before they could cross the pontoons to the other side of the Rappahannock. Artillery shells from both sides damaged almost all the city's buildings, and furniture, clothing, books, and other valuables littered the streets.[32]

The brigade was posted for over three blocks along Caroline Street, its right resting near George Street. After staying there until afternoon, it was moved to a position on the outskirts of the city where the men expected to stay the night, but they were awakened before midnight again and ordered to fall in. Rumors had circulated earlier that their corps would go back across the river, but any hopes of that were dashed when their column began to head not for the bridges, but back to the front.[33]

Colonel Stockton had become ill, and the brigade was now under the command of Strong Vincent, the veteran colonel of the Eighty-third Pennsylvania. As the little band filed silently up Hanover Street, flurries of rain and sleet pelted their faces. Crossing the bridge above the millrace, they filed to the left to the cover of the hill, where so many of their comrades of other commands waited briefly before charging in the hopeless, deadly, blood sacrifice before the stone wall. At the top of the knoll, a quick patch of moonlight revealed long lines of soldiers lying on their arms, facing the enemy. But no answers came to whispered greetings, and with "revolting horror" the marchers realized they were trying to speak with the dead. These frozen sentinels had been placed in rows on the crests of the battlefield, to take the appearance and place of the living. The brigade passed other bodies piled high in grisly, abandoned breastworks. On to the left the brigade went, finally back to the ground it had held before, and relieved the men doing picket duty there.[34]

Since Ames had charge of their part of the line, Chamberlain commanded the regiment, which was alone and out of the sight of the others on either side. In the darkness the men were set to digging rifle pits with tools left by their predecessors, who had warned them that at nightfall the Rebels had placed a battery located to enfilade the whole position in the morning. The last orders were "Hold this ground at all hazards, and to the last," and the young former professor of rhetoric wondered, "Last of what?" Possible answers to that question "reached the infinite," he thought.[35]

Stray gusts of cold wind brought snatches of conversation from the Rebel pickets, whom he could hear digging, and they sounded as apprehensive as their Yankee foes. Scarcely more than a hundred yards from the enemy fortifications, in the dark, cut off from all support, Chamberlain felt isolated and alone in the midst of those who meant to kill him and his men on the dreadful, ghostly battlefield. It presented a situation in which, he mused, "the man of the highest physical courage and the soldier of highest discipline may find that he has something of himself yet to learn."[36]

Chamberlain told his men to get added protection by throwing the dirt to the direction of the Confederates, but as he felt his way along inspecting the line, he saw a man casting it the opposite way. Chamberlain cautioned, "Throw to the other side my man; that's where the danger is!" The man replied, "Golly! don't ye s'pose I know which side them Yanks be? They're right into us now." Careful that his voice and accent not give him away as he posed as a Confederate on grand rounds, Chamberlain quickly replied, as he beat a hasty retreat, "Dig away then, but keep a right sharp lookout!"[37]

Turning back to his own men, he found them pretty well dug in, when a staff officer clattered up on a horse asking for the commander of the men there. After Chamberlain allowed that he was, the man gasped loudly, "Get yourselves out of this as quick as God will let you! The whole army is across the river!" The officer could be clearly heard by the Twentieth Maine men around him, and Chamberlain thought for sure the whole Confederate picket line could hear too and would soon bring the whole force down on them. Pitching his voice for the benefit of all listening, Chamberlain said, "Steady in your places, my men! . . . arrest this stampeder! This is a ruse of the enemy! We'll give it to them in the morning!" The staff officer quickly apologized—he had had a hard time finding and getting up to them. Chamberlain understood; seeking out Ames, he and his colonel quickly formulated a plan to return to the city quickly with some hope of safety.[38]

The men numbered off, one, two, one, two, all down the line. The even numbered men dug with zeal and some noise, while the odd numbered silently withdrew a hundred yards back and faced the front, waiting for the other group to withdraw, pass them, and halt a hundred yards beyond, until they were well near the city. The wind was blowing from the Confederates' direction, muffling all sound from the retreating Yanks as they moved through the dark, guns at a trail. Clouds began scudding fast in the sky, revealing a waning moon whose pale light glinted on the muskets and bayonets, and the men fell flat to the ground. A huge cloud headed toward the moon, and the men held their breaths in fear that the wind might shift it away, but the cloud swung around and darkness closed down again to hide their silent withdrawal. But they caught a glimpse of shadowy figures beginning to follow them, and a shot or two rang out in their rear. In the distance, a bloodhound bayed time and again, the sound coming nearer, a Pennsylvania officer remembered, "as if he too were set upon our tracks."[39]

Returning to the city safely, the brigade found it nearly deserted, the provost guard going from door to door waking stragglers and prodding them toward the pontoon bridges. The city was being evacuated by the Federals, and Stockton's brigade was to be among the last to cross the pontoon bridges. They waited another two hours and then moved through the lower part of the city, deployed as skirmishers and rear guard in their sector, until they reached the same bridge they had crossed before. One of the last officers to leave the city observed, as his horse's hoofs echoed in the street, that "the ghastly dead lay . . . with their pale faces turned toward heaven, while their open eyes, as a stream of moonlight fell athwart their faces, glared at one as if staring from another world." As the dawn began to show the beginning of a new day, and a cold rain soaked their uniforms, the Third Brigade left the terrible battlefield and city behind. They marched again on the swaying pontoons, glad to be returning to the other side of the river at last.[40]

While the regiment rested on the return march to camp near Falmouth, Joshua Chamberlain sat by the wayside, tired and depressed, with his back leaning against a tree. Sometime during the fight on the first day a musket ball had grazed his neck and right ear, but it had done no real harm. Rain dripped from the branches above him, and back across the river in the plain above the city, "death-gardens, haunted by glorious ghosts," were strewn with blue figures. The battle was lost, and the sacrifice of all the men in vain. The Twentieth had made a good name for itself, he thought, "without having once retreated or flinched," and they had not dreamed that the battle had been given up until the order came to retire. The regiment's beautiful blue state flag was torn and rent in several places, the golden crest shot away entirely. He had the Testament that had belonged to the boy whose body had been at his head that night before the stone wall, and he would send it to his family, so they might have some word of his fate.[41]

General Hooker rode by, and seeing the dejected figure slumped against the tree, he called kindly, "You've had a hard chance, Colonel, I am glad to see you out of it." Chamberlain "was not cheerful, but tried to be bright," as he answered, "It was chance, General; not much intelligent design there!" Hooker shot back defensively, "God knows I did not put you in!" "That was the trouble, General," Chamberlain replied. "You should have put us in. We were handed in piecemeal, on toasting-forks." It was straight and plain talk, but Hooker rode on without comment, not rebuking his battle-worn subordinate, who thought he had the right to speak for himself and others who had "put their breasts up to the business."[42]

General Franklin, whose troops had been on the left of the Union position, had his own two corps and part of Hooker's with him. His men made a successful attack on Lee's more vulnerable right, but the advantage was not followed up. On the Union right, Chamberlain thought later, "it seemed more like despair than desperation to order in the Fifth Corps, as Burnside did, to carry that stone-wall front. . . . No main assault should have been made there where the enemy wished and forbade." Burnside had sacrificed thousands of men in the futile assaults on the Rebel left, but still had to be dissuaded from personally leading an attack on Marye's Heights in a last-ditch effort to break through the enemy on Sunday, December 14. After two days of inaction by both sides, on December 15 Burnside ordered barricades and defenses built after nightfall to defend and hold Fredericksburg, but at the last moment he abandoned this plan and ordered the final withdrawal of Union troops back across the river.[43]

Upon the army's return to the camps at Falmouth, the disaster at Fredericksburg weighed on the minds of many soldiers, but Ames was well pleased with his regiment's performance during the battle. He thought it had performed better than any other in the brigade and had earned an excellent reputation. Participating in a battle had taught the officers and men the value of the hard-learned discipline acquired in seemingly endless hours of drill and instruction. A strong and united fighting unit had emerged from a band of green volunteers; Ames also thought that the former feelings of dislike toward him by many in the regiment because of his methods had changed completely. Still not entirely satisfied, however, Ames forced the resignation of some of the regiment's officers, but he liked his lieutenant colonel very much, considering him his "best officer." Ames had been the only colonel in the brigade who went into the charge at Marye's Heights actually leading his regiment, and with Chamberlain also out in front of the men, the fine conduct of the Twentieth may have partially reflected the bravery of its ranking officers.[44]

"Curious people often ask the question whether in battle we are not affected by fear, so that our actions are influenced by it; and some are prompt to answer, 'Yes, surely we are, and anybody who denies it is a braggart or a liar.' I say to such, 'Speak for yourselves.' A soldier has something else to think about. Most men at the first, or a some tragic moment, are aware of the present peril, and sometimes flinch a little by the instinct of nature. . . . But any action following the motive of fear is rare,—for sometimes I have seen men rushing to the front in a terrific fire, 'to have it over with.'

"But, as a rule, men stand up from one motive or another—simple manhood, force of discipline, pride, love, or bond of comradeship—'Here is Bill; I will go or stay where he does.' And an officer is so absorbed by the sense of responsibility for his men, for his cause, or for the fight that the thought of personal peril has no place whatever in governing his actions. The instinct to seek safety is overcome by the instinct of honor."[45]

The weather was particularly cold for Virginia that year, and the men of the Twentieth Maine set to building their first winter quarters along the company streets of their camp. Piling logs about three feet high, they topped high-peaked roofs with the heavy cotton that usually formed their tents. The results of this labor, little more than huts, measured about eight feet square, housed four men, and featured rude stoves fashioned of sod. Wood or sod chimneys were daubed with Virginia mud—ever present in one form or another—and this rude mortar was the only good use the men could ever find for the gooey stuff. Officers had roomier housing built for them, of course, but life for the regiment that first winter was not easy for anyone, and the shelters offered poor protection from the elements. Firewood was very scarce and had to be carried a long distance—several miles as the winter wore on.[46]

Time usually passed slowly and monotonously. Army routine took up some of the empty hours, with drill using up more when the weather permitted. Boredom, the soldier's old affliction, took over but was partially relieved by writing letters, reading, card playing, and other sociable pursuits. Finding that all of his superiors in command and some of his own rank were graduates of West Point, Chamberlain prevailed on the younger of these in the Fifth Corps to start an evening school of sorts for him and other interested officers. This little society studied all aspects of military duties in the field, and Chamberlain participated with his usual intense concentration. He was fulfilling the prophecy he had made to Maine's governor about himself and military matters: what he did not know about them, he certainly knew how to learn.[47]

Christmas brought a new commander for the Fifth Corps, Maj. Gen. George G. Meade, a highly respected career officer. However, it also became apparent by year's end to everyone but General Burnside that the Army of the Potomac had no confidence in its leader and was becoming completely demoralized. New Year's Day of 1863, usually a time for calling and convivial pastimes, found Chamberlain, the Twentieth Maine, and the entire First Division marching back to camp from a cold and miserable three-day reconnaissance to Richards Ford on the Rappahannock. They were learning that soldiers did not ask what or why, they just did their duty, enjoyed simple pleasures, and endured hardships as best they could. Sickness and exposure took a toll on the regiment in that long winter at Stoneman's Switch, and the graveyard on the hill grew larger as time went on.[48]

When General Burnside reviewed the Fifth Corps at the end of the first week in January, old veterans saw the review as a harbinger of a new campaign, and they did not have long to wait. Extensive preparations followed, and Burnside sent some troops downriver to make demonstrations to mask his main movement. On January 20 he pushed his army up the Rappahannock, with pontoons and artillery, intending to cross the river above Fredericksburg and launch another attack on the Confederates. The weather had been dry and cold when the march began that Tuesday, but rain started in the afternoon, and by dark it was falling heavily.[49]

After three days of being under marching orders, the Twentieth struck tents and began their trek, but they stopped after less than three miles and made camp in the rain. They spent the next day mostly waiting for the artillery to pass, a long wait since the Virginia mud when wet becomes viscous and gluey and seems to have no bottom. And wet it was—the rain came down in torrents, soaking everything and everyone. Guns, caissons, and wagons made little headway, and many of them finally sank to the axles and beyond in the glutinous muck. In addition to the teams of animals, lines of stout men pulled ropes attached to the guns and vehicles, but they made little progress. Horses actually fell and drowned in the thick gruel-like ooze. Infantrymen had to slog their way forward as best they could, and the Twentieth covered very little more ground in the next two days. A shortage of rations reached serious proportions; men fell out by the wayside exhausted, and commands became broken and disorganized.[50]

The Confederates had long since caught on to what the Federals were doing, and to the chagrin of the Union men trying to drag pontoons to the river bank, some of the Rebel pickets shouted their intention to come over the next day and help the Yanks build the bridges. Some wags even put up signs in conspicuous places reading "stuck in the mud," or "this way to Richmond," and other professions of helpfulness. One gill of whiskey was ordered served out for each man, a traditional army practice, but the First Brigade of Griffin's division for some reason got a great deal more of the liquor than the regulation amount. Many of the officers and men got drunk, and a donnybrook ensued, eventually involving all the regiments of that brigade. Maine men, some of whom Chamberlain would soon have occasion to know, won out in that fight, however, as one private recalled that "the giants of the Second Maine soon cleared the field."[51]

Under the guise of needing new avenues for supplies, the tired men were put to work on Friday building "courduroy" roads of logs, and the Twentieth Maine was assigned this duty. The distribution of two days' back rations, including fresh meat, must have revived some energies in the regiment. But it soon became apparent, regardless of official explanations, that the campaign was a failure before it had fairly begun and that the roads were built for the return of the artillery and equipment. On Saturday the exhausted army staggered back to their camps; the whole affair was remembered as Burnside's notorious "Mud March."[52]

* * *

In the weeks since the Fredericksburg battle there had been much behind-the-scenes activity in the highest echelons of government. After some general officers, fearing another disaster under General Burnside, had complained to President Lincoln, Burnside journeyed to Washington near year's end to personally tender his resignation from command of the Army of the Potomac. The president had refused to accept it, but immediately after the "Mud March" Burnside presented for his approval an extraordinary course of action: orders that would cashier General Hooker and three other division and brigade commanders from army service and relieve six others, including General Franklin, from their commands. Lincoln did not approve it but instead accepted Burnside's resignation as commander of the Army of the Potomac. In the spring the armies would again be on the move; the president was in great need of military victories, and it was apparent that Burnside could not provide success. Lincoln then appointed General Hooker to Burnside's former command.[53]

Hooker, whose military reputation had earned him the nickname of "Fighting Joe" Hooker, did away with the Grand Divisions and reorganized the army, retaining the corps structure. Consolidating the cavalry into one corps in a move that increased the effectiveness of the mounted men and improved the system of securing information, he appointed an able staff with Gen. Daniel Butterfield as chief. Many other changes moved men and commands, but for the Third Brigade of the Fifth Corps, the structure remained the same, with Colonel Stockton at its head, General Griffin commanding the First Division, and General Meade the Fifth Corps.[54]

Morale rose rapidly under Hooker, a tall, handsome, soldierly looking man who became a familiar sight as he was seen often at the various camps. He had about him an air of dashing authority, and his enthusiasm was somehow infectious. Although assertive and grandiose in manner, his self-assurance, combined with a stern authority, inspired confidence in the men. He added more food and greater variety to the limited diets, and better sanitary procedures were instituted in the camps, which improved the health and spirits of the men. Hooker also introduced reforms that included weeding out many incompetent officers and instituted a system that granted winter leaves for officers and many enlisted men.[55]

* * *

Chamberlain went on leave early in February, traveling to Augusta to see Maine's new governor, Abner Coburn, about filling the officer vacancies in the regiment. Upon returning to the little house on Potter Street in Brunswick, the tall, quiet husband and father must have been welcomed with excitement and love by Fannie and the children. He had longed for this time, being with them again, so often in the past months of separation. Some hours were spent at tea and dinner in the hospitable

Adams home, and the sound of the chatter and laughter of the four little cousins playing together was doubtless a great pleasure for him. The old civilian way of life would have seemed a little strange to a man used to the hard company of men in the winter camps near Stoneman's Switch, where even the sight of a well-dressed gentlewoman was a novelty. But the few days he had at home passed quickly before he again journeyed south.[56]

The Twentieth needed more officers badly, and the problem was addressed when Chamberlain returned from Maine. Eleven vacancies existed in the line, and in six companies lieutenants were acting as captains. Three sergeants, including Tom Chamberlain, had been appointed by Ames as acting second lieutenants before the fight at Fredericksburg and had been serving in that capacity ever since. Tom was doing well in the army; Capt. Ellis Spear asked that he serve under him in Company G, and he was transferred there by order of the colonel. Although being the lieutenant colonel's brother could not have hurt Tom's chances, Chamberlain was careful not to offer suggestions for his brother's advancement, so that the younger man could rise on his own merits. Late in February Ames, through his lieutenant colonel, requested promotion for all three sergeants to commissioned officer status and asked for several other promotions and changes among the officers.[57]

While some days that spring were unseasonably cold, on others March and April brought gentle air to warm the winter-weary Army of the Potomac. Reviews, drills, and a grand review, with President and Mrs. Lincoln present, demonstrated the army's rejuvenated fitness and morale. The reorganized cavalry held mock tournaments, and there were sword presentations to dedicate new and renewed commitments. In their brightly colored dresses, "witching Washington belles" held Chamberlain's attention on "Ladies' Days," fetes organized to brighten the morale in the austere camps.[58]

During the reviews each man wore on the top of his cap the newly ordered corps insignia patch in the color of his division, designed to increase the "esprit de corps," the common spirit, in the ranks. Already there was some of this deep feeling at the company, regimental, and sometimes the brigade level, but with the institution of these cloth badges, corps and division identities were also established that would be a source of pride for the soldiers' lifetimes. The system also provided ready recognition of those engaged with the enemy or in cases of straggling or misconduct. For the men of the Twentieth Maine and the others of their division, the badge was a red Maltese cross, the shape indicating the Fifth Corps and the color its First Division.[59]

Early in April Fannie came to Washington seeking a pass to the Twentieth Maine camp to see her husband. It was likely she reached him, at least with a message, because a day or two later Chamberlain took leave for personal business for the only time in his military career—four days in the capital city and Baltimore. Going about some ordinary tasks a short time after returning to the regiment, he was in especially good spirits, thinking of Fannie, and absentmindedly began humming a little tune, "Sleeping I Dream Love." It was a "very foolish and boyish song," he thought, but it described well his love for his "precious wife," which brightened the otherwise gloomy day in camp.[60]

Chamberlain had reason to be downcast, however. Through some mistake, many men in the regiment had evidently been inoculated with defective smallpox vaccine, causing over eighty cases to develop and several deaths. After confining the sufferers to the hospital, on April 22 the regiment moved camp over a mile to "Quarantine Hill," under orders to keep the men isolated from the rest of the army. Placards announcing the warning "Small Pox" were posted at every entrance to the camp, and the doctors had given their opinion that the regiment could not move for at least two weeks. Chamberlain thought the next battle was not far off, and not only was he afraid he might miss it, but he would be "desperate with mortification" if he did. In the event the regiment would be left behind when the army next moved into battle, he tried but was not able to arrange for his own temporary service on some general's staff.[61]

On the morning of April 27 the soldiers of the Army of the Potomac moved out of their winter quarters in excellent health and spirits, most of them looking forward to battle with their old adversaries in the Army of Northern Virginia. One wit in Griffin's Third Brigade characterized the egress with tongue-in-cheek: "The army commenced its annual movement toward Richmond, this time its route by way of Chancellorsville."[62]

Watching the other regiments of his brigade and division march off without him, Chamberlain felt frustrated and disgusted. Colonel Ames had managed to obtain a place on General Meade's staff, leaving Chamberlain reluctantly in charge of the regiment and "pest house," as he grimly called his quarantined command. He entertained the faint hope that the reason he had not been allowed to go forward in another capacity was that the regiment would soon get orders to move, as Ames had been told might be the case. His optimism apparently faded in the following days as Maine regiments in other corps were seen moving out, Maine's Governor Coburn came and reviewed the regiment, and still no marching orders came.[63]

Finally, after hearing cannonading on two straight days, Chamberlain decided to try to do something about this miserable state of affairs. Riding to general headquarters, he asked that the Twentieth be given something to do, any kind of duty, in the battle. When he was refused, he protested, saying that "if we couldn't do anything else we could give the enemy the small pox." After this remarkable declaration, he rode back to the quarantined camp and spent some free time playing cards with Captain Spear and other officers. Someone at headquarters must have appreciated his memorable verbal sally, because a messenger from Hooker's chief of staff, General Butterfield, woke him hours after midnight with orders for the regiment to be available at Banks and United States Fords on the Rappahannock at daylight. They were to guard the telegraph and signal lines from Hooker's headquarters to various places on the battlefield.[64]

Its men divided, the Twentieth arrived at the fords on the morning of Sunday, May 3, after a daring surprise flank attack by General Jackson's corps had thrown the Eleventh Corps into ignominious flight late the previous day. The disaster marked the first of a series of reverses and maneuvers that ended in a brilliant victory for Gen. Robert E. Lee and his greatly outnumbered Confederates. Dazed by the explosion of a shell and unable to direct the army at crucial times the next day, General Hooker nevertheless failed to retire from duty, which prevented a desperately needed overall direction for the army.[65]

Meanwhile, Chamberlain was in the saddle all the nights, inspecting every inch of the line, since the telegraph wire was broken and tampered with many times each night, and communications had to be kept open. Always on the lookout for some action, under General Griffin's personal supervision Chamberlain joined in a spirited advance of the Second Brigade of his division on May 4, with the result that Prince, his beautiful dappled horse, was shot under him, wounded in the head by a piece of shell.[66]

After making an auspicious beginning to his excellent plan of campaign, Hooker was outmaneuvered and outgeneraled by Robert E. Lee and his audacious subordinate, Stonewall Jackson. The Union general had started the campaign with boasts and bombast, confident of victory to the point of arrogance, and then ended it by withdrawing the army back to its Falmouth camps against the advice of four of his most prominent generals, three of them corps commanders. When the fight was lost and the army retreated back across the river, Chamberlain sat his horse in the rising river torrent caused by heavy rains, steadying the men as they crossed on the surging, insecure pontoons. The Twentieth Maine had done more than had been expected of them with their good, if limited, service during the last part of the battle of Chancellorsville, and in that he could have had some satisfaction as he withdrew his command, the last to cross the river.[67]

Plodding in the mud and heavy rain, the tired and disgusted men of the Army of the Potomac returned to their old camps, their spirits deflated when another defeat followed so unexpectedly after they entertained such high hopes of victory. The Fifth Corps soldiers, who had not done much fighting and had comparatively few losses, could hardly believe it when they were ordered back across the river. Casualties in the army ran high, especially in the Third Corps, and also in the Sixth Corps, where Gen. John Sedgwick was ordered to attack Lee's rear at Fredericksburg. Sedgwick stormed Marye's Heights behind the city, the same field of slaughter of the previous December but with different results: his men overran the stone wall in fierce hand-to-hand combat before their advance toward Chancellorsville was stopped near Salem Church. Lee's great victory, however, was tempered by the calamitous loss of his highly regarded corps commander, Gen. Stonewall Jackson, after the rout of the Union's Eleventh Corps. On the night of May 2, Jackson was mortally wounded by his own troops, who in the dark had evidently mistaken him and his escort for Federal cavalry.[68]

Both Hooker's and Lee's armies prepared for another campaign in the next weeks after the battle of Chancellorsville. For the Twentieth Maine, some duties such as their turn at picket duty were regularly carried out, but it was not until after the middle of May that the smallpox quarantine was lifted and their camp moved to a pleasant location. Chamberlain used some of his time to catch up with his correspondence, including a loving, hand-printed letter to the six-year-old girl he left behind in Brunswick:

May, 1863

My dear little Daisy,

I began a letter to you before the battle, but in the hurry of our moving it was lost. It was night, too, so that we could not see much. I am sorry I lost the letter, for it was almost done. There has been a big battle, and we had a great many men killed or wounded. We shall try it again soon, and see if we cannot make those Rebels behave better, and stop their wicked works in trying to spoil our Country, and making us all so unhappy.

I have looked for the letter a great deal, but I shall enjoy writing another to you. You see I cannot write very well in this way; I believe you could write better if you should try.

I am glad to have so many nice letters from you. I sent the last ones to dear Mamma. I shall want another soon. I suppose Mamma is at home by this time, so I shall have the pleasure of a letter from both of you next time.

Do you and Wyllys have a pleasant time now-a-days? I think dear Aunty must make you very happy. She has such kind ways. I should like to see you all. What a charming little home you have, especially if dear Mamma is with you. Does Master Wyllys call her Fanny yet? You must have a garden to work in. It is very hot here, so that we can hardly bear to have our clothes on. But we do not have any May-flowers here. All the ground is so trampled by the Army that even the grass will not grow much. How I should enjoy a May-walk with you and Wyllys, and what beautiful flowers we would bring home to surprise Mamma and Aunty! I often think of all our paths and sunny banks where we are always sure to find the wild flowers. Do the beautiful birds sing about the trees, and look for places to build nests near the house, as they used to do?

I am suddenly ordered to go to the front to take command of our pickets. Mamma will tell you what they are, so goodbye once more. *Papa*[69]

Within a few weeks after he had taken command of the Twentieth, the ambitious Adelbert Ames had begun actively seeking advancement. Numerous letters in his behalf had been written by ranking army officers and politicians from his home state to the vice president and the secretary of war. Chamberlain and Major Gilmore spoke with Governor Washburn on Ames's behalf when the governor visited their regiment a month before the battle of Fredericksburg, and Washburn wrote to Secretary Stanton immediately.[70]

When Maine's Maj. Gen. O. O. Howard recommended him to General Hooker, he stated that General Griffin considered Ames "his best officer." No doubt Ames was that, and Howard must have known that Griffin's rarely given praise would count highly with any other general officer.

Ames performed so well on General Meade's Fifth Corps staff during the battle of Chancellorsville that Meade did him the honor of mentioning him favorably in his official report; this service probably provided him with the final impetus for promotion. On May 20 his promotion came down through channels, and Brigadier General Ames was transferred to command a brigade in General Howard's Eleventh Corps; Chamberlain proudly became colonel of Maine's Twentieth Regiment.[71]

The new Lt. Thomas D. Chamberlain was the acting adjutant of the regiment in the stead of Lt. John M. Brown, its original and official adjutant. Brown, who had been absent on the staff of Gen. Romeyn B. Ayres, followed Ames to the Eleventh Corps and served on his staff. Tom Chamberlain must have enjoyed his new place on his brother's staff for many reasons, but especially one—the duties entitled him to be a mounted officer, and he would be able to ride horseback on the long marches. Capt. Ellis Spear of Company G soon opened negotiations for a horse, apparently expecting to be named the new major of the Twentieth, Major Gilmore succeeding Chamberlain as lieutenant colonel. Although the smallpox was entirely gone, the regiment also needed surgeons; it was critical that the regiment have new ones. Chamberlain anxiously wrote Governor Coburn asking him to make appointments to fill the vacancies caused by resignation.[72]

After the Sixteenth Michigan's colonel, T. B. W. Stockton, resigned from the service, the Third Brigade had a new commander, the "soldierly and self-reliant" Col. Strong Vincent of the Eighty-third Pennsylvania. Both New York regiments' enlistment times were up, and when they left for their home state, the brigade was reduced in strength from six regiments to four. Similar farewells were repeated in many of the brigades of the Army of the Potomac, causing a serious drain on General Hooker's manpower.[73]

One departing regiment was the Second Maine, which had been recruited from Chamberlain's home area around Bangor and Brewer. Numerically second of Maine's regiments, it was actually the first to leave the state for the "seat of war," in May 1861. Their time up, over two-thirds of the surviving veterans of the Second left the First Brigade of Griffin's division for home on the day Chamberlain became the Twentieth's colonel. However, 120 soldiers whose papers said they had signed up for three years were left behind disconsolate, and about forty of them refused duty and the orders of their brigade commander, Gen. James Barnes.[74]

Four days later a detail of men from the 118th Pennsylvania, with fixed bayonets and loaded muskets, brought the mutineers to Chamberlain. They were assigned to his regiment with orders from General Meade to "make them do duty or shoot them down the moment they refused," an order that Chamberlain was determined not to literally comply with if he could help it. Riding to Meade's headquarters, he sought and received permission to handle the situation in his own way, returned, and dismissed the guard. The men had been badly treated, set apart in a prisoners' camp with no rations in three days, so he first ordered them fed and issued proper clothing and then assigned them in groups to fill out the companies of the regiment, thus breaking up any "esprit de corps" they might have for further rebellion.[75]

Their story was fraught with disappointment and frustration: a recruiting officer had promised, as an inducement to enlist, that they would be discharged with their regiment at the end of its term. In their excitement they had not noticed they were signing papers that obligated them to three years' service. They had not signed up to serve with any other regiment but the Second Maine, and to their bitter disappointment when they found out the mistake, it had gone home without them. Home to their families and friends, and a heroes' welcome in Bangor, and they were still stuck in the army. Understanding their feelings, Chamberlain sympathized with them and thought the whole affair had been clumsily handled. They had been so poorly treated in the past few days that it had given them "time and provocation to work themselves up to such a pitch" that some became mutinous. But these were good men, Maine men, and were from a veteran fighting regiment. It was they who had "cleared the field" in the spectacular brigade brawl on the "Mud March" the previous winter.[76]

Chamberlain knew he had no choice in what he had to do, but he did have some alternatives in the doing. He called his new and reluctant men together and told them that he could not very well treat them as "civilian guests" of the regiment, but he would put them on duty as he was under orders to do, and he would treat them as soldiers should be treated. Assuring them that they would not lose any of their rights by obeying orders, he added that he personally "would see what could be done for their claim." The men wrote to Governor Coburn and Chamberlain wrote to the governor twice in their behalf, but nothing was done. After a few days in which their wise and intuitive commander was first liberal and then firmer with them, all but a few manfully did their duty and became some of Chamberlain's "very best men, worthy of the proud fame of the 2d and the hard earned laurels of the 20th."[77]

On May 28, the ailing General Griffin's First Division of the Fifth Corps, under the temporary command of Gen. James Barnes, broke camp and moved up to guard the fords of the Rappahannock, presaging a new campaign. Fluttering in the breeze near the division and brigade commanders were newly designed flags that bore the Maltese cross of the Fifth Corps in their centers. The crosses blazoned red against white fields, signifying the First Division, the division flag rectangular. Colonel Vincent's mounted orderly rode near him with the staff of the Third Brigade's triangular, blue-bordered ensign braced in his stirrup, lancer style. Somewhere in the blue column following behind them, at the head of his men, rode the Twentieth Maine's Joshua L. Chamberlain. The young colonel's sensitivity, leadership, and sense of responsibility had strengthened his regiment greatly and, unknown to any of them then, would enable him and his men soon to change the course of their country's history.[78]

CHAPTER

Five

GETTYSBURG: TO THE LIMITS OF THE SOUL'S IDEAL

John Chamberlain had wanted to visit the army for some time but had not enough cash for expenses. On June 1, 1863, after being urged to do so by his brothers, he set out to see for himself what life was like at the war front. Arriving at Boston by train, he visited relatives there and learned that the Christian Commission, an organization of hard workers who tended to the physical and spiritual needs of the soldiers and sailors, wanted volunteers to serve for terms of at least six weeks. John soon called upon the agent for the organization and was exhorted by that worthy that it was his duty to enlist in this service. Expenses would be paid, of course, and as a representative, or "delegate," of the commission, John would need only to continue his journey wearing serviceable clothing, sturdy shoes, and with enough spare garments and personal items to fill a small valise. Accordingly, after he received his instructions and some money, John set out again for the front, proceeding on to Washington by way of Philadelphia.[1]

After seeing Independence Hall and other sights in the City of Brotherly Love, John arrived in the national capital on June 5 and reported to his new superiors. He had time to take in the "city of magnificent distances, the glorious National Metropolis" while his travel arrangements were being completed. Making a tour of the Capitol, Smithsonian Institution, White House, and the Patent Office, he found that the latter had many George Washington relics on display, which were much more impressive to John than the president's mansion. Of that house and grounds, John complained, "ordinary city merchants had more," the back was badly neglected, and "the whole garden was very ordinary, lacked care and taste."[2]

Finally, after some tedious delays, he boarded a passenger boat, steamed down the Potomac River, and disembarked on Virginia soil at Aquia Creek. From there he was transported to Stoneman's Station, where, his brothers had written, they would meet him with a horse and escort him the two miles to their camp. Upon inquiry for the Twentieth Maine, John found that the Fifth Corps had moved and was strung for miles up the Rappahannock River. After sending a letter to "the Colonel" by a supply train, and wanting to be useful, he busied himself with Christian Commission tasks. John had the education and training at Bangor Theological Seminary to prepare him for the preaching, prayer, and singing of religious services and for ministering to the needs of the soldiers of the other corps camped near Falmouth. But as he tended to the wounded, wrote letters home for sick boys, and distributed fruit, Bibles, and literature, he was appalled at the suffering and death he saw daily.[3]

John found himself one day at the Fifth Corps hospital and, to his pleasure and gratification, talked with about twenty of the Twentieth Maine's men who were sick enough to be left behind. When the men found out whose brother he was, they became excited and told him they had had hard usage and hard officers, but now "we have as good a Col as in the Army of the Potomac—he is full of military brass but considerate & treats the men like men not dogs as Ames did. He don't say go boys, but come. Why! Would you believe it he had some breastworks to throw up and what does he do but off coat and into it himself . . . every man had the same story to tell of their Col and . . . Adj*t* who was not afraid to speak to a private."[4]

Two days before John Chamberlain left home, the Twentieth Maine left the vicinity of their earlier camps and marched to guard United States Ford on the Rappahannock, and by the time he reached Washington, they had moved farther upriver to Ellis Ford. There, in the warm days of late spring, the soldiers of the regiment and Third Brigade enjoyed a few days of easy duty, the pickets watching their Rebel counterparts on the other side of the river. The usual arrangements for a truce were made between the men of both sides—they saw no need to kill each other when they were only trying to do their duty and no fight was going on. Sometimes when officers were not around, pickets would trade tobacco, coffee, and newspapers by meeting at midstream at a shallow place, or they would send small boats, made of wood with paper sails, across the river. It was understood that they could and would battle each other savagely tomorrow or whenever called upon but would not shoot now unless they gave some notice or prearranged signal that the unofficial truce was over.[5]

Rumors kept circulating that the army would soon move. Cannonading was heard sometimes at night, sometimes by day, and the Confederate pickets opposite the Third Brigade were withdrawn after some firing occurred at the river. The Union high command became aware that Lee, although skillfully engaged in misleading his opponents, was gradually heading north with his army. Leaving the camps near Falmouth and along the Rappahannock, the Army of the Potomac struck tents and began moving in the same direction. On June 13 the Twentieth Maine moved with the rest of the Fifth Corps from Ellis Ford and marched rapidly to Morristown, then Catlett's Station. Although it was hot and the pace tiring, the men were in good spirits. On June 15, at a halt at Manassas Junction near the old Bull Run battlefields, Chamberlain could see clouds of dust following in the rear and thought it portended "a little sport by morning." A third "Bull Run" was probable, he thought.[6]

* * *

Apparently Chamberlain had not heard from Fannie in some time, not an unusual occurrence, and he had no idea where she was. He did hear from Deborah Folsom, however, who was staying with the children in Brunswick, and from Katherine, his sister-in-law in Boston. The latter had taken it upon herself to write that she had been expecting Fannie to visit for weeks to no avail, that Chamberlain's letters had arrived for his wife at both Brunswick and Boston, and that Miss Folsom had heard last from Fannie from New York at the end of April. There was more than a hint of disapproval of Fannie's independent, and perhaps irresponsible, ways in Katie's tone when she commented that she heard that little Wyllys had wondered aloud to Deborah Folsom, "Where Mama's house is now?" Even Sae, who usually did not criticize family members in letters, wrote to Tom at the end of May that Fannie was in New York. "Did you ever *hear* of such a thing?" she asked him. Whatever Tom had heard, he must have thought that it was the better part of valor not to mention the subject to his brother, since Chamberlain evidently did not know that Fannie had been in New York until weeks later.[7]

* * *

The Virginia sun beat down unmercifully as the blue columns toiled along for miles in the heat, and several men went down with sunstroke, including Chamberlain. At Gum Springs he was taken to a nearby house to recover his strength; when the regiment moved on to Aldie, he was left behind. The sounds of firing had been heard in the regiment's front on June 17, when a spirited cavalry battle had taken place near Aldie. Four days later the Twentieth moved out with the First Division to join with the Union cavalry in what became known as the battle of Middleburg. Everything went well—the infantry drove the Confederate horsemen for miles—and the men fell into the chase with a will, although under artillery fire. No doubt Chamberlain was sorry to miss the "sport," but his regiment went out under the command of Lt. Col. Freeman Connor of the Forty-fourth New York, since Lieutenant Colonel Gilmore was also sick. Although feeling somewhat worse, Chamberlain had been brought up to the regiment the day before and could not move from his tent.[8]

The next evening, Ellis Spear was astonished when John Chamberlain rode up, greeted him, and asked for his brothers. John had returned to Washington when the army left Falmouth and, with his friend and fellow Bowdoin man Rowland Howard, brother of Maj. Gen. O. O. Howard, had endured a harrowing ride in a mail wagon through the guerrilla-infested countryside to Eleventh Corps headquarters. This part of the country was known as the famed John S. Mosby's "happy hunting-ground," and prudence required a healthy vigilance. From the Eleventh's headquarters, General Ames had sent him with an escort to the Twentieth's camp a few miles away, where he saw "the Colonel" in his tent. When his unsuspecting younger brother, "the Adjutant," came cantering along on his horse, John recorded later in his diary, Tom expressed his surprise at John's sudden appearance by bantering and joking in the same way young men everywhere and in all eras seem to do: "'Well, take off my pants! What will you go for this, a five-spot?' &c."[9]

Four days later the regiment moved out early in the morning. Chamberlain was still very ill but refused to ride in a wagon when John tried to persuade him. "I'll ride like a man," he told his brother; "Col. Conner will bring the regiment along for me." Rain the previous night had left the roads muddy and the streams swollen, which slowed the progress of the army with its accompanying artillery and wagons. At Goose Creek, Chamberlain, John, and others rode ahead to Leesburg, where a good dinner was obtained from a local family. As in other Virginia towns, the people of this village showed no liking for Yankees, but greenbacks could usually buy some food. Refreshed by their rest and meal, which included fresh green peas and some scarce ice water, the Union men rode on when the army caught up to them.[10]

Sometimes Col. James C. Rice of the Forty-fourth New York rode with the Chamberlains on the long marches. John liked the colonel, whose expansive good humor and patriotic and religious views made him a welcome companion. Rice, just a year or so younger than Chamberlain, had dark, expressive eyes and equally dark hair and beard. A Yale graduate, he was a volunteer officer without military training but had seen hard fighting in the two years he had been with the army. Always concerned with the well-being of his men, he was sometimes criticized by his superiors for being a little too easy on them.[11]

As the Fifth Corps approached Edwards Ferry on the Potomac, they passed under leafy arches made of huge sycamore and walnut trees. At the river the trees bent nearly to the water, and intertwined in their branches were thick grape vines six inches in diameter, a marvel of nature. The army engineers had built a pontoon bridge upon which they crossed the turbulent river to the Maryland side. The next day they crossed the Monocacy at a ford, the men stripping and holding their clothing high over their heads as they waded the stream, the officers and other horsemen curling

Col. James C. Rice
(Massachusetts Commandery, MOLLUS, *and U.S. Army Military History Institute, Carlisle Barracks, Pa.)*

their feet under them as their horses sank deep to get their footing. They camped that night a few miles from Frederick, Maryland.[12]

General Hooker was judiciously taking the whole Army of the Potomac northward, carefully placing his corps as he proceeded in order to protect

Washington, and at the same time attempting to ascertain the movements of Lee's army. Lee by now had invaded Pennsylvania, with his army spread out from York to Chambersburg, while the Army of the Potomac was in Maryland from near Harpers Ferry to Frederick. The battle that Chamberlain, and indeed everyone, was expecting was clearly drawing near. At this juncture of events General Hooker, at odds with the Lincoln administration and feeling that he was not given sufficient authority to use his army effectively, resigned and was replaced early on the morning of June 28 by the commander of the Fifth Corps, General Meade. Command of the Fifth Corps devolved on Gen. George Sykes.[13]

Meade immediately acted, placing his forces to move north in a way that would allow for quick concentration of his seven army corps. Meanwhile, General Lee, learning from a scout that the Union army was north of the Potomac with Meade in command, issued the series of orders that would concentrate his three massive corps. On June 29 the Fifth Corps broke camp and marched through Frederick to the cheers of the populace. This city in the border state of Maryland, although still below Mason and Dixon's line, was pro-Union. How good it was for the men to be met with enthusiasm and the smiles of the townspeople, with flags and bunting displayed, after the sullen receptions south of the Potomac. After a long march of eighteen miles, the soldiers camped, and another day's march of twenty-three miles brought them near Union Mills for the night.[14]

In the early afternoon on July 1, with skirmishers and flankers out and alert, the Fifth Corps crossed the state line into Pennsylvania. The men in many of that state's regiments were happy to be on their own native ground, armed to meet the invader who threatened their homes, and men from other states were glad to be finally on "Northern soil." As the dividing line from Maryland was crossed, the Eighty-third Pennsylvania's color-bearer unfurled the regiment's battered battle flag on order of the brigade commander, Strong Vincent, the fifes and drums struck up "Yankee Doodle," and a tremendous yell went up from hundreds of throats. It was not long before every regiment was shouting, every drum was beating, and every banner flying as men caught the spirit. Spontaneously changing their step from the easier route step to regular order, they presented a most formidable and confident appearance to hearten the inhabitants.[15]

Col. Strong Vincent, now commanding Chamberlain's Third Brigade, was from Erie, Pennsylvania, in the far northwestern part of the state. Having enlisted for service at the beginning of the war, he was promoted colonel of the Eighty-third Pennsylvania Regiment after both its colonel and major were killed at Gaines's Mill in the Peninsula campaign almost exactly a year before. A robust, good-looking man, he had just passed his twenty-sixth birthday and was only a few years graduated from Harvard College. Like Rice and Chamberlain, he had no previous military experience but took to the army with a will. His wife had visited him the winter before, and the soldiers had admired the sight of the handsome young couple as they rode together near the camps and the countryside. Now he assuredly felt good about himself, his life, and his cause as his brigade, made up of good men from four states of the Union, marched with him.[16]

In the afternoon the soldiers heard faraway sounds of guns as the brigades settled into mile after weary mile of marching. Approaching the town of Hanover, they began to see evidence of a cavalry battle between Jeb Stuart's men and Union horsemen, with trampled grain, broken fences, and dead horses in the fields. The tired and worn men had stacked arms and made preparations for supper and camp for the night when a hard-riding messenger brought the disturbing news that the First and Eleventh Corps had fought a desperate battle with the Rebels at Gettysburg, a crossroads town nearly sixteen miles away. Maj. Gen. John F. Reynolds, a much admired leader and commander of the left wing of the army, had been killed, and the orders were to march toward Gettysburg without delay. A bugle sounded "The General," and the hungry men packed up again and quickly formed in marching order.[17]

General Meade was concentrating the entire Army of the Potomac at Gettysburg. The men knew now that they were headed for a great battle, and the cognizance that they were needed by their fighting comrades ahead gave urgency to their steps. When darkness fell and the full moon rose, the bands struck up and colors were unfurled again. Farmers and townspeople came out of the houses and to the roadside, hailing their deliverers and bringing water and food. Young women, all made to seem beautiful by the soft light, sang, waved handkerchiefs, and flirted with young staff officers, who lingered to talk in low, hurried tones and sometimes, perhaps, bent down from their horses to steal a kiss. A group of girls at the wayside began singing "The Star Spangled Banner," and Strong Vincent, inspired by the almost magical mood, looked at his country's flag. Baring his head, he declared to those riding with him: "What death more glorious could any man desire than to die on the soil of old Pennsylvania fighting for that flag?"[18]

Col. Strong Vincent
(Massachusetts Commandery, MOLLUS, *and U.S. Army Military History Institute, Carlisle Barracks, Pa.)*

As the columns marched on, a staff officer appeared from the shadows and whispered a few words to the leading officers. Vincent announced a message from General Barnes that the still popular McClellan was at the head of the army, after which cheer after joyous cheer exploded from the throats of the men and the pace picked up. Catching the enthusiasm, Vincent raised his hand in a wave and exclaimed, "Now boys, we will give 'em hell tomorrow." Of course the report was not true, and it was never known where it had originated. Chamberlain thought that "all things, even the most common, were magnified and made mysterious by the strange spell of night"; and when another rumor was whispered through the ranks that the ghost of George Washington had been seen riding across the fields near Gettysburg, he almost believed it himself. A halt was finally called long after midnight, and the exhausted men sank down at the side of the road to fall asleep almost immediately. Three hours later they were awakened by the bugles and marched the last two or three miles to Gettysburg, without coffee or breakfast.[19]

Reaching the outskirts of Gettysburg about 7:00 A.M., the Fifth Corps halted near Wolf's Hill, southeast of the town. Other corps of the Army of the Potomac had already arrived, and only the Sixth Corps, which had the longest route, was not yet up. The Fifth was placed in rear of the right of the Union line, which resembled a giant, rough, upside-down fishhook. The hook started with its barb southeast of Culp's Hill, curved north, and then ran west to an elevation upon which the town cemetery was located. After proceeding around Cemetery Hill, it plunged south along a low ridge named Cemetery Ridge. Crossing some lower ground, the Union brigades were stretched to the north side of a prominent granite hill known locally as Little Round Top. Beyond it and slightly to the southwest rose the highest prominence in the vicinity, heavily wooded and cone-shaped like a sugar loaf, called Round Top. Behind this fortified line lay strategic thoroughfares to Washington and Baltimore—the Taneytown Road and the Baltimore Pike. Although they did not know it now, Vincent's brigade would form the "eye" of the fishhook for two unforgettable hours before this day was finished.[20]

Dug in behind new breastworks on Culp's and Cemetery Hills were the men of the First and Eleventh Corps, battered survivors of the terrible first day of the battle. The time needed for the Union army to assemble was bought dearly with heavy casualties to these corps the day before, when they were overwhelmed by masses of Confederates coming in from the northwest and north of the little town. Their decimated numbers were now being added to by the Twelfth Corps, some of the latter moving from Little Round Top. Maj. Gen. Winfield Scott Hancock's Second Corps joined them on their left on Cemetery Ridge, and connecting with him farther

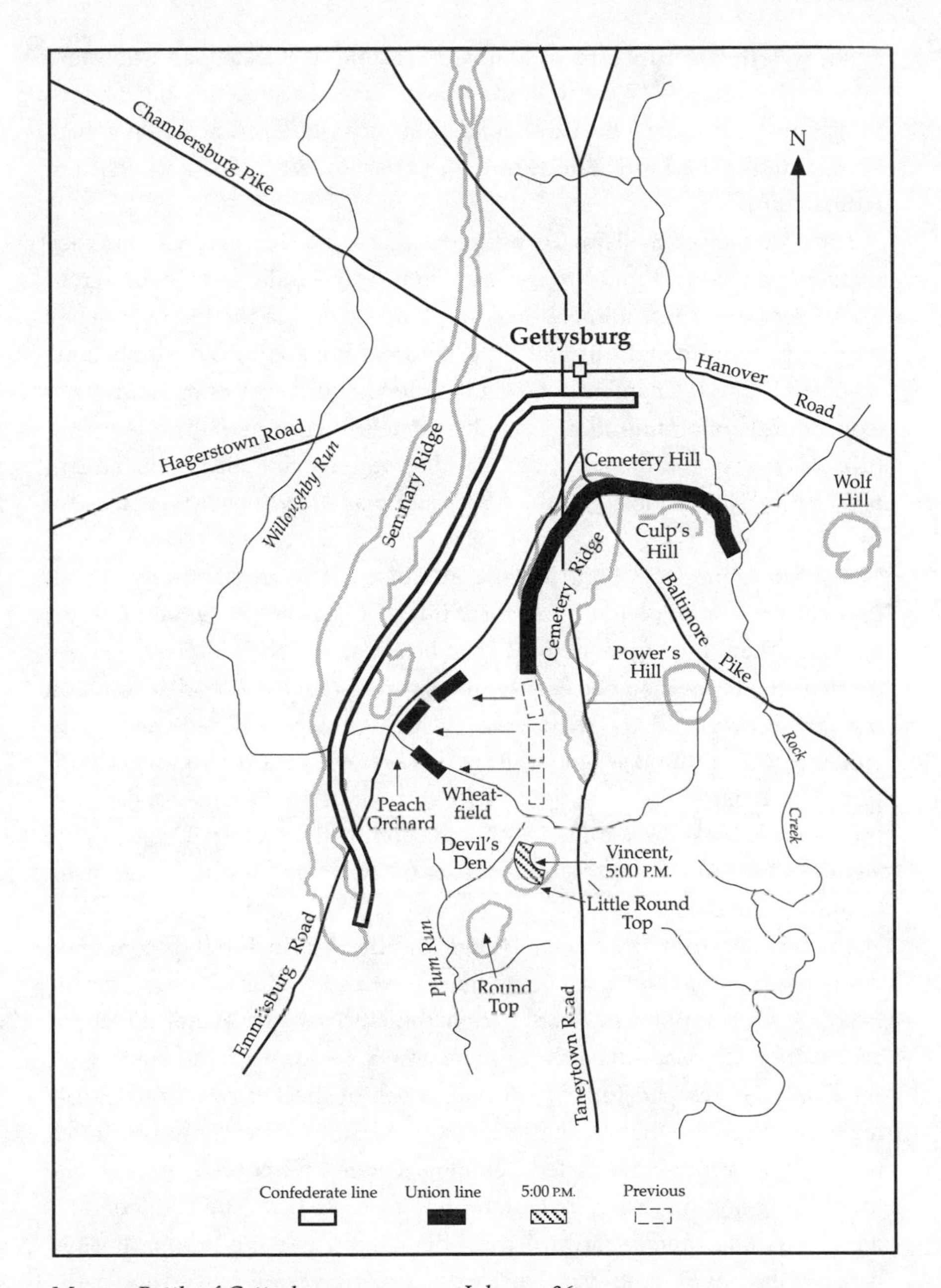

MAP 5. *Battle of Gettysburg, 4:00 P.M., July 2, 1863*

south was the Third Corps of Maj. Gen. Daniel E. Sickles, an important New York politician. General Meade was on the field, directing the disposition of his troops along the excellent defensive ground for the battle, which he had determined to continue and win over Robert E. Lee and his Confederate army.[21]

The tired men of the Fifth Corps tried to get some food and rest, but they were moved several times to the left, then near a mill, and finally across Rock Creek and the Baltimore Pike to a low rise beside the highway. They were expecting to fight at any time, and accompanying noncombatants were left behind. Chamberlain held his men in strict line of battle; twenty extra rounds of ammunition were distributed to each man. The temperature was rising, and the heat humid and oppressive, but many took advantage of the wait to doze, while others rummaged in their haversacks for food.[22]

A sharp cannonade to the left and at a distance shortly before 4:00 P.M. brought new orders and a flurry of action. Quickly, Chamberlain and his staff mounted, the regiment joined the brigade, and with its First Division leading, the corps marched rapidly westward. Soon they headed south on the Taneytown Road and then, leaving the highway, marched west again, crossing some ground where artillerymen were placing their guns in position. The artillery fire from the Confederate batteries became louder, and the rattle of musketry sounded as the division, with its Third Brigade in the advance, passed over the southern part of the ridge onto the more even ground beyond.[23]

The acres in front of Cemetery Ridge and the Round Top hills contained the houses, barns, orchards, fields, pastures, and woods of several farms. Fences built from stones cleared from the land ran in several directions across the once peaceful earth. In the distance to the west and southwest, the Confederates had formed on both sides of the Emmitsburg Road, a main thoroughfare that angled south from the town. Their lines continued north along a low ridge called Seminary Ridge and curved through the town along and opposite the Union line to Culp's Hill. The Confederates were marching rapidly forward from their right, moving in long lines of battle with confident strides. They were striking with a powerful blow at the left of the Union forces.[24]

The brigade finally halted in a column of regiments in a wheat field, in front of and a few hundred yards west of Little Round Top. They may have been among the first to trample the grain planted there, but the end of the day would see that wheat crushed to the ground and bodies by the hundred scattered upon the field. To the south, on a piece of high ground, were scores of huge boulders—some as big as a house—in the midst of which a battery was firing toward the Rebel lines. The townsfolk had given the place the forbidding name, "the Devil's Den." Regiments of Gen. Daniel Sickles's Third Corps were formed roughly along a line running diagonally northwest from near the Devil's Den to a peach orchard on the Emmitsburg Road and then followed the road northeast toward the town of Gettysburg.[25]

General Sickles, on his own, had abandoned the original Federal line and moved to this new salient position, and before General Meade could effect a correction, the Confederate attack began. Sickles's movement not only left Hancock's corps without protection on its left flank, but Little Round Top was left manned only by some Signal Corps men. This prominence, which rose 170 feet from its base, was almost bare of trees on its west side, giving excellent range if artillery were placed on it. It abounded with rocks, in sizes graduating from small to huge, and to the practiced military eye, it was clear that it was the key to the battlefield.[26]

Gouverneur K. Warren, at age thirty-three a brigadier general and a trusted and highly capable engineering officer on Meade's staff, had earlier ascended Little Round Top and had been horrified to find it undefended. Suspecting that the enemy was in place and poised to attack, he directed a battery below him to fire a shot above the woods to the south near the Emmitsburg Road. The Confederate troops sheltered by the trees instinctively looked up when they heard the shell whistling above their heads, and as they moved, the sun glinted on their muskets and bayonets, revealing their presence to the West Pointer. They were in position to advance and far outflanked Sickles's men. Seeing the flashing reflections, Warren commented later in characteristic understatement, "was intensely thrilling to my feelings and almost appalling."[27]

Warren immediately sent his staff officers out to Meade, Sickles, and Sykes for help. Sykes sent one of his aides to find the First Division commander, Gen. James Barnes, with instructions to send a brigade to the endangered hill. Colonel Vincent waited, impatient for orders, near his Third Brigade. He was anxious to deploy his men, but his superior, General Barnes, was away from the command. All around him things were in confusion, as men from the Fifth and Second Corps were rushed in to reinforce Sickles's fragile battle line. Calls for troops sounded in the air over the din of exploding shells, as staff officers hastily made their way carrying messages.[28]

Seeing the approach of one of these officers whom he apparently knew, Vincent rode to meet the courier, calling the question, "Captain, what are your orders?" The aide asked for the division commander: "Where is General Barnes?" Raising his voice in demand, Vincent repeated, "What are your orders? Give me your orders!" The officer replied that General Sykes had sent him to tell General Barnes to send a brigade to "that hill yonder." He was pointing to Little Round Top.[29]

Immediately replying that he would take his brigade there under his own responsibility, Vincent ordered the brigade's senior colonel, James C. Rice, who commanded the Forty-fourth New York, to follow quickly with the brigade. Vincent galloped off toward the hill, his orderly, Pvt. Oliver W. Norton, closely following. Norton carried the triangular white brigade flag, with its dark blue border and red Maltese cross emblazoning the center. The duty of the orderly, who was also the brigade bugler, was to stay near his superior with the flag at all times, so that the brigade commander could be found easily. Vincent needed to ride ahead to reconnoiter the ground, which would enable him to place his brigade in the most advantageous position to defend the hill. An instinctive soldier, he could see its vital position and risked censure or even court-martial to hurry to the defense of it without waiting for the orders to come through his division chief.[30]

Moving to the left at the double-quick, the brigade took a farm road crossing Plum Run, a small stream that flowed north and south through the valley separating the Round Top heights from the Devil's Den. As they advanced, following the route taken by Vincent, they skirted the base of the hill on its north side before finding a place to ascend that was practical for horses. Enemy gunners got the range on the brigade as the soldiers began to climb the lower levels of the rocky, forbidding incline, and shells came crashing around, sending showers of tree limbs and rock splinters among the men.[31]

As Tom rode beside Chamberlain on the lower gradient of the elevation, they saw John Chamberlain galloping up to join them again. Not long after he reached them, a solid shot came in low and swished close to the three brothers' faces. A quick vision of their mother at home in Maine must have flashed in the colonel's mind—she had lost their brother Horace less than two years before. Chamberlain ordered his brothers to separate from him

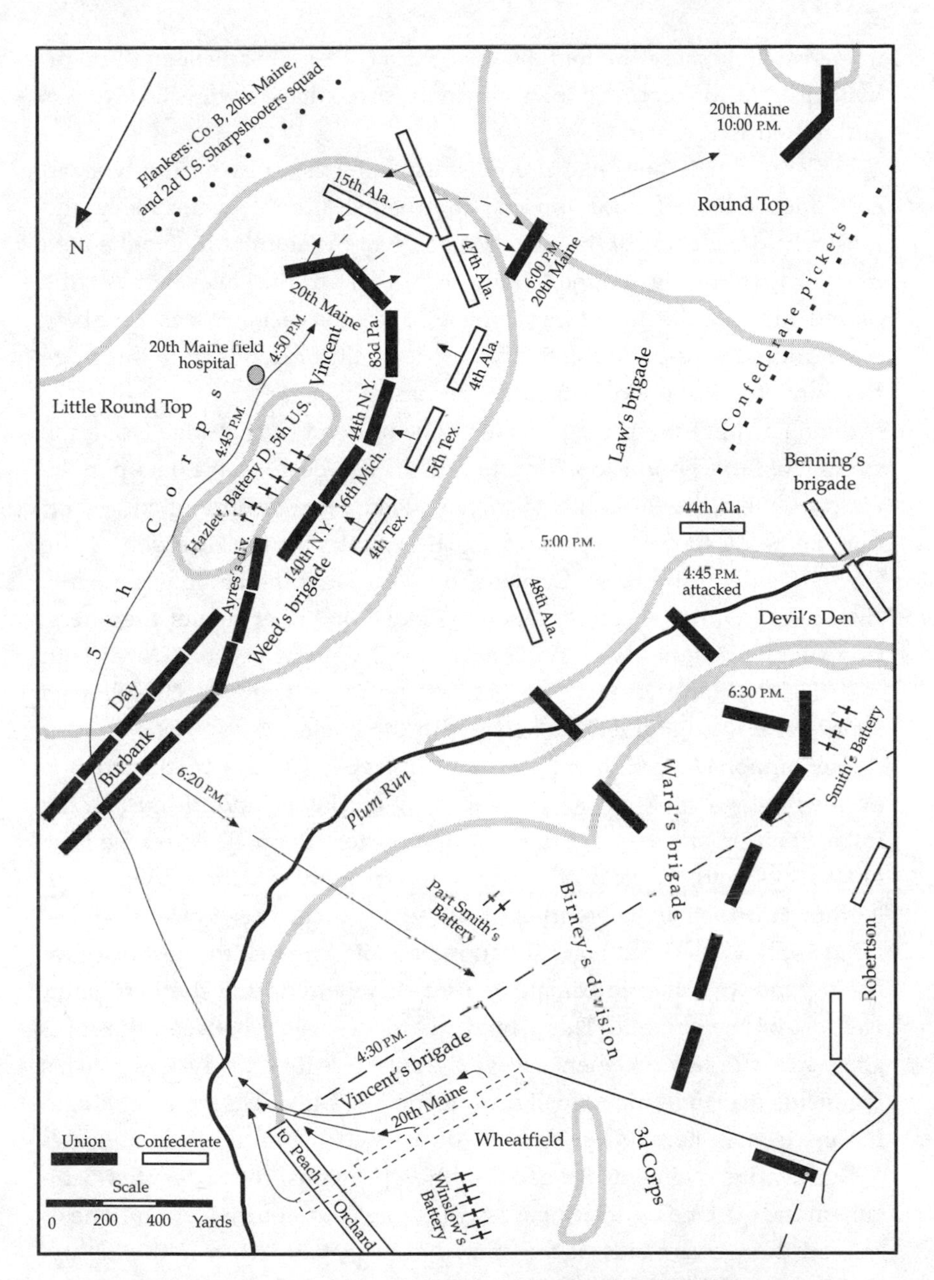

MAP 6. *Routes and Positions Taken by Chamberlain, the Twentieth Maine, and Vincent's Brigade on July 2, 1863, in the Southeast Portion of the Gettysburg Battlefield (adapted from* Maine at Gettysburg*)*

immediately because, he told them laconically, "another such shot, might make it hard for Mother." John hurriedly shook hands with his brothers and retired to the rear.[32]

Vincent, meanwhile, had proceeded behind the crest on the wooded east side of Little Round Top and then came around to the rocky and mostly bald west side of the elevation south of the summit. There the high ridge drops abruptly and the ground slopes toward the valley between the Round Tops. At the end of this slope a ridge runs east and west for about one hundred yards, and the thinly wooded valley extends from this ridge to Round Top itself, along its northern base.[33]

Riding around the great rocks at the south end of the ridge along the summit of Little Round Top, Vincent and his flag-bearer came out upon the plateau where the Sixteenth Michigan Regiment was positioned a short time later. As they looked out over the country in the direction of the Devil's Den and the Peach Orchard, they saw that the battle was raging; two shells in quick succession then exploded on either side of the riders. Confederate batteries were firing at the flag! Vincent yelled: "Down with that flag, Norton! Damn it, go behind the rocks with it!" He followed shortly afterward and left his horse with the bugler.[34]

The cannonade continued, and the hurrying soldiers of the brigade avoided the worst of the danger by moving quickly behind the crest of the hill as their brigade commander had done before them. They reached the great rocks, and the field officers dismounted and left their horses with Norton and their own orderlies. Waiting for them was Vincent, whose rapid appraisal of the military situation had told him that the best place for his brigade was an approximate quarter-circle around the southern spur, well below the summit. This would guard the valley between the hills, allow space for reinforcements, leave the crest free for artillery, and give his regiments maneuvering room if they needed it. The stakes were very high: the place must be held, or disaster threatened the entire Federal line.[35]

Quickly, the regiments formed into their positions, the Sixteenth Michigan on the extreme right facing westward, the Forty-fourth New York next, also on the western side of the spur. Next, to their left, was the Eighty-third Pennsylvania, whose line of battle curved around the southwest turn of the projection, and last was the Twentieth Maine, prolonging the line and facing south and slightly west toward the steep and heavily wooded Round Top, which rose 305 feet above them. Colonel Vincent indicated to Chamberlain the ground that the Twentieth was to defend, impressing on him that it marked the extreme left of the entire Union line. Carefully, Vincent explained that a "desperate attack" was expected at any moment to turn that position. He concluded, intensity giving emphasis to his words, "Hold that ground at all hazards." They were the last words Chamberlain ever heard from that Pennsylvania officer.[36]

Chamberlain understood Vincent, and understood well; the responsibility weighed upon his mind and redoubled his resolve. The military consequences of failure to hold, and to have the left flank of the army turned, meant that the Confederates would seize the Round Top heights, gain the rear of the whole Union position, where large amounts of supplies and ammunition were placed, and "roll up" the Federal line to the north. Meade's army would be faced with defeat, a disaster to the Union cause. The way to Washington, Baltimore, and Philadelphia would be open to a victorious Lee, with incalculable results.[37]

The position must be held then, at all costs. Chamberlain knew that if any could hold it and pay the costs, these Maine men of his could. He had faith in them, even though this would be their first stand-up fight and most of them were hardly more than boys. But they were rugged, disciplined, and tough—veterans of march and battle. They had character and knew what they had to do. He could see the resolve and bravery in their expressive faces as he formed his regiment by a complicated maneuver, "right by file into line." This method took a little longer, but with the Rebels expected momentarily, it had the advantage that the men on the right, nearest the expected direction of the oncoming enemy, would be successively faced to the front, ready to load and fire their weapons first.[38]

Concerned about his exposed left flank, "in the air," as military parlance would have it, Chamberlain sent out Capt. Walter G. Morrill and his Company B as skirmishers on his left front. Numbering only about forty men, they could still guard against any movement of the enemy to flank his main line of battle and gain the rear of his line. This company, mostly from Piscataquis County, were known as excellent marksmen. Morrill, a veteran of the Sixth Maine, had joined the regiment at Antietam. Chamberlain trusted Morrill as an experienced, resourceful man on whom he could count. That day the Twentieth Maine officially contained only 358 men and 28 officers "present for duty, equipped," but a few more men, listed as "absent sick," hurried up to join the fight. To meet the extreme need, Chamberlain released the regimental pioneers, provost guard, and prisoners to take up muskets and join the fight. The drummer boys and chap-

Capt. Ellis Spear (courtesy Abbott Spear)

lains would have to tend the wounded, for the new surgeons had not arrived, and the others had gone.[39]

On the extreme right of General Lee's army, John B. Hood's division of Gen. James Longstreet's corps of Confederate infantry had formed in the

Capt. Holman S. Melcher (courtesy Abbott Spear)

woods on both sides of the Emmitsburg Road. Longstreet's other division, under Lafayette McLaws, was formed to the left of Hood. Orders for the attack were to move *en échelon,* successively by brigade from right to left, up the Emmitsburg Road. Under the fire of Union batteries, Hood's brigades moved in two lines of battle: Alabama, Arkansas, and Texas regi-

Capt. Walter G. Morrill (courtesy Abbott Spear)

Lt. John Marshall Brown
(Massachusetts Commandery, MOLLUS, and U.S. Army Military History Institute, Carlisle Barracks, Pa.)

Capt. A. W. Clark (courtesy Abbott Spear)

ments in the front line and Georgia troops in the second. After considerable maneuvering over the rough ground under heavy fire, two of Gen. Jerome B. Robertson's Texas regiments ended up in line in the midst of Evander M. Law's five Alabama regiments. These seven Confederate regiments were to meet Vincent's brigade on the southern spur of Little Round Top. The others in the division attacked the Federal units near the Devil's Den, including Capt. James E. Smith's Fourth New York Battery.[40]

A battalion of United States Sharpshooters had been acting as skirmishers for Brig. Gen. J. H. Hobart Ward's brigade of Sickles's corps, and while withdrawing from a stone wall in front of Round Top, three of its companies disappeared into the woods up the western slope of that towering landmark and began to fire into the right flank of the enemy line. Col. William C. Oates, commanding the Fifteenth Alabama Infantry, could not allow the sharpshooters' fire to enfilade his right from that hill, so he and his men laboriously climbed over the large rocks, trees, and bushes in their path to exchange fire with the sharpshooters. The Forty-seventh Alabama, commanded by its lieutenant colonel and minus three of its companies, continued his line of battle to the left. The movement up Round Top by these two regiments eventually caused them to be temporarily separated from the other regiments in the gray front line of battle, which continued on to attack the defenders on Little Round Top.[41]

Meanwhile, the sounds of the terrible battle raging to the west of the Round Tops rolled up to the Union brigade waiting on Little Round Top, with the crash of artillery and rattle of muskets almost drowning out the shouts of the fighting men. The soldiers of the other regiments of the brigade to the right of the Twentieth Maine could see the dreadful sight of men in blue being overwhelmed by the vigorous onslaught of lines of figures in butternut and gray. The Union men fought with grim determination in the Devil's Den and the woods and fields around it. As men fell and cannon fired, here and there a horse would gallop away, eyes wild with terror. All seemed a mass of confusion and madness, and then the high, keening sound of the Rebel yell rose above the din and grew "as if all pandemonium had broken loose and joined in the chorus of one universal war whoop."[42]

The men of Michigan, New York, and Pennsylvania could see lines of determined men advancing at the double-quick, to swarm soon into the Plum Run valley and up the hill, bent on occupying their position. The Confederates, too, had seen the importance of Little Round Top and

Col. William C. Oates, CSA
(Oates, The War between the Union and the Confederacy*)*

rushed to gain the advantage. But they arrived a few minutes too late—the timely actions of Warren and Vincent had caused the strategic hill to be seized by the Federals just in time.[43]

On the Confederate far right, Oates and his Alabama men, exhausted from marching about twenty-five miles before the attack began and their steep climb over the rocks and bushes of Round Top, rested for ten minutes at its summit. The Union sharpshooters had disappeared as if into thin air, and Oates did not know their numbers or where they were. Misled by their intense firing from behind rocks and trees and unable to judge their strength as he climbed, the Confederate commander thought he was driving a "heavy force of the enemy." Convinced of the strong tactical position of the summit, he tried to make a case for holding it then and there to a staff officer of General Law, who had caught up with the Alabamians. That officer could only repeat his own instructions to continue the march and turn the Federal left, so Oates had his men move by the flank down the northern side of Round Top, where the Twentieth Maine stood waiting.[44]

All in line and ready, back on the left of the brigade, the officers and riflemen of the Twentieth Maine were deployed along the edge of the ridge facing Round Top and, where it was practicable, placed themselves to take advantage of the shelter of the rocks and trees. Their position was enveloped in young oak and pine trees, and scattered here and there were dark rocks of different sizes mottled with green. The line of battle fell to the right and just short of a giant boulder that marked the end of the ridge. There the ledge turned north, the ground falling away with the earth sloping down gently to the east, marked by great boulders scattered here and there. The men peered through the thinly wooded vale in front of them, which was clear of underbrush but strewn with large rocks, and waited in silence, muskets loaded, for the advance of the enemy.[45]

Chamberlain was concentrating on "the possible and the probable" of the impending attack to prepare himself to meet contingencies, when he became aware of an abrupt stillness: he realized that the enemy artillery shells had stopped flying beyond the regiment or exploding overhead. He knew what the silence meant—the imminent arrival of the Southern infantry. They had to be very near now. The Confederate batteries had ceased fire to avoid hitting their own men as the latter closed in on Little Round Top.[46]

Acting as field officers, Captains Arthur W. Clark and Ellis Spear had taken charge of the right and left wings of the regiment, respectively, leaving subordinates to command their companies. Lieutenant Colonel Gilmore had left the regiment sick at Frederick, and Spear's promotion to major had not come through yet. Officers steadied their men. Capt. Joe Land, who had a reputation for cracking jokes under any kind of danger, made humorous remarks to lighten the tension in the ranks of the strapping members of Aroostook County's Company H. A few soldiers fidgeted with last minute tasks, arranging cartridges, adjusting clothing; sometimes the waiting was as trying to men's minds as actual combat. Many turned their thoughts toward home, and for some, it would be for the last time.[47]

Behind the ranks moved Joshua Lawrence Chamberlain, unaware that all his life experiences had prepared him for this day. This would be the day that his country's destiny would depend on his creativity, courage, and leadership, and upon the discipline, bravery, and tenacity of his officers and men. One of his officers would later describe him just before the fight began: "Up and down the line, with a last word of encouragement or caution, walks the quiet man, whose calm exterior concealed the fire of the warrior and heart of steel, whose careful dispositions and ready resource, whose unswerving courage and audacious nerve in the last desperate crisis, are to crown himself and his faithful soldiers with . . . fadeless laurels."[48]

Musket fire was heard on the right as the advancing enemy drove in the skirmishers of the Forty-fourth New York and the Eighty-third Pennsylvania; then the attacking Texans and Alabamians fell heavily upon the brigade's front. The fire gradually moved around to the left of the brigade with the advance of the Confederates, until the Twentieth was engaged all along its line. Above the crash of musketry, from the rear of the regiment and on the summit, the great boom of belching cannon gave notice to all within hearing and sight, friend and foe, that Little Round Top was in the hands of the Union. Because of the terrain, the guns could not be shotted with canister to directly help Vincent's fighting brigade, but they could employ spherical case, shot, and shell to spew death and destruction in the valley below, giving heart to the embattled Federals on the elevation and in the field.[49]

As Chamberlain watched his firing men from his proper place behind the line of battle, Lt. James H. Nichols, an officer of "dash and fearlessness" who commanded Company K, came to him with the news that something odd was happening behind the enemy battle line engaged by the regiment. Jumping atop a large rock near the center and about fifteen feet in rear of his own line, Chamberlain looked over the heads of his men and saw a long column of Confederate soldiers passing rapidly to his left, its head already far overreaching the left of his line, nearly in position to attack him in flank and rear. Others in the regiment finally saw the moving Rebels, but no one knew how many were coming. It was Col. William C. Oates and his Alabamians, who had descended Round Top and were now moving by the flank along the valley near the base of that elevation.[50]

There was no time to lose. Already the head of the column looked as if it were coming to a front. In this situation, most commanders would choose to "change front" with the entire regiment, adjusting the whole line to face a different direction, but this maneuver would give up too much of the higher defensive ground that Chamberlain needed. Instead, he had the color guard place the flag at the left of the line. He ordered his commanders to have the men keep up a rapid fire to conceal the movement and at the same time to sidestep, taking intervals to the left when they found opportunity, the left wing of the regiment to move to the left and toward the rear. The orders were carried out with energy and precision.[51]

At the colors, which marked the new center, the line now curved to the rear, the left wing bent back at nearly a right angle to the original line. It was extended nearly twice as long as before, the men coming into one rank where the nature of the ground, rocks, and trees enabled them to do so. The maneuver was called "refusing" the line, a particularly difficult movement due to the rough and sloping terrain; the regiment could be proud that it carried it out under fire, as if each man knew what to do and why. Chamberlain marveled at this performance of his regiment in this crisis, but his confidence in his men had allowed him to think of the perfect tactic to defend the Union left. The long study, discipline, and training of the colonel and his troops, together with their indomitable resolution and character, were paying handsome rewards.[52]

"We know not of the future, and cannot plan for it much. But we can hold our spirits and our bodies so pure and high, we may cherish such thoughts and such ideals, and dream such dreams of lofty purpose, that we can determine and know what manner of men we will be whenever and wherever the hour strikes, that calls to noble action . . . no man becomes suddenly different from his habit and cherished thought."[53]

The Forty-seventh Alabama was engaging the Union men on Oates's left, and beyond them, the Fourth Alabama still fought the right of the Twentieth Maine and the Eighty-third Pennsylvania, with the Texans and other

Alabamians on around the slope of the spur to the west. With his Fifteenth Alabama extended far beyond the left of the apparent enemy line, Oates ordered a left wheel of his regiment, a move which he thought would enfilade the Union force and relieve the pressure on the Forty-seventh. Shouting and firing their weapons, the Confederates charged, but as they emerged from their cover, instead of an undefended rear, they encountered a blazing Federal line—the left wing of the Twentieth Maine![54]

Colonel Oates was surprised to receive the blast of withering fire from the low elevation, which he supposed contained only the Federals he had driven over Round Top. It was, he wrote later, "the most destructive fire I had ever seen." The force of it caused grievous losses to his regiment and convinced him that his opponents had fallen back on a second line. But Oates was sure that he had found the Union rear because he had seen, in the distance, the Federal wagons parked east of Little Round Top.[55]

The brave Confederates did not stop; they came to within ten paces of the Union line before retiring in the face of galling fire. It seemed to the defending Federals that they would no sooner beat off one attack when another fresh force would then assail them. Chamberlain thought his adversaries were making their attack in successive advances, or *en échelon*, a natural tactic to be used in this situation. There seemed to be no end to their opponents as the tough Yankees fought off the Rebel charges. Men were falling heavily to the earth as they were hit by the lead minié balls; wounded bluecoats lay sometimes within their own line and other times in front of it. The pressure was intense; the blue line of soldiers would be forced back a few yards and then would push ahead with a huge effort to regain the ground. "The edge of the fight rolled backward and forward like a wave," Chamberlain described the terrible action, as the furious battle went on for long over an hour, probably two.[56]

The acrid battle smoke filled the lungs and stung the eyes of the sweating, grimy officers and men. Powder blackened the faces of the riflemen as they tore the paper cartridges with their teeth and poured it into the hot barrels of the Enfields. The metal rammers clanged and shoved down the lead minié balls into the muskets. On the embattled left, some men laid out their cartridges on the ground before them and stuck their ramrods into the earth when firing, their actions demonstrating that they had come to stay and would not be moved.[57]

"The two lines met and broke and mingled in the shock. The crush of musketry gave way to cuts and thrusts, grapplings and wrestlings. The edge of the conflict

swayed to and fro, with wild whirlpools and eddies. At times I saw around me more of the enemy than of my own men; gaps opening, swallowing, closing again with sharp convulsive energy; squads of stalwart men who had cut their way through us, disappearing as if translated. All around, strange mingled roar—shouts of defiance, rally, and desperation; and underneath, murmured entreaty and stifled moans; gasping prayers, snatches of Sabbath song, whispers of loved names; everywhere men torn and broken, staggering, creeping, quivering on the earth, and dead faces with strangely fixed eyes staring stark into the sky. Things which cannot be told—nor dreamed. How men held on, each one knows,—not I. But manhood commands admiration."[58]

A terrible cross fire cut through the middle of the Twentieth's line, causing frightful casualties in the center companies. Great gaps in the line invited an enemy breakthrough. The colors were still standing in the center; only two members of the color guard, Cpl. William T. Livermore and Pvt. Elisha S. Coan, were left to defend the color sergeant and his precious charge. The twenty-five-year-old color sergeant, Andrew J. Tozier, had transferred into the regiment from the old Second Maine and was a seasoned veteran. His duty was to move the flag when ordered and protect the regimental colors with his life, but as he picked up a musket from one of his fallen comrades he showed his determination that neither the colors nor his life would be given up easily.[59]

Chamberlain peered through the battle smoke toward his center. Suddenly, he saw Tozier standing alone, the smoke curling around his tall frame, his guards unseen in the darkened air and drifting haze. The former farm boy had planted the colors beside him and had them resting inside the curve of his left arm as he rammed a cartridge into his borrowed musket. The sight, in one flashing moment, seemed to Chamberlain to be worthy of a poem or song that commemorated the deeds of ancient heroes, but there was no time then for sentiment—the center was in deadly peril.[60]

Chamberlain quickly ordered his brother Tom, the acting adjutant, to go personally into the fray and repair that breach any way he could, either by rallying the men or pulling up and shortening the line. Doubting that Tom could complete his task without being cut down by the cross fire, he dispatched his special orderly, Sgt. Reuel Thomas, on the same mission. At the same time, he sent to the Eighty-third Pennsylvania to see if its commander, Capt. Orpheus S. Woodward, could spare a company to help fill up his stretched and broken line. When Chamberlain looked again through the lifting smoke after another Rebel assault, the colors and bearer still stood safely, the center forced back and shortened, but solid with unyielding men.[61]

The adjutant and the orderly both came back from the center unhurt but somewhat worse for wear, and the messenger reported Woodward had no troops to spare. The Eighty-third's commander, however, offered to extend his own left, which would allow Chamberlain to close up his line a little more to the left, and this proposal was gratefully accepted. Captain Woodward's cooperation with Chamberlain throughout the fight kept the Twentieth's right flank always guarded.[62]

Later, during a lull that followed a repulse of the Rebels completely down the slope, there was a little time for the men to throw a few stones up here and there for some minimal protection and tend to the severely wounded who lay within reach. Many men had exhausted their allotted sixty cartridges and had to depend on the unneeded supplies of the wounded and dead to replenish their ammunition. In hard-hit Company H, Chamberlain found the recumbent form of Pvt. George Washington Buck. He had a gaping chest wound, and the flowing blood was fast draining his life away. In winter camp at Stoneman's Switch the young soldier had been unjustly reduced to the ranks from sergeant on the word of a bullying quartermaster. As his colonel bent down to him, Buck's face brightened, and he whispered a request that his mother know he had not died a coward. Thinking of a way to right the wrong done Buck and to recognize his bravery too, Chamberlain immediately promoted him again to sergeant for his "noble courage on the field of Gettysburg." The boy, only twenty-one, died knowing he had been exonerated, and his honor restored.[63]

When the battle soon resumed, the brutal fight became again a mixed-up melee, hand-to-hand in places. A Confederate from the Fifteenth Alabama, from a safe vantage place between two large rocks, drew bead on Chamberlain, who was behind his line but fully exposed. The graycoat knew the Maine officer's rank from his uniform and actions, and that it would be a fine prize to bag this Yankee, but something—a strange feeling—caused him to stop. Puzzled and impatient with himself, he tried again to squeeze the trigger but could not. Finally he gave it up, and this perilous moment in Chamberlain's life passed, all unknown to him.[64]

The fighting between the Round Tops on the southern spur of Little Round Top had been going on for nearly two hours—nobody really remembered how long—and exhaustion and the terrible losses were taking a great toll on both sides. Half of Chamberlain's left wing was down, and one-third of the regiment was dead or badly wounded. Spear, Land, and other officers on the left used two hands to hold the flat of their swords to the backs of the men, to help keep the line in place. As the Confederates made another fearful attack, which was barely repulsed by the Maine men, ammunition for many had been used up entirely. By then, Colonel Oates had seen some of his best officers and men shot down, his own brother mortally wounded after being hit with eight bullets. "The blood," he said, "stood in puddles on the rocks." He had almost given up dislodging the tenacious Yankees but decided to sell out dearly if he could.[65]

Chamberlain saw the Confederates seem to fade back, as if gaining strength for a final, overwhelming onslaught. His own troops were virtually out of ammunition, and men turned appealing eyes toward him. Some got ready to club their muskets; others, hesitating, looked to the rear and then resolutely faced the front again. Some officers came to him shouting that they were "annihilated." Brave as his men were, the beset colonel knew his line could not withstand another assault of the enemy, who still had a two-to-one advantage. He would later remember that moment vividly: "My thought was running deep."[66]

Vincent's last order to his junior colonel was to "hold that ground at all hazards," and Chamberlain remembered. He and every man there knew what depended on them. When the term "all hazards" was used, risks or costs did not count. His skirmishers had likely been captured, and over a third of his men were down, either wounded, dead, or dying. As a loud roar of musketry crashed from his rear to the north, he feared that the enemy had almost surrounded Little Round Top and "only a desperate chance was left." Then the answer came to him, and he knew what he would do. He quickly gave the necessary orders.[67]

At that moment, Lt. Holman Melcher rushed up to ask permission to go forward and rescue some of his wounded who were lying on the ground in front of the line. "You shall have the chance," Chamberlain answered the impetuous officer; "I am about to order a charge." He added then, his voice rising over the battle din, "We are to make a great right wheel," and he stepped to the colors. "Bayonet!" Chamberlain shouted. "Forward. . . ."[68]

The rest of his command was unheard as the cry "Bayonet!" went up and down the line, and the clash of bayonets being fixed to muskets sounded in the charged air. Then the word changed into a roar, and a wild yell rose from the regiment, wrung in desperation from two hundred throats. The colors started to move forward, Chamberlain abreast with their bearer, his sword clenched in his right hand. Slowly now, waiting for the left to come nearly even to straighten the line; then—Lieutenant Melcher jumped ahead of the color company, brandishing his sword, and those nearby heard him call, "Come on, . . . come on, boys!" The officers and men on the left moved forward at a run, hurrying to catch up, swinging the left wing even with the right companies to keep the line from breaking at the center, rushing out of the rocks like virtual dervishes upon the astonished Confederates.[69]

The sudden sight of the two hundred hoarsely screaming men surging down the slope with their sharply pointed bayonets of cold steel was enough to strike terror in the hearts of the most courageous of men, and the Confederates in the first line were no exception. Many raised their hands in surrender at once, while some fled to their flank and others to the rear. Groups were isolated and captured in what seemed to be whole companies.[70]

Behind a stone wall that ran across the vale between the Round Tops, cut off from the main fight and about 150 yards away from it, Captain Morrill and his Company B saw many Confederates retreating quickly toward them. To give the unknowing Rebels the impression of a large body of troops on their flank and rear, Captain Morrill started shouting, "Charge! Charge!" as his men stood up and fired a volley into the ranks of the men in gray. Morrill had been joined by a dozen or so of the sharpshooters Colonel Oates had previously driven over Round Top. These men wore different uniforms from the Maine volunteers, giving the appearance of two different bodies of men. Jumping over the low wall, they all joined in pursuit of the Rebels.[71]

Colonel Oates was horrified to find himself in the midst of terrible fire. He saw one of his men shot in the face, another from the side, another from the rear. Others seemed to be hit from all directions. An officer reported to him that he saw Union reinforcements in the rear. Oates, looking through the drifting battle smoke, saw what he thought were two regiments of Yankees firing from behind a stone wall, and other bluecoats were swarming almost everywhere he looked. Later, he wrote that the men around him continued to fight, but that he rapidly assessed the position of his weakened regiment, realized that he had lost half his officers and men, and gave a signal for retreat. As an orderly withdrawal was out of the question, he and his men "ran like a herd of wild cattle."[72]

Meanwhile, the left wing of the Twentieth Maine had caught up with its right, and the whole regiment was swinging in a great arc with the right held firmly in place where it joined with the Eighty-third Pennsylvania. In a wide right wheel, the now sword-straight Union line cut off and compelled the surrender of more Confederates. Others in the Rebel second line stood and fought but then broke, running westward down the valley, while others escaped up the side of Round Top. Chamberlain almost immediately confronted an officer who shot at his face with a navy revolver, but he surrendered quickly when Chamberlain pricked his throat with the point of his sword. Taking the pistol, Chamberlain hastily turned the Confederate over to a Maine sergeant.[73]

As the Union line swept up the Forty-seventh Alabama, its commander, the wounded Lt. Col. Michael Bulger, announced himself Chamberlain's prisoner as the colonel passed. Chamberlain hurriedly gave orders for the Confederate officer's care. The Union men hurried on, taking more prisoners than they could handle as they struck the Texas regiments, allowing some captives to escape up the western slope of Round Top. Men in blue mingled with the butternut-and-gray-clad Rebels of Alabama and Texas as the Twentieth Maine cleared the front of the entire Union brigade to the foreground of the Forty-fourth New York position. There Chamberlain and his officers managed to stop their onrushing and excited soldiers, who declared they were "on the road to Richmond!" They had taken nearly four hundred prisoners, and it looked to Chamberlain as if some of the remaining Texans might rally; he thought he had better reclaim the ground his regiment had first occupied.[74]

But it was over. The fight for Little Round Top was finished. The setting sun left evening shadows as the remaining Confederates near the bottom of the hill withdrew to Round Top, which loomed darkly over the battlefield. When the Twentieth Maine men returned to their original position, they found fifty dead and over one hundred badly wounded Rebels lying among the rocks and trees in front of it. They counted twenty-one of their own who had breathed their last, and the survivors knew that many others would die from their wounds. Details tended to the wounded Maine men and carried off the dead. As some of the exhausted and thirsty men immediately fell asleep on their arms, Fisher's brigade of the Pennsylvania Reserves was brought up. Reinforcements had arrived, but too late to engage the enemy. These troops were then massed in the rear of the Third Brigade.[75]

Chamberlain was met by Colonel Rice and told by him that Strong Vincent had been mortally wounded near the beginning of the battle. The Sixteenth Michigan, which by nature of the ground was exposed more than the other regiments of the brigade, had its right three companies broken, and the Rebels had come pouring through the line on the brigade's right flank. Colonel Vincent had jumped down from a giant rock into the midst of other Michiganders who were trying to stem the tide and was struck down as he was bravely rallying the troops.[76]

Providentially, a few minutes earlier General Warren had intercepted the 140th New York from Weed's brigade column on the Wheatfield Road at the foot of Little Round Top. Led by Col. Patrick H. O'Rorke, this regiment had double-quicked over the summit and plunged down into the breach, the men hurtling their bodies into the opening in the line and using their unloaded muskets as weapons. The right of Vincent's brigade had been saved at a terrible cost in casualties. O'Rorke and twenty-five of his officers and men lay dead, killed in the short, brutal assault to push back the tide of Texans and others that had threatened to gain the Federal rear.[77]

James Clay Rice, who as senior colonel was now the Third Brigade commander, had other problems confronting him. Little Round Top seemed safe for the time being. The rest of Weed's brigade had arrived a short time earlier, securing the summit of the hill to the right of the 140th New York. They had helped fend off any bold Rebels venturing close to the right of the Third Brigade near the end of the battle. All of Capt. Charles E. Hazlett's guns were in place now; some of their carriages had been lifted by hand over rocks up the east side of the rocky elevation. Gen. Stephen H. Weed had been mortally wounded by a sniper's bullet as he stood near Hazlett's guns, and Hazlett himself had been killed instantly by another bullet as he bent over the general's body. But Rice knew that some Union troops had to be sent up Round Top to capture it, or the Confederates there could strengthen themselves advantageously for renewal of the attack at daylight, or even before.[78]

An order to capture Round Top for the Union soon came from the corps commander. It was dusk, and Colonel Rice, whose excitement in battle had earned him the affectionate nickname of "Old Crazy" by his men, asked Col. Joseph W. Fisher to take his brigade of Pennsylvania Reserves up the darkened slope of Great Round Top and seize it. Fisher declined, for some reason judging his men incapable of the effort at the time, and Rice, exasperated, turned to Chamberlain and asked him to capture the hill. Chamberlain called the color guard with their banner to him and then raised his voice and asked his exhausted men for volunteers to ascend the precipitous ground. "I had not the heart to order the poor fellows up," he remembered. A man in the regiment recounted that Chamberlain said, "I am going, the colors will follow me. As many of my men as feel able to do so can follow us," as he led the way, sword in hand, up into the dark.[79]

To a man, the soldiers sprang up to follow their colonel. Bayonets fixed, they entered the woods with orders not to fire. They could not risk an engagement, or any noise that would reveal their small numbers. Soon their eyes became accustomed to the dark, but the moonlight sometimes filtering through the treetops relieved the blackness only a little. They knew not what awaited them, so few against—how many? How many Rebels were up there, ready to fall upon them and finish the job of destruction that three regiments, for all their numbers, could not? One officer, whose bravery could not be questioned, remembered that he was never so scared in his life. Even Chamberlain confessed to an officer that he was "not a little nervous and apprehensive."[80]

The regiment, still reduced to about two hundred men due to casualties and work details, advanced in dispersed order because the large and precipitous rocks on the hill would break an ordinary battle line. Groups of the retreating enemy directed sporadic fire against them as they neared the summit, but most of the shots passed harmlessly over the Federals' heads in the dark. Standing fire without returning it was contrary to a soldier's nature, but the men of the Twentieth obeyed their orders. Near the summit, the regiment fell back for a short time but then gallantly surged forward again.[81]

At the crest, Chamberlain made dispositions of his men. He realized that they were in an isolated and precarious position, open to attack from the Rebels who were apparently present in large numbers a little below him. He sent out some pickets, who captured twenty-five men from Hood's division, including a staff officer of Gen. E. M. Law. From them he learned that Hood's division was massed two or three hundred yards in his front, and they had been sent to find out the strength of the Yankee force before the main body moved to take the ground themselves. Luckily, Chamberlain's men had been more cautious than the Confederates; all of the Rebel party were captured and Law did not hear from his scouts.[82]

Two regiments of Fisher's brigade, ascending Round Top from his right flank and from the direction the enemy might threaten, caused Chamberlain to make preparations "to receive them as such." Before firing,

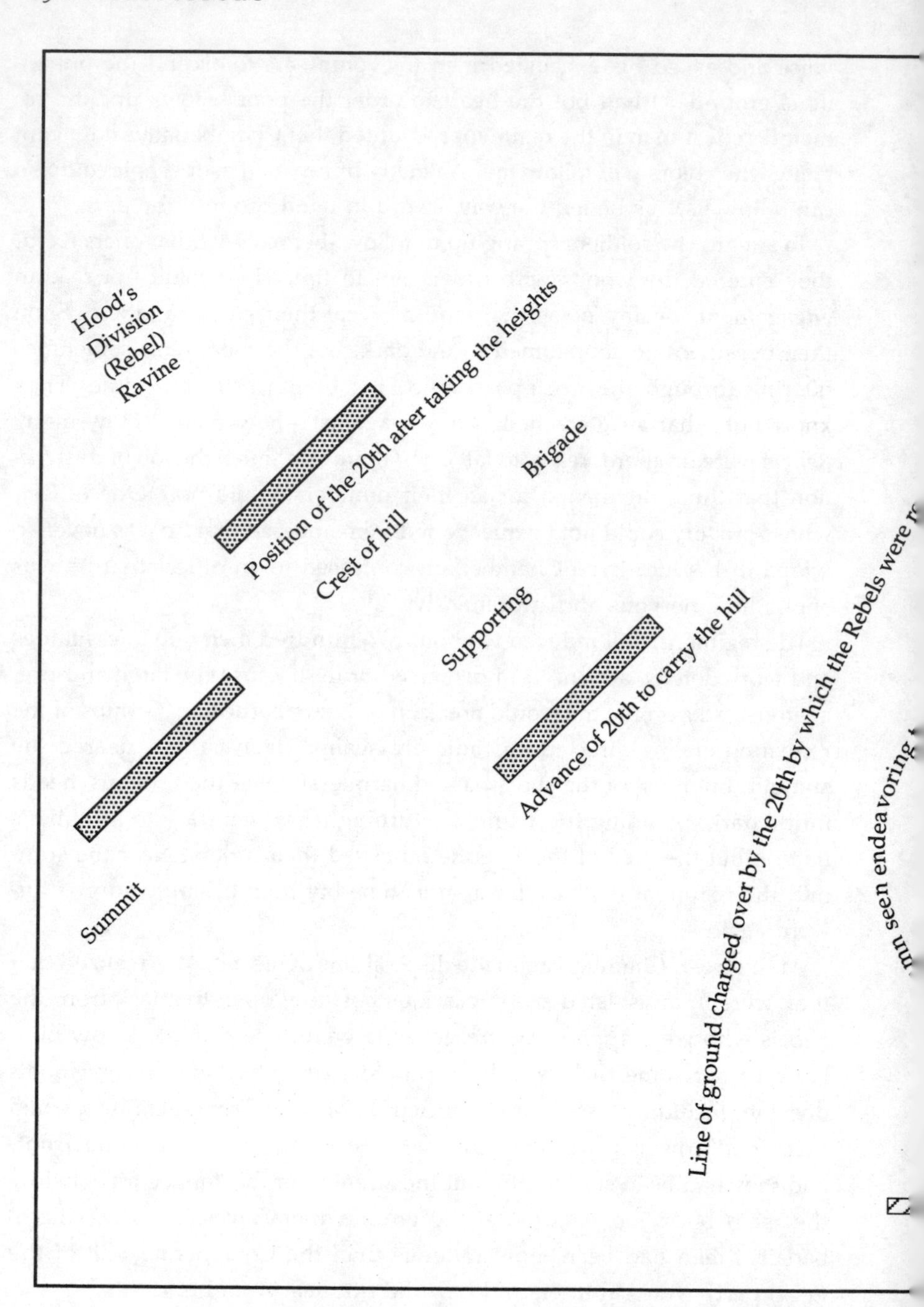

Map 7. *Twentieth Maine Positions on Round Top and Little Round Top as Sketched by Chamberlain (adapted from sketch in Chamberlain Papers, Library of Congress)*

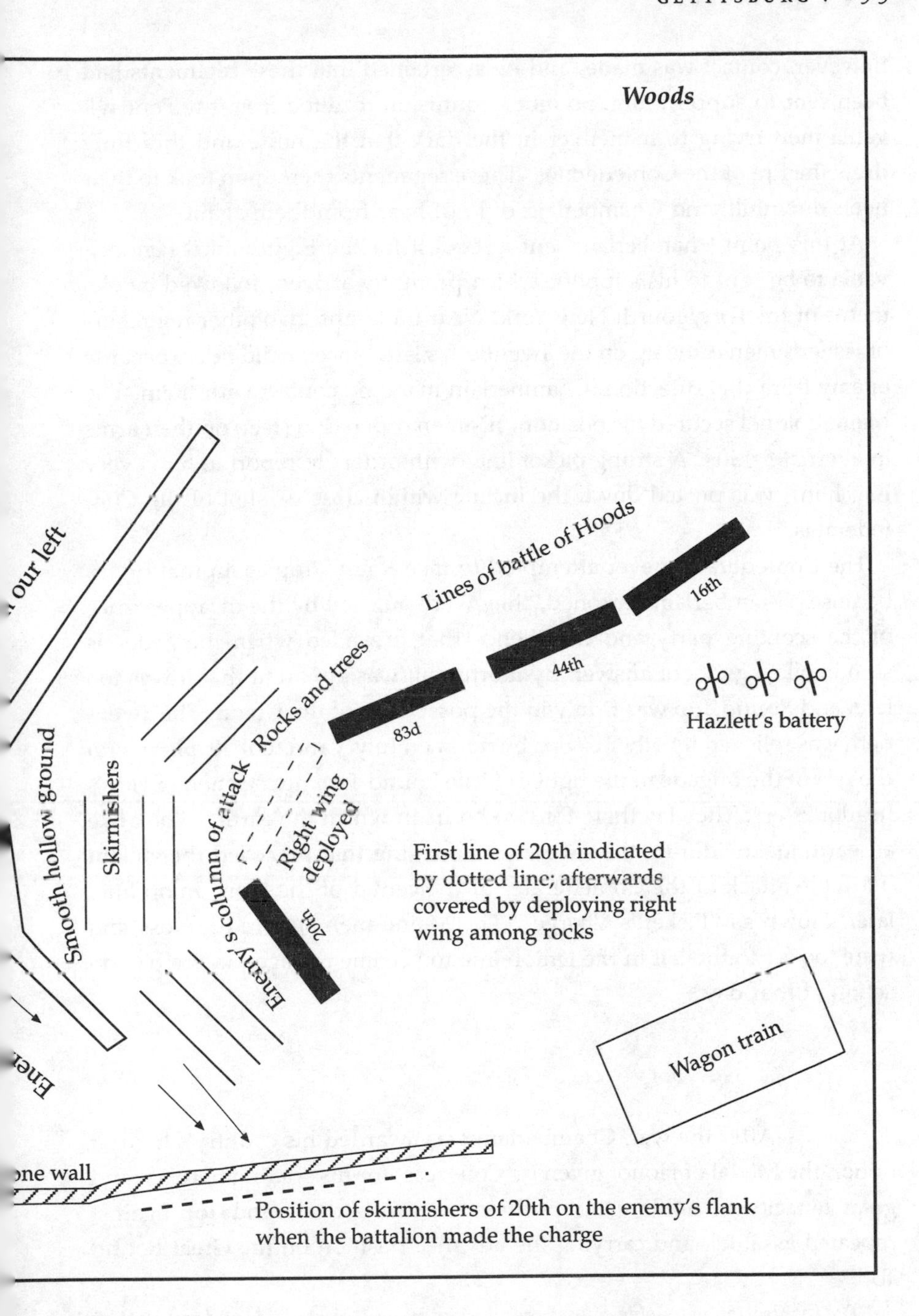

Woods
our left
Lines of battle of Hoods
16th
44th
83d
Rocks and trees
Hazlett's battery
Smooth hollow ground
Skirmishers
Enemy's column of attack
Right wing deployed
20th
First line of 20th indicated
by dotted line; afterwards
covered by deploying right
wing among rocks
Wagon train
Ene
one wall
Position of skirmishers of 20th on the enemy's flank
when the battalion made the charge

however, contact was made, and he ascertained that these regiments had been sent to support him. So much confusion resulted from the Pennsylvania men trying to maneuver in the dark that the noise and thrashing drew the fire of the Confederates. These regiments thereupon took to their heels downhill, and Chamberlain did not hear from them again.[83]

At this point Chamberlain sent a request for the Eighty-third Pennsylvania to be sent to his support, which promptly arrived, followed by elements of the Forty-fourth New York. Near midnight, two other regiments of Fisher's men came up on the Twentieth's left. Since he did not expect the enemy from that direction, Chamberlain made no contact with them. The Maine colonel secured his position, his men ordered to sleep on their arms in alternate shifts. A strong picket line, with orders to report to him every half hour, was posted down the incline within close earshot of the Confederates.[84]

The Confederates never attempted to take Round Top again that night, because, Chamberlain reckoned, they were puzzled by the disappearance of the scouting party and the silence that prevailed when the Federals stood volleys without answer. By morning it was apparent that it was too late, and Round Top was firmly in the possession of the Union. The Twentieth was relieved by other troops by noon on July 3 and took its place with the rest of the brigade to the right of Little Round Top, near General Sykes's headquarters. They lay there for two hours in which the earth "shook like an earthquake" during the severe cannonading that preceded the gallant but futile attack of the Confederates at the center of the long Union line, later known as "Pickett's Charge." The Maine men suffered no loss and were too far to the left in the Union line to become engaged in the bloody action of that day.[85]

* * *

After the war, Chamberlain was awarded his country's highest honor, the Medal of Honor given by Congress, for his "daring heroism and great tenacity in holding his position on the Little Round Top against repeated assaults, and carrying the advance position on the Great Round Top."[86]

"The inspiration of a noble cause involving human interests wide and far, enables men to do things they did not dream themselves capable of before, and which they

were not capable of alone. The consciousness of belonging, vitally, to something beyond individuality; of being part of a personality that reaches we know not where, in space and in time, greatens the heart to the limits of the soul's ideal."[87]

Chamberlain received the thanks of all of his superior officers. General Sykes opined to him that the securing of Round Top was one of the most important achievements of the day, and Colonel Rice took him by the hand and, in his expressive way, exclaimed, "Colonel Chamberlain, your gallantry was magnificent, and your coolness and skill saved us." With tongue in cheek, Chamberlain recounted soon after that he bore all the praise "meekly." He reserved the highest praise for his regiment, stating not only that the Twentieth had "immortalized itself," but that its conduct was "magnificent."[88]

The historian of the Fifth Corps paid this tribute to the regiment's great accomplishment in the hour of their country's peril:

> But the truth of history is, that the little brigade of Vincent's with the self-sacrificing valor of the 20th Maine, under the gallant leadership of Joshua L. Chamberlain, fighting amidst the scrub-oak and rocks in that vale between the Round Tops on the 2d of July, 1863, saved to the Union arms the historic field of Gettysburg. Had they faltered for one instant—had they not exceeded their actual duty . . . there would have been no grand charge of Pickett, and "Gettysburg" would have been the mausoleum of departed hopes of the national cause; for Longstreet would have enveloped Little Round Top, captured all on its crest from the rear, and held the key of the whole position.[89]

* * *

News traveled fast on the battlefield, and the extraordinary reputation of the Twentieth Maine reached the ears of Gen. Adelbert Ames. The man who thought it "a hell of a regiment" less than a year before now wrote to his former lieutenant colonel from his headquarters on July 3: "I am very proud of the 20th and its present Colonel. I did want to be with you and see your splendid conduct in the field. God bless you and the dear old regiment. . . . My love to the officers and men." Ames then visited the regiment that day to congratulate the soldiers in person. "He said he was proud of the 20th," a corporal in the color guard wrote of Ames in his diary, with apparent satisfaction. A day or two later, Ames rode with General Warren in sight of his old regiment and was delighted to see the men swing their hats and hear them give him cheers, "three times three."[90]

The Fourth of July proved dismal as the rain poured hard almost all day, making life miserable for everyone, especially the wounded who lay in open "hospitals" behind the lines and those who had been left on the battlefield. The regiment was sent out on a reconnaissance across the ground in its front where the Third Corps, and parts of the Second and Fifth, had fought two days before. The sights that met their eyes sickened most of the Maine men as they marched in line of battle through the debris of knapsacks, letters, Bibles, clothing, canteens, caissons, and other wrecks of the hell that these farmers' fields and yards had become. Hundreds of bloated, black bodies, both Union and Confederate, lay where they had fallen, and near the Emmitsburg Road over twenty bodies clad in the bright red trousers of Zouave uniforms were counted. Some of the remains of brave men were dismembered by shot and shell. Others, who had died of their wounds more recently, looked as if they had fallen asleep.[91]

Chamberlain put one horse, still alive, out of its misery with the revolver he had taken from the Rebel officer in the charge at Little Round Top. The still-smoldering ashes of a barn, which evidently had been used temporarily as a hospital and had burned after being hit by cannon fire, held the scorched and charred remains of wounded men. Chamberlain said the sights were "too horrible to describe" and thought them completely inconceivable had he not witnessed them himself. The Twentieth was ordered to make breastworks of the stone walls of the lower part of the barn, and when they cautiously pushed on past Willoughby Run, they found the Rebels had gone. Before returning, most of the men exchanged their Enfield rifles for Springfields from the hundreds of muskets lying on the earth. Enfields were known to foul more quickly, and the men were happy to have what they considered the superior Springfields.[92]

Chamberlain bade farewell to the Twentieth's dead. They lay side by side in a "sunny hillside nook" on the east side of Little Round Top, where they had been placed immediately after the battle. His heart ached as he dismounted and looked on their now peaceful faces—young, sun-bronzed, brave warriors cut down too soon. On one boy's "fair young face the sweet mother-look had come out under death's soft whisper." They were buried in a single wide grave, "with touch of elbow still," but rude headboards made of ammunition boxes were carved with each man's name and marked each grave.[93]

Saddened, Chamberlain returned to the regiment. He was limping because during the fight his right instep had been cut through his boot by a piece of shell or a rock splinter, and his left thigh was bruised where a spent minié ball had hit his scabbard, doubling it against his leg. Illness still dogged him; he was weak, and his slight shakiness caused him to appear nervous. He also needed to look after his wounded, now scattered in homes of citizens around Little Round Top and in the hastily improvised corps hospital. The latter had many of the poor fellows out in the open, some with temporary shelter rigged with tents and blankets.[94]

John Chamberlain had spent his time at the Fifth Corps hospital since parting with his brothers, doing what he could to make the wounded more comfortable, and had kept a close eye on the stretchers as ambulances brought in more and more wounded. His heart in his throat, he expected to see "the Colonel" or "the Adjutant" as each new burden appeared. The men of the Twentieth, about fifty at that location, were in dire need of treatment as they had no surgeon, and John sometimes begged attention for them from the surgeons of other regiments.[95]

Finally he could stand it no longer, broke away from his duties, and made his way through the picket line to the Twentieth Maine regimental headquarters. There he found his brothers, Tom with only a few scratches and Joshua only slightly hurt. Relief flooded John's mind, and his joy could scarcely be contained. Later he forgot to think of them as "the Colonel" or "the Adjutant" and exclaimed: "If I ever shook hands heartily, I did so then as I looked on Lawrence and Thomas alive."[96]

As the regiment crossed the terrible field again before it prepared to move out the next day, John Chamberlain was sickened at the sights and appalled at the evidence of looting of the bodies. The nauseating stench of decaying horses and men added to his queasiness. He gave help as much as he could to a few men he found still alive. He was, however, grateful to leave the field when the regiment marched south toward Emmitsburg near the end of the day, his mind filled with scenes that "I never, never shall forget."[97]

"In great deeds something abides. On great fields something stays. Forms change and pass; bodies disappear; but spirits linger, to consecrate ground for the vision-

place of souls. And reverent men and women from afar, and generations that know us not and that we know not of, heart-drawn to see where and by whom great things were suffered and done for them, shall come to this deathless field, to ponder and dream; and lo! the shadow of a mighty presence shall wrap them in its bosom, and the power of the vision pass into their souls."[98]

CHAPTER Six

THE COUNTRY WOULD NOT STAND IT, IF THEY KNEW

The night of July 5 was so black that the Gettysburg veterans of the Twentieth Maine kept bumping into each other, stubbing their toes and falling as they tried to march through dense woods without a semblance of a road much of the way. The horsemen took blows on their heads from limbs on trees that they could not see and bruised their legs on the tree trunks as they felt their way along. Some thought the conditions worse than Burnside's "Mud March" of nearly six months before as they struggled in mire caused by the still-pelting rain. Finally, after much swearing and effort by all, the order to halt gave them time to sleep in the dark midnight near Marsh Creek, only a few miles south of their starting place.[1]

A halt the next day afforded some well-earned rest. Chamberlain and other regimental commanders took the opportunity to draft the inevitable official reports, to start that process up the chain of command. Meade was pursuing Lee by a flanking movement, but the logistics of such movements and the terrain slowed the pace. As Lee struggled to reach the Potomac River and to cross it to comparative safety with his trains and wounded, Union cavalry harassed the Confederate army's rear. The rain gave some heart to the pursuers. They knew if the wet weather continued, the rain-swollen waters of the river would prevent or delay Lee's escape enough to force another fight.[2]

After they turned west near the city of Frederick and crossed Catoctin Mountain, the Maine men found the Maryland scenery familiar from their first long march to Antietam the year before. John Chamberlain, violently sick with nausea and cold chills, bade his brothers farewell and left the regiment to recuperate at Middletown. Recovering his strength, from there he returned to Washington and eventually home to Brewer early in August.[3]

Crossing South Mountain, the soldiers camped near Boonsboro after an eight-mile march. The next morning Colonel Rice ordered the whole brigade out on dress parade, and as an announcement of the promotion of Strong Vincent to brigadier general was read to each regiment, the air resounded with the hearty cheers of the men for their popular brigade commander. Immediately continuing their march, they crossed Antietam Creek and, near Jones's Cross Roads on the Sharpsburg-Hagerstown Pike, bumped into the enemy rear guard. Some heavy skirmishing followed, in which the Twentieth Maine lost two men killed and six wounded or missing.[4]

Two days later the entire brigade was saddened to hear that General Vincent had died from his wounds on July 7. "I grieve for him much," Chamberlain wrote to Fannie. "I am going to write Mrs. V. and I wish you would." Vincent's mourning staff had a jeweler fashion a gift for his widow—a brooch of black onyx inlaid with a wreath of forget-me-nots in diamonds, all edged with tiny pearls affixed with gold-headed pins. The back had a hinged compartment for a lock of hair or other keepsake, and inscribed in flowing letters on it were words of heartfelt remembrance. In a quiet interlude some weeks later, Chamberlain remembered Vincent and felt a deep sadness. He thought the brooch "was a poem—unutterably sad—yet darkly beautiful," an exquisite metaphoric expression of memorial. Nearly entranced, the mystical Chamberlain sat long in dreamy reverie, "gazing with an inner sense on that wonderful memento hours together."[5]

But now the march continued toward the Potomac, where Lee and his men were thought to be delayed at Williamsport, Maryland. When the Army of the Potomac advanced a few miles from the river, it made a splendid sight in its full battle array in the open fields. A soldier wrote that with "each corps in line, each brigade in columns of regimental front . . . the whole line could be seen, with its colors proudly floating in the breeze and bayonets by the tens of thousands gleaming in the sunlight." Morale was high. One boy, writing home during a few minutes of waiting before the last push to Williamsport, exulted: "I am proud to say that I have marched hundreds of miles, gone barefooted and ragged, fought one of the most terrible battles on record, and *whipped—GLORY!!! and chased them by thunder!!!!* We are in line of battle, expecting a battle every moment." But on the morning of July 14, to their disappointment and chagrin, the Federals found that Lee had made good his escape across the river during the night.[6]

Resuming the pursuit by another flank movement, Meade's men moved south on the Maryland side of the Potomac until they went over the river at Berlin on a pontoon bridge. The Fifth Corps crossed on July 17 and then moved down the Loudoun Valley between the Catoctin and the Blue Ridge Mountains in one of the most beautiful parts of Virginia. Some men were barefoot, and one Massachusetts soldier commented that "I never saw the troops so used up and in so destitute a condition as they are now." But there was a little time then to write letters, bathe, and scald out the body lice that infested the clothing and made almost everyone miserable, officers and enlisted men alike.[7]

News of the extensive and violent draft riots in New York City reached the army, and Chamberlain, finally hearing from Fannie that she was in New York, was concerned for her safety. However, he took a dim view of her absence from Brunswick and sharply remarked in a return letter, "I wish you were at home. You should have been there before." When Colonel Rice was placed under arrest the next day for allowing the men to use bundles of wheat to sleep on, Chamberlain took charge of the Third Brigade temporarily.[8]

No doubt Chamberlain thought there were worse things to befall an officer than to be arrested for being good to his men, but sometimes there was a fine line to be drawn between good discipline and indulgence. He was relieved to welcome the new regimental surgeons, Doctors Benson and Shaw, who had reported at last. The regiment had suffered a great deal from lack of medical attention—not only in battle, but on the long and constant marches, which broke down many a man. Chamberlain believed that the strain of being "surgeon & father as well as Colonel" to his regiment caused the serious break in his own health before Gettysburg. His writing supplies available again with his baggage, he wrote personally and unofficially to Governor Coburn about the fighting of the previous month and earnestly thanked him for the "honor you have done me of entrusting to my care this noble Regiment," adding that he grieved the loss of every man who had fallen.[9]

"I consider it an officer's first duty to look after the welfare of his men. To this he is bound no less by the responsibility which the arbitrary nature of his power imposes, than by the regard he should have to the interests of the service in which he is engaged . . . the way to ensure the efficiency of the army is to keep the men in the best possible condition, physically and morally."[10]

Chamberlain kept Maine's governor well informed about its Twentieth Regiment. The state's chief executive had to approve the promotion of all regimental officers and appoint new chaplains and doctors as vacancies occurred. However, it could be more politically advantageous for him to authorize new regiments, with a full complement of officers to appoint, than to fill up the old ones as their numbers dwindled. So it did not hurt to have the governor think well of a regiment and take pride in it, and if he acted on a colonel's recommendations instead of giving into political pressures at home, it helped to run a regiment correctly. In Maine, an election to the governor's office took place once a year, so the whole process was fraught with pitfalls.[11]

The Confederates proceeded south in the Shenandoah Valley across the Blue Ridge Mountains from the Federals. The Army of the Potomac, by its vigorous marching, was in excellent position to concentrate and attack. On July 23, as Lee's long column was passing near Manassas Gap and vulnerable to a flank attack, Meade determined to take the advantage and ordered his leading corps, the Third, to make an assault on this inviting target, with the hope of bringing on a larger conflict. The Fifth Corps waited nearby in support of the action, but the Third Corps commander's lack of boldness wasted the day and a great opportunity.[12]

Early the next morning, the Fifth Corps went on a reconnaissance to the right of the Third and in the direction of the enemy. The men were soon ordered to carry a hill in the distance over some extremely rough country, covered with rocks, ravines, and brush, which they proceeded to do without opposition. The Rebels again escaped; Lee then continued his successful retreat to the vicinity of Culpeper. Before turning back to continue their march, the men of the Third Brigade, short of rations because of supply delays, treated themselves to full stomachs of the wild blackberries that covered the area. So ended the battle of Wapping Heights, as it became known, and although they faced more marching on hot dusty roads before reaching the Rappahannock again, the Gettysburg campaign was essentially ended for the weary soldiers of the Fifth Corps.[13]

But the constant effort had been too much for Chamberlain, who had determinedly held to his tasks while actively campaigning. Unable to perform his duties after July ended, he went to Washington for medical treatment. There he was advised by the doctor that he needed rest and should not resume his duties for at least fifteen days; he was given sick leave for that amount of time. This news must not have been altogether displeasing to the colonel, who immediately entrained for Brunswick, where the weather was considerably more pleasant and the surroundings, in the arms of his family, compatible with recovery. Daisy and Wyllys loved to have their father at home, because life for them then was full of happiness, games, and pony rides.[14]

His health not immediately restored, Chamberlain applied for an extension of his sick leave. A letter from Colonel Rice came soon afterward, however, asking him to return to duty and take the brigade for him if he felt well enough, so that Rice could visit his wife. Still feeling weak, Chamberlain nevertheless did his friend the favor. When he arrived at brigade headquarters at Beverly Ford on the Rappahannock, he learned that Rice had received his long-hoped-for promotion to brigadier general. Rice departed for the First Corps and his new responsibilities a few days later. On August 26, Gen. Charles Griffin gave Chamberlain permanent command of the brigade and, for the remainder of the year's campaigning, resisted any attempt by others to bring in a full general officer from another corps to replace him.[15]

So Chamberlain left his beloved regiment, and his men were sorry to see him go, even though he was still nearby. One private in Company H commented, "Colonel Chamberlain had, by his uniform kindness and courtesy, his skill and brilliant courage, endeared himself to all his men, and had done much to give his regiment that enviable reputation it has since enjoyed." For his part, Chamberlain wrote Governor Coburn that he regretted that he had to leave "the noble Regiment with which I have shared so many hardships & perils, & not a few honors too; but I shall have it still under my eye, & in my care, & shall spare no effort to maintain its high & deserved reputation." Ellis Spear's commission as major had finally arrived, which meant that the Twentieth would fare well, since Lieutenant Colonel Gilmore was seldom present for long. Spear's muster as major left the captaincy of Company G open, which Chamberlain filled by promoting its first lieutenant, Tom Chamberlain. Lt. William E. Donnell, a newly arrived Bowdoin graduate, was appointed adjutant.[16]

It was an unsettling time in the whole country, when hundreds of newly drafted men were filling up the ranks in the old regiments. To fill their draft quotas, cities and towns paid high bounty money to those who would enlist. Drafted men who could afford it and were so inclined could pay $300 to hire substitutes to take their places. Many of these substitutes were good men and made good soldiers, but others would enlist under assumed names, collect the bounty, and then desert, go to another town, and start over again. This practice, called "bounty jumping," attracted "hard cases"—rough, rowdy toughs who would not submit to any discipline, or who would run away before they even reached their assigned regiments.[17]

A few days after Chamberlain took the brigade, five recently drafted soldiers of the 118th Pennsylvania who had deserted were court-martialed and sentenced to be shot. Capital punishment was not usually meted out for desertion except in the face of the enemy, but a great deal of publicity was given the execution of the five deserters. Artists from both *Harper's* and *Frank Leslie's* magazines sketched the scene—a dramatic, nightmarish production conducted before the horrified eyes of the whole Fifth Corps. It was clear that the example to be made of these men was one to be taken very seriously by others both inside and outside of the army.[18]

On the clear, unseasonably cool Saturday afternoon of August 29, the entire corps assembled slowly on the higher ground of a large plain to form the three sides of a hollow square. By the nature of the terrain, every man could see the center field, where five freshly dug graves awaited occupants. A macabre and eerie procession at last came into view, led by a band playing a mournful funeral dirge with muffled drums, followed by the provost marshal with fifty men carrying reversed arms, two coffins borne by four soldiers each, and the first prisoner, a man of the Jewish faith accompanied by a rabbi. Next came twelve more men carrying the other coffins and the other four condemned men in manacles with a Catholic priest and a Protestant clergyman whispering condolences to them. The condemned were dressed in clean blue pants, white shirts, and new caps. An officer and a thirty-man escort brought up the rear.[19]

After the procession had passed with measured tread the front of all the silent and rigid-faced soldiers forming the sides of the open square, the doomed men were seated upright upon their own coffins, which had been placed beside the graves. Oblivious to the irony of the idea, someone thought that the representative of the oldest religious creed should have the "place of honor," which put the man of Zion on the right. Fifty members of the provost guard, chosen from every regiment in the First Division, formed into five subdivisions of ten men each and were placed thirty yards in front of the prisoners to act as executioners. The provost marshal read the orders of execution, the clergymen prayed, and time crawled by slowly but inexorably.[20]

The orders specified that the execution be completed by four in the afternoon, and that hour would be soon reached. Finally, the tension and the interminable delays affected even the First Division commander, General Griffin, the tough Regular Army disciplinarian, who shouted in his high shrill voice, "Shoot those men, or after ten minutes it will be murder. Shoot them at once!" After the condemned men kissed and bade each other good-bye, they were blindfolded, and the provost guard quickly marched up to within six paces of the prisoners. The commands "Ready," "Aim," "Fire" in rapid succession ended the suspense, fifty rifles belched smoke, and the men were dead at last.[21]

In a bizarre ending to the grisly scene, but standard procedure for the times, the band broke into the lively strains of "The Girl I Left Behind Me" as the entire corps marched by the bodies before being dismissed. Undoubtedly reflecting the feelings of most of his fellows, one boy wrote home the next day, "It was the most dreadful spectacle I ever witnessed."[22]

As the month of September wore on in the First Division camps on the Rappahannock, a lull in the war brought forth pleasant times in the late summer days. Tents were laid out in lines, living areas kept clean by constant policing, and pine boughs dressed up camp entrances. The usual duties occupied the men—picket duty, drills, and an occasional dress parade—but there were more free hours to spend in congenial pursuits. Playing cards, gambling, games, and reading were some of the diversions, and the new game of throwing a trusting fellow high in the air and catching him on a blanket stretched tight by several of his comrades had a spell of popularity. Some more intellectual and articulate enlisted men formed a club to debate the issues of the day, and there were preaching and prayer meetings for the religious and the repentant. Food rations improved, with soft bread to be had most of the time, and fresh meat, potatoes, fruit, and vegetables were variously added.[23]

Crowds of excited officers sometimes gathered to race their war-horses. General Griffin's pride in his mare's speed became well known, and he was often coaxed by his fellows into friendly races with their steeds at his headquarters. Presumably, equally friendly wagers were made to add spice to the occasions. Boisterous voices and loud singing at some officers' gatherings betrayed the excessive use of alcoholic beverages to their men, who would exchange knowing looks. Rank had its privileges, that was certain.[24]

For Chamberlain, there was extra time to think and meditate. As he sat under the fly in front of his tent in the evening, he looked down the hill at the wide Rappahannock, watching the mist and foam from a waterfall in the river. The water looked so cool and inviting that he had an impulse to take off his boots and stockings to go wading, as he had in his schoolboy days in the green water of the Penobscot. Dignity prevailing, he contented himself by daydreaming about Fannie, a favorite pastime over the years when he was separated from her. He was in his usual good mood after seeing his wife, and the annoyance he had felt about her extended absence from home and the children had vanished, evidently in the glow of her smiles and attentions.[25]

She reflected her own fondness by writing lovingly to him soon after he left her and then scolding him prettily for losing the box of sweet pickles she had made for him on his trip back to the army. In return, he playfully pointed out her misspelled words, inquired about the extra poufs she used in dressing her hair, called her "pretty butterfly" and "Rogue," and plagued her in any number of ways. Dear Fannie! He loved her so much and so completely and seldom failed to let her know it. He dreamed of her at night, in that tent on the hill beside the flowing water; in one sleeping interlude he thought that she was to be among a group of women coming to visit the camp, and he became excited at the promise of her presence.[26]

But the fresh memories of her with the little boy and precious little girl in the gabled cottage he had provided for them could make him homesick, and his mood would change. He missed them terribly already; even picturing them together in his mind brought a dull, heavy pain to his heart, and tears filled his eyes unbidden. He remembered overhearing Fannie with Daisy, making their bedtime prayer for him, and it comforted him to know that when he was in danger, that prayer had gone up for him, and that even when he nearly neglected God, that same gentle prayer went up to insure that God would not forget him.[27]

After Lee sent Longstreet's corps to the western front temporarily, Meade advanced to occupy the land between the Rappahannock and the Rapidan. On September 16, the camp near Beverly Ford was struck by Chamberlain's men; they crossed the Rappahannock with the Fifth Corps and advanced nearly to Culpeper. Resuming their march the next day, they announced their presence with drumbeats and unfurled flags when they passed through the nearly deserted village. But about two miles beyond Culpeper they halted and made another camp, where they stayed for another few weeks. This early autumn pause from the war gave more opportunity to instruct new recruits and conscripts who were still coming in. It was nearly uneventful except for the public execution of another deserter, and the entire corps was turned out unexpectedly for review by General Meade, which stirred some excitement.[28]

* * *

When General Griffin had returned from sick leave and resumed command of the division again after Gettysburg, he had learned of the heroic exploits of his Maine colonel. He knew Chamberlain, of course, and must have had his eye on him for a long time, or at least since the charge at Chancellorsville where Prince was wounded. After watching the new commander handle the Third Brigade in the weeks following Rice's promotion, Griffin did something that he had never done before: in early October, by his own initiative, he recommended the promotion of one of his colonels to the rank of full brigadier general. Citing Chamberlain's education, ability, quick grasp of military matters, excellent battlefield judgment, and his Gettysburg conduct, Griffin increased the compliment by asking that Chamberlain "may be permitted to remain on duty with this Division." The recommendation was promptly endorsed by General Sykes at corps headquarters, and two days later by Gen. George Meade, who sent it on through regular military channels to the War Department.[29]

Griffin, a West Pointer now thirty-seven, had seen service in Mexico and the western frontier. Commissioned in artillery, he fought with his battery

Bvt. Maj. Gen. Charles Griffin
(Massachusetts Commandery, MOLLUS, and U.S. Army Military History Institute, Carlisle Barracks, Pa.)

at First Bull Run, where he was brevetted major of volunteers for his valor. Although artillery was his delight, he was promoted to brigadier general of volunteers and assigned an infantry brigade under General Porter in 1862. His stout defense of the latter and intemperate words about General Pope caused his temporary suspension from command after Second Bull Run, but he was almost immediately restored. Tall and slim, with piercing eyes, generous mustache, and a jaunty angle to his field cap, he was known for his propensity to correct others, including his superiors. A strict disciplinarian, he appeared cheerfully interested in the welfare of his officers and men and was hugely popular with them. With his head thrown back and his long, pointed chin characteristically thrust forward, the straight-backed general was a welcome figure about the camps. In 1861 he married Sallie Carroll in Washington at a giant society wedding attended by Mrs. Lincoln, cabinet members, and many ranking generals.[30]

Others had been busy in Chamberlain's behalf, adding their recommendations. General Rice, on duty with the First Corps, wrote glowing letters to those he thought had some influence, military or political. Generals Ames, Howard, and Barnes added their praises or endorsements, and Lieutenant Colonel Gilmore, again in command of the Twentieth Maine, forwarded letters of recommendation to Maine's governor with his own complimentary words. Even Vice President Hannibal Hamlin, who hailed from Maine, wrote to President Lincoln asking for Chamberlain's promotion. But nothing happened. Promotions to general officer without active political persuasion were scarce for the Fifth Corps because of a dislike for the corps in Washington, reportedly by Secretary of War Stanton himself and dating back to the days of Fitz John Porter and McClellan. Ames and Rice had gone to other corps upon their advancements. To some disappointment, but surely no surprise to those involved, five of the seven brigades in the corps continued to be commanded by colonels.[31]

* * *

Finally, like opponents on a chessboard, George Meade and Robert E. Lee began a series of moves with their armies, trying to outmaneuver each other to gain advantage before winter set in and serious fighting would cease. Meade was weakened by the loss of his Eleventh and Twelfth Corps, which had been permanently detached and sent to Tennessee. Chamberlain's brigade struck camp again in early October and for the next four weeks joined the rest of the Army of the Potomac in a series of marches and countermarches through sunshine, rain, dust, and mud, back and forth across the Rappahannock, along the Orange and Alexandria Railroad, over Virginia's inhospitable ground. Clashes between the two armies would occasionally break out, but the Fifth Corps was not involved heavily.[32]

During this time a small horse of mixed Morgan and Lexington blood was captured from the Confederates. With his dusty coat marked by wear and sores from use as a pack animal, he was a sorry sight when Chamberlain first looked at him. But there was something appealing about the animal, and the Maine colonel thought proper care would make a great difference in his appearance. Chamberlain bought him from the government at the going rate of $150, and as the little horse's abrasions healed and he was groomed and fed, his chestnut-colored coat became bright and glossy, and his mane and tail of a slightly darker hue sparkled in the sunlight. Chamberlain named him Charlemagne, and an affinity between horse and master developed that caused the desires of the rider almost instantly to be transformed into the action of the horse. Chamberlain, pleased with his purchase, rode the spirited charger in nearly every engagement for the rest of the war.[33]

Somewhere on the road between Fairfax Court House and Centreville, in a rainstorm so heavy that Bull Run was rendered unfordable, Chamberlain's brigade was stumbling along on a dark night in October. The deep Virginia mud was of its usual clayey consistency, and the going was slow as the long lines of men retraced the route they had traveled only the day before. Since it was hard for the men to see their way well enough to stay with their regiments, Chamberlain was concerned that his regiments might lose one another. To cheer the soldiers and guide their steps, he had his bugler peal out the brigade call.[34]

The familiar notes, "Dan, Dan, Dan, Butterfield, Butterfield," had hardly faded when a group of horsemen, barely discernible in the murk, passed the colonel as he sat mounted by the side of the road. A voice called out, "What command is this?" "3d Brigade, First Division, Fifth Corps," Chamberlain answered. "Colonel, your men are strung along the way for a mile back. You could not assemble them for any purpose," replied the same voice, tinged with rebuke. Nettled, Chamberlain replied testily, "Sir, I can conceive of no 'purpose' governing this move, but this bugle-call would bring my men through Hell!" "Sir," came the acerbic rejoinder, "do you know that I am General Sykes?" There may have been a slight pause before Chamberlain answered his corps commander: "I know General Sykes, and he would thank me for showing him through this muddle." The horsemen were past, but the fading voice came back to the colonel through the rain: "You are a little sharp on compliments, but I think you will get your men up." It was well, perhaps, for Chamberlain that spirit and fast thinking were universally admired qualities in a Civil War officer.[35]

October gave way to November, and the days and nights were turning cold. A camp was made three miles from Warrenton Junction that became home for Chamberlain's brigade for more than a week. Great fires warmed and dried the men from the rains that periodically drenched the area as they went through their ritual duties. Lee finally moved the majority of his troops south of the Rappahannock after destroying the Orange and Alexandria Railroad from Warrenton Junction to Rappahannock Station; some Union troops had been rebuilding it behind him. Trying to prevent a Federal advance from penetrating farther into the interior of Virginia before winter set in, Lee left extensive works built on some high ground beside the river at Rappahannock Station to defend the railroad crossing site.[36]

On the north side of the river, lines of rifle trenches buttressed by two earthwork redoubts west of the railroad circled Rappahannock Station from the river above to the river again below it. One redoubt was large enough to be considered a fort, but both contained artillery. Manned by Hoke's and Hays's brigades of the Army of Northern Virginia, these formidable fortifications seemed strong enough to hold off great numbers of the Federal army. On the south bank, another redoubt with eight guns and portions of two Confederate divisions supported the defenders across the river, and a pontoon bridge connected the two.[37]

Taking the offensive on November 7, General Meade had the left wing of his army flank the fortified position by crossing the river a few miles below the railroad at Kelly's Ford, brushing aside the Confederate defenses there. His right wing, consisting of the Fifth and Sixth Corps under the overall command of the Sixth Corps's Gen. John Sedgwick, was given the larger task of capturing the works near the site of the destroyed railroad bridge. Sedgwick had both corps form in woods about two miles from Rappahannock Station, the Fifth Corps on the left of the railroad and the Sixth Corps on the right. A strong skirmish line was placed ahead of the Fifth Corps, with orders to establish a picket line on the river. The right of that line consisted of men detailed from the four regiments of Chamberlain's brigade, including eighty men from the Twentieth Maine, whose right rested on the railroad and who were led by the resourceful Capt. Walter G. Morrill of Company B, now only a few days shy of his twenty-third birthday.[38]

Near three o'clock in the afternoon the Fifth Corps skirmishers, with the First Division supporting them, moved toward the Rappahannock, driving the gray-clad pickets steadily back, and captured the rifle pits on the river and on the left of the railroad. The guns in the Confederate works opened, exploding among the troops and causing some casualties, but the heaviest fire was concentrated on the Sixth Corps, which moved forward in greater force on the right of the railroad where the enemy redoubts were located.[39]

During the advance the Fifth Corps skirmishers had been ordered to keep their right in connection with the left of their counterparts of the Sixth Corps. While obeying this command, that portion of the skirmish line consisting of the men of Chamberlain's brigade managed to cross the railroad to the Sixth Corps side. By happenstance, the skirmish line regiments connecting the two corps were the Twentieth Maine and the Sixth Maine, Walter G. Morrill's old regiment. Several batteries of both corps joined a Federal barrage over the heads of the advancing soldiers, but the artillery fire did not cause the Confederates to abandon their works as the generals had hoped, and the infantry was halted.[40]

At dusk a Sixth Corps storming party of four infantry regiments was organized to attack the Confederate redoubts under the cover of darkness to effect surprise, with an additional four regiments placed for reinforcement and to insure victory. Upon hearing from a Sixth Maine officer that the Sixth had orders to charge, the intrepid Captain Morrill, who had no such order but felt the assault was undermanned, called for volunteers to accompany him and their Maine comrades into the works as the action began. About fifty daring Twentieth Mainers, with some men from the three other regiments of Chamberlain's brigade, immediately responded, yelling "hurrah" and adding a growling "tiger" as they charged the six hundred yards over rough ground to the works.[41]

The defenders finally saw the attackers, and the Federals' last one hundred yards were covered under an intense artillery and musket fire. Without stopping, the men who were not hit ran up the incline and over the top into the enemy works. A deadly hand-to-hand struggle ensued, but the Confederates were eventually subdued in the redoubts and the rifle pits. A special point of pride to the Union officers and men was the overpowering of the enemy with an attacking column of inferior numbers to those defending the strong works. Even the pontoon bridge was captured—along with four guns, over 1,700 men (including 130 officers), two brigade commanders, and eight battle flags.[42]

That night the Third Brigade bivouacked in the woods and fields in the same position they had last held during the day. Although Chamberlain's horse Charlemagne had been shot under him by a minié ball just before the advance began, the colonel escaped injury himself and had the satisfaction of having his men send him seventy Rebels as prisoners, including five officers. Blankets were given to those who had been fished out of the frigid river after they tried to swim to safety. Since their light would attract the fire of the Rebel batteries across the river, no fires were allowed that night, and it was cold and windy in the open. Pvt. Oliver W. Norton, still the brigade bugler, determined to have a cup of coffee to warm him in spite of the "no fires" order. Behind a tree he dug a hole just large enough to hold his coffee pail. In it he built a small fire, inserted the pail, and held his hat over it until his coffee boiled. He gave a cup of the hot, bitter brew to Chamberlain, who agreed that no harm had been done. The spirit of the order, if not the letter, had been followed.[43]

When the morning mist lifted and gray light replaced the dark, it was discovered that the redoubt and rifle pits on the south side of the river were empty—"'nary Reb' was to be seen" was the comment of one Union private. With two Union corps on his side of the Rappahannock, and at least two others directly across, Lee had thought it prudent to pull his army back toward the Rapidan. The next two days found the First Division of the Fifth Corps on a reconnaissance across the Rappahannock at Kelly's Ford and then three miles south in freezing weather. They camped, hungry and cold, and the men blamed their temporary division commander, Brig. Gen. Joseph J. Bartlett, for the lack of food. When he appeared, the men of the entire division yelled "*hardtack*" at him, and the general did not find it amusing. Accordingly, the division was drilled nearly all day as discipline for such insubordination.[44]

When Chamberlain and his brigade recrossed the river, it was long after dark, and there was no wood anywhere to make a fire. They were forced to sleep outside on the frozen ground, making cold beds on the windy plain. Sharing the hardships of his men, Chamberlain slept unsheltered without a fire as a hard sleet storm turned into a blanket of snow an inch deep. In the next few days he began shivering and running a high temperature, presaging a severe attack of the strength-depleting "malarial fever," apparently the illness that had dogged him since late spring. Near the middle of the month, he was put unconscious on a train bound for Washington, D.C., in the only conveyance available, a cattle car. Fearing for his life, the Third Brigade surgeon sent a doctor to accompany him on his journey, and he arrived November 19 at Seminary General Hospital, Georgetown.[45]

In the first week of December, General Meade made one last attempt to give battle to Robert E. Lee before going into winter quarters, but he relinquished the idea after realizing that Lee's defensive position at Mine Run, a stream running below the Rapidan, was too strong to attack with any hope of success. It was fortunate, perhaps, that Chamberlain left the field when he did, because during the Mine Run operations it turned so cold that water froze solid in the canteens; one soldier thought the temperature was below zero. Even the colonel's tough constitution might not then have survived such exposure to the elements. As it was, he spent the next two months recovering from the severe attack of malaria, journeying home in early December to celebrate Christmas and welcome the New Year with his family and friends. In February he was assigned to court-martial duty in Washington, D.C., and Trenton, New Jersey. Fannie joined him in the capital city to nurse him through subsequent, less severe attacks.[46]

Winter encampment for the Twentieth Maine was at Rappahannock Station, where the principal duty was the guarding of the rebuilt railroad bridge. Unlike the previous winter's camp near Fredericksburg, the quarters were snug and comfortable, food and water plentiful, wood nearby, and the location salubrious. The men were healthy and in fine spirits, and one man thought it was the most pleasant time in his army experience. News of his old regiment came to Chamberlain occasionally, and he learned that one of his Twentieth Maine officers had resigned from the service. Earnest and energetic, the man had helped raise the regiment and had proved himself a gallant and brave fighter. Each time Chamberlain had been about to recommend him for promotion, an "unfortunate occurrence" would happen arising out of the officer's habit of drinking to excess. Chamberlain, who did not object to moderate indulgence in alcohol, had held the vacancy open in the hope that the man would overcome his habit to such a degree that he could be promoted.[47]

In his own college days, Chamberlain had decided not to drink alcoholic beverages, needing to give most of his time to his studies. He abstained not because of personal disapproval, but because he felt that if he drank with one friend, he could not refuse to drink with others without giving offense. Over the years, maturity and experience apparently had taught him better ways of meeting social situations, but he was clearly puzzled that a man of the young officer's caliber should continue to exhibit behavior so detrimental to his own self-interest. Tolerant of other men's flaws, even those he did not understand, Chamberlain would formally recommend the officer for the cavalry, hoping that arm of the service "might give him a better opportunity to reform."[48]

Chamberlain found the court-martial duty tedious to the extreme and chafed under the inaction. As the days went by, he was impatient to return to the field, where he was convinced he would recover his health faster and more completely. The modesty in his character did not lessen his ambition, but he was not consumed by the latter as were many of his contemporaries. However, Chamberlain must have known that the absence from his command might prejudice his chances for keeping the command of his brigade. It would be nearly impossible for General Griffin to keep the vacancy when the spring campaign opened.[49]

A new order and widespread changes in the conduct of the war were indicated in early March when President Lincoln made Lt. Gen. Ulysses S. Grant commander-in-chief of the Federal armies. Late that month, the Army of the Potomac's First and Third Corps, battered and understrength after their terrible losses at Gettysburg, were consolidated into the reorganized Fifth, Second, and Sixth Corps. Now the Army of the Potomac consisted of three great infantry corps—the Second, Fifth, and Sixth—with General Meade remaining in command. General Grant elected to take the field and make his headquarters with Meade's army; in April he brought from the western theater of the war a new commander for the cavalry corps—Maj. Gen. Philip H. Sheridan.[50]

Washington that spring of 1864 was the busy scene of the country's capital in wartime. Its streets, deep in mud, were crowded with people and vehicles day and night. National business was conducted by the president, Congress, and the various departments of the Federal government attended by a small civilian army of secretaries, clerks, and functionaries. The newly finished Capitol dome rose majestically above the scores of businesses that catered to the mostly transient population, the solid homes of the rich and middle class, and the shanties of the poor and servants. Many military hospitals were located in the area, and about forty garrisoned forts protected the city's perimeter. With thousands of uniformed soldiers hurrying here and there on leave and official business, Union officers carrying the rank of colonel would have been a common sight.[51]

Chamberlain and Fannie enjoyed the plays and the sights of the city, and the proximity of Gettysburg provided the opportunity for him to take her to see the battlefield, the first of many return visits. Chamberlain had time to think about the details of home again—the making of a new garden, strawberry beds, and placement of the martin house in the yard. When April arrived without a reply to his application to be returned to his command, Chamberlain inquired again about his status, pressing his superiors to be relieved of the court-martial duty. He expected every day to hear affirmatively to his requests, and his anxiety to go back to the army was high.[52]

The return of the wives, sutlers, and other civilians from the winter camps, the influx of sick soldiers from the field hospitals, and the thousands of soldiers passing through the city from furloughs and detached duty to join their units were unmistakable signs to Washington observers that the army was about to move. When reports of the crossing of the Rapidan on May 4 by the Army of the Potomac and subsequent news of the terrible battles in a wild and overgrown area called the Wilderness came back to Washington, Chamberlain was extremely distressed. The knowledge that the army was going on campaign without him for the first time since he had enlisted made this period "one of the most unhappy of my life," he said.[53]

Determined to return to the army, at the end of the first week in May he wired Fannie, who had gone to New York, to return to Washington immediately. He hosted a farewell dinner for his fellow officers on the court-martial board and wrote another letter asking again to return to his command. That letter, to the office of the adjutant general in the War Department, must have unsnarled the red tape, for he was released from the court-martial duty immediately and was soon on his way to the front. Upon his arrival, he resumed his place as colonel of the Twentieth Maine; he would accept the loss of the command of the Third Brigade to General Bartlett philosophically. When the Fifth Corps had been reorganized at the end of March, Bartlett, who had come from the Sixth Corps temporarily to replace the sick General Griffin, had remained with the Fifth Corps and was assigned command of what had been Chamberlain's brigade, which was expanded to contain seven regiments. Gen. Gouverneur K. Warren, who had played such a crucial role in saving Little Round Top at Gettysburg, was the new Fifth Corps commander.[54]

General Warren, a year younger than Chamberlain, was small and slender, with straight black hair and dark eyes. His high cheek bones and prominent nose were salient features of a sensitive, finely drawn face. A West Pointer from New York, he was regarded as a brilliant engineer and had met success as a corps commander the year before when he substituted in command of the Second Corps for the wounded Gen. Winfield S. Hancock. Deep, intense, and conscientious, he was devoted to his duty and respected by his men, who knew he would not spend their lives recklessly. Although known for his calm and understated manner in tense situations, his mood could turn black when things did not go well. One colonel, who thought he had heard the extreme use of profanity in his life and had overheard General Meade in one of his famous passions, was convinced that Warren could outswear anyone in the army.[55]

Brave to a fault, at a battle near Laurel Hill Warren was wearing a new full-regulation uniform complete with sash, mounted on a large white horse, and personally carrying his corps flag to rally his troops. The staff of his flag was shattered in his hands by a bullet, but he continued to hold the shortened shaft. He usually wore a plainer uniform on campaign, but his coolness and visibility served as a splendid example of courage, a quality important to the effectiveness of any Civil War officer, and especially appreciated in a general. Chamberlain learned to like this unpredictable man and became his unswerving champion in the months and years ahead.[56]

On the first day after his return to the army, at the behest of General Warren, Chamberlain headed several regiments on a perilous mission to take an advanced position, which he completed successfully. However, subsequent events left him and his men exposed and without any support on either flank, and they were compelled to withdraw. Chamberlain then temporarily commanded his old brigade while General Bartlett was ill, a task he was to repeat several times in the next three weeks. Then it was back to his dear old Twentieth Maine, but already the faces of many were missing, with Capt. William W. Morrell and Lieutenants Lane and Sherwood dead, Capt. Walter G. Morrill severely wounded in the face, and Lt. Holman Melcher gravely hurt, among the officers. The losses the regiment took in desperate fighting in the Wilderness and Laurel Hill approached

Maj. Gen. Gouverneur K. Warren
(Massachusetts Commandery, MOLLUS, and U.S. Army Military History Institute, Carlisle Barracks, Pa.)

those of Gettysburg, and his men were already dirty and spent from the constant fighting and marching in the dense thickets, woods, and fields south of the Rapidan in the vicinity of Spotsylvania Court House.[57]

The news of the death of his friend Gen. James C. Rice a few days earlier

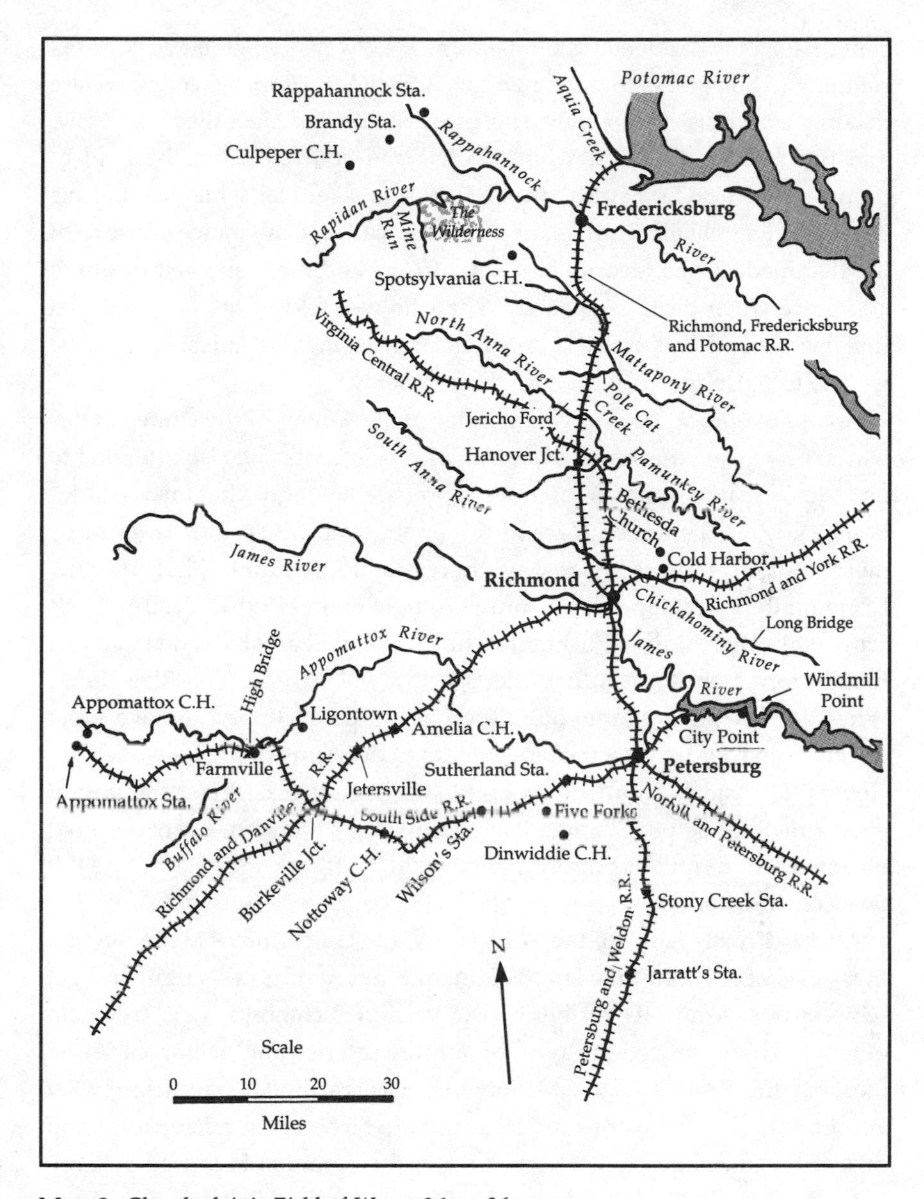

MAP 8. *Chamberlain's Field of War, 1864–1865*

could have only saddened Chamberlain. He always remembered Rice exclaiming to him just before the fight on Little Round Top, "Colonel, we are making world-history today!" The officer Chamberlain called "as brave and true a man who ever went 'booted and spurred' from the field to report to the God of battles" was hit by a musket ball while leading his brigade at Laurel Hill. The gallant Rice, who had an exuberance and love of life that made him a favorite of many officers and men, showed fortitude and grace when death beckoned. When he was told in the field hospital that his wound was mortal, he died after asking his aides, in his last words, to "turn me with my face to the enemy."[58]

Grant's overall strategy as commander of the Armies of the United States was to coordinate the use of those armies on all fronts. He also intended to use "the greatest number of troops practicable" and "hammer continuously against the armed force of the enemy and his resources, until by mere attrition, if in no other way, there should be nothing left to him." Deciding to fight Robert E. Lee unrelentingly in an effort to destroy Lee's army while marching on Richmond, he had told General Meade in almost Biblical terms on April 9 that "Lee's army will be your objective point. Wherever Lee goes, there you will go also." Grant hoped to have great results from coordinating the movements of the Army of the Potomac with General Burnside's Ninth Corps and Gen. Benjamin F. Butler's strengthened army. Just before Chamberlain rejoined his command, Grant declared his intention, despite his heavy loss of men, to "fight it out on this line if it takes all summer."[59]

After the costly battle of the Wilderness, the Union forces made the first in a series of moves by the left flank in an effort to turn Lee's right and get between the Army of Northern Virginia and Richmond. Lee, trying to outguess Grant, moved his army on a more interior line, falling back and blocking the Federals' way. Meanwhile, General Butler had seized City Point on the James River as ordered, but after a series of misfortunes and miscues, he managed to get bottled up in the Bermuda Hundred by Confederate Gen. P. G. T. Beauregard, effectively taking himself out of the action and allowing Beauregard to reinforce Lee.[60]

Grant and Lee then maneuvered their corps and divisions and fought out the rest of a series of bloody contests that would be known as the battle of Spotsylvania Court House. Action in the field was what Chamberlain had wanted, and what he got was enough to make up for his lost time—he and his men got little rest during the next week. They not only had to be on the alert for Rebel attack but were skirmishing, moving the lines, building breastworks, and sleeping in snatches on their arms, their nerves stretched taut. Some soldiers were ready to drop from fatigue, and Chamberlain seized moments under artillery fire to write communications. More casualties were added to the already terrible losses sustained from brutal fighting; as Chamberlain remarked later, "The hammering business had been hard on the hammer." Finally Grant decided that nothing could be gained by continuing to fight in that place and made plans for his next flanking move.[61]

Grant continued his push to turn Lee's right, forcing Lee to keep ahead of him, if he could, on a shorter, interior line to protect the capital city of the Confederacy. On May 21, 1864, the Fifth Corps left the sanguinary battlefields south of the Rapidan and headed south and eastward, the Union corps continuing by different roads on the next segment of Grant's great overland movement to the left. But Lee, anticipating his opponent, headed for the environs of the North and South Anna Rivers, where two vital railroads intersected at Hanover Junction, about twenty-five miles north of Richmond. The two armies skirmished and clashed sporadically as they moved warily through the now open and well-cultivated countryside.[62]

After crossing the Po River at Guiney's Bridge, the Fifth Corps camped long after dark and were off early next morning. Griffin's Third Brigade was in the vanguard with Chamberlain in command, replacing Bartlett who was again on the sick list. Advancing southward on the Telegraph Road and a parallel road beside it, they began picking up Confederate stragglers, and it became apparent that they were pressing the enemy's rear guard. Chamberlain was in advance of the column with his skirmishers, his eyes constantly scrutinizing the terrain, every sense alert. He had developed the habit on the march of anticipating the enemy; he would imagine an attack coming from a nearby woods, or a battery suddenly materializing on a hill, and immediately formulate plans to meet the emergency. His excellent military eye—the ability to see and comprehend a situation in an instant—he attributed to his old technique of intense observation and the scanning of a written or printed page for the troublesome consonant sounds that had caused him to stutter.[63]

Suddenly, a cannon shot whizzed over the heads of the men and exploded. A puff of smoke above some trees on a farther rise betrayed the location of an enemy battery accompanied by some cavalry. After explaining his plan of action to General Griffin, Chamberlain ordered the Sixteenth Michigan and Eighty-third Pennsylvania forward along the road toward the hill as a diversion. Leading the other regiments, he advanced to capture the guns, using the woods and a nearby hollow to gain the flank of the Rebels unseen. He advised his officers to concentrate on shooting the horses, especially the wheel horses, when they neared the battery, so that the guns could not readily be gotten away in the ensuing tangle.[64]

The operation was progressing well when soldiers of a Pennsylvania regiment stopped at the bank of a narrow, deep-looking, muddy stream inelegantly named Pole Cat Creek and refused to budge in spite of their officers' entreaties. Impatient at the delay, Chamberlain urged the men to ford the creek and, when they still hesitated, told them to take down a heavy board fence that was standing nearby and throw it across. Obeying his orders, the men used the fence to successfully cross the water, but the confusion attracted the notice of the Confederates. Giving the oncoming troops a blast of canister, the battery limbered up and dashed away. Chamberlain was disgruntled by the loss of the prize and annoyed whenever he thought of the poor behavior of the regiment that day.[65]

That night a flock of hapless sheep wandered near the Third Brigade camp, and their proximity was too much for the hungry soldiers, whose rations for the past few weeks had been mostly hardtack, coffee, and an occasional bit of beef. When General Bartlett appeared at the scene the next morning, he noticed the piles of pelts and other refuse that were the only remains of the woolly animals. Looking about him, he must have seen some well-fed soldiers with carefully innocent-looking expressions watching him intently, because he imperturbably observed, with inarguable logic, "If sheep attack you, you are obliged to fight."[66]

When they reached the North Anna River the next day, the Fifth Corps crossed at the ford near Jericho Mills in the early afternoon. Griffin's division led the way, wading across in the waist-deep water and climbing the high, precipitous bank on the south side of the river. While a pontoon bridge was built and the rest of the corps with its guns and trains crossed, the division moved inland about three-quarters of a mile. They deployed in a woods with Sweitzer's Second Brigade ahead, Ayres's brigade to the left of Sweitzer, and Bartlett's Third Brigade, which included Chamberlain and the Twentieth Maine, in reserve in rear of the division center.[67]

Late in the afternoon a large force of Confederates of A. P. Hill's corps struck Sweitzer hard after his men had begun to entrench, and Bartlett's brigade rushed forward to reinforce Sweitzer, who gallantly held on. Near that time, Brig. Gen. Lysander Cutler's Fourth Division was just coming into position on Sweitzer's right when it was suddenly attacked by a flanking Rebel brigade. Some of Cutler's men gave way completely, and this break uncovered Griffin's flank, but three regiments of Bartlett's brigade literally ran into the breach handsomely, and with the concentrated fire of several of the corps's well-placed batteries, the Rebels were repulsed.[68]

Three other regiments of Bartlett's brigade hurried to the division left, assigned to hold the interval between two divisions of the corps. One Twentieth Maine man related later that the fire was tremendous there, but Chamberlain had his men lie down while he stood out ahead of them to watch for the right time to strike the enemy. When several of his officers earnestly urged him to take some cover, he was heard to reply, "I am in no more danger than any other person would be here. It is necessary to know what is going on." Chamberlain usually did not expose himself to danger recklessly, but he did not hesitate to incur risk in order to do his whole duty. Now, as darkness set in, the Southerners withdrew with heavy loss. The Fifth Corps, which was separated from the rest of the army, had nearly met disaster, and it was reported that Lee was sorely disappointed in the results of the attack on Warren's corps.[69]

Hancock's Second Corps, meanwhile, attempted to cross the North Anna four miles farther downstream and were opposed so vigorously by the Confederates that all did not reach the other side until the next day. Pushing out then, Hancock found Lee heavily entrenched with artillery positioned about a half-mile upriver, his left on the river and extending along the North Anna up to Ox Ford, and his right resting near the Hanover Marshes; his line was about three miles long running southeast. Hancock's men set about building breastworks within six to eight hundred yards of this line. General Burnside had been ordered to make a crossing at Ox Ford but could not because of the presence of the heavy Confederate force; he finally crossed part of his corps about a mile farther upstream, near the location of the Fifth Corps.[70]

Entrenching their position south of Jericho Mills the night after they crossed the river, the Fifth Corps found the enemy gone from their front as the morning mists rose after dawn the next day. The Sixth Corps crossed the river behind the Fifth, and parts of both were thrown forward to the Virginia Central Railroad on their front and followed it eastward. That day and part of the next were spent developing and examining the enemy line, which was found to run on a heavily fortified diagonal from Ox Ford southwest to Anderson's Mill on the Little River, a distance of a mile and a half. The Fifth Corps proceeded to entrench themselves a few hundred yards from this line, the Virginia soil yielding easily to the efforts of thousands of soldiers, while other work parties tore up the tracks of the railroad for several miles.[71]

One staff officer was constantly amazed at how quickly both armies could throw up fortifications using bayonets, canteen halves, tin plates, and a few shovels. In one day there would be good rifle pits; the second would see artillery placed behind a regular infantry parapet with battle flags flying from the top, and by the third day there would be entrenched batteries with abatis in front. The whole procedure could be condensed into twenty-four hours if need be, the men working hard with little rest for the protection the barricades would afford them. In Virginia, miles of such works ran in every direction, marking the strategic lines of the armies.[72]

Lee had skillfully insinuated his troops between the two wings of the Union army, his lines forming an inverted V with its blunted center on the North Anna and its two ends on either side resting on a river or a swamp. The whole position covered Hanover Junction. If attacked, Lee could easily reinforce his lines from within, while Union forces, except for elements of one corps, would have to cross the North Anna twice to assist each other. Finally, the two armies virtually besieged each other over the barricades, with sharpshooters from each side firing sporadically at any exposed target. Deciding there was little likelihood of success in attacking the formidable Rebel works, on the night of May 26 the Union generals silently withdrew their troops from their entrenchments and recrossed the North Anna. In another move flanking the Army of Northern Virginia, the Twentieth Maine moved with the Fifth Corps east and southward all night and all the next day on a forced march of thirty-five miles before they halted for the night. Early the next morning an eight-mile march brought them to the Pamunkey River, which they crossed at Hanover Town.[73]

With the crossing of the Pamunkey, the Army of the Potomac was again near the 1862 battlefields where veterans of McClellan's failed Peninsula campaign had served in the early summer before the Twentieth Maine was organized. Richmond was only a few miles away, and the rapid movement of his army enabled Grant to change his supply base a second time since leaving Spotsylvania Court House—to White House on the north bank of the Pamunkey where the Richmond and York River Railroad crossed. General Butler held City Point and was still sealed in the Bermuda Hundred at the confluence of the Appomattox and the James Rivers by a small force of Lee's infantry, but he sent to Grant, as ordered, Gen. William F. Smith and his Eighteenth Corps. However, General Lee had no intention of allowing the Union army to gain the rear of his army or to fall back yet into the main fortifications of the Confederate capital; he rushed his troops south again by shorter routes soon after Grant abandoned his lines at the North Anna.[74]

Reconnaissances in force south of the Pamunkey revealed to the Union generals that Lee's army was heavily defending a line north of the Chickahominy River, the latter making a barrier to the outer fortifications of Richmond. With Griffin's division leading Warren's corps, Chamberlain and his men were in almost constant contact with the Rebel army as they contested the ground nearer the Confederate capital. The country was marshy in places, with small streams and the tributaries of larger ones abounding, crisscrossed by a few main roads and innumerable narrow, ill-defined ones. In the oppressive heat, the armies met and clashed in various skirmishes and combats, built entrenchments, and marched on the dusty roads, giving each other little rest.[75]

At the end of May and in the first days of June, Griffin's division was located near Bethesda Church and came under a severe artillery fire. Chamberlain was on the line directing and assisting in building entrenchments, for it was not uncommon for him to take spade or axe in hand to start a work correctly. After the breastwork was finished and the men ordered to take cover, Chamberlain stood aside from the fortifications while watching enemy movements through his field glasses. Concentrating on his task, he paid no attention when a ten-pound Parrott round tore through a tree hardly a foot from his head. His men knew him to be oblivious to danger while he performed what he insisted was his duty, but when some case shot exploded pieces of iron that fell in fragments around him, some of his sergeants could stand it no longer. Rushing into the open, they seized him bodily and carried him to the shelter of the works, risking their lives and possible discipline for such insubordinate action, but demonstrating their affection for him in a way that could not be doubted, only pardoned.[76]

After much movement and repositioning of both Union and Confederate troops with assaults and counterattacks, the armies faced each other across a wide, six-mile front in the vicinity of the strategic crossroads at Cold Harbor.

The Confederate defenses were formidably located upon naturally strong ground with artillery in an excellent position to sweep an oncoming force with both direct and enfilading fire. Grant hoped to dislodge the Confederates and inflict heavy losses as he forced them back across the Chickahominy River, which was at low water at that time, and upon the Richmond fortifications. Finally, at 4:30 A.M. on June 3, a frontal attack ordered by General Grant all along the Union line was executed.[77]

The result was a disaster that forever blemished Grant's record and caused the death and wounding of thousands of some of the Union's best officers and men within an hour of the initial assault. Heavy casualties mounted in the Second, Sixth, and Eighteenth Corps before the attacks were suspended. Losses were comparatively light in the Fifth, which held a long front of over three miles and was too extended for offensive operations. However, Griffin's division on Warren's right cooperated with Burnside's Ninth Corps and made a successful attack on Heth's and Rodes's divisions. Later in the morning when an order went out to renew the assault, each corps to advance without reference to the other, it was reported that no one stirred—the generals made excuses later for the inaction—a silent protest that nothing could be gained from further slaughter.[78]

Ulysses S. Grant later said of the failure of that terrible June day, "I have always regretted that the last assault at Cold Harbor was ever made. . . . No advantage whatever was gained to compensate for the heavy loss we sustained." It was no wonder: on that day at least 5,600 men were killed or wounded, most in the first hour of the desperate attack across open ground or swamp or ravines under withering artillery and musket fire. The valiant Union troops came close to the Confederate works in some places after carrying advance rifle pits but could inflict little loss on the well-protected enemy. The entire campaign from the Rapidan to the Chickahominy cost the Army of the Potomac at least 55,000 casualties, while Lee's losses were estimated to be much less.[79]

"The Wilderness, Spotsylvania, the North Anna, Cold Harbor . . . unspoken, unspeakable history. Call back that roseate May morning, all the springs of life athrill, that youthful army pressing the bridges of the Rapidan, flower of Northern homes, thousands upon thousands; tested in valor, disciplined by experience, hearts swelling with manly courage, confident trust, and supreme devotion,—to be plunged straightway into hell-like horrors; the murderous maze where desperate instinct replaced impossible tactics; men mowing each other down almost at hand-reach, invisible each to each other till the flaming muzzles cut lurid windows

through the matted brush and bramble walls, and underneath the darkened woods low-lying cannon and bursting shells set the earth itself on fire, and wrapped in winding sheets of flame unnumbered, thick-strewn bodies of dead and dying, never to be found or known on earth again.

"Then the rushing, forced flank movements, known and overmatched by the ever-alert enemy; followed by reckless front attacks, where highest valor was deepest loss . . . all the way down to the fateful Chickahominy . . . morning reports at last not called for, and when we asked explanation our superiors answered,—confidentially, lest it seem disloyal: 'Because the country would not stand it, if they knew.'"[80]

CHAPTER

Seven

IN THE HANDS OF PROVIDENCE

On June 5 General Warren reorganized the corps. This time he changed the entire First Brigade of General Griffin's First Division from mostly Regular Army to all volunteer soldiers. Five veteran Pennsylvania regiments of the old First Corps—the 121st and 142d from Rowley's brigade and the 143d, 149th, and 150th from Roy Stone's Bucktail Brigade—were combined with a large, new regiment, the 187th Pennsylvania. Chamberlain received the gratifying news that he was to be the commander of the new outfit, although there were colonels senior to him eligible for the command. One soldier in the Twenty-second Massachusetts was unhappy with General Warren's decision because his colonel, William S. Tilton, was the ranking colonel of the division and should have been given the brigade.[1]

After bidding farewell to his beloved Twentieth Maine, the next day Chamberlain called on Gen. Lysander S. Cutler, the Fourth Division com-

Sgt. Patrick DeLacy

mander. Cutler, veteran of the old First Corps, was very reluctant to give up one brigade of his division of First Corps men to another command, but he obeyed orders and turned the brigade over to Chamberlain. Commanding a brigade with a colonel's rank and allowances caused certain staffing problems and other inconveniences, but Chamberlain must have felt both satisfaction and challenge in his new assignment. However, his prior expe-

Capt. John Bigelow
(Massachusetts Commandery, MOLLUS, and U.S. Army Military History Institute, Carlisle Barracks, Pa.)

Brig. Gen. Lysander Cutler
(Massachusetts Commandery, MOLLUS, *and U.S. Army Military History Institute, Carlisle Barracks, Pa.)*

Lt. Ransford B. Webb

rience in brigade command had been with the Third Brigade, which included his own regiment and other familiar units and faces. Now, all were strangers to him.[2]

The men of the five old regiments were ragged, dirty, and lousy, but they were unmistakably seasoned fighters. Survivors of the past terrible month since the army crossed the Rapidan, their regiments had taken awful losses, and Chamberlain knew their reputations. At Gettysburg they had fought with the First Corps between the Chambersburg Pike and the Hagerstown Road on the first day of the battle. When the corps was at last overwhelmed, the Bucktails had been among the last to leave the field; their orderly retreat into the town had found them nearly surrounded by the enemy, but most escaped. Now their ranks were depleted, with some companies numbering little more than squads and led by enlisted men. They were tired, worn down, and needed rest badly.[3]

In contrast, the new regiment, the 187th Pennsylvania, had its beginnings as a six-month battalion organized the year before, when Lee invaded Pennsylvania. Most of the soldiers had never seen action and had been transported by boat up the Rappahannock to Port Royal, Virginia, where they burned their surplus clothing and headed south. They joined Chamberlain's brigade on June 6, after a hot, five-day march. Like all green soldiers, they took much more than they could carry; much of the superfluous gear they started with was strewn from Cold Harbor back to Port Royal. The Virginia sun blazed, but they did no fighting, had ample water, and even had the opportunity to bathe. Their ranks contained the regulation number of officers, who had drilled and trained the men, but they lacked the precision and discipline required for the kind of service that soon would be asked of them. However, Chamberlain considered them "a fine new regiment" and was satisfied with his command.[4]

Calling together all of the officers of the new brigade, Chamberlain told them that although he might be a stranger to them, he was no stranger to their excellent reputations and fighting qualifications. He hoped that their confidence in each other would be mutual, and he would do his best to "fill the measure" of his duty. One officer was so impressed with this short speech that he went back to his regiment and reported that it had a "trump" for a brigade commander, whatever might happen. Chamberlain's superiors also shared this high opinion of him.[5]

On that same day, General Warren asked General Griffin to "make out a recommendation for the promotion of Colonel Chamberlain." General Bartlett promptly wrote a glowing letter of recommendation for Chamberlain's promotion to brigadier general, and Griffin's endorsement requested its quick approval. General Warren, in turn, "earnestly recommended" it, with the observation that Chamberlain was entitled to the promotion, and added in his own handwriting this unusual statement: "I am sure his appointment would add to my strength even more than the reinforcement of a thousand men." It was forwarded at once, and three days later General Meade included Chamberlain's name on a short promotion list sent to the War Department.[6]

Very early in the morning of June 7, Griffin's and Cutler's divisions moved to the north bank of the Chickahominy River to guard the crossings and picket its banks from the left of the Second Corps to the railroad bridge. Their orders were to hold the latter with some force, and if they found any Rebels on the north side of the river, they were to drive them across the stream. Chamberlain's "Keystone Brigade," as they would proudly call themselves in honor of their native state, settled into their duties. The veterans washed an extra pair of stockings if they had any, which would set them up for at least two more weeks of campaigning. The line officers, who on the march could hardly strip by the roadside to bathe in front of the men and still keep their positions of authority, now were able to get rid of their accumulated dirt. As the new men bustled about their daily tasks, rumors reaching their ears of the battles and losses of the previous month may have increased their apprehension of the fighting to come.[7]

After sunset one day when Chamberlain was the general officer of outposts, he set out along the Chickahominy inspecting his picket line. The river was low, with small sluggish streams wandering near its edges, confusing directions. Crossing a pool by a handy log, Chamberlain froze when he heard a noise on his right. Men of a Rebel picket reserve of twenty to thirty soldiers a short distance away had seen him and were making excited gestures in his direction. He thought then that Libby Prison was his probable destination, but his mind worked quickly to formulate a plan of escape.[8]

Fortunately he was wearing a faded old coat that appeared a nearly neutral color in the gathering dusk and had buttoned it high, which gave him an air of extra dignity. He could hear the voices of the Confederates speculating that he was one of their own officers making his rounds. Straightening up to his full height, he called, "Never mind the guard, its after sunset!" Placing his sword under his arm, he saluted smartly and then turned his back and rode away, expecting a bullet every second before reaching the safety of some trees. Just as at Fredericksburg, Chamberlain's cool thinking and a bold accent again got him out of a perilous predicament.[9]

Grant's final flanking move to the south of the James River and on to

Petersburg, a city lying twenty-three miles south of Richmond, was an audacious and risky strategy. Petersburg was a hub of rails and roads that supplied Richmond and Lee's army from the south; if Grant could seize the city and cut these supply routes, he would force the evacuation of Richmond, and Lee would have to flee or fight on open ground. Grant believed that the Confederate government would place the defense of Richmond as the first priority and that Lee would have to agree. Since Grant had a large number of other troops north of the James, Lee would not realize, if the move was made skillfully and quickly enough, that Grant's objective was the capture of Petersburg instead of Richmond, and he would not be able to shift the main force of his army away from the defenses of the Confederate capital until it was too late. Finally, after several of the usual false alarms, the Federal army moved on June 12.[10]

Toward evening, Chamberlain's six regiments started their march in the rain, crossing the Chickahominy at Long Bridge on pontoons the next morning. The task of the Fifth Corps was to screen the movement around Richmond, block the roads, and confuse the Confederates as much as possible as other corps preceded them toward Petersburg. The Keystone Brigade was never out of range of the sounds of fighting on the whole miserable march toward the James. The ground was swampy, the water brackish, and the mosquitoes buzzed. Marching was punctuated only by short rest periods, which offered no opportunity for unbroken sleep. When they reached sight of the broad James, the cool breezes and open air gave heart to the veterans who had been fighting through the humid inlands of enemy country for six weeks.[11]

Early in the morning of June 16, the men of the Fifth Corps were ferried by steam transports across the James at Windmill Point. A nearly half-mile-long bridge of a hundred pontoon boats had been built downstream by the army engineers for the use of the wagons and the artillery. All were protected by gunboats ordered by Grant. Once on the south side of the James, the men were ordered to bathe in the river, an especially welcome duty. One old soldier described how the men removed their shoes, then jumped into the river, clothes and all. They soaped all over, working the suds through their uniforms, and took off as many layers of dirt as they thought safe. Rinsing by floating blissfully and playing in the water, they then clambered onto the bank and dried themselves in the hot sun. When the order came to fall in for the march, their clothes were nearly dry, and their spirits revived mightily.[12]

Chamberlain, however, did not share their sense of well-being. He could not overcome a nagging feeling that he would be wounded in the abdomen. The feeling of personal harm to come was new to him, but he met it by taking his blanket roll from behind his saddle and strapping it in front of him for what little protection it might provide. He also made it a point to see his old friends in the division.[13]

Petersburg's strategic importance had long been recognized by the Confederates. Accordingly, they had constructed a semicircular ring of formidable fortifications and gun emplacements from the James River on the northeast around the city to the James again on the northwest. These main works consisted of redoubts and high breastworks, fronted with ditches and wooden abatis and other defensive devices designed to allow a small number of defenders to hold the line indefinitely. By the time the Fifth Corps crossed the James, poor generalship and bad luck had cost the other Union corps their best opportunities to capture the city. With less caution, Petersburg could have been captured with very little loss on either side. Confederate generals Henry A. Wise and P. G. T. Beauregard had skillfully managed the few troops on hand. Beauregard then brought in more reinforcements, as Lee vainly tried to ascertain the location of the bulk of the Federal army.[14]

Heading southwest toward Petersburg, the Fifth Corps marched all night; the dust constantly boiled up around the men and horses, almost choking them. Canteens were soon empty, and the only surface water was shallow and covered with green slime. The soldiers quickly learned that in the arid country below the James, where many of the streams were all but dried up from drought, the first thing to do at a new place was to dig for cover and then dig for water.[15]

Approaching Petersburg on June 17, Chamberlain's brigade could hear the sound of guns and small arms fire as Gen. D. B. Birney's Second Corps and Gen. Ambrose Burnside's Ninth Corps charged against the enemy defenses, sustaining heavy losses. The attacks were fitful and uncoordinated, however, and no assault produced a breakthrough of the Confederate line that would capture the city. Coming into position near the left of the other corps, the Fifth Corps was held in reserve. Meanwhile, General Lee had sent some reinforcements in response to General Beauregard's urgent requests. It was not until June 18, however, that he determined that Grant was across the James with the main part of his army and committed the Army of Northern Virginia to the Petersburg defenses in force.[16]

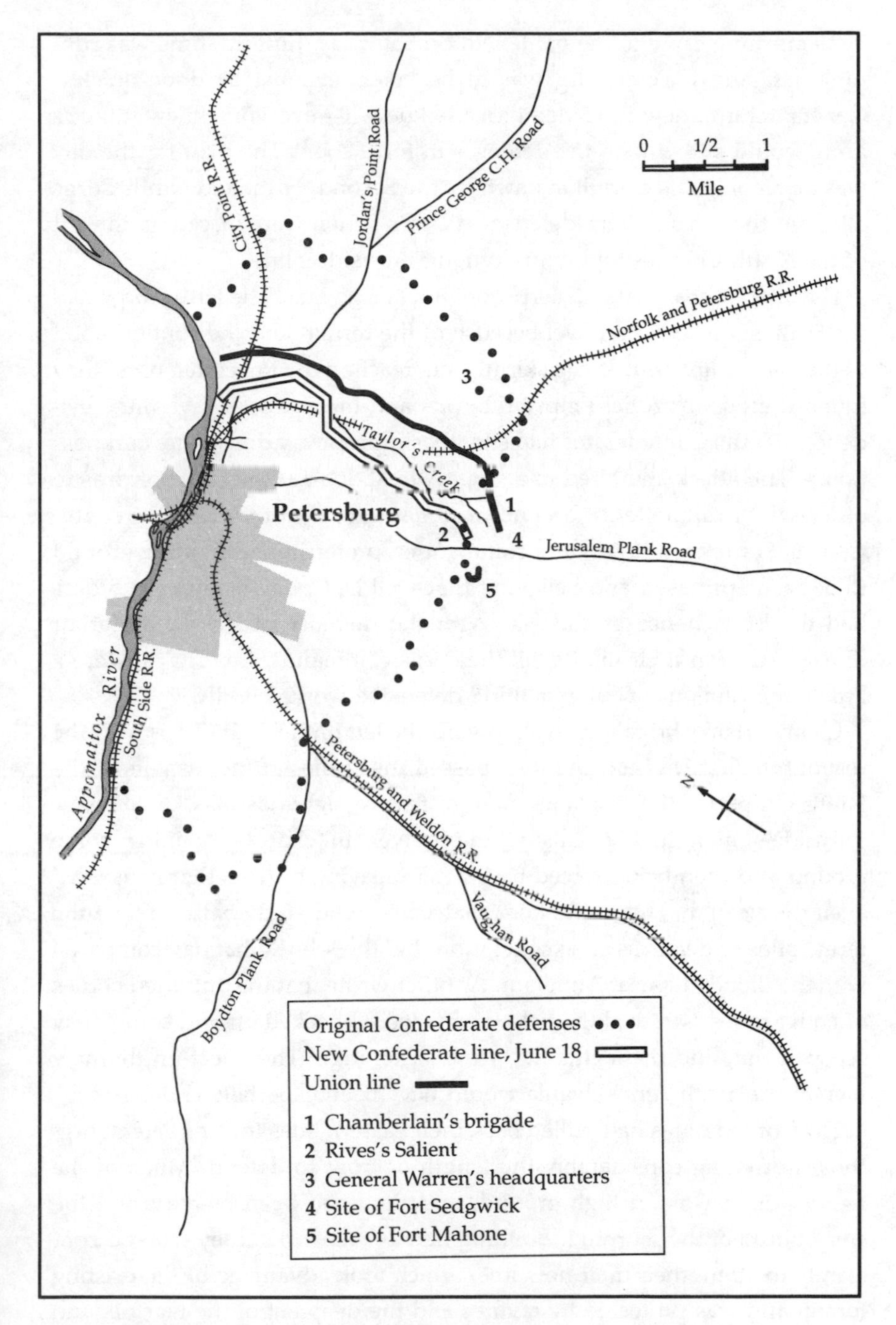

MAP 9. *Union Attack at Petersburg, June 18, 1864, 3:00 P.M.*

As morning came to the battlefield on Saturday, June 18, time was running out, and if Petersburg was to be taken, it must be done quickly. General Grant knew it, General Meade knew it—everyone knew it. Lee's army would surely man the defenses in force soon. The plan for the day was for a concerted assault at dawn by the Second, Fifth, and Ninth Corps all along the city's eastern defenses. Warren's men were placed on the left of the Ninth Corps, roughly prolonging Burnside's line.[17]

The attack began with all corps moving at 4:30 A.M. The Fifth Corps had the farthest distance to travel because of the terrain and the configuration of the enemy line. But as the skirmishers reached the Rebel defenses, they found the enemy gone! Empty rifle pits and breastworks gave mute evidence that the Confederates had silently slipped away during the darkness hours. The attack sputtered to a stop. A fresh look at the situation was in order, with reconnoitering and new estimates to take of the Rebel strength. General Warren was a prudent commander, preferring his fighting ground to be well appraised and believing that well-laid plans within his orders had the best chance of success. With the memory of the Cold Harbor disaster fresh in their minds, all the corps commanders, perhaps, were a little more cautious about assaulting defensive works blindly.[18]

Chamberlain's brigade moved toward the left of the Fifth Corps with the rest of the First Division. As they passed the scenes of the assaults of the Ninth Corps on the previous day, grotesque sights assailed their eyes. Burnside's men had exhausted themselves in charges, gaining some ground and then being forced back again, leaving horrors that nauseated even the veterans. One said later that many who study battles reject the term "piles of dead" as an exaggeration, but the scenes that day compared with the Bloody Lane at Antietam. Another wrote that the unburied bodies of both armies "strewed the field, heads were knocked off and completely scooped out, and the sights . . . were sickening." The effect on the new men of the 187th Pennsylvania would have been especially chilling.[19]

The Confederates had pulled back their eastern lines toward Petersburg, thus shortening considerably the length of front to defend. Much of the new position was on high ground, and they had been busy during the small hours of the morning. Building new breastworks, they worked constantly to strengthen their new line, which took advantage of the existing terrain and was protected by ravines and the deep cut of the Norfolk and Petersburg Railroad. At a bluff in the high ground, called Rives's Salient, the line turned abruptly west and intersected with the redans and forts of the original entrenchments.[20]

Several hundred yards west of the angle, the Jerusalem Plank Road ran southeast from the town, crossing the defensive line. Beyond the road, a large earthen fort, bristling with guns, jutted down from the main line. Its cannon could sweep the ground to the east in front of Rives's Salient to decimate any assaulting force. Around the salient stretched a ravine, three to four hundred yards wide, with sloping sides to its floor. Even in the dry weather the waters of Taylor's Creek still flowed through the narrow valley, with several forked rivulets running into it. To the south and east of the salient, the ravine sloped upward to a plateau of high ground.[21]

As these new conditions were being studied by the Federal generals, the troops halted and made coffee. To mask the movement of Union batteries going into position behind them and preparing for action, the men were placed along the far side of the railroad, many within plain sight of the enemy. Sitting his horse near his men, his mounted brigade flag-bearer beside him, Chamberlain saw that the Rebels had left a battery with infantry supports several hundred yards south of their main works, across the wide ravine and near the Jerusalem Plank Road. Besides discouraging a Union advance, this battery was dropping shells on the Fifth Corps men, killing some and wounding more. The men were understandably on edge—standing under artillery fire without cover stretched nerves taut. General Warren rode up to Chamberlain and remarked in his characteristic understated, offhanded manner that the fire was "very annoying" and asked if Chamberlain thought he could silence it. Chamberlain allowed that he could and sent his aides with orders for his waiting regiments.[22]

Sgt. Patrick DeLacy of the 143d Pennsylvania hurried toward the front, where thousands of soldiers in blue uniforms marked the location of the Federal lines. His right knee had been injured on the forced march from the James River, and he had just talked the doctor into allowing him out of the field hospital. He limped gamely on as some skulkers, seeing the red Maltese cross on his cap, called, "Your division is about to charge and you had better not go up." DeLacy was disgusted. He felt contempt for those cowards who deliberately fell behind if they could when real fighting was at hand. He was also worried about his own Company A. It had no officers left, and he was needed there to lead the boys. At the age of twenty-eight, he was older than many enlisted men and had left a wife and two little girls back in Pennsylvania.[23]

Before reluctantly allowing him to leave the hospital tent, the doctor had given DeLacy a large jolt of "commissary." The whiskey had warmed his stomach, but he needed no bolster to his courage. His colonel once called him "the man who never goes to sleep, and is always where he should be." He was not afraid of much, especially not after that day almost a year ago at Gettysburg, when he and Capt. M. L. Blair had rallied the men to the regimental flag. They had held the Johnnies off once more in desperate action when the Rebs closed in on their front and right as the brigade prepared to retreat along the Chambersburg Pike.[24]

Just a few weeks before, in the Wilderness, he had personally captured an enemy battle flag after a charge against entrenchments. Now, if his regiment was to "go in" again, he was going to be with it. Up ahead, he saw the rectangular white flag with the red Maltese cross that marked the location of his division. It was easy then to find his brigade and regiment. The boys were glad to see him, and the lieutenants commanding Companies F and K greeted him with relief. DeLacy was back, and Company A would be all right now.[25]

About ten-thirty in the morning the brigade formed in column of fours, marched by the left flank along the side of the deep part of the railroad cut, and then crossed over it on a bridge muffled by grass. Chamberlain could see the church spires of Petersburg as he rode, and he quickly got his bearings. Under cover of woods on the other side of the cut, the brigade formed two lines of battle, the old regiments in front except for the 142d Pennsylvania. While still in the woods, the commanding officer of the 187th made an error in aligning the regiment, and it almost doubled in on itself before another officer could extricate it from its predicament. Maneuvering under combat conditions was quite different than drilling in camp.[26]

The blue lines of battle emerged from the woods about fifty yards apart, skirmishers in front, into the clearing ahead, which could be raked by enemy guns in Fort Mahone, across the Jerusalem Plank Road to the west. The offending battery that was the object of Chamberlain's advance was located on the other side of this open space, but a Rebel line of infantry now protected it. The front lines of the Federal infantry and the Rebels began firing at each other, and the Southerners soon began falling back.[27]

Chamberlain quickly noticed that the enemy line of battle overlapped his front line and ordered the 142d Pennsylvania to double-quick forward and to the right of the first line. The 142d accomplished this maneuver under fire with the precision and grace of a drill field review, although it required two flank moves. Now all the veteran regiments were in the front line of battle, the 187th Pennsylvania making up the second line and Chamberlain and his staff riding between the two. A large shell from the Confederate fort burst suddenly near the brigade commander, and the whole staff was unhorsed. Charlemagne was wounded severely through the haunch and Chamberlain's flag-bearer went down. Gaining his feet and not stopping, Chamberlain caught up the staff of the triangular white brigade flag with its red Maltese cross emblazoning the center. Though more artillery and musket fire threatened death with each step, Chamberlain continued on foot carrying the flag, encouraging his men forward.[28]

The Confederate battery fled to avoid capture, along with its infantry supports beating a hasty retreat into the narrow valley in front of Rives's Salient and then back to the protection of the Confederate works. Now Chamberlain's brigade was very exposed, out far ahead of the rest of the Union army. The location of the battery that the brigade had successfully silenced was near the place where the Union Fort Sedgwick, renamed "Fort Hell" by the men, would be constructed. Pulling the brigade back a bit, Chamberlain had the men lie down behind a crest, taking advantage of the protection offered by the knolls and uneven ground of the ridge facing the main Confederate entrenchments.[29]

Across the valley some three or four hundred yards away, muskets gleamed in the sun from behind the well-constructed works that had been completed the previous year to defend the city. Cannon were placed in embrasures behind them, with abatis in front. On the farther slope, trees had been felled in places to clear the range for the Confederate guns, and a small field of stunted corn grew raggedly below. Through the vale a narrow stream, fed by rivulets, flowed slowly through soft, marshy ground with a low growth of ash, briers, and bushes near it. It appeared to Chamberlain that the number of infantrymen was increasing in the enemy line across the small valley. He knew that his position needed to be fortified to prepare for the expected general assault by the Union army. Meanwhile, his brigade could hold off a counterattack by the enemy if they should try.[30]

While Chamberlain's brigade drove off the Confederate guns, Capt. John Bigelow's Ninth Massachusetts Battery, along with Capt. Patrick Hart's Fifteenth New York, had crossed the railroad; another battery had started and then stopped. Later, Col. Charles Wainwright, the Fifth Corps Artillery Brigade commander, ordered Capt. Almont Barnes's Battery C, First New York, across the cut and to a position seventy-five yards to the left of Bigelow's and Hart's batteries. After slight lunettes were dug in back of the crest away from the Rebel main works, the guns were placed in them, their muzzles lying on the grass. The recoil from firing would force the guns back where they could be reloaded and then run up to the ridge line and fired again. This procedure offered some protection for the gun crews, who were plagued by sharpshooters in trees behind the Confederate lines. Some cannon were arranged so that they could aim a slant fire to disable enemy batteries. The battery positions were at Chamberlain's right and rear; the deep railroad cut behind them would make escape difficult should the assault fail and the Rebels counterattack.[31]

During the morning the Confederates had been busy. Finally convinced that Beauregard's opinion of the location of the Army of the Potomac was probably correct, General Lee had arrived in the city at 11:30 A.M. Two of his divisions, led by Generals Joseph B. Kershaw and Charles W. Fields, had preceded him with their cannon and about 10,000 men. Kershaw's division had first reinforced the shortened Rebel line, with its right on or near the Jerusalem Plank Road, and Fields's was then placed on the right of Kershaw's.[32]

At army headquarters, General Meade was in a terrible temper, lashing out at his staff with caustic remarks and fault-finding comments. General Burnside was angry about the performance of some of his infantry the day before and said so to anyone who would listen. General Griffin arrived at Fifth Corps headquarters storming and swearing about some matter, not caring that his outspokenness had gotten him into trouble before. During the first day at the Wilderness, General Grant, who did not know Griffin or of his rough manner, had wanted to arrest him for his mutinous language when he rode up cursing several other generals because his men had not been supported. Only Meade's explanation to Grant that "it's only his way of talking" saved him. Now General Warren seemed to be the only high-ranking officer calm and diplomatic enough to soothe ruffled tempers.[33]

Pressures mounted as Meade impatiently urged his corps commanders to make a unified assault on the new Confederate lines. To keep himself closely informed, he had assigned two aides to Burnside's and Warren's headquarters. Grant's high-ranking staff members went in and out of Meade's and the corps commanders' headquarters on the same duty. They and their orderlies added to the confusion; communications sometimes became erratic, and orders ran behind at critical junctures.[34]

While Chamberlain kept watchful eyes through his field glasses on the enemy fortifications, his officers and men rested quietly behind the crest of the ridge, where an old rail fence entwined with bushes and briers ran across the top. More enemy guns were coming into position, and more and more Confederate infantry were ominously filling the breastworks across the wide ravine. Then a staff officer with the silver oak leaves of a lieutenant colonel on his shoulder straps came up to Chamberlain and informed him that his brigade was to assault the enemy works, by order of the general commanding the army. Chamberlain was astonished; the officer was a man he did not recognize and seemed not to have come through the usual chain of command. It was very strange.[35]

"Do they send a verbal order, and say nothing about whether I am to make the attack alone, or with the whole army?" The officer replied, "I understand you are to attack alone." Chamberlain was sure there must be some mistake. Attacking with his lone brigade meant nothing less than a suicide charge. When he had last looked at the enemy works, huge cannon frowned down upon him, and at least 3,000 muskets gleamed in the hazy sunlight. He took out a pencil and a piece of notepaper and wrote in his scrawling hand:

Lines before Petersburg
June 18, 1864

> I have just received a verbal order not through the usual channels, but by a staff officer unknown to me, purporting to come from the General commanding the army, directing me to assault the main works of the enemy in my front.
>
> Circumstances lead me to believe the General cannot be perfectly aware of my situation, which has greatly changed within the last hour. I have just carried a crest, an advanced post occupied by the enemy's artillery, supported by infantry. I am advanced a mile beyond our own lines, and in an isolated position. On my right a deep railroad cut; my left flank in the air, with no support whatever. In my front at close range is a strongly entrenched line of infantry and artillery with projecting salients right and left, such that my advance would be swept by a cross fire, while a large fort to my left enfilades my entire advance, (as I experienced in carrying this position.) In the

hollow along my front, close up to the enemy's works, appears to be bad ground, swampy, boggy, where my men would be held at a great disadvantage under a destructive fire.

I have got up three batteries and am placing them on the reverse slope of this crest, to enable me to hold against expected attack. To leave these guns behind me unsupported, their retreat cut off by the railroad cut—would expose them to loss in case of our repulse. Fully aware of the responsibility that I take, I beg to be assured that the order to attack with my single brigade is with the General's full understanding. I have here a veteran brigade of six regiments, and my responsibility for these men warrants me in wishing assurances that no mistake in communicating orders compels me to sacrifice them. From what I can see of the enemy's lines, it is my opinion that if an assault is to be made, it should be by nothing less than the whole army.

Very respectfully,
Joshua L. Chamberlain
Colonel Commanding 1st Brigade,
1st Div. 5th Corps[36]

Chamberlain knew that sending this reply was an audacious thing to do, but after the staff officer had gone, it finally occurred to him that he had also risked his shoulder straps. The staff officer soon returned. Expecting to be put under arrest, Chamberlain watched him approach with some apprehension. Would the brigade still have to make a lonely, hopeless, deadly charge on the waiting enemy? To his relief, the officer said that the whole army would move to the attack, but because of his brigade's advanced position, it would be necessary for Chamberlain to lead.[37]

Many preparations were made for the advance. Parts of General Ayres's Second Division, and all of General Cutler's Fourth, crossed the railroad several hundred yards in Chamberlain's rear. Cutler formed under cover of woods, the same woods in which Chamberlain's brigade had formed before driving off the enemy guns in the morning. The First Division's Second Brigade, under Col. Jacob B. Sweitzer, moved across the railroad and to Chamberlain's right. New orders came and went. Told that General Cutler had been ordered to support his exposed left, Chamberlain decided to see Cutler and talk with him about coordinating the movements of their commands in the coming action.[38]

Brig. Gen. Lysander Cutler was a brave veteran of many fiery battlefields. Originally he was the colonel of the Sixth Wisconsin, a regiment of the renowned Iron Brigade. One brigade of his present division consisted of that regiment and others from that fabled old First Corps organization. Overly sensitive to the prerogatives of rank, however, Cutler was known to be gruff, arbitrary, and tyrannical. His disposition was not sweetened any when General Warren's aide-de-camp brought him orders, and he opened the folded paper to find it completely blank![39]

When Chamberlain approached General Cutler and told him of his own orders and his understanding that Cutler would support his action on the left, Cutler listened. When the Maine colonel said earnestly that he felt the charge to be a desperate one, but that he was going into it with all his might, Cutler apparently did not react. But when Chamberlain went on to propose that Cutler move in echelon with him to divert the fire of the fort on their left front, so that his men would not be "mown down like grass," Cutler acted amazed and exploded: "I do not take orders from you," he declared. "I am your senior. You had rather take orders from me!" This outburst unsettled Chamberlain, but he tried again: "I have my orders, General, and I suppose you have yours. We are to work together, and I think it well we should have an understanding." Concluding the conversation, Cutler asserted, "I shall know what to do when the time comes." Returning to his brigade, Chamberlain could only hope that Cutler would see to his left, or the consequences would be more severe for him and his men.[40]

Calling his regimental commanders together, Chamberlain advised them that when the charge was made, they should have their men double-quick down the slope, jump the stream near the bottom, and hurry up the other side of the vale without stopping to fire. For some the stream bed would be too wide to jump, so those men were to proceed in any kind of order, and to reform again when they reached the other side. The object of the advance would be to create a breach in the enemy line through which the other divisions could follow. He then told them to return to their regiments, show their officers and then their men what they faced, and explain the orders to them so that all would be fully informed. Horatio N. Warren, who commanded the 142d Pennsylvania, was especially pleased with the instructions. Since the campaign began in the Wilderness over six weeks ago, neither he nor his men usually knew what was going on beyond a very small segment of the battle. He thought his men would fight better if they knew the importance and the objective of the action.[41]

As the afternoon progressed, Generals Warren and Burnside proposed to General Meade that an attack be made at about three o'clock, when they could finally overcome difficulties of coordinating with the Second Corps on their right. General Meade, highly agitated and exasperated, wired back that he was "greatly astonished at your dispatch. . . . What additional orders to attack you require I cannot imagine. My orders have been explicit and are now repeated," he continued testily, "that you each immediately assault the enemy with all your force, and if there is any further delay the responsibility and the consequences will rest with you." The attack was set for three o'clock.[42]

Sgt. Patrick DeLacy lay on the grass just behind the ridge with the rest of the 143d Pennsylvania. They were at the brigade right, and not a yard separated him from the cluster of officers and the triangular flag that marked brigade headquarters, such as it was. Their new commander, Col. Joshua Chamberlain, was talking with his staff officers about charging the Reb lines. The day was overcast and hot, and DeLacy was so near he could not help eavesdropping a little. The colonel asked the officers for a drink of water.[43]

"Colonel, here's a drink," said DeLacy, slipping the string of his canteen over his head and handing the container over to Chamberlain. "Keep it, thank you," replied the brigade commander. "I would not take a drink from an enlisted man going into battle. You may need it. My officers can get me a drink." At first DeLacy was offended at this refusal, but as he thought longer about it, he came to the conclusion that the colonel really meant what he said and was only showing consideration for him. Anyway, the sergeant's leg still hurt, and this day was far from over. The seasoned soldier had taken a look at the enemy works and knew there was real trouble ahead.[44]

All the officers of the regiments looked over the crest of the ridge. Maj. George W. Merrick of the new regiment, the 187th Pennsylvania, showed his officers the enemy fortifications. "We are to charge those works," he said quietly. Second Lt. Ransford B. Webb, commanding Company I, had served with Major Merrick in the old Pennsylvania Reserves and knew that the major had nerve. He also thought he had a little of that quality himself.

As he looked across the narrow valley to the fortifications, big guns loomed on his right front, most of them trained on the brigade's position. From these cannon, running one-half mile in a semicircle, were breastworks containing at least ten more field pieces. On the far left a large fort bristled with guns. Over the top of the Rebel fortifications he could see at least 3,000 bayonets shining, and he knew there was a Johnnie behind each one of them! "My heart dropped to my shoes," Lieutenant Webb recounted. "Cold drops stood on my forehead. I could still use my eyes, and turned them to the rear. Over a broad plain . . . not a bluecoat was in sight. By this time my blood was frozen solid."[45]

After everyone had taken their views of the forbidding objective, the brigade adjusted, forming the same lines of battle as in the morning. The old regiments would be in front again, with the 187th following about fifty yards in rear of them, its line of battle as long as the other five regiments combined. The 143d Pennsylvania, Patrick DeLacy's regiment, was on the right of the first line. To its left were the Bucktail regiments—the 149th and 150th Pennsylvania, whose men had bucktails proudly displayed on the front of their caps. The 142d and 121st would complete the line—experienced men who could be counted on.[46]

Capt. M. L. Blair was in charge of the 143d's color company, and for the first time he was afraid for the performance of the men of his company. They had never failed him before—at Chancellorsville, Gettysburg, or in any of the harrowing battles since. But now they seemed nervous, and he wondered how far they would go when the order came to assault those apparently impregnable lines in their front. The soldiers lay in position, prone on the ground. Chamberlain walked easily down the line in front of them speaking in a kind voice, but loud enough to be heard by some. Blair and DeLacy could hear every word and remembered him as saying: "Comrades, we have now before us a great duty for our country to perform, and who knows but the way in which we acquit ourselves in this perilous undertaking may depend the ultimate success of the preservation of our grand republic. We know that some must fall, it may be any of you or I; but I feel that you will all go in manfully and make such a record as will make all our loyal American people grateful. I can but feel that our action in this crisis is momentous, and who can know but in the providence of God our action today may be the one thing needful to break and destroy this unholy rebellion."[47]

This short speech put new life and determination into the brigade. The soldiers were ready to spring forward on command. But a few minutes remained, and in the suspense before the charge, minutes seemed like hours. It was nearing three o'clock, the time set for the general assault. Chamberlain assembled his staff. He thought it his duty to lead the charge in person, starting midway between the two lines of battle as he did in the morning action, but this time on foot. Sweitzer's brigade of his own First Division was now across the railroad and on his right. As he walked in the back of his lines, field glasses in hand and surveying the ground to the rear, General Cutler's brigades were nowhere to be seen. Where was the Fourth Division? He stopped between Companies D and I of the 187th. Lieutenant Webb was reassured by Chamberlain's cool and calm demeanor. He could distinctly hear his own heart beating. His eyes were on the brigade commander.[48]

Chamberlain looked at his watch and then at his brigade's two lines of battle that stretched about two hundred yards each way from him, in all about a quarter of a mile in length. Everyone was in readiness, bayonets fixed. General Griffin said later that Chamberlain had a quality that marked a great soldier: "his absolute indifference to danger . . . in the field his mind worked as deliberately and as quietly as it would in his own study." The Maine professor was living up to his reputation as he stepped a few paces to the front, faced about, and, drawing the cavalry saber he was wearing that day, shouted the commands: "Attention! Trail Arms! Double-quick, march." The bugler sounded the advance. Over thirty years later, one soldier thought he could still hear the notes of that bugle. All of the men started forward, although none of them, not even the veterans, could remember when they thought sure death awaited them more. As the men went over the crest, they yelled "like a pack of infuriated devils," the deep-throated shout reverberating in the air as they started down the slope.[49]

Drawing his sword and starting to run, Lieutenant Webb tried to keep up with Chamberlain as hell broke loose from the Confederate lines. The brigade was in the plain view of every gunner in the forts and in front, with thousands of muskets firing at the charging lines. At once many cannon belched forth exploding shells, case shot, and whirring deadly canister. Bullets darkened the air as acrid black smoke filled the lungs of the advancing soldiers. Down the incline they ran, into the shadowed valley, now a maelstrom of death. Some men were hit and went down. Their companions, heedless and intent, ran on. Torn and furrowed with shot and shell, the earth shook with artillery concussion; seeing was difficult. The Union guns on the high ground to the rear of the infantrymen fired over their heads, and the batteries farther back across the railroad opened on the Confederate defenders.[50]

"Shaking asp," briers, and brush dotted the incline in places. At the bottom of the slope, Chamberlain could see that the ground was cluttered with more brush, sweet briers, and alder trees, becoming swampy and hard to traverse for forty or fifty yards. His men would be slowed there and nearly helpless in the enemy fire. They needed to move and move quickly, closer up under the Rebel defenses where guns could not be depressed enough to reach them. The onrushing troops needed to oblique to the left, but commands were impossible to hear above the din of battle.[51]

Out in front of all his men now, Chamberlain half turned toward his line, motioning with his saber to the left. Enough of the men understood the gesture so that the line was obliqued, but just then a ricocheting minié ball hit their brigade commander with a staggering blow. The soft lead bullet entered below Chamberlain's right hip and went through his body, expanding and tearing as it traveled diagonally to his other side at the left hip before stopping near the surface. The first pain Chamberlain felt was in his back, and he thought, "What will my mother say, her boy, shot in the back!" Then he saw the blood gushing from his sides and somehow felt better. His brain continued to work smoothly and clearly. Instantly realizing that if his men saw him go down they might falter, he would not give up, because he knew that soldiers would follow an officer who displayed personal bravery. Thrusting his sword point into the ground in front of him, he balanced himself above the hilt and stood rigidly upright, facing his troops as if inspecting them. The expressions on the men's faces as they leaned into the battle wind were impressed forever into his memory.[52]

Loss of blood finally weakening him, Chamberlain went down on one knee, then the other. After he finally slumped to the ground, two of his staff officers, Lieutenants West Funk of the 121st Pennsylvania and Benjamin Walters of the 143d, managed to lift and pull him back from his perilous position. The new location was not much better, because the enemy fire was coming in a murderous enfilade and cross fire. He ordered his aides to get word to the senior regimental commander, Lt. Col. John Irwin of the 149th Pennsylvania, to take charge of the brigade and to protect the batteries if the Confederates counterattacked. West Funk was himself a courageous man, but he would later describe Chamberlain's actions in the fatal charge and characterize himself only as "a Soldier who had the honor to serve on the Staff of as brave a man as ever drew a sword in defence of his Countrie's rights." Chamberlain believed himself to be mortally wounded and lay in the dirt for the better part of an hour, watching the carnage of his men around him. Feeling the blood spread through his trousers, he thought his very life was ebbing away into the Virginia soil, and like many dying men he thought of his mother, who gave him life.[53]

Most of the first line of veteran soldiers had run across the bottom of the wide ravine and up the incline of the enemy works. They needed support to go on up and over the crest and to pierce the strong defenses. Throwing themselves on the ground, they hugged close to the incline. Here cannon could not be depressed enough to fire at them blindly, and the irregularities of the ground protected them from the sight of the Confederate musket handlers in their entrenchments above. An enemy battery, however, maneuvered enough to send a hail of canister down the ravine behind them, cutting off escape.[54]

In the brigade's second line of battle, the men of the 187th Pennsylvania followed bravely into the valley, which had become a smoking caldron of destruction. Hit with the fury of the concentrated fire of case shot, canister, and minié balls, some of the men faltered; then panic set in and their line broke. Their officers tried frantically and valiantly to rally them. Some went forward again into the galling fire, but the thrust of the charge was broken. The survivors streamed to the rear, toward the railroad cut and Union cannon on the ridge, the only directions that they thought promised any semblance of safety.[55]

The success of the charge and the best chance for safety depended upon the ability of the soldiers to move quickly across the space between them and the defending line. Any pause or delay would effect more casualties, and the break of the 187th caused it to suffer great losses. The recoil of this second line of battle held many of the first line trapped under the enemy breastworks. Seeing the break in their rear, these men knew that to go into the fortifications would mean failure and certain death or capture. Maj. H. N. Warren of the 142d, however, had a difficult time stopping his men even under those circumstances. Hurling themselves into the charge with fierce abandon, the experienced soldiers could hardly be restrained. They stayed down finally, hoping to stay alive until nightfall when the obscuring darkness could cloak their escape. They hoped that Rebels would not move forward and capture them.[56]

The First Division's Second Brigade, to the right of Chamberlain's, was also made more vulnerable by the break of the First Brigade's second line of battle. Although his regiment was held out of the action, one private of the Twenty-second Massachusetts bitterly blamed the Pennsylvanians for the heavy casualties incurred by his brigade. He erroneously thought that Chamberlain's men had failed to move forward at all, placing his brigade in an untenable position. Men of the 155th Pennsylvania advanced to within twenty feet of the fortifications on the right, and some were trapped there.[57]

General Cutler, meanwhile, had not received his orders to advance at three o'clock until ten minutes before that hour, and it was three o'clock before an order arrived that the advance was general. Gen. Romeyn B. Ayres, who commanded a division of Regular Army, Maryland, and New York troops on Cutler's left, had also received his orders late and did not move simultaneously with Cutler's division. Since it took some time for his command to get into position, Cutler did not begin his advance until twenty minutes after the appointed hour. His Fourth Division formed in column by brigades, with J. William Hofmann's brigade in front and Col. Edward S. Bragg's Iron Brigade following in the second line. Confederate cannon immediately opened, with shot and shell descending on the hapless division as it came out of the cover of the woods. Under the withering artillery fire, General Cutler sought to strengthen the charging column and moved Bragg's brigade by the right flank to bring it directly in rear of Hofmann's. They advanced into the valley under a hail of minié balls and canister, taking many casualties. When the order to advance was given again, only a part of the division went forward. The others fell back under cover of a rise in the ground.[58]

Col. Charles S. Wainwright, commanding the Fifth Corps Artillery Brigade, had been with General Cutler before the advance. Later he rode in rear of the crest of the ridge across from Rives's Salient and saw a mass of soldiers there. In the absence of infantry officers above the rank of lieutenant, he was advised by a man of the latter rank that the men might follow an officer of high rank in a rally. The artillery colonel impulsively decided to lead them himself and appealed vainly to the men he took to be Cutler's veterans to follow him and return to the terrible lowland, "for the honour of the old First Corps." Only about two dozen would budge, which probably saved Wainwright's life, since in the excitement he actually tried to lead on horseback.[59]

Capt. John Bigelow, another hero of Gettysburg, and his Ninth Massachusetts Battery had been firing over the heads of the blue-coated infantrymen, trying to silence the Confederate artillery that was wreaking so much havoc with the assaulting lines. Suddenly he saw Union soldiers coming toward his position and knew a repulse of the charge had likely happened. His guns were in a bad position, since the nature of the terrain and the railroad cut in his rear would make it difficult to retreat to safety if the enemy should come out of his works and take the offensive. Bigelow and his other officers strenuously worked to halt the infantrymen, who looked dazed from their rough experience, and gathered about a hundred of them in front of the guns for defense. Many were too frightened to speak and obeyed promptly, even in their panic docilely following orders of anyone in shoulder straps.[60]

One man came up to Bigelow and reported that his brigade commander was down and seriously wounded. Sending to his ambulance for a stretcher, the captain ordered four of his men to bring the officer back. His informant then led them to Joshua Chamberlain. Chamberlain lay in the dirt, showers of soil dusting him when shells hit nearby; he heard the cries and moans of his fallen men. "Men had gone down like scythe-swept grain," he remembered later. As Bigelow's men reached Chamberlain's side, he told them to leave him be. He was mortally wounded, he said, and they should take others who were less seriously hurt. "You are not in command, sir," one artilleryman replied. "Captain Bigelow's order to us was to bring you back, and that is what we must do."[61]

Hurriedly placing him on the stretcher, the men had not gone four yards when a huge shell from the left, probably from Fort Mahone, fell close to them, almost covering them with dirt. Bursting shells and flying missiles filled the air, and the ground was plowed with furrows. Carrying Chamberlain safely through the barrage, the artillerymen placed him behind Bigelow's guns. Darkness fell, but the shelling continued from both sides, and smoke hung over the field. One wounded man thought the shells bursting high in the air looked like a beautiful display of fireworks.[62]

Under cover of darkness, Patrick DeLacy twice left the men of his regiment close to the enemy works to get help for the wounded and new orders. Shrapnel and canister fell around him, but he remained unscratched. Stopping to give water from his canteen to the suffering wounded, he was grateful to Chamberlain, the brigade commander who would not drink an enlisted man's water just before a battle. If anyone had to be thirsty, it would be an officer. It was a fine gesture, and DeLacy had not expected it, because many officers were not as considerate of the ordinary soldier. He heard somewhere that Colonel Chamberlain had been badly wounded. The last time DeLacy had seen the colonel, he was waving his sword and gesturing for the line to oblique; then he disappeared. DeLacy was sorry—another brave officer gone. But it was the way of things too many times.[63]

The battered Fifth Corps regrouped and prepared for another last-ditch effort to force the Confederate lines. Finally, after more heavy losses to the other Union corps on the right, Generals Meade and Grant decided nothing more could be done and called off any further attacks. Grant decided now to "rest the men and use the spade for their protection until a new vein can be struck." Weary men began to dig and build up breastworks and carry the wounded out of the ill-fated valley. Dawn found the Confederates looking at Union fortifications that signaled the start of a nine-month siege of the city of Petersburg. Fitful, bloody battles at critical supply routes would later allow the Union siege lines to stretch westward for miles.[64]

That night Colonel Wainwright wrote in his diary that he hoped it would be the last attempt to attack entrenchments by a general advance in line. He felt that "the stupidest private" knew now that it could not succeed, and the men would be extremely reluctant to move. As it was, Cutler's division was cut up badly, losing about one-third of its officers and men. One Wisconsin sergeant complained that his regiment "lost forty-four men and never fired a shot." Another man in the same regiment wrote home: "Yesterday afternoon in another hopeless assault there was enacted a horrible massacre of our corps. Our brigade charged half a mile over an open field, under the musketry fire of the enemy."[65]

Many thousands of lives had been lost since the Army of the Potomac crossed the Rapidan on May 4 and waged the series of sanguinary battles that brought them to this juncture in a little over six weeks. Many more lives would be lost because Petersburg was not taken on those June days, and the war was prolonged considerably. But as both sides entrenched, the future was hazy and stretched unknown before them all. Now there would be more heat, dust, flies, misery, blood, and death.[66]

"Desperate valor could accomplish nothing but its own demonstration. Our veterans were hurled back over the striken field, or left upon it—I too, proud witness and sharer of their fate. I am not of Virginia blood; she is of mine."[67]

Because it was held in reserve with the rest of the division's Third Brigade, the Twentieth Maine had not participated in the direct assaults on the Petersburg lines, but Capt. Tom Chamberlain finally learned that his brother had been badly hurt in the charge on Rives's Salient. Accompanied by the Twentieth's respected surgeon, Dr. Abner O. Shaw, who had become Chamberlain's friend, and Dr. Morris W. Townsend, the handsome young surgeon of the Forty-fourth New York, Tom searched for his brother for hours. Other corps had also sustained bloody casualties that day, and there were many field hospitals, all with more wounded than they could handle.[68]

Chamberlain had been carried to the division hospital three miles behind the Union lines. He bade good-bye to his faithful staff officers, but his mind was on his brigade. He entreated his aides to tell his men, for his sake and "for the honor of the name of the state they represent," not to allow themselves to lose the reputation they had gained while under his command. It was not until seven o'clock that the field surgeon, Dr. R. A. Everett, was able to determine the extent of Chamberlain's wounds. A private of the 143d Pennsylvania, one of Chamberlain's own men who had been wounded in the morning charge on the Confederate guns, was on the operating table prepared for amputation of his leg when his brigade commander was brought in. He heard Chamberlain ask to be laid to one side, saying that he was all right and they should take care of his boys. No attention was paid to his protests, however, and the private was put by for later attention.[69]

When Tom Chamberlain and the two physicians, Shaw and Townsend, arrived at the field hospital, they were told that Chamberlain had no chance of surviving. The minié ball had torn through his whole body from right thigh to left hip, severing blood vessels, nicking the urethra and bladder, and crushing bone before it stopped. Generals Warren and Griffin both visited Chamberlain that night and told him that their recommendation for his promotion to brigadier general would be forwarded immediately. Chamberlain, pleased by the thought of this recognition on this and previous fields, replied that he wished it especially for the gratification of his family and friends.[70]

In the operating tent, the doctors labored through the night to save the dying general. At one point they stopped, thinking that all they were doing was prolonging his terrible pain, but he urged them to go on, with a determination to live that transcended his agony. They removed the bullet, and at last they managed to patch up and connect things enough that they concluded there might be a chance for recovery.[71]

The next day, glad to be alive, but in great pain and still believing himself to be on his deathbed, Chamberlain wrote a farewell note to Fannie, in pencil, on both sides of a small piece of notepaper:

"My darling wife I am lying mortally wounded the doctors think, but my mind & heart are at peace Jesus Christ is my all-sufficient savior. I go to him. God bless & keep & comfort you, precious one, you have been a precious wife to me. To know & love you makes life & death beautiful. Cherish the darlings & give my love to all the dear ones Do not grieve too much for me. We shall all soon meet Live for the children Give my dearest love to Father, mother & Sallie & John Oh how happy to feel yourself forgiven God bless you evermore precious precious one Ever yours Lawrence"[72]

The June sun burned down hotly as eight enlisted men taking turns hand carried a stretcher bearing Chamberlain to City Point on the James River. There he was placed on the hospital ship *Connecticut* by Dr. Townsend and was taken to the Naval Hospital at Annapolis with 60 other officers and 462 enlisted men, all severely wounded.[73]

General Meade promptly endorsed General Warren's telegraphed request for Chamberlain's promotion. General Grant had had the authority granted him to promote officers on the field for special acts of gallantry before he had left Washington, D.C., to start the campaign. On June 20 he used this authority to issue Special Orders No. 39, promoting Chamberlain, and forwarded the papers to the secretary of war for approval of the president and confirmation by the Senate. "Colonel Joshua L. Chamberlain . . . is, for meritorious and efficient services on the field of battle, and especially for gallant conduct in leading his Brigade against the enemy at Petersburg, Virginia . . . appointed Brigadier General of Volunteers, to rank as such from the 18th of June, 1864."[74]

It was a full brigadier's commission, not by brevet, and later Grant told Chamberlain that he had never made a promotion on the field of battle before. Grant also wrote of his high opinion of Chamberlain: "Col. J. L. Chamberlain, of the 20th Maine, was wounded on the 18th. He was gallantly leading his brigade at the time, as he had been in the habit of doing in all the engagements in which he had previously been engaged. He had several times been recommended for a brigadier-generalcy for gallant and meritorious conduct. On this occasion, I promoted him on the spot . . . and at last a gallant and meritorious officer received partial justice at the hands of his government, which he served so faithfully and so well."[75]

Arriving at the Naval Hospital at Annapolis the next day, the new general was given priority care and treatment by several physicians. Fannie

Brig. Gen. Joshua L. Chamberlain
(Brady Collection, National Archives)

arrived with friends shortly thereafter to help care for him. The following day, a wire reached his hometown of Brewer, where the news of his critical condition nearly prostrated his mother and threw the rest of his family and friends into consternation. Helen Adams, visiting friends in Bangor while

Brig. Gen. Joshua L. Chamberlain
(Brady Collection, National Archives)

Dr. Adams was attending a church convention, came to the Chamberlain home immediately upon hearing the news. Crying together at length, she and Sae and Mrs. Chamberlain prayed that Chamberlain might recover, and for the "grace to endure if it should be otherwise." But the subsequent wires and newspaper reports came at agonizingly spaced intervals, and the tension was almost unbearable to the general's waiting family. It was all they could do to restrain themselves from leaving for Annapolis.[76]

On the day before the Fourth of July holiday, Lieutenant Colonel Gilmore of the Twentieth Maine, who was still on general court-martial duty in Washington, hand delivered to Chamberlain at Annapolis his commission as brigadier general from the secretary of war. He also brought along a copy of the Senate resolution confirming the appointment. Still in very serious condition, Chamberlain nevertheless made the effort to recommend promotions for field officers of the old regiment. "He had earned this promotion long ago," Gilmore wrote to Maine's adjutant general. "He has been a most gallant and worthy Officer and the state of Maine should be proud to own him as one of her sons."[77]

Scarcely ten days later, the suffering Chamberlain wrote "a thoughtful and considerate letter" to Governor Samuel Cony of Maine further recommending promotions, including posthumous recognition for Capt. Samuel T. Keene, who was killed by a Confederate sharpshooter in the lines before Petersburg. Governor Cony answered promptly, happy at the receipt of the unexpected communication, and reported his approval of the recommendations. The governor recalled a conversation they had had in Washington shortly before Chamberlain had returned to the army, in which Cony had offered his "aid in a certain direction gratifying to your ambition," and went on to add, "But you have illustrated the general truth that real merit seldom requires extraneous helps."[78]

Not long after he wrote to the governor, a severe crisis came in Chamberlain's condition, which sent John Chamberlain hurrying to Annapolis from Bangor. By the time John arrived, however, his brother had passed the turning point, and he started to heal rapidly the following week. The most excruciating pain ceased then, and the left side healed almost entirely. John noted that Joshua held his physical and mental strength, impassively enduring his wounds with patience and calmness, and even confidently expecting that he would be able to return to the field. The surgeon finally declared, a little over a month after the ill-fated charge, that the danger was considered past, and the general's recovery certain.[79]

Chamberlain heard from many of his old friends as he became stronger, and by the end of August, he felt well enough to write letters in his own hand. Able to sit up a good part of his day, he spent some of his time looking up Maine soldiers in the hospital to ensure that those who warranted were sent home when able to convalesce—and, incidentally, to vote in the upcoming elections. But he was impatient at the time it took his body to mend and told Governor Cony, "I long to be in the field again doing my part to keep the old flag up, with all it's stars."[80]

From far away in Brunswick, where Daisy and Wyllys waited with Cousin D for their parents to come home, the president of Bowdoin sent word that not only was Chamberlain's position thère open to him at any time he wanted to claim it, but he would be greeted with great appreciation if he chose to return. But for Chamberlain himself, the near future seemed to hold a return to the army, if his wounds would allow it. In a letter to his mother he wrote:

"Not a selfish ambition: for I assure you not all the honor & titles that can be given or won, would tempt me to hazard the happiness and welfare of my dear ones at home, nor would they be any equivalent whatever, for these terrible wounds as must cast a shadow over the remainder of my days, even though I should apparently recover.

"But what it is, I can't tell you. I havn't a particle of fanaticism in me. But I plead guilty to a sort of fatalism. I believe in a destiny—one, I mean, divinely appointed, and to which we are carried forward by a perfect trust in God. I do this, and I believe in it. I have laid plans, in my day, & good ones I thought. But they never succeeded. Something else, better, did, and I could see it as plain as day, that God had done it, & for my good.

"So I am right, be sure of that, happen what may. Not for any merit of mine, but for divine & loving mercy all is bright with me, in this world and beyond."[81]

Finally, on September 20, although still very weak, Chamberlain was furloughed home to Brunswick to regain his strength with the help of his family and friends. Sometimes he ventured out for short periods, including an appearance at a meeting to raise money for the Christian Commission, and after only a month, he thought he would soon take the field again. On November 18, in what represents a triumph of the human spirit, and before he was able to mount a horse without help or walk a hundred yards, he arrived back for duty with his command in front of Petersburg.[82]

Upon his return, Chamberlain found his old brigade broken up and scattered, five of the Pennsylvania regiments incorporated into the Third Division of the Fifth Corps, and the 187th Pennsylvania returned to the Keystone State. He had command of these regiments only a short time, but he was remembered with affection. One man later told him that not only had he been popular with both the officers and men in the brigade, but that they "loved you as a father and you in return loved them like your children and treated them as equals and was not afraid to lead them." They were "not afraid to follow you or go wherever you ordered them to go, having implicit confidence in your judgment and ability as a commander." In their place were two new regiments, the 185th New York and the 198th Pennsylvania, the latter an oversize regiment of fourteen companies. Even though it was titled the same, his First Brigade had gone from being the largest brigade in the Fifth Corps to the smallest.[83]

More than this had changed. After the unsuccessful attempts to capture the city of Petersburg in June, the Union army had fought its way farther west, cutting the Rebels' important Weldon Railroad supply line and lengthening the siege lines with trenches and forts. The Confederates strengthened their existing fortifications ringing the city. Both sides faced each other, sometimes only a few hundred yards apart, hurling death across a no-man's-land in the form of mortars, artillery shells, and almost incessant sniping. The price for these gains had been high casualties, especially for the Union.[84]

The Fifth Corps also had been sifted down more and more as enlistments ran out for many regiments and men went home. Some regiments had enough men reenlist to keep their regimental identities, but others broke up, and their reenlisted veterans and leftover men whose service times were not completed were consolidated with those who kept their identities. New regiments were added, which were numbered in the regular order of their states and consisted of some veterans and many recruits. A military railroad had been built from City Point and extended to the far left of the Union lines, efficiently carrying provisions and men to and from the supply base on the James River. As Chamberlain took command in the field for the first time as a general officer, it was with the knowledge that his new brigade was a fine one with experience from the previous few months, and that they were ready to fight again.[85]

The presidential election held just a few days before had given the citizens, including the citizen soldiers of the Army of the Potomac, an opportunity to evaluate the war and the necessity for its continuation. Many veteran soldiers thought the issue boiled down to a question of whether their many sacrifices in toil, blood, and property would be for nothing if Abraham Lincoln, who stood for continuing the war, were not reelected. Their old idol, George McClellan, removed by Lincoln as commander of the Army of the Potomac after the battle of Antietam, was the nominee of the Democrats and still had great personal popularity in the army. But the soldiers voted overwhelmingly for Lincoln, by a margin of three to one by some accounts, in spite of the personal sacrifices that they thought would soon be required of them because of it. When the Confederates learned the size of the victory, one soldier reported, a gloom came over them, and he thought that Lincoln's winning by such a majority was one of the most important Union victories of the war.[86]

It would have been with a feeling of great personal satisfaction that Chamberlain took the field again leading a brigade, this time as a full brigadier general. He was the kind of man to whom recognition of his ability and valor would be a source of gratification, and he would regard his new status as an opportunity to better serve the Union cause. However, he surely took care, as he did after Gettysburg, that he bore the honor "meekly." Col. Horatio G. Sickel of his own brigade and Col. Edgar M. Gregory of the Second Brigade, now both brevet brigadiers, had been senior to him as colonels, but they accepted the new situation and his superior rank with courtesy and good will.[87]

The month of November was one of comparative rest for the Fifth Corps, except for the usual work on the entrenchments, and Chamberlain settled down to the myriad duties of the army, getting acquainted with his new command, while renewing old ties with friends and associates. However, just as the men thought that active campaigning had ceased for the winter, new orders came through. Early on the mild and lovely morning of December 7, the Fifth Corps with four batteries of its artillery, Gregg's division of cavalry, and Mott's division of the Second Corps moved south under the command of General Warren. This large assemblage of about 26,000 infantry and cavalry started on an expedition that would be known as the Weldon Railroad Raid. Its object was to destroy the railroad and bridges below the Nottoway River to Hicksford on the Meherrin River, forty miles below Petersburg near the North Carolina state line.[88]

Confederates brought the supplies for Petersburg up the Weldon Railroad to Stoney Creek Station, a point below Federal army control. They then unloaded and transported the cargo in wagons by other routes into the beleaguered city. Destroying the Weldon Road would further cripple the lines of supply to the South that Lee must have to hold Petersburg and would leave only the Petersburg and Lynchburg, or "South Side," Railroad open to the south and west from Petersburg.[89]

Except for cavalry skirmishing, the Yankee force met no resistance on the march south, although there was apprehension that enemy infantry might be detached from Lee to fight, and defensive measures were strictly followed. On the evening of December 8, having struck the railroad below the Nottoway, the infantry began the systematic destruction of the railroad track, working by moonlight until midnight.[90]

Each brigade lined up on one side of the track, and in one motion the men would lift the rails with cross ties attached and push them up and over, raising a portion from the ground. When this part came up, it would be seized by the men and passed along for a mile or more in one continuous swell. The rails were pried from the ties and their joints broken by a swaying motion. So that the weight of the ends would bend the rails when they were heated, the ties were heaped into triangular-shaped piles with the rails balanced crosswise on top. Then the ties would be set on fire, and when the pitch-pine bonfires died down and the metal cooled, the rails would be useless. Sometimes the men would bend the red-hot rails into fantastic shapes, including the Maltese cross symbol of the Fifth Corps. However tired from the forced marching, the men still fell willingly to the work.[91]

Continuing their work the next day, the Federals destroyed nearly twenty miles of track below the Nottoway. When they reached the Meherrin River, they found that the Confederates had fortified the south side of the river at Hicksford with artillery and entrenchments. General Warren decided that to go farther would not be worth the casualties and ordered the expedition to return as scheduled. The Southerners would be unlikely to rebuild the railroad, especially when they saw how easily it could be destroyed again.[92]

The men foraged the entire trip. At almost every house, quantities of apple or peach brandy could be found. In the Third Brigade of the First Division, which included the Twentieth Maine, many men, lacking experience with the strength of the applejack, filled their canteens with it and became drunk—some uproariously and others to insensibility. The provost guards were called; they poured out barrels of the delicious-tasting liquor onto the ground, but not before the applejack had announced itself, with loud voices and hilarity, and the uproar had spread to the cavalry. When one regiment of cavalry was sent to suppress disorder in another, it was no help—it joined in the revelry too.[93]

Just a few days before, Tom Chamberlain had been appointed provost marshal of the First Division, and the confusion must have kept him very busy. Joshua Chamberlain had the infantry rear guard then; many of his men were engaged in trying to keep those drunken soldiers who could march in the column and not left behind. When the casualties for the expedition were totaled up, General Griffin found that his First Division had no men missing in Chamberlain's First Brigade, but the other two brigades had fifty-eight stragglers missing. General Warren attributed the missing men to the effects of the applejack, a serious matter since those left behind would probably be killed or captured—or die of exposure.[94]

On December 10 the soldiers began the march back, very tired from their exertions and lack of sleep. It had begun to snow the night before, followed by rain and falling temperatures. In the morning every tree and blade of grass was covered with ice—a beautiful sight, but the men suffered much because the roads were in terrible shape, and progress was slow. When the mud froze, marching became very hard, and soldiers were seen walking barefooted over the icy ground to ease their blistered feet. Worst of all, bodies of stragglers from the march down were found; they had been stripped and their throats cut by bushwhackers. The news spread quickly through the ranks, and the men could not be restrained from burning, in retaliation, almost every building for a half mile on either side of the return route for miles below Petersburg. Black smoke rolled skyward from blazing fires as the army passed.[95]

"This was a hard sight. Our men got very much exasperated & one day when I brought up the rear, I [had] some sad work in protecting helpless women and children from outrage, when the Rebels had been firing from their houses on us, and the men were bent on revenge. I invariably gave them my protection which any man of honor will give any woman as long as she is *a woman. But I have no doubt they were all 'burnt out' before the whole army got by. It was sad business. I am willing to fight men in arms, but not* babes in arms.*"*[96]

After six days the weary Federals returned, somewhat the worse for wear. An expected challenge from part of Lee's infantry had not materialized, and General Warren considered the operation a resounding success. In spite of the hardships, Chamberlain had withstood the march well; Tom Chamberlain thought he appeared better than ever. He continued to do full duty but reluctantly came to realize that he had returned to the field too soon. He did not yet feel right and steeled himself to the knowledge that he would have to undergo further surgical treatment. Even with that eventuality, Chamberlain thought he might again command the Third Brigade for the first time since November of 1863. General Bartlett was "going away," leaving him as the senior brigade officer, and he felt confident that

General Griffin would not let anyone come in and rank him while he was gone.[97]

At dawn on January 15, 1865, Chamberlain headed north again for surgery at Philadelphia. A little later, his brigade staff sat down to breakfast, silent and sad, in contrast to the cheerful faces presented on previous days when their general was with them. Tears welled in the eyes of Capt. Francis B. Jones when he thought how he had learned to love Chamberlain as a child loves his father, "who not only feels that he has a protector, but a confidant." The staff really did not expect Chamberlain back and thought that they had lost forever the best commander the brigade had ever had or was likely to have. Chamberlain was accompanied north by the faithful Lt. Benjamin Walters, still his aide from the 143d Pennsylvania in his old First Brigade. At Philadelphia, he was treated by Dr. Pancoast, whom he would later characterize as "the most skillful surgeon in the United States" and who not only relieved his disabilities but helped him to a more rapid recovery. Then it was home to Brunswick to recover his strength.[98]

January and February are deep-freeze months for Maine. Snow is frequent, and though many days are sunny, the cold is penetrating. In that winter of 1865, when Chamberlain came home again to Fannie and the children, he found another baby girl had been born into his family on the day after he left Petersburg. Fannie had been carrying the promise of this newest life when he was so grievously wounded. In the uncertain weeks immediately afterward, she undoubtedly had despaired of his ever looking on the face of their fifth child, whom she named Gertrude Loraine. At home and content with his dearest ones, he stayed in his room most of his sick-leave time and did not leave the warm house.[99]

A tempting position as collector of customs for the district of Bath was offered to Chamberlain. This Federal office enjoyed great respect in the state, with the position at Bath second in prestige only to that held at Portland by former governor Washburn. In Chamberlain's absence, changes at Bowdoin had finally settled its religious character, and the college was anxious to have him resume his professorship. After thinking about all of his alternatives very carefully, Chamberlain finally made some decisions. He would return to the army if possible, where he felt his services were needed in the coming campaign. Later that year he would probably resign from the college and "be ready to throw myself on the current of affairs, and either remain in the military service (as is most congenial to my temperament) or strike into some other enterprise of a more bold and stirring character than a college chair affords."[100]

Chamberlain wanted to see his parents and Sae again—John was living in New York—but a trip to Brewer was not possible. By the time he recovered enough to travel, he was impatient to get back to the army. His parents were against his decision to decline the collectorship opportunity and return to the field. He was not surprised at their opposition but rather expected it. In her New Year's letter to him, his mother had begged her "dear child" to take care of himself. "Surely, you have done & suffered & won laurels enough in this war to satisfy the most ambitious," she had continued. Not too confidently, she added, "Not that I would say you were eager for the praise of man alone but moved by nobler motives I trust." She was "not wishing to dictate," she added in her usual disclaimer, "yet daring to hope" that he would retire and avoid the coming battles.[101]

Written the day before his return to the army, a part of Chamberlain's explanation to his parents stands as a statement of faith and courage from an extraordinary man who knew his duty:

"I owe the Country three years service. It is a time when every man should stand by his guns. And I am not scared or hurt enough yet to be willing to face the rear, when other men are marching to the front.

"It is true my incomplete recovery from my wounds would make a more quiet life desirable, & when I think of my young & dependent family the whole strength of that motive to make the most of my life comes over me.

"But there is no promise of life in peace, & no decree of death in war. And I am so confident of the sincerity of my motives that I can trust my own life & the welfare of my family in the hands of Providence."[102]

Chamberlain went on to discuss his military prospects but made one assurance to his parents: "At all events I must return to the army, and if I find I cannot stand it I shall not be foolish about it but shall take proper care of myself."[103]

It was near the end of February before Chamberlain could report back for active duty, and then he had been compelled to extend his sick leave longer than he had thought prudent to hold his position. Since General Bartlett was still with the division and in charge of the Third Brigade, Chamberlain returned to his same place with his First Brigade. Spring came much sooner to Virginia than to Maine, and he had to prepare for the new campaign. He knew it would open strong—a confrontation with Lee that could destroy the hopes of the Rebel cause once and for all. Desertions had increased across the lines from the Army of Northern Virginia, and virtually everyone sensed the approaching end of the failing Confederacy.[104]

As the Federal troops waited and the weather warmed in March, high-ranking officers, government officials, and their ladies came by the Military Railroad from City Point to watch the grand reviews presented by several divisions of the different corps. At one such review early in March, to the admiration of the watching visitors, Capt. Tom Chamberlain gave a display of daring horsemanship, recovering on his feet "light as a cat" when his horse fell and rolled several times. Tom liked being the division's provost marshal; he considered the job an easy one with the important consideration that there was less chance of being killed in the performance of his duties.[105]

Tom had also been home on leave during the winter, and his behavior there had been so "restless and roving" that his parents were worried that he had been indulging in "incorrect habits." Chamberlain tried to reassure them, telling them their youngest son's chief annoyance to him was his sensitivity—"allowing a few cowardly fellows disturb his peace of mind. It is more creditable and more safe to have such men enemies than friends, & in my opinion it will be a good thing for him to have to stand his hand among men just as they come." Tom had some maturing to do; his oldest brother had had his excellent judgment formed in large part by standing his own hand among men, just as they came.[106]

Chamberlain still intended to keep his promises to his family and take care of himself, even if his physical limitations caused him to give up the idea of fighting again. Within ten days of his return, however, being in the field gave his whole personality such "a tonic" that he felt strong and ready to lead. This kind of life, he enthusiastically believed, promoted his recovery greatly, and he could now "ride as fast and far as the best, and ask no favors."[107]

"I do not in the least regret my choice. I shall not feel obliged to lead any more charges, unless it becomes necessary, and hope to escape any further injuries. I have no insane desire to deprive my little family of my protection & support. . . . On the contrary I look forward with delight to a speedy return to the happiness and affection of my little home. No man's ever was dearer or more blest. And to no man could it be a greater sacrifice to leave them far away and face the dangers which in threatening me threaten them tenfold. Still . . . the course I take is not only that

which honor and manliness prompt, but the one which will prove best for them & for all who belong to me or to whom I belong."[108]

The cause of preserving the Union was too great to consider the personal good of one man or his family above its call, Chamberlain thought. And indeed, the lengthening of the war with its attendant sacrifices seemed to the young general a necessary process: "The winnowings of life and death must go on till the troubles be sifted to the core." If peace had been negotiated sooner with the South when some had called for it, or had military success occurred too early, compromise might have brought it "at cost of the vital point of the whole contention, the supremacy of its announced ideal—the guarantee of human rights."[109]

During Chamberlain's absence, the regiments of his brigade had earned another battle inscription for their colors under the command of Bvt. Brig. Gen. Horatio G. Sickel of the 198th Pennsylvania. The Confederates were found to be bringing in supplies to Petersburg by wagon train as they did before the Weldon Railroad Raid two months before, only by a much longer route up the Meherrin River and the Boydton Plank Road through Dinwiddie Court House. When Union forces set out to destroy wagons and disrupt this supply route, the Confederates disputed the Federal advance spiritedly in the resultant Hatcher's Run battles of February 5, 6, and 7, 1865. Chamberlain's brigade participated in the action along with the rest of the Fifth Corps, the Second Corps, and Gregg's cavalry, but suffered only thirty-eight casualties.[110]

Now, as spring was heralded by the warmer air of March, General Grant devised a plan to force Lee and his army from the defenses of Petersburg by mounting a great offensive. Grant would cut the South Side Railroad, and perhaps the Richmond and Danville Railroad also, with Maj. Gen. Philip Sheridan's two divisions of cavalry and the Fifth and Second Corps as infantry support. The severing of General Lee's communications and supply lines and the resultant thinning of his already stretched center and left to repel the Union attack on the Confederate right would leave his siege entrenchments undermanned and open to attack by other elements of Grant's armies. If Lee were successful in escaping with his army, he would certainly head west in an effort to join forces with Confederate Gen. Joseph Johnston, but he would have Federal cavalry and infantry in pursuit. Maj. Gen. William T. Sherman and his army were now at Goldsboro, North Carolina, and Sherman would move north to catch Lee in a pincers movement if Lee outdistanced Grant's eastern troops. The collapse of the Petersburg defenses would guarantee the fall of Richmond, with the Confederate government forced to flee that city.[111]

Awaiting the arrival of General Sheridan and his cavalry on March 27, Grant completed the plans for the disposition of his various corps so that the new campaign could begin. On March 24 he issued an order for the movement of many Union forces to the left, with the main offensive scheduled to begin on March 29. Grant was most anxious that Lee not make a dash to join with Johnston by his own volition before Sheridan was up and Grant's forces in position to give pursuit.[112]

The next days were filled with preparations for what the war-weary old soldiers of the Army of the Potomac hoped would be their last campaign. Chamberlain knew that his proper position in battle would be 150 yards in rear of the center of his command, but he also knew that when his brigade got into action, he could go any place he thought his presence was needed. Previous experience showed the latter to be "anywhere but in the rear." Shortly after his last return from sick leave, he had resolved not to lead any more charges unless it became necessary, but given the opportunity, combined with his bravery, sense of duty, and inclination toward impetuosity, "necessary" would surely become "essential" before much more time would pass.[113]

In his usual third-person writing style, Chamberlain later recounted his feelings on the night before the beginning of that last campaign:

"So when . . . each one who could dashed off his little farewell message home, there was in his heart a strange mingling of emotion, the vision of a great joy, in which, perhaps, he was to lie silent and apart, a little shadow on the earth, but overhead a great light filling the sky. This lifted him to the surpassing joy that, however it should be with him, his work and worth had entered into the country's life and honor."[114]

And so it would come to pass.

CHAPTER

Eight

SOUL OF THE LION

The Fifth Corps moved out before dawn on March 29, 1865. A long procession of over 17,000 officers and men, with a large complement of horses, artillery, and ambulances, wended its way south through Arthur's Swamp southwest of Petersburg. They were carrying twelve days' rations and seventy rounds of ammunition per man in knapsacks, ammunition boxes, and wagons. On their right advanced Maj. Gen. Andrew A. Humphreys's somewhat larger Second Corps. Gen. Philip Sheridan's force of cavalrymen, nearly as large as the Fifth Corps, swung in an even wider arc to the south and west. Their objective was the South Side Railroad to the north, but their route was a circuitous one to mask their intentions. Now they headed to Dinwiddie Court House, on the left of the Fifth Corps.[1]

Chamberlain's brigade moved near sunrise, at the head of the First Division. There had not been much sleep for anyone the past twenty-four hours, but excitement and anticipation quickened the senses in the mild morning air. At the Monk's Neck Bridge over Rowanty Creek, a pontoon bridge was quickly laid, and the infantry and artillery filed onto the Stage Road and then to the Vaughan Road, which led to Dinwiddie Court House. Just two miles short of that small Virginia crossroads town, judicial seat of sprawling Dinwiddie County, the brigade halted in the vicinity of the Chapple house. Only a few enemy cavalry pickets had been seen.[2]

Receiving an order from General Meade to retrace his route a short distance, General Warren sent his corps north on the Quaker Road. Griffin's division led the corps's advance, and in the vanguard Joshua Chamberlain rode on his war-horse up the Quaker Road, flanked by his aides. Charlemagne was back with his master, a scar on his chestnut-colored haunch marking his near-fatal wound the previous June in the first charge at Rives's Salient. Chamberlain sat erect, his position in the column, accompanying flag, and commanding presence virtually the only indications of his rank. In his worn field uniform—its old coat a relic of hard service and faded to a pale, steely color—he would hardly appear a dashing figure to the casual observer.[3]

The nondescript coat had helped save him from capture by Confederate pickets the year before on the Chickahominy, where quick thinking and the neutral hue of the jacket had allowed him to make a hasty getaway. Now he was on campaign again, looking ahead to see when the Confederates would appear. They were known to be entrenched in heavy force a mile north of the junction of the Quaker and Boydton Plank Roads, where the White Oak Road met the Plank Road near Burgess's Mill. Almost parallel to these works and only a few miles north lay the South Side Railroad, and a few miles farther west on the White Oak Road was another strategic location, a hub of roads called Five Forks. Chamberlain certainly expected the Rebels to dispute the Union advance soon. It was afternoon, and Lee knew now that large numbers of the Union army were moving toward his right defenses.[4]

Spring had come, with new life giving a freshening smell to the air. Violets could be seen along the roadway; the buds on the trees were swollen, and some had burst into green. A peach tree blazed with bloom in the distance. The blue column had proceeded nearly a mile and a half up the Quaker Road when skirmishers reported that the bridge over a branch of Gravelly Run ahead had been destroyed, with an advance force of the enemy entrenched on the other side. Chamberlain and General Griffin took a look at the situation, and the younger man proposed a plan that the division commander approved. Griffin ordered General Gregory, commander of the Second Brigade, to give support to the First Brigade's left as Chamberlain should instruct him.[5]

Chamberlain picked a battalion of six companies from the 198th Pennsylvania, commanded by Maj. Edwin A. Glenn, and placed them in skirmishing order across the road. Behind them he formed the other troops in line of battle, the 185th New York on the left of the road and the remaining eight companies of the 198th Pennsylvania on its right. While the right of his brigade started firing rapidly to create a diversion, Chamberlain and the left wing plunged into the waist-deep stream and struck the Rebel line on its right flank. A hand-to-hand fight began there, but Major Glenn's men swiftly forded the run; suddenly the whole brigade was across the water, the New Yorkers and Pennsylvanians closing on Major Glenn's left and right. The Rebels quickly retreated, but their numbers constantly increased as they withdrew. The ground on both sides of the road was mostly in woods, and the going was hard in places, but Chamberlain's brigade went forward with dispatch, Glenn's skirmishers moving faster and far ahead of the line.[6]

Over a mile from Gravelly Run the trees opened into a large clearing, measuring roughly 1,000 yards on a side. It contained the Lewis farmhouse and outbuildings set back about two to three hundred yards from the right of the road; a large pile of sawdust trailed about two to three hundred yards beyond the farmstead where a steam sawmill had stood. The retreating enemy made a stand near the farmhouse, but after a sharp encounter, they were driven back by Glenn's men until they joined a large body of their troops stationed behind breastworks in the woods.[7]

A full volley from the woods started a slow Union retreat. The Federal skirmishers were soon followed by Confederates leaving the cover of their breastworks, and they were also harassed by Rebel sharpshooters stationed in the trees of the woods. Some of Glenn's Pennsylvanians managed to bring out their wounded, and others grabbed Confederates and dragged them along as prisoners. Meanwhile, the sun had disappeared behind clouds, and the air had become humid and moist. Combined with the rifle smoke into a dank mixture and carried by a south wind, it blew back into the eyes of the Confederate marksmen and made their fire unsteady. Chamberlain brought his line of battle to within supporting distance, and perhaps into view, as Glenn's men turned and made another

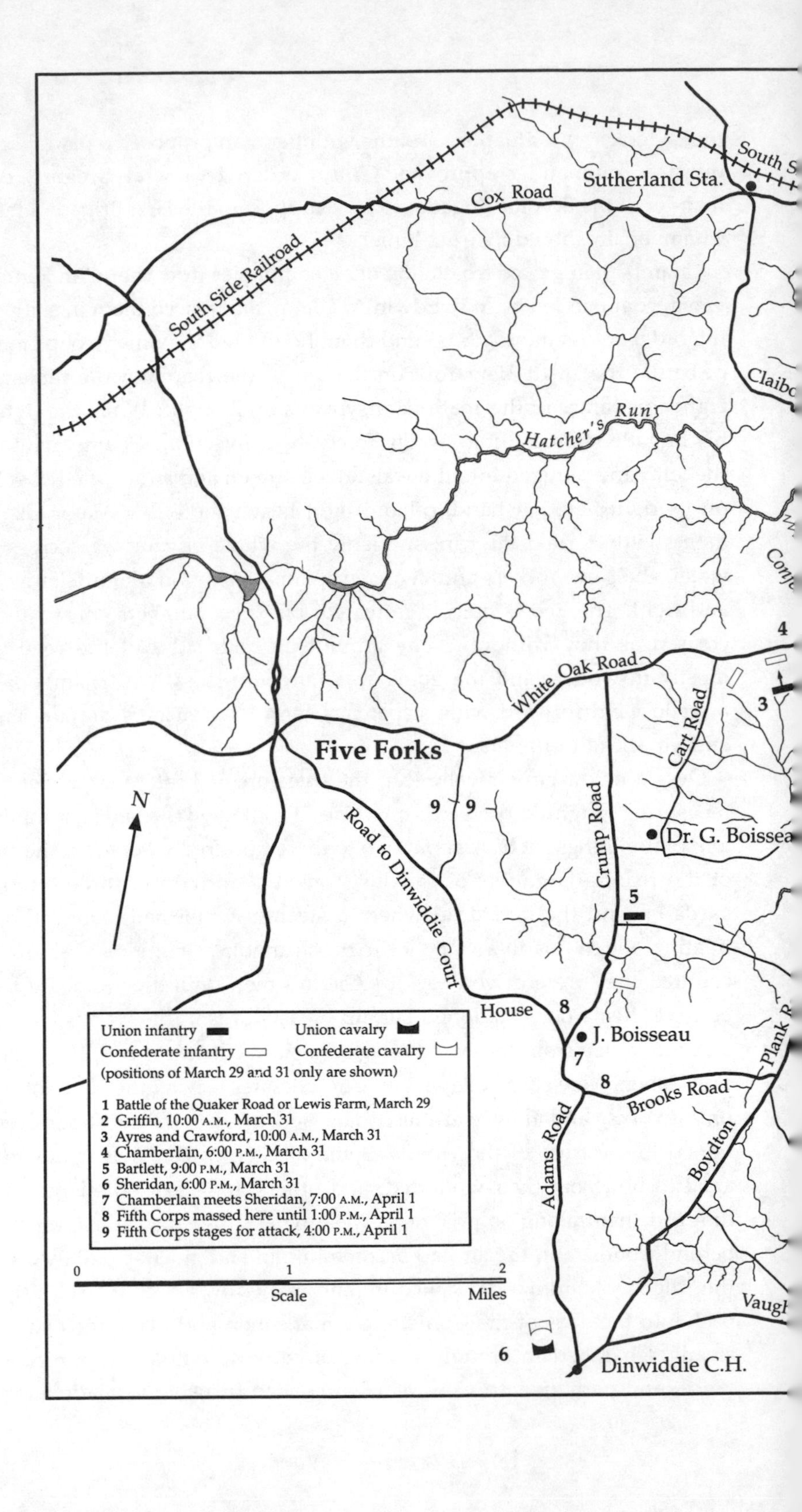
South Side Railroad
Cox Road
Sutherland Sta.
Hatcher's Run
White Oak Road
Five Forks
Cart Road
Crump Road
Dr. G. Boissea
Road to Dinwiddie Court House
J. Boisseau
Brooks Road
Adams Road
Boydton
Dinwiddie C.H.
N
Union infantry
Union cavalry
Confederate infantry
Confederate cavalry
(positions of March 29 and 31 only are shown)
1 Battle of the Quaker Road or Lewis Farm, March 29
2 Griffin, 10:00 A.M., March 31
3 Ayres and Crawford, 10:00 A.M., March 31
4 Chamberlain, 6:00 P.M., March 31
5 Bartlett, 9:00 P.M., March 31
6 Sheridan, 6:00 P.M., March 31
7 Chamberlain meets Sheridan, 7:00 A.M., April 1
8 Fifth Corps massed here until 1:00 P.M., April 1
9 Fifth Corps stages for attack, 4:00 P.M., April 1
0
1
2
Scale
Miles

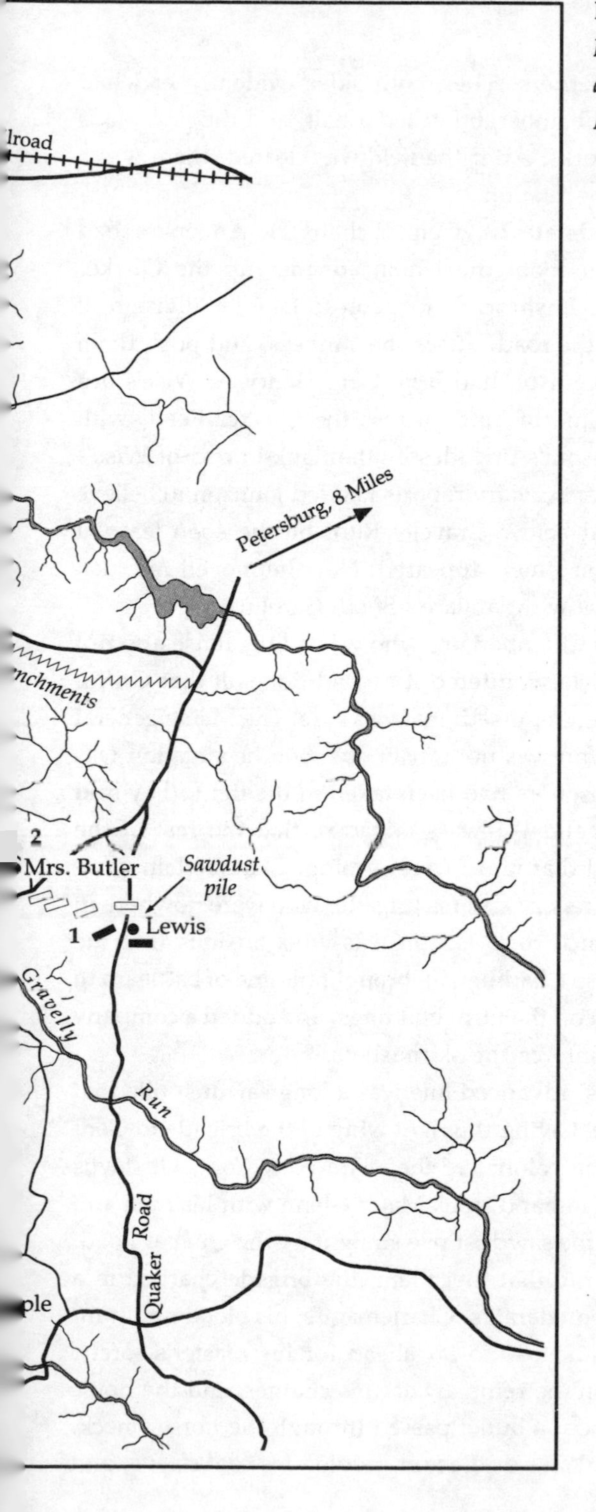

Map 10. *Actions at the Battles of the Quaker Road and the White Oak Road, March 29 and 31, 1865*

dash at the following Southerners. Then both sides evidently had had enough for the time being. Chamberlain called a halt, and the gray-clads joined their fellows in the works. After the field was cleared, there was a pause and time to assess the situation.[8]

Earlier in the day, Confederate Lt. Gen. Richard H. Anderson had learned from cavalry reports about the Union advance up the Quaker Road. He ordered Maj. Gen. Bushrod R. Johnson to take his division of four veteran brigades down the road, attack the Yankees, and push them back to the Vaughan Road. Johnson had Brig. Gen. Henry A. Wise's brigade form and advance in line of battle across the Quaker Road, with Wallace's, Moody's, and Ransom's brigades by the flank in rear of Wise's Virginia regiments. Subsequent cavalry reports had led Johnson to believe that the Federals had retired below Gravelly Run, but he soon learned differently when Chamberlain's men appeared. Now he moved to crush the Federals, reinforcing Wise with Wallace's South Carolinians.[9]

General Griffin rode up to Chamberlain, who was a little tense and not certain of Griffin's reaction. He wondered if he had done all that Griffin thought he could. He had been repulsed, that was sure. The Maine general was relieved to find that Griffin was not censorious, but the situation was crucial. About a hundred prisoners had been taken in the fight; they said that they were from Wise's and Wallace's brigades, that the rest of the division was with them, and that more were coming. Chamberlain wondered what had become of Gregory and his brigade, who were nowhere in sight and had not been heard from. Griffin was most anxious that the enemy's position be carried, so Chamberlain brought his line of battle up to the skirmish line, reformed it on the farm buildings, and added a company of the 185th New York to reinforce the skirmishers.[10]

At the center of the Rebels' advanced line was a long sawdust pile that formed a natural breastwork. Giving the right wing of the brigade to General Sickel and the left to the colonel of the 185th New York, Gustavus Sniper, Chamberlain, sword in hand, took Major Glenn with his men and led them in a charge toward the sawdust pile straight up the Quaker Road. With no time to return the fire that met them, the brigade charged in a headlong rush to rout the Confederates. Charlemagne, his blood up, thundered ahead of the foot soldiers—too far ahead for his master's safety. Chamberlain gave a check on the reins to curb his charger, and the horse reared slightly. At that moment a bullet passed through the horse's neck, painfully wounded Chamberlain's bridle arm, riddled his coat sleeve, and hit the general a terrible blow just below the heart. Fortunately, it was deflected by a sheaf of field orders and a brass-backed pocket mirror, but it moved around his coat, went out its back seam, and then knocked his aide, Lieutenant Vogel, from his saddle. Charlemagne stopped, bleeding profusely, and the unconscious Chamberlain slumped onto his horse's neck.[11]

Soon afterward, he regained consciousness in time to hear General Griffin say, with great concern and his arm around his subordinate's waist, "My dear General, you are gone." Chamberlain, the teacher of rhetoric, thought the word "you" was meant in the military sense and, hearing the high-pitched scream of a Rebel yell, dazedly looked in the direction of his right wing. He saw his Pennsylvania battle line break and start a hurried retreat before a surging mass of men in gray and butternut uniforms. "Yes, General, I *am* gone," he replied. Grazing Charlemagne's flank with his heel, the Maine general rode down the line, waving his sword and yelling, exhorting his men to turn and face the enemy.[12]

General Griffin would later comment that "it is a magnificent sight to see Chamberlain in battle," and his subordinate was giving him reason for the praise now. Chamberlain had lost his cap and was covered with blood, both his own and Charlemagne's. As he dashed among his men, his battered figure was an odd and inspiring sight. At the far right of his line he came upon Maj. Charles Maceuen and General Sickel, both valiantly urging the men to reverse their backward motion. In the next minutes he was horrified to see Sickel go down with a shattered arm and Maceuen shot dead a few feet from him in the whirling struggle. The stalwart Pennsylvanians, heeding the entreaties of their leaders, turned and, with a mighty shout, pushed back the charging Rebels. Satisfied, Chamberlain headed back toward his proper place in the center. As he rode, his men cheered him vigorously, and when he came into the view of the Confederates, they cheered too! "I hardly knew what world I was in," he later recalled.[13]

When he reached the center, Charlemagne could go no farther, and there was some fighting and confusion at the sawdust pile, where Major Glenn was having a bad time. Pushing to the front on foot to better see what was going on, Chamberlain was suddenly confronted by several Rebels, who lowered their muskets, crossed their bayonets, and demanded his surrender. The specter of Libby Prison rose before him. Thinking fast, and remembering that the faded coat he wore helped him get out of a similar scrape the year before, he replied, presumably in a Southern accent: "Surrender? What's the matter with you? What do you take me for?

Don't you see these Yanks right onto us? Come along with me and let us break 'em." He waved his sword in the direction of the Union soldiers as he turned back. Caught off guard, the Confederates followed him and were captured themselves.[14]

Just then, Maj. Ellis Spear, his old friend from the Twentieth Maine, now a staff officer for General Bartlett, appeared in front of him seemingly out of nowhere. Chamberlain always suspected the major of making it his personal business to look after him, and now Spear, with a ceremonious manner, as if preparing to confer an honor on him, offered a "swallow" from a flask of excellent wine he had been saving. Chamberlain took a swallow all right, but he judged the word had an indeterminate definition. When Spear took the bottle back and held it up to the light to see how much of the drink was left, his face took on a "melancholy, martyr-like look." Amused and embarrassed, Chamberlain was glad he would not have to face Spear at headquarters that night.[15]

But the pause was only a short one, for trouble flared on the left. Colonel Sniper had fought the enemy into the woods and had tried to carry the breastworks there. The enemy, heavily reinforced, gave forth such a withering fire that the soldiers could not stand up to it and survive. The Confederates poured out of their works, and the New York regiment fell back until its line was turned and nearly parallel to the Quaker Road. Someone helped Chamberlain mount a mud-spattered, pale horse; then he and his staff had all they could do to hold the men to their duty. Later Chamberlain thought that he "must have looked more than ever like a figure from the Apocalypse."[16]

The anxious Chamberlain knew that the position of his left wing could not be maintained for long without some assistance. He sent a message to General Gregory, who he thought was up near the First Brigade's left by now, asking him to attack the enemy right; this action would enfilade the flank of the Confederates' new alignment. Instead, General Griffin came on the line and assured him that if he and his men could hold for ten minutes, he could have a battery up. Heartened, Chamberlain made his way toward the embattled Colonel Sniper, who had seized his regimental flag from the third color-bearer to go down and was carrying it forward himself. Yelling to Sniper so that the men could hear, Chamberlain shouted, "Once more! Try the steel! Hell for ten minutes and we are out of it!"[17]

Behind him, Chamberlain had noticed a spot of higher ground, and he meant to save that position for the promised artillery. Inspired by their officers, the men pushed the enemy back into the woods with a herculean effort. As the Rebels regrouped, Chamberlain strained his eyes down the Quaker Road, praying for the guns to come into view. Finally, there they were: "B of the 4th Regulars . . . with headlong speed, horses smoking, battery thundering with jolt and rattle, wheeling into action front . . . while the earth flew beneath the wheels,—magnificent, the terrible Napoleons."[18]

Lt. John Mitchell, a Regular Army man, had served with Battery B, Fourth United States, in every capacity for eleven years and now was commanding it for the first time in combat. He had fought with these guns in many battles, including close-quarter fights at Antietam and Gettysburg. Knowing his business well, the Irishman was as tough as they came. Even in this tight place, however, he could not help but smile at the sight of Chamberlain, who looked ragged, bloody, and unlike a general officer. Intent on pointing out the ground to Mitchell and forgetting his appearance, Chamberlain somehow did not see anything funny. "Mitchell," he shouted abruptly above the din, "do you think you can put solid shot or percussion into those woods close over the rebels' heads, without hurting my men?" "Yes, Sir! if they will keep where they are," Mitchell replied. "Well then, give it to them. . . . But stop quick at my signal, and fire clear of my men when they charge!"[19]

Divided into sections of two, the four twelve-pound smoothbores wheeled into action. Their muzzles belched forth shot and shell into the trees and brought branches and sharpshooters down upon the heads of Bushrod Johnson's surprised men, who were bent on charging again. The screaming Rebel yells broke off suddenly and were immediately replaced by the deep hurrahs of the heartened Yankees when they heard the voices of their own guns. It was none too soon, because the men in gray recovered rapidly and massed ominously, spilling over and again flanking Chamberlain's bent-back left wing.[20]

The left section of Battery B was in danger of being captured. Sniper maneuvered his men to his left to meet the Rebel flanking move, leaving the field clear on his right. Lieutenant Mitchell, his guns loaded with case shot, then canister, fired point-blank into the charging Southern infantrymen. Chamberlain was near the guns and saw Mitchell, who was coolly mounting a recoiling gun carriage to see the result of his last shot, go down, wounded in his right elbow. The artillery and infantry succeeded in holding Chamberlain's left, but then the enemy renewed the attack on the

Federal center and right. Almost out of ammunition, the Pennsylvanians began to retire slowly and lose ground.[21]

The situation was desperate now. Chamberlain sent one of his aides to General Gregory for a regiment, hoping that Gregory would finally have his men within reach on the left. Coming back on the field, General Griffin thought that his brigade commander looked ready to expire and exclaimed, "General, you must not leave us. We cannot spare you now." Startled, Chamberlain replied, "I had no thought of it, General." Griffin immediately ordered up three regiments from Bartlett's Third Brigade. Chamberlain worked to repair his broken line in order to save Mitchell's guns, now under the command of Lt. William P. Vose; his men were falling back in front of the Lewis house.[22]

Lt. Col. Isaac Doolittle, 188th New York Infantry, received an urgent order from General Gregory to "report to General Chamberlain." He moved his regiment by the right flank until his two right companies came to the open field, where he saw a Union line of battle advancing on his right. Without orders, he connected his troops with the battle line and went forward with it toward the enemy on the right of Chamberlain's struggling left wing.[23]

Coming up behind the advancing line in fine style was Col. Alfred L. Pearson with his colorful 155th Pennsylvania Zouaves. At Chamberlain's direction, Pearson's regiment swept to the center to aid their fellow Pennsylvanians. Ahead was the sawdust pile that the enemy was now using as breastworks. Seizing his regimental flag from his color sergeant, the colonel shouted, "Follow me men, or lose your colors," and then courageously charged up onto the long sawdust pile that sheltered some of the Confederates. Cheering loudly, the men followed him, passing through and in front of the line of the tired fighters of the First Brigade.[24]

Seeing reinforcements arrive, the Confederates withdrew rapidly, and at least one of their officers thought they were fighting huge numbers of Yankees. Most were able to retreat in some order, but others surrendered, and their badly wounded and dead fell into the hands of the victorious bluecoats. As the Rebels fell back toward their main entrenchments on the White Oak Road, Lieutenant Vose positioned the battery on either side of the Lewis house. Chamberlain then stationed his own 185th New York on both sides of the battery, right and left, and had the 198th Pennsylvania collect in front of the farm buildings.[25]

It had been a fine victory and an important one. Bartlett's brigade, which contained the Twentieth Maine and was accompanied by General Warren himself, immediately moved forward to the junction of the Quaker and Boydton Plank Roads. They worked far into the night building breastworks near there, less than a half-mile from the Confederates' advance entrenchments and not a mile below their stronghold near Burgess's Mill on the White Oak Road. Word came that the Second Corps, after being delayed most of the day, was up but had not connected with the Fifth Corps's right. Sheridan was at Dinwiddie Court House.[26]

Numbering less than 1,700 officers and men, the First Brigade's two regiments had fought and held much larger numbers of Confederates in the two hours before help came. Chamberlain calculated that the battery and reinforcing regiments added only about 1,000 men more to his complement. General Griffin had allowed him to fight his own battle through to its conclusion; when reinforcements were available to finish the fight and drive the enemy from the field, Griffin brought in units to operate under his subordinate's command. He could have easily ordered up General Bartlett, who ranked Chamberlain, with his whole brigade, which would have taken the credit from Chamberlain and his men. Griffin's decision not to do so, Chamberlain thought, demonstrated the power of a commanding officer to make or break lives and reputations, to inspire loyalty, and to bring out the best in his soldiers. With faith in the fairness and sensitivity of such a commander, men were inspired to extend themselves and give the best they had to their duty.[27]

Personally gratifying to Chamberlain were the words of General Warren, his corps commander, who came to him and said, "General, you have done splendid work. I am telegraphing the President. You will hear from it." A short time afterward, Chamberlain did hear from it: he was given a brevet promotion to major general "for conspicuous gallantry in action on the Quaker Road, March 29, 1865."[28]

But Chamberlain's command had sustained over 400 casualties; he had lost some of his best officers, and many of his men were lying dead or badly wounded in the gray twilight. The Confederates had also suffered terribly with 130 dead, nearly 200 taken prisoner, and an unknown number of their wounded scattered about the fields and in the woods. During the time the battle raged, clouds had gathered and the air became permeated with moisture; now the setting sun was obscured from view by the overcast. As it began to grow dark, lingering battle smoke combined with mists rose to envelop the bloody ground like spirits newly freed from their

Bvt. Maj. Gen. Joshua L. Chamberlain
(Alice Rains Trulock and James A. Trulock)

earthly clay. Anguished, his own responsibility for the carnage lying like a pall upon his mind, Chamberlain rode slowly in the damp, chill air across the body-strewn field.[29]

"But we had with us, to keep and to care for, more than five hundred bruised bodies of men,—men made in the image of God, marred by the hand of man, and must we say in the name of God? And where is the reckoning for such things? And who is answerable? One might almost shrink from the sound of his own voice, which had launched into the palpitating air words of order—do we call it?—fraught with such ruin. Was it God's command we heard, or His forgiveness we must forever implore?"[30]

Giving over his borrowed horse, Chamberlain looked in on Charlemagne at one of the farm buildings. Then on foot, weak, bent, and barely able to walk from the pain of his old and new wounds, he searched for familiar forms and faces. A cold rain began to fall, and groups of men moved over the ground, the rays of their lanterns shining out into the gathering darkness. In one place a chaplain intoned prayers for the dead above a burial trench as soldiers stood by patiently waiting to finish their sad task. Chamberlain looked into one tired face, then another, and spoke words of encouragement. At last he knelt in sorrow beside the body of Major Maceuen, "where God's thought had folded its wing." He remembered the day when the young man's father had taken him by the shoulders and implored him to take care of his only son. Grief bowed Chamberlain's head and shrouded his spirit.[31]

Nearby lay the wounded General Sickel, who had refused to be taken from the field before his turn and had watched the poignant scene from the shadows. "General," he said, smiling benignly on his commanding officer, "you have the soul of the lion and the heart of the woman." Chamberlain, the Cartesian Victorian, considered the comment a high compliment and asked Sickel to take the remark as his own description.[32]

His uniform soaked with the rain, but feeling fortunate to be alive, Chamberlain finally turned and made his way to the Lewis farmhouse, which was crowded with wounded. He sat in the kitchen using a cracker box for a desk and, by the light of a guttering candle, wrote a letter to Major Maceuen's father telling him how heroically his boy had died. He reflected on the Rebel wounded, lonely and helpless in the hands of their enemies. They would be cared for; "indeed," he thought, "in the hour of sorrow and disaster, do we not all belong to each other?" Rain continued to pour down outside, the wind sighing in the trees. Some soldiers on picket duty that night noticed that the rain sometimes turned to snow. Many snatched a few hours of exhausted sleep, the trees their only shelter.[33]

At his headquarters near the Vaughan Road crossing of Gravelly Run, General Grant decided to change his original purpose of making the destruction of the railroads the principal objective of General Sheridan's movements. He wired Sheridan that he was modifying his plans—that he felt "like ending the matter." Sheridan should not cut loose and go for the railroads but should push around the enemy and get on his right rear. "We will all act together as one grand army here until it is seen what can be done with the enemy," Grant declared.[34]

All through the night and the next day it continued to rain steadily; the swamps filled up with water, and the roads became virtually impassable until corduroyed. The Virginia mud, a combination of clay and sand in that area, became a quagmire and acted as a kind of quicksand. Chamberlain's brigade remained on the field at the Lewis house. While the rest of the Fifth Corps dug in along the Boydton Plank Road, at Grant's initiative Warren had General Ayres's division move west of the Boydton Road and establish a chain of pickets opposite the fortified Confederate works on the White Oak Road. General Humphreys's Second Corps connected on the right of the Fifth Corps. Chamberlain, suffering from his wounds, was not out on March 30, but he issued a congratulatory order to the troops of his brigade for their gallant conduct in the Quaker Road battle.[35]

At Grant's headquarters that morning, there was talk of withdrawing and starting over when the weather was better, but Grant thought differently: once the skies cleared the roads would dry quickly. General Sheridan arrived, his horse sinking to the knees at every step in the sticky mire. Cheerfully, his sun-browned face beaming, the little general dismounted. Energetically, he expounded that if he were given some infantry to add to his command of cavalry, he could crush Lee's right or force him to weaken his lines before Petersburg until the Union troops could pierce them. Pacing "like a hound on a leash" and bouncing up and down reminiscent of a sailor, he exclaimed, "I tell you, I'm ready to strike out tomorrow and go to smashing things."[36]

Grant and Sheridan then had a private conversation in which an understanding was reached between them about Sheridan's immediate movements. Answering only to Grant so far, Sheridan had been acting as an independent commander and would continue to do so. General Meade, commanding the Army of the Potomac, was Sheridan's senior in rank; this

Maj. Gen. Philip H. Sheridan
(Massachusetts Commandery, MOLLUS*, and U.S. Army Military History Institute, Carlisle Barracks, Pa.)*

would lead to awkward situations later when the infantry and cavalry were "acting together as one grand army," but Sheridan would never serve under Meade's orders during the entire campaign. Grant decided to extend his lines no farther, but at the right time to reinforce Sheridan with a corps of infantry. Sheridan would then be expected to turn the enemy's right flank, and the other Union corps, now ready and waiting eastward, would assault the Petersburg lines. The main business was to turn Lee's right and break up his army; perhaps Grant realized that he had in Sheridan not a hound but a mastiff, and he was prepared to unleash him, with little restraint.[37]

Aware of the peril on the right of his long defensive line, Robert E. Lee kept his men busy on the rain-sodden day as the Union generals planned their strategy. He reinforced the Confederate defenses on the White Oak Road near Hatcher's Run with additional infantry and strengthened breastworks that would run about two miles west from the Boydton Plank Road, ending in a "return" angle north, nearly paralleling the Claiborne Road. He also sent his newly appointed cavalry chief, Gen. Fitzhugh Lee, to take possession of Five Forks, the strategic crossroads about four and a half miles west on the White Oak Road from the Claiborne. Five Forks had a road running north three miles to the South Side Railroad, and one of the southerly roadways led six miles to Dinwiddie Court House. Fitzhugh Lee and his single cavalry division arrived on the thirtieth and, in sharp skirmishing, successfully prevented Sheridan's cavalry from occupying Five Forks.[38]

Confederate Maj. Gen. George E. Pickett and his infantry division reached the White Oak Road stronghold at daylight. Leaving one of his brigades with the other Confederate defenders in the works on the White Oak Road, he then marched by the White Oak Road to Five Forks, arriving at sunset on the thirtieth with five brigades from his own and Johnson's divisions. Additional cavalry divisions under Generals Rosser and W. H. F. Lee joined Fitzhugh Lee that night, and Pickett assumed command of an infantry and cavalry operation planned against Sheridan to begin the next morning. To further protect the South Side Railroad, General Lee also intended to use some of his troops in the White Oak Road entrenchments to get on the left flank of the Fifth Corps and roll it up in conjunction with Pickett's attack on Sheridan. Sheridan was soon aware of Pickett's arrival and reported it to Grant.[39]

Near the end of the day, Grant told Sheridan that if his situation the next morning could "justify the belief that you can turn the enemy's right with the assistance of a corps of infantry, entirely detached from the balance of the army, I will so detach the Fifth Corps, and place the whole under your command for the operation." Sheridan answered that morning as requested. He did not want the Fifth Corps; he wanted the Sixth, and given it he could turn the enemy's right or break through his lines. The enemy's right was by then at Five Forks. But the Sixth was too far away for practicality, and Grant told his cavalry chief so; he could alternatively give Sheridan the Second Corps. There the matter rested until events intervened.[40]

Before dawn on March 31, the Fifth Corps's other two divisions, Griffin's and Maj. Gen. Samuel Crawford's, joined Ayres west of the Boydton Plank Road, while elements of General Humphreys's Second Corps took the places of Warren's men in their entrenchments. Commanding the smallest division in the Fifth Corps, General Ayres moved his whole force to the left and about six hundred yards south of the White Oak Road near the S. Dabney place. Crawford's division was in rear and to the right of Ayres about five hundred yards, and Griffin's was out of sight but within supporting distance of both on the south or east side of a branch of Gravelly Run near Mrs. Butler's. Warren had suggested the movement to Meade the afternoon before, with the intention of advancing to block the White Oak Road, and the move was approved by Grant. Grant later ordered Meade to have Warren keep strong and guard against an attack after he was in place, and Meade had answered that he would not let Warren advance unless Grant directed it.[41]

Still hurting from his accumulated wounds, Chamberlain was resting on a heap of straw when he was summoned to take command at the far left of Griffin's division. This critical position was not only the left flank of the division, but also that of the entire Fifth and Second Corps, and enough was known of Lee's position to fear a sudden attack there. Facing his own brigade toward Ayres's position on the other side of Gravelly Run, Chamberlain put Gregory's brigade on the left and had Gregory bend back his line at right angles, facing west along a country road. Two batteries of the division artillery strengthened his lines. Grant had pointed out the Fifth Corps's exposed position in a dispatch to Sheridan the night before and had advised the cavalry commander to be prepared to assist Warren with all his force if an attack did occur. Later learning that Sheridan had not reached the White Oak Road as he had wished, however, Grant advised Meade to warn Warren to look out for his own left flank.[42]

Because of the nearly impassable conditions of the roads and country, Grant sent an order to Meade at 7:40 A.M. that his troops should stay substantially where they were. Warren telegraphed Meade that Ayres had reported that the enemy pickets were on the south side of the White Oak Road, so that the Confederate communications were continuous along it. As a precaution, he had directed Ayres to drive the enemy pickets from the White Oak Road or find out in what force the Confederates held it. Meade answered that if Ayres could get possession of and hold the White Oak Road on this reconnaissance, he should do so, notwithstanding the directive suspending movement for the day. But things would get out of hand now in very short order.[43]

Chamberlain could imagine, in tantalizing vision, the results of Grant's grand strategy, if it worked: The Fifth Corps across the White Oak Road just west of the Claiborne Road and menacing the Confederate works in front; Sheridan sweeping around on the Fifth Corps's wheeling flank, cutting communications, enfilading the Claiborne entrenchments, followed by the Second Corps assaulting on the right and taking the main works; the other Union corps then smashing the Petersburg defenses, and Lee's army broken and scattered! But the Fifth Corps would first have to effect a lodgment on the White Oak Road, cutting off the Confederate forces on Lee's right flank from each other. As it was, the Fifth Corps generals had no idea that Grant had changed his original purpose to have Sheridan cut loose and first destroy Lee's communications.[44]

In the vanguard of the Fifth Corps reconnaissance to the White Oak Road, Ayres advanced in a wedge formation without skirmishers, although he expected his movement might bring on a battle. Chamberlain, who liked and respected him, thought Ayres resolute and fearless, but "in truth not fearing enough." Meanwhile, McGowan's, Gracie's, and Hunton's brigades had been ordered by Robert E. Lee in person out of the White Oak Road defenses to smash in the Fifth Corps on its left. Not expecting to meet the Federals so soon, the Confederates, hidden from the view of the Union division, were surprised to see Ayres's advance. When his lead brigade got to within fifty yards of the White Oak Road, the Rebels rose up, appearing to materialize out of the woods. An impulsive lieutenant in Brig. Gen. Eppa Hunton's brigade jumped in front of his line, waving his sword and shouting, "Follow me boys!"—and Hunton's men attacked. The two brigades on Hunton's right were immediately ordered in, and the entire Confederate detachment charged into the open and struck Ayres's leading brigade on the left and front with overwhelming force.[45]

Caught off guard and not in position, Bvt. Brig. Gen. Frederick Winthrop's brigade still faced about and marched across the field in good order.

In spite of the efforts of the officers and some of the men to stand and make a fight of it, their supports behind them broke. Then followed a phenomenon that sometimes seized even veteran troops of both armies—a panic ensued as succeeding lines broke, like dominoes falling, and exposed other units behind them to annihilation or capture before the driving enemy. Ayres, alarmed and mortified, "like a roaring lion" in Chamberlain's descriptive phrase, tried vainly to stem the tide, although enough men rallied for at least two distinct stands. The disorganized soldiers ran back on General Crawford's large division, and as Crawford's lines became broken and exposed, a general rout ensued.[46]

As the late morning sun began to shine through the clearing clouds, the men in Griffin's division were cooking coffee and peacefully spreading their sodden clothing and blankets out to dry. Suddenly they heard a tremendous uproar—cannon, cheers, and the crash of musketry—sounding about a mile to their front and rolling louder toward them. Bugles screamed, "Fall in, Fall in." Griffin's men grabbed their stacked rifles and double-quicked toward Gravelly Run. Reaching the crest of a rise of ground overlooking the stream, they went into line and could see hordes of Second and Third Division men struggling across the swampy, waist-deep stream, which was swollen to about sixty feet wide. "For God's sake, let them through, or they will break our line," General Griffin yelled above the noise. In plain sight of Griffin's men, the Rebel line was advancing in close pursuit down a lower crest onto the level ground on the other side of the stream. One Federal private remembered that "the bands played, the cannons roared; our muskets crashed with awful force; the hill itself shivered as if with fear." The Confederate movement was checked.[47]

General Warren rode toward the point of conflict and tried to stem the tide of fleeing fugitives of his retreating divisions. Failing in this, he returned across the branch of Gravelly Run and helped re-form them in rear of Griffin's stalwart lines. Chamberlain, sharply watching the left against flank attack even more now because he knew that the enemy was aware of the corps's situation, looked up to see Generals Griffin and Warren bearing down on him. Both were out of breath from their exertions of stopping the flight of the other divisions. Griffin burst out: "General Chamberlain, the Fifth Corps is eternally damned!" Quickly, Chamberlain rejoined with a pleasant voice, "Not 'til you are in Heaven." Not a flicker of a smile revealed that Griffin had even heard; he rushed on: "I tell Warren you will wipe out this disgrace, and that's what we're here for."[48]

General Warren, his face grave, his tone intense but compressed and strange, asked, "General Chamberlain, will you save the honor of the Fifth Corps?" Save the honor of the Fifth Corps! How could Chamberlain refuse a request expressed in that manner? But he thought of his own worn and fought-out men and instead mentioned to his superiors Bartlett's Third Brigade, the division's largest and best, which had been hardly engaged. It contained veteran regiments, including his old Twentieth Maine, with the remnants of Butterfield's Light Brigade and Porter's division, which became the nucleus of the Fifth Corps. Warren was unmoved. "We have come to you; you know what that means."[49]

"I'll try it General," Chamberlain replied, and thinking that the way things had been going, he had reason to say so, he added, "Only don't let anybody stop me except the enemy." Warren proposed building a bridge over the swampy Gravelly Run branch; it would take only an hour, and he thought Chamberlain could not get his men across in any kind of order otherwise. Apparently not wanting to allow the enemy more time than was absolutely necessary to regroup and prepare a hot welcome for him, Chamberlain demonstrated a great deal of faith in the capabilities of his men. "It may do to come back on, General," he replied, referring to the bridge. "It will not do to stop for that now. My men will go straight through."[50]

Maj. Edwin Glenn of the 198th Pennsylvania took its right wing through the soft, mud-bottomed stream, the men carrying their cartridge boxes on the bayonet sockets of their muskets to keep them dry. The fire of the regiment's second battalion kept the enemy at bay until the intrepid Glenn and his men, who had also spearheaded the advance on the Quaker Road, formed in skirmishing order on the other side. Chamberlain brought over the rest of the First Brigade and formed in line of battle, followed by General Gregory's Second Brigade in column of regiments. After the Fifth Corps reformed, the Third Brigade accompanied by General Griffin acted as a reserve for Chamberlain, and Ayres followed on the division's left rear, *en échelon* by brigade and fronted by First Division skirmishers. Crawford was to the right and rear, out of sight and reach after they crossed the stream. Now the Fifth Corps had Chamberlain on its cutting edge as it advanced northwest, with a visible enemy in his front.[51]

Meanwhile, his Second Corps poised on the right of the Fifth Corps, General Humphreys had heard the sounds of the original clash with the Confederates and learned from an increasing number of stragglers from the rout that Warren needed support. General Lee had apparently ordered Wise's brigade out of the entrenchments on Hunton's left to protect his other three brigades, and Humphreys immediately ordered Gen. Nelson A. Miles's division to attack Wise. Miles hit Wise in front and flank, while Humphreys's other divisions began attacking the Confederate entrenchments east of the Boydton Plank Road, keeping the Confederates busy on their left. Chamberlain pushed forward, driving the Rebels fighting in his front, and much farther on the Union right, Humphreys's men drove back Wise's lines.[52]

Chamberlain's troops, opposed only by a skirmish line, pressed the enemy back at first without much resistance. Then the Rebels fell back on supports and made stand after stand for a mile or so on the broken, ravine-marked ground. Finally coming to the field where the Rebels had struck Warren's other divisions with such resounding shock that morning, Chamberlain's men drove the enemy into some ordinary breastworks. These had been hastily thrown up from logs and earth in advance of the Confederate main defenses; from them and from some woods on each flank the Rebels formed a strong line pouring a galling fire into the advancing Yankees, causing the right of Chamberlain's line to waver. Under the slight protection of a rise in the open field, Chamberlain was making quick preparations for a final charge when a staff officer rode up with orders, apparently from Warren, to halt and take the defensive until the Fifth Corps commander could take a look at the conditions in the front.[53]

Not liking the stop because his men were in a bad place to stay, Chamberlain joined Warren and Griffin back at the edge of some woods. Now the question of whether to cross the White Oak Road or not had to be decided. The Fifth Corps had been vindicated, with the lost ground completely regained, but Grant had indicated the road's importance, and Meade had just given positive instructions. Chamberlain was all for it. It would cost him as many men to withdraw from his precarious position as it would to carry the enemy fieldworks, and he advanced a plan that his superiors approved. As things turned out, Chamberlain would later regret his own "youthful impetuosity" for pressing to go beyond the ground lost by the other divisions and placing the Fifth Corps in a position from which it could not be easily withdrawn. But he truly believed that what was wanted—the object of all the fighting since the morning of March 29—was the enemy right at the White Oak Road entrenchments, and his superiors apparently agreed. Years later, after he realized Grant had "suddenly changed his tactics and resolved to concentrate on Sheridan," he mused, "How could we then know Grant's change of purpose?"[54]

On Chamberlain's right flank, obscured by woods, were the Confederates' main entrenchments. Now he asked General Gregory to move quickly into the woods on the right, "by battalion in echelon by the left," and with two batteries of artillery to take in flank and reverse any attack on his own First Brigade. When Gregory struck opposition, he was to fire with musketry and artillery and make all the demonstration he could; Chamberlain would seize the moment to charge the enemy advance works. General Ayres's division was located in a piece of woods on Chamberlain's left and rear. Putting his plan into effect, Chamberlain brought his brigade together in one line, stretching across the field. Later Chamberlain would write, no doubt with a twinkle in his eye, "Had I known of the fact that General Lee himself was personally directing affairs in our front, I might not have been so rash, or thought myself so cool!"[55]

At the crash and boom of Gregory's guns, the First Brigade's bugles sounded the "Forward!" and Chamberlain with his Pennsylvanians and New Yorkers rushed to the charge, the men with muskets at right shoulder. The line moved rapidly over the ground with open front, not heeding alignment or ranks, toward the Confederate fieldworks. Chamberlain raced across the field, riding again on Charlemagne, heedless that both of them were worn and hurt from wounds. "We belonged together," Chamberlain declared about his hardy steed. "He knew that as well as I. . . . His Morgan endurance was under him, and his Kentucky blood was up." Met with a huge storm of musketry and artillery promising death at every step, the Union men charged on, "every color flying, officers leading, right in among the enemy," one eyewitness characterized the sweeping charge. A Confederate general officer watched, struck with the sight, and later recounted, "I thought it was one of the most gallant things I had ever seen."[56]

The New York and Pennsylvania regiments hit the enemy in a torrent. Up and over the breastworks Chamberlain went with his men, in the swirling, cutting fight, carrying all before them. Then, after a short struggle, the whole fighting mass rolled back. In the confused, hand-to-hand fighting, Lt. Amos W. Seitziger saw Pvt. Augustus Zeiber of Company D of the 198th Pennsylvania snatch away the flag of the Fifty-sixth Virginia on the parapet and give it to his general. Handing it right back, Chamberlain told the private to keep it and take the credit for himself, a magnanimous gesture certainly typical of the earnest professor turned general. Almost the whole Virginia regiment was captured besides its battle flag, and Private Zeiber later took the flag to General Warren.[57]

Chamberlain's brigade then swung to the right and, with Gregory's brigade, sent the enemy flying into their main works at the Claiborne and White Oak Roads. Establishing the lines of his own brigade on a diagonal facing northeast toward the Confederate angle, with Gregory's south of the White Oak Road facing north, Chamberlain could finally pause for a short rest. After three hours of almost continuous fighting, the line of his brigade placed the Fifth Corps three hundred yards across the White Oak Road.[58]

Chamberlain posted pickets close up to the enemy works and found that his losses, though comparatively small in numbers, included some of his best officers and men. After he finally dismounted, he stood on a small knoll, a solitary figure wrapped in thought, as he listened a little anxiously to the sound of heavy firing some distance away from the Fifth Corps's exposed left flank. Heard as soon as the Fifth's battle had ceased, from a direction where Sheridan should be, the sounds now seemed to be moving away. It was evening, and although the day had been long and hard, Charlemagne waited with his girth unslackened, ready for instant action. Just then General Warren rode up and with earnest concern asked Chamberlain if he thought the sounds of firing were nearing or receding.[59]

It was Chamberlain's opinion that the firing was moving away from them toward Dinwiddie, and Warren concurred. The corps commander discussed the situation a few minutes with Chamberlain, considering what action would be best to take in the absence of orders. Chamberlain's opinion was that Grant would probably not want to draw Warren's corps from its present strategic position and would rather send General Miles of the Second Corps to help Sheridan. However, Warren might be blamed if he did not go to the cavalry general's support if he believed Sheridan were in trouble. "Well, will you go?" Warren asked his brigade chief. "Certainly, General, if you think it best; but surely you do not want to abandon this position," Chamberlain replied.[60]

Now Griffin joined the conversation, and Warren asked him to immediately send Bartlett's brigade, which had not been engaged that day, across country to threaten the rear of the enemy engaged with Sheridan. This soldierly decision to assist the cavalry chief would begin a sequence of events that would prove the undoing of the gallant Fifth Corps commander. After sunset, General Warren came out again to Chamberlain's headquarters, and together they crawled on their hands and knees within two hundred yards of the Confederate works to examine the strength of the enemy defenses. A commotion on the picket line with resultant musket and cannon fire told them all they needed to know—the Rebels could get a cross fire with their big guns on any troops within range. Chamberlain was pushing his battered body hard in this campaign: leading charges, nursing new wounds, crawling on his hands and knees on muddy ground. And he would fight yet another battle and endure over twenty-four hours more with little or no sleep in the name of duty.[61]

Chamberlain ordered most of his men into bivouac so that they, at least, could get some uneasy rest. But he and General Gregory, realizing the distinct possibility of an enemy attack, and later expecting to move, were up all the long dark night, mostly on the picket line. General Griffin joined them at intervals with more news. Sheridan was indeed in trouble at Dinwiddie Court House. That morning, part of Sheridan's cavalry on its way to Five Forks had met Confederate cavalry, and Confederate infantry under Pickett left Five Forks soon after. Battles between the two sides continued all day, as the forces ranged over the rough and wooded country between Five Forks and Dinwiddie on either side of the Chamberlain Creek and south of Gravelly Run, over to the Boydton Plank Road. The combined Confederate forces proved too strong for Sheridan. At nightfall his troopers were facing lines of Rebel infantry with cavalry on each flank a mile north of the county seat at Dinwiddie Court House. They badly needed infantry reinforcement.[62]

General Meade, from his headquarters at the Vaughan Road crossing of Hatcher's Run, about six miles away from Chamberlain's position, mistakenly judged the firing as moving north and ordered Warren to push out a brigade west on the White Oak Road to meet Sheridan. This misunderstanding, later rectified after Meade finally heard from Sheridan, was the first of the communication problems of the ensuing night. Far from the actual scene of action, Grant and Meade at their separate headquarters issued orders to subordinates with poorly coordinating efforts. Meade's and Warren's headquarters were nearly five miles apart, and Grant's, near Dabney's Mill, was about two miles from Meade's and six miles from Sheridan's at Dinwiddie. The telegraph was working badly, and no telegraph communications were in place to Sheridan. Even when the wire service was working, much time elapsed in the transmittal and execution of orders over the widely scattered commands. Staff officers rushed over the muddy roads in the dark night carrying hurriedly written messages.[63]

As events rapidly transpired, Meade informed Warren of Sheridan's situation, which left Warren's and Humphreys's corps open to the enemy by the Boydton Plank Road from Dinwiddie, and instructed him to be concerned for his right and rear. Warren reported his troop dispositions to headquarters, and also his opinion that the enemy was in an untenable position and would fall back on Five Forks if Sheridan kept fighting. Advancing a plan for part of his corps to move down the Boydton Plank Road to attack the enemy on one side with Sheridan on the other, Warren proposed an open field fight while Bartlett was in rear of the Confederates. Meade, a diminished and apparently intimidated commander, presented the plan to Grant but did not say that it was initiated by Warren, an omission that would later contribute to grief for the Fifth Corps commander. Meade gave no orders unless they were initiated by Grant or cleared through him.[64]

Soon afterward, Warren was ordered to contract his lines, pull his divisions from the hard-fought-for position on the White Oak Road, and send Griffin's division down the Boydton Plank Road to Sheridan. Warren immediately complied, ordering Griffin to recall Bartlett and then to march to Dinwiddie, and Ayres and Crawford to withdraw to the Boydton Road. After his orders were dispatched, Warren learned that Gravelly Run at the Boydton Plank Road was suddenly bank full or more and not fordable for infantry, but he determined to have the broken bridge rebuilt by the time Griffin's reunited division reached it, and he so informed Meade. However, a downed telegraph line prevented Meade and therefore Grant from receiving this crucial information for hours, and their subsequent orders to Warren were based on faulty assumptions.[65]

The following hours became a nightmare for Warren as orders came in confused sequence. An order from Meade came telling him to give Griffin another good brigade instead of Bartlett. Since Warren knew from the wording that his dispatch about the bridge had not been received, he assumed that when it was, Meade would know that Bartlett could arrive and rejoin Griffin by the time the bridge was repaired. However, later he was concerned to get another order that showed his broken bridge message was still not received. The order told Warren to send Griffin promptly as ordered and bring Ayres and Crawford by the same road Bartlett was on and strike the enemy in rear. Not only that, but its contents also showed a complete misapprehension of the enemy position. Warren's topographer had conducted Bartlett when the Third Brigade first marched and had returned to report the exact location of the Confederates.[66]

Meade immediately let Sheridan know that Griffin's division would come by way of the Plank Road and that he had asked Grant to authorize sending the two divisions of Warren's corps to the rear of the Confederates, "down the dirt road past Crump's to hold and cover that road and to attack at daylight." But Grant sent a misleading dispatch to Sheridan promising him part of Warren's corps on the Plank Road by midnight, a physical impossibility under the existing conditions.[67]

Warren's orders contracting his lines had been gone an hour and a half, and he thought the movements of his corps in obedience to them would be thrown into confusion and delay if the new orders were literally followed. Writing new instructions to his subordinates, Warren had Ayres proceed down the Boydton Road to Sheridan and ordered him to send a report to him upon arrival. Griffin and Crawford were instructed to mass where his staff officers reached them and wait for further orders. Warren then telegraphed Meade all he had done. Meanwhile, an hour before midnight Chamberlain noticed that the Rebels in his front had put out their fires, which Griffin took as a prelude to an attack and so informed Warren. The Fifth Corps commander was between two bodies of Rebels with his corps in motion and vulnerable to disaster, not knowing if the enemy might attack on his front or arrive on the Plank Road from the rear. But he worked with all his might to make things right and do as he was told.[68]

Finally receiving, just before midnight, a partial transmission of Warren's message about the bridge being out, Meade wired Warren that "Sheridan cannot maintain himself at Dinwiddie without reinforcements," and that he should get troops to Sheridan by the Quaker Road or any way he could, even if he had to give up the rear attack. Grant was getting impatient with the delay and wanted his orders obeyed without questions or discussion. Warren did not receive this message until one o'clock in the morning of April 1, and at that time he expected the bridge over Gravelly Run to be finished soon. Considering this order discretionary under the circumstances, Warren rejected the Quaker Road option as too lengthy for Ayres to get to Sheridan in time and decided that the quickest and best way to carry out his responsibilities would be to continue his present course.[69]

Shortly after 2:00 A.M., about an hour after Warren had received Meade's nearly frantic message, Ayres's division moved down the Boydton Plank Road to Dinwiddie, having had little, if any, delay. A new bridge had been built in record time by almost superhuman effort. However, the long process of withdrawing in the face of the enemy, with each man awakened individually, had consumed much time, and Griffin had only ordered Chamberlain to get ready to move while they were waiting for Bartlett to return. At 3:00 A.M. Chamberlain pulled his pickets quietly off the White Oak Road, and they were replaced by Crawford's men. Warren, his quick mind racing with all possibilities, and still concerned that Sheridan had been forced to retreat, waited for Ayres's message that he had reinforced Sheridan before he started Griffin's movement. It arrived at 4:30 A.M. Years later, Chamberlain characterized Warren correctly when he observed, among other complimentary comments: "He was a good fighter, but he thought of too many things."[70]

At 4:50 A.M., nearly an hour before sunrise, when Warren was about to join Griffin and Crawford, a cavalry officer brought a message from Sheridan, dated April 1, that he was still holding at Dinwiddie and would fight at daylight if the enemy remained. Stating that he understood Warren had a division at J. Boisseau's in rear of the enemy, Sheridan wanted it to attack at daylight to capture the enemy between the two Federal forces. Of course, there had been no division, only Bartlett's brigade, which had been north of J. Boisseau's but was withdrawn hours before by Meade's order. But Ayres had already reinforced Sheridan, and daylight was not far away.[71]

This dispatch immediately changed Warren's understanding of the situation, since he knew now that Sheridan still held at Dinwiddie; he moved right away to get Griffin and Crawford started. Warren expected that the Confederates would be gone because of the threat posed earlier by Bartlett, but he cautioned Griffin to anticipate a fight when his division moved to that vicinity and to report to General Sheridan when the situation allowed. Warren himself supervised the ticklish removal of Crawford's division from in front of the White Oak Road. Expecting the enemy to pursue him from their works after his movements were discovered, Warren had Crawford's men retire in line of battle and ordered his personal cavalry escort down the Boydton Road to take back any men or supplies found there because of ignorance of change of plan.[72]

But the enemy in front of Sheridan was gone after all. The arrival of Bartlett's brigade early in the evening on Pickett's left flank and rear, "magnified by the magic lens of night," had made Fitzhugh Lee and Pickett fear that the whole Fifth Corps was arriving to attack them. Confederate artillery and supply wagons rolled, followed near midnight by the infantry and cavalry, in retreat northwest to Five Forks. Ayres had seen the last picket of their cavalry rear guard in the distance at earliest dawn when he arrived at the Brooks Road, and he marched on and massed his men near the intersection of the latter and the road from Dinwiddie Court House to the White Oak Road. Chamberlain thought later that Warren's decision to send Bartlett's brigade to the left rear of Pickett's division was a master stroke that would have been considered "Napoleonic" in other circumstances.[73]

Despite his later allegation that Warren's tardiness in coming to his support lost him the opportunity to trap the Confederates, Sheridan could not have really expected Warren's reinforcements by midnight, although Grant's dispatch the previous night stated so. Shortly after Grant forwarded his dispatch, Meade sent a message by staff officer to Sheridan. A Fifth Corps brigade was ordered down the Plank Road to attack the enemy, Meade wrote, and Grant had been asked to authorize sending Warren's other two divisions down the dirt road past Crump's behind the Confederates, with orders to attack at daylight. Meade's returning messenger, who would have left Dinwiddie shortly after midnight, reported to headquarters that Sheridan thought the Confederates were withdrawing at that time. And more than an hour before daybreak, General Ayres's relieving division arrived so much sooner on the Boydton Road than Sheridan expected that his staff officer sent to conduct the column apologized for intercepting it so late. Because of this error, Ayres's division had to turn around and retrace its steps for a mile to the Brooks Road turnoff, delaying it an hour.[74]

Although he felt that perhaps Warren could have done better in the White Oak Road affair, Chamberlain later thought that Grant's partiality to Sheridan was vastly unfair to Warren. When Sheridan attacked with only one division, was driven back by an inferior force, and failed to take Five Forks on March 30, Grant did not blame him. Grant only reproved the cavalryman when he did not get into position to smash the Confederate rear on March 31 when Lee's men drove Ayres and Crawford. Now Sheridan had been driven back, and Grant not only had high praise for his generalship, but actually accepted as true Sheridan's malicious and ridiculous allegation that Confederate troops that had fought the Fifth Corps on the White Oak Road withdrew from that front, moved to Five Forks, and helped push him back to Dinwiddie. But for Warren there was only censure and impatience, when he had done all that his commander General Meade had asked, under the most trying circumstances.[75]

At five o'clock in the morning of April 1, 1865, Chamberlain and his men proceeded across country to an old cart road and followed it to the Crump Road near Dr. Boisseau's, turning south. Somewhere in the lightening dawn, Bartlett's brigade joined the rest of Griffin's division and for the third time that night stumbled tiredly over the same rough country. Preparing to meet Confederates in force, at Dr. Boisseau's Chamberlain formed part of his brigade as an advance guard and moved cautiously with it; General Griffin followed with the leading brigade of his division. They came to the south branch of Gravelly Run, where Bartlett had been the night before. A new day was dawning, but Warren and the Fifth Corps were under the shadow of the old, and it would not be a good one for Warren.[76]

CHAPTER

Nine

FORWARD TO THE NATION'S SECOND BIRTH

Dawn came slowly, clear and cold. Tired and bone weary, the soldiers of the Fifth Corps advanced carefully and silently like ghosts through the gray mist of morning. As the sun rose, Chamberlain detected movement and the flash of sabers and brass buckles a mile away in his front. His men positioned themselves to fire, but Chamberlain told them to hold on—maybe it was Sheridan's cavalry. They moved forward cautiously, but when the blue uniforms of the approaching horsemen became visible, the pressure eased. Contact was made with Sheridan at seven o'clock just south of the J. Boisseau house.[1]

General Sheridan himself rode up to greet the two approaching Fifth Corps divisions, and Chamberlain, at their head, reported to the Federal commander. With no preliminaries, Sheridan angrily demanded to know where Warren was. Chamberlain said he understood he was with Crawford's division in the rear. "That is where I should expect him to be," Sheridan roared, the affront to Warren's courage exploding shockingly into the morning air. He demanded to know why the Fifth Corps had not advanced sooner, and Chamberlain told him quickly of the heavy engagement of the day before, the night in the presence of the enemy, and the withdrawal in the early morning with a strong rear guard faced in line of battle. For the present this seemed to pacify Sheridan, and he rode up the Five Forks Road.[2]

The Fifth Corps halted where they were, about three miles below Five Forks, the strategic crossroads on the White Oak Road, which was about four miles east of their battle the day before. Griffin's division rested close to the J. Boisseau house, Crawford's division was nearby, and Ayres's men were nearly a mile south near the intersection of the Dinwiddie Court House and Brooks Roads. Chamberlain did not sleep, but finally there was some for the men, and some food and coffee. Packing their haversacks with three days' rations, the men added an extra twenty rounds of ammunition, the usual amount issued before a battle. While they waited, the Union cavalry pressed the enemy cavalry and made reconnaissances of the Confederate position at Five Forks.[3]

Sheridan was unhappy. He knew that he must fight a battle today or much of the effort of the previous days would be lost, presumably including the opportunity to restore the polish to his reputation. Reproved by Grant for not being in position to fall on the Confederate rear when Ayres and Crawford were repulsed on the White Oak Road, he had also disappointed Grant's hope that he could assist Warren when the infantry general regained the lost ground. He had been forced back to Dinwiddie Court House the day before, and Warren had not then magically produced his corps on the flank and rear of the Confederates to extricate Sheridan from this humiliation. The cavalryman was about to be armed with the means of retribution for this failure.[4]

Although he considered himself already under the immediate command of Sheridan, at nine o'clock Warren received a directive from General Meade reminding him of that change. Not long before noon, Sheridan received a verbal message from General Grant, sent by Col. Orville E. Babcock of Grant's staff, telling him "that he was authorized to relieve General Warren if, in his judgment, it was for the best interests of the service to do so." As his commanding officer, Sheridan already had the authority to relieve Warren, so this was an extraordinary message. Warren did not hear of it, but word spread to the Fifth Corps general officers of Sheridan's new emphasized authority over Warren. Chamberlain and Griffin talked about what could be expected. There would certainly be a battle today—no one doubted that. Anxious for Warren, the two generals resolved that they would do their parts to make things go right.[5]

Sheridan was finally ready and at one o'clock ordered Warren to bring up his troops; orders to march came to the infantry generals a short time later. The divisions moved out, Crawford's in the lead, followed by Griffin's, then Ayres's, turning up a narrow road that ran north by a small church and intersected the White Oak Road over a mile east of Five Forks. South of the church, on either side of the road, the corps formed in battle lines over rough terrain, both cleared and thinly wooded, out of sight of enemy eyes. Muddy and obstructed by the led horses of dismounted cavalry, the road was badly broken up; the men slipped and cursed, halted, and then went on. It was a march of a little over two miles, and it took about two hours altogether—a good rate under the conditions.[6]

As Chamberlain and his men arrived near the little Gravelly Run Church, he began to form them in three lines, with each regiment deployed in line of battle and forming a column of regiments, so as to be easily handled when the expected movement of attack should begin. In the vicinity of the church officers were scattered in small groups either talking or busy with the formation of the corps. Near three o'clock, about twenty minutes after his arrival, Chamberlain walked with Griffin over to where other infantry officers were gathering around Sheridan near the church. Sheridan impatiently waited the necessary time for the infantry to arrive and form, striding tensely up and down. It seemed to him that it was taking too long to get the Fifth Corps up to the staging area, and time was getting short to fight a battle. He thought Warren "wished the sun to go down before dispositions for the attack could be completed."[7]

Phil Sheridan began to outline what he had already told Warren. Confederate Gen. George Pickett's infantry had built strong breastworks along the White Oak Road, he explained, beginning a mile to the west of the junction at Five Forks and extending east until the enemy left rested near the junction of the White Oak and Gravelly Run Church Roads. The latter was located about 450 yards north of the church, where the attentive group was standing. Sheridan took his sword and drew the battle plan in the dirt.

It was simple and blunt, and it would crush the Confederates. Deployed in front of the Rebel line, the Union cavalry would engage the Confederates on their right and center to divert and hold them in their works. Then the Fifth Corps would strike at the enemy's left flank and rear and advance westward toward Five Forks, rolling up the enemy along his White Oak Road defenses.[8]

About twenty yards across the road from Sheridan, General Warren sat like a "caged eagle," pale and quiet but, to Chamberlain, obviously full of intense thought. This demeanor of Warren's could be mistaken for indifference or apathy, but Chamberlain had seen it too many times to believe that. The Fifth Corps commander was constantly busy, writing orders for his subordinates, sending aides to expedite the movement of his men. He was working under a strain: the atmosphere had become tense between him and Sheridan almost from the first moment they had met that morning. Warren was also forced to translate Sheridan's attack plan into proper orders without making his usual personal reconnaissance of the enemy objective. He had to rely entirely on what Sheridan had told him about the location and nature of the Confederate defenses when he had explained in detail what he wanted Warren to accomplish.[9]

Warren wrote out the attack orders and, because it was a difficult movement to make, drew a diagram that showed the expected position of the Confederate works and the corresponding movement of the three divisions of the corps. He showed both the diagram and orders to Sheridan to be sure that they conformed to his directions, and they received Sheridan's approval. As the battle preparations continued, Warren explained the plans to his division and brigade commanders, impressing upon his subordinates the importance of their part in the attack. He especially took time with the commander of his Third Division, Maj. Gen. Samuel W. Crawford. Several generals in the corps considered Crawford incompetent, but he was a man of considerable political influence. Everyone was impatient by now. They knew they had to fight the battle before dark. When Ayres's division finally came up, Chamberlain went back to his command.[10]

Chamberlain was with his brigade and not yet mounted when the commander of Ayres's leading brigade came to him with a personal appeal. It was Col. Frederick Winthrop, and he had not eaten anything all day. Could Chamberlain spare some food? Chamberlain sent an orderly to find whatever he could, and he came back shortly with what poor victuals were at hand. Chamberlain and Winthrop sat on a log and shared their meager

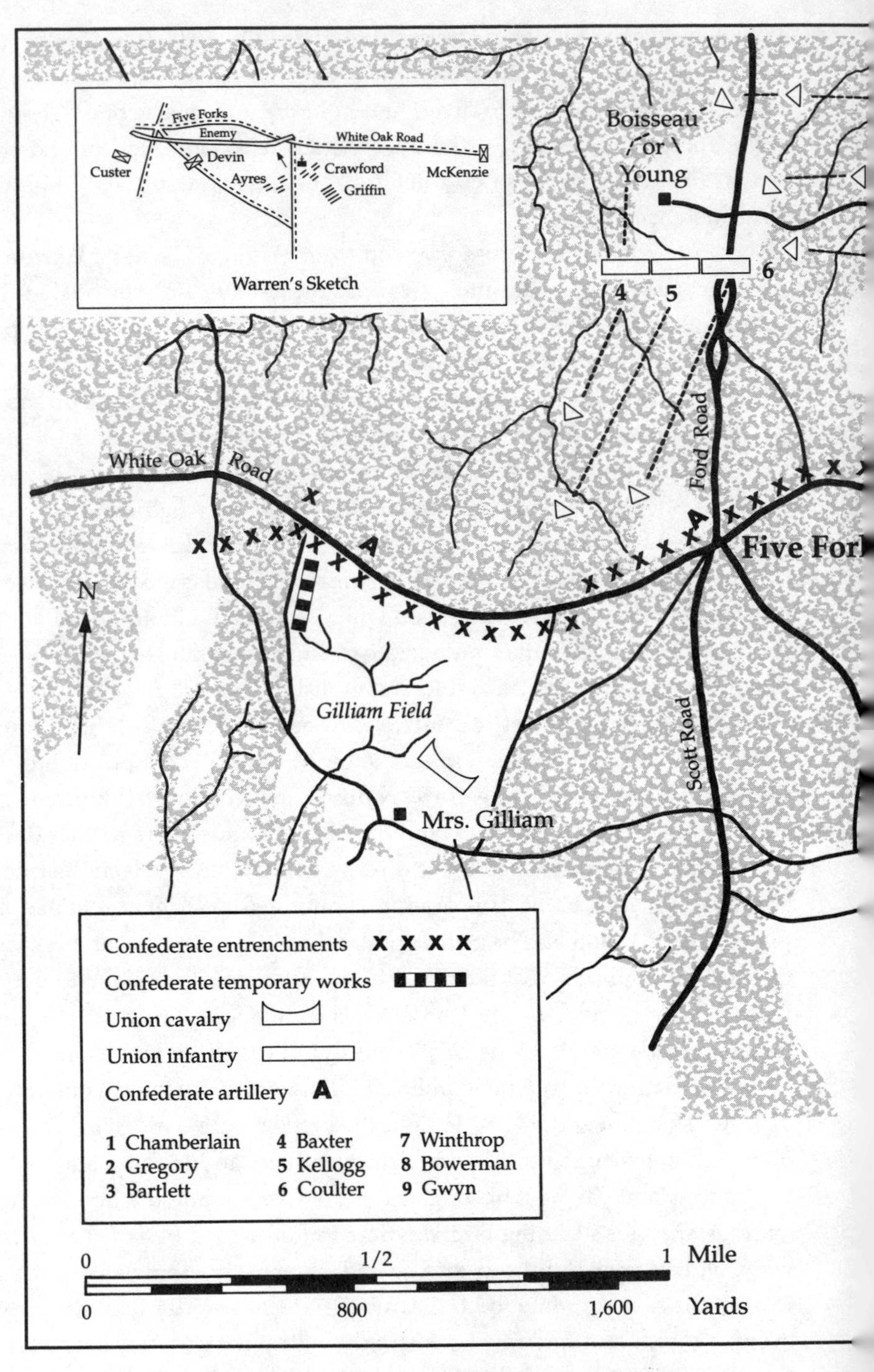

MAP 11. *Battle of Five Forks: Sheridan and the Fifth Corps Attack*

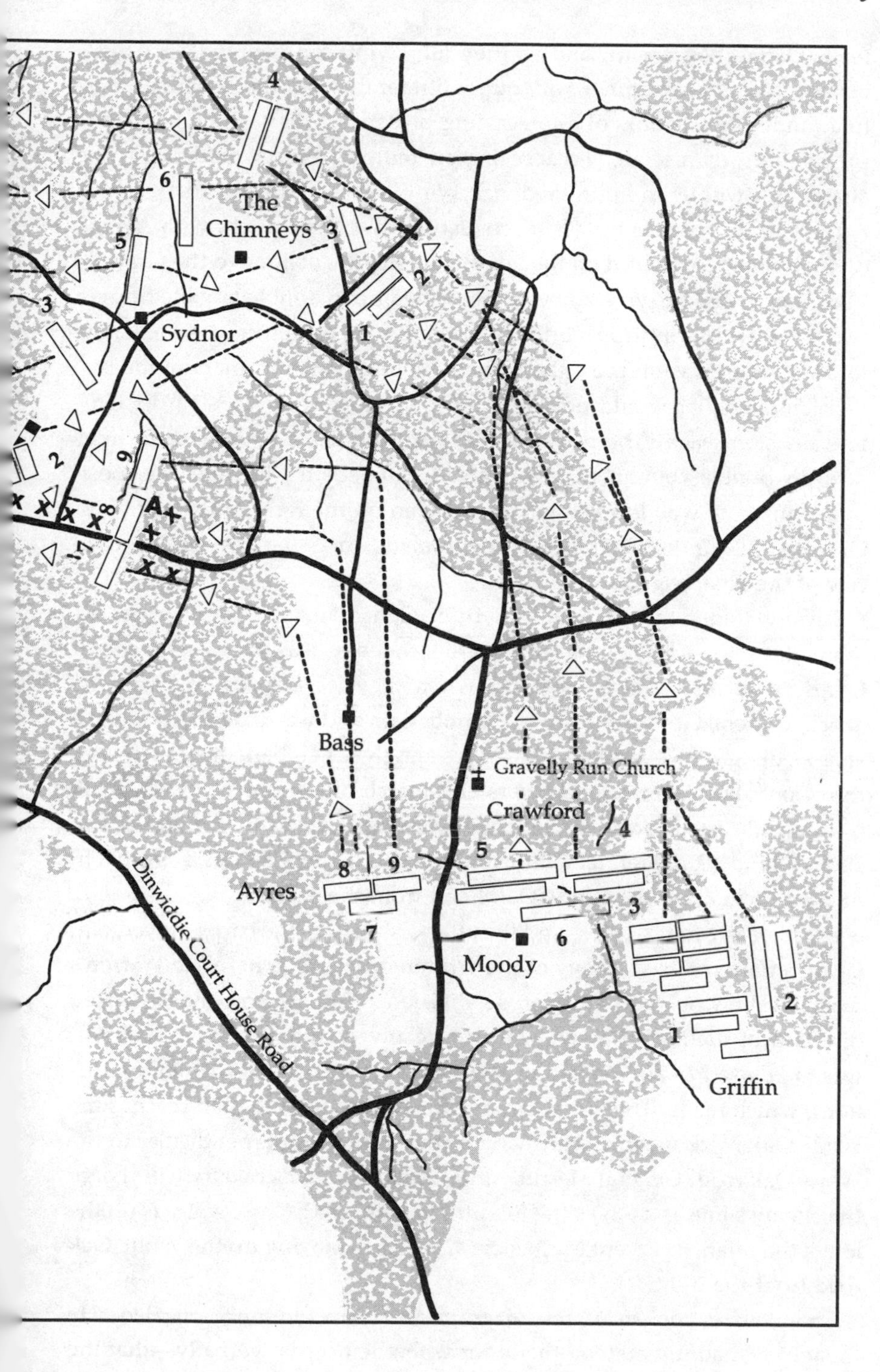
The Chimneys
Sydnor
Bass
Gravelly Run Church
Crawford
Ayres
Moody
Griffin
Dinwiddie Court House Road

feast. Danger lay ahead, and as they ate, Winthrop confided in Chamberlain "as men sometimes will, quite differently from their common custom, under the shadow of a forecasting presence." Perhaps he had some premonition of his fate, because in ten minutes they would begin the attack, and within an hour, Frederick Winthrop would be dead.[11]

The Fifth Corps was now in place just south of the church, with Ayres's division on open ground on the left of and slightly oblique to the Gravelly Run Church Road. Ayres's division was lined up in double brigade front in two lines, with Winthrop's brigade in rear of his center in reserve. Crawford's division was on the right of the road in a similar formation; the two divisions together would present a formidable front of 1,000 yards. Griffin's division was in the rear of Crawford's, Bartlett's brigade three lines deep in double column of regiments. Chamberlain's brigade was positioned in some woods somewhat in echelon on the right of Bartlett, with Gregory, still under Chamberlain's command, massing his regiments in rear of the First Brigade.[12]

Cavalry under the command of Brig. Gen. Ranald S. Mackenzie, acquired from the Army of the James earlier that day, was to protect the Fifth Corps's right flank. However, just when they were ready to begin the attack, General Griffin rode up to Chamberlain and warned him to "keep a sharp lookout for your own right." Accordingly, Chamberlain had Gregory throw out skirmishers and flankers and march one regiment by the flank on the right ready to turn and give warning, especially if General Lee should send Confederate reinforcements from the Claiborne entrenchments attacking up the White Oak Road from the east.[13]

It was nearly four o'clock, and the attack began. As the corps moved out, Chamberlain received a copy of the written orders together with Warren's diagram showing the Fifth Corps's division positions and the proposed direction of their movement, with the relative position of the cavalry. It was to be used as an illustration and enhancement of the written instructions, which read: "The line will move forward as formed till it reaches the White Oak road, when it will swing round to the left perpendicular to the White Oak road. General Merritt's and General Custer's cavalry will charge the enemy's line as soon as the infantry get engaged. The cavalry is on the left of the infantry, except Mackenzie's, which is moving up the White Oak road from the right."[14]

Chamberlain looked at the diagram and was suddenly puzzled. He thought he had understood the order when he heard it verbally—that the

Bvt. Brig. Gen. Edgar Gregory
(Massachusetts Commandery, MOLLUS, *and U.S. Army Military History Institute, Carlisle Barracks, Pa.)*

Bvt. Maj. Gen. Romeyn B. Ayres (National Archives)

whole corps would reach the White Oak Road before swinging to the left. The drawing, however, showed the corps obliquing at half of a right angle and crossing the Church Road, so that Ayres's small division would strike the breastworks in front, and Crawford's division, the largest in the corps, would strike at the left flank of the enemy works before swinging around.

Bvt. Maj. Gen. Joseph J. Bartlett
(Massachusetts Commandery, MOLLUS, *and U.S. Army Military History Institute, Carlisle Barracks, Pa.)*

Bvt. Maj. Gen. Samuel W. Crawford (National Archives)

Feeling uneasy, he rode over to General Griffin to ask for some clarification. Griffin set the matter straight. Chamberlain was told not to worry about diagrams. They were to follow Crawford and hold themselves ready to act where they were needed. "Circumstances will soon develop our duty," Griffin said. Like many situations in life, the map is not the territory;

Maj. Edwin A. Glenn (Library of Congress)

Chamberlain calmed himself with the thought "that the earth certainly was a known quantity, and the enemy susceptible to discovery, whatever be true of roads, diagrams, or understandings."[15]

Because of a northerly bend in the White Oak Road, Crawford reached it first; Griffin's division also crossed it before Ayres's did. Crawford now began to come under a sharp fire on his right front. This fire was coming from the dismounted Confederate cavalry division of Maj. Gen. Fitzhugh Lee, now commanded by Col. Thomas T. Munford. He had about 1,500 men posted in the woods north of the road, some behind a breastwork of hastily thrown up rails. They gave ground reluctantly to the advancing Union infantry and continued to harass them. Chamberlain, riding with Griffin near the left front of his command, went quickly over to the right to check on his flank. The right flank, guarded by Gregory's men, was secure, but Chamberlain got a glimpse through the woods of some Confederate cavalry farther off to the right.[16]

The skirmish firing along Crawford's right front tended to draw the men toward it, and Chamberlain stayed at the right of his command, on the fast-moving flank. He and his officers urged the men to gain toward the left, away from the fire, and to keep closed on Bartlett. They had been out about fifteen minutes now and were nearly a mile past the Gravelly Run Church. Suddenly Chamberlain heard sharp, intense, and growing fire off to his left, becoming very heavy. Ayres had found the Confederate works.[17]

As Ayres approached the White Oak Road in an open field, his division received some scattering fire from the woods in his front. Soon after crossing the road, his left flank was enfiladed by a full volley of raking musketry coming from some woods to the west. The experienced old soldier now knew about where the Rebel line was—and it was far to the left of where it was expected to be. The enemy's entrenchments actually extended only three-quarters of a mile east along the north side of the White Oak Road from the Five Forks crossroads, ending in a refused section, or "return," about 1,200 yards west of the Gravelly Church Road. Entirely situated in dense woods, the return line ran almost perpendicular to the road for at least 100 yards. To cover this flank, another breastwork ran still farther east of it for about 160 yards on the south side of the White Oak Road. When Ayres quickly changed front to the west to meet the fire and begin his attack, Crawford failed to swing around to come in on Ayres's right. Ayres was left to fight alone as Crawford's division, with Griffin's following, continued to march north and westerly through the woods.[18]

Upon hearing the gunfire toward the south, on a prolongation of his line to the left as he was advancing in the woods, Chamberlain halted his men. The concentrated fire seemed to "hang in one spot," and he rode toward it to some high ground at a corner of a large, irregularly shaped, open area called the Sydnor field. Catching a glimpse of Warren's flag in one direction, in another Chamberlain could also see Griffin's flag in a ravine half-way to Ayres. Something was terribly wrong. Griffin's location and the spirit of the whole movement were order enough for the decisive Chamberlain; he knew his place was to go to his left, to help Ayres.[19]

Chamberlain ordered his brigade out of the woods into the open by the left flank. He told General Gregory to bring in his skirmishers and follow him with the Second Brigade; then he sent an aide off to find General Bartlett to let him know what he was doing. Bartlett had continued on, following Crawford. When Chamberlain halted his brigades, he had let Bartlett's brigade pass, and his subsequent movement put Chamberlain on Bartlett's left instead of the opposite. Now Chamberlain and his command were the nearest of Griffin's men to Ayres's division.[20]

The brigade pushed across a muddy little stream; the men then forged in column up a ravine filled with catbriers and blackberry bushes in a south-west direction. Chamberlain saw General Griffin again but did not get close enough to speak. Griffin nodded approval as Chamberlain signaled to let him know where he was headed; then Griffin gestured to indicate that he wanted Chamberlain to attack on his right after gaining the head of the ravine. The division commander then rode off toward Bartlett.[21]

Fronting his brigade without halting, Chamberlain brought his men into line when they reached the head of the gulley. The firing on the left died suddenly, and he thought that Ayres's initial attack was over. Chamberlain and his men were near some woods that lined the east side of the southern part of the Sydnor field. Hidden in them to the southeast was the angle of the Confederate return line on the White Oak Road, which Ayres was just carrying. But at the edge of some other woods across the field on its west side, other Confederates, joined by hundreds of their comrades retreating from the east, had hastily thrown up a low barrier made of rails, logs—anything they could find. About eight hundred feet long, these works joined the White Oak Road perpendicularly. Behind them, men in gray were making a stand and sending a hot cross fire toward Ayres.[22]

Meanwhile, General Bartlett had heard Ayres's musketry fire, too. General Griffin joined him, and together they managed to recover three of Bartlett's regiments, including the Twentieth Maine, from the rear of the advancing Third Brigade and wheeled them to the left and into the field. Chamberlain's men advanced toward the enemy return on the west side of the Sydnor field, while Bartlett's regiments eventually followed and came in on their right. While the sight of Federals bearing down on them from the north caused some Confederates to run toward Ayres to surrender, others fled west on the White Oak Road to join their fellows. Chamberlain's line swept over the crest of the ridge dividing the Sydnor field, drawing the Rebel fire away from Ayres, and struck the enemy return obliquely, in flank and reverse. Part of the First Brigade, Sniper's 185th New York and Glenn's battalion of the 198th Pennsylvania, crossed the Confederate works, while the rest of the Pennsylvania regiment swung down in front of them.[23]

Fighting their way up the line of makeshift works, Chamberlain's men and Bartlett's on their right were staggered by heavy flank fire poured in on them from Rebels farther back in the woods. Some of Chamberlain's men were forced to take refuge in the works from which they had driven the enemy. The fighting became hard and in places hand-to-hand. Gregory was dispatched to help Bartlett, along with some First Brigade men, and many of the commands became mixed. Some members of Chamberlain's brigade fought beside men from his old regiment, the Twentieth Maine, which was under the command of the former captain of its Company B, Lt. Col. Walter G. Morrill.[24]

Just at that time, the embattled Chamberlain saw Ayres's Third Brigade emerge from the woods behind him. Earlier, in the advance from Gravelly Run Church, this brigade had become unsteady and had drawn Sheridan's criticism, but now it appeared in good order. It was commanded by a First Division man, Bvt. Brig. Gen. James Gwyn of the 118th Pennsylvania. Gwyn rode up and down in front of his brigade, making a good show, but the brigade was not moving forward. When questioned, Gwyn replied that he was cut off from Ayres, had no orders, and did not know what to do. Chamberlain directed him to go in on the First Brigade's right and attack the force of enemy in the woods that was flanking his men. Gwyn gladly agreed, and his men greeted Chamberlain with cheers as he rode down their front. He shouted out the order: "Forward, right oblique!" Gwyn's men plunged into the woods to attack the Confederates.[25]

Chamberlain had begun to swing his left wing around to avoid firing into other Union troops when a huge body of Confederates, apparently caught by Gwyn's men, came up on his left battalions from the flank and rear. They held their arms in a manner Chamberlain described as "something like a ready," and he thought it was his turn to be "caught between two fires." Ignoring the enemy in front, he ordered his men to fire by the rear rank. As his men turned around to obey the order, the menacing mass of Rebels threw down their weapons and surrendered. They outnumbered Chamberlain's men, and the amazed captors were much relieved when these men were marched to the rear and given to a cavalryman assigned to take charge of prisoners. Chamberlain's and Gregory's brigades captured over 1,500 men in the battle, most of them taken in this encounter.[26]

Chamberlain then struggled to re-form his own line. He and Bartlett worked together, forming all the First Division men they could find into a line perpendicular to the White Oak Road. When Chamberlain rode back over the scrubby field toward two or three hundred men behind his line, he met Phil Sheridan himself. Riding with Ayres in the early part of the action, Sheridan had seemed to be everywhere, shouting, giving orders, riding among and encouraging unsteady skirmishers in the early part of the fray. Suddenly attacked on his left, Ayres had changed front with two of his brigades to meet the challenge, separating them from Gwyn's brigade, without sending word to Gwyn. Sheridan stayed with Ayres in the rush to the angle of the enemy works and ordered Ayres to halt after it was carried. Poor Fred Winthrop, Chamberlain's lunch mate, had been mortally wounded and was carried back to the green-shuttered Gravelly Run Church, now a field hospital. He died on the stretcher before he got there, deliriously giving commands. "Straighten the line," Winthrop shouted. They were his last words.[27]

Sheridan had apparently seen Chamberlain putting in his men. After asking Chamberlain who he was, Sheridan exclaimed, "By God, that's what I want to see! General officers at the front. Where are your general officers?" Chamberlain told him he had seen Warren's flag in the north of the Sydnor field; he had seen Ayres in trouble and had come to help by Griffin's order. "Push out for the Five Forks," fiery Phil told Chamberlain. "Then you take command of all the infantry around here and break this dam- . . . " Chamberlain did not wait for the rest of the sentence but rode off to carry out the order.[28]

Gathering up all the troops he could find, Chamberlain worked to assemble the men, with the help of a member of Griffin's staff. If he could, Chamberlain tried to convince men to do what needed to be done by persuasion. Seeing a man down on all fours, hiding not very successfully behind a tree stump with look of terror on his face, Chamberlain shouted to him, "Don't you know you'll be killed here in less than two minutes? This is no place for you. Go forward!" The man replied, "But what can I do? . . . I can't stand up against all this alone!" "No, that's just it," Chamberlain replied. "We're forming here. I want you for guide center. Up, and forward!" Chamberlain and the other officers formed about two hundred men on him, and the proud soldier led them against the enemy's makeshift work where it met the White Oak Road.[29]

Sheridan rode up in a frenzy, his face dark with anger, shouting that Chamberlain was firing into his cavalry. Chamberlain wondered what Sheridan would have him do; if the cavalry was there, it seemed to have "got into the rebels' place." Although it was Chamberlain's opinion that the bullets were all coming from the west, he suspected that his men might have fired obliquely across that return line into the woods south of the White Oak Road. Sheridan repeated the accusation as General Ayres rode up and argued instead of Chamberlain. Ayres had told Sheridan before that the bullets flying around them were not from carbines, and he did so again. "We flanked 'em gloriously," Sheridan smiled, greeting Griffin as he joined the little group.[30]

After Chamberlain told him what had become of Gwyn's brigade, Ayres went back to his two brigades in the woods near the angle. They had taken care of their many prisoners and were re-forming to march. Griffin joined Bartlett and quickly rode off; suddenly Chamberlain was left with Sheridan, who sat his famous black horse, Rienzi. Apparently attracted by Sheridan's distinctive red and white, double-starred pennon, the bullets came so hot and heavy then that Chamberlain was worried for Sheridan's safety. It occurred to him that the poet's phrase "darkening the air" was more than a metaphor, and he was emboldened to tell Sheridan that he should go to a safer place. With comical expression, Sheridan looked at him and, giving a peculiar twist to his head said, "Yes, I think I'll go!" Bolting off toward the west, Sheridan rode straight up the White Oak Road, heedless of the buzzing bullets.[31]

Meanwhile, Crawford's division had continued its march north while obliquing to the west after crossing the White Oak Road. After it was clear that Ayres had found the enemy works, General Warren sent a staff officer to General Griffin with orders to change direction quickly to help Ayres. He then went personally to Crawford's left brigade and ordered its colonel, John A. Kellogg, to face to the left and hold in place so that Crawford's other brigades could turn and guide on his, forming a new line of battle.[32]

Warren then went into the woods but, unable to find Crawford, returned to the field, where he sent other staff officers to intercept Crawford and Griffin. Going back to the place where he had left Kellogg, Warren was appalled to find that Kellogg and his brigade had vanished. One of Sheridan's staff officers had found the brigade apparently idle and had ordered Kellogg to march south and west. In the words of Colonel Kellogg, an "italicized conversation" followed, but Kellogg finally headed west and came under fire from Munford's Confederate cavalrymen.[33]

Crawford's Third Brigade commander, Bvt. Brig. Gen. Richard Coulter, whose brigade was the reserve of the division, found himself alone after Kellogg's brigade was halted. He understood that his orders were to march west after changing his direction, so he proceeded on that basis without further orders. Coulter and Kellogg acted independently, their brigades under fire, until they were reunited.[34]

Meanwhile, anxious for Ayres, Warren sent out messengers to Crawford and Griffin until he had none left. Returning to the field north of the White Oak Road, he met Sheridan, who was in high spirits and exulted, as he would to Griffin, "We flanked them gloriously!" Sheridan had sent out staff officers to Griffin and Crawford, too, and also became concerned when neither of them appeared. Warren then rode north, saw Griffin, and gave him instructions personally before returning to Ayres's part of the field, where he found that Ayres had carried the angle and was doing well. In a move that would contribute to his undoing, Warren then determined to find Crawford himself and rode northwest, following a trail of the Third Division dead and wounded.[35]

Crawford was riding with Brig. Gen. Henry Baxter's brigade on the far right of the division. Along with some of Bartlett's other regiments that had continued to follow Baxter, they had swung in a wide arc and marched in a westerly direction. Crawford had told each messenger from Sheridan and Warren that he was following his orders. "I told General Sheridan's staff officer that he could see that I was fighting and that I would do what I could," he remarked later. Although Crawford's failure to turn soon enough was at least a poor reading of his orders, his division was now moving in echelon by the left. It was somewhat like the intended movement, except that Griffin's division had turned and was the first to fall on the enemy's rear instead of Crawford's after Ayres struck the angle. Baxter, Coulter, and Kellogg were moving westward, fighting as they went. Finally, everyone was going the right way.[36]

Farther south, Chamberlain's entire fight had lasted only twenty minutes to half an hour. Now the battle moved due west. Somewhat ahead of Ayres's men, stretched from left to right, were regiments of Chamberlain's,

Gregory's, and Bartlett's brigades, the men from different commands sometimes mixed together. They swept along the line of works parallel to the White Oak Road. It was fitting somehow that in the last great battle of the war in which he was heavily engaged, Chamberlain recognized Twentieth Maine men in his line. Pressing the Confederates before them, they fought on over wooded ground west toward Five Forks, where the Ford Road met the White Oak Road perpendicularly and led north to the South Side Railroad.[37]

About halfway to the Ford Road, Capt. R. M. Brinton, aide-de-camp to General Griffin, dashed up to Chamberlain with the astonishing news that Griffin had been given the command of the Fifth Corps. Chamberlain's first thought was that Warren had been killed, but Brinton told him that on the White Oak Road near the Sydnor field, General Sheridan had asked some assembled officers, "Where is Warren?" Everyone had looked around and at each other—General Griffin, some of his staff, Sheridan's staff, and others were present—but no one answered. The little general did not wait. According to Brinton, he called across to the First Division commander: "General Griffin, I place you in command of the Fifth Army Corps." Chamberlain did not quite believe Brinton. Since Sheridan had told him to take command of all the infantry he could find in the Sydnor field, he thought it likely that Sheridan had told General Griffin to take in hand parts of other divisions. Things would surely sort themselves out.[38]

After a rapid ride on his prized bay horse, General Warren found General Crawford west of the Ford Road in a farm clearing south of Hatcher's Run. Seeing Crawford's brigades reunited and the division in good order, Warren detailed two regiments of Bartlett's brigade to guard the Hatcher's Run crossing of the Ford Road and then directed Crawford to move his troops south on a line with the road toward the sound of artillery firing. The men were turned south, most deployed on the right side of the Ford Road, and faced directly into the Confederate rear. Pounding their way toward the White Oak Road, Crawford's troops cut off the principal road of retreat to the South Side Railroad for the Confederates.[39]

Gen. George E. Pickett, overall commander of the Confederate forces at Five Forks, tardily reached the battlefield on the Ford Road. Arriving near the Forks, he found his left gone, the survivors in retreat and pursued by Warren's Fifth Corps west along the White Oak Road, and more Fifth Corps infantry coming up from the north. In a desperate attempt to resist Crawford's advance, Pickett ordered several regiments from the center of his

White Oak Road line to move two hundred yards north on the Ford Road. The line of infantry formed across the road facing north, with part of it refused on the right, facing northeasterly. Ahead of them a battery of four cannon wheeled from other parts of the entrenchments fired at the approaching Federals.[40]

Leading Crawford's division up the Ford Road was Maj. West Funk, Chamberlain's former aide-de-camp. He now commanded both the 121st and 142d Pennsylvania Infantry, the only regiments remaining with the Army of the Potomac of the brigade that charged with Chamberlain at Rives's Salient the previous June. Deploying his command on either side of the road, Funk had his men shoot at the Confederate battery personnel and horses from behind trees, keeping up a continual fire that finally silenced the guns. Funk then saw Griffin's men come from the left and south of him, advancing through the trees from the east. Without direct orders, Funk decided to act, and he and his men rushed the guns and captured them. Realizing the futility of further resistance, Pickett quickly gave up the fight on the Ford Road and ordered his brigade commander, Col. Joseph Mayo, "to get out the best way you can."[41]

Meanwhile, moving on with his men near the Five Forks junction, Chamberlain guided his horse into a little clearing. Seemingly from nowhere, General Sheridan suddenly appeared, riding beside him "like an apparition." Chamberlain felt uneasy being by himself in his superior's presence. Sheridan seemed to be the embodiment of "incarnate will," but he was friendly to Chamberlain, and they spoke easily about the way the battle was going. As they rode into the midst of a group of officers and men, General Bartlett galloped up in great excitement and reported the capture of enemy guns on the Ford Road. Sheridan yelled, "I don't care a damn for their guns, or you either, sir! What are you here for? Go back to your business, where you belong! What I want is that Southside Road." Bartlett, mortified, did not waste an instant in obeying the order.[42]

Expecting that the unpredictable Sheridan would turn his wrath on him, Chamberlain waited silently as the other men present looked amazed at the scene they had witnessed. The sun was getting low: it touched the treetops now. Phil Sheridan rose up in his stirrups, waving his hat, "face black as his horse, and both like a storm-king," and shouted: "I want you men to understand we have a record to make, before that sun goes down, that will make hell tremble!—I want you there!" The men scattered quickly, evidently thinking that any place away from this commander would be safer for them. For his part, Chamberlain realized that there was much more to be done before this day was finished.[43]

The fighting intensified just before Chamberlain and other First Division men reached the Ford Road. A major holdup came in front of Chamberlain's left center opposite the 198th Pennsylvania regiment, commanded by Maj. Edwin A. Glenn. Chamberlain saw Major Glenn and Colonel Sniper, "with their flags close together," on the flank of enemy guns in the Five Forks works. A hero of "fiery courage" in the battles of the Quaker and White Oak Roads, Glenn was overdue for promotion. Riding up to his subordinate, his mind focused with intense concentration on the problem at hand, Chamberlain impulsively cried, "Major Glenn, if you will break that line you shall have a colonel's commission!" Glenn looked into Chamberlain's eyes and, without a word of reply, turned and spurred his horse, waving his sword above his head. Not looking back to see who was following, Glenn cried, "Boys, will you follow me?" Cheering, his men went with him into the deadly vortex.[44]

While pressing his men on from his position on the left of Glenn's action, Chamberlain could catch glimpses of the beautiful war-torn flag of the 198th Pennsylvania in the whirl of battle. Passed from hand to hand as its bearers went down, the flag fell and came up again three times. Then the 198th seemed to go up and over the defenses in a wave, and the Pennsylvanians carried the line. Snatching a moment from the rushing action in his front, Chamberlain rode over to congratulate Major Glenn and his regiment.[45]

As he reached a particularly dense section of the woods Chamberlain saw two men carrying a blanket dripping blood. In the makeshift stretcher was Major Glenn, struck down, his bearers said, as he snatched away a Rebel battle flag from its rallying regiment. Chamberlain bent down from his horse over Glenn's recumbent body. Sorrow welled up in him, helpless now as Glenn's life began to ebb away. All Glenn could manage to whisper was, "General, I have carried out your wishes!" Glenn's words cut through Chamberlain with the force of a bullet. His mind raced in the anguish of responsibility for the order and promise he had given the major. Why had he not allowed the advance on the enemy to take its usual course and let Glenn take his natural chances? By interfering, it was as if he had singled the major out for death. Bending down from his horse and bringing his face low, Chamberlain told the dying man what he could: "*Colonel*, I will remember my promise; I will remember *you*!"[46]

This encounter, remembered with crystalline clarity, would always have a hold on Chamberlain. He would tell of it into the twentieth century, the memory of Maj. Edwin A. Glenn haunting an old man's thoughts. Even now, in the furor of battle, he felt he had an additional reason to stay alive: to fulfill his promise. When the battle was over, he sent by special messenger his recommendation for Glenn's brevet promotion. Glenn, thirty years old and leaving a wife and two daughters, died three days later, a brevet colonel of United States Volunteers.

"War!—nothing but the final, infinite good, for man and God, can accept and justify human work like that!"[47]

When General Pickett was forced to order his troops on the Ford Road to retreat after only a few minutes of fighting, he knew that the battle was lost. All organized Confederate opposition to the Federal onslaught ceased except for a later holding action to cover the retreat. The cannon in the Five Forks crossroads were abandoned by their crews, and except for determined little groups of men who fought on until they were overwhelmed, the Rebel infantry began to flee west on the White Oak Road and northwest through the woods. As the mixed divisions of Ayres and Griffin nearly reached the Five Forks crossing, two brigades of dismounted Union cavalry, which had kept up a fire on the Confederate front, charged out of the trees from the south and over the works. Bartlett's men, followed by some of Crawford's, came down from the north, penning in those defenders who had not escaped and taking them prisoner.[48]

Along the White Oak Road, some of the First Division infantry spilled over the breastworks south of the line and were forging ahead in the road. Riding on the south side of the Rebel fortifications himself, Chamberlain saw Griffin galloping his horse past him as they neared the Five Forks junction. The First Division commander headed right for the works and jumped his mount over them. Chamberlain followed and, although he considered himself a good horseman, decided to go over at a lower point in the barricade. As his horse prepared to leap, it was struck by a bullet in a hind leg, giving it extra impetus. Chamberlain gave his animal full rein, and over they went, landing almost on top of one of the enemy's still hot guns. This was the sixth and last time a horse was shot under Chamberlain during the war.[49]

At about six o'clock, near sunset, after he had changed Crawford's direction southward, Warren sent his adjutant general, Col. Frederick T. Locke, to Sheridan with his compliments. Locke reported that everything was going well; Warren had gained the enemy's rear, cutting off his retreat, had taken many prisoners, and was putting in a division as fast as he could. When Locke asked Sheridan if he had any orders for Warren, Sheridan barked, "By God, sir, tell General Warren he wasn't in the fight!" Locke was stunned at these words and asked Sheridan if he required him to say that to Warren. "Tell him that sir!" rejoined Sheridan emphatically. Locke hardly knew what to do; he would not like to take such a verbal report to his commander. He asked Sheridan if he might put the message in writing. "Take it down sir," Sheridan replied. "Tell him, by God, he was not at the front!"[50]

Locke wrote it all down—the words, the oaths, and a gesture Sheridan made. He then found Warren on the Ford Road not far north of the Five Forks junction and handed him the piece of paper. Even fifteen years later, Warren's cold, mortified anger at the insults, the affront to his bravery, was clearly evident in his words when he spoke of the episode. The effect on him at the time would have been devastating. But Warren, his emotions under control, continued his duties as corps commander.[51]

Griffin, Ayres, and Chamberlain were riding together discussing the battle when the still-driven Sheridan, hell-bent on making every advantage, came to them and instructed, "Get together all the men you can, and drive on while you can see your hand before you!" Since many men of the First Division were scattered and mingled with other commands, Griffin ordered Chamberlain to collect all of the First Division he could find and assemble them on the White Oak Road. With his bugler at his side sounding the division's various brigade calls, Chamberlain rode down the Ford Road. There he met General Warren, reported, and explained to him what he was doing. Undoubtedly having heard the rumor concerning Griffin's change of status, Warren said Chamberlain was doing exactly right but added, in a statement that must have been more of a question, that he was no longer in command of the corps. Carefully cheerful, Chamberlain replied that he had heard that, but since Sheridan had been assigning general officers command of everything near to hand, everyone surely would be back in his own place when the battle was over.[52]

To cover the retreat of his infantry, General Pickett ordered the brigade commander of the troops on his far right, Brig. Gen. M. D. Corse, to form his men into a line perpendicular to the White Oak Road and facing east. Some dismounted cavalry joined Corse's men on the part of the line south of the road, and they quickly threw up some fieldworks along the western wood line of a large open space in front of the home of the Widow Gilliam, called the Gilliam field. Soon to oppose them was Kellogg's brigade of Crawford's division, which had advanced southwest through the woods west of the Ford Road, crossing the White Oak Road at the northeast corner of the Gilliam field. But as they swung around to face west, some confusion developed among them and others who had reached the clearing. Bullets were coming in from the gray line across the field, and although some of the Federals were firing back, the Union officers could not assemble an effective infantry line to charge the Confederates.[53]

Shortly after leaving Chamberlain, General Warren turned west on the White Oak Road. Pausing only long enough to order General Crawford to turn his men westward to pursue the enemy, he hurried forward past throngs of enthusiastic troops who were happy and enjoying their success. It was indicative of his state of mind, however, that although he was usually observant of detail, Warren did not see General Sheridan when he passed close to him. Coming upon the scene at the northeast corner of the Gilliam field, Warren saw that a great many men were shouting to go forward, but no one was advancing. It was obvious to him that the troops needed the colors out and someone to lead them from the relative safety of the shadowed woods at the east side of the field. Personally seizing his Fifth Corps headquarters flag, Warren galloped to the front and, oblivious to the enemy fire, started walking his horse west across the northern part of the field, calling for those near him to follow.[54]

Lt. Col. Hollon Richardson, intrepid commander of the veteran Seventh Wisconsin Regiment, brought up the rear of Kellogg's brigade and had just arrived on the field. Ordered by General Griffin to lead his regiment in an advance on the enemy, Richardson, regimental flag in hand, rode quickly down in front of his men just as Warren sprang out to lead the charge. Richardson soon caught up with his corps commander, some of whose staff now joined in the forward movement. Other color-bearers jumped to their duty, and a solid battle line of blue-clad soldiers eagerly began to move forward. When they were about halfway to the Confederates, Maj. Gen. George A. Custer and his mounted cavalry, "sabres drawn," with dismounted skirmishers in front, joined Warren's line to the south. Infantry and cavalry swept together across the field toward the Southerners. Bullets came flying, the flashes from the guns glowing red in the enveloping dusk and, Warren remembered, "the balls striking down on the ground like big drops of rain, all around."[55]

The Confederates gave the approaching Yankees a full volley as they neared the Rebel line, killing several men; one bullet struck Warren's horse. Immediately afterward, some Confederates threw down their weapons and gave themselves up, but when the Union officers went over the breastworks, Colonel Richardson noticed a Confederate rifleman aiming at General Warren. Throwing himself in front of the general and taking the ball himself, Richardson nearly lost his own life to save Warren's. The last stand of the Confederates at Five Forks melted away in the deepening twilight. Warren continued on until there was no one in sight to pursue; as Chamberlain later observed: "In that last reckless onset in the charge in the Gilliam field, he would let Sheridan see whether he was in the fight or not."[56]

It was seven o'clock, and the bugles were sounding the recall. In an open space not far beyond the Gilliam field, at the end of what he thought was one of the most glorious day's work of his life, the commanding general of the Fifth Corps was handed an official order by Sheridan's chief of staff, Bvt. Brig. Gen. James W. Forsyth. Warren took the small piece of paper that was to change his life forever, turned in the saddle, and, holding the note above his head to catch the sun's dying light, began to read: "Major-General Warren, commanding Fifth Army Corps, is relieved from duty, and will report at once for orders to Lieutenant-General Grant, commanding Armies of the United States. By command of Major-General Sheridan: Jas. W. Forsyth, Brevet Brigadier-General and Chief of Staff."[57]

The dismissed commander rode back down the White Oak Road to find Sheridan. Seeing him near the Forks, Warren asked him to reconsider his order. Sheridan snapped, "Reconsider. Hell! I don't reconsider my decisions. Obey the order!" Warren turned away, and as Chamberlain would later comment, "The iron . . . entered his soul." Gouverneur Kemble Warren then took "his lonely way over that eventful field, along that fateful White Oak road, which for him had no end on earth."[58]

"I am by no means sure but that injustice must be taken by a military officer as a necessary part of his risks, of the conditions and chances of his service, to be suffered in the same way as wounds and sicknesses, in patience and humility. But when one feels that his honor and the truth itself are impugned, then that larger personality is concerned wherein one belongs to others and his worth is somehow theirs. Then he does not satisfy himself with regret,—that strange complex feeling that something is right which is now impossible,—and even the truth made known becomes a consolation."[59]

By now it was too dark to "see your hand before you." As the corps gathered near the Five Forks crossroads, officers and men began to let down from the work of this day. Warren was gone, under circumstances no one in the corps understood; the knowledge of his dismissal dimmed somewhat the elation of his soldiers for the glorious victory. Right at the crossroads, Chamberlain and others grouped around General Griffin, who carried his now official promotion with characteristic modesty. The new corps commander was well liked by his men. Virtually exhausted, the officers sat on the ground and leaned against the empty breastworks and nearby trees. Introspection and weariness overtook them, and little was discussed. Chamberlain wondered if the right things were done, if it had all been worth it, and what would be in store for them tomorrow. The Confederates had been dealt a terrible defeat. He knew that he and these comrades had lived through the beginning of the end of the war and the killing.[60]

Suddenly, out of the dark, appeared Gen. Philip Sheridan; he showed a side of himself Chamberlain had not seen before. "Gentlemen, I have come over to see you. I may have spoken harshly to some of you to-day; but I would not have it hurt you. You know how it is: we had to carry this place and I was fretted all day till it was done." Expansive now, Sheridan continued: "You must forgive me. I know it is hard for the men, too; but we must push. There is more for us to do together. I appreciate and thank you all." Chamberlain was astonished at this short speech, but he began to understand this impetuous and volatile man a little better. And he admired Sheridan's driving and energetic style of fighting, infused with color, verve, and emotion.[61]

After Sheridan had joined the group by the Forks, a correspondent for the *New York World* stepped into the firelight. Chamberlain, whom he had met before, greeted him, and to the reporter's delight Sheridan himself explained the strategy and tactics of the battle to him. The newspaperman talked with several of the officers who were willing to give him more background, and a detailed article was soon published in the *World*, with its "Dispatches" repeating it in smaller newspapers in Maine and elsewhere. Some of the highest praise the journalist saved for the Fifth Corps's First Brigade commander. "What shall I say for Chamberlaine," he began, misspelling the name slightly in his haste, "who, beyond all question, is the first of our brigade commanders, . . . the hero of both Quaker Road and Gravelly Run, and in this action of Five Forks making the air ring with the applauding huzzas of his soldiers, who love him?" The writer then made this prediction: "His is one of the names that will survive the common wreck of the shoulder straps after the war."[62]

Isolated now from the rest of the Union army, the Fifth Corps divisions and the cavalry were reassembled in defensive positions around the Five Forks, to guard against possible attack. Gen. Robert E. Lee could still send an assault force from the right of his Petersburg lines to fall upon the tired Yankees. Crawford's and Ayres's divisions moved back down the White Oak Road to camp near the Gravelly Run Church Road. Griffin's old division, now under the command of the senior division officer, General Bartlett, was assigned to positions along the Ford Road, with Chamberlain and his men left in reserve near the Forks.[63]

By midnight they were alone at the battleground's center. The inevitable ambulances creaked back and forth, and men with flickering lanterns and candles searched for fallen comrades. Quiet had replaced the roar of battle, broken eventually by the faint sound of cannon far off toward Petersburg. "Their flashes in the dim distance, so close together, pierced the heavens like the bursts of an aurora."[64]

General Grant had received the news of the great victory at Five Forks from his aide, Bvt. Brig. Gen. Horace Porter, who galloped in from the battlefield with glee and excitement about nine o'clock. Grant immediately gave orders for a general assault along the Petersburg lines but modified them half an hour later to a general bombardment, with the assault set for four o'clock the following morning.[65]

Shortly after midnight on April 2, General Humphreys ordered Gen. Nelson A. Miles's division of his Second Corps west on the White Oak Road to reinforce Sheridan, as earlier directed by Grant. Later that morning, after sending his cavalry north to attack the enemy cavalry, Sheridan took two divisions of the Fifth Corps and followed Miles's division east on the White Oak Road, planning to attack the Confederates at the Claiborne Road intersection. The latter were still entrenched from there to the Boydton Plank Road, although in much fewer numbers than had been present in the battle with the Fifth Corps two days before, on March 29. Wise's, Gracie's, Hunton's, and Fulton's brigades had been ordered out of the Claiborne Road defenses the evening before; using routes north of Hatcher's Run, they had joined Pickett's scattered command near the South Side Railroad.[66]

At break of day, Union forces attacked along the Petersburg defenses, and desperate fighting marked gains and breakthroughs. General Humphreys's two other divisions forced the remaining Confederates out of their stronghold along the White Oak Road, and Humphreys planned to pursue the enemy north and close in on their rear with his whole corps, expecting Sheridan's forces also to attack them in flank and front. Humphreys wanted to destroy or capture not only those fugitives, but other Confederate brigades cut off by the breakthroughs of Federal corps on the right. When Miles came to the intersection of the Claiborne and White Oak Roads, he began to pursue the retreating Rebels by the Claiborne Road toward the Sutherland depot of the railroad.[67]

General Meade, meanwhile, disapproved of Humphreys's plan and ordered him to take his other two divisions up the Boydton Plank Road northeast toward Petersburg and have Miles to turn east toward Petersburg at the first road he came to on his right after crossing Hatcher's Run. But when Humphreys arrived on the Claiborne Road to retrieve Miles and found that Sheridan "had not intended to return General Miles' division to my command," he "declined to assume further command of it, and left it to carry out General Sheridan's instructions."[68]

For his part, Sheridan reported that not only had he given Miles permission to attack, but "receiving notice from General Meade that General Humphreys would take command of Miles' Division, I relinquished it at once, and facing the Fifth Corps by the rear . . . returned to Five Forks." Undaunted, Miles continued northward on the Claiborne Road alone and attacked the entrenched enemy at Sutherland Station.[69]

Because of Sheridan's delay, it was about noon on that bright Sunday before Chamberlain started with his command in the vanguard of the Fifth Corps as it marched down the Ford Road toward the South Side Railroad. At Hatcher's Run a Confederate rear guard was brushed aside. After a short march, Chamberlain heard the noise of a train approaching from the east and pushed his skirmishers forward to catch it. When the men in his main line heard the piercing, unbroken shriek of a loud steam whistle, they rushed forward to find the officer in charge of the skirmishers in the cab of the engine, triumphantly holding the whistle open to announce the capture of the last Confederate train to leave Petersburg. The civilian passengers were let go, but several Rebel officers and men aboard were made prisoner.[70]

Chamberlain was ordered by General Bartlett, who now commanded the First Division since Griffin had become Corps commander, to push on to the Cox Road, now defended by Fitzhugh Lee's dismounted cavalry. After a short fight the Rebels fell back, and Chamberlain secured that important road, which led into Petersburg. Moving east along the Cox Road, he stopped at a creek just a mile short of Sutherland Station. In his rear the rest of the Fifth Corps engaged in tearing up the South Side Railroad between his command and Cox's Station.[71]

As he approached on the flank and rear of the Confederates fighting Miles, Chamberlain could hear the fire from the fight a mile distant at Sutherland Station die away. In three assaults Miles had defeated and routed the enemy, taking six hundred prisoners. The threatening presence of the Fifth Corps on the Rebel flank and rear, keeping Fitzhugh Lee's cavalry from joining the fray, undoubtedly helped the situation, but Miles had a brilliant victory with his lone division. Shortly afterward, the Federal cavalry came up in rear of the infantry, and Sheridan pursued the escaping enemy northwest.[72]

Chamberlain turned into the Namozine Road, marched two miles, and camped for the night at the intersection of the Namozine with the River Road, south of the Appomattox River. His men had been marching in line of battle for most of the afternoon and evening over difficult country, and this, together with the almost continuous marching and fighting of the previous two days, had nearly exhausted them. They set about making their campfires, boiling coffee, and eating a few bites of food, and those not on picket duty turned in for as much sleep as the night would allow.[73]

"Sic vos non vobis—not you for yourselves—says Virgil to his bees and birds building nests and storing up food, mostly for others. Strange shadows fall across the glamour of glory. The law of sharing for the most of mankind seems to be that each shall give his best according to some inner commandment, and receive according to the decree of some far divinity, whose face is of a stranger, and whose heart is alien to the motives and sympathies that animate his own."[74]

General Lee had determined by midmorning of April 2 that he could probably do no more than hold his position until night, if that, and accordingly warned his government to prepare to leave Richmond. In the afternoon he notified the Confederate secretary of war that the Richmond and Danville Railroad, which ran southwest from the capital city and met the South Side Railroad at Burkeville, would be safe until the next day. By evening he wired that he had to abandon his position that night, and that the troops had been directed to Amelia Court House.[75]

During the night of April 2, after hard fighting all day at many points, the Confederates evacuated their Richmond and Petersburg defenses, and the westward pursuit of Lee's army by the Federals began in the early morning hours of April 3. The cavalry and Fifth Corps under Sheridan headed for the Danville Railroad, followed by the Second and Sixth Corps, which were accompanied by General Meade. The Ninth Corps followed General Ord and the Army of the James in the direction of Burkeville, by a route nearly paralleling the South Side Railroad.[76]

At daylight Sheridan's force continued west, following that part of the Confederate army that remained south of the Appomattox River. The cavalry was in front of the Union infantry, which made marching in the mud unpleasant for the foot soldiers in more ways than one. But the news of the Confederate government's flight from Richmond by the Danville Railroad and of the full retreat of Lee's army, proclaimed in "exultant and wildly exaggerated phrase" by the bearers, gave vigor and excitement to the advance. The cavalry had a sharp encounter with the Rebels about dusk; then the whole command camped near Deep Creek on the Namozine Road for the night.[77]

Sheridan learned that General Lee was collecting his army at Amelia Court House, and at 5:00 A.M. on April 4, the Fifth Corps moved at a rapid pace toward Jetersville, eight miles below Amelia Court House, to cut the Danville Railroad. Federal cavalry were ordered by another route to strike the railroad south of Jetersville and then move up to join the infantry. Darkness had fallen before the Fifth Corps arrived at its destination, thirty-five long miles from the starting point, and formed a line of battle across the railroad below Jetersville. It was midnight before the men were entrenched and works thrown up. The tired soldiers worked with a will, for they expected to be attacked by Lee's entire army and would have to hold their position until the Second and Sixth Corps could come up. All the next day, as they waited under arms, the tension grew. They felt alone and vulnerable, because the concentrated Army of Northern Virginia, that fine body of fighters made desperate by their present situation, could overwhelm them with their numbers. But most of the old soldiers slept all they could, since they did not know when they would get another chance.[78]

The other two corps began to arrive at midafternoon, the Second Corps first, forming on the left of the Fifth Corps, and then the Sixth on the right. Not long before the arrival of the reinforcements, Chamberlain's command was ordered to support the cavalry, which was under attack coming in from a raid. What fight there had been was over on Chamberlain's arrival, but the cavalrymen had captured artillery, a long train of wagons, and many prisoners. With silver pots and sugar bowls strapped to their saddles, and wearing odd pieces of clothing, hats, ribbons, and other unidentifiable objects plundered from the wagons, the troopers disdained military discipline. Chamberlain thought dubiously that they looked as if "a company of troubadours had dismounted a squadron of crusaders between Joppa and Jerusalem." That night Sheridan ordered General Griffin to report to General Meade and released the Fifth Corps, which he had not wanted in the first place, from his command.[79]

On the next day, April 6, all three corps moved together several miles across country toward Amelia Court House to attack Lee, but they were halted when it was learned that the Confederates had left in the night on roads leading toward Lynchburg and Danville. Before turning west again, the Fifth Corps was detoured north, from the extreme left to the far right of the army. Sheridan was finally granted his wish to have the Sixth Corps as his infantry arm: the Sixth was placed on the Union left to operate with the cavalry. Humphreys's Second Corps headed west between the other corps, but not far from the Sixth. After harassing and destroying enemy wagon trains, the cavalry then joined with the Sixth Corps at Sailor's Creek for a desperate battle with Ewell's corps, resulting in the capture of thousands of Confederates, many flags, and several general officers. The Second Corps also fought that day, capturing over a thousand prisoners and several flags. Although the Fifth Corps soldiers had thirty-two miles of hard marching to Ligontown Ferry, they did not encounter the enemy in force.[80]

In the vanguard of the Fifth Corps, Chamberlain's men destroyed all military materiel that the Confederates had left behind and built bridges for the wagons and artillery. They waded streams so high that they had to hold their guns above their heads, and then they marched again with the water sloshing in their shoes. Always they had to be cautious—keeping skirmishers and flankers out as they marched—because sometimes the Rebel rear guard would turn and fight to give time for their comrades ahead to overcome some obstacle. They captured 150 Rebels, many of whom were exhausted and had given up the struggle to keep ahead of the ever-following bluecoats. Sometimes ammunition wagons, abandoned and fired by the Rebels, were still burning when the Federals arrived, and care had to be taken that unexploded powder did not blow up in the pursuers' faces. Other times the carts and wagons of hundreds of civilians fleeing before the Yankees, "as if they were the scourge of God," slowed the advance.[81]

Since Lee had not received the supplies he expected at Amelia Court House, he lost a precious twenty-four hours trying to collect food in the countryside. When he found the Union force at Jetersville and heard that a large body of Yankees were approaching Burkeville, he realized the latter junction of the South Side and the Danville Railroads would be closed to him, and he could no longer hope to supply his army by rail from Danville. He decided to turn toward Farmville, where he could order supplies to be sent to his hungry men from Lynchburg.[82]

After the Confederate disaster at Sailor's Creek, the remaining divisions of Lee's army were organized as much as possible. Some provisions were distributed at Farmville on April 7, but not to everyone, since the approach of the Union army required that the supply trains be moved. The great Army of Northern Virginia was now reduced to two corps of exhausted and half-starved men under General Longstreet and Maj. Gen. John B. Gordon. Some of the men straggled and fell behind, but there was still plenty of fight left in those who continued west.[83]

On the same day, the Fifth Corps moved out at five in the morning, but four hours later, near the High Bridge of the South Side Railroad over the Appomattox River, orders came for them to move in rear of the Sixth and Second Corps again and proceed with all possible speed to Prince Edward Court House. This time they tramped from the right of the army back to the extreme left and camped for the night after a march of twenty miles. At early light on the morning of April 8, they marched toward the Lynchburg Road, Ayres's division leading, and were ordered to press forward rapidly on Lee's left flank in rear of the Twenty-fourth Corps of General Ord's Army of the James. General Sheridan and the cavalry were hurrying ahead to get in front of Lee, while the Second and Sixth Corps followed a more direct route behind the fleeing enemy.[84]

Crossing the Buffalo River that morning, Chamberlain absentmindedly allowed his horse to wade knee-deep into the river while taking a drink of water. Charlemagne took another step and, without warning, slipped into the main channel of the stream, horse and rider plunging headlong into the water. Both surfaced and managed to get to the muddy bank, the general in the lead, slipping and sliding in the mire and half carrying his mount. Chamberlain finally climbed out of the river, covered with mud, but it took three hardy men to finish Charlemagne's rescue. Chamberlain's dripping, bedraggled appearance was hardly suitable for a general officer, and surely his assistants could barely, if at all, contain their amusement at such a sight. Chamberlain later acknowledged that the joke was on him, explaining with some chagrin: "What they had to do for us both afterwards, official dignity prevents explaining."[85]

General Ord, with Gen. John Gibbon's Twenty-fourth Corps and Birney's division of U.S. Colored Troops of the Twenty-fifth Corps, had left Petersburg on April 3, marched through Burkeville, and was ordered by General Grant to pick up the Fifth Corps. At Prospect Station the Fifth Corps met Ord's corps at noon and fell in behind Gibbon's men. The next fourteen hours were a nightmare for Griffin's corps. Ord's men were weary, and their column straggled out farther and farther. The infantrymen of the Fifth Corps had to stop and wait, march a little, and wait again, standing in place fully loaded down or creeping along at a snail's pace. If a commanding officer allowed them to fall out and rest until the congestion cleared, a staff officer was sure to see it and report to headquarters that the officer was not following orders and had halted.[86]

Another outcome was that this tediousness made it so hard on the tired men that they "fretted . . . almost to mutiny," and good soldiers who generally respected and even loved their officers would "greet the luckless officers believed to be leading the column with very insubordinate and wholly impracticable advice as to the merits" of the march. They pointed out the duty of the officers to use some good sense in language that would be intolerable in ordinary situations. At the head of the column, a mob of soldiers took matters into their own hands and moved the road-blocking wagons; after dark, even offending artillery and horses were moved to the side. A brawl began when the drivers defended the horses with their whips, and there came a barrage of blows, threats, and oaths from the enraged men. The generals brought the bands up to the front, hoping that the commotion would be drowned out by the music, but the strains of "The Girl I Left Behind Me" did not help—and only seemed to egg everybody on until things finally settled down.[87]

The Fifth Corps endured this kind of punishment for twenty-nine miles, marching exhausted until after midnight, when human endurance failed; they could go no farther. A halt was called, and the men almost fainted in the roadway. Like other officers, Chamberlain slid from his saddle, loosened his horse's girth, and fell immediately to sleep at the side of the road.

Charlemagne lowered his head and dozed, his nose near his master's face. They were six miles away from the Appomattox Station of the South Side Railroad, where earlier in the night Sheridan's cavalry, commanded by Gen. George A. Custer, had captured four of Lee's supply trains with locomotives, hundreds of prisoners, wagons, and thirty pieces of artillery. Unknown to the prostrate sleepers of the infantry, the end of the chase was at hand.[88]

About four o'clock in the morning of April 9, a messenger galloped up, and Chamberlain's orderly shook him by the shoulder: "Orders, sir, I think." Groggy, Chamberlain propped himself on an elbow and, through sleep-watered eyes by the light of a flickering match, read Sheridan's message to the infantry commanders. The cavalryman told of his position at Appomattox Station and concluded, "If you can possibly push your infantry up here tonight, we will have great results in the morning."[89]

The bugles blew, and the soldiers roused. There was no time to be lost; the men had gone supperless the night before, but they were given only a short time to eat what little food they could quickly gulp down. "Almost with one foot in the stirrup," Chamberlain grabbed a few bites of food, washed down with black coffee seeped from grounds. Most of the men were on their feet when the "Forward" sounded, and by sunrise on that soft, misty Palm Sunday morning, they had marched to Appomattox Station. Near there, they were directed to turn right by a staff officer, and they hurried toward the booming sounds of horse artillery and the distinctive crack of cavalry carbines, answered by the rattle of infantry muskets and thunder of field artillery.[90]

Sheridan's cavalry was across the enemy's front and holding on gamely, waiting for the Union infantry to come up. It was what everyone had been waiting for, and Chamberlain and the other veterans were aware that there were high stakes now. Ord's and Griffin's other men were also rushing toward the front, in double column and at double-quick, the wheeled vehicles taking the road and soldiers on either side. Then Chamberlain's wondering eyes saw something he would remember always: "Birney's black men abreast with us," he exclaimed, "pressing forward to save the white man's country."[91]

Ord's men led, the Fifth Corps following with Ayres's division in the lead. Chamberlain had the advance of the First Division, and Crawford's division brought up the rear. General Bartlett threw out a "division" skirmish line when he thought the front was near, which he and General

Griffin followed intently. A cavalry staff officer dashed from the right and addressed Chamberlain, asking if he commanded the column. Quickly, he answered: "Two brigades of it, sir, about half the First Division, Fifth Corps." The cavalryman replied urgently: "Sir, General Sheridan wishes you to break off from this column and come to his support. The rebel infantry is pressing him hard. . . . Don't wait for orders through the regular channels, but act on this at once." Not hesitating, Chamberlain ordered his brigades to leave the column and follow him and his guide.[92]

On the far left of what would be Chamberlain's new front, part of Ord's infantry moved to cross the Lynchburg Pike to relieve the cavalry that was blocking the head of Confederate Gen. John B. Gordon's corps; Ayres's division came up on Ord's right. The rear of Gordon's formidable force was trying to break through not far from the village of Appomattox Court House, and one division of Sheridan's cavalry was holding it there. Since cavalry was never a match for infantry for very long, Chamberlain's troops pressed through a woods to relieve the horse soldiers. Suddenly, on the border of an open field, Sheridan's red and white swallow-tailed battle pennon came into view, the smoke of firing batteries swirling around it. And there was Sheridan himself, looking powerful as a coiled spring, on his black war-horse Rienzi, both appearing dark and forbidding, "terrible to look upon, as if masking some unknown powers."[93]

Sheridan smiled grimly at Chamberlain, giving no orders but an impulsive gesture. Chamberlain's men formed rapidly in double lines of battle, the 198th Pennsylvania now commanded by Bvt. Lt. Col. Ellis Spear. Gregory's brigade came up on the left in the space between the First Brigade and the Third Brigade, which was coming out of the woods and forming on Ayres's right. Chamberlain and his command went forward on this new front on the Confederates' left flank past Sheridan, relieving the cavalry in successive waves as enemy shells burst high in the air in puffs of white smoke.[94]

It was a beautiful scene in motion for a moment, revealing to the disbelieving eyes of Gordon's men the sight of blue lines of Union infantry, with the flags that they had seen on other battlefields, across the field in front of them again. With grace and precision, as the cavalry bugles sounded, the cavalrymen left the field to the Federal infantry in successive squadrons to the Union right, which was closing in on the Confederate left. As Sheridan rode away, an inspiring and fearsome figure, he struck his hands together and shouted to the Federals, "Smash 'em, I tell you; smash 'em!"[95]

Gordon's men hesitated, their last glimmering of hope nearly gone when they saw that the Federal infantry had accomplished a tremendous feat of marching and had caught up to the Union cavalry. Ord's and Ayres's men were across the Lynchburg Pike on the far left, and so the trap was sprung—the Sixth and Second Corps were in Longstreet's rear a few miles away. The Confederates began to fall back, but halfway up the low ridge behind them, some started to rally at a stone wall. Chamberlain ordered a battery to fire, to send the Rebels retreating over the crest behind them, and prepared his men for a quick advance. The Maine general was all concentration and intensity, but General Griffin came up and teasingly accused him of mistaking a peach tree in full bloom for a Confederate flag and firing on it! Chamberlain realized then that he was too tense, pushing too hard, so he relaxed a little sheepishly with a humorous remark about being nearsighted and not used to long-range fighting. Griffin, he thought ruefully, had a "way of hitting off our weak points when we get a little too serious."[96]

After a few minutes, Griffin rode up to Chamberlain again, agitated and his manner considerably changed. General Crawford had not appeared with his division, and the corps commander was afraid that Crawford would somehow cause him to be dismissed, as Warren had been. He ordered Chamberlain to go back and bring Crawford's troops up and verbally gave Chamberlain command of the Third Division, saying he would follow the action up with a written order. A little shocked, Chamberlain quickly talked his superior out of pursuing such a course of action; he reminded Griffin that Crawford was a man of considerable political influence, that his friends could block Griffin's next promotion, and then too, that "I do not desire the position." In a tone of finality, he finished: "I think General Baxter of the Third Division is my senior; that must settle it."[97]

Concerned that the enemy's massed guns might rake the top of the ridge, General Ord arrived and cautioned Chamberlain about exposing his men on its crest. But Chamberlain thought he saw a "qualifying look" in Ord's eye as he turned away. His men were in a poor position where they were, and Chamberlain disliked being literally the "under dog." Then he thought of Sheridan's calling out, "Smash 'em," as he rode away; Chamberlain decided that it must have been meant as an order, and he wanted to obey its spirit. It did not take long for his men to rush quickly to the crest; only a single shot went past their front, hardly noticed.[98]

At the top of the rise, a wonderful scene beyond adequate description appeared before them—the Army of Northern Virginia, in a stirring panorama on the landscape below. The narrow headwaters of the Appomattox River flowed in the distance, and the town of Appomattox Court House nestled in some trees not far away. The hilly, rolling ground seemed filled with thousands of gray-clad soldiers formed in masses, with horses, wagons, artillery, fleeing civilians, and all sorts of animals milling around. From his vantage place at the Fifth Corps right, Chamberlain could see the blue infantry, muskets gleaming as the morning sun came out from the gloomy clouds, sweep in concave cordon—20,000 men visible from flank to flank. It was like a dream, and when awakening to reality, finding the dream was true.[99]

Advancing down the gentle slope in imposing full array, the Fifth Corps, uniforms blue against the bright, velvet-soft, new green grass, moved toward a small stream that wandered by the village. Battle flags in advance of each regiment made splotches of color in reds and blues, while the white stripes and stars on the "old flags" proclaimed the national cause. General Griffin and his staff rode proudly between the skirmishers and the battle lines, the flag-bearer displaying the rectangular Fifth Corps headquarters emblem with its Maltese cross. General Bartlett, with his aides and division flag, kept pace with the skirmish line, and Chamberlain rode on the extreme right between the lines with his skirmishers, staff, and triangular white flag with the red Maltese cross, all moving inexorably toward the Confederates. The Confederates backed slowly, seemingly giving only token resistance, as if from force of habit.[100]

Joy surged in the hearts of the Union soldiers, but it was mixed with uneasiness. It would be a tragedy to kill or be killed now, with the end so near, but necessity and duty might require it. Moving through a swamp and across the stream, Chamberlain and his men reached the outskirts of the village. A great show of fighting was made as some of the antagonists met, but little damage was done. Everyone took it easy as the skirmishers entered the town. Unable to contain himself, Chamberlain's young orderly got permission to go forward and, to Chamberlain's amusement, "dashes in, sword-flourishing as if he were a terrible fellow,—and soon comes back, hugging four sabers to his breast, speechless at his achievement."[101]

Overwhelmed and recognizing the futility of further resistance, some Confederate units surrendered. Others fired some shots in desperate feeling. But it was not over yet. Chamberlain was keenly aware that his right flank was in the air and vulnerable to attack by some infantry he could see a mile distant near the river. As he looked to his far right from his vantage point on "quite an eminence," he saw the Union cavalry forming there and hoped that they would save him from a flank attack. Just then, his eye caught the movement of a single horseman, immediately joined by another, riding between the lines nearly a mile away. They had disappeared into a copse of trees when suddenly a Confederate staff officer carrying a white flag appeared in Chamberlain's front and came toward him at a diagonal. The flag was actually a white towel, and Chamberlain found himself wondering irrelevantly where a clean towel could be found in either army. When the man dismounted, he announced that he was from General Gordon and that General Lee wished a truce until he could hear further from General Grant about the "proposed surrender."[102]

Having no idea that Generals Lee and Grant had been exchanging notes through the lines for the past two days, Chamberlain's senses reeled. Surrender? The long-awaited word rang in his mind like a peal from heaven! He pulled himself together and had the messenger wait while he sent word to his corps commander; then he sent the Confederate officer along the line to the left where Sheridan and Ord were. Soon after, the two horsemen he had seen before galloped up. Chamberlain recognized Colonel Whitaker, one of Gen. George Custer's staff officers, followed by a Confederate officer bearing another white flag. "This is unconditional surrender! This is the end!" Whitaker shouted excitedly.[103]

Barely taking the time to introduce his companion in gray, Whitaker added, "I am just from Gordon and Longstreet. Gordon says 'For God's sake, stop this infantry, or hell will be to pay!' I'll go to Sheridan," and spurred his horse away. Chamberlain was not quite sure what to do. He could not halt without orders, but he did not push—no one did much after flags of truce were seen all along the line. There was a final cannon shot from the edge of town, and the shell killed Lt. Hiram Clark of the 185th New York, a young officer whom Chamberlain liked, after the flag of truce was in. Chamberlain lamented that "it seemed a cruel fate for one so deserving to share his country's joy."[104]

Finally the order came down to cease fire and to halt, and the men excitedly surged forward toward the front to see for themselves what was going on. For them, Chamberlain declared, it was "forward still,—forward to the end, forward to the new beginning; forward to the Nation's second birth!" When their officers finally stopped their eager motion and ordered them to keep their positions, stack arms, and plant the colors, the men cheered, threw their caps in the air, and jumped upward, arms and legs flying. Jubilation filled most hearts as the expectation that the end of the war was near spread to all ranks. When he heard the news of the truce, General Gregory, the usually grave, white-haired parson, shouted "Glory to God!" Then he nearly sent himself and Chamberlain falling to the ground from their horses as he grabbed for his superior's hand, which still held an upraised sword.[105]

Near the courthouse, Chamberlain joined several generals of both sides, including Sheridan and Gordon, who gathered to talk. They spoke mostly of commonplace things—many of them were friends and acquaintances from West Point and old army days. Some whiskey was found by one Union general and passed around. The general officers, old enemies and new friends, mingled and talked together cordially in great shows of cheerful manners, the Confederates mostly able to mask their emotions of sadness, hostility, or mortification, and the Federals generally careful of wounded feelings.[106]

When he approached the courthouse after the truce, Sheridan had been fired upon by mistake, and he was suspicious and sure that the truce was a Rebel trick. He was for unconditional surrender, and Chamberlain thought he would have continued the fight if it had been left to him. Some firing out on the Lynchburg Pike broke the stillness. General Gordon jumped up and looked toward Sheridan, who had sent some of his men to stop anyone who tried to get away. "Oh never mind! I know about it," Sheridan declared disdainfully. "Let 'em fight!" He concluded with an oath that really meant that he was very satisfied with his men—"damn them!"[107]

As the end of the agreed-upon time of the temporary truce came, there was a final shaking of hands, and Chamberlain turned to leave. General Griffin murmured to him the order, "Prepare to make, or receive an attack in ten minutes!" The thought of more killing was appalling to the Maine general and to many of the others. To take up arms again with the armies so close to each other and at such a time would be little short of murder in the eyes of the former theologian. But the order was only to "prepare," so the men made themselves ready.[108]

His advanced line positioned across the main road of the town, Chamberlain was mounted and tensely waiting when he began to feel an uneasy discomfort. A feeling of the presence of an invisible power or portent came over him. Perhaps it was only the sound of hoofbeats in a sudden, curious silence following the intake of the breaths of hundreds of men that caused him to turn in his saddle toward the rear. There he beheld the splendid figure of the general-in-chief of the Armies of the Confederate States, Robert E. Lee himself, riding between his lines. Accompanied by his chief of staff, General Lee was resplendent in his best dress gray uniform richly trimmed in gold braid, sword at his side. The white-bearded face was sad, but his bearing was strong and commanding. Chamberlain, mindful of the momentous meeting for which Lee had come and of his brilliant reputation, felt "a certain awe and admiration" as he watched the already legendary figure pass between his lines.[109]

But the sight that filled Chamberlain with wonder a short time later was the appearance, by another road, of Lt. Gen. Ulysses S. Grant. To Chamberlain, Grant conveyed all the power and dignity of the United States in his intense face and quiet, calm presence, regardless of his modest attire. Grant was swordless, the three tarnished stars of his rank lay dully on the blue blouse of a private soldier, his trousers were tucked into muddy high boots, and his old felt hat rested shapelessly on his head. Chamberlain mused later: "He seemed greater than I had ever seen him,—a look of another world about him. No wonder I forgot to salute him. Anything like that would have been too little."[110]

As Grant and Lee retired to the parlor of the Wilmer McLean house for the last conference on terms and then the official surrender of the Army of Northern Virginia, a few ranking generals and aides were asked into the room, while others lounged in the McLean yard. It was agreed by the two commanders that all Confederate officers were to be paroled individually, and company or regimental commanders were to list and sign for the parole of their men, who were not to take up arms again until properly exchanged.[111]

Supplies, arms, and ammunition were to be surrendered as captured property. Grant, with an eye on Lee's sword, amended the latter stipulation to provide that officers were to keep their sidearms and, with more thought, their horses. He verbally agreed to Lee's later request that horses not belonging to the Confederacy were to be kept by their owners, whether officers or ordinary soldiers. Lee was relieved that some of his men would have the means of making a crop and remarked that the terms would have a good effect on his men and go a long way toward "conciliating our people." While the terms were being copied, Lee raised the subjects of the freeing of Union prisoners and the feeding of his starving army. Grant agreed to send over 25,000 rations, which would relieve the immediate need.[112]

"It was reserved for Lee to be confronted by a man as magnanimous as himself, and guided by a better star. He had to go down, honored and beloved indeed for the man he was, but the more lamented for the unhappy choice he made when he cast in his lot with those who forsook the old flag for a new one, which did not recognize the fact that old things had become new,—that even constitutions move with the march of man, with wider interpretations and to their appointed goals, and that the old flag borne forward by farther-seeing men held its potency not only in the history of the past but for the story of the future."[113]

The Union troops near the village waited expectantly. They were almost sure that the surrender would take place, given the hopeless position of the Southern army. A few miles away, impatiently looking for messengers of the latest news, was General Meade, to whom no invitation came to join the momentous proceedings at Appomattox Court House. With him was General Humphreys, whose Second Corps, which had done much long war service and a great deal of fighting the past nine days, was halted in rear of Longstreet's corps.[114]

Not far away from them, Confederate Col. Robert M. Powell of the Fifth Texas Regiment could barely keep control of his men. He had been exchanged after his wounding and capture at Little Round Top at Gettysburg and was now nearing the end of the war as the last commander of Hood's Texas Brigade. As the stark fact that their army might be surrendered crashed in on their incredulous minds, the ragged men obeyed the order to stack arms only with great difficulty. Finally they did so by throwing their muskets together in an unsoldierlike manner undreamed of before. They spoke of their feelings and their fears in tight, emotion-packed voices. Many wanted to fight until the death; others imagined "a great triumphal procession to Washington with General Lee chained to the victor's car and his ragged rebels trailing behind" or all of them cold-bloodedly slaughtered in a hellish spectacle of ringing bells and cheering populace. All except the chaplain seemed to turn bitterly from their faith in "the 'signs and wonders and the strong hand and the stretched out arm,' in which they had believed the Lord had so often been manifest."[115]

After the surrender was officially announced, the Federals' hurrahs rent the heavens, and caps, canteens, bodies—everything—went into the air. A band posted near Chamberlain, which had earlier played "Auld Lang Syne," began a patriotic tune but broke into discordant notes in the excitement. Giving no sign that he felt left out of the surrender proceedings, General Meade galloped around waving his cap with the best of them while his men went "perfectly crazy" and hopped up and down with joy. The bands played, flags waved, and artillery guns fired until another message from Grant stilled the voices of the guns. Sounds of cheering Rebels were heard by the Union forces, but it was suspected that they were cheering their beloved leader General Lee as he made his way back through his faithful soldiers.[116]

Settled down at last, the men made camp, and rations were distributed to the famished men in gray and to the hungry troops of the Fifth Corps. For the next two days, curious soldiers visited across the lines, mostly in the Union camps, eager to trade for souvenirs, food, coffee, and wearing apparel. Good discipline became a problem for both sides, however, and steps had to be taken by both commands to avoid complete confusion.[117]

Nearly everyone, officers and men alike, enjoyed the strange sensations of peace. The campfires of nearly 100,000 men twinkled in the night, making a beautiful sight. All was quiet; no sounds of picket firing broke the stillness. As the virtual certainty of the end of the war became apparent, thoughts winged through the darkness to thousands of homes and families left behind. Many Confederates had thought it "treason to our convictions and duty to our country to think of home" as the war wound down, but now thoughts of their loved ones came easily to mind. Men of both armies slipped into sleep untroubled by the threat of violent death for the first time in years and dreamed their separate dreams.[118]

When accolades were written later, few exceeded those given the Maine professor turned soldier. One from ordinary soldiers particularly recalled the momentous last twelve days of the Appomattox campaign, from the Quaker Road to the surrender: "The chances that came to General Chamberlain during this campaign," began the veterans of one Pennsylvania regiment, "came to one of conceded high soldierly abilities, whose unswerving sense of honor and justice impelled him to the exercise of those abilities fully and fairly, no matter what the duty, what the danger, what the fatigue." The old soldiers of the Keystone State concluded with this high tribute: "If any one in the Fifth Army Corps maintained a spotless name and won enduring fame during the operations of that corps from the 29th of March to the 9th of April, 1865, more than commensurate with the range of the command he held, that one was Joshua L. Chamberlain."[119]

CHAPTER

Ten

THE PASSING OF THE ARMIES

As the telegraph wires hummed the news northward, the rejoicing began. Early on Monday morning at Brunswick, Dr. Adams heard shouts in the streets, bells ringing, and firecrackers exploding and knew they heralded the long-awaited news of the surrender of Lee's army. That night the entire town was aglow from the lighted candles placed in every window as an "illumination" celebrated the great victory. At Brewer, after the initial excitement, someone put up a huge kite nearly a half mile into the air with a large American flag dangling twenty feet below it. From across the river in Bangor it looked as if "the beautiful flag . . . was supported by unseen hands in the heavens."[1]

To formulate and facilitate the details of the surrender agreements, commissioners were appointed by Grant and Lee. Grant, Sheridan, and Ord were to depart the field soon, and so for the Union, Grant picked Generals Wesley Merritt, John Gibbon, and Charles Griffin, of the cavalry, Army of the James, and Fifth Corps, respectively. Much had to be done in a short period of time, including making up, filling out, and signing parole lists and passes to enable the Confederates to be honorably paroled. Joshua Chamberlain was called to headquarters and told by commissioners Griffin and Gibbon that he had been chosen by General Grant to command the surrender ceremonies of the infantry of the Army of Northern Virginia.[2]

Pleased with the honor, Chamberlain asked for, and received, permission to command again the First Division's Third Brigade, the old brigade he and the Twentieth Maine had started with before Antietam and which he had later commanded after Gettysburg. Although winnowed down by losses over the years, and with ranks periodically fleshed out with new recruits, what was left of the old Fifth Corps was embodied in this brigade. "It's the most magnificent Brigade in the army, beyond all question," Chamberlain believed. He wanted these deserving men at his side to directly share the honor, and in a larger sense he saw them as representing all of the members of the Army of the Potomac, who had struggled, fought, and died to bring about this momentous event. He was also keenly cognizant that Generals Meade, Humphreys, and Wright and their men of the Second and Sixth Corps of that great army had been ordered to march away, without participating in or witnessing, even by token representation, any of the historic events of the actual surrender.[3]

General Griffin told Chamberlain that General Grant wanted a simple ceremony, one that would not "humiliate the manhood" of the officers and men of the vanquished army. He confided that the Confederate generals had "begged hard" to allow their men to leave their arms and colors in their camps, then disperse to their homes. However, Grant thought that would be a too lenient policy, "not quite respectful enough to anybody, including the United States of America," and insisted on a formal observance. Near noon on the eleventh of April, the First Division relieved Bvt. Maj. Gen. John W. Turner's men of the Army of the James, who had received the surrender of the Confederate artillery, and lined up to begin the surrender ceremony of the infantry. The infantry parole lists and certificates were not finished, however, and the official parade had to be postponed until the next day.[4]

"What was surrendered? Whatever was surrendered and laid down, it was not manhood, and not honor. Manhood arose, and honor was plighted and received. No, but that army, the organized expression of the power of the rebellion, surrendered, and with it the whole prestige and paraphernalia and pretext and privilege of secession went down. It was the doctrine of absolute State sovereignty, the right of the State over the people of the United States. . . . Those officers and men who surrendered with Lee, I am very sure, so understood it. When they gave their parole of honor never again to assail the authority of the United States, they did not take it to mean that they were to keep the peace till they could get another chance to fight, but that henceforth they were in all ways to receive, support and maintain the integrity and rightful supremacy of the United States of America. I know that they so understood it. They are men of honor, and they meant it, and their word of honor is good.

"Well, there was indeed another thing surrendered, though not included in the terms of the surrender, nor yet plainly set forth in the issue that was joined, but something that was an ally and accessory of secession, and so went down with it by the force of the situation, as a military necessity, or rather by a certain divine ordering and ordinance—slavery. Slavery and freedom cannot live together. Had slavery been kept out of the fight, the Union would have gone down. But the enemies of the country were so misguided as to rest their cause upon it, and that was the destruction of it and of them. We did not go into that fight to strike at slavery directly; we were not thinking to solve that problem, but God, in his providence, in His justice, in his mercy, in His great covenant with our fathers, set slavery in the forefront, and it was swept aside as with a whirlwind, when the mighty pageant of the people passed on to its triumph."[5]

Very early in the morning of Wednesday, April 12, Chamberlain assembled his men at the courthouse. Although he technically commanded only the Third Brigade of the division, General Griffin had directed that the First and Second Brigades line up also as witnesses to the surrender of Lee's army, with Chamberlain as ranking officer. The Third Brigade proudly aligned along the Richmond-Lynchburg Road east of the courthouse in line of battle, facing the valley to the north where Lee's men could be seen on an opposing hillside, moving through the morning mists, folding their tented shelters and breaking camp for the last time. Behind the Third stood the First Brigade, consisting of the 198th Pennsylvania and the 187th New York, now commanded by Bvt. Brig. Gen. Alfred Pearson of the 155th Pennsylvania. Across the road, facing them, was Gregory's Second Brigade. Chamberlain and his staff positioned themselves at the Third Brigade's extreme right. They would be the first Federals the Confederates would pass on their dolorous march.[6]

Behind the mounted Chamberlain and his officers, the "old flag"—its white stars in their dark blue field and red stripes intermingled with its white ones—showed conspicuously. Beside it, the triangular ensign of the Third Brigade in like colors, with its red Maltese cross displayed brightly on the white field bordered in dark blue, fluttered from its staff when a stray gust of wind would stir it. It was a handsome and colorful sight indeed, as the growing morning light brightened the chilly day, with the officers and men in blue uniforms and full battle array, muskets gleaming, the regimental flags interspersed among them. The Union soldiers stood at "order arms," awaiting the approach of the Confederate fighting men.[7]

Across the valley, the figures in gray came together in marching columns, their bodies swinging with practiced ease in the old route step. They forded the Appomattox River, now narrow and shallow near its headwaters, and neared the waiting Federals. Although it had seemed almost like treason to do so in the days and nights of early April, since the hostilities had ceased most had turned their thoughts toward home and what awaited them there. The future held dreadful uncertainties for them all. In what must have seemed a lifetime ago, many had dreamed of a glorious homecoming to a new country, their army greeted with the huge parades, bands, cheers, flowers, and adulation due conquering heroes. Now, all had turned to ashes, the dreams dashed, and the hardships and blood and death seemed for naught.[8]

The thin survivors' most terrible imaginings had been allayed somewhat by the unexpected magnanimity of Grant's terms and the friendly way they had been treated by his soldiers in the informal visitations. But what would happen now? Would the victorious Yankees jeer or make fun, humiliating them with words or gestures? These were proud men, still unbowed. Some were resentful and unreconciled to defeat; others were accepting, impassive, or jocular. But the last bitter duty remained, and they marched resolutely to the final encounter with their old foes of the Army of the Potomac.[9]

At the head of the army rode Maj. Gen. John B. Gordon, thin and young, but the commander of a corps, the very epitome of a fine-looking general officer. Now his head was bowed, eyes cast down, expression dejected. The flag of the Confederacy preceded the column behind him, with its solid white field and familiar design of red background and crossed blue bars with white stars in the upper left corner. The canton—the familiar "stars and bars"—was repeated alone in oversized replica in the tattered array of worn battle flags following at intervals behind. One officer, noting that the flags marked units small in comparison to their former sizes, described Gordon's infantry as looking, "like marching gardens blooming with cockscomb, red roses, and poppies."[10]

As Gordon reached the right of the Federal column where Chamberlain and his officers waited, a bugle sounded. Immediately, the whole Union line snapped to attention, and the slapping noise of hands on shifting rifles echoed in the stillness as regiment after regiment in succession down the Union line came into the old manual of arms position of "salute" and then back to "order arms" and "parade rest." It was not the "present arms," that expression of highest possible honor, because when Chamberlain earlier considered his idea of ordering such a controversial gesture to show respect for the bravery of the Confederate soldiers, he decided that it would be too much recognition. He felt that the "carry arms"—the old marching salute—with the musket held by the right hand and perpendicular to the shoulder, would be more fitting.[11]

When Gordon heard the sounds of the drill, he instantly recognized their significance and wheeled to face Chamberlain. As he did, his spurs touched the sides of his horse, causing it to rear, and as his horse's head then came down in a bow, the gallant young general dropped his sword point to his boot toe in a graceful salute to the man whom he would call "one of the knightliest soldiers of the Federal army."[12]

Turning to his men, the Confederate leader gave an order, which was repeated back through the ranks, and the large Confederate banner dipped. The men of the vanquished army then answered with the same salute given them as they marched by, "honor answering honor," as Chamberlain described it. "On our part not a sound of trumpet more, nor roll of drum; not a cheer, nor word nor whisper of vain-glorying, nor motion of man standing again at the order, but an awed stillness rather, and breath-holding, as if it were the passing of the dead!"[13]

Down the full Union line the Rebels marched; then, as each division halted in turn, they faced the Federals at a distance of about twelve feet and carefully dressed their lines, every man and officer in his proper place. This last march of the Army of Northern Virginia would reflect the soldierly pride of its men, defeated and tattered as they were. They fixed their

Maj. Gen. John B. Gordon, CSA
(Massachusetts Commandery, MOLLUS, *and U.S. Army Military History Institute, Carlisle Barracks, Pa.)*

bayonets and stacked arms, placing their cartridge boxes beside them. The color-bearers then folded their battle flags, nearly all torn, dark splotches showing only a small part of the blood spilled in the effort to preserve them. They were their owners' most precious possessions, symbols of their

Bvt. Maj. Gen. Joshua L. Chamberlain
(Alice Rains Trulock and James A. Trulock)

valor. The banners were tattered tokens of a cause they would have done almost anything to save, and for which so many of their comrades had died. They gave them up slowly, painfully, some kissing them, as unashamed tears rolled down browned cheeks. And there were tears, too, on the rigid faces of many of the men in blue, who, with tremulous, compressed lips, could imagine how they would have felt if their places were changed with those of their former enemies.[14]

As Chamberlain watched the grim procession stop to repeat the sorrowful scene again and again, he thought he could recognize these men "almost . . . by face." There was the Stonewall Brigade, whose flags he had

Brig. Gen. Henry A. Wise, CSA
(Massachusetts Commandery, MOLLUS, and U.S. Army Military History Institute, Carlisle Barracks, Pa.)

seen only three days before as he strained toward that last crest before the truce was called; Cobb's Georgia men, who had held the stone wall at Fredericksburg before which he and his men had piled a breastwork of bodies; Laws's Alabamians, whom he had met at Little Round Top and later at Petersburg's Rives's Salient. What was left of Hood's old Texas Brigade came by, men whom he had also seen at Gettysburg, and many more from Spotsylvania Court House to Five Forks passed with heavy tread as the day wore on. As the terrible memories of past battles flooded over him, he wondered: "How could we help falling on our knees, all of us together, and praying God to pity and forgive us all!"[15]

Riding around with his staff and the division flag, General Bartlett, whose whole division was turned out for the parade under the temporary command of Chamberlain, talked with Confederate officers as he found the opportunity. Although Bartlett had complied with the changed arrangements, Chamberlain thought the situation "troubled . . . Bartlett a little, but he was a manly and soldierly man and made no comment." Chamberlain also was able to talk with some of the Confederates during lulls. One remarked that he was "astonished with your generosity; we should have not done the same to you." Others expressed relief that the war was virtually over, and some were prepared to declare their loyalty to the Union again.[16]

As the day wore on, some of the discipline must have worn off. Confederate Brig. Gen. Henry A. Wise, looking much older than his age with his wrinkled face and thick shock of white hair, was having a hard time and reprimanded some of his command in a high, hectoring voice. His spare figure was a strange sight, dressed in gray except for a blue coat covered with gold braid, as he energetically scolded his men. Perhaps, as their part in the grand design of war was nearly over, they thought the old man held no more authority over them, for they taunted, "Look at him! He is brave enough now, but he was never so near the Yankees before in his life!"[17]

Overcome by curiosity, some men of the 118th Pennsylvania asked the men in gray, "Who is he? Who is he?" When informed of the name, some instantly recognized the man who, as governor of Virginia, had officiated at the hanging of abolitionist insurrectionist John Brown six years before. "Who killed John Brown?" one cried out. Calls of "Where did you steal your coat?" and "Hang him to a sour apple tree!" could be heard from the Yankee lines by the disgusted Wise.[18]

Undoubtedly, Chamberlain would have disapproved had he heard the exchange, but he only heard voices raised and rode down the line to find the red-faced Wise, tobacco juice trickling from one corner of his mouth, bickering with some of his men. Thinking to help the situation, Chamberlain made a comment that the good conduct of the troops of both sides boded well for the future of relations between the two sections. "You are mistaken, sir, we won't be forgiven, we hate you, and that is the whole of it!" the belligerent Virginian replied.[19]

Calming down some, and perhaps a little regretful, Wise remarked with concern on the condition of Chamberlain's coat, the same disreputable coat used in the previous campaigns of last year and this, and asked where he got the ugly tears in its breast and sleeve. Chamberlain said that he had received them in his and General Wise's last encounter when Wise had left him the field on the Quaker Road. Stung, Wise challenged, "I suppose you think you did great things there, but I stopped you until I saw I was fighting three divisions." Upon being told that three regiments were his opponents, Wise replied, "I know better, you go home and take those fellows home, and that will end the war!"[20]

With perhaps a smile and a little edge to his voice now, in exaggerated courtesy Chamberlain replied, "We are going, General, but first let us escort you home!" "Home," Wise countered bitterly; "we have no homes; you have destroyed them!" The Union commander replied, "You should have not challenged us then; we expected somebody would get hurt when we came down here!" The scene had become comical. Many of the staff officers on both sides were laughing, and the overhearing men smiled too, as the generals parted.[21]

But the sad business at hand went on all day, and it was sunset before all was finished. A small group, evidently the remainder of a regiment used as some headquarters guard, came in last and late, after their comrades had marched away. As they gave up their flag, stained by the blood and smoke of battle, its color-bearer burst into tears and said to the Union soldiers, "Boys, this is not the first time you have seen that flag. I have borne it in the front of the battle in many a victorious field, and I had rather die than surrender it now." Chamberlain knew that the banner was "dearer than life to them—dear as manhood and honor." "Brave fellow," Chamberlain answered, "I admire your noble spirit and only regret that I have not the authority to bid you keep your flag, and carry it home as a precious heirloom." Chamberlain's kind words were repeated to others, and the story became widely known throughout the South.[22]

At dusk, after the last Confederate had marched away, lines of ammunition in the road were set on fire. As they were consumed with flame, they flared and writhed, making weird shadows, and a kind of sadness settled over Chamberlain, an emptiness, a sense of loss. It was as if he were leaving a part of himself there too, and he did not quite want to leave. He did not hate these men. Great changes had taken place in himself and the country in a few short years, and he knew that life would never be the same again for him as well as for them. The future was still to be seen through a glass, darkly.[23]

"Nor blame them too much . . . nor us for not blaming them more. Although, as we believed, fatally wrong in striking at the old flag, misreading its deeper meaning and the innermost law of the people's life, blind to the signs of the times in the march of man, they fought as they were taught, true to such ideals as they saw, and put into their cause their best. For us they were fellow-soldiers as well, suffering the fate of arms. We could not look into those brave, bronze faces, and those battered flags we had met on so many fields where glorious manhood lent a glory to the earth that bore it, and think of personal hate and mean revenge. Whoever had misled these men, we had not. We had led them back, home."[24]

Morning saw the exit of the Confederates, singly and in groups, on horseback and on foot, headed in all directions toward their homes. They carried passes that guaranteed their undisturbed passage by Federal authorities, and most had little else to take with them. But the sun was shining, and these were resourceful men who were used to living outdoors with a minimum of comforts, and if they could beg or forage a little food on their journeys, it would do.[25]

Collecting and loading the rest of the Confederate war materiel and other like "housekeeping" duties occupied the Union soldiers that day and the next. All the rations had been shared with the Confederates, and food was very short. Officers and men alike were reduced to eating meagerly of hard corn, well soaked for softening; some lucky ones got food from sympathetic former slaves in the countryside.[26]

On the day after the surrender ceremony, General Griffin wrote a lengthy request recommending Joshua Chamberlain for the brevet of major general in the most glowing terms. Citing his "conspicuous gallantry" in the last campaign, Griffin said Chamberlain "particularly distinguished himself" at the battle at the Quaker Road and commended his actions at Five Forks and at Appomattox. Chamberlain was gratified to receive the brevet and would remark a short time later that he would rather have it than the regular rank of major general, because a brevet was a permanent honor. However, Griffin determined that his talented subordinate should have that rank also, and two weeks afterward recommended him for full major general, mentioning Chamberlain's "distinguished and gallant conduct" in the battles of the Quaker Road, White Oak Road, and Five Forks.[27]

As reaction to peace finally set in, the mood among the Union soldiers was generally somber. Without the existence of the Army of Northern Virginia, the Army of the Potomac was thrown off balance, as if all the weight had suddenly been removed from one side of a scale. The soldiers now felt incomplete somehow, a little disoriented perhaps. The army seemed to have lost its purpose for being, to have been transformed into something different—a fighting machine without a fight or near prospect of one. When they left Appomattox Court House for Burkeville on April 15, Chamberlain found himself scanning the countryside in his usual way, alert for any indication of "the familiar forms that had long so firmly held our eyes, until they almost demanded the sight of them for their daily satisfaction."[28]

The last few hours of the march were spent in a pouring rain, and the familiar Virginia mud was ankle-deep again. Camp was made in cold, wet misery, empty stomachs and men growling alike as promised rations failed to arrive again. But the night finally ended, and at six o'clock on that rainy Easter Sunday morning, 1865, the Fifth Corps set out toward Farmville. The weather cleared and the soldiers' mood changed. After all, the war was as much as over, and their army was triumphant! Arriving to make camp near Farmville in glorious afternoon sunshine, they ate heartily of newly drawn rations and dried out soaked clothing and blankets.[29]

That evening, Chamberlain was feeling good about the past ten eventful days. He was listening happily to the fine German band of his old First Brigade, which had come to his headquarters to serenade him, when a mud-spattered cavalryman came galloping up to the headquarters in a hurry. Telling Chamberlain's chief of staff that he thought that "the General would wish to treat this as personal," the courier handed Chamberlain a yellow telegram of thin tissue paper, which read, as Chamberlain recalled: "Washington, April 15, 1865. The President died this morning. Wilkes Booth the assassin. Secretary Seward dangerously wounded. The rest of the Cabinet, General Grant, and other high officers of the Government included in the plot of destruction." Shock nearly paralyzed Chamberlain as he read the telegram.[30]

"In the midst of all this triumph—in this hour of exaltation, in this day of power & joy & hope, when our starry flag floats amid the stars of Heaven, suddenly it falls to half-mast—'darkness sweeps athwart the sky,' & the President of the United States, with his heart full of conciliation & charity & forgiveness is struck down by the assassin's hand—Words will not tell the feeling with which this army receives this blow."[31]

Acting immediately, without explanation and with conscious calm, Chamberlain quietly issued orders: a double guard was to be placed around the whole camp; then regimental commanders were to get in their men, allow no one to leave, and afterward report to him. This done, he thanked and dismissed the German band. When the regimental officers arrived with serious and questioning faces, he told them all of the "appalling news." His first actions had been taken to insure strict discipline. He trusted his men but could not predict the reaction of those stalwart soldiers when they heard the news of their beloved president's death. "What if now," he thought, "this blackest crime should fire their hearts to reckless and implacable vengeance?" He feared that their initial, intense sorrow might break into rage and wreak itself on the nearby town of Farmville, which was reportedly full of goods, stores, and many civilian refugees.[32]

"It seemed as if the darkest things might be yet to come; as if, now that men of honor had given up the fight, it had fallen to baser hands; as if victory, magnanimity, and charity, accepted by those who had lost in the manly appeal of arms, were all to avail nothing against the sullen treacheries that lurked in the shadows of the capital."[33]

Deciding to seek the company of his superior officers, Chamberlain mounted his horse and soon met General Griffin, who had been on the way to see him. Both rode to see Ayres, and then they all proceeded to General Meade's headquarters. In the general conference that followed, it was agreed that if the worst fears of the generals were realized, if the government of the United States became completely inoperable and the nation was thrown into anarchy, then they might have to march on Washington and make Grant military dictator until constitutional government could be restored.[34]

Fortunately, none of these apprehensions came true, and the regular march resumed. On Wednesday, April 19, the day of Abraham Lincoln's funeral, all military duties were suspended. Chamberlain ordered a "funeral in the field" observance on his own responsibility, scheduled at the same time the Lincoln funeral procession was to pass the Capitol in Washington, and it was attended by the entire First Division of the Fifth Corps. The solemn men formed into a large hollow square, with ammunition boxes placed on the open side of it to serve as a speaking platform. Drooping flags, draped in black cloth obtained by dipping handkerchiefs or other material into ink, stood in front of the regiments, the stacked muskets shining in line behind them. Black signs of mourning were also displayed on the headquarters tents and on the officers' swords and left sleeves, all reflecting the spirit of the day.[35]

At noon the toll of the minute guns began, and as the last sounds of the cannon died away the German band played mournful dirges, including the familiar and stirring "Russian Hymn." Griffin and some of the other generals of the corps and their staffs were gathered near their respective flags, which were clustered on the platform. Chamberlain stood near Father Egan, the senior chaplain of the First Division and a well-known orator. His "Celtic soul took fire," Chamberlain recounted, as the priest loudly voiced the words from his text, *"Give me the head of John the Baptist in a charger!"* The good father's passionate rhetoric in memory of the murdered president affected the assembled men powerfully. Mainly because they did not know what else to do, they became agitated enough to reach for their weapons. Almost spellbound himself, but suddenly aware of the chaplain's effect, Chamberlain intervened with a touch on the priest's arm and a few whispered words, just quickly enough to avert any unplanned demonstration. A prayer by the fiery man of God, and an oath of "new consecration to the undying cause of freedom and right," brought everyone to earth again and ended the ceremonies.[36]

That night Chamberlain's thoughts turned toward home, his spirits raised from receiving loving letters from Fannie. Writing a letter to her, he declared in it a passion and love and longing for her reminiscent of the days when they were first married. He had last begun a letter to her shortly after the first "and the fiercest" battle of the campaign on the Quaker Road. His mind filled with the events of the past three weeks, which seemed like months or years to him, he recounted briefly the "tremendous scenes" in which he had participated. "It will take a lifetime to tell you all I have to tell," he said, confiding that he had received many congratulatory letters about the surrender parade and that he had also heard that many of the newspapers had commended him. After telling of the Lincoln funeral in the field, he affirmed again his abiding faith and optimism: "These are terrible times, but I believe in God, & he will bring good at last."[37]

The end of the week found the Fifth Corps under new orders to relieve the Ninth Corps and the First Division with a new commander. General Bartlett had been transferred to a command in the Ninth Corps, and Griffin had named Chamberlain to succeed him. The corps's divisions were posted for miles along the South Side Railroad from Nottoway Court House to Petersburg. Chamberlain made his headquarters at Wilson's Station and originally, through some mistake, had responsibility from that point on the railroad all the way to Petersburg. His First Division was finally ordered to pull back to Sutherland Station, but Chamberlain still had charge of seventeen miles along the road and the adjacent territory, which included the old battlegrounds in Dinwiddie County—Five Forks, the White Oak Road, and the Quaker Road. This desolated countryside contained the local white inhabitants and property owners, newly freed slaves with no homes, occupations, or food, and freewheeling stragglers and marauders from both armies.[38]

Chamberlain was kept busy for nearly two weeks with the countless tasks of attending to the problems of the area. Food was distributed from army commissaries to civilians who would take the oath of allegiance to the Union, and other food given according to need. Many former slaves, homeless either voluntarily or otherwise, were "especially unruly," according to Chamberlain. When Lee's army suddenly left the area, the "floodgates were opened to the rush of animal instinct. The only notion of freedom apparently entertained by these bewildered people was to do as they pleased." However, he thought he understood how they acquired such an idea: "That was what they had reason to suppose white men did. To act according to each one's nature was liberty, contrasted with slavery." In the absence of their usual patterns of life and without food, "they not unnaturally banded together; and without any serious organization and probably without much deliberate plotting of evil, they still spread terror over the country."[39]

Using soldiers on almost constant patrol and detailing guards, Chamberlain restored order and set up a temporary military court to settle disputes. But because he thought there was no other way to deal with it, he ordered a "process more summary than that authorized by courts" in cases of "personal violence or outrage." The countryside was not under martial law, but "military law, which admits of some discretion." Chamberlain construed his orders to protect life and property very liberally and resorted to a kind of dictatorship—a step he thought was necessary. He allowed some commerce in necessities to open on a limited basis.[40]

Meanwhile, Tom Chamberlain fell in love, at least temporarily, with an enchanting young lady considered "the belle of Dinwiddie," he confided to his older brother. Joshua admitted later, since he "was not then on the superannuated list myself," that even he was almost dazzled by her beauty and charm when Tom introduced them. When the corps began its march toward Washington, D.C., a short time later, however, Tom's infatuation apparently had to end. Some citizens were so pleased with Chamberlain's short tenure in their county that a deputation of gentlemen was sent to the general proposing to give a public dinner in his honor before he left. While appreciating the sentiment, Chamberlain declined courteously and warmly, believing that they had better keep their small stores of food for themselves and their families.[41]

Gathering itself up by having the farthest division on the South Side Railroad march eastward first, the Fifth Corps began its march toward Richmond on May 1, 1865. The Second and Third Divisions reached Chamberlain's First Division headquarters at Wilson's Station that night, and early on May 2, Chamberlain proceeded to pick up his brigades in succession along the seventeen-mile stretch of railroad to Sutherland Station. As they passed the place where, exactly one month before, the last Confederate train to leave Petersburg was captured, memories of that incident and of battles on fields that lay south of the return route flooded back to him. At Sutherland's the entire corps massed and spent the night.[42]

The next day they advanced toward Petersburg along the Cox Road, seeing for the first time the inside of the long lines of enemy works and forts that had stood in their way for so long, now deserted and gloomy. In the distance they saw the signal tower erected by their engineers near Hatcher's Run and their own old lines. It was a somber march, with all colors and the officers' sword hilts still draped in mourning, but finally they entered the city of Petersburg. Nearly a year of fighting and dying had passed since the Union soldiers had first seen its spires in the distance on that hot, dusty June day in 1864. As Chamberlain rode toward the center of the town, his thoughts strayed back to that day, when so many lives had been lost in the terrible charge at Rives's Salient, now just beyond his view. The wound that would subdue his youthful vigor and cast its shadow on the rest of his life was the price he had paid for his first attempt to enter the city.[43]

Since General Warren was commanding troops in Petersburg, General Griffin sent word that his old corps wanted to salute him as they passed through the city. Warren stood on the balcony of the Bolingbrook Hotel with his wife and staff to review his former command. A great, dramatic scene unfolded in the heart of the "Cockade City" as the arbitrarily dismissed Fifth Corps commander was paid homage by his successor and all his former officers and men. Giving him some of the recognition he deserved, in celebration of the victory he had done so much to bring about, the bands played enthusiastically, officers saluted with swords, drums rolled, and colors dipped as the thousands of marchers hailed their old chief.[44]

As each unit came opposite the hotel, the men threw their caps in the air with unbridled enthusiasm as they gave rousing cheers. Chamberlain's division of bronzed veterans contained the 155th Pennsylvania. Formed in open order with their guns carried on their knapsacks, their bright Zouave uniforms dulled somewhat by campaign wear, the soldiers cheered loudly and repeatedly, adding "tigers" in such numbers that their officers had to order them to move on. The tribute ended, the men marched on through the town, through throngs of townsfolk lining the streets, followed by miles of artillery, ambulances, and supply trains. Turning north, they were finally and literally "on the road to Richmond," five miles before they camped.[45]

An easy march the next day brought the corps almost to the capital of the Confederacy, but rain stopped the procession for a day. On May 6 they crossed over the James River on the upper pontoon bridge, at last into Richmond, "the famed city which the newspapers had ordered us 'on to' since 1861," Chamberlain remarked humorously. The First Division having the honor of leading the Fifth Corps, it passed along the front of the Twenty-fourth Corps, which presented arms to each general officer as he came by, and simultaneously was reviewed by Generals Henry W. Halleck and Meade. The corps's considerable reputation had to be lived up to mostly with pride and military precision; the threadbare and tattered appearance of the men would otherwise have given an entirely different impression.[46]

Former slaves greeted them in the streets with joy, and some of the white populace turned out to watch them pass. Closed doors and shrouded windows showed plainly the regard other inhabitants held for them. There was time for only a fleeting glimpse of the sights of the city, but a cursory look at Richmond's extensive defenses convinced the soldiers that they were glad they had not been required to enter the city by force the year before.[47]

A schedule set by "high headquarters" called for a hard and long march, as if they were still pursuing the Rebels. Since the leading general usually sets the pace, Chamberlain was discomforted by many sour looks from soldiers who thought he was responsible. At ten that night, the tired soldiers camped near Hanover Court House. If he had been in charge of the march from the James to the Potomac, Chamberlain mused, he would have taken an extra day and gone by altered routes, allowing the men to have the satisfaction of seeing again their battlefields of previous campaigns.[48]

About midnight Chamberlain was awakened to find his horse, which had been tethered in some pines, nervous, noisy, pawing the ground, and snorting. Investigating, he was horrified to find half-buried human skeletons, with skulls strewn about in the darkened wood. By initials cut into breastplates and other recognizable objects, some veterans near daylight were able to identify the remains of missing comrades who had fallen there nearly three years before. The bones were gathered up, laid into empty hardtack boxes, and placed in supply wagons. The soldiers traveled on toward Washington with their sad, strange burden—dead heroes returning home in cracker boxes—borne in solemn procession.[49]

The days came and went on the journey, each marked by memories of earlier years, from the North Anna to Fredericksburg. The dreamy forms of long lost or scattered men and women were seen in fleeting glimpses by the mystical mind of the Maine professor turned fighter: the blue-clad bodies on the terrible Marye's Heights, winter quarters in 1862 with Ames's war schools, Hooker's grand reviews and Ladies' Day parties. Memories of the "Mud March," smallpox hospital tents, and more appeared in Chamberlain's mind's eye in rushing numbers as the corps toiled onward. In a sudden, violent thunderstorm, the lightning flashed from musket to musket along the long lines of plodding men, looking like a long "river of fire" to Chamberlain, who could see the entire corps from the top of a high hill.[50]

At last, on May 12, the weary soldiers reached their assigned permanent campgrounds on Arlington Heights, near the Lee mansion. Chamberlain recognized with a new flood of memories that also nearby was the First Division's old campground from September of 1862, when the newly mustered Twentieth Maine had first joined the Army of the Potomac. As the corps reached the crest of the heights, fog obscured the view; it soon disappeared in the bright sunlight, revealing the wide, silvery Potomac below and the city of Washington lying splendidly beyond. Although he had seen the magnificent sight before, one Maine private thought he knew the feelings of the Crusaders as they stood on the hills above Jerusalem and "for the first time obtained a view of the holy city."[51]

In the next few weeks, however, much would have to be accomplished. The war was virtually over, and the government did not want the expense of keeping men under arms any longer than necessary. General Sherman came to the city with several corps of his men, and final grand reviews were scheduled for both armies. Energies formerly used in the planning, logistics, and carrying on of war were now employed in preparing for the reviews and attending to the myriad of details and paperwork required for the mustering out and transportation of hundreds of thousands of men. A multitude of clerks labored under the shelter of giant hospital tents. Chamberlain's division had grown to number 10,000 men, but there was plenty of everything—tents, equipment, food, and long-forgotten niceties that made the men happy as they busied themselves making elaborate camps. Some received passes and visited the points of interest in Washington and the surrounding countryside. Blooming peach trees, colorful flowers, and green grass in fields nearby lifted all spirits as the pleasant days passed.[52]

For Chamberlain and the other officers there was also some time for socializing and entertaining visitors to the camps. Lonely and homesick after the cessation of hostilities, Chamberlain was glad to see his father-in-law, who came by train to Washington a few days after the arrival of the army. Dr. Adams, by his own appraisal, was relaxed and had less tendency to worry and fret than in the past. After giving him news of Fannie and the children, Dr. Adams pressed Chamberlain eagerly for details of his experiences of the past weeks. They crossed Long Bridge and arrived at Chamberlain's headquarters tent, where the good pastor was greatly impressed with his son-in-law's large staff, which now included Capt. Tom Chamberlain and Lt. Col. Ellis Spear. Staying in a house nearby, he occupied himself sight-seeing and talking with the many high-ranking officers in the camps.[53]

On Saturday, May 20, Chamberlain went into Washington to see Sheridan on behalf of General Griffin, who was afraid that he might be displaced as commander of the corps. Dr. Adams was told that General Meade was hostile to Griffin because of Griffin's "habit of severe criticism." When Chamberlain returned, Dr. Adams's concern turned to pride when he learned that not only had "Sheridan seemed delighted to see a Fifth Corps man," and "that Griffin would not be disturbed," but that Chamberlain had also seen General Grant.[54]

The next day they attended Sunday church with Colonel Spear and General Gregory, and Dr. Adams noted with satisfaction that the chapel was full. Monday was the day before the scheduled grand review of the Army of the Potomac, and Chamberlain was constantly busy, going here and there, signing passes, listening to complaints, and approving paperwork. In addition, he was overseeing arrangements for a large ceremony planned for that night to honor General Griffin. Dr. W. R. DeWitt, the First Division's chief surgeon, commented to Dr. Adams that he had never seen a man who would continue to work as Chamberlain did when he had been really unable to move.[55]

That evening First Division officers with their invited guests gathered for a ceremony and farewell party to show their high regard for their corps commander. Hundreds gathered under the spacious cloth of four hospital tents put together; bugles rang out "The Retreat," followed by the far away booms of the sunset gun. For presentation to General Griffin, Chamberlain had designed, and Tiffany's in New York had fashioned, a pin in enameled gold of a red Maltese cross against a white ground, a miniature of the division flag. The cross was outlined in diamonds, with a center diamond that cost, it was said, $1,000.[56]

Chosen by his fellow officers to make the presentation speech, Chamberlain carried out this duty with his customary eloquence. Griffin, in short answering acceptance, spoke in tribute to the valor of his officers and gratitude for the honor they paid him. Chamberlain then pinned the badge to his commander's uniform, and Griffin, nearly overcome with emotion, silently bowed to the assemblage.[57]

After the applause began, men turned to each other with tears in their eyes and clasped hands; shouts and cheers rang out then until the band played "Hail to the Chief," and all gathered around Griffin. The sentimental "Auld Lang Syne," sung by the entire company, ended the evening. As the ceremonial party broke into small groups and drifted away in the peaceful night, light shone through thousands of tents on the hills above the Potomac, where the corps of two armies were gathered, waiting, for the first of the grand reviews to take place on the morrow.[58]

There was not much sleep for anyone. Reveille was at two o'clock on the morning of May 23, 1865, and the Fifth Corps left camp to cross Long Bridge from Arlington Heights to Washington at four o'clock. The Ninth Corps, with a division of the Nineteenth, the cavalry, and some smaller, specialized units that were to precede them in the order of march, crossed before the Fifth, and the Second Corps brought up the rear behind them. The Sixth Corps had not yet returned to the capital, and that fighting organization had to miss being part of the great spectacle on that day. Morning dawned clear, bright, and softly warm as the Fifth Corps crossed the bridge to the city. Rain had settled the dust in the capital, making the Washington streets pleasant and the air clear and invigorating.[59]

Since the return of the army, the worn uniforms of men and officers alike had been replenished, and much thought given to appearances for the grand review. Some soldiers in other divisions may have dressed more gaudily—indeed, other hardy veterans were resplendent—but the standard in Chamberlain's division was to be the same as for regular field inspection: dress and equipment clean, with bright brasses and muskets. Officers would not wear sashes or epaulets; service uniforms with shoulder straps, belts, plain scabbards, boots, and spurs would be the rule. Horses would have only simple saddles and trappings.[60]

Chamberlain wondered humorously if the manner in which his soldiers turned away from such finery might demonstrate "a scornful pride more sinful than that of vanity." After all, sometimes splendid dress reflected a personal worth that had been tested in battle. And they could not appear to be proud of their humility! "Perhaps we thought we could not look equal to what we deemed our worth and our reputation," he reflected, acknowledging no real way out of this minor moral dilemma; "so we resolved to do nothing for show, but to look just what we were, and be judged by what we wore, letting our plainness tell its own story."[61]

After passing the south end of the Capitol, the Fifth Corps divisions arrived at their staging area about six o'clock, and waited several hours until it was time to move out on parade. The black mourning crepe for Lincoln's death was gone from the city, and the flag above the White House flew at the top of its staff for the first time since that terrible day the month before. The Capitol, now finished, was hung with flags, and other pennants with mottoes decorated it, too. "The only debt we can never repay; what we owe to our gallant defenders," proclaimed one of the banners grandly. Schoolchildren waving little American flags came to fill the staging erected on the north side of the Capitol, the girls all dressed in white and poised with quantities of flowers to toss at the passing heroes. Singing patriotic songs, they delighted passersby. All along Pennsylvania Avenue from the Capitol to the White House, spectator stands decorated with the national colors, banners, and streamers lined the route, and by the time the parade began, they were thronged with thousands of enthusiastic men, women, and children.[62]

Washington was packed with visitors—never had there been so many—and housing was so scarce that some had to sleep in the parks. Every window and balcony and rooftop of the buildings lining the broad avenue were filled with people, the women in colorful dresses, waving handkerchiefs and flags. Dr. Adams, who had been given a ride into the city in a wagon filled with ladies who were guests of General Gregory, took his seat in the Fifth Corps stand. A ticket from his son-in-law gained him admission to this choice location.[63]

At nine o'clock the signal gun sounded to begin the last review of the Army of the Potomac. President Andrew Johnson, General Grant, Secretary Stanton, General William T. Sherman, and other dignitaries were assembled in the president's covered reviewing stand, where some high-ranking officers would join them after they saluted and passed the stand. Leading the 80,000 fighting men who would march this day was General Meade with his staff, the old victor at Gettysburg receiving his rightful honors after the humiliations of the last campaign.[64]

"It is the Army of the Potomac. After years of tragic history and dear-bought glories, gathering again on the banks of the river from which it took its departure and its name; an army yet the same in name, in form, in spirit, but the deep changes in its material elements telling its unspeakable vicissitudes; having kept the faith, having fought the good fight, now standing up to receive its benediction and dismissal, and bid farewell to comradeship so strangely dear."[65]

The cavalry came next, colorful with horses' hoofs clattering, sabers flashing, and bugle calls renting the air, taking an hour to pass. Gen. Wesley Merritt was at its head, with the flamboyant Gen. George A. Custer pleasing the crowd. To the disappointment of many spectators, Sheridan was not to be seen in all this glory. He had left three days before for official duties in Texas, but one general in the Army of the Potomac was sure

Sheridan's absence was caused by his unwillingness to appear under his ranking officer, George Gordon Meade.[66]

Now the Engineer Corps passed, accompanied by lumbering pontoons on their wheeled conveyances. Chamberlain remembered the many times he and his men had crossed rivers on swaying bridges made from the ungainly wooden boats: at Fredericksburg, ducking under the hot breath of the swishing cannon shot; on the retreat from Chancellorsville, nearly losing footing and life in the dark night; at the North Anna; and over the Potomac at several crossings. He mused:

"And where are the brave young feet that pressed your well-laid plank at Germanna and Ely's Ford of the Rapidan on that bright morning a summer ago? To what shores led that bridge?"[67]

Following the engineers was the Ninth Corps, together with a division of the Nineteenth, their ranks containing many valiant Mainers and some Bowdoin men. Then it was the turn of the Fifth Corps. Surrounded by his staff, Gen. Charles Griffin quickly mounted his horse and sat it easily. Chamberlain watched his friend and commander's familiar figure, "straight and slender, chin advanced, eyes to the front, pictured against the sky!" Not yet forty, Griffin would live little beyond the end of the war before disease struck him down where bullets could not.[68]

Chamberlain's division bugle sounded. As commander of its First Division, he had the honor of leading the advance of the Fifth Corps, at close interval behind his corps commander. His staff accompanied him, including Colonel Spear and Tom Chamberlain, "my brave young brother." Nearby, Chamberlain's color-bearer held proudly aloft the rectangular, white flag of the First Division of the Fifth Corps, its centered Maltese cross glowing blood red in the morning sun. Then the column moved, intervals between regiments, brigades, and divisions shortened, company fronts an equal twenty files each, across wide Pennsylvania Avenue. With rifles at right shoulder arms, the veterans of many a fiery field swung in route step up the thoroughfare.

"My division that left Appomattox five thousand strong now mustered twice that number. The ranks stood full—what there were of the living—for one more march together, one last look and long farewell."[69]

Thundering waves of sound hit the marchers and riders as the crowds roared their welcome to the returning heroes. Flags, banners, flowers, and costumes swirled everywhere in bright, drenching color. When a tattered and torn regimental color would precede a regiment, loud applause welcomed its followers. Throngs of people pressed close to the striding soldiers, at times almost impeding their way. Chamberlain sat straight on the chestnut-colored Charlemagne, his sword upraised in his right hand as he received the plaudits of the multitude. The pair surely made a fine sight: the handsome, gallant Chamberlain astride his mount, stars gleaming from the shoulder straps of his general officer's uniform and sunlight sparkling in his war-horse's dark-hued mane and tail.[70]

Suddenly a young woman dressed in white moved quickly toward them with the purpose of giving Chamberlain a braided garland of flowers, "fit for viking's armring or victor's crown." Charlemagne had never been so close to a woman before, and the startled horse reared, his master struggling with his bridle arm to control the animal. As the horse's front hoofs came back down, close to the girl but not injuring her, Chamberlain bowed so low he could almost touch the young woman's cheek, his sword point near her feet. "Was it the garland's breath or hers that floated to my lips?" Chamberlain asked himself. Only his distrust of the wildly trembling horse held back his impulse to find out! "I might have solved the mystery could I have trusted him," he recounted with some amused regret later, adding, "From that time my horse was shy of girls . . . I dare say for his master's peace and safety!" The moment passed quickly as Chamberlain righted Charlemagne and rode on; one of his dashing young aides following gladly took the fragrant blossoms for himself.[71]

The tumult and cheers and flowers swirled around Chamberlain and his men as they continued up the avenue, General Griffin on ahead triumphantly leading the Fifth Corps. Bands played popular songs—"When Johnny Comes Marching Home," "Tramp! Tramp! Tramp!," and "When This Cruel War Is Over"—with the crowd singing the choruses.

"At the rise of ground near the Treasury a backward glance takes in the mighty spectacle: the broad Avenue for more than a mile solid full, and more, from wall to wall, from door to roof, with straining forms and outwelling hearts. In the midst, on-pressing that darker stream, with arms and colors resplendent in the noon-day sun, an army of tested manhood, clothed with power, crowned with glory, marching to its dissolution!"[72]

The avenue turned again at the State Department building, and the procession took a "guide left." Now the bugle warned of the impending review, the bands changed the beat, and the men began the cadence march, their rifles at the shoulder arms, the ceremonial "carry." Lines straightened, company fronts took perfect dress: ahead was the president, who was the reviewing officer, with Lieutenant General Grant, General Sherman, ambassadors, governors, judges—so many high-ranking officers and officials it was impossible to count. The balconies of the public offices and fine residences were filled with women waving handkerchiefs, some of whom, Chamberlain fancied, strained to look for some beloved face.[73]

In one of the stands sat a hero who was not receiving the plaudits of his adoring countrymen that day, but he was noticed just the same. Many spectators could not help looking toward Maj. Gen. Gouverneur K. Warren on the sidelines as the men of the Fifth Corps approached his place. Warren was "seen, recognized, and uproariously cheered by the men of the Fifth as they marched by," a newspaper reporter wrote. "The affection and admiration of those cheers were unmistakable, whatever may have been thought of the infraction of military discipline which was thus committed."[74]

Finally the corps neared the patriotically decorated reviewing stand; the culmination of this day and many others was at hand for Chamberlain and his men. For this review, drums were to ruffle and colors dip, but only mounted officers were to salute the chief reviewing officer. President Johnson stood leaning forward in recognition, and for a fleeting moment Chamberlain remembered and missed the tall, thin form and "deep sad eyes" of that other president who on so many other occasions, in less auspicious times, reviewed this army. Wheeling Charlemagne, Chamberlain saluted with his sword and, with light spur and touching rein, brought his war-horse's head and scarred neck to share the gesture.[75]

On the sidewalk a few yards away, a man in civilian dress watched with pride as Chamberlain saluted the president. He had stood for hours at that spot and had recognized many Bowdoin men passing with their various regiments. But there was only one who excited his admiration enough to mention later by name in his account of the marvelous review in a letter printed in his hometown newspaper: "The cheers for Gen. Chamberlain, who looked finely, were very marked."[76]

After riding past the reviewing stand, at the invitation of the president Chamberlain dismounted and joined the dignitaries there. As he made his way to the front of the stand to take his place and watch the rest of the parade, he could hear excited and admiring remarks as his men marched by. "This is Porter's old Division!" "This is the Fifth Corps!" "These are straight from Five Forks and Appomattox!" The review of the soldiers of the great First Division of the Fifth Corps would be an emotion-charged experience of the highest order for their commander.[77]

"For me, while this division was passing, no other thing could lure my eyes away, whether looking on or through. These were my men, and those who followed were familiar and dear. They belonged to me, and I to them, by bonds birth cannot create nor death sever. More were passing here than the personages on the stand could see. But to me so seeing, what a review, how great, how far, how near! It was as the morning of the resurrection!"[78]

Leading the division was his old Third Brigade, which Chamberlain had given the advance, the place of honor. Brevet Brigadier General Pearson commanded it today; the brigade flag—the familiar white triangle bordered in blue with the red Maltese cross in its center—dipped as the mounted officers of the brigade saluted the reviewing officer. These ranks contained the dear old Twentieth Maine, which still included men of the old Second Maine. Memories of Antietam, Fredericksburg, Chancellorsville, and Gettysburg filled Chamberlain's mind as he proudly watched this regiment pass. In swift succession came the 118th, Eighty-third, and 155th Pennsylvania; then the Sixteenth Michigan and Thirty-second Massachusetts passed quickly by. In his mystic and perhaps truer vision, Chamberlain saw marching with the living the fallen of Gettysburg, the Wilderness, Spotsylvania, Cold Harbor, and beyond.[79]

The shades of the indomitable men he had known well as young colonels—Strong Vincent, James C. Rice, and Norval E. Welch—rode silently by in Chamberlain's illusionary view. Vincent's soul had been taken up at Gettysburg, Chamberlain imagined later, "in a chariot of fire," and brave, exuberant Rice was gone in the terrible battle at Spotsylvania Court House with his face still turned to the enemy. Welch, leading his Sixteenth Michigan in a charge up and over the parapet of works at Peebles farm near Petersburg in the bloody autumn of 1864, died sword in hand on the battlements. They were accompanied in phantomlike procession by other fallen colonels, companions of the winter officers' school at Fredericksburg—Winthrop, O'Rorke, Jeffords, Cross, and the brave Prescott, who died near Chamberlain in the field hospital at Petersburg.[80]

General Gregory and his three New York regiments, veterans of the last campaign, followed with the Second Brigade of the division. Chamberlain thought not only of them but of the other, earlier Empire State regiments that had fought so illustriously to bring about the triumphant victory, especially the Forty-fourth New York. Bringing up the rear of the First Division under the white, three-sided brigade flag with its red Fifth Corps insignia were the 185th New York and 198th Pennsylvania, Chamberlain's old First Brigade. Colonel Sniper still commanded the New York regiment, but the 198th Pennsylvania was bereft of field officers. Gone from it in body but not in spirit were its brave majors, Maceuen and Glenn, killed on the Quaker Road and at Five Forks; General Sickel was still recovering from his shattering wound. And gone too were scores of the brave men, dead and severely wounded, that he led to battle on those March and April days. But Chamberlain remembered them all.[81]

"Each of these brigades had been severally in my command; and now they were mine all together, as I was theirs. So has passed this First Division,—and with it, part of my soul."[82]

With his Second Division flag proudly aloft, its dark blue background setting off the white Maltese cross in the center, the hard-fighting Gen. Romeyn Ayres, adopted son of Maine and career army man, rode at the head of his soldiers. As his veteran Maryland, Delaware, and New York brigades came by, only two regiments, the 140th and 146th New York, represented the soldierly Ayres's three brigades that fought on that second July day at Gettysburg not far from Chamberlain's own embattled band.[83]

Then came Gen. Samuel Crawford and his Third Division, which contained regiments from the storied First Corps, melded into the Fifth before the Wilderness. Their rectangular, white division flag had a blue Maltese cross, the color of drifting battle smoke. Survivors of the valorous Iron Brigade paraded by, few in numbers now. Chamberlain's eyes rested on one of that brigade's bravest—Lt. Col. Hollon Richardson, riding at the head of the Seventh Wisconsin. Richardson had recovered from his wound received on that sunset field at Five Forks, saving the reckless Warren, who was leading a charge for the last time.[84]

Near the rear of the Third Division, Chamberlain caught sight of the men who had charged with him into that valley of death at Petersburg. But only two regiments of the original six remained to receive the applause of their countrymen and witness the pride of their former commander: the 121st and 142d Pennsylvania Volunteers. Chamberlain broke the courtesies of the occasion; without apology and before the president, he proudly saluted his companions of that day, remembering the final surge, from that crest named "'Fort Hell,' down past the spewing dragons of 'Fort Damnation' into the miry, fiery pit before Rives' Salient of the dark June 18."[85]

Bringing up the rear of the Fifth Corps were seven of the batteries that had belched fury and death with it in fierce battle. Gen. Charles S. Wainwright, head held high and saber drawn, preceded his men, handpicked for their soldierly appearance. Cannoneers rode on now-empty ammunition chests, their cannon and brasses gleaming from much polishing, horses rubbed to a sheen and accoutred with hand-blackened harness. Chamberlain noticed especially those batteries with which he had shared fierce fighting. He recognized Battery D, Fifth United States, the fire of which had let all know at Gettysburg that Little Round Top was still in the hands of the Union. Hart's New York Battery, which had blazed over the heads of his men at Rives's Salient was there, but he missed the presence of Capt. John Bigelow and his Ninth Massachusetts, whose men had recovered his broken body from that blood-soaked ground. Battery B, Fourth United States, with the Napoleons Chamberlain had last seen smoking on the Quaker Road, was led by its old commander, James Stewart, instead of the wounded John Mitchell.[86]

Chamberlain stayed to see the Second Corps march that day, too, and watched Sherman's western army parade on the next. In June he would admire the Sixth Corps review. Many years later, alone and lonely, he wrote an account of the last grand review of his army; it is plain to see in its poignant words that no other body of men could compare for him with his magnificent Fifth Corps. So many of its laughing young officers and men would be gone by then—some to honored graves during the war, others since. After more than four decades, they again marched by in Chamberlain's memory, dreamlike and yet alive, and the past, the present, and the shadowy beyond seemed to come together as he questioned:

"Have they all passed,—the Fifth Corps? Or will it ever pass? Am I left alone, or still with you all?"[87]

A pleasant month followed the review, marked by dinners, entertainments, and sightseeing in the city of Washington for both officers and men, as the work of mustering out the regiments went on apace. Near the end of May, Col. Charles Gilmore, who had been absent from the Twentieth Maine most of the war and led it into battle only once, resigned after a talk with Chamberlain, and the long-deserving Ellis Spear was commissioned the last colonel of the regiment. On June 5 most of the officers were discharged, and the men of the Twentieth whose enlistments were up before October were mustered out. Spear sent them home to the Pine Tree State under the command of Lt. Col. Walter G. Morrill. At last, their numbers greatly thinned, what was left of the original band who had left Maine for the "seat of war" nearly three years before joyfully returned by rail and boat to their homes and families. The war was truly over for them, but their lives and their country were unalterably changed.[88]

Fannie's usual propensity to write infrequently did not help Chamberlain's homesickness, but he had plenty of work to do. His promotion to full major general had been endorsed by Generals Meade and Grant but still languished in the War Department that June. Chamberlain privately thought that anyone else with half his record or high recommendations would certainly get the appointment, but since the "political gentlemen of Maine" showed no special interest in him, he was not optimistic. Apparently somewhat discouraged by the politics of the military promotional process, he began to think that he was better known in New York or Pennsylvania than in Maine.[89]

His brevet for major general had needed no political assistance, and since he had been recommended because of his performance in several battles, Chamberlain later made efforts to see that the brevet he really wanted, for valor on the Quaker Road, was confirmed by Congress. Although his wounds still troubled him, for the time being, at least, he planned to stay with the army, and trusted Providence to "both open and guide" his way in the future.[90]

On July 1 Chamberlain received an order that moved him deeply, although it was expected. Dated June 28, 1865, it declared that the great Army of the Potomac, as an organization, "ceases to exist." Chamberlain thought rhetorically, "Ceases to exist! Are you sure of that?"

"The splendor of devotion, glowing like a bright spirit over those dark waters and misty plains assures us of something that cannot die! . . . The War Department and the President may cease to give the army orders, may disperse its visible elements, but cannot extinguish them. . . . This army will live, and live on, so long as soul shall answer soul, so long as that flag watches with its stars over fields of mighty memory, so long as in its red lines a regenerated people reads the charter of its birthright, and in its field of white God's covenant with man."[91]

The Army of the Potomac was disbanded, but because he was chosen as a brigade commander in the new Provisional Corps, Chamberlain remained in camp. It was whispered confidentially that the provisionals were selected to go with Sheridan to Mexico to help the French get their army out of that country, but international events made their mission unnecessary, and the new corps was short-lived.[92]

Upon the disbandment of the Provisional Corps in the middle of July, the remainder of the Twentieth Maine was finally mustered out of the United States Army. Col. Ellis Spear, with his newly commissioned lieutenant colonel, Thomas D. Chamberlain, accompanied the regiment home. Tom, according to Spear, had risen "by force of his own character from the ranks, and filled a variety of difficult positions with marked ability and success." Colonel Spear also thought that no other officer of Tom's rank had given service more valuable to the government. Spear was closely associated with Tom throughout the war, and he was a precise man not given to idle compliments; Tom seemed to have a bright future ahead of him.[93]

Chamberlain came home to Brunswick later that month too, brown and fit-looking, but he had applied for relief from duty to have his wounds surgically treated again. He arrived in time for Bowdoin's commencement, scheduled for August 2 that year. A feature of the occasion was to be a gala reunion of surviving graduates who had been in the war, for which hundreds of them were expected to return. When Chamberlain learned that General Grant was to be in the city of Portland at the same time, he invited his former commander to attend.[94]

News of Grant's acceptance caused much excitement in Brunswick, for the general was the idol of the nation at the time. Upon his arrival by train, he and his wife, accompanied by a crowd of well-wishers, proceeded immediately to the Chamberlain house, where the two comrades in arms warmly greeted each other and exchanged amenities. During his visit Grant was considered the guest of Chamberlain, a deserved recognition for the hometown hero, and certainly a happy and exciting time for Fannie.[95]

At commencement ceremonies, the college conferred an honorary doctorate on the modest leader of the Union armies, and afterward a large dinner was held, attended by many prominent dignitaries and the homecoming military graduates. Dr. Adams offered prayer, and Chamberlain, Gen. O. O. Howard, and others made speeches. Throughout the affair, the guest of honor was agreeable to all, affably laughed at the jokes, and acknowledged the cheers and applause. However, when urged to say a few words himself, Grant smilingly bowed and shook his head. Popular with the ladies, Grant was completely surrounded later by a bevy of crinoline-clad figures at President Woods's levee. A great military reception held in the evening filled the flag- and bunting-draped First Parish Church to overflowing; one citizen reported that it occasioned "the greatest jam I ever saw in this place."[96]

When the memorable day was over and the guests had departed, Chamberlain could finally draw near to his family; Fannie and the children could enjoy the presence of their dear husband and "Papa," as Daisy and Wyllys called him. More gray streaked his hair than when he had left Brunswick three years before, and his blue eyes sometimes seemed to mirror the memories of far away battlefields. But only a few days of happiness remained before a heart-wrenching event cast a new shadow over the lives of the reunited family, and in quick succession another blow would fall. After a short sickness Gertrude Loraine, the youngest and last child of Joshua and Fannie Chamberlain, died at the age of seven months, and Dr. Adams conducted the funeral for another baby granddaughter. Several days later, Chamberlain was notified that he had been mustered out of the army with the first group of generals, while he still needed surgery for his Petersburg wounds.[97]

With his health and future uncertain, Chamberlain resumed his professorship at the college, again in rhetoric and oratory, but apparently was not able to fulfill a complete schedule of his duties. Thanksgiving that year was celebrated as usual with Dr. Adams's family, and the holiday happened to fall on the Chamberlain's tenth wedding anniversary. Chamberlain's gift to Fannie was a beautiful enameled gold and diamond bracelet engraved with her name and their anniversary date, which he had personally designed and had fashioned by Tiffany jewelers in New York. Its design incorporated Chamberlain's rank and war service and, reflecting the custom of the time, symbolized the link of those accomplishments to Fannie and his devotion to her. Fannie, who apparently enjoyed being the wife of a general and war hero, prized it and liked showing it to friends. The ten years of their marriage had been filled with changes and events that would have filled ordinary lifetimes, but their love still burned strong.[98]

That autumn Chamberlain met Governor Samuel Cony, and the governor, who held the young general in high esteem, inquired enough to learn about his condition. Unknown to Chamberlain, Cony wrote to Senator Lot Morrill about Chamberlain's situation, with the hope that the government could see him through his difficulties. The letter prompted action by Maine's congressional delegation. By December both senators and most of

Frances Caroline Adams Chamberlain, 1865
(courtesy Bowdoin College, Hawthorne-Longfellow Library, Special Collections, Joshua L. Chamberlain Collection)

the representatives from the state had petitioned the president to restore Chamberlain to army service. Chamberlain's discharge with surgery on his wounds pending and consequent inability to return fully to civilian life had been contrary to military policy. The secretary of war required General Grant's approval, which the lieutenant general gave with pleasure, and Chamberlain's rank was restored, his former muster-out date revoked, and he was mustered out effective January 15, 1866.[99]

The brief army career of Joshua Lawrence Chamberlain ended quietly, without fanfare, although he was considered the "beau ideal" of a soldier and would be described rightly as "one of the most remarkable officers in the history of the United States." He commanded troops in twenty-four battles, eight reconnaissances, and countless skirmishes. He was wounded "by shot or shell" six times, and soldiers under his command captured 2,700 prisoners and eight battle flags in the nation's most tragic war. With his intelligence, education, and character, he epitomized the best of America's citizen soldiers, a volunteer standing with millions of other volunteers risking all for their country's cause.[100]

From listening to the first chapters of *Uncle Tom's Cabin* in Mrs. Stowe's parlor to presiding over the surrender ceremony of the South's finest army, Chamberlain was a witness to a beginning and an ending of his country's greatest struggle. Distinguishing himself in battle, he transcended death to become a true hero in the romantic and classical tradition that stretches back through chivalric times to epic deeds of ancient warriors. The American Union was saved, and the institution of slavery no longer darkened the luster of its shining ideals, but the great travail brought forth new challenges to a reborn nation. Still confidently placing the welfare of himself and his family in the hands of Providence, Joshua Lawrence Chamberlain, like his beloved country, faced a future shadowed by the continuing pain of terrible wounds, slow, if ever, to heal.[101]

CHAPTER

Eleven

AND OTHER SONGS IN OTHER KEYS

As the country struggled with economic and social postwar problems in the new year 1866, Joshua Chamberlain was restless and recurrently depressed after his final discharge from the army. In addition to his teaching, he spent the late winter and spring speaking around the state about his war experiences, and he intended to write a history of the old Fifth Corps. It became increasingly clear that a college professorship was too confining and narrow a role for him now, but no acceptable alternative appeared. Then it occurred to some Republican party leaders that an educated, well-known, wounded war hero of proven leadership ability and spotless reputation would be attractive to the electorate, and he was approached to head the state ticket as candidate for governor of Maine in the fall election.[1]

At first Chamberlain considered the prospect reluctantly, but the field of politics certainly offered a greater scope for his talents, and at the time Maine elected its governors for only one-year terms. His mother, who had been a little worried about her oldest son, was gratified to hear of it but cautioned in her usual manner that she would not have him "yield your conscientious convictions of *right* to gain any position earth can give." Finally, he decided to take the risk of entering the political arena. Although he did not attend the party convention in Bangor that June, he allowed his name to be placed in nomination for governor and accepted when he was chosen by the delegates as their candidate.[2]

The month after the Republican convention, Dr. Leonard Woods, the president of Bowdoin College who had almost suspended Chamberlain as a student fifteen years before, resigned his office. Still a member of the faculty, Chamberlain agreed to serve temporarily as the college's acting president, his prior political obligation surely preventing him from being a candidate for the position permanently. Another opportunity came too late for Chamberlain's serious consideration in August, when he received a note from Gouverneur K. Warren, now a lieutenant colonel in the Regular Army. On being solicited to make recommendations to General Grant for field officers of new army regiments, Warren had placed Chamberlain at the top of the list. Warren knew that his former subordinate was not likely to accept, but he left it to Chamberlain to write to General Grant and let him know his decision.[3]

After the Republican and Democratic state conventions, debates on the issues were held that summer in Augusta, Bangor, and Portland. James G. Blaine, the powerful Maine congressman and rising star of the House of Representatives, home during congressional adjournment, usually spoke for the Republicans. The main issue of the national campaign became the approval of the Fourteenth Amendment to the United States Constitution, a compromise between radicals and moderates passed that summer by the Republican Congress over the objections of President Johnson. Besides the usual congressional seats to be filled, the voters would choose many of the state legislators who would vote on its ratification.[4]

In the summer and fall of 1865 most of the former Confederate states had reestablished state governments under lenient conditions set by the president. While all but one, at Johnson's insistence, had ratified the Thirteenth Amendment to the Constitution abolishing slavery, many states also enacted repressive new laws governing race relations. These "black codes" were designed to provide control of the black labor force and ensure white supremacy; in states that provided for public schools, no provision was made for black children. Many citizens concerned with the fate of the freedmen were convinced that under these new laws, blacks would be placed in a condition very near to slavery.[5]

When the Thirty-ninth Congress had convened in December 1865, the presidentially reconstructed states sent their chosen representatives to be admitted. Included were former high-ranking Confederate leaders, asking to be seated and take their places in the affairs of the nation as if nothing had happened. Besides residual war rancor, issues such as confiscation of abandoned lands and the Federal administration of black labor, education, and provision for the welfare of the former slaves caused hostility for the Union throughout the white South. Race hatred and violence were widespread. The House of Representatives categorically refused to seat any representative from the seceded states and with the Senate convened a Joint Committee on Reconstruction to investigate whether any of them were entitled to seats in Congress.[6]

Congressional hearings were held on the social and political conditions in the South, and impassioned debates ensued. The Joint Committee report declared the Southern states not ready for the readmission of their representatives to either house, and relations between Congress and the president rapidly deteriorated. The extent of popular interest in these issues in the North is exemplified by Chamberlain's mother, who for the first time had taken an interest in "politics" and had read all the political speeches that came her way. She agreed with Congress rather than President Johnson and was afraid that the freed slaves "now must suffer unless they are protected from the rage or violence of their former masters and put in the right way of taking care of themselves."[7]

Two of the major results of the congressional debates were the passage of the Civil Rights Act of 1866, over Johnson's veto, and passage of the Fourteenth Amendment to the Constitution of the United States. This revolutionary amendment, with other important provisions, defined American citizenship for the first time and included former slaves, guaranteed the right to due process and equality under the law for all citizens, changed the basis of apportionment for state representation in the House of Representatives, and provided penalties to states for refusing suffrage to otherwise eligible males because of race or color. Some former Confederate officers and officeholders were excluded from holding state or Federal office unless approved by a two-thirds vote of Congress. The amendment was sent to the state legislatures for ratification in June 1866, just five days before the Maine state convention that nominated Chamberlain for governor. Three states immediately ratified the measure before Congress adjourned, and the timing allowed its provisions to be weighed and discussed by the people before the fall elections.[8]

In September of 1866 Chamberlain was elected governor of Maine by the largest majority in the state's history. Since voting in other states followed Maine's early balloting, after his election he took an active part in at least one national veterans' convention to build support for the Republican party and the Fourteenth Amendment. The Republicans virtually swept the fall elections in the North. By quickly ratifying the Fourteenth Amendment, Tennessee regained its right to representation in Congress, but ten other Southern state legislatures reconstructed under presidential conditions had overwhelmingly rejected it by January. When Chamberlain gave his first address to the Maine legislature as governor of the state in January of 1867, with his usual eloquence he called upon the people's representatives to ratify the Fourteenth Amendment:[9]

"We are struck with amazement, and thrown upon our guard when we see those who with scorn and contumely spurned the Constitution, and defied the Government, and sought with violence and cruelty to destroy the Union, now demanding, with equal effrontery and the same spirit of violence, without an apology for the past, without a guaranty for the future, the unconditional restoration of their rights under the Constitution, their place in the Union and their prestige in the Government."[10]

Declaring that Congress was the rightful authority in the policies of Reconstruction, Chamberlain thought that the terms it had proposed for the South were neither "hard nor humiliating" and reflected a "magnanimity without parallel." Since Congress's first measures had been thwarted, he went on, "the duty is still before us of securing the great results which Providence, and not our own foresight, has placed in our hand, and of which the same great Power will hold us to strict account." Chamberlain believed that the consequences of the South's resort to war involved the "suspension of certain privileges, the abandonment of certain rights, the forfeiture of certain claims." New agreements had to be made before the old relations could be restored:

"War is not a game where there is everything to win and nothing to lose. Those who appeal to the law of force, should not complain if its decision is held as final."[11]

In the new governor's opinion, however, the wording of the Fourteenth Amendment was still deficient, "hazarding one of the very fruits of our victory by placing it in the power of the South to introduce into the Constitution a disability founded on race and color," but it was "at least a step in the right direction." Three years later, the third and last constitutional amendment enacted as a result of the Civil War also became law. The Fifteenth Amendment removed the disability Chamberlain had cited, by making it illegal for a state to deny the right to vote because of race, color, or previous condition of servitude. While Maine previously had been one of only six Northern states to allow the vote to its free black men, Chamberlain himself was more conservative when it came to allowing the vote to recently freed slaves. He opposed such an early and sweeping reform.[12]

When President Johnson was impeached by the House of Representatives in 1868, Chamberlain supported Maine's more conservative senator, William Pitt Fessenden, who voted against the president's removal from office. Chamberlain's stands on the Fifteenth Amendment and Johnson's impeachment were contrary to those of the leaders of the Republican party. Chamberlain was certainly not a practical party politician, although he remained demonstrably popular with the people, who elected him Maine's governor for four one-year terms. On his first reelection bid, his majority fell off somewhat, but in 1868, when General Grant was elected for the first time as president of the United States in a noisy, parade-filled campaign, Chamberlain garnered an even higher number of votes than his 1866 record-breaking total.[13]

Two other controversial issues, enforcement of the state liquor laws and capital punishment, confronted Chamberlain in Maine and caused him a great deal of criticism from those who felt strongly about them. He opposed the establishment of a special constabulary to enforce the prohibition laws because he thought the powers given these special police would infringe greatly the constitutional rights of Maine's citizens to be secure in their persons and homes. Because the issue was likely to come to him officially, he also refused to attend a public meeting called by temperance advocates for the purpose of influencing the legislature in the matter. The capital punishment issue arose because, although Maine law required that the governor order the execution of criminals sentenced to death by the courts, it specified no time limit in which the warrant should be issued except that it be after one year of sentence. A series of Chamberlain's predecessors had not signed death warrants, but Chamberlain considered it his duty to carry out the law.[14]

Repeatedly bringing this problem to the attention of the legislature, he recommended that the laws either be changed or enforced: "If we cannot make our practice conform to our law, to make our law agree with our practice." When the legislature subsequently voted down a bill abolishing capital punishment, Chamberlain felt that he was forced to act. He commuted two death sentences to life imprisonment, but ordered the execution of a former slave by the name of Harris, a rapist and murderer who boasted of his guilt. Chamberlain stressed that his own views on the subject did not affect "in the least" his duty to carry out the law, but he made it clear that he believed that the death penalty deterred high crimes and felt that it should be retained in the law. "Many are bitter on me about capital punishment," he wrote to his mother, "but it does not disturb me in the least." Continuing his lifelong custom, he tried "to seek wisdom and strength from above."[15]

Furious denunciations came upon Chamberlain from church groups and others. He made some lasting enemies during his tenure by turning up irregularities when the war debts to the cities and towns in Maine were settled, and he received threats against his life and personal safety. "I do not think I have a particle of fear in me of anything that walks or flies," he reassured his mother. "I go on in the strength of conscious rectitude & you can't scare me." But many citizens supported Chamberlain's position on these subjects, and he also provided strong leadership in affairs concerning veterans, war widows and orphans, education, improving jails and insane asylums, promoting industry and agriculture, reorganizing the state militia, and many other far-reaching matters beneficial to Maine.[16]

* * *

Just after Chamberlain's first election as governor, Deborah Folsom, Fannie's "Cousin D," had died in Brunswick at age sixty-nine; Dr. Adams conducted the funeral service for his former sister-in-law. A younger member of the family would also die a few months later. John Chamberlain had returned to Bangor Theological Seminary in 1863 after his brief stint with the Christian Commission and graduated the next year. He was appointed chaplain of the Eleventh Maine Infantry late in the war but declined the commission, working instead as an inspector at Internal Revenue in New York City and establishing himself in business. In April 1865 the harbinger of his fatal illness appeared as a hemorrhage from his lungs; apparently recovering, however, he married Delia F. Jarvis of Castine and Bangor the next year. But his health worsened considerably in early 1867, and on August 10, at Castine, Maine, Sarah Chamberlain's "good boy Johnny" died at the age of twenty-nine from the same pulmonary disease that had claimed Horace Chamberlain nearly six years earlier.[17]

* * *

Chamberlain believed that "war is for the participants a test of character; it makes bad men worse and good men better." Tolerant of veterans who had fought so bravely, as governor he investigated their applications for clemency and issued many pardons for those whose "extravagance of satisfaction at their safe return home carried their frolics to the extent of crime." But typical of his own lifelong inclination for thoroughness and hard work, Chamberlain gave innumerable speeches around the state and presided at many official ceremonies, although his war wounds continued to trouble him, as they would throughout his life. The old Petersburg wounds became inflamed, causing him a great deal of pain throughout his abdomen and in both hips. In late 1868 he applied for a government pension and was awarded a total disability pension of $30 a month, the disability dating from the date of his discharge.[18]

Fannie had been loving and understanding of Chamberlain's depression and restlessness when he returned from the war. Though the future was unsettled, life in Brunswick was much the same before he was nominated for governor, and she had resumed her customary travels alone. But with the pain from his wounds undoubtedly limiting the couple's conjugal relations, Fannie must have lost a great deal of what little influence a wife had in their typical Victorian marriage. She had disliked her husband's years in the army and began to care little for those when he was governor. Continuing to make their home in the familiar surroundings of Brunswick, Fannie entertained for her husband and joined him in Augusta for various events, while Chamberlain came home as he could, his days and nights filled with many demands on his time. The stresses and separations of Chamberlain's busy years as governor, with all the other problems facing them, apparently took a great toll on the Chamberlain marriage.[19]

Near the end of 1868, at a time when Chamberlain was being attacked by opponents of capital punishment and militant temperance men and his war wounds were causing him a great deal of pain, he learned that Fannie was actually contemplating filing suit for divorce. Appalled and saddened, he asked her not to bring such "wretchedness" to their families, and if she was serious, only to quietly effect a separation. He had already ignored hints from her and others that all was not well, preferring to concentrate on warning her about her choice of friends, who, he heard on good authority, spread damaging lies and gossip about their marriage. Extremely upset, he still lectured her like a young girl, saying that she perhaps did not realize the life a divorced woman might lead and that any problems she brought upon him, she would likewise bring on herself. The episode apparently blew over, and adjustments satisfactory to both were made, but the war must have taken more from the Chamberlains than was generally known.[20]

It may have been partly because of his personal concerns that Chamberlain's address to the Maine legislature just over a month later, in January 1869, made it clear that he expected his third term as governor to be his last. In the regular Federal senatorial election in January of that year, Chamberlain was mentioned in the preelection talk as the man to whom the Maine legislature could turn if the vote was deadlocked between Hannibal Hamlin and the present senator, Lot M. Morrill, an event which appeared likely. Hamlin, vice president in Lincoln's first term and a popular former senator from Maine, won out. But later that year the death of Senator William Pitt Fessenden caused another vacancy in that office, and Chamberlain appointed Morrill to fill out the remainder of the term. Friends pointed out that he could appoint another candidate who would gladly make way later for Chamberlain, but he refused to take such a self-promoting action.[21]

After being persuaded to run again for governor, however, Chamberlain was easily reelected and completed his fourth and last term of office at the end of 1870. In early September of that year, hundreds of his friends in the Bangor area signed a public invitation to a political rally to urge the election of state representatives who would champion him as senator at the next senatorial election. While there is little doubt that he would have liked to have the office and surely acquiesced in his friends' efforts in his behalf, Chamberlain was hesitant about declaring himself openly. He told one supporter that he did not "like the idea of seeming to *ask* the people for something & being denied." Morrill remained senator. Several years later Morrill resigned as senator to become a member of Grant's cabinet, with the understanding that Chamberlain would take his place. However, Maine party head James G. Blaine, who had been speaker of the United States House of Representatives and was defeated in that post after the Democrats regained their majority in the 1874 elections, was appointed instead.[22]

While governor, Chamberlain had continued his close ties with Bowdoin College and had been elected to its Board of Trustees in 1867. At the commencement of 1869 his alma mater had conferred upon him the honorary degree of doctor of laws, his second; Pennsylvania College had given him the same distinction three years earlier. Providentially, in 1871 Bowdoin's president, Samuel Harris, wearied of his heavy executive duties, especially the necessary fund-raising part, and resigned to accept a professorship in theology at Yale. Chamberlain, who was then free of his political commitments, was at once elected unanimously to the presidency by the trustees of the college, and the vote was ratified by the overseers. When the election was immediately announced to a meeting of the Alumni Committee chaired by the new president-elect, the result was greeted by great applause.[23]

With the concurrence of the governing boards of the college, Chamberlain set about making sweeping changes in the everyday life of the college and considerably broadening the curriculum. His experience as a Bowdoin student and professor brought a particular insight to the requirements of the school, and his subsequent years of leadership in the army and state gave him the confidence, presence, and prestige to help carry out his ideas. One of the first traditions to change was the assignment of class ranking and honors on the basis of both deportment and scholarship; Chamberlain determined that records of the two should be kept separate. Perhaps he remembered the earnest and conscientious young student from Brewer who wanted to be liked by his fellows at college but was not allowed even a little mischievous fun if he wanted class honors.[24]

Tuition was raised to $75, and room rent, which for fifty years had been a flat rate of $10, was now changed to reflect the desirability of the room. To make the college schedule more efficient, morning prayers were held after breakfast, with the recitations of the day immediately following; no recitations were held on Saturdays, and evening prayers were discontinued except for Sundays. Library hours were greatly lengthened to make the books more available to the student body. Commencement was to be held in June instead of August, and the long vacation shifted from winter to summer. These were marked changes, undoubtedly startling to the more conservative alumni and boards members, but their new president had even bolder plans.[25]

Chamberlain had made it a condition when he accepted the presidency that a policy of expansion be adopted for the school. He felt that to avoid obsolescence and meet the challenge of the expansive postwar era, with its burgeoning industry and business, Bowdoin had to change with the times. No longer would it do to offer only the traditional classical education that would provide a man with the foundation of habits, discipline, and knowledge to fit him for further professional studies. There was also need for a course of study in the practical sciences and engineering to attract those students who would desire to begin their careers at once upon graduation. While the idea was not new to Bowdoin, Chamberlain proposed and obtained the support of the governing boards to add a separate scientific department for studies leading to a bachelor of science degree. Additional funds would have to be raised until enough students were attracted to meet the new expenses. He was also concerned that the undergraduates were kept too much separate from the world around them and proposed that anyone who had a desire to pursue independent study be able to take advantage of the college facilities.[26]

For those who had misgivings about the effect of the new scientific advances on religious belief, Chamberlain had heartening words:

"I do not fear these men of science, for after all they are following in God's ways, and whether they see him now or not, these lines will surely lead to him at the end. Sooner or later, if not now, they will see and confess that these laws along whose line they are following, are not forces, are not principles. They are only methods. And those powers which they so triumphantly behold are not primal but transmitted powers; not creating but only reproducing. . . . I would say that Laws are God's ways seen by men, *while Principles are* God's thoughts to himself, . . . *Now the* knowledge of these Laws *I would call* Science, *and the* apprehension of Principles *I would call* Philosophy, *and our men of science may be quite right in*

their science and altogether wrong in their philosophy. . . . So I do not fear the advance of science . . . for I know that all true working and real discovery . . . can rest in no other theory than truth, and no other goal than God.

"So now I say this is a good age, and we need not quarrel with it. We must understand it, if we can. At least we must do our work in it. We must have the spirit of reverence and faith, we must balance the mind and heart with God's higher revelations, but we must also take hold of this we call science, and which makes knowledge power."[27]

Speaking personally, Chamberlain raised the issue of the possibility of some students, especially those who would be enrolled in the new courses for bachelor degrees in science, acquiring the classics in modern form rather than in the ancient tongues. And although he did not go so far as to propose that women be admitted to Bowdoin, he advocated their higher education so that they too could "rise to these high harmonies of spiritual science in which . . . true life lies." In a statement that was fairly liberal for his time, but still reflected Victorian attitudes toward women, he declared: "Women too should have part in this high calling. Because in this sphere of things her 'rights,' her capacities, her offices, her destiny, are equal to those of man. She is the Heaven, appointed teacher of man, his guide, his better soul. By her own right, however, she inherits here, not as the sister of man but as the daughter of God!"[28]

In Bowdoin's earlier days rules had been strict, students were treated as children, and the faculty acted as policemen. When forbidden mischief, which usually consisted of "robbed hen roosts, translated livestock, greased blackboards, and tormented tutors," was found out by the alert and ever-patrolling professors, they solemnly met over any infraction and then acted swiftly and severely. The resulting lack of freedom and the scent of danger in the air only seemed to encourage acts of deviltry by the undergraduates. One of Bowdoin's presidents later observed that the years between 1839 and 1866, when President Woods's leniency somewhat offset the strict and paternalistic behavior of the old professors, were "the best years for boys to be boys" in the history of the college. President Harris, Chamberlain's immediate predecessor, was not as tolerant as Woods, and his four years in office were reminiscent of the old days.[29]

By the time Chamberlain became president, all the old professors were no longer active. Remembering his college experiences as student, tutor, and professor, Chamberlain dealt with the students differently. Treating them as gentlemen, he took their word of honor before the testimony of outsiders, did not let suspicion come between him and them, and would "not abandon my confidence in them until they were false to themselves." However, Chamberlain viewed untruthfulness as a heinous act, and he thought a man who would lie to him "good for nothing." Honor was a conscious watchword with Chamberlain, whose own was beyond question; he would mete out discipline firmly and fairly.[30]

But there would still be problems, and at least one graduate thought that a more boisterous and trying kind of collegian came to Bowdoin in the decade following the Civil War. Immature young men would sometimes take advantage of change and mistake more freedom for license. Disciplinary incidents, some serious, continued to plague Chamberlain's tenure as president of Bowdoin before the good effects of some of his innovations came to fruition; then there were better ways for the collegians to assert themselves and release their high spirits.[31]

"Oh my young countrymen, into whose hands we commit these sacred trusts, remember well, and do not forget, but face to the front. That flag shall be the beckoning signal for human eyes in many a good fight yet. Men will love it and die for it and glorify it on many a field to come. Great things are coming on—I know not what. Be ready. God is before us as well as behind. Nations are borne onward to their destiny. In the shock of empires, the world moves, and from the smoke and flame comes forth redeemed, regenerate man."[32]

Chamberlain believed that future wars were inevitable as America moved forward to its "appointed ends" with "new interests to guard and keep." Every generation would undoubtedly have to come to the defense of its country, he thought, and the educated and cultured men should be prepared to lead others should the nation's need arise. An episode that became known as Bowdoin's great "Drill Rebellion" made Chamberlain one of the earliest—if not the first—college presidents required to handle a student revolt against compulsory military training. Recognizing the important part played by volunteers in the Civil War, the Federal government had made an instructor and equipment available to eligible colleges to teach military science and drill, and Bowdoin took advantage of the opportunity under the urging of its president.[33]

An army major duly arrived in early 1872 as instructor, and the drill was a popular success. By June there were four infantry companies numbering nearly two hundred student privates, noncommissioned officers, and officers, many fitted out in uniforms resembling those used at West Point. With the use of four Napoleon cannon lent by the state, some students even learned artillery drill. The sudden, near-deafening sounds of the guns at special demonstrations sometimes terrified nearby horses, which promptly reared or bolted, causing confusion and dismay. Besides the fun of it all, one young man thought that the marching and handling of the rifles in the manual of arms was "splendid exercise for the body, tending to make one erect and strong and of easy carriage."[34]

As the novelty wore off, however, dissatisfaction over time spent drilling began among the upperclassmen, and in the fall of 1873, when purchase of a modest uniform at a cost of just under $6 became mandatory, great opposition developed. Letters to each trustee and overseer on the boards, signed by all students of the higher classes except one senior, five juniors, and one sophomore, asked that the drill be abolished due to its unpopularity, expense, and time taken from study. Although a committee met briefly with student representatives, no action was taken by the boards, and by spring disorders broke out at drill, including shouting, profane language, and organized moaning, groaning, and jeering by the junior class. Insulting inscriptions appeared on the chapel walls.[35]

Discipline and suspensions followed these disorders, with the result that the juniors voted never to drill again. The sophomores and freshmen eventually voted the same, and only two students turned out for the next scheduled drill. The rebellion was on. Lights burned late as Chamberlain and the faculty met, undoubtedly in surprise and consternation. The issue dragged out for several days, punctuated by student and faculty meetings, with rain preventing drill sessions that would have provoked a showdown. Finally all the underclassmen signed class statements that they would never again drill and that if any were disciplined because of it, each class would consider all of its members disciplined and act accordingly; the juniors also refused to drill. After each individual was asked to comply with the rules of the college and refused, nearly all of three classes were suspended and sent home to await the action of the faculty. Chamberlain soon sent a letter to the parents of the strikers promising that students who did not return within ten days pledging to obey all college rules and participate in the drill would be expelled.[36]

Newspapers from Maine to New York carried stories about the unusual, almost shocking goings-on at Bowdoin. Letters to the editors poured in, some antimilitary, excoriating the drill, the faculty, and the college. Others lamented the student behavior. Rumors were rife that Dartmouth College would take in the miscreants, a notion Chamberlain squelched by obtaining and publicizing a letter to the contrary from Dartmouth's president, who also supported Chamberlain's stand. In the end, all but three of the suspended students returned within the time limit, and the uproar ended. However, after intense discussions at their commencement meeting that year, the boards made the drill voluntary, and it continued with gymnasium exercise until the subject was abolished in 1882.[37]

One graduate of the class of 1875, looking back at the incident, concluded, "Of course we were wrong, and we all went back and submitted to the rules of the college, but the backbone of the drill was broken, and it died a speedy and unregretted death as a Bowdoin institution." A committee report on the responsibility for the whole affair and the handling of the emergency had criticism for all of the authorities at Bowdoin, including the president, faculty, and even the boards. About the first, the committee said, "The President of a college must deal both with Faculty and Students face to face with unswerving directness of statement, and in the manner of one doing the duties of his station, because they are duties and not because his station is superior." The habit of command Chamberlain had acquired in the army may have emerged strongly in the crisis and contributed to this observation of his performance. In the end, Chamberlain was disappointed but philosophical that military science was one of his innovations that did not turn out as he had hoped.[38]

* * *

Chamberlain had apparently been successful in his investments and business ventures during the postwar years. In May of 1871, confident of his permanent location in Brunswick, he realized an ambition to own a yacht and purchased a six-ton, twenty-six-foot sloop, which he named *Wildflower*. Now he could enjoy cruises with family and friends in coastal waters, and he often sailed to and from Portland. Sometime afterward he established a large summer home by the sea that he called Domhegan, about four miles from Brunswick at a five-acre projection of land named Simpson's Point. The place had been a favorite of the Indians because a vessel could be landed at all tides, and it had later been the site of a shipyard. Chamberlain rebuilt the wharf there for his use. In his later years, he owned a ten-ton schooner, the *Pinafore*, which was also to bring him a great deal of pleasure.[39]

In the spring of 1867 Chamberlain had moved his house a short distance

Chamberlain house, Brunswick, Maine

east to a more desirable location facing the wide main street of Brunswick, across from First Parish Church. The year before, he had considered selling it and buying the stately and spacious Upham house a few doors from Dr. Adams's home, but because of his unsettled future then, he had done nothing. At that time he had also thought of raising the whole building and constructing under it a new first floor with high ceilings, which would make the house more suitable for the entertaining Fannie and he enjoyed. Deciding against so great a change after the move, however, he contented himself with some remodeling of the house to enlarge it at its new location.[40]

When he was sure that he would remain in Brunswick, and with a $300 housing allowance in addition to his salary, in the autumn of 1871 Chamberlain went ahead with his more elaborate plan. The finished house, including a two-story ell, had twenty rooms, with the first floor providing ample space for entertaining guests and the two upper stories of the main house containing the family sitting room and bedchambers. Sae Chamberlain had lamented Fannie's lack of front stairs when the Chamberlains first bought the house and could have only been impressed at her brother's remedy to that situation. Chamberlain personally designed the grand entrance hall spanned by a Gothic arch of heavy oak and featuring a spiral staircase winding down from the second floor. At the foot of the stairs hung an elaborately framed portrait of his mother dressed in the black silk dress trimmed with Spanish lace that she had worn to her son's inauguration as governor. Heavy oak doors leading to other main rooms of the first floor, woodwork imported from England, fine stenciling near the ceiling, and a hanging brass lamp gave visitors a handsome first impression as they entered the home.[41]

Fannie eventually filled the home with fine furniture; antiques abounded, some of which had been in her family since colonial days. Paintings almost covered the walls in some rooms, including some from her own hand. One of the most valuable was a portrait of her maternal grandmother by the noted artist John Trumbull. Oriental carpets lay everywhere on the floors. In the large, formal, blue and white drawing room, the ceiling was ornately decorated. There the general's bass viol leaned against Fannie's beautiful piano, and a lute that had been in her family for generations rested nearby, all evidence of their owners' love for music. A crystal candelabra designed by Fannie reflected in a mirror above the fireplace and lighted the faces of the hundreds of guests entertained by the hospitable couple over the years.[42]

When Henry Wadsworth Longfellow returned to Bowdoin for his fiftieth anniversary class reunion, he was shown the rooms upstairs where he had brought his first wife to live as a bride. Longfellow wept and declared that the rooms looked the same as in his day; he then told the Chamberlains that he had composed several poems while gazing into the fireplace in the sitting room. The couple took great pride in their home, although Chamberlain, like many husbands, grumbled sometimes about the amount Fannie spent on its furnishings. The frame building was painted a fashionable stone beige trimmed in dark red, with the window sashes in deep green. A graceful iron fence ran along the front lawn. A garden and barn were in back, and the old martin house so prized by Chamberlain was located in the side yard. By spring of 1873 there were nearly fifty different kinds of flowers blooming from their greenhouse or conservatory, which Chamberlain described as the "wonder of the town."[43]

Chamberlain very often could be found in his comfortably furnished library, with its 2,000 books, or its attached study. Many a Bowdoin undergraduate considered it the highlight of his college career to be interviewed by President Chamberlain in one of these two rooms, and in them visitors could see the general's memorabilia from the war. In the library an American flag was suspended across the stenciled ceiling, and above the fireplace against the patterned, dark red, French wallpaper was a Twentieth Maine battle flag, folded to display the stars on its blue field of the national colors. The bugle sent to Chamberlain after the death of General Griffin hung below it, along with the sword and scabbard Chamberlain had given Griffin after he had lost his own in the last campaign of the war. A pair of crossed swords hung above the doorway. In a corner, three stacked muskets with bayonets stood on a small bookcase behind a large, white bust of General Grant. These were flanked by a smoke-stained division flag with a red Maltese cross and a Confederate battle flag—the latter captured in a "racing charge" just before Appomattox.[44]

Another Confederate flag—the one given up by the last Confederate regiment to surrender its arms and colors—was displayed in Chamberlain's smaller study where he did most of his writing in later years. Here, too, was the Colt revolver that Chamberlain took from the Confederate officer who had tried to kill him in the charge at Little Round Top. On the wall a tapestry depicted the general's old war-horse, Charlemagne, who had been sent to Brunswick after the war, became the pet of the Chamberlain children, and was later buried at Domhegan.[45]

In what must have been a severe blow for Fannie and Chamberlain, Dr. George Adams died on Christmas Day, 1875, in East Orange, New Jersey. Certain that God was calling him to new work, over six years previously Dr. Adams had resigned his ministry, over the protests of his parishioners, and moved from Brunswick. In the last summer of his life, in poor health, he had visited Brunswick after resigning his successful New Jersey pastorate. This last appearance among his old people seemed to some "like the visit of an angel," but that autumn after returning home, the old minister's health declined rapidly until his death. Beloved by generations of college boys and parishioners he had served for over forty years, Dr. Adams was buried in Brunswick as members of his old congregation had asked. His funeral service was held in the black-draped interior of First Parish Church, with his wife Helen and his two young daughters among the many mourners. Seven years later, Chamberlain gave the church its first and largest memorial stained-glass window in memory of his father-in-law. The beautiful window, designed under Chamberlain's personal attention, was installed centrally, behind the pulpit.[46]

* * *

The year 1876 marked the one hundredth anniversary of the independence of the United States, and a great international exhibition in celebration of that milestone was held at Philadelphia, the city where the bells had first rung out proclaiming the new nation. Chosen by Maine's governor to give an oration there in honor of his native state, Chamberlain responded that November with a well-received, elaborate oration titled "Maine, Her Place in History." The centennial year also saw a disputed presidential election that plunged the nation into crisis. A hard-wrought political compromise early in 1877, which counted the electoral votes in three Southern states in favor of the Republican Rutherford B. Hayes, presaged the end of Reconstruction in the South.[47]

By the time Chamberlain left office as Maine's governor, all of the former Confederate states had been reconstructed, ten under strict rules set by Congress. They all had ratified the Fourteenth Amendment, and their representatives were readmitted to Congress. As the years went on, many people in the North began to weary of the unending economic and racial problems of the South. Some of the great radical congressional leaders who had championed the cause of the freedmen were gone, and the nation had other matters to engage its attention: the Panic of 1873 plunged the country into a lasting economic depression, and scandals rocked Grant's administration. In 1872 Congress voted amnesty to most of those Confederates barred from public office under the terms of the Fourteenth Amendment, which helped to allow the leadership of the old antebellum Democratic party to be reestablished in the Southern states.[48]

A decreasing army presence could not provide enough protection for honest elections in the South. Violence and the deaths of hundreds in state after state were common over the years in what were ultimately successful attempts to keep the former slaves, who virtually all voted Republican, and their sparse white allies from voting. Hayes's "Southern policy," reportedly the price he paid for his election victory, subsequently removed almost all of the remaining Federal troops from the South, and the return of political control there to white state and local officials was complete. The Union was indeed united again, regardless of the fate of the freedmen, who were abandoned to the rule of their former masters.[49]

In a lecture given in Boston a year later, Chamberlain's defense of the

Joshua L. Chamberlain, ca. 1875 (National Archives)

status quo demonstrated that some of his attitudes also had changed since the war and offered some surprising insights into his thinking. Lauding the end of slavery and the power of the people over that of states in matters "pertaining to the general welfare," he declared his faith that those who lay down their arms at Appomattox were men of honor who would "support and maintain the integrity" of the country. Chamberlain rejoiced in the establishment, once and for all, of the reality of the nation—"the Being of the people of the United States of America." To him, that definition of the word *nation* also meant "fidelity to the past, honesty to the present, faith for the future. It means inviolable honor everywhere." It also meant keeping faith with all races in it and "new and unheard of chivalry that scorns to do dishonor no less than to suffer it."[50]

That said, and having been pleased by Hayes's election, Chamberlain defended the president's policies and said that Hayes was correct in "declining to maintain the surveillance of the United States army over local affairs." Individual wrongs done freedmen could not be redressed by the national government, but only by state and local laws, he said, making it clear that he supported this limitation of Federal power. Considering otherwise, he thought, would be a "usurpation" of states' rights and dangerous to liberty in the long run, however benefiting justice in particular cases. "Look to it, men of New England," he admonished, "or you may bitterly rue the day. Some other issue may arise and we be the ones who want our rights respected."[51]

Those in public life who said there could be no peace because "the negroes did not have good treatment in the South and the rebels are back again in Congress" drew Chamberlain's disagreement. Acknowledging only that blacks were "abused" in the South, he apparently believed they were treated no differently than other less fortunate groups, adding "so are the Chinese in California, so are 40,000 poor girls in London, and so are the Indians. We must do the best we can for the negroes." While he was "sorry" that blacks could not vote "without interruption," Chamberlain wondered rhetorically if that was the reason for all the sacrifice of the war and for which "the best blood in all the land made those mountains and rivers and streams immortal, that negroes might have no one to stop them in going to the polls."[52]

Believing that the country had a "divine commission to hold the van in the great but slow marching enfranchisement of man," Chamberlain thought the sacrifice was made for "the whole country. . . . The free country—first the men who made it so, then those who are cast upon it." Elucidating further, and apparently openly voicing what others would not, he added, "Yes, I say it. The men who have made a country what it is, given it character and built their very lives into its history are to have the foremost hand if we would keep the country true to its mission, true to its ideal." Chamberlain reassured his audience: "The voting business in the South will regulate itself. As for the presence of rebel Generals in Congress, you yourself took back the States which they represent, and besides they have sworn to support the Constitution and laws of the United States."[53]

Chamberlain seemed to have an abiding faith in the future of a reunited country led by an elite class of men of honor much like himself, and the speech gives further insight into the kinship he felt with the Southerners he had fought. Like other good men, perhaps he was convinced that any excesses during Reconstruction were committed by "baser hands" in the Southern population, something he suspected when he heard the first news of Lincoln's assassination. And it is small wonder that many years later Chamberlain would remember as extraordinary the sight of black men "pressing forward to save the white man's country" in the rush to the front just before the Confederate surrender at Appomattox. The white man's country it was, and the white man's country it remained.[54]

A story told by Chamberlain after the war and his answer to it may have some relevance here. It concerned a Virginia father who lost not only his home and nearly all he had in the conflict, but also two dearly loved sons. One had died fighting for the Union, the other for the Confederacy. The father raised a memorial to them and inscribed an epitaph on the stone, ending in "God only knows which was right!" Chamberlain saw a double meaning in the father's question as to which of the boys was right: the motives of the young men were one thing, the justice of the causes another. In his own later views concerning treatment of the former slaves, he well might have heeded his own admonition and judgment:[55]

"God alone knows the heart, and he alone can judge men's motives. . . . the best of feelings are sometimes enlisted in the worst of causes, and the worst of feelings in the best of causes. You cannot always judge the moral value of an act merely from its surface, nor can you judge it merely from its motive. But men are responsible for their motives which they have allowed to control them, and for their use of the light they might have had if they would open their eyes to it."[56]

In the last year of Grant's second term, friends of Chamberlain pursued an appointment for him as minister to England without success; others were at work the next year to influence President Hayes for him, this time to the French mission. Chamberlain himself was open to accepting such important positions but actually cared more about having the offer as the office itself. He stood well with President Hayes, who consulted him for his opinion of candidates for Federal patronage posts in Maine. As it would happen, Chamberlain did go to Paris, not as minister but as a prestigious United States commissioner of education to the 1878 Paris Universal Exposition. The long-ago dream of the European trip that he had given up to serve his country sixteen years earlier finally became a reality, and he would be able to take Fannie and his now-grown children to enjoy it with him.[57]

Sailing on the steamer *England* from New York in June 1878, Chamberlain looked forward to a nearly five-month stay in Europe. He planned to first visit Britain for three weeks and then take a house in Paris, staffed with a French housekeeper, for the rest of the time. From there the family could travel the rest of the Continent. He had to raise a considerable sum of money to finance so long a journey with his family, but it was an eventful one, full of sight-seeing and amusing incidents. "Many funny things happen in this family, I assure you," Grace wrote to a friend about the happy and relaxed Chamberlains near the end of their stay.[58]

A European tour was exciting, but the grand ball held in the famous Hall of Mirrors at Versailles was unforgettable, a bright memory to be handed down to the grandchildren. Chamberlain would write an official report of the Paris exposition for Congress, and for his services he would be awarded a medal from the French government, but when he danced with his daughter in the pleasure palace of the kings of France, he was indeed a long way from his birthplace in Maine. In years past, only looking in at a ballroom had caused consternation and censure in Brewer.[59]

As the new year of 1880 began, a disputed Maine election, which was mismanaged by governmental and political party officials to the point of nearly plunging the state into civil war, embroiled Chamberlain as a military commander again. Since 1876 a major general of the state militia, Chamberlain had been recently appointed military commander of the state. The outgoing governor summoned him formally to the state capital just as his term was ending and ordered Chamberlain to "protect the public property and institutions of the State until my successor is duly qualified." When he arrived in Augusta, Chamberlain found the statehouse occupied by an armed force of about a hundred men answering only to the governor. The city was rapidly filling with various rival claimants to seats in the legislature, their political champions, and fighting men arriving by the hour. Feelings ran high and the threat of violence was almost electric in the air.[60]

In the 1878 elections, the populist Greenback-Labor party advocating monetary reform had elected ten representatives to Congress, two of whom were from Maine. The "Greenbackers," as they were called, were strong enough in Maine to poll more votes for governor than the Democratic candidate and cause the ballot-leading Republican candidate to receive less than the needed majority of votes cast to be elected. The divided Maine legislature then elected the Democrat Alonzo Garcelon as governor, all the Republicans voting for him rather than electing a Greenbacker. The next year's election had similar results, but this time the Republicans apparently had won a majority in the legislature, which would give the state a Republican governor when the new legislature convened in January 1880.[61]

However, upon receiving reports of irregularities at the polls, the outgoing Governor Garcelon and his council had canvassed the votes from the cities and towns and in mid-December announced changes in the outcome based on technicalities in the reporting of votes. By this new count, the Republican majority in the legislature had turned into a majority by the "Fusionists"—Democrats and Greenbackers voting together—and twelve vacancies. At the request of the Republican party's national leader and Maine's senator James G. Blaine, Chamberlain both telegraphed and wrote Garcelon to submit the whole question to the Maine Supreme Court for a decision, as requested publicly by the respected former senator Lot M. Morrill. Shortly thereafter, Blaine called indignation meetings all over the state to protest the "count-out" of Republican ballots. These rallies raised emotions to a high pitch by suggesting that Maine men might have to literally fight for their rights. Chamberlain was asked by Blaine to call such a meeting in Brunswick, but fearing violence, he refused.[62]

Setting up his headquarters in a small office in the statehouse after his arrival in the city, Chamberlain and his small staff, headed by his former student and regimental adjutant John Marshall Brown, alerted his militia commanders in other parts of the state and made arrangements with the railroads for transportation of arms and men if needed. His telegrams were to have the highest priority. Not wishing to provoke the tense situation further by a show of force, Chamberlain decided not to call out the militia. Enlisting the help of Augusta's mayor Charles A. Nash, Chamberlain hoped the civilian police would provide the only visible means of the enforcement of law and order that he would need.[63]

Succeeding in disarming and dismissing Garcelon's force in the statehouse, Chamberlain locked up the governor's and council's offices and secured the records. He also limited access to the legislative chambers to those with certificates of election from the Garcelon canvass of the election or those candidates who had legitimate claims to seats. The Republican party leaders and their growing band of armed zealots were headquartered nearby at the Blaine house, and the Fusionist leaders and their fighters at an office and hotel downtown, ready to settle the dispute by force. Each side distrusted the other. Chamberlain and his cool judgment were all that stood between Maine and possible civil war, and he was acutely aware that violence and bloodshed could occur at any time.[64]

Chamberlain made calming proclamations explaining his purposes to the people, asking them not to rush to Augusta. His orders left him to decide for himself what constituted a legal government, and he repeatedly declared that the Maine Supreme Court was the only body that could decide the questions involved. In the tense days that ensued, Chamberlain adhered to that position despite many attempts to dissuade him. Representatives of both of the Fusionist parties formally offered to elect him United States senator, due to be chosen by the new legislature, if he would uphold the Fusionist majority there. Shortly thereafter, the eminent and respectable Mr. Morrill brought word that James G. Blaine would step aside from his U.S. Senate seat in favor of Chamberlain if the general would support the Republican organization of both legislative houses. Incapable either of being bribed or of making a decision that would give the appearance of taking personal advantage of a trust, Chamberlain answered negatively to both propositions.[65]

The fact that Blaine and leaders in his own party seemed to be pursuing both violent and nonviolent strategies in order to gain their ends made Chamberlain particularly unhappy. But his nonpartisan stance pleased neither side in Augusta, and newspapers of both parties heaped vituperation on him. Democratic papers called him a traitor, usurper, and tool of Blaine, while those favoring the other party called him a Republican renegade and Fusionist sympathizer. Many people had confidence in Chamberlain's integrity, however, and letters of support came to him from ordinary citizens and old friends throughout the state. One private soldier, who had lost one leg in the charge at Little Round Top, wrote to him at the height of the crisis that he could raise a company of good, reliable men for Chamberlain on very short notice and would be glad to risk his other leg in the defense of his old commander![66]

One major claimant to the governor's chair whom Chamberlain would not recognize sent his self-styled staff officer to arrest Chamberlain near midnight one night. Chamberlain politely declined to be arrested, causing a somewhat awkward, if comical scene. But serious plots abounded to get rid of Chamberlain. Mayor Nash assigned police to follow the general for a time, when he learned of a plan to assassinate him, and Chamberlain had Wyllys bring him two pistols from home that had seen good service in other years. One memorable day near the end of the crisis reminded Chamberlain of "another Round Top." Great excitement had prevailed all day, with ugly crowds and threats against him following an attack in a Bangor paper calling on the people to send Chamberlain to a traitor's doom. Men begged him to call out the militia, and others threatened violence, but Chamberlain kept his own counsel and did not reveal his plans. A scheme to kidnap him and detain him away from the action caused him to change his room at night, but still, he wrote to Fannie, "I had the strange sense again of sleeping inside a picket guard."[67]

One incident he did not recount to her at the time was that of a narrow escape with his life. A thoroughly alarmed aide rushed into Chamberlain's office in the statehouse to warn that an ugly crowd of twenty-five or thirty men bent on killing him were outside. Donning his coat and walking rapidly to the rotunda, Chamberlain ascended two steps of the stairs and faced the menacing mob:

"Men, you wished to kill me, I hear. Killing is no new thing to me. I have offered myself to be killed many times, when I no more deserved it than I do now. Some of you, I think, have been with me in those days. You understand what you want, do you? I am here to preserve the peace and honor of this State, until the rightful government is seated,—whichever it may be, it is not for me to say. But it is for me to see that the laws of this state are put into effect, without fraud, without force, but with calm thought and sincere purpose. I am here for that, and I shall do it. If anybody wants to kill me for it, here I am. Let him kill!"[68]

With a gesture both dramatic and fearless, Chamberlain threw back his coat and looked his threateners straight in the eyes. The daring words and action had the desired salutary effect: in the sudden, startled silence, an old veteran pushed his way to the front of the crowd shouting, "By God, old General, the first man that dares to lay a hand on you, I'll kill him on the spot!" Muttering and fuming, the mob dispersed and seemed to melt away.[69]

Finally the situation became so perilous that even the great Blaine, U.S. senator and leading presidential contender, asked Chamberlain repeatedly to call out the militia. Chamberlain demurred, giving his reasons: "Whoever first says '*take arms!*,'" he wrote, "has a fearful responsibility on him, & I don't mean it shall be me who does that." On January 16 the Maine Supreme Court decided in favor of the Republicans, and that party's gubernatorial candidate, Daniel F. Davis, was elected governor the next day. Upon receiving a certified copy of the court's decision, with great relief Chamberlain formally declared, "The trust devolved on me . . . is at an end." After thanking by name those who had helped him, he added, "The General also thanks the citizens of Maine, who, without distinctions of party, . . . have strengthened his hands in the trying task laid upon him, of protecting property and rights in what might be called the absence of civil government."[70]

Near the end of his twelve eventful days in Augusta, Chamberlain had written Fannie that "my main object is to keep the peace & to give opportunity for the laws to be fairly executed." As a military commander, he accomplished that seemingly impossible task without calling out his troops or shedding blood, using only his judgment, courage, and the force of his personality.[71]

Encouraged by the unsolicited assurance of support from all over the state, that autumn Chamberlain actively explored the idea of placing his name as a candidate for the office of U.S. senator. But that high position always remained out of his reach. Chamberlain had never seemed at ease temperamentally with practical politics, and his conduct during the 1880 crisis made him many political enemies, including the most powerful men of the Republican party. Eugene Hale, a close friend of Blaine and a Republican leader during the "count out" crisis, was elected senator by the Maine legislature to succeed the retiring Hannibal Hamlin. Blaine resigned his Senate seat the following year to enter President James Garfield's cabinet, but the ensuing vacancy was filled by the legislature this time with longtime House of Representatives member and Blaine man, William P. Frye. Both Hale and Frye served in the Senate from Maine until the second decade of the twentieth century.[72]

That spring of 1880 Chamberlain journeyed to New York to testify at the official court of inquiry into the case of Gen. Gouverneur K. Warren. Fifteen years after the battle of Five Forks, Warren would finally get his hearing investigating his removal as commander of the Fifth Corps. Gen. Philip H. Sheridan, present also to give his testimony, greeted Chamberlain in a very friendly fashion, as did Gen. Winfield Scott Hancock, the famed former commander of the Second Corps, who originally sat on the court. Sheridan must have either forgotten or ignored an incident that had occurred nearly eleven years before, in 1869, at the founding of the Society of the Army of the Potomac in New York.[73]

Chosen as the principal orator for that occasion, Chamberlain at one point in his speech had spoken out boldly to the large audience containing members of that army, including many high-ranking officers and Sheridan, who was elected president of the new organization. Undoubtedly thinking of General Warren, and probably Fitz John Porter, Chamberlain had spoken for himself and others: "Nor do they forget to-night those officers, once the favorites of fortune, whom misunderstanding, impatience, or jealousy has stricken from our rolls." Continuing in this risky vein, he continued, "Pardon me, comrades, if I venture here to express the hope, knowing all the pains and penalties of so doing, that tardy justice (if that can be called justice which is tardy) may be done to officers whose character and service in behalf of the Republic, deserv[e] something better than its hasty and lasting rebuke." Chamberlain had been interrupted frequently by applause during his eloquent speech, which was so well received that he was given "prolonged cheers" at its close.[74]

"We are bound to have the true history of this thing out now," Chamberlain wrote to Fannie just before he gave his witness at the Warren hearing, and he was not disappointed. Warren was exonerated when the whole truth was known. Chamberlain was concerned enough for the vindication to be preserved, and his own opinion of Sheridan's actions made evident, that he would make the battles of the White Oak Road and Five Forks the subjects of the first war papers he prepared for the Military Order of the Loyal Legion. Eventually they would be included in his only book about the war.[75]

Toward the end of summer that year, the elder Joshua Chamberlain died at the age of seventy-nine. He and Chamberlain's mother still lived in the old family home in Brewer, together with Sae and her family. In 1867 Sae had married Charles O. Farrington, a prosperous young banker and store owner; they and their children provided companionship and help for the aging Chamberlains. But now the first of the older generation was gone, and Sarah D. B. Chamberlain would follow her husband in death eight years later at the age of eighty-five.[76]

Chamberlain's tie with his parents had remained close throughout the years, and he felt their deaths deeply. As a mature man and an army general he had confessed to his sister, "I could not bear to lose Father or

Mother any more than if I was a boy of 10," and two years before his father's death he had written to Mrs. Chamberlain that "my respect and affection for you & father increase the longer I live, & the more I know." Each year on his birthday Chamberlain made a point of writing to his mother, thanking her for the love and care she had given him and assuring her of his continued faith in God's guidance of his affairs. Many of the qualities of both of these two God-fearing people, the taciturn, commanding authority of Joshua Chamberlain and the cheerful, loving sensitivity of Sarah D. B. Chamberlain, lived on in their oldest son.[77]

His own children grew to adulthood during Chamberlain's years as Bowdoin's president. Although he must have endured with some amusement her breezy way of addressing him as "dear old papa" and "darling boy" in her adolescence, Grace Chamberlain was her father's special joy. Chamberlain looked forward to "bright glimpses of companionship" with her when she was not away at school, and he felt that she responded to him with "kindred thought and feeling." He could depend on her thoughtfulness in little ways—she would straighten and put his papers away after he left them spread around from his desk to the floor and on the mantelpiece. At a later time and in a serious mood, he expressed his deep love for her and said, "I love you because you are a splendid soul and belong to eternity."[78]

In the spring of 1881 Grace married Horace Gwynn Allen, a Boston lawyer, in the church where her parents had been married. Allen was the son of Stephen M. Allen, the old friend of Fannie's who had given her advice so many years before about her decision to marry Chamberlain. It was a love match, and Chamberlain grew fond of his daughter's husband. Allen was able to give Grace a life of luxury, and his affable good nature never seemed to flag, even though it must have seemed at times that at least one member of his wife's family was a guest in their home almost continuously. Chamberlain's love for Grace seemed to grow as the years went by. He visited Boston often and after the three granddaughters came, delighted in their company.[79]

Harold Wyllys Chamberlain graduated from Bowdoin in 1881 and, though he was not the scholar his father was, later completed his master's degree and then studied law at Boston University Law School. For a few years he practiced law in Florida and helped oversee some of his father's business interests there and later in Maine, but he never seemed to become truly independent of his parents. Returning north, Wyllys finally turned to inventing as a vocation and for years centered on electrical experiments and work in New York, Brunswick, Boston, and Portland, usually living with members of his family. Fannie relied heavily on him, especially in her later years, and she was probably his greatest influence, although Wyllys sought the approval of his father. Chamberlain tried to keep up appearances, donating money to the college in both his and Wyllys's names, but while loving him and showing his concern, he seemed disappointed in his son's lack of success in the world. Life in the shadow of his famous father must have been very difficult for Wyllys.[80]

Gradually increasing new business interests had begun to take more of Chamberlain's time. Returning from a visit to Florida in early 1882, he extolled its climate and its promise of opportunity for him—for health, wealth, and for service to his fellow man. "It would cure Fanny of all her ills," he enthusiastically wrote to Sae. That year he became president of the Florida West Coast Improvement Company.[81]

After protracted suffering from his old wounds, Chamberlain finally was persuaded to have surgery for them in April 1883. He resigned the presidency of Bowdoin after commencement that year, when it became clear that his recovery would be long and slow. He also felt that his political enemies in influential positions would act against the best interests of Bowdoin as long as he stayed at its head. His bold initiative in adding the scientific department to the college had never had the unqualified support of Bowdoin's governing boards, and he had offended some of the extreme Congregationalists. But with untiring efforts Chamberlain had raised the prodigious sum of $200,000 for the college, despite the great depression that fell over the country for years in the wake of the Panic of 1873. And when money was scarcest, for five years he had taught the important and taxing course in mental and moral philosophy himself. But the scientific department had failed to attract the number of students necessary to sustain it and, as a distinct department, was officially discontinued in 1880. However, the prescribed course of study at Bowdoin was remodeled and broadened to include some electives and provide more opportunities for the teaching of science.[82]

Despite the controversy that surrounded him during much of the twelve years of his presidency, Chamberlain liberalized Bowdoin, making its benefits available to the community and turning it "outward instead of inward." Memorial Hall, built to honor Union soldiers from the college, was finished, and the dormitories refurbished. His successor later lauded

Chamberlain's vision, stating: "His views of educational policy were broad and progressive." As a professor and through his years as president, "he advocated the very reforms, using often the very phrases," that were, years later, "the commonplaces of progressive educational discussion." Chamberlain dared "to plant his standards far in advance of present and sustained achievement. . . . Gen. Chamberlain never hauled down his flag to the low level of what he or any man could easily do or habitually be."[83]

After his resignation, at the urging of the boards, Chamberlain agreed to continue as lecturer in his popular course in political science and public law, which included political economy and both constitutional and international law. In the latter, he stressed that the object in life was not wealth but human welfare and weal. At the end of two years, however, he ended even this reduced schedule to devote his full time to his business interests in Florida. Three other colleges offered presidencies to him, which he declined, but he served his beloved Bowdoin as an active trustee until his death.[84]

* * *

On his way back from his 1882 trip to Florida, Chamberlain had stopped at Petersburg, Virginia, and reconnoitered the old battleground around Rives's Salient, which he had last seen that unforgettable June 18, 1864. All was changed—the woods from which he had led his men was now a cleared field, and the hillside, which had been smooth, was grown up with clumps of trees. Finally finding the place where he must have fallen, Chamberlain thought of "all those who had stood there on that day . . . & what it was all for, & what would come of it—& of those who on the one side & the other thought there was something at stake worthy of dearest sacrifice." On another trip, as his train skirted the battlefield at Fredericksburg, he remembered all that had happened there and exclaimed, "All along the route are haunted fields!"[85]

Chamberlain returned to Petersburg again in 1903, and old Confederate officers opened their "hall of war records and relics" for him and later talked hours away before he returned for the first time to Appomattox. But he most often spoke about the war to former Union soldiers. A speaker in great demand, he was invited over and over again to various reunions, large and small, of the boys in blue, and nearly every Memorial Day service found him speaking eloquently of the fallen heroes. At these observances,

Twentieth Maine Reunion, Gettysburg, 1889
(courtesy Theodore S. Johnson)

veterans greeted him and renewed old acquaintances and old times. Active in many veteran organizations, Chamberlain was both Maine department commander of the Grand Army of the Republic, the largest of the Union veteran associations, and commander for Maine's Military Order of the Loyal Legion commandery. Occasionally he gave a talk for the Brunswick chapter of the Grand Army. At Gettysburg in 1888, attending the reunion at the twenty-fifth anniversary of the battle, he was surprised and extremely pleased to be elected president of the Society of the Army of the Potomac although he had not been officially a candidate. "There were candidates who 'ranked' me out of sight," he commented.[86]

On the beautiful day of October 3 in the following year, the survivors of all the Maine regiments who had fought at Gettysburg dedicated their monuments at the battlefield. Two monuments of Maine granite marked the ground where the state's Twentieth Regiment had fought on Little Round Top and its position on Great Round Top, and Chamberlain spoke of the battle and the fallen heroes to his veterans. He was "President of the day" and addressed the assembly of all the Maine regiments at the dedicatory exercises that evening in the town courthouse. Touching upon his now familiar themes of the battle for the Union and the proper functions of the Federal and state governments, he titled his eloquent speech "The State, the Nation, the People." He also took the occasion to speak out against a widely used expression that troubled him:

"There is a phrase abroad which obscures the legal and the moral questions involved in the issue,—indeed, which distorts and falsifies history: 'The War Between the States.' There are here no States outside of the Union. Resolving themselves out of it does not release them. Even were they successful in intrenching themselves in this attitude, they would only relapse into territories of the United States. Indeed, several of the States so resolving were never in their own right either States or Colonies; but their territories were purchased by the common treasury of the Union, and were admitted as States out of its grace and generosity. . . . There was no war between the States. It was a war in the name of certain States to destroy the political existence of the United States."[87]

"Loyalty" was the theme of the major speech Chamberlain had given at the founding meeting of the Military Order of the Loyal Legion of the United States at Philadelphia February 22, 1866. In later years he was to read five war papers for the Maine commandery of that organization, and one for the New York commandery. On February 12, 1909, the centennial of Lincoln's birth, he was invited to the Pennsylvania commandery and delivered the primary oration of the observance, "Abraham Lincoln," which eulogized the martyred president in the most soaring terms and which his friends regarded as his masterpiece. But some friends agreed also that he was at his best in impromptu addresses discussing a particular theme of a meeting, where he "spoke 'winged words' that thrilled the hearts of his hearers."[88]

* * *

On July 23, 1885, the nation mourned the death of its former president and legendary Civil War hero, Ulysses S. Grant; the funeral was held early the next month in New York City. It was a huge affair organized and conducted by General Hancock, the commander of the army's Atlantic Division. Over a million and a half mourners packed the streets of the city, and the funeral procession, as it moved from City Hall toward a temporary tomb on Morningside Heights in Riverside Park, was eight miles long. The most distinguished men of the land attended, including President Grover

Cleveland and his cabinet, Supreme Court justices, and delegations of senators and representatives. Thinking with typical modesty that he did not quite belong in such exalted company, Chamberlain rode in his carriage with the group of cabinet ministers, in line with the senators chosen as chief mourners, and far ahead of state governors and many officers of the army.[89]

When Hancock's staff officer directed Chamberlain's carriage to the prominent place in the column that the commanding general had ordered, Chamberlain's surprised protestation that he was only a private citizen was brushed aside. "I would not have chosen that position because it was too much," Chamberlain wrote to Fannie after the magnificent pageant was all over, but he sounded pleased, nevertheless. During the burial service, he stood not ten feet from the casket in front of the tomb door. In the rushing emotions of mourning, it all seemed so strange to him:

"That emblem of strength & stubborn resolution yielding to human weakness & passing helplessly to dust. . . . The great men of the nation were there. But nothing seemed great to me—but what was gone; . . . Grant himself seemed greater now than ever. And he is."[90]

As the ceremony was completed, the notes of the "Tattoo! The evening roll call . . . the end of the day—the signal of silence and darkness" filled the air. Chamberlain's eyes searched nearby faces in vain for some sign that the old bugle call brought forth emotions corresponding to his own. Finally his gaze fell on the countenances of Generals Sherman, Hancock, and Sheridan, as they stood over the bier; there he saw the same response as his in their expressions, and his own feelings deepened. "What thoughts—what memories—what monitions passed through those minds!" Asking Fannie not to think him "egotistic," Chamberlain apologized for speaking so much of himself in his letter: "But you know I have had great & deep experiences—& my life has gone into the history of the days that are past. . . . It was the last of the great scenes. At least for this generation."[91]

Chamberlain spent the next several years dividing his time between Florida, where he had many financial interests, his Wall Street offices, where he raised money and cultivated investors in New York, and his home in Brunswick. He was president of several companies including a New Jersey railroad construction company, the Kinetic Power Company, which made motors for street cars, and the Mutual Town and Bond Company. He also sat on boards of directors for textile mills and other companies. As president of another railroad construction company in Florida, he sometimes acted as "master and pilot" of a steamboat that ran from Cedar Key to Homosassa. A hotel in Ocala and orange groves near there were other investments, and he was later president of the Ocala and Silver Springs Company, with offices in seven cities. Chamberlain evidently provided work in Florida for his brother Tom, or helped him find it, for a few years, after which Tom returned to Bangor. Fannie joined her husband sometimes in Florida and frequently in New York, and he took an apartment in "uptown" New York City when it was apparent he would spend a great deal of his time there.[92]

Malaria and his old wounds continued to beset Chamberlain, but he usually was able to go on, with his customary combination of strength and indifference to pain. However, infection from the wounds made him bedfast, sometimes for months, in the early 1890s. In 1893 he was awarded the Medal of Honor by Congress for his gallantry at Gettysburg. Chamberlain was gratified by the honor but was extremely modest about receiving praise for it. Returning an 1896 request that he give a full description of how he got the medal for a projected book about its recipients, Chamberlain complied. However, he then suggested that the author confine the book description to a short statement saying only that he had led a bayonet charge in person against an overpowering enemy assault. The author, himself a Mainer, assured him that the third person would be used, but "it would be impossible for you to say anything . . . that would savor of boasting, for your record as a brave soldier is so well known that self praise would necessarily fall far below what those who remember the dark days know to be true of you."[93]

Chamberlain's Florida investments proved unsuccessful. When his businesses suffered reverses, his concern for others was primary; one reason undoubtedly was that he knew that his name at the head of an enterprise encouraged others to invest in it. Wyllys summed up Chamberlain's business dealings very well in a letter to his mother: "Two of Father's companies are coming to the front, three of them in fact, and I hope he will see that he gets something for himself out of them," Wyllys wrote from New York. "But I am coming to realize better than ever what you have seen so long, that our man can't be best at *everything*, and Father cannot ever be relied upon to look out for himself, but always for the other fellow." There were other concerns and a silver lining: "Father has sunk so much money, and gotten his property[,] most of it[,] all tied up besides. . . . However, Father stands it very well, on the whole, and his reputation is still bright in every way."[94]

* * *

In 1896 Tom Chamberlain died at the age of fifty-five. Soon after the war he had settled in Brooklyn, New York, working as a clerk for his brother John and then continuing there in business for himself after John's death. On December 14, 1870, Tom had married John's widow, Delia, in Boston. Returning to Maine, he was a merchant in Bangor for a time; from 1879 to 1886 he worked in a "pension office," away from Bangor and perhaps in Washington. However, his parents' distress over his "restless and roving" conduct when he returned home on leave from the army in early 1865 sadly seemed to portend a pattern of behavior in his later years.[95]

While Tom was employed in the pension office his wife lived apart from him, and he was so remiss in his support of her that Delia had to ask her mother-in-law, the aged Mrs. Chamberlain, for money to pay her board and other necessary expenses. Sae Chamberlain Farrington, distressed over Tom's failures, irresponsibility, and future, darkly confided to her older brother that she had more fears about Tom than she wanted to state in a letter, hinting that his improvidence might have something to do with dissipation. And Fannie compared Tom with a relative of hers whose openly inebriated states caused her much embarrassment, although she said Tom made a better appearance. In addition, reports came to Chamberlain from acquaintances in Florida complaining of Tom's "strange and unbusinesslike" activities and "laziness" there.[96]

Whatever his other difficulties, Tom suffered from chronic lung and heart disease before he was fifty, and in the summer of 1896 his health utterly failed. Nursed day and night for weeks by the loyal Sae and loving Delia, he suffered such continuous nausea, chills, fever, and breathlessness that Sae thought his death would be a blessed relief if she were sure of his "acceptance of Christ." In later years Chamberlain would remember Tom fondly as his "brave young brother" who served his country faithfully in his youth. But Thomas Davee, the youngest of Joshua and Sarah Chamberlain's five children, died on August 12, 1896, and now only Lawrence and Sae were left of their original family.[97]

* * *

Befitting his interest in education and art, Chamberlain became president of the Artist-Artisan Institute in New York and was a close friend of Gen. Alexander S. Webb, president of the College of the City of New York. Chamberlain was named editor-in-chief and wrote a lengthy introduction to a large historical and biographical work on prominent universities, joined many civic and benevolent organizations, and lectured on a variety of themes to wide audiences. When the nation went to war with Spain, Chamberlain immediately offered his services to his country but received only a polite reply. At the same time, he dispatched a more detailed and enthusiastic letter to Maine senator William P. Frye in hope of a field command, but apparently to no avail. He was nearing his seventieth birthday, and although old friends, notably Adelbert Ames, and old enemies, such as Confederate William C. Oates of Little Round Top memory, received commissions as general officers, they were both several years younger than he. Chamberlain's age and perhaps his lack of political support must have been the real factors against him, if his old wounds were not taken into account.[98]

Finally, after a great deal of effort by his friends, in the spring of 1900 Chamberlain was appointed surveyor of the port of Portland by President McKinley. He had wanted the position of collector there, a post that had a great deal more status and responsibility, but the political realities were such that he was fortunate to have the surveyorship. His friends strongly advised him to accept the latter. There was no doubt that he needed the income, and the new post would give him ample opportunity for rest and leisure since the work was not taxing.[99]

A disappointed Chamberlain accepted the appointment, although he privately thought he was qualified to fill a more challenging job and said that a description of his new position "suggests a free bed in a hospital." But the arrangement seemed to work well for him. Portland was within easy commuting distance from Brunswick, and he could spend time at home, continue his service to the college, speak, write, travel, and enjoy an occasional abstemious drink and cigar with friends. Still loving the sea, he sailed with the *Pinafore* on the Maine coast, especially to Domhegan and back, in good weather.[100]

Fannie had continued to suffer with her eyes throughout the years, as she vainly sought relief from various doctors. Before she was seventy, she not only had pain in both eyes, but was totally blind in one of them. Chamberlain, Grace, and Wyllys began to speak of her in the diminutive—"little Ma," "little Mama," or "little one." Her husband's long absences from Brunswick on business or pleasure seemed to cause her to feel neglected, but many a long winter evening was made pleasant for them both when he read aloud to her. She visited Grace and the grandchildren often and enjoyed Sae's hospitality in Brewer. But as time passed, she became more and more reclusive, sometimes refusing Chamberlain or her son-in-law when they tried to coax her to come away with them from the confines of the Brunswick house. She had the company of her housekeepers and some friends in Brunswick, but Chamberlain worried often that she would fall into despondency. By the turn of the century she had lost her sight completely.[101]

When Chamberlain embarked on a lengthy trip to Italy and Egypt late in the year 1900, he left Fannie in the care of Grace and her family, promising to see things for her and describe them while he was away. He wrote to her just before he sailed: "You remember we are 'engaged' again," he said, surely referring to some fanciful whimsy between them, "not to sink down under any evils in our absence, but to keep whole and well for other days to come." Then, saying that he was nearly, but not quite, quoting Dante, he added, "'*And other songs in other keys, God willing.*'" Fannie was still waiting when he came back, although he had become so seriously ill in Europe that his own return was doubtful for a time, and convalescence delayed his homecoming.[102]

Ever the romantic, Chamberlain wrote love letters to his wife throughout all their years together, and if toward the end they were not so passionate and yearning as at the first, they still brimmed with love. And he sometimes caught glimpses of the old Fannie. In 1901, accompanied to Portland by Chamberlain and her companion and housekeeper, Lillian Edmunds, Fannie delightedly shopped for several silk skirts and shirtwaists to replenish her wardrobe. Chamberlain then selected another black and white print dress for her that he thought set off her gray hair attractively, which completed the purchases. Before they left the store, however, Fannie's attention was somehow drawn to another expensive and elaborate skirt of rich black silk, for which there would be few, if any, opportunities for wearing. "But of course the dear little woman," Chamberlain wrote fondly to Grace, "following her old and indulged habit, . . . insisted that she wanted that, too."[103]

On most Sunday evenings late in her life, Fannie could be seen slowly making her way down the middle aisle of First Parish Church, supported and led to their pew by her husband and son. After the service, friends would stop to talk with her, and with a beautiful smile she would turn her sightless eyes toward the sound of the greeting voices. She would never formally unite with the church as a full member, because, her pastor said, she was "unable to assent to propositions beyond comprehension," a reason which he took to be the manifestation of a scrupulous conscience.[104]

In midsummer of 1905 Fannie fell and broke her hip. A short time later Chamberlain wrote a cheering letter to her on her eightieth birthday, in which he sent his love and thanks for their long life together. After reviewing the happy attributes of her life, he declared, "Your husband and children 'rise up and call you blessed'—as the old scriptures represent the crowning grace of a good woman." He signed it as he did in the days of their youth, "Lawrence." On October 18, Chamberlain's beloved Fannie died in their Brunswick home. She was buried three days later in the family plot in Pine Grove Cemetery after a funeral in the church where they had been married nearly fifty years before.[105]

Chamberlain mourned his loss. He set about gathering Fannie's paintings and other mementos into a special place in their home as a memorial to her, and in later years he would proudly show them to visitors. In the past he had allowed only short references to his personal life in accounts about him meant for public consumption, but the next spring, when preparing a war paper about the last review of the Army of the Potomac for a meeting of Maine veterans, he penned an eloquent last tribute to his dear wife. The homage was placed so that the casual listener or reader would not realize that it was not a part of the description of the last assemblage of that great army and its spectators forty years before; Fannie had not been present in Washington on that long-ago day. Following a section of the discourse that described onlooking women who had nursed the suffering wounded during the war, he penned a paragraph that surely reflected his current feelings:

"You in my soul I see, faithful watcher by my cot-side long days and nights together through the delirium of mortal anguish,—steadfast, calm, and sweet as eternal love. We pass now quickly from each other's sight; but I know full well that where beyond these passing scenes you shall be, there will be heaven!"[106]

In his later years, Chamberlain's terms as governor of the state were mostly forgotten, but his war service was not: he was repeatedly called "the Hero of Little Round Top," and sometimes Maine's "Grand Old Man." "A general, first, last and always!" his last secretary said of him, and feature stories about him and texts of his speeches appeared often in the state's newspapers. Although he kept his Brunswick home, opening it mostly for summer use, Chamberlain bought a pleasant, two-story house on Ocean Avenue in Portland and lived there much of the time. Behind it, over a bright splash of red poppies and gradually sloping land, he enjoyed a clear view of Portland's "Back Bay" and, farther on, Tukey's Bridge and the ocean.[107]

He became a familiar and distinguished sight in the city—a straight, upright figure with white hair and flowing white mustache, "his personal dignity made doubly impressive by his soldierly bearing," as a long-time friend described him. Making his way by trolley to his office in the Customs House on Portland's docks, Chamberlain spoke to longshoremen and clerks as well as colleagues and friends he would meet. His dress seldom varied: a nearly black suit, blue shirt with a starched white collar, black tie, a sturdy cane, and on cold days, a long, black overcoat reaching to his high-topped shoes. When he was in Brunswick, young men from the college seemed to accompany him everywhere he went, and he courteously greeted and introduced to others even the youngest of acquaintances he would meet on the street.[108]

The three daughters born to Grace and Horace Allen in the second decade of their marriage were a delight to Chamberlain. For many years everyone had addressed him as "General," but the granddaughters' pronunciation of it, "Gennie," became the favorite of the family. "Gennie's coming, Gennie's coming," the little girls would titter and giggle, in happy anticipation of his frequent visits to them in Boston or to their summer home in Duxbury, and they looked forward to their own trips to Maine. To the youngest granddaughter, the brown-eyed Rosamond, he once wrote a letter in a style reminiscent of the young colonel's letter to his daughter after the battle of Chancellorsville: "How lovely and dear your letter to Gennie is! . . . You must come to me in the summer, with the birds and flowers, when all brown-eyed things are building nests. We will build one too!" He remained an optimist, and his keen observation of the everyday beauties of nature filled his last years with enjoyment.[109]

In October 1912 the editor of the popular *Cosmopolitan Magazine*, his curiosity piqued by an extremely complimentary passage in another periodical about Chamberlain and his part in the Appomattox surrender, asked

Joshua L. Chamberlain, ca. 1905
(National Archives)

Chamberlain to write an article about his experiences at the battle of Fredericksburg. He promptly obliged in the emphasized first-person style requested by the editor. "My Story of Fredericksburg" was the result; it was published just after the fiftieth anniversary of the battle. Very happy with the Fredericksburg piece, the editor quickly asked for another, longer, article. "Through Blood and Fire at Gettysburg" appeared in the June 1913 issue of another monthly with the same owner, *Hearst's Magazine*, although considerably shortened from the original. Both articles, copiously illustrated and accompanied by photographs of Chamberlain, reached a national audience. Chamberlain intended to write a full-length narrative about the battle of Gettysburg, but first he nearly finished preparing the book that he tentatively titled "The Last Campaign of the Armies," which was ultimately published posthumously as *The Passing of the Armies*.[110]

Since he first went back to Gettysburg with Fannie in the spring of 1864, Chamberlain had returned many times to that battlefield. He went back again in the middle of May 1913 to help make final preparations for the grand reunion commemorating the fiftieth anniversary of the battle, although the state of his health was so poor it was a hardship for him to do so. Accompanied by Dr. Abner O. Shaw, who saved his life on the night of the Petersburg charge and was still his physician in Portland, Chamberlain carried out his arduous duty to attend as Maine's representative to the anniversary planning committee.[111]

The May trip became the last time Chamberlain would see the storied and hallowed ground. He could not attend the great reunion six weeks later after all—traveling in the summer heat then would tax him more than even he could stand. But he gamely saw the Maine contingent off at the Portland train station, undoubtedly wishing he could go with them one last time to see the great assemblage of over 50,000 Confederate and Union veterans, there clasp the hands of his old comrades again, and on the night of July 3 enjoy the spectacle of the rocky heights of Little Round Top lighted up in the splendid colors of a gigantic fireworks display.[112]

In August Chamberlain visited the Allens at their summer home with Wyllys, enjoying sailing and the company of his family. Later that month he was still thinking about writing a book about Gettysburg, but by October a letter of advice from him to his son suggested some recognition of his own mortality. Soon afterward he fell ill again, and a worried Grace came from Boston to be with him in early December. The new year of 1914 found Chamberlain bedfast in the house at Portland, suffering greatly with infection of his old wounds. Attending him, as he had that long, hard night at Petersburg, and recommending the specialists and nurses the patient required, was the faithful Dr. Shaw.[113]

Later in the month Chamberlain began to rally enough that he could

Joshua L. Chamberlain
(courtesy Pejepscot Historical Society, Brunswick, Maine)

sometimes sit up in a chair and required less care, but the toll on his strength had been great. In a dictated letter to his sister, he discarded his long habit of using minimizing euphemisms in describing his recurring bouts with infection to others and acknowledged his pain as "unspeakable agony." But, he assured Sae, "if the dear Lord has appointed me to live a little longer, I am resolved it shall be of good to me and others. I am trying to get a little closer to God and to know him better."[114]

By the middle of February Chamberlain seemed partially recovered and expected to return soon to his work in the Customs House, but another attack that his depleted strength could not withstand overwhelmed him. Near half past nine in the morning of Tuesday, February 24, 1914, with the outside temperature plunging below zero, life left the painfully injured body of Joshua L. Chamberlain at his Portland home. Nearly fifty years after the minié ball tore through him on that unforgettable June 18, 1864, at Petersburg, Virginia, the culminated effects of it finally killed him. Both of his children were at his bedside at the time of his death, and Horace Allen came that afternoon to help comfort Grace, who was prostrate with grief.[115]

Word that the "Hero of Little Round Top" was dead spread quickly by word of mouth from homes to offices and shops in Portland, and a friend there reported that wherever the news went, "there was a feeling of profound sorrow." In Brunswick, similar regrets were expressed as the news went over the wires to more distant cities and towns. Thousands of words of praise for his life and deeds filled the Maine newspapers for days. Later, Grace received callers at the Portland house with the help of friends, including Dr. Adams's two daughters. Their aged mother, Helen Root Adams, then in her ninetieth year, would attend the funeral of her old friend, as would Sae Chamberlain Farrington and her family from Brewer. With her brother's death, Sae became the last of the family, and she would live another seven years.[116]

Chamberlain had made his wishes concerning his funeral known to his family before his death, but it was well known that the general "hated all ostentation." A military funeral under the charge of the Military Order of the Loyal Legion with brief services in Portland and Brunswick, impressive but "almost severe in their simplicity," was the result. On the morning of February 27 a platoon of police, four companies of Maine's old militia, now reorganized as the National Guard, with Chandler's band playing funeral dirges, accompanied the funeral cortege from the general's residence on Ocean Avenue to Portland's City Hall. Throngs of people with bared heads lined the sidewalks. At ten o'clock 2,000 people crowded into City Hall to pay homage to Maine's famous son. Dignitaries present included Maine's governor, representatives of the governor of Massachusetts, officers of Bowdoin College, and an impressive array of other high-ranking officials,

Joshua L. Chamberlain
(courtesy Pejepscot Historical Society, Brunswick, Maine)

besides large contingents of members of the Military Order of the Loyal Legion and Grand Army of the Republic.[117]

Chamberlain's sword rested on the casket, which was attended by an honor guard. After Beethoven's funeral march, "Upon the Death of a Hero," and Chamberlain's favorite, "The Death of Asa" from Grieg's *Peer Gynt* suite, were played on the organ, a eulogy given by the Reverend Jesse M. Hill emphasized that it was no ordinary man who was being mourned that day. "There was a texture to his mind, a color to his soul, a certain quality to his personality that would have made him conspicuous and lovable without the titles and robes of the earth," the minister declared. "He was the incarnation of the best and manliest qualities of the American character." A prayer followed, and then the bugle call "Taps" rang out from the upper gallery before the casket, draped in an American flag, was removed from the hall by the guard of honor to the strains of Chopin's "Funeral March." Muffled drums and the funeral honors by the band accompanied the placing of the casket in the hearse.[118]

More crowds of solemn citizens lined Portland's snowy streets to view the funeral procession as it made its way to the railroad station, where a special train waited to take the remains of the old warrior home to Brunswick. The police, band, and National Guard companies, together now with units of the Coast Artillery and the U.S. Naval Reserve, preceded the long funeral cortege, which included the hearse with a marching guard of honor and the carriages of the honorary pallbearers and the family. Full honors were paid at Railway Square as the escort drew up in line while the funeral party passed.[119]

As the train carrying the body of Maine's honored son arrived at Brunswick, all town businesses shut their doors for the afternoon, and all classes at Bowdoin were suspended. By proclamation of the governor, all national flags in the state flew at half-staff in respect to the general's memory. Over a thousand people watched the funeral procession as it proceeded the short distance from the Maine Central station to the First Parish Congregational Church across from the Chamberlain home. Members of the Brunswick post of the Grand Army acted as honor escorts, and the mourners, headed by the Bowdoin students as a body, filled to overflowing the church that had been the scene of so many great events in Chamberlain's life.[120]

In that immense old church, with its "beautiful arches, braces and pillars" rising fifty feet to the ridgepole of the roof, Chamberlain had married

Frances Caroline Adams and attended church services for many years. There he had taken part in literally scores of Bowdoin commencements as graduate, speaker, professor, president, and trustee of the college that was so dear to him. There he, General Grant, and other Union army survivors had been feted at the end of the war, and there he had spoken at many a funeral and mourned the deaths of his own young children and his wife. Bowdoin undergraduates acted as pallbearers and ushers at Chamberlain's final service, and Bowdoin's president, Dr. William DeWitt Hyde, reviewed his life and accomplishments in a long and glowing eulogy. Strains of cello music reminiscent of Chamberlain's own bass viol wafted in the solemn air, and two of his favorite hymns, "Abide with Me" and "Nearer My God to Thee," were sung by a soloist. The casket was then borne from the church to the sound of the organ playing Chopin's "Funeral March."[121]

Out the Bath Road the great, sad procession wended its way easterly the short distance to Pine Grove Cemetery. There the mourners stood with uncovered heads as the National Guard escort fired a salute of three volleys. Then the body of Maine's great hero was consigned to the earth a few yards from a stand of stately pine trees behind Bowdoin College. His daughter Grace, who stood that day desolate from the loss of her beloved father, and his son Harold Wyllys would later follow their parents to lie in the family plot.[122]

On another cold February day sixty-six years before, a sleigh bearing the apprehensive and hopeful young Chamberlain to Bowdoin College had passed this same graveyard on the Bath Road, but from the opposite direction as this day's mournful procession. The cemetery was much smaller then, and the wind had sighed and whispered, as it does now, through the grove of tall pines that stand near the burial ground. When a tempest blows, at times it still comes up from the shores of Harpswell Neck, whirls around the college buildings through the wind-driven pines, and fills the cemetery with its mighty roar. And as the sun shines down in early spring through nearby maples, a thin blanket of brown pine needles covers his grave. It is marked by a plain and modest headstone of pale rose Maine granite, inscribed only with the name of Joshua L. Chamberlain and the years of his birth and death. He wanted nothing more.[123]

EPILOGUE: 1913 REVISITED

"I went—it is not long ago—to stand again upon that crest whose one day's crown of fire has passed into the blazoned coronet of fame; to look again upon the rocks whereon were laid as on the altar the lives of Vincent and O'Rorke."

For nearly fifty years, it was to Little Round Top at the battlefield of Gettysburg that Joshua Lawrence Chamberlain always returned. His footsteps on its southern spur led him away from the bronze statues and stone monuments back to the place where a memorial of hard granite marked the ground where Maine's Twentieth Regiment had fought and triumphed.

"And farther on where my own young heroes mounted to fall no more—Billings, the valor of whose onward-looking eyes not death itself could quench; Kendall, almost maiden-sweet and fair, yet heeding not the bolts that dashed his life-blood on the rocks; Estes and Steele, and Noyes and Buck, lifted high above self . . . and far up the rugged sides of Great Round Top, swept in darkness . . . where the impetuous Linscott halted at last before the morning star."

Inscribed on the stone were the names of those Maine heroes who had sacrificed their young lives on that July day long ago, and in the mystic vision of their old commander, they returned for one brief moment more.

"I sat there alone on the storied crest, till the sun went down as it did before over the misty hills, and the darkness crept up the slopes, till from all earthly sight I was

buried as with those before. But oh, what radiant companionship rose around, what steadfast ranks of power, what bearing of heroic souls. Oh, the glory that beamed through those nights and days. Nobody will ever know it here!—I am sorry most of all for that."

Then, in lofty tribute to their lives, and paean unaware to his own:

"The proud young valor that rose above the mortal, and then at last was mortal after all . . . "[1]

APPENDIX

Command Organization of the Fifth Army Corps, Army of the Potomac Antietam through Appomattox in Conjunction with the Army Career of Joshua L. Chamberlain

---

Maryland Campaign, September 11–30, 1862
Maj. Gen. FITZ JOHN PORTER, Commander
Escort—1st Maine Cavalry (detachment), Capt. George J. Summat

First Division

Maj. Gen. GEORGE W. MORELL

First Brigade

Col. JAMES BARNES

2d Maine, Col. Charles W. Roberts; *18th Massachusetts*, Lt. Col. Joseph Hayes; *22d Massachusetts*, Lt. Col. William S. Tilton; *1st Michigan*, Capt. E. W. Belton; *13th New York*, Col. E. G. Marshall; *25th New York*, Col. C. A. Johnson; *118th Pennsylvania*, Col. C. M. Prevost; *2d Co., Massachusetts Sharpshooters*, Capt. L. E. Wentworth.

Second Brigade

Brig. Gen. CHARLES GRIFFIN

2d District of Columbia, Col. C. M. Alexander; *9th Massachusetts*, Col. P. R. Guiney; *32d Massachusetts*, Col. Francis J. Parker; *4th Michigan*, Col. J. W. Childs; *14th New York*, Col. James McQuade; *62d Pennsylvania*, Col. J. B. Sweitzer.

Third Brigade

Col. T. B. W. STOCKTON

20th Maine, Col. Adelbert Ames; *16th Michigan*, Lt. Col. N. E. Welch; *12th New York*, Capt. William Huson; *17th New York*, Lt. Col. N. B. Bartram; *44th New York*, Maj. Freeman Conner; *83d Pennsylvania*, Capt. O. S. Woodward; *Brady's Co. Michigan Sharpshooters*, Lt. J. H. Titus, Jr.

Artillery

Massachusetts Light, Battery C, Capt. Augustus P. Martin; *1st Rhode Island Light, Battery C,* Capt. Richard Waterman; *5th U.S., Battery D,* Lt. Charles E. Hazlett.

Sharpshooters

1st U.S., Capt. John B. Isler.

Second Division

Brig. Gen. GEORGE SYKES

First Brigade

Lt. Col. ROBERT C. BUCHANAN

3d U.S., Capt. John D. Wilkins; *4th U.S.,* Capt. Hiram Dryer; *12th U.S., 1st Battalion,* Capt. M. M. Blunt; *12th U.S., 2d Battalion,* Capt. T. M. Anderson; *14th U.S., 1st Battalion,* Capt. W. H. Brown; *14th U.S., 2d Battalion,* Capt. D. B. McKibbin.

Second Brigade

Maj. CHARLES S. LOVELL

1st and 6th U.S., Capt. Levi C. Bootes; *2d and 10th U.S.,* Capt. John S. Poland; *11th U.S.,* Maj. De L. Floyd-Jones; *17th U.S.,* Maj. George L. Andrews.

Third Brigade

Col. GOUVERNEUR K. WARREN

5th New York, Capt. C. Winslow; *10th New York,* Lt. Col. J. W. Marshall.

Artillery

1st U.S., Batteries E and G, Lt. Alanson M. Randol; *5th U.S., Battery I,* Capt. Stephen H. Weed; *5th U.S., Battery K,* Lt. William E. Van Reed.

Third Division

Brig. Gen. ANDREW A. HUMPHREYS

First Brigade

Brig. Gen. E. B. TYLER

91st Pennsylvania, Col. E. M. Gregory; *126th Pennsylvania,* Col. James G. Elder; *129th Pennsylvania,* Col. Jacob G. Frick; *134th Pennsylvania,* Col. M. S. Quay.

Second Brigade
Col. PETER H. ALLABACH

123d Pennsylvania, Col. John B. Clark; *131st Pennsylvania*, Lt. Col. William B. Shaut; *133d Pennsylvania*, Col. F. B. Speakman; *155th Pennsylvania*, Col. E. J. Allen.

Artillery

1st New York Light, Battery C, Capt. Almond Barnes; *1st Ohio Light, Battery L*, Capt. L. N. Robinson.

Artillery Reserve

1st Battalion New York Light, Battery A, Lt. Bernhard Wever; *1st Battalion New York Light, Battery B*, Lt. Alfred von Kleiser; *1st Battalion New York Light, Battery C*, Capt. Robert Langner; *1st Battalion New York Light, Battery D*, Capt. Charles Kusserow; *5th Battalion New York Light*, Capt. Elijah D. Taft; *1st U.S., Battery K*, Capt. William M. Graham; *4th U.S., Battery G*, Lt. Marcus P. Miller.

Organization of the Fifth Army Corps, Army of the Potomac by Maj. Gen. Ambrose E. Burnside, November 9, 1862 for the Fredericksburg, Virginia, Campaign

Brig. Gen. DANIEL BUTTERFIELD, Commander

First Division

Brig. Gen. CHARLES GRIFFIN

First Brigade
Col. JAMES BARNES

2d Maine, Lt. Col. George Varney; *18th Massachusetts*, Lt. Col. Joseph Hayes; *22d Massachusetts*, Lt. Col. William S. Tilton; *1st Michigan*, Lt. Col. Ira C. Abbott; *13th New York*, Col. E. G. Marshall; *25th New York*, Capt. Patrick Connelly; *118th Pennsylvania*, Lt. Col. James Gwyn; *2d Co., Massachusetts Sharpshooters*, Capt. L. E. Wentworth.

Second Brigade
Col. JACOB B. SWEITZER

9th Massachusetts, Col. P. R. Guiney; *32d Massachusetts*, Col. Francis J. Parker; *4th Michigan*, Lt. Col. G. W. Lumbard; *14th New York*, Lt. Col. T. M. Davies; *62d Pennsylvania*, Lt. Col. J. C. Hull.

Third Brigade

Col. T. B. W. Stockton

20th Maine, Col. Adelbert Ames; *16th Michigan*, Lt. Col. N. E. Welch; *12th New York*, Lt. Col. R. M. Richardson; *17th New York*, Capt. John Vickers; *44th New York*, Maj. Freeman Conner; *83d Pennsylvania*, Col. Strong Vincent; *Brady's Co., Michigan Sharpshooters*.

Artillery

Massachusetts Light, 3d Battery (C), Capt. Augustus P. Martin; *Massachusetts Light, 5th Battery (E)*, Capt. Charles A. Phillips; *1st Rhode Island Light, Battery C*, Capt. Richard Waterman; *5th U.S., Battery D*, Lt. Charles E. Hazlett.

Sharpshooters

1st U.S., Capt. John B. Isler.

Second Division

Brig. Gen. George Sykes

First Brigade

Lt. Col. Robert C. Buchanan

3d U.S., Capt. John D. Wilkins; *4th U.S.*, Capt. Hiram Dryer; *12th U.S., 1st Battalion*, Capt. M. M. Blunt; *12th U.S., 2d Battalion*, Capt. T. M. Anderson; *14th U.S., 1st Battalion*, Capt. J. D. O'Connell; *14th U.S., 2d Battalion*, Capt. G. B. Overton.

Second Brigade

Maj. Charles S. Lovell

1st and 2d U.S. Battalion, Capt. S. S. Marsh; *6th U.S.*, Capt. Levi C. Bootes; *7th U.S. Battalion*, Capt. D. P. Hancock; *10th U.S.*, Capt. H. E. Maynadier; *11th U.S.*, Capt. Charles S. Marshall; *17th and 19th U.S.*, Capt. John P. Wales.

Third Brigade

Col. Gouverneur K. Warren

5th New York, Capt. Cleveland Winslow; *140th New York*, Col. Patrick H. O'Rorke; *146th New York*, Col. Kenner Garrard.

Artillery

1st Ohio Light, Battery L, Lt. Frederick Dorries; *5th U.S., Battery I*, Lt. M. F. Watson.

Third Division

Brig. Gen. ANDREW A. HUMPHREYS

First Brigade

Brig. Gen. E. B. TYLER

91st Pennsylvania, Col. E. M. Gregory; *126th Pennsylvania,* Col. James G. Elder; *129th Pennsylvania,* Col. Jacob G. Frick; *134th Pennsylvania,* Lt. Col. Edward O'Brien.

Second Brigade

Col. PETER H. ALLABACH

123d Pennsylvania, Col. John B. Clark; *131st Pennsylvania,* Lt. Col. William B. Shaut; *133d Pennsylvania,* Col. F. B. Speakman; *155th Pennsylvania,* Col. E. J. Allen.

Artillery

1st New York Light, Battery C, Lt. W. H. Phillips; *1st U.S., Batteries E and G,* Capt. A. M. Randol.

Organization of the Fifth Army Corps, Army of the Potomac for the Chancellorsville, Virginia, Campaign
May 1–4, 1863
Maj. Gen. GEORGE G. MEADE, Commander

First Division

Brig. Gen. CHARLES GRIFFIN

First Brigade

Col. JAMES BARNES

2d Maine, Col. George Varney; *18th Massachusetts,* Col. Joseph Hayes; *22d Massachusetts,* Col. William S. Tilton; *2d Co., Massachusetts Sharpshooters,* Lt. Robert Smith; *1st Michigan,* Col. Ira C. Abbott; *13th New York,* (battalion), Capt. William Downey; *25th New York,* Col. Charles A. Johnson; *118th Pennsylvania,* Col. Charles M. Prevost.

Second Brigade

(1) Col. JAMES MCQUADE
(2) Col. JACOB B. SWEITZER

9th Massachusetts, Col. P. R. Guiney; *32d Massachusetts,* Lt. Col. L. Stephenson; *4th Michigan,* Col. H. H. Jeffords; *14th New York,* Lt. Col. T. M. Davies; *62d Pennsylvania,* Col. J. B. Sweitzer and Lt. Col. James C. Hull.

Third Brigade
Col. T. B. W. STOCKTON
20th Maine, Lt. Col. Joshua L. Chamberlain; *16th Michigan*, Lt. Col. Norval E. Welch; *12th New York*, Capt. William Huson; *17th New York*, Lt. Col. N. B. Bartram; *44th New York*, Col. James C. Rice; *83d Pennsylvania*, Col. Strong Vincent; *Brady's Co., Michigan Sharpshooters*.

Artillery
Capt. AUGUSTUS P. MARTIN
Massachusetts Light, 3d Battery (C), Capt. Augustus P. Martin; *Massachusetts Light, 5th Battery (E)*, Capt. Charles A. Phillips; *1st Rhode Island Light, Battery C*, Capt. Richard Waterman; *5th U.S., Battery D*, Lt. Charles E. Hazlett.

Second Division
Brig. Gen. GEORGE SYKES

First Brigade
Brig. Gen. ROMEYN B. AYRES
3d U.S., Companies B, C, F, G, I, and K, Capt. John D. Wilkins; *4th U.S., Companies C, F, H, and K*, Capt. Hiram Dryer; *12th U.S., Companies A, B, C, D, and G (1st Battalion), and A, C, and D (2d Battalion)*, Maj. Richard S. Smith; *14th U.S., Companies A, B, D, E, F, and G (1st Battalion), and F and G (2d Battalion)*, Capt. J. B. Hager.

Second Brigade
Col. SIDNEY BURBANK
2d U.S., Companies B, C, F, I, and K, Capt. S. S. Marsh and Capt. S. A. McKee; *6th U.S., Companies D, F, G, H, and I*, Capt. Levi C. Bootes; *7th U.S., Companies A, B, E, and I*, Capt. D. P. Hancock; *10th U.S., Companies D, G, and H*, Lt. E. G. Bush; *11th U.S., Companies B, C, D, E, F, and G (1st Battalion), and C and D (2d Battalion)*, Maj. De L. Floyd-Jones; *17th U.S., Companies A, C, D, G, and H (1st Battalion), and A and B (2d Battalion)*, Maj. George L. Andrews.

Third Brigade
Col. PATRICK H. O'RORKE
5th New York, Col. Cleveland Winslow; *140th New York*, Lt. Col. Louis Ernst; *146th New York*, Col. Kenner Garrard.

Artillery
1st Ohio Light, Battery L, Capt. Frank C. Gibbs; *5th U.S., Battery I*, Lt. Malbone F. Watson.

Third Division

Brig. Gen. Andrew A. Humphreys

First Brigade

Brig. Gen. E. B. Tyler

91st Pennsylvania, Col. E. M. Gregory and Lt. Col. J. H. Sinex; *126th Pennsylvania,* Lt. Col. D. W. Roe; *129th Pennsylvania,* Col. Jacob G. Frick; *134th Pennsylvania,* Lt. Col. Edward O'Brien.

Second Brigade

Col. Peter H. Allabach

123d Pennsylvania, Col. John B. Clark; *131st Pennsylvania,* Maj. R. W. Patton; *133d Pennsylvania,* Col. F. B. Speakman; *155th Pennsylvania,* Lt. Col. J. H. Cain.

Artillery

Capt. Alanson M. Randol

1st New York Light, Battery C, Capt. Almont Barnes; *1st U.S., Batteries E and G,* Capt. A. M. Randol.

Organization of the Fifth Army Corps, Army of the Potomac
June 30, 1863
for the Battle of Gettysburg, Pennsylvania
July 1–3, 1863
Maj. Gen. George Sykes, Commander

First Division

Brig. Gen. James Barnes

First Brigade

Col. William S. Tilton

18th Massachusetts, Col. Joseph Hayes; *22d Massachusetts,* Col. William S. Tilton; Lt. Col. Thomas Sherwin, Jr.; *1st Michigan,* Col. Ira C. Abbott; *118th Pennsylvania,* Lt. Col. James Gwyn.

Second Brigade

Col. Jacob B. Sweitzer

9th Massachusetts, Col. P. R. Guiney; *32d Massachusetts,* Col. G. L. Prescott; *4th Michigan,* Col. H. H. Jeffords; *62d Pennsylvania,* Lt. Col. James C. Hull.

Third Brigade
Col. STRONG VINCENT
20th Maine, Col. Joshua L. Chamberlain; *16th Michigan*, Col. Norval E. Welch; *44th New York*, Col. James C. Rice; *83d Pennsylvania*, Capt. O. S. Woodward.

Second Division
Brig. Gen. ROMEYN B. AYRES

First Brigade
Col. HANNIBAL DAY
3d U.S., (6 cos.), Capt. H. W. Freedley; *4th U.S., (4 cos.)*, Capt. Julius W. Adams, Jr.; *6th U.S., (5 cos.)*, Capt. L. C. Bootes; *12th U.S., (8 cos.)*, Capt. T. S. Dunn; *14th U.S., (8 cos.)*, Maj. G. R. Giddings.

Second Brigade
Col. SIDNEY BURBANK
2d U.S., (6 cos.), Maj. A. T. Lee; *7th U.S., (4 cos.)*, Capt. D. P. Hancock; *10th U.S., (3 cos.)*, Capt. William Clinton; *11th U.S., (6 cos.)*, Maj. De L. Floyd-Jones; *17th U.S., (7 cos.)*, Lt. Col. J. D. Greene.

Third Brigade
Brig. Gen. STEPHEN H. WEED
140th New York, Col. Patrick H. O'Rorke; *146th New York*, Col. Kenner Garrard; *91st Pennsylvania*, Lt. Col. J. H. Sinex; *155th Pennsylvania*, Lt. Col. J. H. Cain.

Third Division[1]
Brig. Gen. SAMUEL W. CRAWFORD

First Brigade
Col. WILLIAM MCCANDLESS
1st Pennsylvania Reserves, (9 cos.), Col. William C. Talley; *2d Pennsylvania Reserves*, Lt. Col. George A. Woodward; *6th Pennsylvania Reserves*, Lt. Col. W. H. Ent; *13th Pennsylvania Reserves*, Col. Charles F. Taylor.

Third Brigade
Col. JOSEPH W. FISHER
5th Pennsylvania Reserves, Lt. Col. George Dare; *9th Pennsylvania Reserves*, Lt. Col. J. McK. Snodgrass; *10th Pennsylvania Reserves*, Col. A. J. Warner; *11th Pennsylvania Reserves*, Col. S. M. Jackson; *12th Pennsylvania Reserves*, *(9 cos.)*, Col. M. D. Hardin.

Artillery

Capt. AUGUSTUS P. MARTIN

Massachusetts Light, 3d Battery (C), Lt. A. F. Walcott; *1st New York Light, Battery C*, Capt. Almont Barnes; *1st Ohio Light, Battery L*, Capt. Frank C. Gibbs; *5th U.S., Battery D*, Lt. Charles E. Hazlett; *5th U.S., Battery I*, Lt. Malbone F. Watson.

Organization of the Fifth Army Corps, Army of the Potomac Reorganized to Include the First Corps for Grant's Overland Campaign Beginning May 4, 1864[2]

Maj. Gen. GOUVERNEUR K. WARREN, Commander

Provost Guard—12th New York Battalion, Maj. Henry W. Rider

First Division

Brig. Gen. CHARLES GRIFFIN

First Brigade[3]

Brig. Gen. ROMEYN B. AYRES[4]

140th New York, Col. George Ryan; *146th New York*, Col. David D. Jenkins; *91st Pennsylvania*, Lt. Col. J. H. Sinex; *155th Pennsylvania*, Col. Alfred H. Pearson; *2d U.S., (6 cos.)*, Capt. James W. Long; *11th U.S., (6 cos.), 1st Battalion*, Capt. Francis S. Cooley; *12th U.S., (10 cos.), 1st and 2d Battalions*, Maj. Luther B. Bruen; *14th U.S., (1st Battalion)*, Capt. E. McK. Hudson; *17th U.S., (8 cos.), 1st and 2d Battalions*, Capt. James F. Grimes.

First Brigade[5]

Col. JOSHUA L. CHAMBERLAIN[6]

121st Pennsylvania, Capt. Nathaniel Lang; *142d Pennsylvania*, Maj. H. N. Warren; *143d Pennsylvania*, Maj. James Glenn; *149th Pennsylvania*, Lt. Col. John Irvin; *150th Pennsylvania*, Maj. George W. Jones; *187th Pennsylvania*, Lt. Col. Joseph F. Ramsey.

Second Brigade

Col. JACOB B. SWEITZER

9th Massachusetts, Col. P. R. Guiney; *22d Massachusetts, (2d Co., Mass. Sharpshooters attached)*, Col. William S. Tilton; *32d Massachusetts*, Col. G. L. Prescott; *4th Michigan*, Lt. Col. George W. Lumbard; *62d Pennsylvania*, Lt. Col. James C. Hull.

Third Brigade
Brig. Gen. JOSEPH J. BARTLETT
20th Maine, Maj. Ellis Spear; Col. Joshua L. Chamberlain;[7] *18th Massachusetts,* Col. Joseph Hayes; *1st Michigan,* Lt. Col. William A. Throop; *16th Michigan,* Maj. Robert T. Elliot; *44th New York,* Lt. Col. Freeman Conner; *83d Pennsylvania,* Col. Orpheus S. Woodward; *118th Pennsylvania,* Col. James Gwyn.

Second Division
Brig. Gen. JOHN C. ROBINSON

First Brigade
Col. SAMUEL H. LEONARD
16th Maine, Col. Charles W. Tilden; *13th Massachusetts,* Capt. Charles H. Hovey; *39th Massachusetts,* Col. Phineas S. Davis; *104th New York,* Col. Gilbert G. Prey.

Second Brigade
Brig. Gen. HENRY BAXTER
12th Massachusetts, Col. James L. Bates; *83d New York (9th Militia),* Col. Joseph A. Moesch; *97th New York,* Col. Charles Wheelock; *11th Pennsylvania,* Col. Richard Coulter; *88th Pennsylvania,* Capt. George B. Rhodes; *90th Pennsylvania,* Col. Peter Lyle.

Third Brigade
Col. ANDREW W. DENISON
1st Maryland, Maj. Benjamin H. Schley; *4th Maryland,* Col. Richard N. Bowerman; *7th Maryland,* Col. Charles E. Phelps; *8th Maryland,* Lt. Col. John G. Johannes.

Third Division
Brig. Gen. SAMUEL W. CRAWFORD

First Brigade
Col. WILLIAM MCCANDLESS
1st Pennsylvania Reserves, Col. William C. Talley; *2d Pennsylvania Reserves,* Lt. Col. P. McDonough; *6th Pennsylvania Reserves,* Col. W. H. Ent; *7th Pennsylvania Reserves,* Maj. LeG. B. Speece; *11th Pennsylvania Reserves,* Col. S. M. Jackson; *13th Pennsylvania Reserves,* Maj. W. R. Hartshorne.

Second Brigade

Col. JOSEPH W. FISHER

5th Pennsylvania Reserves, Lt. Col. George Dare; *8th Pennsylvania Reserves,* Col. S. M. Bailey; *10th Pennsylvania Reserves,* Lt. Col. Ira Ayer, Jr.; *12th Pennsylvania Reserves,* Lt. Col. Richard Gustin.

Fourth Division

Brig. Gen. JAMES S. WADSWORTH

First Brigade

Brig. Gen. LYSANDER CUTLER

7th Indiana, Col. Ira G. Grover; *19th Indiana,* Col. S. J. Williams; *24th Michigan,* Col. Henry A. Morrow; *1st New York Battalion, Sharpshooters,* Capt. V. J. Shipman; *2d Wisconsin,* Lt. Col. John Mansfield; *6th Wisconsin,* Col. Edward S. Bragg; *7th Wisconsin,* Col. William W. Robinson.

Second Brigade

Brig. Gen. JAMES C. RICE

76th New York, Lt. Col. John E. Cook; *84th New York (14th Mil.),* Col. E. B. Fowler; *95th New York,* Col. Edward Pye; *147th New York,* Col. F. C. Miller; *56th Pennsylvania,* Col. J. W. Hoffman.

Third Brigade

Col. ROY STONE

121st Pennsylvania, Capt. Samuel T. Lloyd; *142d Pennsylvania,* Maj. Horatio N. Warren; *143d Pennsylvania,* Col. Edward L. Dana; *149th Pennsylvania,* Lt. Col. John Irvin; *150th Pennsylvania,* Capt. George W. Jones.

Artillery Brigade

Col. CHARLES S. WAINWRIGHT

Massachusetts Light, Battery C, Capt. Augustus P. Martin; *Massachusetts Light, Battery E,* Capt. Charles A. Phillips; *1st New York Light, Battery D,* Capt. George B. Winslow; *1st New York Light, Batteries E and L,* Lt. George Breck; *1st New York Light, Battery H,* Capt. Charles E. Merik; *4th New York Heavy, 2d Battalion,* Maj. William Arthur; *1st Pennsylvania Light, Battery B,* Capt. James H. Cooper; *4th U.S., Battery B,* Lt. James Stewart; *5th U.S., Battery D,* Lt. B. F. Rittenhouse.

Organization of the Fifth Army Corps, Army of the Potomac in the Appomattox Campaign
March 29 to April 9, 1865
Maj. Gen. GOUVERNOR K. WARREN, Commander
Bvt. Maj. Gen. CHARLES GRIFFIN[8]
Escort—4th Pennsylvania Cavalry, (Co. C), Capt. Napoleon J. Horrell
Provost Guard—104th New York, Capt. Wm. W. Graham

First Division

Bvt. Maj. Gen. CHARLES GRIFFIN
Bvt. Maj. Gen. JOSEPH J. BARTLETT[9]

First Brigade

Brig. Gen. JOSHUA L. CHAMBERLAIN
185th New York, Col. Gustavus Sniper; *198th Pennsylvania*, Bvt. Brig. Gen. Horatio B. Sickel;[10] Maj. Edwin A. Glenn;[11] Capt. John Stanton.

Second Brigade

Bvt. Brig. Gen. EDGAR M. GREGORY
187th New York, Lt. Col. Daniel Myers; *188th New York*, Lt. Col. Isaac Doolittle; *189th New York*, Lt. Col. Joseph G. Townsend.

Third Brigade

Bvt. Maj. Gen. JOSEPH J. BARTLETT
Bvt. Brig. Gen. ALFRED L. PEARSON[12]
1st Maine Sharpshooters, Capt. George R. Abbott; *20th Maine*, Lt. Col. Walter G. Morrill; *32d Massachusetts*, Lt. Col. James A. Cunningham; *16th Michigan*,[13] Bvt. Col. Benjamin F. Partridge; *83d Pennsylvania*, Col. Chauncey P. Rogers; *91st Pennsylvania*, Lt. Col. Eli G. Sellers; *118th Pennsylvania*, Bvt. Lt. Col. Henry O'Neill; *155th Pennsylvania*, Bvt. Brig. Gen. Alfred L. Pearson; Maj. John A. Cline.

Second Division

Bvt. Maj. Gen. ROMEYN B. AYRES

First Brigade

Bvt. Brig. Gen. FREDERICK WINTHROP[14]
Col. JAMES GRINDLAY
Brig. Gen. JOSEPH HAYES[15]
5th New York (Veteran), Capt. Henry Shickhart; Lt. Col. William F. Drum;[16] *15th New York Heavy Artillery*, Lt. Col. Michael Wiedrich;[17] Maj. Louis Eiche; *140th New York*, Lt. Col. William S. Grantsynn; *146th New York*, Col. James Grindlay; Lt. Henry Loomis; Col. James Grindley.

Second Brigade
Bvt. Brig. Gen. ANDREW W. DENISON[18]
Col. RICHARD N. BOWERMAN[19]
Col. DAVID STANTON
1st Maryland, Col. David L. Stanton; *4th Maryland*, Col. Richard N. Bowerman; Maj. Harrison Andreon; *7th Maryland*, Lt. Col. David T. Bennett;[20] Maj. Edward M. Mobley; *8th Maryland*, Lt. Col. Ernest F. M. Faehtz.

Third Brigade
Bvt. Brig. Gen. JAMES GWYN
3d Delaware, Capt. John H. Cade; *4th Delaware*, Capt. William H. McClary;[21] Bvt. Lt. Col. Moses B. Gist; *8th Delaware, (3 cos.)*, Capt. John N. Richards; *157th Pennsylvania, (4 cos.), 190th Pennsylvania, 191st Pennsylvania*, Bvt. Col. Joseph B. Pattee; *210th Pennsylvania*, Col. William Sergeant;[22] Lt. Col. Edward L. Witman.

Third Division
Bvt. Maj. Gen. SAMUEL W. CRAWFORD

First Brigade
Col. JOHN A. KELLOGG
91st New York, Col. Jonathan Tarbell; *6th Wisconsin*, Lt. Col. Thomas Kerr;[23] Capt. Edward A. Whaley; Capt. Lewis A. Kent; *7th Wisconsin*, Lt. Col. Hollon Richardson.[24]

Second Brigade
Brig. Gen. HENRY BAXTER
16th Maine, Col. Charles W. Tilden; *39th Massachusetts*, Lt. Col. Henry M. Tremlett;[25] Capt. Jos. J. Cooper; *97th New York*, Lt. Col. Rouse S. Eggleston;[26] *11th Pennsylvania*, Maj. John B. Overmeyer; *107th Pennsylvania*, Col. Thomas F. McCoy.

Third Brigade
Bvt. Brig. Gen. RICHARD COULTER
94th New York, Maj. Henry H. Fish;[27] Capt. Albert T. Morgan;[28] *95th New York*, Capt. George D. Knight; *147th New York*, Maj. Dennis B. Dailey;[29] Capt. James A. McKinley; *56th Pennsylvania, 88th Pennsylvania*, Maj. Henry A. Laycock; *121st Pennsylvania*,[30] Maj. West Funk; *142d Pennsylvania*,[31] Lt. Col. Horatio N: Warren.[32]

Unattached
1st Battalion, New York Sharpshooters, Capt. Clinton Perry.

Artillery Brigade

Bvt. Brig. Gen. CHARLES S. WAINWRIGHT

1st New York Light, Battery B, Capt. Robert E. Rogers; *1st New York Light, Battery D,* Lt. Deloss M. Johnson; *1st New York Light, Battery H,* Bvt. Maj. Gen. Charles E. Mink; *15th New York Heavy, Co. M,* Capt. William D. Dickey; *4th U.S., Battery B,* Lt. John Mitchell;[33] Lt. William P. Vose; *5th U.S. Batteries D and G,* Lt. Jacob B. Rawles.

NOTES

ABBREVIATIONS

BC	Special Collections Room, Hawthorne-Longfellow Library, Bowdoin College, Brunswick, Maine.
CSA	Confederate States of America.
FPC	First Parish Church, Brunswick, Maine.
FPYU	Frost Family Papers, Manuscripts and Archives, Yale University Library, New Haven, Connecticut.
GNMP	Gettysburg National Military Park, Gettysburg, Pennsylvania.
JLC	Joshua Lawrence Chamberlain.
LC	Library of Congress, Washington, D.C.
MAGR	Maine Adjutant General. *Annual Reports of the Adjutant General of the State of Maine*, 1861–1867. Augusta, 1862–68.
MHS	Joshua L. Chamberlain Papers, Collection 10, Maine Historical Society, Portland, Maine.
MOLLUS	The Military Order of the Loyal Legion of the United States.
MSA	Maine State Archives, Augusta, Maine.
NA	National Archives, Washington, D.C.
OR	U.S. War Department. *The War of the Rebellion: A Compilation of the Official Records of the Union and Confederate Armies*. 70 vols. in 128 pts. Washington, D.C., 1880–1901. *OR* citations take the following form: volume number (part number, where applicable): page number(s). All citations are to series 1, unless otherwise indicated.
PHS	Pejepscot Historical Society, Brunswick, Maine.
PWCI	U.S. Army. Adjutant General's Office. *Proceedings, Findings, and Opinion of the Court of Inquiry in the Case of Gouverneur K. Warren*. 3 pts. Washington, D.C., 1883.
RBHC	Rutherford B. Hayes Presidential Center, Fremont, Ohio.
RC	Chamberlain-Adams Family Correspondence, Arthur and Elizabeth Schlesinger Library, Radcliffe College, Harvard University, Cambridge, Massachusetts.
UMO	Special Collections Department, Raymond H. Fogler Library, University of Maine, Orono.
WP	In writer's possession.

Note: All manuscript repository collections are Joshua L. Chamberlain collections or papers unless otherwise noted.

PROLOGUE

1. Quotations, JLC, "Through Blood and Fire at Gettysburg," p. 909.

CHAPTER ONE

1. Furbish, *Facts about Brunswick*, p. 9; newspaper clipping, "Presentation to Brunswick Officers," JLC Letterbook, PHS; JLC, "My Story of Fredericksburg," p. 148; Gerrish, *Army Life*, p. 2; Whitman and True, *Maine in the War*, p. 7. Quotation, Furbish, *Facts about Brunswick*. The JLC Letterbook, an unfinished scrapbook of newspaper clippings and handwritten memorabilia of JLC's wartime experiences, was owned by Dr. Arpad A. Warlam of Saddle River, New Jersey, and was first shown to the writer by JLC's granddaughter Rosamond Allen (1898–) in the summer of 1983. Dr. Warlam later donated it to the Pejepscot Historical Society for their Chamberlain Civil War Museum at JLC's home in Brunswick, Maine. It had been given to Dr. Warlam by the late Eleanor Wyllys Allen (1893–1980), JLC's eldest granddaughter. A third granddaughter was Beatrice Lawrence Allen Patten (1896–1943). JLC has no other descendants. John Furbish's chronicle of the "brief accounts of various events, changes, and interesting incidents connected with the history of the town of Brunswick . . . Maine" was begun June 27, 1862, and published in facsimile by the Pejepscot Historical Society in 1976. Gerrish was a private in the Twentieth Maine.

2. Newspaper clipping, "Presentation to Brunswick Officers," JLC Letterbook, PHS. JLC's state of mind can be inferred from his subsequent speech.

3. Ibid.; "Early Memoirs, J. L. Chamberlain," pp. 62, 63, BC; *In Memoriam*, p. 12; *MAGR, 1863*, app. C, p. 3. Quotation, newspaper clipping, "Presentation to Brunswick Officers," JLC Letterbook, PHS. "Early Memoirs" is a typed manuscript corrected in JLC's hand and numbered pages 41 to 77. *In Memoriam* is a tribute to JLC written by his old friends Selden Connor, Franklin M. Drew, and Abner O. Shaw. The Twentieth Maine numbered 979 officers and men when mustered for duty August 29, 1862.

4. Fox, *Regimental Losses*, p. 62; JLC to Frances Caroline Adams (hereinafter Fannie), Nov. 3, 1854, LC; Gerrish, *Army Life*, p. 347. Quotation, ibid.

5. JLC to Fannie, Nov. 3, 1854, LC; JLC to Secretary of State, Oct. 25, 1900, FPYU; newspaper clipping, "Commencement at Bowdoin," JLC Letterbook, PHS; Catherine T. Smith interview, *Brunswick Times-Record*, Sept. 7, 1976; Copeland, Mrs. Catherine Smith interview, PHS. Although Mrs. Smith, JLC's last secretary, remembered him as having "twinkling blue eyes, no matter how badly he felt, always snapping right out at you" (ibid.), he gave their color as blue-gray in his application for a passport in 1900. In the same application he gave his height as 5 feet 9 inches, but forty-six years before, as a much younger man, he gave his height as 5 feet $10\frac{1}{2}$ inches in a mock deed to his person sent as a joke to Fannie, then his fiancée. The description

of JLC's physical appearance is taken from a *carte de visite* depicting him in a lieutenant colonel's uniform, with "August, 1862" written in ink on the back of the copy in FPYU, and a comparison of it with other, younger civilian photographs in Bowdoin yearbooks, 1857–61, BC, a daguerreotype, PHS, and an older photograph in the Brady Collection, NA. Because of the lighting in old photographs, it is difficult to determine JLC's hair color. Earlier photos show him with very dark hair and, in one, with a startling narrow white streak in front, but in the August 1862 *carte de visite,* it appears dark blond, probably the result of a combination of lighting and his mixed gray and dark hair. The "Commencement at Bowdoin" newspaper clipping cited above, describing the events of August 2, 1865, remarked that JLC was "grayer than four years ago." Rosamond Allen has stated to the writer that she and her mother, Grace Chamberlain Allen, began to gray quickly in their early thirties and that their hair eventually became white, as did JLC's.

6. Newspaper clipping, "Presentation to Brunswick Officers," JLC Letterbook, PHS; Haythornwaite, *Uniforms,* pp. 104–6, 141, 142, pl. 12; JLC's lieutenant-colonel *carte de visite,* "Wm. Pierce, Photographer, Brunswick, Me." stamped on reverse, WP.

7. JLC's lieutenant-colonel *carte de visite,* WP; Haythornwaite, *Uniforms,* p. 142, pl. 12.

8. JLC to Gov. Washburn, July 14, 1862, MSA.

9. Ibid.; Whitman and True, *Maine in the War,* pp. 2–8; *MAGR, 1861,* Gen. Order No. 43, July 27, 1861, app. A, p. 10. Quotation, ibid. The usual Civil War infantry regiment at full strength consisted of, for field and staff: three field officers (colonel, lieutenant colonel, and major), one adjutant, one quartermaster, one surgeon, two assistant surgeons, one chaplain, one sergeant major, one quartermaster's sergeant, one commissary-sergeant, one hospital steward, two principal musicians; and, for each of ten companies: one captain, one first lieutenant, one second lieutenant, one first sergeant, four sergeants, eight corporals, two musicians, one wagoner, and eighty-two privates, for a total of 1,025 officers and men (Fox, *Regimental Losses,* pp. 4, 5). A popular Stephen Foster song of the period was inspired by Lincoln's call for troops in July 1862: "We are Coming Father Abraham, 300,000 More" (Taylor et al., *Treasury of Stephen Foster*).

10. Little, *Genealogical History,* 1:132–33; Thayer and Ames, *History and Families,* p. 244; JLC to Gov. Washburn, July 14, 1862, MSA. A publisher's proof of the Little entry on JLC is in PHS, indicating either JLC's authorship or his approval of the facts in the article. Among the contributors to Thayer and Ames, before her death in 1960, was Alice M. Farrington, JLC's niece.

11. JLC to Gov. Washburn, July 14, 1862, MSA; JLC to Gov. Washburn, July 17, 1862, MSA. Quotation, JLC to Gov. Washburn, July 14, 1862.

12. JLC to Gov. Washburn, July 14, 1862, MSA. JLC did not tell the governor that he was sacrificing a European tour, only that "I am expecting to have leave, at the approaching Commencement, to spend a year or more in

Europe." That he was willing to leave his comfortable position for the war was remarked upon in the newspapers. The enlistment of prominent men was used as an example for others to support the volunteer enlistment effort.

13. Joshua Chamberlain, Jr., to JLC, n.d. (but probably early September 1862), RC; Catherine T. Smith interview, *Brunswick Times-Record*, Sept. 7, 1976, PHS; A[mericus] Fuller to "My Dear Chum," June 15, 1861, Oliver O. Howard Papers, BC; "Early Memoirs," pp. 41, 75, 76, BC; Chamberlain Association, *JLC: A Sketch*, p. 4; Hatch, *Bowdoin College*, pp. 116, 120. First quotation, Joshua Chamberlain, Jr., to JLC, n.d.; second, "Early Memoirs," p. 76. Bowdoin had 144 students in 1861 (Hatch, *Bowdoin College*, p. 121). Joshua Chamberlain, Jr., (1801–80) was JLC's father. A 1942 article from the *Lewiston Journal* in BC ("Chamberlains, Maine History Fame, Were Opposed in Politics," *Lewiston Journal*, Oct. 31, 1942) characterized him as a Democrat who was adamantly opposed to the Civil War. JLC's paternal grandfather (1770–1857) was also named Joshua. The Chamberlain Association's purpose was apparently genealogical; *JLC: A Sketch* was prepared for their report and then expanded and printed as a pamphlet. It appears to have been written for the society by someone using biographical information only JLC himself could provide. "Early Memoirs" seems to be a portion of a much longer manuscript that was undoubtedly the basis for *JLC: A Sketch*.

14. Hatch, *Bowdoin College*, pp. 115–17. President Woods's war position earned him the enmity of many and contributed to his decision to resign in 1866 (ibid., p. 123). A relative of JLC's wife, writing to JLC in the fall of 1863, called Woods "our Copperhead president" and described an incident at a social gathering where the hostess refused to take Woods's hand because of it (Deborah Folsom to JLC, Oct. 25, no year [but from contents, 1863], RC). JLC, as a member of the small Bowdoin faculty, certainly met Jefferson Davis at the 1858 commencement.

15. Horace B. Chamberlain to JLC, July 7, 1858, RC; JLC to Sarah D. B. Chamberlain, Jan. 31, 1860, BC; A[mericus] Fuller to "My Dear Chum," June 15, 1861, Oliver O. Howard Papers, BC; JLC to Nehemiah Cleaveland, Oct. 14, 1859, BC. Sarah D. B. Chamberlain (1803–88) was JLC's mother.

16. JLC to Nehemiah Cleaveland, Oct. 14, 1859, BC; Chamberlain Association, *JLC: A Sketch*, p. 9; JLC to Fannie, Oct. 10, 1862, LC. Quotation, JLC to Nehemiah Cleaveland, Oct. 14, 1859.

17. Chamberlain Association, *JLC: A Sketch*, pp. 9–10; A[mericus] Fuller to "My Dear Chum," June 15, 1861, Oliver O. Howard Papers, BC; "Early Memoirs," p. 76, BC; JLC to Sae [Sarah B. Chamberlain], "Tuesday noon," n.d. (but no doubt early March 1862), UMO; Sae to JLC, Mar. 11, no year (but from contents, 1861), RC; JLC to Gov. Washburn, July 14, 1862, MSA; Cleaveland, *Bowdoin College*, p. 671; handwritten statement signed by JLC, Aug. 28, 1862, LC. The latter shows that JLC had not received any of the $500 bonus, although its payment was not conditional upon his going to Eu-

rope. JLC's brother Horace, an 1857 Bowdoin graduate, counseled him to continue with the rhetoric post. But his family knew how much the trip meant to him: shortly after the war, his brother John wrote to him about the lost "continental tour" and thought that perhaps then, with his war service, he could be rewarded with a "foreign appointment." Under the common belief that Providence would provide a "reciprocation," John added, "And how suitable that the same agent for which you sacrificed those plans which had been culminating for a life time should now become the direct means of consummating them . . . specific things which in heroic self sacrifice we turn our backs upon, we are startled in the end to find before our eyes and within our grasp" (John C. Chamberlain to JLC, July 12, 1865, RC).

18. JLC to Gov. Washburn, July 17, 1862, MSA.

19. Ibid.; Chamberlain Association, *JLC: A Sketch*, pp. 4, 10; JLC to Gov. Washburn, July 22, 1862, MSA; *MAGR, 1862*, pt. 2 of app. D, pp. 541, 570, 598, 625. Some of what transpired between the governor and JLC is inferred from JLC's letters.

20. Diaries of Dr. George E. Adams (hereinafter Dr. Adams diary), July 19, 1862, FPC; Furbish, *Facts about Brunswick*, p. 5; *MAGR, 1864–1865*, 1:391; Warner, *Generals in Blue*, p. 237; Wilder, "Stars on Their Shoulders"; JLC to Gov. Washburn, July 22, 1862, MSA. Quotation, Wilder, "Stars on Their Shoulders." Dr. Adams (1801–75) was the foster father of Frances Caroline Adams, JLC's wife. His diaries were not kept by using a notebook for each year but were continuous in mostly undifferentiated volumes.

21. Newspaper clipping, "Colonel of 20th Regiment," JLC Letterbook, PHS; JLC to Gov. Washburn, July 22, 1862, MSA; "Early Memoirs," pp. 76, 77, BC; JLC to Sarah D. B. Chamberlain, Jan. 31, 1860, BC; Ashby, *First Parish Church*, p. 302; Hatch, *Bowdoin College*, pp. 57, 103, 115; JLC to Fannie, Oct. 26, 1862, LC. Quotations, ibid. In his letter to his mother JLC wrote, "We have our usual amount of diplomacy this term—plotting and counterplotting. The game now is Professor of Modern Languages in which curious developments of human nature appear in full relief—& how it will turn out I can't predict." Bowdoin was a Congregational school, but its charter said nothing about its denomination, and the denominational fight, including moderates and ultraconservatives, had been raging on and off for many years in the Board of Overseers and Board of Trustees. The overseers had a majority of Congregationalists and veto power over the trustees; the trustees usually had a majority of moderates, including Unitarians and Episcopalians. The division extended to the faculty: in 1857 a professor of modern languages had been reelected by the trustees but rejected by the overseers because he was a Unitarian (Hatch, *Bowdoin College*, pp. 111–15).

22. "Early Memoirs," pp. 76, 77, BC; Josiah Drummond, Attorney General of Maine, to Gov. Washburn, July 21, 1862, MSA; Ashby, *First Parish Church*, p. 294; Dr. John D. Lincoln to Gov. Washburn, July 17, 1862, MSA. First quotation, "Early Memoirs," pp. 76, 77; second, Josiah Drummond to Gov.

Washburn, July 21, 1862; last, Dr. John D. Lincoln to Gov. Washburn, July 17, 1862.

23. *MAGR, 1862*, General Order No. 26, Aug. 7, 1862, app. A, p. 9; Gov. Washburn to JLC, Aug. 8, 1862, LC; JLC to Gov. Washburn, Aug. 8, 1862, MSA; JLC to "My Dear Loring," Aug. 11, 1862, BC; Cleaveland, *Bowdoin College*, p. 671. JLC wrote to the governor twice on August 8, one letter before he received the governor's commission by mail, and then his hurried acceptance. Both are used here. His and Ames's commissions dated from August 8, 1862 (*MAGR, 1862*, app. D, p. 653).

24. JLC to Gov. Washburn, Aug. 8, 1862, MSA; JLC to Col. Eugene Hale, Aug. 15, 1862, MSA; JLC undirected recommendation, Aug. 15, 1862, MSA; Furbish, *Facts about Brunswick*, p. 5; *MAGR, 1862*, General Order No. 26, Aug. 7, 1862, app. A, p. 9; ibid., General Order No. 31, Aug. 14, 1862, app. A, p. 12; ibid., General Order No. 32, Aug. 16, 1862, app. A, p. 15. Maine had enrolled all men between the ages of eighteen and forty-five into the state militia previously that year (ibid., app. A, pp. 24–29). No state or U.S. bounty was to be paid for nine-month men, even for volunteers, and the adjutant general asked towns not to pay bounty, except for up to $20 for volunteers to substitute for drafted men. However, by August 30 Brunswick voted to pay a $100 bounty to nine-month volunteers to help fill their quota (Furbish, *Facts about Brunswick*, p. 7).

25. Spear, "Regiment"; Furbish, *Facts about Brunswick*, pp. 4, 5; *MAGR, 1864–1865*, 1:513; JLC to Gov. Washburn, Aug. 8, 1862, MSA; *MAGR, 1862*, pp. 6, 7, 26; ibid., General Order No. 31, Aug. 14, 1862, app. A, p. 12; ibid., General Order No. 22, July 17, 1862, app. A, p. 8; JLC recommendation for Lt. J. H. Nichols, Mar. 10, 1864, MSA. Quotation, Furbish, *Facts about Brunswick*, p. 4.

26. JLC to Col. Eugene Hale, Aug. 15, 1862, MSA; Spear, "Regiment," pp. 5, 6; Gerrish, *Army Life*, p. 56; *MAGR, 1862*, app. D, pp. 653–77. Quotation, Spear, "Regiment," p. 6. *MAGR, 1864–1865*, 1:526, gives general categories of occupations for Maine volunteers; in addition, occupations of several individuals in the regiment are available from various records and sources.

27. Spear, "Regiment," p. 7; *MAGR, 1864–1865*, 1:370; *MAGR, 1862*, app. D, p. 653.

28. *MAGR, 1864–1865*, 1:302; Ames, *Adelbert Ames*, p. 1; U.S. Congress, *Medal of Honor Recipients*, p. 365; Spear, "Regiment," pp. 8, 9. Quotation, ibid., p. 9.

29. Spear, "Regiment," pp. 5, 7. Quotation, p. 7.

30. Ibid., p. 9; *MAGR, 1862*, app. G, p. 21; Gerrish and Hutchinson, *The Blue and the Gray*, p. 64. Quotation, ibid.

31. Spear, "Regiment," p. 9; Pullen, *Twentieth Maine*, p. 34. Small, inexpensive books containing the elements of basic infantry tactics were in widespread use and were studied along with the more complete volumes as

many enlisted men as well as officers struggled to learn the intricate drill movements.

32. Spear, "Regiment," pp. 8, 10, 11. Quotation, p. 8.

33. Ibid., pp. 11, 12. Quotation, p. 11.

34. *MAGR, 1862*, app. C, p. 3; Billings, *Hardtack and Coffee*, p. 44; Dr. Adams diary, Sept. 1, 1862, FPC; newspaper clipping, "Brunswick Officers," JLC Letterbook, PHS. Quotation, Billings, *Hardtack and Coffee*.

35. Little, *Genealogical History*, p. 140; Dr. Adams diary, Sept. 1, 1862, FPC; information provided to the writer by Rosamond Allen. A double daguerreotype taken of the Chamberlain children, ca. 1862, shows them both wearing dresses made of the same fabric, and another pose of Harold Wyllys shows him wearing a different dress. A letter from Fannie to JLC (Dec. 2, 1861, RC) describes Wyllys's "long sleeved aprons." For a similar boy's costume of the period, see an early photograph of President William Howard Taft, who was a year older than JLC's son, in *The American Heritage Pictorial History of the Presidents of the United States*, 2:662. Although most of her correspondents used the spelling "Fanny," Mrs. Chamberlain apparently preferred "Fannie."

36. Dr. Adams diary, Sept. 1, 1862, FPC.

37. Ibid.; Gerrish, *Army Life*, p. 2; *MAGR, 1862*, General Order No. 26, Aug. 7, 1862, app. A, p. 9; ibid., app. C, p. 5; *Maine at Gettysburg*, p. 273; Pullen, *Twentieth Maine*, p. 16, citing *The Lincoln County News*, Jan. 18, 1877. Quotation, Pullen, *Twentieth Maine*. *MAGR, 1862*, app. D, pp. 653–77, gives the hometowns of the original Twentieth Maine officers and men.

CHAPTER TWO

1. *MAGR, 1862*, p. 113; Little, *Genealogical History*, 1:133; Thomas D. Chamberlain Military Pension records, NA; Tom Chamberlain letter (no addressee, but probably to his brother John), Feb. 2, 1863, UMO; Tom Chamberlain to JLC, July 21, 1862, RC; Tom Chamberlain to JLC, Aug. 22, 1862, RC. Tom's physical appearance is also drawn from contemporary photographs of him in uniform. He was born April 29, 1841.

2. *MAGR, 1864–1865*, 1:337; *MAGR, 1862*, app. D, p. 673; Joshua Chamberlain, Jr., to JLC, n.d. (but certainly early September 1862), RC. Quotation, ibid. The latter was addressed "Hall's Hill, Virginia," and sent with Tom, undoubtedly when he reported to the regiment after recovery from his illness, a violent attack of indigestion or other intestinal disorder.

3. Little, *Genealogical History*, 1:132, 133. Quotation, ibid., p. 132. The family may have removed from Danvers instead of Cambridge (ibid).

4. Thayer and Ames, *History and Families*, pp. 17–23, 30–39. This volume was published for the 150th anniversary of the towns of Brewer, Orrington, Holden, and Eddington.

5. Ibid., pp. 50, 51, 54, 69; Little, *Genealogical History*, 1:133; Lord, "Early Church Records," p. 62, Brewer Public Library, Brewer, Maine. "Early Church Records" is a 1942 typed manuscript from the original records of the First Congregational Church of Brewer, Maine.

6. Little, *Genealogical History*, 1:133; Thayer and Ames, *History and Families*, p. 35, and Genealogical section, p. xxiv; *Bangor Historical Magazine* 2 (1886–87): 135–37.

7. Chamberlain Family Bible, Brewer Public Library, Brewer, Maine; JLC to Fannie Hardy Eckstorm, Apr. 28, May 5, and May 20, 1909, Fannie Hardy Eckstorm Papers, UMO; Lord, "Early Church Records," p. 63, Brewer Public Library, Brewer, Maine; JLC's penmanship copy book, BC; interview with Alice Farrington, in newspaper clipping, "Brewer's Forgotten Hero," WP. First quotation, Chamberlain Family Bible; second, Wallace, *Soul of the Lion*, p. 18. JLC's birthplace is now number 350 Main Street, Brewer. Another half story was added to the house after the turn of the century. One of JLC's earliest memories was here: "The odor of the roses at the door. That abides" (JLC to Fannie Hardy Eckstorm, Apr. 28, 1909, Fannie Hardy Eckstorm Papers, UMO). In later life, JLC entitled an address "Joshua as a Military Commander" (Chamberlain Association, *JLC: A Sketch*, p. 41). He signed letters in various combinations of his given names and their initials up to 1855. Family correspondence never addressed him as "Joshua," always "Lawrence." His name appears as Lawrence Chamberlain in the "Early Church Records," when he joined the church in 1845, and appeared in the catalogues of Bangor Theological Seminary as "J. Lawrence Chamberlain" (*Catalogue of the Theological Seminary, Bangor*, 1853–55).

8. JLC to Sarah Shepard, Feb. 8, 1847, UMO; *Bangor Historical Magazine* 6 (1890–91): 82; *Farrington Memorial*, p. 66; Wilder, *Catalogue*, p. 106. Sarah Shepard was JLC's cousin. Horace, Beriah, Thomas, and, of course, Sarah Brastow were all names from Mrs. Chamberlain's family (Thayer and Ames, *History and Families*, Genealogical section, pp. xxiii, xxiv), and Davee must have been also. The Chamberlain family home still stands at 80 Chamberlain Street in Brewer.

9. Chamberlain Association, *JLC: A Sketch*, p. 3; JLC to Sarah D. B. Chamberlain, Sept. 8, 1872, BC; Sarah B. Chamberlain to JLC, Sept. 12, 1863, RC; Alice M. Farrington to Rosamond Allen, Oct. 26, 1954, WP. Sarah B. Chamberlain is JLC's sister, afterwards Sae here to differentiate from her mother, Sarah D. B. Chamberlain. Mrs. Chamberlain's letters to JLC give insight into the thoughtful, persuasive influence the mother had on her son. Alice Farrington, Sae's daughter, described her grandmother to JLC's granddaughter Rosamond Allen in the 1954 letter; Alice remembered her grandmother well, having lived with her from the time of her birth in 1869 until the elder woman died in 1888.

10. Chamberlain Association, *JLC: A Sketch*, pp. 4–6; "Early Memoirs," pp. 49, 63, 66, 67, 70–72, BC.

11. "Early Memoirs," p. 53, BC; Chamberlain Association, *JLC: A Sketch*, pp. 3, 4; Charlotte Adams to Fannie, Apr. 19, 1845, MHS. Charlotte Adams was Fannie's sister; she sometimes visited relatives in Bangor and penned descriptive letters laced with humor.

12. Chamberlain Association, *JLC: A Sketch*, p. 5; "Early Memoirs," p. 73, BC; Little, *Genealogical History*, 1:133.

13. Sae Chamberlain to JLC, May 8, 1859, RC; Alice M. Farrington to Rosamund Allen, Oct. 26, 1954, PHS; Munson, *Penobscot*, p. 344. Quotation, ibid.

14. "Early Memoirs," pp. 43–46, BC. First quotation, p. 45; last two, p. 46.

15. Ibid., p. 46.

16. Ibid., pp. 41, 46. All quotations except the last, p. 46; the last, p. 41. The correspondence reveals that Mr. Chamberlain was particularly indulgent with money when cash was available, providing financial help in the form of loans, gifts, and opportunities to his adult children. He and his wife were quick to offer their home and hospitality for long periods of time to their children and grandchildren.

17. Chamberlain Association, *JLC: A Sketch*, pp. 5, 6.

18. Ibid., p. 5; Thayer and Ames, *History and Families*, pp. 47, 49, 238; "Early Memoirs," pp. 46, 48, BC. Manly Hardy, a fur trader of the area who was four years younger than JLC, was known to say that in his boyhood the local Indians used the birch shelters, but that by the time he was a young man, they mostly used canvas tents (Thayer and Ames, *History and Families*, p. 47, and Genealogical section, p. clviii).

19. "Early Memoirs," p. 51, BC; Chamberlain Association, *JLC: A Sketch*, p. 3; Ashby, *First Parish Church*, p. 48; Thayer and Ames, *History and Families*, pp. 77, 78; Lord, "Early Church Records," p. 63, Brewer Public Library, Brewer, Maine. Quotations, "Early Memoirs." It was the custom for baptized individuals, all of whom were counted as members of a church, but not full members, to come forward if it was their intention to unite with the church in full membership and lead a Christian life, publicly describe the experiences that led to their decisions, and then be accepted by the congregation. Ashby states that the full members were always in the minority in a congregation (Ashby, *First Parish Church*, pp. 55, 56). The records of the Brewer church show JLC's full membership ended only at his death; ordinarily, when parishioners established themselves with another Congregational church, they transferred by "letter" and were so shown on the records. Apparently JLC did not remove his membership to Brunswick's First Parish Church, which he attended and was active in all his life, both during and after his college years, also owning a pew there. A search of the membership rolls of the latter church by Robert M. Cross for his 1945 Bowdoin senior essay failed to find JLC's name ("Joshua Lawrence Chamberlain," p. 68, BC).

20. "Early Memoirs," p. 41, BC; Cleaveland, *Bowdoin College*, p. 570; Little, *Genealogical History*, 1:133; Sarah D. B. Chamberlain to JLC, Oct. 21, no year

(but certainly 1856), RC; Tom Chamberlain to JLC, July 21, 1862, RC; John Chamberlain to JLC, Oct. 20, 1862, RC. Quotation, "Early Memoirs." Mrs. Chamberlain's letters in RC show her as helpful, giving her opinions, counsel, and suggestions and having faith in her children's good judgment and right action. She rarely scolded, and when she admonished she did so in gentle or amusing ways. JLC described her in military metaphor as a "chasseur" ("Early Memoirs," p. 41, BC).

21. "Early Memoirs," pp. 41, 42, BC; Sae to JLC, Mar. 11, no year (but from contents, 1861), RC; Thayer and Ames, *History and Families*, p. 79. Quotation, "Early Memoirs," p. 41.

22. "Early Memoirs," pp. 42, 43, BC.

23. JLC to Sarah Shepard, Feb. 8, 1847, UMO; Chamberlain Association, *JLC: A Sketch*, p. 7.

24. Chamberlain Association, *JLC: A Sketch*, p. 7; JLC to Sarah Shepard, Feb. 8, 1847, UMO; Ashby, *First Parish Church*, pp. 52, 352. A bass viol was commonly used to accompany singing, especially where no piano or organ was available.

25. JLC to Sarah Shepard, Feb. 8, 1847, UMO; Sarah D. B. Chamberlain to John Chamberlain, attached to a letter to JLC, Oct. 8, 1855, RC; "Early Memoirs," p. 49, BC. Quotation, JLC to Sarah Shepard, Feb. 8, 1847.

26. "Early Memoirs," pp. 49, 50, BC; Cleaveland, *Bowdoin College*, p. 570. Lemon Bennett of Waterville heard JLC's Greek recitations.

27. "Early Memoirs," pp. 51, 52, BC. Quotation, p. 51. The railroad did not come to Brunswick until 1849 (Ashby, *First Parish Church*, p. 241).

28. "Early Memoirs," p. 51, BC; Hatch, *Bowdoin College*, pp. 403, 407, 409, 418, 419, photograph facing p. 107.

29. Little, *Catalogue*, pp. xvii, lxxxiii; Cleaveland, *Bowdoin College*, p. 2; Hatch, *Bowdoin College*, p. 305, photograph facing p. 107; Rand, "Chums at Bowdoin," pp. 14, 15.

30. "Early Memoirs," pp. 52, 53, BC; JLC to "My Dear Pastor," May 5, 1848, BC.

31. JLC to "My Dear Pastor," May 5, 1848, BC; "Early Memoirs," pp. 54, 55, BC. Quotations, ibid., p. 54.

32. "Early Memoirs," pp. 55, 56, 63, BC. Quotation, p. 63.

33. Ibid., p. 64; Cleaveland, *Bowdoin College*, p. 302; JLC to Sarah Shepard, Feb. 8, 1847, UMO.

34. "Early Memoirs," pp. 55–58, BC. Quotations, pp. 55, 58.

35. Ibid., p. 58; Hatch, *Bowdoin College*, p. 92.

36. "Early Memoirs," p. 59, BC.

37. Ibid., p. 60.

38. Ibid., pp. 60, 61, 63. Quotation, p. 63.

39. Ibid., pp. 60–63; *In Memoriam*, p. 12. Quotations, "Early Memoirs," pp. 60, 63.

40. "Early Memoirs," pp. 63–65, BC.

41. Ibid., pp. 65, 66. Quotation, p. 66.

42. Ibid., pp. 66–68; Ashby, *First Parish Church*, p. 225.

43. "Early Memoirs," p. 69, BC; Stowe, *Harriet Beecher Stowe*, pp. 149, 156, 159; Ashby, *First Parish Church*, pp. 227, 230. JLC called Mrs. Stowe the professor's "genius of a wife" ("Early Memoirs," p. 67, BC).

44. Ashby, *First Parish Church*, pp. 230, 231, 271; "Early Memoirs," p. 69, BC; Little, *Genealogical History*, 1:140; newspaper clipping, "Mrs. Chamberlain's Funeral," PHS. From material in the Stowe book, other biographies, and church records, Ashby was able to establish the date of Mrs. Stowe's vision of the death of Uncle Tom as March 2, 1851. She was sitting in pew number 23, which is so marked today with a brass plate.

45. Dr. Adams to Mrs. H. C. Knight, Aug. 24, 1875, FPYU; Eleanor Wyllys Allen, Adams family genealogy drafts, RC; Amelia Adams to Fannie, Apr. 3, 1838, RC; Charlotte Adams to Fannie Adams, Mar. 12, 1833, BC; Amelia Adams to Fannie, Feb. 19, 1844, RC. Quotations, Dr. Adams to Mrs. H. C. Knight, Aug. 24, 1875. Amelia Adams was also called Emily (Allen, Adams family genealogy drafts, RC). (Fannie probably came to live with her cousin at about the age of five. Fannie's given name may have originally been "Caroline Frances," according to Eleanor Allen's genealogy drafts and Cleaveland, *Bowdoin College*, p. 672. Fannie's Boston family sent art supplies to Brunswick for her, and her half-sister Catherine taught art (Amelia Adams to Fannie, Apr. 3, 1838, RC). Her brother, George Wyllys Adams (1815–60), was an accomplished artist—a handwritten book about his European tour, beautifully illustrated with ink drawings, is in the JLC Collection, LC.

46. Helen R. Adams to JLC, Nov. 26, 1905, BC; Amelia Adams to Fannie, Apr. 3, 1838, RC; Allen, Adams family genealogy drafts, RC; Deborah G. Folsom headstone, Pine Grove Cemetery, Brunswick, Maine; Fannie to Cousin D, Apr. 14, 1864, MHS; Ashby, *First Parish Church*, p. 157; Anna D. Davis to Fannie, Mar. 10, 1852, MHS; Fannie to Dr. Adams, Aug. 31 and Sept. 11, 1838, RC. Quotation, ibid. Fannie's education also contained a study of the French language, in which Deborah Folsom was proficient (Fannie to Dr. Adams, Aug. 31, 1838, RC). The relationship of Deborah Folsom to the first Mrs. George E. Adams, Sarah Ann Folsom, is surmised.

47. Wheeler and Wheeler, *History of Brunswick*, p. 711; Cleaveland, *Bowdoin College*, p. 80; Dr. Adams to JLC, Sept. 6, 1864, RC; Dr. Adams to Fannie, July 9, no year (but from contents, certainly 1852), MHS; Dr. Adams diary, Oct. 14, 1856, FPC; newspaper clipping, "Mrs. Chamberlain's Funeral," PHS.

48. Fannie to Charlotte Adams, Feb. 8, 1849, RC; Fannie to Deborah Folsom, Feb. 17, 1853, MHS; Ashby, *First Parish Church*, pp. 157, 235; Ellen M. Bacon to Fannie, Sept. 28, 1849, MHS; Allen, Adams family genealogy drafts, RC. Comments concerning Fannie's inability to see things to Dr. Adams's satisfaction are numerous in his diaries.

49. Anna D. Davis to Fannie, Mar. 10, 1852, MHS; "Saturday morn," note

to Lawrence in Fannie Adams's hand, n.d. (but ca. 1851), RC; "Early Memoirs," pp. 67–69, BC; Ashby, *First Parish Church,* p. 234; JLC to Fannie, May 16, 1852, RC; JLC to Fannie, June 7, 1852, RC; JLC to Fannie, "*Evening Edition,* Monday evening 8 o'clock," MHS. The "Saturday morn" note indicates that Fannie may have given private music or art lessons.

50. Ashby, *First Parish Church,* pp. 234, 235; Pejepscot Historic Survey, Card u-13 188, PHS; Dr. Adams diary, Feb. 11, 1855, FPC; Deborah Folsom to Fannie, Feb. 17, 1853, MHS; S[tephen] M[errill] Allen to Fannie, Jan. 9, 1852, RC; S. M. Allen to Fannie, Feb. 8, 1852, MHS; information provided to the writer by Rosamond Allen; additional information provided by Sally W. Rand, Pejepscot Historical Society. The address of Dr. Adams's former home is now number 167 Park Row, Brunswick.

51. S. M. Allen to Fannie, Jan. 9, 1852, RC; S. M. Allen to Fannie, Feb. 8, 1852, MHS; JLC to Fannie, May 16, 1852, RC; George E. Adams to Fannie, July 9, [1852], MHS. Quotations, S. M. Allen to Fannie, Jan. 9, 1852. Thirty years later, Allen's son Horace married the Chamberlains' daughter Grace.

52. "Early Memoirs," pp. 69, 70, BC; Meyer, *The Instructed Conscience,* p. 4; Hatch, *Bowdoin College,* pp. 304, 305; Wilder, *Catalogue,* p. 98. Professor Thomas C. Upham was head of the department of mental and moral philosophy at Bowdoin for many years. His three-volume *Elements of Moral Philosophy,* used extensively as college textbooks, were undoubtedly the three books JLC studied (Cleaveland, *Bowdoin College,* pp. 131–33).

53. JLC to Fannie, May 16, 1852, RC.

54. JLC to Fannie, May 28, no year (but certainly 1852), MHS.

55. JLC to Fannie, June 7, 1852, MHS; "*Evening Edition,* Monday evening 8 o'clock," MHS; Fannie to JLC, June 23, 1853, RC; JLC to Fannie, Apr. 27, 1854, RC; Deborah Folsom to Fannie, Jan. 12, 1854, MHS. First quotation, JLC to Fannie, June 7, 1852; others, "*Evening Edition.*" "*Evening Edition*" is probably an addition to the JLC to Fannie letter, June 7, 1852. The young couple may have visited Brewer before commencement. Fannie's and JLC's future plans are partially inferred from subsequent actions. Fannie's debt to her father must have been for education and travel expenses. According to Cousin D, these funds were expended on Fannie with the understanding that they were to be returned. Apparently Fannie later considered the amount a "fine" instead of a debt (Deborah Folsom to Fannie, Jan. 12, 1854, MHS).

56. Pejepscot Historic Survey, Card u-13 188, PHS; "Limited Power of Attorney" from Deborah G. Folsom to A. C. Robbins, Mar. 14, 1853, BC; JLC to Fannie, June 7, 1852, MHS; George E. Adams to Fannie, July 9, [1852], MHS; Deborah Folsom to Fannie, Feb. 17, 1853, MHS; Deborah Folsom to Fannie, Jan. 12, 1854, MHS.

57. JLC to Fannie, June 7, 1852, MHS. JLC's June 7, 1852, letter showed him to be very possessive toward Fannie. His unfamiliarity with his new betrothed status and Victorian custom may have accounted for some of his at-

titude. Anna Davis was apparently away from Brunswick until July 1852 (Anna Davis to Fannie, Mar. 10, 1852, MHS; Geo. Adams to Fannie, July 9, [1852], MHS).

58. Hatch, *Bowdoin College*, pp. 253–55; Ashby, *First Parish Church*, pp. 188–90, 212–13; "Early Memoirs," pp. 70–71, BC; Chamberlain Association, *JLC: A Sketch*, p. 29; JLC to Sarah D. B. Chamberlain, Aug. 6, 1852, UMO. Quotations, "Early Memoirs," p. 71. The first ("certain friends," etc.) is a reference to Fannie. JLC habitually used oblique phrases to allude to personal matters in any nonprivate writings. Bowdoin College commencement exercises were held in First Parish Church until 1966, except for a few small commencements during World War II in the smaller Bowdoin Chapel (*The First Parish*). JLC's college honors besides First Class Oration were: "Announced first rank in Greek. First Assistant Librarian; First Honor in French. German Junior Part at Exhibition. Prize for Declamation. Prize for English Composition. Test Problem Higher Mathematics, Junior Examination. First Assistant in Chemistry; Honorary Appointment. Original Problem in Astronomy; Senior Examination. First Class Oration; Bachelor's Degree. Master's Oration; Master's Degree" (Chamberlain Association, *JLC: A Sketch*, p. 29). JLC's diplomas are in UMO.

59. JLC to Fannie, "Tuesday p.m.," n.d. (but ca. August 1852), FPYU; "Early Memoirs," pp. 71, 72, 75, 76, BC; *Catalogue of the Theological Seminary, Bangor*, 1853. First quotations, "Early Memoirs," p. 72; last quotation, Chamberlain Association, *JLC: A Sketch*, p. 8. The seminary in 1852–53 had forty-three students and four professors; JLC's class had thirteen members. Dr. Adams was a trustee. See *Catalogue of the Theological Seminary, Bangor*, 1853.

60. JLC to Fannie, Oct. 8, 1854, RC; Mrs. Abby Orme to Fannie, Dec. 9, 1852, RC; Fannie to Charlotte Adams, Jan. 10, 1853, MHS; Fannie to JLC, Apr. 1, 1853, RC. George F. Root had a school for teachers of music in New York City. Both Dr. Adams, in his July 9, 1852, letter to Fannie (MHS), and Mrs. Orme, in the letter cited above, mentioned "Professor Root" as the recommender of Fannie for her music teaching position. Root later moved to Chicago, where he became famous as a composer, writing several well-known Civil War songs including the hugely popular "Battle Cry of Freedom" and "Just Before the Battle, Mother." It is very likely that JLC knew Root through Helen Root Adams. Root later built a summer home near Brunswick. See Johnson and Malone, *Dictionary of American Biography*, 8:147–48; Pejepscot Historic Survey, Card U-28-7, PHS.

61. "Early Memoirs," p. 50, BC; Thayer and Ames, *History and Families*, p. 131; JLC to Martha, Sept. 5, 1855, RC; Chamberlain Association, *JLC: A Sketch*, pp. 8, 9. Quotation, ibid., p. 8. Martha was another cousin of JLC. Students were charged only $2 annually for rooms at the Bangor Theological Seminary and a nominal amount for board at private homes, with no charge for instruction. Indigent students could apply for scholarship help. JLC had room number 2 his first and second years there, and number 22 his last. He

probably boarded at home. See *Catalogue of the Theological Seminary, Bangor,* 1853–55.

62. Unsigned letters to Fannie in JLC's hand, one starting "N.B. Perhaps the preservation of this note will not . . . you would do well to consecrate it to the fire," and another, evidently a postscript to the first, n.d., (both, from contents, early 1853), RC. Quotations, "N.B." letter. Most of the letters from JLC to Fannie during the time she was in Georgia were love letters.

63. JLC to Fannie, beginning "I don't know when I have laughed so much," n.d., RC; Fannie to JLC, Feb. 22, 1854, RC; JLC to Fannie, "*Evening Edition,* Monday evening 8 o'clock," MHS; JLC to Fannie, Sept. 28, 1854, RC; JLC to Fannie, Mar. 27, 1855, RC; JLC to Fannie, Apr. 6, 1855, RC. First quotation, JLC to Fannie, "I don't know when I have laughed so much," n.d.; second quotation, JLC to Fannie, Apr. 6, 1855.

64. A letter from Dr. Adams to JLC a few years later about the situation of a young man known to JLC casts considerable light on the attitudes of the community toward couples in a predicament. Clearly neither a prude nor unsympathetic to young people, Dr. Adams asks questions about the previous character and reputation of the man and his new wife that would clarify and perhaps mitigate the degree of censure toward them (Dr. Adams to JLC, Mar. 30, 1860, RC).

65. JLC to Fannie, "Tuesday p.m.," [Aug. 1852], FPYU; Fannie to JLC, Apr. 1, 1853, RC; JLC to Fannie, Oct. 8, 1854, RC; Charlotte Adams to Fannie, Mar. 12, 1833, RC. Quotation, ibid.

66. Deborah Folsom to JLC, Oct. 25, no year (but certainly, from contents, 1863), RC; Deborah Folsom to Fannie, July 30, 1853, RC; JLC to Fannie, "Tuesday p.m.," [Aug. 1852], RC; Deborah Folsom to Fannie, Feb. 17, 1853, and Mar. 4, no year (but from contents, 1854), MHS; Deborah Folsom to Fannie, Mar. 15, no year (but probably 1854), MHS; Deborah Folsom to Fannie, June 22, no year (but probably 1856), MHS. Fannie had expensive tastes, even with Cousin D's frugal shopping, paying $20 or $30 for dresses of silk and fine muslin. Her winter coat in 1855 had dark sable cuffs and tippet; additional trim to match them would cost $40. For comparison, Cousin D rented a comfortable room with a fire at $1.75 per week. Cousin D was very critical of Fannie and instructed her sometimes as if she was a child; she complained often, as did JLC, of Fannie's not writing. She also fretted that Fannie never thanked anyone and that her letters were only about "business." Although she certainly loved Fannie, it is difficult to get a completely fair view of Fannie through Cousin D's eyes. It is also unlikely that any second wife of Dr. Adams would have been liked by Deborah Folsom. She had a small income of her own and gave up her half financial interest in the parsonage in 1853 (Deborah Folsom to Fannie, July 7, no year, MHS; "Limited Power of Attorney" from Deborah G. Folsom to A. C. Robbins, Mar. 14, 1853, BC).

67. Fannie to JLC, Feb. 22, 1854, RC. Fannie was afraid to trust her

thoughts on their most personal relations to paper. In spite of JLC's assurances of privacy, she feared that if she used other than the most oblique phrases about personal matters, her reputation would be finished forever with an unauthorized reader of her letters. Her tastes, she said, were called "extravagant and *gorgeous*" by her brother George (ibid.).

68. Ibid.; JLC to Fannie, Sept. 21, no year (but certainly 1855), RC; JLC to Fannie, Apr. 27, 1854, RC; JLC to Fannie, May 30, 1854, RC; Fannie to JLC, Oct. 27, no year (but from contents, 1854), RC; JLC to Fannie, Oct. 31, 1854, RC; JLC to Fannie, Oct. 8, 1854, RC; JLC to Fannie, Nov. 6, 1854, RC. Quotation, JLC to Fannie, Apr. 27, 1854.

69. JLC to Fannie, Sept. 28, 1854, RC; Ashur Adams to JLC, Oct. 14, 1854, RC; JLC to Fannie, Oct. 17, 1854, RC; Deborah Folsom to Fannie, Oct. 3, no year (but from contents, certainly 1854), MHS; Fannie to JLC, Oct. 27, [1854], RC. Charlotte Adams died in 1855 at the age of thirty-eight, and Fannie's natural mother, Amelia Wyllys Adams, died in 1854 (Allen, Adams family genealogy drafts, RC).

70. Deborah Folsom to Fannie, Oct. 21, no year (from contents, 1856), MHS.

71. "Early Memoirs," p. 72, BC; Cleaveland, *Bowdoin College*, p. 671; George E. Adams to JLC, "Saturday morning," n.d. (but surely August 1855), RC; Fannie to JLC, Feb. 22, 1854, RC; JLC to Fannie, Mar. 27, 1855, RC; JLC to Fannie, Apr. 6, 1855, RC. Quotations, ibid. According to a form filled out in JLC's hand for Bangor Theological Seminary's projected "Historical Catalogue," during his seminary course he received "calls to pastorate" to Belfast, Maine, and Wolfeboro, New Hampshire (Bangor Theological Seminary Historical Catalogue inquiry form, Bangor Theological Seminary Library, Bangor, Maine). JLC graduated from the seminary and was licensed to preach but was not ordained a minister (Cleaveland, *Bowdoin College*, p. 671).

72. Dr. Adams diary, July 30, 1855, FPC; JLC to Fannie, Apr. 6, 1855, RC; Little, *Genealogical History*, 1:133; "Early Memoirs," p. 72, BC.

73. "Early Memoirs," pp. 72, 73, BC; Fannie to JLC, Aug. 12, 1855, RC; Little, *Genealogical History*, 1:133. Quotation, "Early Memoirs," pp. 72, 73.

74. Fannie to JLC, Sept. 20, 1855, RC; JLC to Fannie, Sept. 21, [1855], RC; JLC to Martha, Sept. 5, 1855, RC.

75. "Early Memoirs," p. 73, BC; Dr. Adams to JLC, "Saturday morning," [1855], RC; Fannie to JLC, Aug. 12, 1855, RC; Little, *Catalogue*, pt. 1, p. 133; Sarah D. B. Chamberlain to son John Chamberlain, Oct. 8, 1855, RC; JLC to Sarah D. B. Chamberlain, Aug. 6, 1852, UMO. Quotation, Sarah D. B. Chamberlain to John Chamberlain, Oct. 8, 1855. Horace Chamberlain was apparently in Europe at the beginning of the term (ibid.; Sarah D. B. Chamberlain to JLC, Oct. 8, 1855, RC; Fannie to JLC, Aug. 12, 1855, RC). Horace was born November 14, 1834, and John, August 1, 1838. The tutorship paid $400 a year. Dr. Adams thought that if JLC worked hard and gave good sermons occasionally in addition to grading themes and tutoring, he could pos-

sibly make $700 to $800 a year at Bowdoin. The college was small and could offer only about $1,000 annually for a full professorship. A large house could be rented then for $75 to $100 a year, and a showy horse and carriage was $600 (Stowe, *Harriet Beecher Stowe*, pp. 129, 130).

76. Sarah D. B. Chamberlain to JLC, Oct. 8, 1855, RC.

77. JLC to Fannie, Sept. 21, [1855], RC; Deborah Folsom to Fannie, Dec. 3, 1855, MHS; Dr. Adams diary, Nov. 7, Nov. 13, Nov. 25, and Dec. 6, 1855, FPC. Quotation, ibid., Nov. 13, 1855. Deborah Folsom would make her home with Anna and her new husband (D. Folsom to Fannie, Dec. 3, 1855, MHS).

78. Dr. Adams diary, Dec. 7, 1855, FPC; Ashby, *First Parish Church*, p. 367; Dr. Adams to JLC, Jan. 14, 1856, RC. Quotation, Dr. Adams diary, Dec. 7, 1855. Helen Adams did not come downstairs in her home until Christmas 1855 (Dr. Adams to JLC, Jan. 14, 1856, RC). Cousin D, who did not attend the wedding but "would be glad to hear that the deed is done," was happy to hear that Fannie was "really and truly married" and sent her best wishes for the young couple's happiness (Deborah Folsom to Fannie, Dec. 3, 1855; Deborah Folsom to Fannie, Dec. 19, no year [but certainly 1855], MHS).

79. Fannie to JLC, Feb. 8, 1857, RC; JLC to Fannie, Feb. 1, 1856 (misdated; from contents, Feb. 1, 1857), RC. First quotation, Fannie to JLC, Feb. 8, 1857; others, JLC to Fannie, Feb. 1, 1856.

80. Dr. Adams diary, Dec. 8, 1855, and Jan. 24, Feb. 1, 1856, FPC; Dr. Adams to JLC, Jan. 14, 1856, RC; JLC to Fannie, Apr. 27, 1854, RC; JLC to Fannie, Friday Morning, Aug. 22, no year, but [1856] penciled in, RC; "Early Memoirs," p. 73, BC. Several letters or letter fragments with no dates have notations of months and/or years in brackets marked on them. These appear to have been made by someone knowledgeable with the dates of the original or missing parts of the letters and usually appear on those written by Fannie or JLC.

81. Dr. Adams diary, Oct. 17, 1856, FPC; Sarah D. B. Chamberlain to JLC and Fannie, Oct. 21, no year (but certainly 1856), RC; "Early Memoirs," p. 74, BC; Little, *Genealogical History*, 1:140. First quotation, Sarah D. B. Chamberlain to JLC and Fannie, Oct. 21, no year; second, "Early Memoirs." Grace Dupee Chamberlain was born October 18, 1856, but Fannie did not name her for over six months (JLC to Fannie, Feb. 25, 1857, RC; Annie [Chamberlain] to Fannie, "Middle of May, 1857," RC).

82. Fannie to JLC, Jan. 31, no year (but from contents, 1857), RC; JLC to Fannie, Feb. 1, 1856 (misdated; from contents, 1857), RC; Fannie to JLC, Feb. 8, 1857, RC. The Chamberlains bought the Wilde house two years later and lived in it all their lives. Deborah Folsom, in a letter dated Oct. 21, [1856], MHS, verifies this when she refers to having always associated that house with Mrs. Fales, with whom she passed many pleasant hours. Mary Ann Fales was the second owner of what became the Chamberlain house, and a "John Wild," certainly the "Mr. Wilde" mentioned in the letters, who rented

rooms to the Chamberlains, held the mortgage on it from 1856 to 1859. See Rand, "Chamberlain House," p. 2, PHS. Ms. Rand prepared the manuscript for the Pejepscot Historical Society, Brunswick, after an extensive study of the deeds, photographs, census records, and maps of Brunswick. The society has restored the house and some of the furnishings, and part of it is now the Joshua L. Chamberlain Civil War Museum.

83. Fannie to JLC, "Tuesday morning," in Fannie's hand, with [Feb. 1857] penciled in, RC. A fragment of a letter in JLC's hand, beginning "so if you want to know how your husband really feels," MHS, seems to answer Fannie's "Tuesday morning." In part, JLC explains that he would not have written the "terrible words" if he had not loved her. Quotation, Fannie to JLC, "Tuesday morning."

84. Three fragments of a letter in Fannie's hand, beginning "Does Mrs. Wilde," "Well darling," and "be almost impossible to retract," n.d. (ca. spring 1857, from contents), RC; Fannie to JLC, May 17, 1857, RC; Fannie to JLC, May 1857, RC; Fannie to JLC, Mar. 6, 1857. Quotation, Fannie to JLC, "be almost impossible to retract," n.d.

85. Sarah D. B. Chamberlain to JLC, "Boston, Aunt Susan's, Friday," n.d., RC; JLC to Fannie, May 20, 1857, MHS; Joshua Chamberlain, Jr., to JLC, Apr. 2, 1858, RC. Quotation, JLC to Fannie, May 20, 1857. JLC's father undoubtedly helped the young couple financially, as he surely did off and on since their marriage. Deborah Folsom, expressing surprise after Fannie asked for baby clothes shortly before Daisy's birth, asked, "Does not Mr. Chamberlain still have access to his Father's inexhaustable purse?" (D. Folsom to Fannie, Oct. 21, [1856], MHS).

86. Wilder, *Catalogue*, p. 106; Cleaveland, *Bowdoin College*, p. 714; Deborah Folsom to Fannie, Oct. 3, [1854], MHS; Horace Chamberlain to JLC, May 8, 1858, RC; JLC to Sae Chamberlain, Feb. 4, 1862, BC; "Early Memoirs," p. 75, BC; Dr. Adams diary, Nov. 19, 1857, and all Dec. 1856 entries, FPC; Ashby, *First Parish Church*, p. 236. Quotation, Dr. Adams diary, Nov. 19, 1857. Dr. Adams's diary is the only place a record of the birth of this Chamberlain child has been found. Apparently he was not given a name. The Chamberlain family plot in Pine Grove Cemetery at Brunswick has a marker inscribed with the names of other Chamberlain children who did not survive infancy, but it does not include that of a boy.

87. "Early Memoirs," p. 74, BC; Fannie to "My dear Lawrence," n.d. (but from contents, spring 1859), RC; Hatch, *Bowdoin College*, p. 107; JLC to Nehemiah Cleaveland, Oct. 14, 1859, MHS. Photographs in the Bowdoin College Archives class photograph albums, BC, of JLC as a young professor show his appearance.

88. JLC to Horace Chamberlain, Apr. 30, 1858, UMO; Little, *Genealogical History*, 1:140; Joshua Chamberlain, Jr., to JLC, Jan. 3, 1858, (year misdated; from contents, 1859), MHS; Joshua Chamberlain, Jr., to JLC, Feb. 13, 1859, RC; Sae Chamberlain to JLC, attached to ibid., RC. Harold Wyllys was Fan-

nie's biological mother's brother (Allen, Adams family genealogy drafts, RC). He was fond of Fannie (Fannie to JLC, Sept. 20, 1855, RC) and was the uncle Deborah Folsom referred to as "your bachelor Uncle, the rich Carolina planter" (D. Folsom to Fannie, Oct. 3, no year [but from contents, 1854], MHS).

89. "Early Memoirs," p. 75, BC; Horace Chamberlain to JLC, Feb. 14, 1859, RC; Sae Chamberlain to JLC, May 8, 1859, RC; Cleaveland, *Bowdoin College*, pp. 310–11; newspaper clipping, "Old Longfellow House," *Lewiston Journal*, Aug. 1907, PHS; Rand, "Chamberlain House," pp. 1–3, PHS. Quotation, Sae Chamberlain to JLC, May 8, 1859.

90. "Early Memoirs," pp. 74, 75, BC; Furbush, *Facts about Brunswick*, p. 18; JLC to Fannie, Apr. 24, 1863, LC.

91. Cleaveland, *Bowdoin College*, p. 735; Hatch, *Bowdoin College*, p. 214; Helen R. Adams to JLC, n.d., RC; "Early Memoirs," p. 75, BC; Dr. Adams diary, Sept. 26, 1860, FPC; Allen, Adams family genealogy drafts, RC; Wilder, *Catalogue*, p. 74; Deborah Folsom to JLC, Apr. 18, no year (but from contents, after 1858), RC; Ashur Adams to JLC, July 28, 1858, RC. Quotation, "Early Memoirs." Dr. Adams's diary also notes that Emily Stelle was four months old when she died, which would fix her birth month as May 1860. The 1860 census, taken in Brunswick on June 19, 1860, lists a daughter "Mary," age one month, at the Chamberlain house. Mary was undoubtedly a temporary name, perhaps given only for census purposes. Little Emily died on September 23, 1860; her name appears on a marker in the family plot. Ashur Adams and George Wyllys Adams also died in 1860, Amelia Adams in 1854, Charlotte and Mary Adams in 1855 and 1858, respectively. Only Katherine, Fannie's married half-sister, and Samuel Adams were left of her Boston family. Anna Davis Atkinson probably died between 1859 and 1861.

92. Cleaveland, *Bowdoin College*, p. 714; Fannie to JLC, Dec. 2, 1861, RC; Fannie to JLC, Dec. 8, 1861, RC; JLC to Sae Chamberlain, Feb. 4, 1862, BC. Quotation, ibid. Horace Chamberlain died on Dec. 7, 1861, of "a pulmonary affection" (Cleaveland, *Bowdoin College*, p. 714), undoubtedly tuberculosis. Two letters from Sae to JLC ("Mary's kitchen, March 11, Monday afternoon," no year [but certainly 1861], RC, and "Brewer, April 28," no year [but certainly 1861], RC) describe his illness. He had married Mary Ann Wheeler of Bangor in 1859; no children are known (Little, *Genealogical History*, 1:133).

93. JLC to Sae Chamberlain, Feb. 4, 1862, BC.

94. JLC, "Loyalty," BC. The only other known copy of this lecture, given in 1866 to the the Military Order of the Loyal Legion of the United States, is at the MOLLUS Museum, Philadelphia. The Loyal Legion, a large organization of Union officers, later including their sons and descendants, was organized into state commanderies, of which the Pennsylvania Commandery was the first. JLC was a founder of the Maine Commandery a few years later. In "Loyalty" JLC outlined some reasons for the war, the constitutional

implications, etc. Later he was to teach a college course in public law that included international, constitutional, and parliamentary law (Hatch, *Bowdoin College*, p. 178).

95. McPherson, *Battle Cry of Freedom*, pp. 232–36, 279, 282, 283; JLC, "Loyalty," BC. Quotation, ibid.

96. McPherson, *Battle Cry of Freedom*, pp. 273–75, 854.

97. "Early Memoirs," p. 75, BC.

98. Hatch, *Bowdoin College*, pp. 117, 119, 120; Curtis, "Bowdoin under Fire," p. 268.

99. Hatch, *Bowdoin College*, p. 118; A[mericus] Fuller to "My Dear Chum," June 15, 1861, Oliver O. Howard Papers, BC; JLC to Gov. Washburn, July 22, 1852, MSA; "Early Memoirs," p. 76, BC; Sae Chamberlain to JLC, Mar. 11, no year (but from contents, 1861), RC; Chamberlain Association, *JLC: A Sketch*, pp. 9, 10; JLC to Gov. Israel Washburn, July 14, 1862, MSA. Quotation, "Early Memoirs."

100. *MAGR, 1862*, app. C, p. 5; "Early Memoirs," pp. 75–76, BC; Annie [Chamberlain] to JLC, July 5, 1856, RC; JLC to Annie [Chamberlain], Nov. 10, 1854, RC; JLC, *Armies*, p. 55. Quotation, Annie [Chamberlain] to JLC, July 5, 1856.

101. *Dedication of the Twentieth Maine Monuments*, JLC's address, p. 30.

CHAPTER THREE

1. Gerrish, *Army Life*, p. 13.

2. Ibid., pp. 13–16; Spear, "Regiment," p. 14. Quotations, Gerrish, *Army Life*, p. 15.

3. Gerrish, *Army Life*, pp. 15–18; *MAGR, 1862*, p. 113; E. M. Woodward, *One Hundred and Ninety-eighth Pennsylvania*, p. 3.

4. *MAGR, 1862*, p. 113; Spear, "Regiment," p. 14; Gerrish, *Army Life*, pp. 18, 19; Quarterly Return of Ordnance and Ordnance Stores, ending Dec. 31, 1862, signed by JLC, LC. Quotation, Spear, "Regiment."

5. Gerrish, *Army Life*, p. 19; Pullen, *Twentieth Maine*, p. 19. First quotation, Gerrish, *Army Life*; second, Pullen, *Twentieth Maine*.

6. Gerrish, *Army Life*, p. 19; Powell, *Fifth Corps*, pp. 17, 18, 184, 244, 260, 273; *History, 118th Pennsylvania*, p. 71.

7. *OR* 19(1):24–26; Swinton, *Army of the Potomac*, pp. 182–93, 197.

8. *OR* 19(1):338; Gerrish, *Army Life*, pp. 20, 24, 25; Swinton, *Army of the Potomac*, p. 197.

9. Gerrish, *Army Life*, pp. 25, 26; Pvt. John Lenfest to his wife, Sept. 29, 1862, and Oct. 29, 1862, Lenfest Letters, PHS; *History, 118th Pennsylvania*, pp. 29, 30.

10. *History, 118th Pennsylvania*, p. 30.

11. Carter, *Four Brothers*, pp. 105, 106; Swinton, *Army of the Potomac*, pp. 198–201; Judson, *Eighty-third Pennsylvania*, p. 53. According to an article writ-

ten by Judson in 1893, he wrote the history of his regiment early in 1865 and published it the same year (*Proceedings of the Third Brigade Association, 1893*, p. 91). The Eighty-third Pennsylvania was brigaded with the Twentieth Maine until the end of the war. Carter's book is a compilation of letters written by four brothers in the Union army who were originally from Maine. The letters are connected with a narrative written later by the youngest, Robert, who was sixteen when he joined the army as a replacement recruit in the Twenty-second Massachusetts with his eighteen-year-old brother Walter. The Twenty-second Massachusetts was in another brigade in the First Division of the Fifth Corps, and its movements usually coincided with the Twentieth Maine's during this part of the war.

12. O. W. Norton to Sister L., Sept. 23, 1862, in Norton, *Army Letters*, p. 119; Gerrish, *Army Life*, p. 27; Carter, *Four Brothers*, p. 106; Judson, *Eighty-third Pennsylvania*, p. 53; Fox, *Regimental Losses*, p. 540. Quotation, Gerrish, *Army Life*. Fitz John Porter, the Fifth Corps's commander, had crossed South Mountain with Brigidier General Sykes's brigade of Regulars on September 15 on the "direct road to Sharpsburg" through Fox's Gap (*OR* 19[1]:338; Powell, *Fifth Corps*, p. 266). Norton was a private in the Eighty-third Pennsylvania from 1861 until November 1863 and was Third Brigade bugler much of that time.

13. Carter, *Four Brothers*, p. 109; Lt. Eugene Carter to his parents, Sept. 17, 1862, in ibid., p. 107; O. W. Norton to Sister L., Sept. 23, 1862, in Norton, *Army Letters*, p. 120; Powell, *Fifth Corps*, p. 304; Gerrish, *Army Life*, p. 27.

14. Gerrish, *Army Life*, pp. 27, 28; Nolan, *Iron Brigade*, pp. 121–27; JLC, Memorial Day address at Somerville, Mass., 1881, in the *Somerville Journal*, June 4, 1881. Quotation, ibid. Gibbon's famous brigade earned their sobriquet, "the Iron Brigade," in Turner's Gap at the battle of South Mountain on the evening of September 14, 1862.

15. *OR* 19(1):338; Swinton, *Army of the Potomac*, pp. 208, 209; Powell, *Fifth Corps*, pp. 268–70, 272–73; Sears, *Landscape Turned Red*, p. 169. McClellan has been faulted for not moving the Union army aggressively after a fortunate chance on September 13 brought the Union commander an intercepted set of orders that revealed Lee's plans. If he had immediately broken through the South Mountain passes before they could be heavily defended by Confederate infantry, McClellan could have fallen on and perhaps defeated Lee's then divided forces and relieved the beleaguered Union force at Harpers Ferry. Later, McClellan took too much time completing preparations. As it was, Lee's army, except for A. P. Hill's division, was given time to concentrate before the battle began.

16. *OR* 19(1):338; Gerrish, *Army Life*, p. 28; Powell, *Fifth Corps*, pp. 273–74; Carter, *Four Brothers*, pp. 109, 110.

17. Carter, *Four Brothers*, p. 110; Walter Carter to his parents, Sept. 23, 1862, in ibid., p. 129; U.S. Secretary of War, *U.S. Infantry Tactics*, pp. 32–54. Two examples of green regiments going untrained into battle with disastrous

results are those of the Sixteenth Connecticut on the Union left at the battle of Antietam and the 118th Pennsylvania at Shepherdstown Ford shortly afterward on September 20, 1862 (*History, 118th Pennsylvania*, pp. 54–70; Johnson, Buel, *Battles and Leaders*, 2:655, 656; *OR* 19[1]:453, 454).

18. Powell, *Fifth Corps*, pp. 272–75; Carter, *Four Brothers*, pp. 110, 111; Gerrish, *Army Life*, pp. 30, 31.

19. Letter written by JLC, "Camp opposite Fredericksburg, Dec. 17, 1862," in newspaper clipping, JLC Letterbook, PHS; Gerrish, *Army Life*, pp. 32, 33; Carter, *Four Brothers*, p. 111; Walter Carter to his parents, Sept. 23, 1862, in ibid., p. 130. Quotation, ibid.

20. Carter, *Four Brothers*, pp. 112, 131; Swinton, *Army of the Potomac*, p. 197; *History, 118th Pennsylvania*, p. 42.

21. *OR* 19(1):31, 419–21; Johnson and Buel, *Battles and Leaders*, 2:648–56.

22. *OR* 19(1):31, 32, 142, 339, 349; Gerrish, *Army Life*, pp. 37, 38; Fox, *Regimental Losses*, p. 540; Frassanito, *Antietam*, pp. 288, 289; Carter, *Four Brothers*, p. 115; Swinton, *Army of the Potomac*, pp. 222–25; *History, 118th Pennsylvania*, pp. 46, 47. Morell's division relieved Burnside's corps, but only one of Morell's brigades was sent over the Antietam that day (Johnson and Buel, *Battles and Leaders*, 2:659, 660). Fox (*Regimental Losses*, p. 540) establishes Antietam as the bloodiest single day in America's Civil War, and Frassanito (*Antietam*, pp. 288, 289), after a comparison of the total of Antietam's killed and wounded with single-day figures in America's other wars, has concluded that September 17, 1862, retains that dubious distinction for all the nation's wars to date. Livermore (*Numbers and Losses*, pp. 92, 93) gives the losses: Army of the Potomac: killed in action, 2,108, wounded, 9,549, captured or missing, 753, total, 12,410; Army of Northern Virginia: killed in action, 2,700, wounded, 9,024, captured or missing, 2,000; total, 13,724; both armies total: 26,134. McClellan has been severely criticized for not renewing the fight the next day.

23. *History, 118th Pennsylvania*, pp. 51, 52; O. W. Norton to Sister L., Sept. 23, 1862, in Norton, *Army Letters*, p. 121; Gerrish, *Army Life*, p. 40; Walter Carter to his parents, Sept. 23, 1862, in Carter, *Four Brothers*, pp. 131, 132; Carter, *Four Brothers*, pp. 116–18; Judson, *Eighty-third Pennsylvania*, p. 54.

24. Gerrish, *Army Life*, pp. 40–42; Powell, *Fifth Corps*, pp. 295–99; Judson, *Eighty-third Pennsylvania*, p. 54.

25. Gerrish, *Army Life*, p. 42; Powell, *Fifth Corps*, p. 301; Judson, *Eighty-third Pennsylvania*, p. 54; newspaper clipping, "Army Correspondence," Oct. 23, 1862, JLC Letterbook, PHS; list of horses and wounds in JLC's hand, JLC Letterbook, PHS. First quotation, Gerrish, *Army Life*; second, from list of horses, JLC Letterbook. *OR* 19(1):204 gives the Twentieth Maine wounded as 3. Not so fortunate were the men of the division's other new regiment, the 118th Pennsylvania. Armed with defective rifles, they stood up to the Rebels before the order to retire reached them and had 3 officers and 60 men killed, 4 officers and 97 men wounded, and 3 officers and 102 men captured or

missing. Some of the green troops were literally driven over the sharp inclines of the bluffs near Boetler's mill, and others were shot as they tried to return on a low dam over the river.

26. *Maine at Gettysburg*, p. 275; Gerrish, *Army Life*, p. 47; *OR* 19(1):69–71, 93, 341; U.S. War Department, *Atlas*, pl. 29, map 2; JLC to Fannie, Oct. 10, 1862, LC; Carter, *Four Brothers*, pp. 121, 122; Nash, *Forty-fourth New York*, p. 107; newspaper clipping, "Army Correspondence," Oct. 23, 1862, JLC Letterbook, PHS.

27. JLC to Fannie, Oct. 10, 1862, LC; JLC to Fannie, Oct. 26, 1862, LC. First two quotations, JLC to Fannie, Oct. 10, 1862; the last two, JLC to Fannie, Oct. 26, 1862. A lieutenant colonel of infantry's pay, with ration and expense allowances for himself and two servants, plus forage for three horses, was $198 per month; a colonel's was only $24 higher (U.S. Secretary of War, *Revised Regulations*, p. 525). Maine had an allowance system for soldiers; perhaps JLC made arrangements through it for Fannie's income from him.

28. JLC to Fannie, Oct. 10, 1862, LC; Hatch, *Bowdoin College*, pp. 411, 412. First quotation, JLC to Fannie, Oct. 10, 1862; second, Hatch, *Bowdoin College*, p. 411.

29. Adelbert Ames to his parents, Oct. 10, 1862, in Ames, *Chronicles*, 1:14; JLC, *Armies*, p. xiii; Pullen, *Twentieth Maine*, p. 36.

30. Gerrish, *Army Life*, pp. 45, 46.

31. Newspaper clipping, "Army Correspondence," Oct. 23, 1862, JLC Letterbook, PHS; Hardee, *Hardee's Tactics*, pp. 1–152; Pullen, *Twentieth Maine*, pp. 34–36. Both quotations from Pullen, *Twentieth Maine*, p. 36, citing Tom Chamberlain to Sae, Oct. 26, 1862, and Tom Chamberlain to John Chamberlain, Oct. 30, 1862, respectively.

32. "The Army of the Potomac," speech given by JLC at the founding meeting in New York of the Army of the Potomac Association, 1869, in newspaper clipping, "Army of the Potomac, the Address of Governor Chamberlain," LC.

33. Hardee, *Hardee's Tactics*, pp. 32–36.

34. Newspaper clipping, "Army Correspondence," Oct. 23, 1862, JLC Letterbook, PHS; Coggins, *Arms and Equipment*, p. 38; Norton, *Army Letters*, pp. 323–25; U.S. Secretary of War, *Revised Regulations*, pp. 58–61; Hardee, *Hardee's Tactics*, pp. 72–73, 84–86.

35. JLC to Fannie, Oct. 26, 1862, LC. Using advanced manuals, JLC mastered the intricate movements of the regiment, brigade, and undoubtedly the division.

36. Adelbert Ames to JLC, Oct. 18, 1864, LC; newspaper clipping, "Army Correspondence," Oct. 23, 1862, JLC Letterbook, PHS; Pvt. George W. Carleton to the Adjutant General of Maine, Jan. 8, 1866, FPYU. First quotation, Adelbert Ames to JLC, Oct. 18, 1864, LC; second, newspaper clipping, "Army Correspondence," Oct. 23, 1862.

37. Adelbert Ames to his parents, n.d. (but probably late December 1862),

and Jan. 14, 1866, in Ames, *Chronicles*, 1:16 and 28, respectively; Ames to JLC, Oct. 18, 1864, LC; Ames, *Adelbert Ames*, flyleaf quotation by Col. Henry C. Lockwood, and pp. 1, 3, 4, 23, 24, 59; Nevins, *Diary of Battle*, p. 242. Ames ended his 1864 letter to JLC, which contained advice and pointed, joking references to his own lack of success with women, "With love, your friend, A. Ames."

38. Powell, *Fifth Corps*, p. 309; JLC, "My Story of Fredericksburg," p. 148; JLC, "Abraham Lincoln," p. 22. First quotation, JLC, "My Story of Fredericksburg"; second, JLC, "Abraham Lincoln."

39. JLC, "Abraham Lincoln," p. 23; JLC, "My Story of Fredericksburg," p. 148. Quotations, JLC, "Abraham Lincoln."

40. JLC, "My Story of Fredericksburg," p. 148; Carter, *Four Brothers*, p. 121; Pvt. John Lenfest to his wife, Oct. 5, 1862, Lenfest Letters, PHS. Quotation, ibid.

41. JLC to Fannie, Oct. 10, 1862, LC; newspaper clipping, "Whipped for Chewing Tobacco," [ca. 1908], PHS; JLC to Fannie, May 30, 1854, RC. Quotations, ibid.

42. JLC to Fannie, Oct. 10, 1862, LC.

43. JLC to Fannie, Oct. 26, 1862, LC.

44. JLC to Fannie, Nov. 3, 1862, LC; *MAGR, 1864–1865*, 1:331. Quotations, JLC to Fannie, Nov. 3, 1862.

45. JLC to Fannie, Oct. 26, 1862, LC; JLC to Fannie, Nov. 3, 1862, LC; Billings, *Hardtack and Coffee*, pp. 112, 113; Nevins, *Diary of Battle*, pp. 407, 408. Quotation, JLC to Fannie, Oct. 26, 1862.

46. Gerrish, *Army Life*, pp. 66, 67; Billings, *Hardtack and Coffee*, pp. 110–12, 121, 122, 125, 225. The sutler was a civilian businessman allowed to follow the army with his wagon and stores and set up business in a tent, with one sutler allowed per regiment. His stock was mainly foodstuffs, including cookies, pies, canned goods, sugar, flour, cakes, and other delicacies, but he also carried ink, paper, and other supplies. His prices were high, but his risks were high also. Besides the usual wartime hazards, it was not unknown for a large body of men to swoop down on a sutler at night and clean out his entire stock, with the culprits uncaught and unpunished. See Billings, *Hardtack and Coffee*, pp. 224, 225, 228–29.

47. Billings, *Hardtack and Coffee*, pp. 113–20; Gerrish, *Army Life*, pp. 64, 67. Quotations, ibid., p. 67.

48. Thomas D. Chamberlain Military Pension records, NA; Tom Chamberlain to [John Chamberlain], Feb. 2, 1863, UMO; Gerrish, *Army Life*, pp. 47, 48; *Maine at Gettysburg*, p. 275; *MAGR, 1862*, app. D, pp. 653–77.

49. JLC to Fannie, Oct. 26, 1862, LC; JLC to Fannie, Nov. 3, 1862, LC; *OR* 19(1):341.

50. *OR*, ser. 3, 2:584–85; Catton, *Terrible Swift Sword*, pp. 446, 461, 462. Quotations, *OR*, ser. 3, 2:584–85. Lincoln released the preliminary text of the Emancipation Proclamation on September 22, 1862. It was published to the

Army of the Potomac on September 24, 1862, in General Orders No. 139 (*OR*, ser. 3, 2:584–85). The full Emancipation Proclamation is in ibid. 3:2–3.

51. JLC, *Armies*, p. 31; *OR* 19(2):395, 396. Quotation, JLC, *Armies*.

52. JLC, "Loyalty," BC.

53. Gerrish, *Army Life*, pp. 50, 51; Carter, *Four Brothers*, p. 52; Judson, *Eighty-third Pennsylvania*, p. 55; JLC to Fannie, Nov. 3, 1862, LC; *OR* 19(1):87, 88. One of the army's favorite marching songs honored the fiery martyr. The first line, "John Brown's body lies a moulderin' in the grave," was familiar to every soldier.

54. Fannie to JLC, Sept. 20, 1855, RC; JLC to Fannie, Nov. 3, 1862, LC; *MAGR, 1864–1865*, 1:509. Quotation, JLC to Fannie, Nov. 3, 1862.

55. JLC to Fannie, Nov. 3, 1862, LC; Rand, "Chums at Bowdoin," pp. 3, 4. Quotations, JLC to Fannie, Nov. 3, 1862.

56. JLC to Fannie, Nov. 3, 1862, LC; Judson, *Eighty-third Pennsylvania*, p. 55; JLC to Fannie, Oct. 26, 1862, LC.The first and last quotations are from JLC's November 3 letter; the second, from October 26.

57. Gerrish, *Army Life*, p. 51; JLC to Fannie, Nov. 4, 1863, LC. Quotation, JLC to Fannie, Nov. 4, 1863.

58. Warner, *Generals in Blue*, p. 62; Norton, *Army Letters*, pp. 323–29. Butterfield's "Taps" is the same that is in use today, probably as well known as any music in America. His brigade bugler was Pvt. Oliver W. Norton.

59. Gerrish, *Army Life*, p. 68; JLC to Fannie, Oct. 26, 1862, LC; JLC to Fannie, Nov. 3, 1862, LC; JLC to Fannie, Nov. 4, 1862, LC; JLC to Daisy, May [13,] 1863, BC; Fannie to Cousin D, Apr. 14, 1862, LC; Hatch, *Bowdoin College*, p. 400.

60. Fannie to JLC, Dec. 8, 1861, RC; JLC to Fannie, Nov. 3, 1862, LC; JLC to Fannie, Oct. 26, 1862, LC; JLC to Fannie, Nov. 4, 1862, LC. First quotation, JLC to Fannie, Nov. 3, 1862, LC; "good frolic," JLC to Fannie, Oct. 26, 1862, LC.

61. JLC to Fannie, Nov. 4, 1862, LC. A daguerreotype of Mrs. Chamberlain, probably taken in 1862 and much worn on the velvet edges of the double frame, shows her looking extremely sad. A thumbnail-sized daguerreotype image of her, evidently taken at the same time, looks drawn and hostile. Rosamond Allen lent the larger, which is now in the Pejepscot Historical Society's Chamberlain Civil War Museum, to the writer for publication in this book and gave her the smaller, along with daguerreotypes of the children. Fannie had a penchant for travel in an age when a "change of scene" was believed to lift spirits, and other examples of Fannie's behavior that might indicate a depressive reaction to her life situations are indicated in or inferred from letters throughout her life. Ms. Allen, who is familiar with most of the letters in the collections, some no longer extant, has strongly agreed in conversation with the writer that this observation undoubtedly elucidated some of her grandmother's attitudes and behavior.

62. *OR* 19(1):5, 88; ibid. 19(2):545; Carter, *Four Brothers*, pp. 155–57; Powell, *Fifth Corps*, pp. 316, 319.

63. Powell, *Fifth Corps*, pp. 320–22, 353, 354; Judson, *Eighty-third Pennsylvania*, p. 55. A few days afterward, General Porter was arrested in his hotel at Washington and court-martialed under charges of "shameful" misconduct and disobeying General Pope's orders at the second battle of Bull Run, with the effect of causing the disastrous defeat. Found guilty, he was cashiered and barred from holding any government office for life. Convinced that Porter was not guilty, the soldiers of the Fifth Corps considered this action a slur on their organization. Porter, always maintaining his innocence, was finally given a review hearing in 1878, in which new evidence was introduced. He was completely exonerated by the military board, the ban on holding government office was revoked, and he eventually was restored to the retired list of the army under his Regular Army commission. JLC apparently talked with President U. S. Grant in 1874 concerning a new hearing for Porter, and he and Porter became friends. Porter later wrote one of the letters of recommendation for JLC's Medal of Honor. JLC was invited to serve as pallbearer at Porter's funeral after his death on May 21, 1901. JLC also had the honor of accepting an invitation of the Association of Graduates of the Military Academy at West Point to speak on the life and character of Fitz John Porter. It was considered unusual for a civilian officer to speak to this group. See Powell, *Fifth Corps*, pp. 322–51; Porter to JLC, May 23, 1874, LC; Porter affidavit describing JLC physical condition, Feb. 9, 1893, JLC Military Pension records, NA; Fitz John Porter to Secretary of War, May 19, 1893, JLC Military Personnel file, NA; funeral invitation as pallbearer for Porter, MHS; Chamberlain Association, *JLC: A Sketch*, p. 42.

64. Swinton, *Army of the Potomac*, pp. 230, 231; *OR* 19(2):552–54, 583, 584; Powell, *Fifth Corps*, pp. 19, 354–56. Quotation, *OR* 19(2):552.

65. *OR* 21:46–48.

66. Judson, *Eighty-third Pennsylvania*, p. 56; Gerrish, *Army Life*, pp. 62, 63; Simonton, "Recollections," pp. 248, 249; Billings, *Hardtack and Coffee*, pp. 51–53; *Maine at Gettysburg*, p. 275. Quotations, Simonton, "Recollections," p. 248. Full rations were issued the next day, November 28 (Simonton, "Recollections," p. 248). Each shelter half measured about 4½ by 5 feet and had three sides edged with a row of buttons and buttonholes. Simonton was a sergeant in Company G of the Twentieth Maine at the time of the battle. An 1861 Bowdoin graduate, he was promoted to second lieutenant in January 1863 and transferred to U.S. Infantry in July 1863. See *MAGR, 1863*, p. 590; *MAGR, 1864–1865*, 1:495, 514.

67. Fannie to JLC, Nov. 27, 1862, RC; JLC to Fannie, Nov. 4, 1862, LC; Dr. Adams to JLC, Nov. 27, 1862, RC. First quotation, Fannie to JLC, Nov. 27, 1862, RC; "particulars," from JLC to Fannie, Nov. 4, 1862, LC.

68. Powell, *Fifth Corps*, p. 366; letter to the editor dated Dec. 19, 1862, signed "W," in newspaper clipping, JLC Letterbook, PHS; *OR* 21(1):399.

CHAPTER FOUR

1. *OR* 21:63, 399; Nash, *Forty-fourth New York*, p. 112; Carter, *Four Brothers*, p. 192; JLC letter dated Dec. 17, 1862, in newspaper clipping, JLC Letterbook, PHS; letter to the editor dated Dec. 19, 1862, signed "W," in newspaper clipping, JLC Letterbook, PHS. These letters were no doubt printed in a Portland newspaper, first "W" and then—as explained by the editors under a headline of "The Twentieth Maine at Fredericksburg"—"from a private letter. We are not permitted to use the writer's name, but few, who guess, will miss it." It was common for soldiers in the Civil War to write the newspapers about their experiences, and editors gladly printed the more descriptive or articulate accounts. Some of them used pen names or letters: "W" in this case is certainly the Twentieth's adjutant, John Marshall Brown, a former student of JLC's. It is also abundantly clear that the second writer is JLC. These two letters hereinafter will be referred to as Adj. Brown letter, Dec. 19, 1862, and JLC letter, Dec. 17, 1862, respectively.

2. *OR* 21:221–22; JLC letter, Dec. 17, 1862, PHS; Swinton, *Army of the Potomac*, p. 238; Johnson and Buel, *Battles and Leaders*, 3:71, 74.

3. *OR* 21:218–19; JLC letter, Dec. 17, 1862, PHS. JLC heard a staff officer ask a battery commander to avoid hitting a tall, slim, white monument that marked the grave of Mary Washington, George Washington's mother (JLC, "My Story of Fredericksburg," p. 150). Nevertheless, the marker was damaged by Union artillery on that day (December 11); years after the war, a new monument was raised (Frassanito, *Grant and Lee*, pp. 66, 69, 70).

4. JLC Letter, Dec. 17, 1862, PHS; Johnson and Buel, *Battles and Leaders*, 3:72–74. JLC must have used field glasses to examine the Confederate positions.

5. Johnson and Buel, *Battles and Leaders*, 3:97, 131; *OR* 21:99, 262; Swinton, *Army of the Potomac*, pp. 235–36; Powell, *Fifth Corps*, p. 366; Carter, *Four Brothers*, p. 192; Adj. Brown letter, Dec. 19, 1862, PHS. Quotation, *OR* 21:99.

6. Johnson and Buel, *Battles and Leaders*, 3:88, 89; *OR* 21:219, 399, 404, 449; Gerrish, *Army Life*, pp. 73, 74; JLC letter, Dec. 17, 1862, PHS. Quotation, ibid. JLC included some exerpts from his notebook (now apparently lost) in his December 17 published letter. No fires were allowed to the Federals in the city, to conceal their presence from the Confederates (Johnson and Buel, *Battles and Leaders*, 3:109).

7. Johnson and Buel, *Battles and Leaders*, 3:76, 78–79; Warner, *Generals in Gray*, pp. 151–52; Carter, *Four Brothers*, p. 196.

8. Johnson and Buel, *Battles and Leaders*, 3:78–79. Quotation (from CSA Brig. Gen. E. P. Alexander), ibid., p. 79. The infantry brigades were those of Brig. Gen. Thomas R. R. Cobb's Georgians and Brig. Gen. Joseph B. Kershaw's North Carolinians. General Cobb was mortally wounded December 13.

9. Ibid., p. 79.

10. JLC to Gov. Washburn, Dec. 17, 1862, PHS; Adj. Brown letter, Dec. 19, 1862, PHS; JLC, "My Story of Fredericksburg," pp. 151–52. Quotation, ibid., p. 152. The letter to Governor Washburn appeared in the newspaper; a clipping of it is in the JLC Letterbook, PHS.

11. JLC letter, Dec. 17, 1862, PHS; JLC, "My Story of Fredericksburg," p. 152; Quotation, JLC letter, Dec. 17, 1862.

12. JLC, "My Story of Fredericksburg," p. 152; *OR* 21:399, 404–5; Simonton, "Recollections," p. 252. Quotation, ibid.

13. Simonton, "Recollections," p. 252; letter of anonymous Twentieth Maine officer dated Dec. 15, 1862, in newspaper clipping, JLC Letterbook, PHS (hereinafter referred to as Twentieth Maine officer letter, Dec. 15, 1862); Hill, "Last Charge at Fredericksburg," p. 43, map. Quotation, Twentieth Maine officer letter, Dec. 15, 1862. The letter by "an officer of the Maine 20th," extracts of which were permitted to be published in the newspaper, was written before the battle was over, possibly by Adjutant Brown. He ended the letter by saying "He [Colonel Ames] behaved splendidly, so did Lieut. Col. Chamberlain." The Hill article is a copy of a talk given to the Third Brigade Association on December 21, 1892. This association may have been short lived; only one other publication of its meetings, that of 1893, has been found by the writer. JLC was not in attendance in 1892, but the Fifth Corps commander, Gen. Daniel Butterfield, and men from every regiment in the brigade that served at Fredericksburg, including Ellis Spear of the Twentieth Maine, were there. Favorable reaction to the publication of the proceedings from other wartime participants, including Amos Judson, historian of the Eighty-third, was recorded in a letter section of the brigade's 1893 meeting publication, *Proceedings of the Third Brigade Association, 6 September 1893*. It is clear that Hill, in preparation for writing his talk, had read the official records of the battle, made careful measurements of the positions of the brigade in relation to the stone wall, the river, etc., and checked on the time of sunset and sunrise that December. The description in this paragraph of the brigade movements and positions are from the map that accompanied Hill's article, which is accepted as substantially accurate.

14. Simonton, "Recollections," p. 252; Hill, "Last Charge at Fredericksburg," p. 134; Judson, *Eighty-third Pennsylvania*, p. 58; JLC letter, Dec. 17, 1862, PHS; Twentieth Maine officer letter, Dec. 15, 1862, PHS; *OR* 21:404; Adj. Brown letter, Dec. 19, 1862, PHS; Walter Carter to his parents, Dec. 24, 1862, in Carter, *Four Brothers*, p. 213. Quotation, ibid.

15. Adj. Brown letter, Dec. 19, 1862, PHS; Twentieth Maine officer letter, Dec. 15, 1862, PHS; Hill, "Last Charge at Fredericksburg," p. 35.

16. JLC letter, Dec. 17, 1862, PHS; JLC to Gov. Washburn, Dec. 17, 1862, PHS; *OR* 21:411. Ames quotations, JLC letter, Dec. 17, 1862. The officers of the Twelfth and Seventeenth New York Regiments realized their error and caught up "promptly," according to Colonel Stockton.

17. Hill, "Last Charge at Fredericksburg," p. 35; Adj. Brown letter, Dec.

19, 1862, PHS; Pvt. George W. Carleton to the Adjutant General of Maine, Jan. 8, 1866, FPYU. Quotation, ibid.

18. Hill, "Last Charge at Fredericksburg," pp. 34–36; Judson, *Eighty-third Pennsylvania*, p. 58; *OR* 21:411, 413; Twentieth Maine officer letter, Dec. 15, 1862, PHS. Quotation, ibid. Hill believed the charge of the Third Brigade to be the last charge made at Marye's Heights in the battle. However, he stated that the charge began at 6:30 P.M., after full dark, a conclusion apparently arrived at from the time of sunset (4:42 P.M. by his information) and other unknown data. A careful comparison of all the accounts made within a few days of the battle, including the division and brigade *Official Records* reports and the letters of JLC, Adjutant Brown, and the anonymous Twentieth Maine officer, plus deductions from other observations, leaves little doubt that the charge began at or near sunset. When the brigade aligned for the charge in the brickyard (850 yards from the stone wall, according to Hill), the Eighty-third Pennsylvania, on the left, and the Twentieth Maine composed the first line of battle, and the Sixteenth Michigan, also on the left and behind the Eighty-third, and the Forty-fourth New York composed the second line (Hill, "Last Charge at Fredericksburg," p. 43, map). *OR* includes only an incomplete report at the regimental level, that of Col. Strong Vincent of the Eighty-third Pennsylvania, which confirms Hill's account by referring to the Sixteenth Michigan's position (after dark) as "then in my rear" (*OR* 21:413).

19. Carter, *Four Brothers*, p. 196; *OR* 21:405; JLC letter, Dec. 17, 1862, PHS. First quotation, Carter, *Four Brothers*; second, JLC letter, Dec. 17, 1862. The area over which the Third Brigade had to charge was to the left of the action that JLC had watched from across the river. One man thought later that the Confederates had to have been firing high, or the advancing men would have been nearly annihilated. As it was, casualties were comparatively light in the regiment and brigade. Capt. Amos M. Judson, author of the Eighty-third Pennsylvania's regimental history, on several occasions points out, sometimes with humor, the low ratio of wounds or deaths to the amount of lead expended. The Civil War soldiers were not exaggerating the storm of fire; the aim was notoriously bad, and in the case of artillery, the ammunition was sometimes defective.

20. Johnson and Buel, *Battles and Leaders*, 3:125; Twentieth Maine officer letter, Dec. 15, 1862, PHS; JLC, "My Story of Fredericksburg," pp. 153–54; Adj. Brown letter, Dec. 19, 1862, PHS; Carter, *Four Brothers*, p. 208; JLC to Gov. Washburn, Dec. 17, 1862, PHS; Hill, "Last Charge at Fredericksburg," p. 37; *OR* 21:400, 411. Quotation, JLC, "My Story of Fredericksburg," pp. 153–54. W. H. Powell, who served on the staff of Lt. Col. R. C. Buchanan during the battle, described the positions of Andrews's and Buchanan's brigades of Regulars from Sykes's division. Andrews's right connected with Buchanan's left, Buchanan's right resting on the Telegraph Road, and extended to the left about eighty yards from the stone wall (Powell, *Fifth*

Corps, p. 392. See also *OR* 21:418–29). Stockton's brigade was to the left of Andrews. Simonton ("Recollections," pp. 254–55) describes the Regulars as on the same line and "near neighbors." These three brigades moved into position late at night—near midnight, according to the various reports. Stockton does not mention the move in his official report, but General Butterfield does (*OR* 21:400). Since the Twentieth Maine, by the contempory accounts, was in advance of the brigade, they likely held their ground, or did not move much farther up, when the brigade was later ordered to the extreme front.

21. JLC, "Night on the Field," p. 128; JLC letter, Dec. 17, 1862, PHS. First quotation, JLC, "Night on the Field"; second, JLC letter, Dec. 17, 1862. "Night on the Field at Fredericksburg" was originally published in the *Congregationalist and Boston Recorder* on December 25, 1884, before being reprinted in King and Derby, *Camp-fire Sketches*. A copy is in LC.

22. JLC, "Night on the Field," p. 130; Adj. Brown Letter, Dec. 19, 1862, PHS.

23. JLC, "Night on the Field," pp. 129, 130; JLC, "My Story of Fredericksburg," p. 154. First quotation, JLC, "Night on the Field," p. 130; second, JLC, "My Story of Fredericksburg." Oliver W. Norton, in a talk given in 1876, said that the "Confederate forts" were "80 or 100 yards away" (*Army Letters*, pp. 318–19). JLC said the enemy was so near that night he could hear "the voices of the Rebels in their lines" (JLC letter, Dec. 17, 1862, PHS); Simonton stated, "We were separated from the rebel intrenchments by a narrow vale, or field, only some one hundred yards across" ("Recollections," p. 253); Hill further stated that enemy batteries were two hundred yards away ("Last Charge at Fredericksburg," p. 37).

24. Twentieth Maine officer letter, Dec. 15, 1862, PHS; Adj. Brown letter, Dec. 19, 1862, PHS; Johnson and Buel, *Battles and Leaders*, 3:123. Quotation, ibid.

25. JLC letter, Dec. 17, 1862, PHS; JLC, "My Story of Fredericksburg," p. 156; Judson, *Eighty-third Pennsylvania*, p. 58; *OR* 21:400. Quotation, ibid. In 1869 one of Capt. John B. Ames's distinct memories of the war was of the Confederates that morning. The official report of his regiment (Seventeenth U.S. Infantry, Andrews's brigade) stated that it was located seventy-five yards from the stone wall (*OR* 21:429). The Twentieth's position was on the last "crest" before the stone wall, on the side away from the Confederates. On that part of the field, especially on the brigade's extreme left where the Eighty-third Pennsylvania was positioned, the land was apparently very irregular and broken.

26. *OR* 21:411; JLC letter, Dec. 17, 1862, PHS; Adj. Brown letter, Dec. 19, 1862, PHS.

27. JLC, "Night on the Field," p. 130; Adj. Brown letter, Dec. 19, 1862, PHS; *OR* 21:411–12; Judson, *Eighty-third Pennsylvania*, p. 59; JLC, "My Story of Fredericksburg," p. 156. Quotations, ibid.

28. Judson, *Eighty-third Pennsylvania*, p. 59; ibid., Introduction by Trulock and Trulock. Quotation, Judson, *Eighty-third Pennsylvania*.

29. Hill, "Last Charge at Fredericksburg," p. 39; JLC, "Night on the Field," p. 130; JLC letter, Dec. 17, 1862, PHS. Quotation, ibid.

30. JLC letter, Dec. 17, 1862, PHS. JLC's stirring description of the northern lights on the night of December 14, 1862, was in his letter written only three days later. It was a passionate and eloquent tribute to the first of his men that he had seen shot down in battle. A similar description was unaccountably cut out of "My Story of Fredericksburg" by the editor of *Cosmopolitan Magazine*, according to the author's proof sheets of the manuscript in UMO. Douglas Southall Freeman called one chapter of his book *Lee's Lieutenants* (vol. 2, chap. 23) "The Night of the Northern Lights," referring to the night of December 13. He noted (ibid., 2:374n) that "other writers" had fixed the date for the aurora as December 14, but he relied on the manuscript diary of Maj. Jedediah Hotchkiss for the date of December 13. Perhaps implying his recognition that diaries were sometimes filled in at a later date and could be in error, Freeman qualifies Hotchkiss's date by stating that it "seems to fix the time"; he does not name the other writers, but it is unlikely that he read any of JLC's accounts of the aurora. It is more unlikely that JLC was wrong about the date.

31. JLC letter, Dec. 17, 1862, PHS; Judson, *Eighty-third Pennsylvania*, p. 59; Nash, *Forty-fourth New York*, p. 116; Simonton, "Recollections," p. 256; Gerrish, *Army Life*, p. 80. Quotation, Simonton "Recollections."

32. Twentieth Maine officer letter, Dec. 15, 1862, PHS; Johnson and Buel, *Battles and Leaders*, 3:108, 125; Judson, *Eighty-third Pennsylvania*, p. 59; Powell, *Fifth Corps*, p. 398; Walter Carter to his parents, Dec. 24, 1862, in Carter, *Four Brothers*, p. 203; JLC letter, Dec. 17, 1862, PHS. Quotation, Twentieth Maine officer letter, Dec. 15, 1862. In his December 17, 1862, letter, JLC acknowledged the damage done the city but defended his own men by stating they had taken only what was needed for their own use and "no wanton mischief was done there under my eye." "I do not attempt," he continued, "to palliate the possible charge of pillage. I simply deny it, and think that our men showed a great deal of forbearance, considering that the houses were used as a cover for rebel sharpshooters, and that they were shelling the town more or less all the time." Simonton's description of the Twentieth's activities in the city ("Recollections," pp. 257–58) verifies JLC's statements. In "My Story of Fredericksburg," JLC did not address the subject or the aftermath, in which nearly all of the Union dead were stripped bare by the Confederates, perhaps in retaliation for the despoilment of the city. See Col. John R. Brooke's report, *OR* 21:261–62, for the account of the Union burial detail on December 17 and 18.

33. Judson, *Eighty-third Pennsylvania*, p. 59; Hill, "Last Charge at Fredericksburg," pp. 39, 43 (map).

34. *OR* 21:412; JLC, "My Story of Fredericksburg," p. 156; Hill, "Last

Charge at Fredericksburg," p. 41. Quotation, ibid. Several instances of bodies used as protection for the living in front of the stone wall appear in the Fredericksburg literature and official reports.

35. JLC letter, Dec. 17, 1862, PHS; JLC, "My Story of Fredericksburg," p. 156. Quotation, ibid.

36. JLC letter, Dec. 17, 1862, PHS; JLC, "Last Night at Fredericksburg," pp. 131, 132. Quotation, ibid., p. 132. The latter is the second and last of the *Congregationalist and Boston Recorder* articles by JLC about Fredericksburg, this one published on March 26, 1885. A partial copy of it is in LC. When Stockton became ill, the command of the brigade devolved on Col. Strong Vincent (*OR* 21:412). Colonel Ames had charge of three regiments, including his own (JLC to Gov. Washburn, Dec. 17, 1862, PHS). JLC must have used the newspaper clippings of the letters written by himself, Adjutant Brown, and the anonymous Twentieth Maine officer cited above when he wrote of his experiences at Fredericksburg twenty-three years later, printed in King and Derby, *Camp-fire Sketches*, and fifty years later, for "My Story of Fredericksburg" in *Cosmopolitan Magazine*. The latter contained the information given in the letters and was expanded to place the battle in historical context, with a few incidents from his memory, both from the Fredericksburg battle and the Antietam campaign. When writing his accounts, JLC usually did not rely on his memory alone but kept careful records for accuracy.

37. JLC, "Last Night at Fredericksburg," pp. 132, 133; JLC, "My Story of Fredericksburg," pp. 156–57; Chamberlain Association, *JLC: A Sketch*, p. 38. Quotation, JLC, "My Story of Fredericksburg," p. 157.

38. JLC, "My Story of Fredericksburg," pp. 157, 158; JLC, "Last Night at Fredericksburg," p. 133. Quotation, JLC, "My Story of Fredericksburg," p. 157.

39. JLC, "My Story of Fredericksburg," p. 158; Judson, *Eighty-third Pennsylvania*, p. 60. Quotation, ibid.

40. JLC, "My Story of Fredericksburg," p. 158; Hill, "Last Charge at Fredericksburg," pp. 42–43 (map); Powell, *Fifth Corps*, p. 397; Nash, *Forty-fourth New York*, p. 117. Quotation, Powell, *Fifth Corps*. The Fifth Corps was given the task of the defense of the city about 10:00 P.M. on December 15, and General Butterfield was directed to relieve the pickets on the left of Hanover Street; at about 3:30 A.M. the order came for the withdrawal from the city (*OR* 21:401). Hill thought Stockton's brigade was the last to cross on the lower pontoon bridge at the steamboat wharf. Powell rode through the deserted streets of the city alone as an aide to Colonel Buchanan, whose brigade was the last to cross the river on a pontoon bridge (which one was not specified) from the city, at about 8:00 A.M. on December 16 (*OR* 21:401).

41. JLC letter, Dec. 17, 1862, PHS; list of wounds in JLC's hand, JLC Letterbook, PHS; JLC, "Night on the Field," pp. 127, 130; JLC from M. S. Morse, Aug. 3, 1863, BC. First quotation, JLC, "Night on the Field," p. 127; second, JLC letter, Dec. 17, 1862. The Morse letter, from Rockville, Connecti-

cut, was from a brother or sister of the dead soldier thanking JLC. The family had never heard from the brother after the battle of Fredericksburg, had "long since mourned him for dead," and was grateful to get definite word of the soldier's fate. Morse's body was probably one of the 913 that Colonel Brooke buried in an unknowns' grave after the battle.

42. JLC, "My Story of Fredericksburg," p. 158; author's proof, "My Story of Fredericksburg," portion omitted by *Cosmopolitan* editor, UMO. Hooker and Chamberlain conversation quotations, JLC, "My Story of Fredericksburg"; last quotation, author's proof, "My Story of Fredericksburg." Hooker, whose Center Grand Division had been divided and much of it thrown into the battle piecemeal, could hardly be blamed for the debacle, a fact JLC acknowledged in "My Story of Fredericksburg." The *Official Records* give the following casualty figures (*OR* 21:572, 635): Twentieth Maine, 4 killed, 32 wounded, all enlisted men (*MAGR, 1862*, app. D, pp. 881–82, gives the further information that one of the wounded subsequently died and another was missing); Stockton's brigade, 18 killed, including 1 officer, 158 wounded, including 15 officers, and 25 enlisted men missing, for a total of 201. Griffin's division accounted for almost half of the Fifth Corps' casualties with 926, and Barnes's First Brigade accounted for over half of Griffin's at 500. Franklin's Left Grand Division, below the city, suffered heavy casualties also, a total of 3,787, of which the First Corps accounted for 3,337. By far, Sumner's Right Grand Division casualties exceeded all: 5,444, which with the Fifth Corps's 2,175 constituted a rough figure of 7,619 casualties in and behind the city. For the entire Army of the Potomac, there were 124 officers and 1,160 men killed, 654 officers and 8,946 men wounded, and 20 officers and 1,749 men missing, for a total of 12,653. Some of the wounded would later die of their wounds, and many of the missing were probably dead. Confederate Brig. Gen. Robert Ransom, Jr., walked over the field containing the Union dead in front of the stone wall on December 16. His summation of what he saw there, at the end of his official report, was in one descriptive sentence: "The havoc was appalling" (*OR* 21:628). Confederate casualty numbers are incomplete, but CSA Gen. James Longstreet reported 18 officers and 233 men killed, 102 officers and 1,414 men wounded, and 7 officers and 120 men missing, for a total of 1,894. CSA Gen. Thomas J. "Stonewall" Jackson reported his losses at 26 officers and 318 men killed, 195 officers and 2,350 men wounded, and 18 officers and 508 men missing, total 3,415. For these two corps, then, the loss total was 5,309.

43. Author's proof, "My Story of Fredericksburg," UMO; Swinton, *Army of the Potomac*, pp. 244–48; Johnson and Buel, *Battles and Leaders*, 3:117, 118, 127; *OR* 21:400–401, 429–30. Quotation, author's proof, "My Story of Fredericksburg." An aside to JLC's "My Story of Fredericksburg" that may be of interest is that a photograph run with the article by the *Cosmopolitan* editors and identified as JLC showed a three-quarters standing pose, in profile, of a young Union general who somewhat resembled JLC but was in actuality

Brig. Gen. Edwin H. Stoughton. In 1984 at the National Archives, Brady Collection, the original photo was found in the Chamberlain file, the original misfiling evidently the source of the editor's mistake. The archivist recognized the photo as that of Stoughton and corrected the error of some long-ago clerk.

44. Powell, *Fifth Corps*, p. 405; Adelbert Ames to his parents, n.d. (but probably late December 1862), and Ames to his parents, Jan. 10, 1863, both letters in Ames, *Chronicles*, 1:16, 17. Quotation, Ames to his parents, Jan. 10, 1863.

45. JLC, *Armies*, pp. 19, 20.

46. Gerrish, *Army Life*, p. 63; Billings, *Hardtack and Coffee*, pp. 51–56.

47. Powell, *Fifth Corps*, p. 405; Carter, *Four Brothers*, pp. 222, 224; Ellis Spear diary, Jan. 25–Feb. 6, 1863, in possession of Abbott Spear, Warren, Maine; Chamberlain Association, *JLC: A Sketch*, p. 11; Little, *Genealogical History*, 1:134; JLC to Gov. Washburn, July 14, 1862, MSA.

48. *OR* 21:882, 887; Nash, *Forty-fourth New York*, p. 118; Gerrish, *Army Life*, p. 63; Swinton, *Army of the Potomac*, pp. 256–57.

49. Powell, *Fifth Corps*, pp. 406, 407; Nash, *Forty-fourth New York*, p. 122; Swinton, *Army of the Potomac*, p. 258; *OR* 21:68–69.

50. Spear diary, Jan. 17–21, 1863; Nash, *Forty-fourth New York*, p. 123; Powell, *Fifth Corps*, pp. 407–9; *History, 118th Pennsylvania*, p. 161.

51. Swinton, *Army of the Potomac*, p. 260; Nash, *Forty-fourth New York*, p. 123; Powell, *Fifth Corps*, p. 409; Carter, *Four Brothers*, pp. 226, 228; *History, 118th Pennsylvania*, pp. 161–63. Signboard quotations from Nash, *Forty-fourth New York*, and Powell, *Fifth Corps*; other quotation from Carter, *Four Brothers*, p. 226. Although Powell, in the Regular Army, reported the whiskey was issued on January 23, both Carter and the 118th Pennsylvania's regimental history state that their whiskey rations were distributed on January 22. Carter's regiment was the Twenty-second Massachusetts, and both the latter regiments belonged to the First Brigade of Griffin's division, which had the near riot featuring the men and some officers. All versions may be correct, and the Regulars' ration given out a day later.

52. Carter, *Four Brothers*, p. 226; Billings, *Hardtack and Coffee*, pp. 378–79; Spear diary, Jan. 23, 1863; Judson, *Eighty-third Pennsylvania*, p. 61.

53. Swinton, *Army of the Potomac*, pp. 261–66; *OR* 21:998, 999, 1004–5; *OR* 25(2):4. Despite his questionable competence, Burnside seemed to be well liked among his superiors and subordinates. Although at least one called him "crazy," others excused his shortcomings with expressions of sorrow (*OR* 25[2]:1008; Johnson and Buel, *Battles and Leaders*, 3:106, 117). He was reassigned in the western theater of operations but returned to his old command of the Ninth Corps in March 1864.

54. *OR* 25(2):6, 51; Powell, *Fifth Corps*, pp. 416–20, 423–24; Swinton, *Army of the Potomac*, p. 268.

55. Swinton, *Army of the Potomac*, pp. 268, 269; *History, 118th Pennsylvania*, pp. 165, 166; Gerrish, *Army Life*, pp. 85, 86; *OR* 25(2):10–12, 57, 239–40.

56. JLC to Gov. Coburn, Feb. 26, 1863, MSA; Twentieth Maine Regimental Records, NA; Tom Chamberlain to John or Sae Chamberlain, Feb. 2, 1863, UMO; Spear diary, Feb. 6, 1863; Dr. Adams diary, Feb. 12 and 13, 1863, FPC; Powell, *Fifth Corps*, pp. 405–6; Pvt. G. W. Carleton to the Adjutant General of Maine, Jan. 8, 1866, FPYU.

57. JLC to Gov. Coburn, Feb. 26, 1863, MSA; JLC, *Armies*, p. xiii.

58. Norton, *Army Letters*, p. 148; Carter, *Four Brothers*, pp. 235–38; JLC, *Armies*, p. 311. Quotations, ibid. Spear's diary entries for the period show several reviews and frequent drill.

59. *OR* 25(2):152; Norton, *Army Letters*, pp. 330–32. The men became so attached to their insignia that veterans' organizations and reunion badges after the war rarely failed to display a corps badge insignia and the division colors, if appropriate. Chamberlain had a red-brick Maltese cross built into one of his house chimneys, the latter white brick. The badges of the corps other than the Fifth in the Army of the Potomac on the date the order was issued, March 21, 1863, were First Corps, sphere (circle); Second, trefoil (called "Ace of Clubs"); Third, lozenge (diamond); Sixth, cross (Greek); Eleventh, crescent; Twelfth, star. The color of the first division of a corps was red, the second division, white, and third division, blue. The badges measured about two inches in length and width. Gen. Daniel Butterfield devised this system, although Gen. Philip Kearney first had the idea of a distinguishing patch for his division in 1862, to identify the men of his command. Other corps outside the Army of the Potomac later adopted corps insignia. See Billings, *Hardtack and Coffee*, pp. 254–58.

60. E. B. French to Lt. Col. Conrad, Apr. 9, 1863, WP; JLC Military Service records, NA; *MAGR, 1864–1865*, 1:337; JLC to Fannie, Apr. 24, 1863, LC. Quotation, ibid.

61. *MAGR, 1864–1865*, 1:331; Pullen, *Twentieth Maine*, p. 74; Gerrish, *Army Life*, p. 86; JLC to Fannie, Apr. 24, 1863, LC; Spear diary, Apr. 22, 1863. Quotation, JLC to Fannie, Apr. 24, 1863. Pvt. George W. Carleton was convinced, and no doubt it was a widespread belief in the Twentieth, that the Rebels had somehow diabolically introduced smallpox into the regiment, hoping it would spread to the rest of the army (Carleton to Adjutant General of Maine, Jan. 8, 1866, FPYU).

62. *History, 118th Pennsylvania*, p. 165; Judson, *Eighty-third Pennsylvania*, p. 61; JLC to Fannie, Apr. 24, 1863, LC; JLC to Fannie, Apr. 27, 1863, appended to ibid.; Spear diary, Apr. 27, 1863. Quotation, Judson, *Eighty-third Pennsylvania*.

63. Spear diary, Apr. 28–May 1, 1863; [Gen. Daniel] Butterfield to Ames, Apr. 21, 1863, in Ames, *Chronicles*, 1:19; JLC to Fannie, Apr. 24, 1863, LC. JLC used the term "pest house" in his April 24 letter to Fannie.

64. Spear diary, May 1–3, 1863; *OR* 25(1):518; *MAGR, 1864–1865*, 1:331. Quotation, ibid. Powell states that Hooker arrived at Chancellorsville on April 30, leaving his chief of staff, General Butterfield, at his headquarters at

Falmouth "to facilitate communications with both wings of his army" (*Fifth Corps*, p. 434). The Twentieth's situation must have been well known, since General Butterfield wired Hooker on May 3 that he had "put every officer and man here in use during the operations even to the Twentieth Maine" (*OR* 25[2]:377).

65. Spear diary, May 3, 1863; Powell, *Fifth Corps*, pp. 448–70.

66. JLC to Gov. Coburn, May 25, 1863, MSA; Powell, *Fifth Corps*, p. 471; *MAGR, 1864–1865*, 1:331; *OR* 25(1):508, 518; "Horse[s] shot under me," list in JLC's hand, JLC Letterbook, PHS. JLC apparently joined in the rapid advancement of a "reconnaissance in force" of the Second Brigade of his division on the afternoon of May 4, which its commander, Colonel McQuade, describes as occurring "under the personal supervision of Gen. Griffin" (*OR* 25[1]:518). Griffin had commanded this brigade during the 1862 Peninsula campaign. JLC, in his Letterbook, PHS, labels the action "Griffin's charge." Prince's ultimate fate is unknown. John Chamberlain expected to ride "a grey horse" when he came to visit his brothers in the army a month after the battle of Chancellorsville (John Chamberlain diary, p. 1, PHS) and described taking his brother's "valuable horse" to be shod at Frederick, Maryland, after Gettysburg (ibid., p. 74), but he does not say it was Prince. John Chamberlain's diary, apparently undisturbed and filled with newspaper clippings about the war from 1863 to 1865, was found in the late summer of 1986 at the summer cottage of JLC's granddaughter Rosamond Allen when she removed the cottage's contents and prepared to close it for the last time. She and her sister Eleanor had disposed of the contents of the old Chamberlain home in Brewer in 1962 after the death of their cousin and JLC's niece, Alice M. Farrington. The diary must have come into Miss Allen's possession at that time, apparently preserved.

67. Swinton, *Army of the Potomac*, pp. 269–75; Powell, *Fifth Corps*, pp. 471, 495; Little, *Genealogical History*, 1:134; Judson, *Eighty-third Pennsylvania*, p. 62. The Fifth Corps recrossed the Rappahannock at United States Ford, acting as rear guard for the whole army, with Griffin's division bringing up the rear (*OR* 25[1]:508).

68. Judson, *Eighty-third Pennsylvania*, p. 62; *History, 118th Pennsylvania*, pp. 201–8; *OR* 25(1):185, 191, 557–62, 798–99, 999; ibid. (2):791.

69. Powell, *Fifth Corps*, pp. 488–89; Spear diary, May 7–16, 1863; JLC to Daisy, May 1863, BC. Quotation, ibid. The letter was probably written May 13. A later JLC letter (JLC to Aunty, June 15, 1863, LC) was written on the back of an order dated May 13, 1863, asking JLC to relieve Lieutenant Colonel Welch of the Sixteenth Michigan Regiment, who had reported himself ill, and detailing JLC as commander of outposts (i.e., pickets) (Lt. F. M. Kelly, AAG, Third Brigade Hdqtrs, to JLC, May 13, 1863, LC).

70. Ames to his parents, Sept. 21, 1862, Maj. Gen. Joseph Hooker to Vice-President Hamlin, Nov. 16, 1862, Brig. Gen. H. G. Berry to Vice-President Hamlin, Nov. 14, 1862, Ames to his parents, n.d. (but probably late Decem-

ber 1862), Brig. Gen. Charles Griffin to Gen. Hooker, Apr. 5, 1863, Maj. Gen. O. O. Howard to Maj. Gen. Hooker, Apr. 19, 1863, in Ames, *Chronicles*, 1:13–19; Carter, *Four Brothers*, pp. 162–63; Gov. Israel Washburn to JLC and Major Gilmore, Nov. 21, 1862, LC.

71. O. O. Howard to Gen. Hooker, Apr. 19, 1863, in Ames, *Chronicles*, 1:18–19; *OR* 25(1):509; *MAGR, 1864–1865*, 1:302, 331. Quotation, O. O. Howard to Gen. Hooker, Apr. 19, 1863, p. 19. Ames distinguished himself later in the war and kept in touch with JLC, his letters showing the affection and high regard he held for his former subordinate. After the war he served as provisional governor of Mississippi under the Reconstruction Acts; he was later senator and then governor from that state. In 1870 he fell in love with and married Blanche Butler, the surprisingly beautiful auburn-haired daughter of the decidedly ugly Benjamin F. Butler, Massachusetts politician and former Union major general. No radical, and at first indifferent to the plight of the freedman in the South, Ames was changed by his firsthand experience to a position of black advocacy. In 1876, after white-supremacist Democrats won election through intimidation and violence, Ames was forced to resign under threat of impeachment by the Mississippi legislature. Successful in business later, he served as brigadier general of volunteers in the Spanish-American War. He died April 13, 1933, at the age of ninety-seven, the oldest survivor of general officers of either side in the Civil War.

72. JLC, "Blood and Fire," p. 899; John Chamberlain diary, p. 1, PHS; U.S. Secretary of War, *Revised Regulations*, p. 525; Spear diary, Mar. 8–22, May 30, June 28, 1863; Houston, *The Thirty-second Maine*, p. 52; JLC to Gov. Coburn, May 25 and May 27, 1863, MSA. The officer promotion process in the Civil War was often so cumbersome and political that soldiers would act in various capacities, sometimes for months, before finally receiving their rank, if then. Although Adjutant Brown was not officially transferred from the regiment until June 29, 1863 (*MAGR, 1863*, p. 571), he had in fact been long gone from the Twentieth. The text of John Chamberlain's diary shows that when he left home on June 1, 1863, he knew, presumably from letters, that JLC was the new colonel and Tom the adjutant of the Twentieth.

73. Nash, *Forty-fourth New York*, p. 135; JLC, "Blood and Fire," p. 898; *OR* 25(2):531, 532, 579. Quotation, JLC, "Blood and Fire." Hooker was expecting a total loss of 18,760 from regiments whose terms of service ended from May 22 through July 7, 1863 (*OR* 25[2]:532).

74. Whitman and True, *Maine in the War*, pp. 37, 38, 54–55; *MAGR, 1864–1865*, 1:331–32; Spear diary, May 24, 1863; JLC to Gov. Coburn, May 25, 1863, MSA. Quotation "seat of war" is from Whitman and True, *Maine in the War*, p. 37, but is an expression in common use during the war.

75. Spear diary, May 24, 1863; Little, *Genealogical History*, 1:135; JLC, "Blood and Fire," pp. 899, 900. Quotation, ibid., p. 900.

76. JLC, "Blood and Fire," p. 899; JLC to Gov. Coburn, May 25, 1863, MSA; Carter, *Four Brothers*, p. 226. Quotation, JLC to Gov. Coburn, May 25,

1863. Tom Chamberlain shortly thereafter received a letter from his sister describing the wild celebration of the citizens of Bangor on the return of the Second Maine; she and her mother were acquainted with some of the returning men and joined the celebration (Sae to Thomas, May 26, 1863, RC). Tom Chamberlain also knew men from the Second, and one asked later to be placed in his company of the regiment (Thomas D. Chamberlain Military Pension records, NA). Sae also acknowledged the receipt of Tom's new photographs in his officer's uniform, although she thought one so bad it made him look like a "scape-grace" (Sae to Thomas, May 26, 1863, RC).

77. JLC, "Blood and Fire," p. 900; JLC to Gov. Coburn, May 25, May 27, and Sept. 19, 1863, MSA; *MAGR, 1864–1865*, 1:332. First quotation, JLC, "Blood and Fire"; second quotation, *MAGR, 1864–1865*. Only a few Second Maine soldiers refused duty in the Twentieth; all but two finally came around, and after the latter's cases went to courts-martial, their sentences were remitted by JLC's efforts (*MAGR, 1864–1865*, 1:332; Twentieth Maine Regimental Records, NA).

78. *OR* 25(2):470, 535–36; Oliver W. Norton to Cousin L., Apr. 2, 1863, in Norton, *Army Letters*, p. 146; Norton to Sister L., May 27, 1863, in ibid., p. 155; ibid., pp. 331–32.

CHAPTER FIVE

1. John Chamberlain to JLC, Mar. 6, 1863, RC; Christian Commission information for delegates, Boston, May 1863, UMO; John Chamberlain diary, pp. 1–3, PHS.

2. John Chamberlain diary, pp. 3, 4, PHS. First quotation, p. 3; second and third, p. 4.

3. Ibid., pp. 5–21; Powell, *Fifth Corps*, p. 496; Little, *Genealogical History*, p. 133. John also was entertained by a "Negro slave genuine howler faces up elbows wiggling and swinging their bodies." This was evidently a religious revival in a tent characterized by loud singing of the call and response variety, using Old and New Testament lines and verses. Later he attended another "howler" with sick white soldiers: "Such earnestness & grappling on G[od] in prayer . . . the most Methodistical revival." Although John spoke of blacks as "negroes," he also unfortunately referred to them in the cruder form of the word characteristic of the widespread racism shared by the country as a whole. His older brother, to his credit, apparently did not use the coarse term.

4. John Chamberlain diary, pp. 16, 17, PHS.

5. *MAGR, 1863*, p. 90; Ellis Spear diary, June 5–12, 1863, in possession of Abbott Spear, Warren, Maine; Judson, *Eighty-third Pennsylvania*, p. 63; Nash, *Forty-fourth New York*, p. 322; Pvt. John Lenfest to his wife, May 31, 1863, Lenfest Letters, PHS; Carter, *Four Brothers*, p. 191; Nolan, *Iron Brigade*, p. 191.

6. Spear diary, June 5–12, 1863; Powell, *Fifth Corps*, pp. 490–92; JLC to "Aunty" [Deborah Folsom], June 15, 1863, LC. Quotation, ibid.

7. JLC to "Aunty" [Deborah Folsom], June 15, 1863, LC; JLC to Daisy [Grace], May [13], 1863, BC; Katie to JLC, June 1, 1863, RC; Sae Chamberlain to Tom Chamberlain, May 26, 1863, RC; JLC to Fannie, July 17, 1863, LC. Deborah Folsom's letter to JLC is inferred from JLC's note to her on June 15, 1863, LC. First quotation, Katie to JLC, June 1, 1863; second, Sae Chamberlain to Tom Chamberlain, May 26, 1863. Mail service was erratic at that time (JLC to the Maine Adjutant General, July 11, 1863, MSA).

8. Spear diary, June 16–21, 1863; John Chamberlain diary, p. 42, PHS; Powell, *Fifth Corps*, p. 495; *OR* 27(1):614; Judson, *Eighty-third Pennsylvania*, pp. 63, 64. The Twentieth Maine lost one man killed and seven wounded at the battle of Middleburg (*OR* 27[1]:172).

9. Spear diary, June 22, 1863; John Chamberlain diary, pp. 26–42, PHS; *History, 118th Pennsylvania*, p. 228. First quotation, ibid.; second, John Chamberlain diary, p. 42. When John Chamberlain left Washington for the front, either on the night of June 21 or morning of June 22, he went so abruptly that he forgot the notebook containing his diary. He did keep some notes, however, and immediately wrote the story of his adventure from that time on after his return to Washington on July 16.

10. Judson, *Eighty-third Pennsylvania*, p. 64; John Chamberlain diary, pp. 43–45, PHS. Quotation, ibid., p. 43.

11. John Chamberlain diary, p. 43, PHS; Warner, *Generals in Blue*, pp. 400–401; Nash, *Forty-fourth New York*, pp. xiv, 20, 87–89, 161, 162, 223; Norton, *Army Letters*, pp. 174, 280–81.

12. John Chamberlain diary, pp. 45, 46, PHS; Spear diary, June 26, 1863.

13. Johnson and Buel, *Battles and Leaders*, 3:265–70; Warner, *Generals in Blue*, p. 493.

14. Johnson and Buel, *Battles and Leaders*, 3:250, 270–71; Nash, *Forty-fourth New York*, pp. 140–41. Col. William L. Tilton gave this mileage in his account of the march: left Frederick on June 29, marched fifteen miles through Liberty, Maryland; June 30, marched a twenty-five-mile forced march through Johnsville, Union, and Frizelburg to Union Mills, Maryland, reaching there at 5:00 P.M. On July 1, left Union Mills at "11¾ A.M." and arrived near Hanover, Pennsylvania, at 3:00 P.M. Men roused to march again at 8:00 P.M. (William L. Tilton to JLC, Oct. 6, 1865, LC). Tilton commanded the First Brigade of the Fifth Corps's First Division.

15. *History, 118th Pennsylvania*, p. 245; Judson, *Eighty-third Pennsylvania*, p. 66; Nash, *Forty-fourth New York*, p. 141.

16. Warner, *Generals in Blue*, pp. 527–28; Judson, *Eighty-third Pennsylvania*, pp. 21, 42; Norton, *Little Round Top*, pp. 281, 285.

17. Powell, *Fifth Corps*, pp. 505, 506, 510; John Chamberlain diary, pp. 48, 49, PHS; Nash, *Forty-fourth New York*, p. 141; JLC, "Blood and Fire," pp. 895, 896.

18. JLC, "Blood and Fire," p. 896; Powell, *Fifth Corps*, pp. 511–13; John Chamberlain diary, p. 49, PHS; Norton, *Army Letters*, p. 281. Quotation, ibid. Norton wrote an account of his 1863 experiences for his sister in the summer of 1864. Vincent's words about the flag are from that account.

19. John Chamberlain diary, pp. 49, 50, PHS; JLC, "Blood and Fire," p. 896; Gerrish, *Army Life*, p. 101; *OR* 27(1):621. Vincent quotation, John Chamberlain diary, p. 50; JLC quotation, JLC, "Blood and Fire." The night march of July 1–2 was a memorable one for the Fifth Corps. Many descriptions of it are extant, but most describe the McClellan rumor as being spread by unknown staff officers. However, John Chamberlain stated, "General Barnes, commanding the Division, announced through Col. Vincent . . . that McLellan [*sic*] was appointed to the command of Halleck." Col. Joseph Hayes, who commanded a regiment in the First Brigade of Barnes's division, sent JLC extracts from his diary. On July 1 he wrote: "During the night march a Staff Officer brought me word from the division commander that McClellan had been appointed General in Chief, and was then at Gettysburgh. I halted my men . . . and told them the news. One grand hurrah arose" (Hayes to JLC, Oct. 23, 1865, LC). Gerrish estimated that the Twentieth Maine marched thirty miles on July 1 and the early morning of July 2.

20. *OR* 27(1):115–16, 622; Fremantle and Haskell, *Two Views of Gettysburg*, pp. 114–17; Powell, *Fifth Corps*, p. 519; Swinton, *Army of the Potomac*, pp. 335–37; Norton, *Little Round Top*, pp. 128, 129. Round Top was also called "Sugar Loaf" (Powell, *Fifth Corps*, p. 527), and Colonel Rice, in his official report, called it "Wolf's Hill."

21. *OR* 27(1):115, 116, 252; Swinton, *Army of the Potomac*, pp. 329–34.

22. Judson, *Eighty-third Pennsylvania*, p. 66; *OR* 27(1):622; Haskell, "Battle of Gettysburg," p. 113; Johnson and Buel, *Battles and Leaders*, 3:294; *Dedication of the Twentieth Maine Monuments*, Capt. Howard L. Prince's address, pp. 9, 10.

23. *OR* 27(1):593, 610, 622–23; Norton, *Little Round Top*, p. 238.

24. Swinton, *Army of the Potomac*, p. 342; Johnson and Buel, *Battles and Leaders*, 3:306, 320; Norton, *Little Round Top*, p. 309; Georg, "Our Principal Loss Was in This Place," p. 4. Seminary and Cemetery Ridges were from approximately one-half to one mile apart.

25. *Maine at Gettysburg*, pp. 251, 276 (map); JLC, "Blood and Fire," p. 898; *OR* 27(1):623; Swinton, *Army of the Potomac*, p. 345; Coddington, *Gettysburg*, map no. 7, facing p. 333; Johnson and Buel, *Battles and Leaders*, 3:305.

26. *OR* 27(1):116; Warren to Porter Farley, July 13, 1872, in Norton, *Little Round Top*, p. 309; Johnson and Buel, *Battles and Leaders*, 3:307; Coddington, *Gettysburg*, p. 331. Both Round Tops were important for the Union to hold and the Confederates to sieze, but Little Round Top had the advantage of an unwooded western face and, at that time, was the more critical height.

27. E. G. Taylor, *Warren*, pp. 4, 119, 120; Warner, *Generals in Blue*, p. 541; Warren to Porter Farley, July 13, 1872, and Dec. 6, 1877, in Norton, *Little*

Round Top, pp. 309, 325. Quotation, ibid., p. 309. Warren was promoted to major general on August 8, 1863, to date from May 3, 1863. The battery that Warren ordered to fire was Smith's Fourth New York, posted in and near the Devil's Den (Warren to Farley, Oct. 3, 1877, in Norton, *Little Round Top*, p. 313).

28. Norton, *Little Round Top*, pp. 263, 264; JLC, "Blood and Fire," p. 898. Oliver W. Norton, brigade bugler and flag-bearer for Col. Strong Vincent that day, did a thorough study of the battle of Little Round Top, published in 1913 as *The Attack and Defense of Little Round Top*. There were conflicting reports of how Vincent's brigade was ordered to Little Round Top, but since Norton's duty was to stay near the brigade commander with the flag, he witnessed Vincent's hailing the staff officer. He concluded, after much study and correspondence, that the messenger was General Sykes's aide.

29. Norton to JLC, May 8, 1901, MHS; Norton, *Strong Vincent*, p. 6. Quotations, ibid. This short book is Norton's earlier, greatly abbreviated version of the 1913 volume.

30. Norton, *Strong Vincent*, pp. 6, 7. Norton held Strong Vincent in the highest esteem. He wrote his books principally to make sure that history recorded the contribution Vincent made in the saving of Little Round Top for the Federals by his prompt response to the immediate need for troops and his proper selection of the part of the hill to defend. The lower, southern part of Little Round Top defended by his brigade is sometimes called "Vincent's Spur."

31. *OR* 27(1):623; Norton, *Strong Vincent*, pp. 7–8; Norton to JLC, May 8, 1901, MHS; JLC, "Blood and Fire," p. 899.

32. John Chamberlain diary, p. 51, PHS; JLC, "Blood and Fire," p. 899. Quotation, ibid.

33. Norton, *Strong Vincent*, p. 7; Norton, *Little Round Top*, p. 264.

34. Norton, *Strong Vincent*, p. 7; O. W. Norton to Sister L., July 21, 1863, in Norton, *Army Letters*, p. 167. Quotation, ibid.

35. *OR* 27(1):623; Norton, *Little Round Top*, pp. 265–67; *Dedication of the Twentieth Maine Monuments*, Capt. Howard L. Prince's address, p. 12; *Maine at Gettysburg*, p. 251, map.

36. Judson, *Eighty-third Pennsylvania*, p. 67; Coddington, *Gettysburg*, p. 331; *OR* 27(1):623; Norton, *Little Round Top*, pp. 265–66. Quotations, *OR*.

37. Powell, *Fifth Corps*, p. 531; Johnson and Buel, *Battles and Leaders*, 3:303; G. K. Warren to his wife, July 2, 1863, in E. G. Taylor, *Warren*, p. 130.

38. *Dedication of the Twentieth Maine Monuments*, JLC's address, pp. 29, 30; *OR* 27(1):623; U.S. Secretary of War, *Infantry Tactics*, pp. 114–15.

39. *OR* 27(1):623; *Maine at Gettysburg*, pp. 254, 264; *MAGR, 1862*, app. D, pp. 134, 656; JLC, "Blood and Fire," pp. 899, 900; John Chamberlain diary, p. 57, PHS; JLC to Gov. Abner Coburn, May 25, 1863, MSA; JLC to Gov. Abner Coburn, July 21, 1863, MSA. Quotation, *Maine at Gettysburg*, p. 254.

40. Johnson and Buel, *Battles and Leaders*, 3:320; Norton, *Little Round Top*,

pp. 253–60. The Forty-fourth Alabama was detailed by Law to attack Smith's battery. Its commander does not mention ascending Little Round Top (*OR* 27[2]:393–94). However, the report of the commander of the Fourth Texas mentions that his regiment was reinforced by the Forty-eighth and the Forty-fourth Alabama on his last charge upon Little Round Top (*OR* 27[2]:411).

41. Norton, *Little Round Top*, p. 256; *OR* 27(2):392, 395; ibid. (1):518–19; Oates, "Gettysburg—The Battle on the Right," p. 174. Colonel Oates published three versions of his July 2 fight. The first and second were his short official report and the article cited above, the latter published in 1878 and adding more detail. The third and final version was in his 1905 book about himself and his men (Oates, *The War*).

42. JLC, "Blood and Fire," p. 900; Judson, *Eighty-third Pennsylvania*, p. 67. Quotation, ibid.

43. Judson, *Eighty-third Pennsylvania*, p. 67.

44. Oates, "Gettysburg—The Battle on the Right," pp. 174–75; *OR* 27(2):392. Quotation, ibid. In his 1903 letter to the secretary of war (Oates to Elihu Root, June 2, 1903, Oates Correspondence Scrapbook, GNMP, copy in LC), Oates stated for the first time that General Law had ordered him also to direct the Forty-seventh Alabama if they were separated from the rest of the brigade. This statement so startled the Confederate representative on the Gettysburg Park Commission that he wrote to General Law to confirm it (William Robbins to Evander Law, June 20, 1903, Oates Correspondence Scrapbook, GNMP). No reply from Law is extant in the battlefield files. Oates, in a November 13, 1903, letter to Col. John Nicholson, said he had a letter from Law confirming his order to Oates to turn the left of the Union line.

45. *OR* 27(1):623; *Dedication of the Twentieth Maine Monuments*, Capt. Howard L. Prince's address, pp. 12, 13, 15; ibid., JLC's address, p. 27; *Maine at Gettysburg*, pp. 254, 261, 277. The regimental monument was placed, and now stands, on the giant boulder beyond the left of the original Twentieth Maine line (*Dedication of the Twentieth Maine Monuments*, JLC's address, p. 27).

46. JLC, "Blood and Fire," p. 900; Johnson and Buel, *Battles and Leaders*, 3:323. Quotation, JLC, "Blood and Fire."

47. *Maine at Gettysburg*, pp. 257–58; John Chamberlain diary, p. 75, PHS; Spear diary, June 28, 1863; *Dedication of the Twentieth Maine Monuments*, Capt. Howard L. Prince's address, pp. 13, 17.

48. *Dedication of the Twentieth Maine Monuments*, Capt. Howard L. Prince's address, p. 17.

49. Judson, *Eighty-third Pennsylvania*, p. 67; Nash, *Forty-fourth New York*, pp. 144, 145; Warren to Capt. Porter Farley, July 13, 1872, in Norton, *Little Round Top*, p. 310; *OR* 27(1):623, 659; ibid. (2):394; Rittenhouse, "The Battle of Gettysburg," p. 522; JLC, "Blood and Fire," p. 902; Coan manuscript, p. 11, Elisha S. Coan Papers, BC.

50. *OR* 27(1):623; JLC, "Blood and Fire," p. 902; JLC to Gov. Coburn, Oct.

28, 1963, MSA; Coan manuscript, pp. 10, 11, Elisha S. Coan Papers, BC; *Dedication of the Twentieth Maine Monuments*, Capt. Howard L. Prince's address, p. 18; ibid., JLC's address, p. 27; *Maine at Gettysburg*, pp. 255–56. Quotation, JLC to Gov. Coburn, Oct. 28, 1863. Although JLC's official report stated that "an officer from my center" first called his attention to the flanking Confederates, years later his friend Ellis Spear apparently contended that he was the man (Spear to JLC, May 22, 1895, LC, and *Dedication of the Twentieth Maine Monuments*, Capt. Howard L. Prince's address, p. 18). JLC maintained it was Lt. James H. Nichols but, trying to reconcile the two claims, recalled that Spear came to him later about the flanking column (*Dedication of the Twentieth Maine Monuments*, pp. 27, 28; JLC, "Blood and Fire," p. 902). Pvt. Elisha S. Coan, a member of the regimental color guard, was a witness, and his manuscript (in the Elisha S. Coan Papers, BC) seems to support JLC's recollection, describing JLC as already on the large rock behind Coan, with bullets coming in from the left, when "an officer from the left" rushed up. The Forty-seventh Alabama had crowded in to the right of the Fourth Alabama and was engaging the Twentieth (JLC, "Blood and Fire," p. 902; Oates, "Gettysburg—The Battle on the Right," p. 176). Before the 1889 Gettysburg reunion to dedicate the regimental monuments, JLC did not know that Spear and Nichols both claimed to have warned him of Oates's flanking movement (*Dedication of the Twentieth Maine Monuments*, JLC's address, p. 27). Regardless of JLC's official report and memory of the incident, Spear apparently resented this conclusion, which may have been the start of serious consequences for the friendship many years later.

51. JLC to Gen. James Barnes, Sept. 3, 1863, Gen. James Barnes Papers, New-York Historical Society, copy at GNMP; *OR* 27(1):623; *Maine at Gettysburg*, p. 255; *Dedication of the Twentieth Maine Monuments*, JLC's address, p. 27. Spear also contended later that he originated the idea of the refusal of the line, went to JLC for approval, and then bent back slightly the two left companies (Ellis Spear to John Bachelder, Nov. 15, 1892, John B. Bachelder Papers, New Hampshire Historical Society, copy at GNMP). In a letter from Spear to JLC, Spear stated that he had received orders "directly from you to bend back a little the two left companies, when I had reported to you that the enemy was extending beyond our left. I did so" (Spear to JLC, May 22, 1895, LC). But Spear wrote to the *Portland Press* soon after the battle, described it, and said, among other things highly complimentary to JLC, "The Colonel perceiving that their object was to gain our rear, bent back the left wing until it was nearly perpendicular to the first line and facing the enemy" ("20th Maine at Gettysburg," clipping of letter pasted in John Chamberlain diary, PHS, with "Capt. Spear's letter" inscribed in John Chamberlain's hand). JLC first described his refusing of his left wing in his official report.

52. *Dedication of the Twentieth Maine Monuments*, JLC's address, p. 28; *OR* 27(1):623; JLC, "Blood and Fire," p. 902; JLC to John Bachelder, Jan. 25, 1884,

John B. Bachelder Papers, New Hampshire Historical Society, copy at GNMP. The order of companies in the line, from right to left, was E, I, K, D, F, A, H, C, G, the colors at the left of F, the color company (*Maine at Gettysburg*, p. 254n). The left wing had only four companies (A, H, C, and G) since the other, B, was detached as skirmishers. The ground where the Twentieth's left wing was deployed after the line was refused was disturbed greatly near the turn of the century when a road, Chamberlain Avenue, was built around the Twentieth's position on Little Round Top. In the early 1930s the avenue was removed, causing more damage and the loss of the left flank marker. It is difficult today to visualize some of the ground where the Twentieth's left wing fought as it was on the day of the battle. The old roadbed can still be faintly seen.

53. *Dedication of the Twentieth Maine Monuments*, JLC's address, p. 30.

54. Ibid.; Maj. William Robbins to Col. John Nicholson, Feb. 26, 1903, Oates Correspondence Scrapbook, GNMP; *OR* 27(1):623; ibid. (2):392–93; Oates, "Gettysburg—The Battle on the Right," p. 176; JLC to Gen. Barnes, Sept. 3, 1863, Gen. James Barnes Papers, New-York Historical Society, copy at GNMP.

55. Oates, "Gettysburg—The Battle on the Right," p. 176.

56. JLC to Barnes, Sept. 3, 1863, Gen. James Barnes Papers, New-York Historical Society, copy at GNMP; *OR* 27(1):624; JLC to Gov. Abner Coburn, July 21, 1863, MSA. Quotation, *OR*.

57. Gerrish, *Army Life*, p. 108; Ellis Spear, speech at Warren, Maine, Memorial Day, 1888, typescript in possession of Abbott Spear.

58. JLC, "Blood and Fire," p. 903.

59. Ibid., p. 904; *Maine at Gettysburg*, pp. 261, 270–72; William T. Livermore to JLC, May 22, 1899, MHS; *MAGR, 1861*, app. D, p. 94. The two center companies, F and A, with the color guard added, sustained casualties of thirteen killed, thirty-four wounded in the terrible cross fire (*Maine at Gettysburg*, pp. 270–72). Tozier had been wounded at Gaines's Mill the year before (*MAGR, 1862*, app. D, p. 21). Unlike Fredericksburg, there is no direct evidence of which colors the Twentieth was fighting under at Gettysburg, but circumstantial evidence points to the national flag. A photograph in the possession of Abbott Spear, taken ca. 1883, shows the national flag accompanying JLC, Spear, and others standing on the rock upon which the monument was later placed. A lithograph of the same scene is in JLC's papers in LC. Mr. Spear owns another photograph of the flag taken at the dedication of the Twentieth Maine monument on Little Round Top in 1889. Holman S. Melcher, in his opening remarks on that occasion, said, "We stand here, today, under the same battle-torn and blood stained flag that was carried to victory in the struggle for this key-point, to dedicate this monument" (*Dedication of the Twentieth Maine Monuments*, p. 7). A reference in Hamlin, *Nineteenth National Encampment*, p. 77, states: "The Twentieth Regiment assembled . . . and formed a line of about one hundred and twenty men in front

of City Hall. The old flag which they defended at Round Top was brought to the front and the column." Civil War veterans referred to only one flag as the "old flag," and that was the Stars and Stripes; another choice of words would have been used to denote any other.

60. JLC, "Blood and Fire," p. 904; Twentieth Maine Regimental Records, NA; *Maine at Gettysburg*, p. 256. In August 1898 Tozier was awarded the other Medal of Honor given a Twentieth Maine man at Gettysburg, with this citation: "At the crisis of the engagement this soldier, a color bearer, stood alone in an advanced position, the regiment having been borne back, and defended his colors with musket and ammunition picked up at his feet" (U.S. Congress, *Medal of Honor Recipients*, p. 595). JLC apparently thought that Tozier stood alone, but Sgt. W. T. Livermore wrote him to correct this after reading the account in *Maine at Gettysburg*, which was published in 1898. Livermore, from Company B, was a color guard that day and was horrified to wonder what his comrades in his company might think about him when they read it. He said that he and Elisha Coan, who died in 1896, were still guarding the colors and suggested that battle smoke had obscured JLC's vision (W. T. Livermore to JLC, May 22, 1899, MHS). JLC worded the incident differently in his 1913 "Blood and Fire" to reflect Livermore's version. JLC's accounts of actions sometimes differed in detail; the voluminous correspondence in the manuscript collections shows that he was willing to amend his statements when other information warranted and was substantially correct. He also went out of his way to reconcile seemingly contradictory accounts where possible.

61. *Maine at Gettysburg*, p. 256; *Dedication of the Twentieth Maine Monuments*, JLC's address, p. 28. In 1882 Ellis Spear visited Oates in Washington, D.C., where Oates was serving as U.S. Congressman from Alabama. It was then that Oates learned, apparently for the first time, that the men he fought were only one regiment—the Twentieth Maine (Spear to JLC, July 2, 1882, LC). Over twenty years later, in a letter to the secretary of war concerning a monument he wanted to erect, Oates gave a differing account of the action than he had recounted in his official report and in his "Gettysburg—The Battle on the Right," including a claim that he had "turned the Union flank, and drove the right of the 20th Maine back on its left, and attacked the 83d Penna., and 44th New York" (Oates to Elihu Root, June 2, 1903, Oates Correspondence Scrapbook, GNMP).

The Oates Correspondence Scrapbook in Gettysburg National Military Park contains a fascinating series of letters by Chamberlain and Oates in which Oates makes more assertions and includes a nearly incomprehensible sketch of the positions of his men. He gave the impression that except for the short-time help of the Forty-seventh Alabama, he fought Vincent's brigade isolated and alone during the battle. However, the Confederate representative on the Park Commission, Maj. William Robbins, who fought with the Fourth Alabama on the left of the Forty-seventh Alabama, stated in a letter to the Park Commission chairman, Col. John Nicholson, that during the fight at Little Round Top, the Fifteenth Alabama was about one hundred yards from the Fourth, the Forty-seventh in between and in touch with the Fourth, and that the Fifteenth Alabama had fought only the left wing of the Twentieth Maine. Robbins added that the Forty-seventh fought JLC's center, and the Fourth fought the right of the Twentieth Maine, plus the Eighty-third Pennsylvania. He also stated that the rock on which JLC stood to see the Fifteenth's flanking move was only fifty yards from where he (Robbins) was during the battle (Robbins to Nicholson, Feb. 26, 1903, Oates Correspondence Scrapbook, GNMP). Robbins seemed to be put off by Oates's allegations in the controversy, and his letter effectively negates virtually all of Oates's claims. Oates in 1904 was so confused about battlefield directions that he sent to the park for maps (Oates to Nicholson, Apr. 4, 1904, Oates Correspondence Scrapbook, GNMP). Again, Oates sent for a blueprint of Little Round Top, "because I get confused on directions" (Oates to E. B. Cope, Aug. 6, 1904, Oates Correspondence Scrapbook, GNMP). In 1905 he published his book (*The War between the Union and the Confederacy and Its Lost Opportunities*), which materially differed from many of his previous published and unpublished statements.

62. *Maine at Gettysburg*, p. 256–57; JLC, "Blood and Fire," p. 904; *OR* 27(1):624; Judson, *Eighty-third Pennsylvania*, p. 68. JLC ordered one of his right companies to relieve his hard-pressed left wing but soon countermanded the order because of the confusion the movement would cause (*Dedication of the Twentieth Maine Monuments*, JLC's address, p. 28).

Colonel Oates claimed in his book (*The War*, p. 219) that at and southwest of "the point or angle of the rocky ledge where the right marker of his [JLC's] regiment stands," he "lost the greatest number of my men"; Oates then described action at a large boulder "about forty steps up the slope." This assertion disregards the presence of the Eighty-third Pennsylvania and the Fourth Alabama. In his official report, JLC complimented the Eighty-third's commander for cooperating closely, making "his movements conform to my necessities, so that my right was at no time exposed to a flank attack" (*OR* 27[1]:624). Over the years, JLC stated several times that the Twentieth Maine and the Eighty-third Pennsylvania were connected during the fight. At the present time on the Gettysburg battlefield, and on an 1893 GNMP blueprint of Little Round Top, the right flank marker of the Twentieth Maine is placed approximately eighty yards southeast of the left flank marker of the Eighty-third Pennsylvania. The main road over Little Round Top runs between them (Gettysburg Battlefield Commission Map, Blueprint, 1893, GNMP). On August 23–28, 1869, many commanding officers or ranking members of each regiment met at Gettysburg to place stakes at the spots on the battlefield where the flank markers of each regiment should be located. JLC was present at that meeting, besides a representative of the Eighty-third Pennsylvania, and the right flank marker of the Twentieth Maine and the left of the Eighty-third were represented by only one stake (Gettysburg Battlefield Memorial Association, "Report of the Reunion of the Officers of the Army of the Potomac, August 23–28, 1869," John Nicholson Papers, Huntington Library, Art Gallery, and Botanical Gardens, San Marino, Calif., typescript, GNMP). Unfortunately, a corresponding blueprint or map cannot be found. Why the flank markers are placed as they are now is not known.

His other allegations notwithstanding, however, if Oates had designated JLC's *left* flank marker instead of the right, his description of the fight at and near the large boulder where he lost the greatest number of his men would be plausible and tie in perfectly with the preceding paragraph in his book and the correspondence in the GNMP files. A large boulder is described in a letter to JLC in 1909 about a wholly unrelated matter; in 1909 this boulder was "10 feet in diameter and 3 feet high, *just opposite the LF of the 20th Maine* [emphasis supplied], where from the curve in the avenue . . . would be seen in front and on each side" (Henry S. Burrage to JLC, Nov. 22, 1909, BC). This prominent boulder stands alone, can be seen today, and is positioned where Oates described if he meant JLC's *left* flank marker. On the 1893 blueprint of Little Round Top at GNMP, the position of the now missing left flank marker is located east of Chamberlain Avenue, perhaps one hundred feet. Oates's "forty steps" from JLC's left flank marker to the boulder would be just over ninety-three feet in military steps of twenty-eight inches each. It therefore follows that Oates may have also reversed JLC's right and left when he claimed that he "drove the right of the 20th back on its left" (Oates to Elihu Root, June 2, 1903, Oates Correspondence Scrapbook, GNMP). JLC not only denied Oates's claim but estimated that the angle of the Twentieth's refused line was not less than a "quarter circle" (JLC to William C. Oates, May 18, 1905, Oates Correspondence Scrapbook, GNMP).

63. Gerrish, *Army Life*, pp. 69, 70, 109; *Maine at Gettysburg*, p. 256; *MAGR, 1862*, app. D, p. 672; JLC, "Blood and Fire," pp. 904–5. Quotation, ibid., p. 905. George Washington Buck was one of the first in the Twentieth Maine to enlist, on July 4, 1862; he died on July 3, 1863 (Twentieth Maine Regimental Records, NA). During the battle the regiment only had time to hastily throw up a few stones here and there for protection. The stone walls now at the Twentieth's position on the Gettysburg battlefield were built that night or the next day by others. JLC complained about their presence prior to his last known visit to the battlefield in May 1913 and said his men might consider them as an "excresence" should they find them at the reunion in July (JLC to John Nicholson, Apr. 14, 1913, MHS).

64. *OR* 27(1):624; JLC, "Blood and Fire," p. 905.

65. JLC to Gen. James Barnes, Sept. 3, 1863, Gen. James Barnes Papers, New-York Historical Society, copy at GNMP; *OR* 27(1):624; JLC to Gov. Abner Coburn, July 21, 1863, MSA; *Dedication of the Twentieth Maine Monu-*

ments, Capt. Howard L. Prince's address, p. 23; Oates, "Gettysburg—The Battle on the Right," pp. 176–78. Quotation, ibid., p. 178.

66. *OR* 27(1):624; *Maine at Gettysburg*, p. 257; JLC to Gen. Barnes, Sept. 3, 1863, Gen. James Barnes Papers, New-York Historical Society, copy at GNMP; JLC, "Blood and Fire," p. 905. Quotation, ibid.

67. *OR* 27(1):623–24. First quotation, p. 623; second, p. 624.

68. *Dedication of the Twentieth Maine Monuments*, JLC's address, pp. 28, 29; JLC, "Blood and Fire," p. 906. Quotations from second and third sentences, ibid.; last, from ibid. and *Dedication of the Twentieth Maine Monuments*, JLC's address, p. 29. JLC thought the time of the charge was "about sunset" (JLC to John Bachelder, Jan. 25, 1884, John B. Bachelder Papers, New Hampshire Historical Society, copy at GNMP).

69. JLC, "Blood and Fire," p. 906; *OR* 27(1):624; *Dedication of the Twentieth Maine Monuments*, Capt. Howard L. Prince's address, p. 23; ibid., JLC's address, pp. 28, 29; Gerrish, *Army Life*, p. 110; *Maine at Gettysburg*, p. 257. Quotation, Gerrish, *Army Life*. Gettysburg was a historic battle and has generated more controversy, perhaps, than any other in the Civil War. JLC's friend Ellis Spear, acting as major for the Twentieth that day, declared nearly thirty years later that he received no order from JLC to charge. He stated that although he could not personally vouch for it, there was a story among the men that JLC never gave the order, but that they spontaneously charged when men in Company K shouted to advance and recover some downed men; the left wing followed when ordered by Spear after he heard the "shout" and the whole line started to move (Ellis Spear to John Bachelder, Nov. 15, 1892, John B. Bachelder Papers, New Hampshire Historical Society, copy in GNMP). These assertions were contrary to JLC's official report and statements after the war and Spear's own account shortly after the battle. In the *Portland Press* clipping pasted in John Chamberlain's diary, with "Capt. Spear's letter" inscribed in John Chamberlain's hand, Spear described the battle and said that at "the hottest part of the fight . . . the Colonel ordered a charge!" Spear went on to state that the "men encouraged by the order, rushed down over the slope with yells," and he concluded: "Col. Chamberlain handled the regiment in a splendid manner. Though constantly exposed to the hottest of the fire, no officer could be cooler, or more skilled and prompt to make use of favorable opportunities."

70. JLC, "Blood and Fire," pp. 906–7; *OR* 27(1):624; JLC to Gen. Barnes, Sept. 3, 1863, Gen. James Barnes Papers, New-York Historical Society, copy at GNMP.

71. *OR* 27(1):624; Capt. Walter G. Morrill to JLC, report, July 8, 1863, John B. Bachelder Papers, New Hampshire Historical Society, copy at GNMP; JLC to John Nicholson, Aug. 14, 1903, Oates Correspondence Scrapbook, GNMP; Gettysburg Battlefield Commission Map, Blueprint, 1893, GNMP. Quotation, Capt. Walter G. Morrill to JLC, July 8, 1863, report.

72. *OR* 27(2):393; Oates, "Gettysburg—The Battle on the Right," pp. 177, 178. Quotation, ibid., p. 178.

73. *OR* 27(1):624; JLC to Gen. Barnes, Sept. 3, 1863, Gen. James Barnes Papers, New-York Historical Society, copy at GNMP; *Maine at Gettysburg*, p. 258; JLC, "Blood and Fire," pp. 906–7.

74. JLC, "Blood and Fire," p. 908; JLC to Gen. James Barnes, Sept. 3, 1863, Gen. James Barnes Papers, New-York Historical Society, copy at GNMP; *OR* 27(1):625. Quotation, ibid. Bulger told Oates that he had been captured by Colonel Rice (Oates, *The War*, p. 217). JLC's official report stated: "Four hundred prisoners, including two field and several line officers were sent to the rear." In his September 1863 letter, he wrote to Barnes that the count of prisoners was 368 taken in the charge, including a lieutenant, lieutenant colonel, and a dozen other officers, plus an additional 25 taken on Round Top that night.

75. JLC to John Bachelder, Jan. 25, 1884, John B. Bachelder Papers, New Hampshire Historical Society, copy in GNMP; JLC to Barnes, Sept. 3, 1863, Gen. James Barnes Papers, New-York Historical Society, copy in GNMP; *OR* 27(1):617, 618, 625; JLC, "Official Report," July 6, 1863, MSA; Norton, *Little Round Top*, p. 269; Gen. James C. Rice to Rev. Dr. M. Jacobs, Nov. 21, 1863, in the *New York Times*, Nov. 28, 1863. A shorter version of JLC's official report, differing slightly in detail, was sent by JLC to Maine's adjutant general (JLC to Adj. Gen. Hodsdon, Nov. 4, 1863, MSA) and is in MSA. In it JLC said his men were "heated and thirsty almost beyond endurance." A story arose that a portion of Fisher's Pennsylvania Reserves joined in Chamberlain's charge; indeed, Fisher's official report seems to indicate just that (*OR* 27[1]:658). According to Coddington (*Gettysburg*, pp. 743–44 n. 48), Chamberlain refused to accept an explanation presented to him by John Bachelder years after the war that the Union infantry Colonel Oates saw coming up just before he retreated was Fisher's brigade. It could not be settled satisfactorily because Colonel (then General) Rice was killed May 10, 1864, and could not give his witness. Another, more animated version of the story was given publicity in the quickly published *Notes on the Rebel Invasion of Pennsylvania and the Battle of Gettysburgh*, a short book written by a professor, Rev. M. Jacobs, which inspired General Rice to write Jacobs an open letter on November 21, 1863, that appeared in the *New York Times* on November 28, 1863. This letter left no doubt that Fisher's brigade had come up too late to join in the fight or the charge, as Chamberlain stated to Bachelder. Rice quoted parts of Jacobs's allegations about the actions of the Pennsylvania Reserves and then commented, "This reflects credit upon the fancy and imagination, but it is not history." O. W. Norton, in a 1888 letter, states that Fisher's brigade came on to the ground, but after the fight was all over (Norton to Frank Appleton, Sept. 28, 1888, in *Gettysburg, Historical Articles of Lasting Interest*, July 1989, p. 43).

76. *OR* 27(1):625; Norton, *Little Round Top*, pp. 259–60, Norton, *Strong Vincent*, p. 8; Judson, *Eighty-third Pennsylvania*, p. 67.

77. Fox, *New York at Gettysburg*, 3:956, 957.

78. *OR* 27(1):618, 625, 651, 652; Norton, *Little Round Top*, pp. 300, 310, 311, 312; Rittenhouse, "Battle of Gettysburg," pp. 7, 8.

79. JLC to Bachelder, Jan. 25, 1884, John B. Bachelder Papers, New Hampshire Historical Society, copy GNMP; Norton, *Army Life*, p. 65; *OR* 27(1):618, 625; Coan manuscript, Elisha S. Coan Papers, BC; Pvt. J. W. Carleton to the Adjutant General of Maine, Jan. 8, 1866, FPYU; Rice to Jacobs, Nov. 21, 1863, in *New York Times*, Nov. 28, 1863. First quotation, JLC to Bachelder, Jan. 25, 1884; second, Coan manuscript. Fisher claimed credit in his official report for the capture of Round Top and thirty prisoners (*OR* 27[1]:658), a claim which was echoed in his division commander's report (Brig. Gen. S. W. Crawford, in ibid., p. 654). The content of Rice's November 21 letter to Jacobs in the *New York Times* refuted this claim by Fisher. On the same date, Rice wrote a strongly worded letter to General Barnes, rejecting the story and giving full credit for the capture of Round Top to "the gallant Col. Chamberlain" (Rice to Barnes, Nov. 21, 1863, New-York Historical Society, copy at GNMP). Rice's wording gave no doubt that he knew the historical importance of the battle and wanted to set the record straight. Apparently Crawford took the matter to the Fifth Corps commander, Gen. George Sykes. Sykes replied in a testy and impatient letter to Crawford that Fisher's brigade was "only assisting in taking forcible possession of Round Top Mountain, but the merit and result of that achievement, [is] due to Colonel, now General Rice, and especially to Colonel Chamberlain and his regiment" (Sykes to Crawford, Dec. 17, 1863, typed copy in LC, signed by John Nicholson as a true copy).

80. Coan manuscript, Elisha S. Coan Papers, BC; JLC to Bachelder, Jan. 25, 1884, John B. Bachelder Papers, New Hampshire Historical Society, copy at GNMP; Pvt. J. W. Carleton to the Adjutant General of Maine, Jan. 8, 1866, FPYU; *OR* 27(1):625; *Dedication of the Twentieth Maine Monuments*, Lt. Samuel L. Miller's address, p. 34. Quotation, ibid.

81. *Dedication of the Twentieth Maine Monuments*, Lt. Samuel L. Miller's address, p. 32; JLC to Bachelder, Jan. 25, 1884, John B. Bachelder Papers, New Hampshire Historical Society, copy at GNMP; *OR* 27(1):625; JLC, "Official Report," July 6, 1863, MSA; Gettysburg manuscript in JLC's hand, BC. Contents of ibid. indicate that it was probably a draft text of an early JLC lecture on Gettysburg used shortly after the war, but part of it is apparently missing.

82. Gettysburg manuscript in JLC's hand, BC; JLC to Gen. Barnes, Sept. 3, 1863, James Barnes Papers, New-York Historical Society, copy at GNMP. E. S. Coan remembered a story that went the rounds: "As our skirmishers proceed down the western slope of Round Top in the darkness of the woods

they wer challinged by some one Halt! Who comes there. 'fifteenth Alla.' 'All right' was the response 'we thought the d—d yanks had gobbled you up' Quietly our men surround and captured 34 more prisinors without firing a gun" (Coan manuscript, Elisha S. Coan Papers, BC). Another version of the same story had it as a Texas regiment instead of the Fifteenth Alabama.

83. *OR* 27(1):625.

84. Ibid., pp. 625–26; Norton, *Little Round Top*, p. 270; *Maine at Gettysburg*, p. 261; Gettysburg manuscript in JLC's hand, BC.

85. JLC to Gen. Barnes, Sept. 3, 1863, New-York Historical Society, copy at GNMP; *OR* 27(1):626; *Maine at Gettysburg*, p. 260; Judson, *Eighty-third Pennsylvania*, p. 70. Quotation, ibid.

86. U.S. Congress, *Medal of Honor Recipients*, p. 401.

87. JLC, "The State, the Nation, and the People," in *Maine at Gettysburg*, p. 552. This was a speech given by JLC at the dedication of the Maine monuments at Gettysburg, October 3, 1889.

88. JLC to Fannie, July 17, 1863, LC; JLC to Fannie, July 4, 1863, LC. First quotation, JLC to Fannie, July 17, 1863; the others, JLC to Fannie, July 4, 1863.

89. Powell, *Fifth Corps*, pp. 530–31. Colonel Oates also had praise for the Twentieth and Chamberlain: "There never were harder fighters than the Twentieth Maine men and their gallant colonel. His skill and persistency and the great bravery of his men saved Little Round Top and the Army of the Potomac from defeat" (Oates, *The War*, p. 219).

90. Ames to JLC, July 3, 1863, typed copy in JLC Military Personnel file, NA, handwritten original in JLC Letterbook, PHS; William T. Livermore diary, in *Lincoln County News*, LC; Adelbert Ames to his parents, Aug. 1863, in Ames, *Chronicles*, 1:20–21. First quotation, Ames to JLC, July 3, 1863; second, William T. Livermore diary; third, from Ames, *Chronicles*, p. 21.

91. John Chamberlain diary, p. 54, PHS; *OR* 27(1):626; Gettysburg manuscript in JLC's hand, BC; Livermore diary, in *Lincoln County News*, LC. The Zouave regiment was the 114th Pennsylvania (Nicholson, *Pennsylvania at Gettysburg*, 2:600–609; Haythornwaite, *Uniforms*, pl. 26).

92. Gettysburg manuscript in JLC's hand, BC; *OR* 27(1):626; Livermore diary, in *Lincoln County News*, LC; William to Charles Livermore, July 6, 1863, copy at GNMP. Quotation, Gettysburg manuscript. The barn was undoubtedly the Sherfy barn located near the intersection of the Emmitsburg Road and the Wheatfield Road.

93. Gettysburg manuscript in JLC's hand, BC; John Chamberlain diary, p. 72, PHS. Quotations, Gettysburg manuscript.

94. *Maine at Gettysburg*, p. 261; John Chamberlain diary, p. 59, PHS; *OR* 27(1):626; J. B. Westcott to JLC, Feb. 1896, LC. JLC did not count his own wounds in the returns of regimental wounds in the battle (*Maine at Gettysburg*, p. 270).

95. John Chamberlain diary, pp. 53–58, PHS. Quotations, p. 55.

96. Ibid., pp. 58, 59; *Maine at Gettysburg*, p. 261. Quotation, John Chamberlain diary, p. 59, PHS. John Chamberlain incorrectly stated that he returned to the regiment July 5, instead of July 4 (John Chamberlain diary, pp. 58, 59, PHS). He recounted that he spent a rainy night with his brothers, and then they left Gettysburg (on the evening of July 5). Because he left his notebook in Washington, his journal entries after June 20 were written after his return to that city on July 16.

97. John Chamberlain diary, pp. 65–70, PHS; *OR* 27(1):621. Quotation, John Chamberlain diary, p. 70. John said they found notes from the retreating Rebels to "the d—d Yankees." Because of apparent discrepancies in contemporary letters and diaries, some confusion exists about the date the Twentieth Maine crossed the terrible battleground on reconnaissance. JLC gives the date as July 4 in his official report, which is accurate and matches Captain Woodward's Eighty-third Pennsylvania report. The regiment crossed the ground again on the morning of July 5 and must have stopped there for some time before heading south about 5:00 P.M. by a route following the Emmitsburg Road away from the battlefield (*OR* 27[1]:621, 626, 632; A. E. Fernald to JLC, Mar. 4, 1897, BC). Sights seen on both crossings of the ground are generally described as if only one crossing of the field occurred.

98. JLC, "The State, the Nation, and the People," in *Maine at Gettysburg*, pp. 558–59. Losses in the Twentieth Maine were high, with the official records (*OR* 27[1]:179) showing 29 men killed, 6 officers wounded, 85 men wounded, and 5 prisoners, a total of 125. Of the wounded, of course, many died. In his official report Chamberlain estimates his loss at "136—30 of whom were killed, and among the wounded are many mortally" (ibid., p. 626). *MAGR, 1863*, p. 91, gives the losses as "3 commissioned officers killed or mortally wounded, and 134 men killed and wounded." The Twentieth Maine monuments at Gettysburg, dedicated in 1889, cite 38 killed or mortally wounded of 358 engaged, which would not include officers (the latter numbered 3 wounded mortally). The monuments also count 92 wounded of 358. Three other officers were wounded, for a total of 95. Combined, the figures would reflect 41 killed or mortally wounded, 95 wounded, total 136. *Maine at Gettysburg*, pp. 270–72, gives a total of 130 casualties; of these, 41 officers and men were killed or ultimately died of their wounds.

Confederate losses are almost impossible to assess. In his official report for the Fifteenth Alabama, Oates gave "killed 17; wounded, 54, missing, 90, total 161." In 1878 Oates stated, "Of 644 men and 42 officers, I had lost 343 men and 19 officers" ("Gettysburg—The Battle on the Right," p. 178). He also gave these figures to Ellis Spear in 1882 (Spear to JLC, July 2, 1882, LC) and added, "Its [the Fifteenth Alabama] effectives numbered nearly 700 officers and men. Now 225 answered at roll call." However, in his 1905 book Oates retracted his earlier statements and declared that his Fifteenth Alabama went into the assault with "less than 400 officers and men," due to detachments, captures, and straggling. He also said that the Forty-seventh

Alabama had only 154 men. Couching statements about his losses in ambiguity, Oates cited a published report that there were 50 Confederate dead and 100 badly wounded Confederates lying in front of the Twentieth Maine position; he agreed that approximately 45 of the Fifteenth Alabama were killed outright, with 4 or 5 from the Forty-seventh, but said only 84 of the Fifteenth Alabama men were captured unwounded and denied that there were 100 badly wounded Confederates captured from both regiments. He accused Chamberlain of "seeing double" on the number of prisoners he captured. See Oates, *The War*, pp. 215, 216, 222, 225. First quotation, p. 222; second, p. 216. Since his book version of the battle completely ignored the presence of the other Texas and Alabama regiments on Little Round Top, giving the impression that he fought Vincent's brigade alone, Oates could not recognize that others besides those from the Fifteenth or Forty-seventh Alabama were captured. Coddington (*Gettysburg*, p. 743n) estimated the Forty-seventh's original strength as roughly from 210 to 290 men, plus 21 officers. Fox gives the total Union losses at Gettysburg as 23,001 and Confederate as 20,448 (*Regimental Losses*, pp. 541, 550).

CHAPTER SIX

1. John Chamberlain diary, pp. 72–73, PHS; *OR* 27(1):627.
2. *OR* 27(1):622, 627, 630; Powell, *Fifth Corps*, pp. 563–68; Johnson and Buel, *Battles and Leaders*, 3:379–80, 422–29; Swinton, *Army of the Potomac*, pp. 366–67. Meade used indirect routes to follow Lee with the bulk of his army, fearing being bogged down indefinitely in the mountain passes by a comparatively small number of Confederates. Lee, using direct routes, reached the Potomac more quickly.
3. *History, 118th Pennsylvania*, pp. 278–79; John Chamberlain diary, pp. 79, 80, 108, 110, PHS. John Chamberlain returned to Bangor Theological Seminary after his brief stint with the Christian Commission (Little, *Genealogical History*, 1:133).
4. *OR* 27(1):627; Judson, *Eighty-third Pennsylvania*, p. 73; JLC to John Hodsdon, Maine Adjutant General, July 11, 1863, MSA; JLC to Fannie, July 17, 1863, LC. Quotation, ibid. It came back to JLC that Strong Vincent's promotion had been read to him on his deathbed, but he was not conscious to hear it (ibid.). Vincent's only child, a daughter, was born that autumn, but the baby lived only a year. A marble slab, erected on Little Round Top by the Strong Vincent post of the Grand Army of the Republic (*Nelson's Erie County*, p. 551), marks the place where he fell. The monument of the Eighty-third Pennsylvania, placed in rear of the center of his brigade position, is surmounted by a bronze statue of Vincent, eternally facing the direction of the oncoming Confederates on July 2, 1863.
5. *OR* 27(1):620; JLC to Fannie, July 17, 1863, LC; JLC to Fannie, Sept. 12,

1863, LC. First quotation, JLC to Fannie, July 17, 1863; last two, JLC to Fannie, Sept. 12, 1863.

6. Powell, *Fifth Corps*, p. 567; Pvt. Robert G. Carter to his parents, July 14, 1862, in Carter, *Four Brothers*, p. 334. Quotation, ibid.

7. *OR* 27(1):118; Judson, *Eighty-third Pennsylvania*, p. 75; Norton, *Army Letters*, pp. 165–66; Nash, *Forty-fourth New York*, pp. 161–62; Carter, *Four Brothers*, pp. 333, 336. Quotation, ibid., p. 336.

8. Carter, *Four Brothers*, pp. 336, 337; JLC to Fannie, July 17, 1863, LC; Nash, *Forty-fourth New York*, pp. 161–62. Quotation, JLC to Fannie, July 17, 1863. A $40 receipt for jewelry made to Fannie from Tiffany Jewelers in New York, dated July 8, 1863, is in MHS.

9. Nash, *Forty-fourth New York*, p. 162; JLC to Gov. Coburn, July 21, 1863, MSA; JLC to Gov. Coburn, Aug. 7, 1863, MSA. Quotations, JLC to Gov. Coburn, July 21, 1863.

10. JLC to Gov. Coburn, July 21, 1863, MSA.

11. Inferred from correspondence. JLC showed some political acumen in his letters to Maine's governors. While straightforward and honest, his letters were deferential and showed understanding of the governor's problems.

12. Swinton, *Army of the Potomac*, pp. 374–75; *OR* 27(1):118, 595.

13. *OR* 27(1):595, 622, 627; Swinton, *Army of the Potomac*, p. 375; Nash, *Forty-fourth New York*, pp. 162–63; Judson, *Eighty-third Pennsylvania*, p. 76; JLC to Gov. Coburn, July 29, 1863, MSA.

14. JLC Military Service records, NA; Dr. Adams diary, Aug. 6, 1863, FPC; JLC to Fannie, Sept. 12, 1863, LC; D. G. Folsom to JLC, Oct. 25, [1863], RC.

15. James C. Rice to JLC, Aug. 16, 1863, LC; Nash, *Forty-fourth New York*, p. 164; JLC to Fannie, Sept. 12, 1863, LC; Warner, *Generals in Blue*, p. 401; *MAGR, 1864–1865*, 1:332.

16. Gerrish, *Army Life*, p. 122; JLC to Gov. Coburn, Aug. 25, 1863, MSA; *MAGR, 1864–1865*, 1:514. Quotations, Gerrish, *Army Life*, and JLC to Gov. Coburn, Aug. 25, 1863, respectively. The reason for the delay in commissioning Spear is unknown, but Capt. A. W. Clark was senior captain and had at least one important political ally who wished his promotion to major (The Hon. J. H. Rice, U.S. Representative, to Gov. Coburn, May 28, 1863, MSA). Until JLC could be promoted to brigadier, no vacancy existed in the regiment for the rank of colonel.

17. Judson, *Eighty-third Pennsylvania*, pp. 75–77; *History, 118th Pennsylvania*, pp. 292–93; Norton, *Army Letters*, p. 180; Nevins, *Diary of Battle*, p. 281. Sae wrote disapprovingly to JLC that a prominent young man at Brewer had been let out of the draft supposedly because of weak lungs, and "that ended it, no substitute or $300 offered to the country" (Sae to JLC, Sept. 12, 1863, RC).

18. *History, 118th Pennsylvania*, pp. 294–96; Nash, *Forty-fourth New York*, p. 164; Norton, *Army Letters*, p. 179.

19. *History, 118th Pennsylvania*, pp. 298–99; Nash, *Forty-fourth New York*, p. 165; Gerrish, *Army Life*, p. 126; Carter, *Four Brothers*, p. 347.

20. *History, 118th Pennsylvania*, pp. 299, 300.

21. Ibid., p. 300; Nash, *Forty-fourth New York*, p. 336. Griffin quotation, *History, 118th Pennsylvania*. One musket in every ten was loaded with a blank so that each of the executioners who wished to avoid personal responsibility could think that perhaps his was the one with the blank cartridge (Nash, *Forty-fourth New York*, p. 165).

22. Carter, *Four Brothers*, p. 347; Pvt. Carter to his parents, Aug. 30, 1863, in ibid., pp. 347, 348. Quotation, ibid, p. 347. JLC's opinion is not known directly but can be inferred from Sae's answer to a letter he wrote to his family in Brewer about it: "What a dreadful thing to witness the execution of those deserters was! It occasioned many a sigh from Aunt Susan, not to say *groan*" (Sae to JLC, Sept. 12, 1863, RC). In a letter to Governor Coburn later, JLC stated that more officers were needed for the Twentieth to handle new conscripts—he did not want Maine men shot (JLC to Gov. Coburn, Sept. 19, 1863, MSA). He wrote to Fannie on the night of the executions, but the letter is not extant in any known collection. The execution of the five deserters illuminates the times in many ways. It was apparently approved of by members of the rank-and-file as needed for discipline, and any excess was made more palatable to the majority by the general belief that all five were "foreigners" and only one could speak English (*History, 118th Pennsylvania*, p. 295). "It is one thing," a man from a Pennsylvania regiment said later, "when soldiers with heated blood and inflamed passions . . . in fierce conflict, inflict horrid wounds or death upon others. It is a very different thing," he continued, "to look forward to a scene in which men are to be done quietly to death without any of the circumstances which rob war of half its terrors and hide its real character" (*History, 118th Pennsylvania*, p. 298).

23. Carter, *Four Brothers*, pp. 348–49; Norton, *Army Letters*, pp. 177–79.

24. *History, 118th Pennsylvania*, p. 303.

25. Norton, *Army Letters*, p. 281; JLC to Fannie, Aug. 31, 1863, LC; JLC to Fannie, Sept. 12, 1863, LC.

26. JLC to Fannie, Sept. 12, 1863, LC; JLC to Fannie, Aug. 31, 1863, LC. Quotations, JLC to Fannie, Sept. 12, 1863. Contents of Fannie's letter inferred from JLC's September 12 letter.

27. JLC to Fannie, Aug. 31, 1863, LC.

28. Swinton, *Army of the Potomac*, p. 375; Nash, *Forty-fourth New York*, p. 166; *History, 118th Pennsylvania*, pp. 307, 308; Judson, *Eighty-third Pennsylvania*, p. 76; Norton, *Army Letters*, p. 180; JLC to Gov. Coburn, Sept. 19, 1863, MSA.

29. *MAGR, 1864–1865*, 1:331; *OR* 25(1):508, 518; ibid. 27(1):605; C. B. Mervine, AAG, to JLC, Oct. 7, 1863, MSA; Gen. Charles Griffin to Gen. Seth

Williams, AAG, Oct. 7, 1863, MSA. The original recommendation, endorsed on the back, is in NA. A copy accompanied by the note from Griffin's assistant adjutant general Mervine, sent "sub rosa" to JLC, is in MSA. Mervine was not specific as to why the promotion was the first Griffin had made, and the text is inferred from other Griffin promotions. Ames's promotion was probably initiated elsewhere, with Generals Meade or Howard; Griffin wrote a letter of recommendation, which he would have done as Ames's commanding officer, whether he initiated it or not (Ames, *Chronicles*, p. 17).

30. Powell, *Fifth Corps*, pp. 18, 19; Warner, *Generals in Blue*, pp. 190, 191, 623; *OR* 19(2):188; Gerrish, *Army Life*, pp. 345, 346; Meade, *George Gordon Meade*, 1:235. After Union cannon posted on the Maryland side of the Potomac drove Confederate cannoneers opposite them away from their guns on September 19, 1862, near the Shepherdstown Ford, the river was crossed by a handpicked Michigan regiment. Griffin, then Second Brigade commander in Morell's division, was directing the operation. Driving off the Rebel infantry support, the attacking party captured two Confederate cannon and some caissons, and Griffin was elated to find that one of the big guns recovered had been lost to the Rebels from his battery at the first battle of Bull Run over a year before. He had been a captain then, and a lieutenant serving under him at that time, who was wounded and still fought his guns, was Adelbert Ames, who must have been as happy as Griffin when he heard that the field piece was regained. Artillerymen take a great liking to their guns, and to have one captured under any circumstances is an affront to their pride. It was sweet revenge. See *OR* 19(1):339, 340, 349, 350; Powell, *Fifth Corps*, p. 19; Ames, *Adelbert Ames*, pp. 67, 68; U.S. Congress, *Medal of Honor Recipients*, p. 365; Nolan, *Iron Brigade*, p. 143.

31. James C. Rice to Hon. Mr. P. Fessenden, Sept. 8, 1863, MSA; Gen. James Barnes to JLC, Sept. 1, 1863, MSA; Lt. Col. Charles Gilmore to Gov. Coburn, Oct. 8, 1863, MSA; H[annibal] Hamlin to "Mr. President" [Lincoln], Oct. 16, 1863, BC; JLC, *Armies*, p. xiv; *OR* 29(1):221–22. The timing of the promotion attempt may have been very poor. Only two to three weeks before, a circular went around the army soliciting funds from officers and men for a testimonial for General McClellan as a token of the esteem of the Army of the Potomac. This was taken as a political move in Washington, causing a stir in the newspapers and reportedly making Secretary of War Stanton angry enough to draw up an order summarily dismissing several high-ranking officers from the service, including the Fifth Corps's General Sykes. This order was never issued, but the circular was discontinued as contrary to army regulations. See Nevins, *Diary of Battle*, pp. 282–86.

32. Powell, *Fifth Corps*, pp. 576–79; Judson, *Eighty-third Pennsylvania*, pp. 77, 78; Swinton, *Army of the Potomac*, pp. 375–85.

33. Charlemagne description, typed manuscript on Surveyor, U.S. Customs Service stationery, UMO.

34. Powell, *Fifth Corps*, p. 578; Nash, *Forty-fourth New York*, p. 168.

35. Nash, *Forty-fourth New York*, pp. 168–69. JLC and Sykes quotations, p. 168, except their last, p. 169.

36. *History, 118th Pennsylvania*, pp. 333, 334; Nash, *Forty-fourth New York*, p. 171; *OR* 29(1):610; Swinton, *Army of the Potomac*, pp. 386–87.

37. Swinton, *Army of the Potomac*, p. 387; Nash, *Forty-fourth New York*, 171; *OR* 29(1):587, 588, 609, 610.

38. *OR* 29(1):11, 578, 583–86; Swinton, *Army of the Potomac*, pp. 386–87; Beyer and Keydel, *Deeds of Valor*, 1:276; *MAGR, 1863*, p. 91; newspaper clipping, Lt. Holman S. Melcher to the *Portland Press*, Nov. 13, 1863, in John Chamberlain diary, PHS. Two other officers from the Twentieth, Lieutenants Keene and Morse, were also in the storming party (ibid.).

39. Judson, *Eighty-third Pennsylvania*, p. 78; *OR* 29(1):577–78, 585.

40. *OR* 29(1):578, 585; *Pittsfield Advertiser*, Apr. 14, 1898, cited in Vickery, "Walter G. Morrill," pp. 137–38. That the Third Brigade men crossed the railroad during the advance to maintain their connection is the official explanation in the report of Brig. Gen. Kenner Garrard, who was in charge of the entire Fifth Corps skirmish line (*OR* 29[1]:578). It is more likely that Morrill and his brave band crossed the railroad later, when the assault on the works began; Morrill himself says so in the newspaper article. In the Beyer and Keydel account (*Deeds of Valor*, 1:276), with material apparently provided by Morrill, it was stated again that the Fifth Corps men crossed the railroad at the beginning of the charge. General Bartlett, who had come over from the Sixth Corps to replace the absent General Griffin as First Division, Fifth Corps, commander (Carter, *Four Brothers*, p. 361), had his report sent back to him by General Sykes with a request to identify the units of those men who entered the redoubt with the Sixth Corps (*OR* 29[1]:580). Bartlett added the names of Chamberlain's regiments (*OR* 29[1]:579). In his report, JLC referred to General Garrard as the proper authority to account for the movements of the skirmish line but added, "Several of my men fell inside the enemy's works, and they sent to me 70 prisoners" (*OR* 29[1]:582). There was no censure, however. In their reports, the Sixth Corps officers, from the regimental through the corps level, gave Morrill and the Twentieth Maine the credit due them.

41. Vickery, "Walter G. Morrill," p. 138; *OR* 29(1):586, 588, 589, 590; Beyer and Keydel, *Deeds of Valor*, 1:276. For his "dash and gallantry" in leading his men in the storming party, Walter G. Morrill was awarded the Medal of Honor by Congress (U.S. Congress, *Medal of Honor Recipients*, p. 522).

42. *OR* 29(1):575, 586; Pvt. O. W. Norton to Sister L., Nov. 13, 1863, in Norton, *Army Letters*, p. 190; Vickery, "Walter G. Morrill," p. 138.

43. *OR* 29(1):582; Nash, *Forty-fourth New York*, p. 172; Norton, *Army Letters*, p. 293; *MAGR, 1864–1865*, 1:332. Casualties for the Twentieth Maine were 1 killed, 7 wounded; for Chamberlain's brigade: 4 killed, 16 wounded; overall casualties, Fifth and Sixth Corps: 83 killed, 330 wounded, 6 missing, total

419 (*OR* 29[1]:558–60). General Lee reported 6 killed, 39 wounded, and 1,629 missing; of the latter, undoubtedly many were killed and wounded. Lee characterized the battle as "this unfortunate affair," but Gen. Jubal Early called it "a disaster that has befallen this division" (ibid., pp. 613, 616, 626). The Third Brigade bugler, Pvt. Oliver W. Norton, who had enlisted soon after the fall of Fort Sumter in 1861, left the Fifth Corps a few days after the battle to accept a commission as a first lieutenant of U.S. Colored Troops, where he proudly served until November 1865. Later he became a successful businessman in Chicago, and after the turn of the century, though blind, he published three books about the war. See Norton, *Army Letters*, p. 313; Norton to JLC, May 8, 1901, MHS. Charlemagne recovered from his wound.

44. *OR* 29(1):11, 610, 611; ibid. 51(1):1115; Norton, *Army Letters*, p. 292; Ellis Spear diary, Nov. 9, 1863, in possession of Abbott Spear, Warren, Maine; *History, 118th Pennsylvania*, p. 347; Carter, *Four Brothers*, p. 364. Quotation, Norton, *Army Letters*.

45. O. W. Norton to Sister L., Nov. 11, 1863, in Norton, *Army Letters*, p. 190; Lt. Wm. E. Donnell to Fannie, Nov. 16, 1863, LC; *MAGR, 1864–1865*, 1:332–33; Dr. M. W. Townsend, Surgeon's Certificate, Nov. 16, 1863, and Hospital Medical Certificate, Nov. 28, 1863, JLC Military Service records, NA; Dr. Adams diary, Nov. 21, 26, 1863, FPC.

46. Swinton, *Army of the Potomac*, pp. 390–98; Carter, *Four Brothers*, pp. 372–73; Mrs. J. H. Robinson to JLC, May 30, 1888, FPYU; *MAGR, 1864–1865*, 1:333; JLC Military Service records, NA; Dr. Adams diary, Dec. 9, 1863, Jan. 15, 1864, FPC; Fannie to Cousin D, New York, [ca. early May 1864], LC.

47. Gerrish, *Army Life*, pp. 135–36; C. C. Hayes to JLC, Dec. 26, 1863, LC; JLC to Gov. Coburn, Oct. 28, 1863, MSA; JLC handwritten "Testimonial," Washington, Mar. 10, 1864, MSA; [Edgar O. Achorn], "General Chamberlain," n.d., typescript, BC. Quotation, JLC to Gov. Coburn, Oct. 28, 1863. The author of "General Chamberlain" is deduced from contents.

48. [Edgar O. Achorn], "General Chamberlain," n.d., typescript, BC; "Early Memoirs," pp. 57, 58, BC; JLC to Gov. Coburn, Oct. 28, 1863, MSA. Quotation, ibid.

49. JLC to Auntie, in Fannie to Auntie, Apr. 14, 1864, MHS.

50. *OR* 33:663, 669, 717, 722, 723, 798. The Army of the Potomac numbered 97,273 present for duty, equipped, on May 4, 1864 (Humphreys, *Virginia Campaign*, p. 409; JLC, *Armies*, p. 6).

51. Brooks, *Washington, D.C.*, pp. 13, 14, 20, 21, 22.

52. JLC to Auntie, in Fannie to Auntie, Apr. 14, 1864, MHS; Fannie to Cousin D, n.d. (but ca. early May 1864), LC; Fannie to JLC, Mar. 8, 1866, RC; JLC to Col. E. D. Townsend, AAG, May 9, 1864, JLC Military Personnel file, NA.

53. Leech, *Reveille in Washington*, pp. 318–19; JLC to Col. E. D. Townsend, AAG, May 9, 1864, JLC Military Personnel file, NA; JLC to Gov. Cony, May 18, 1864, MSA. Quotation, ibid.

54. Telegram, JLC to Fannie, May 7, 1864, FPYU; newspaper clipping, "Captain [*sic*] Chamberlain, 20th Maine," John Chamberlain diary, PHS; JLC, *Armies*, p. 255; *OR* 33:717, 738, 1040; ibid. 51(1):1115; JLC's Military Personnel file, NA. The latter shows JLC released from the court-martial duty May 10. Fannie's undated letter to Cousin D from New York showed a great deal of ambiguity. She had left JLC in the Trenton train station, where he was to entrain for Washington, even though JLC "was very anxious" for her to go with him. "I thought it was not best" she said of her decision not to return to Washington with him. She said he had been sick again with that "miserable *malaria*," but she would not rejoin him unless he took very sick or "insist upon my going back." Although anxious to go home, she intended to shop and wait at the St. Germain Hotel to hear from him, as he wished her to do (Fannie to JLC, n.d. [but ca. early May 1864]). It is likely that she went to Washington in response to JLC's urgent summons before he returned to the field.

55. Nevins, *Diary of Battle*, pp. 338, 339, 405; E. G. Taylor, *Warren*, pp. 4–8, 135, 144–45; Agassiz, *Meade's Headquarters*, pp. 42, 58; *OR* 29(1):696–98; JLC, "Petersburg and Appomattox," p. 171; *History, 118th Pennsylvania*, pp. 655–56.

56. *History, 118th Pennsylvania*, pp. 655–66; Nevins, *Diary of Battle*, p. 364; *Under the Maltese Cross*, p. 264. Warren, Meade, Griffin, and Grant usually wore plain uniforms in the field, some the worse for wear. Warren's dressing in a new uniform on May 10 (rumored presented to him on the march) was so unusual that General Humphreys, in his *Virginia Campaign*, p. 81, uncharacteristically remarked that Warren "was wearing his full uniform" that day.

57. Chamberlain Association, *JLC: A Sketch*, pp. 11–12; *MAGR, 1864–1865*, 1:333; Spear diary, May 15, 1864; Gerrish, *Army Life*, pp. 163, 166, 178, 193–95; *OR* 36(1):150, 573, 574. JLC apparently rejoined the Fifth Corps on May 14, 1865. The corps had been on a seven-mile, all night march to the left of Burnside's Ninth Corps and were placed near the village of Spotsylvania Court House. It took all of May 14 for the entire corps to get up and together again, and JLC may have taken part in actions by the Second Brigade of the First Division, commanded by his friend Gen. Romeyn B. Ayres and described in Warren's official report and Ayres's "Itinerary" (*OR* 36[1]:542, 554). Ayres, when commanding a division, asked for JLC to command his brigade of Regulars, but JLC declined, preferring to command volunteers and at General Griffin's request that he remain with the First Division (Chamberlain Association, *JLC: A Sketch*, p. 13; JLC, *Armies*, p. 256). Spear's diary entry of May 15 stated that "Col. Chamberlain came, and Gen. Bartlett being ill, took command of the brigade," which marked the earliest that Spear knew JLC had returned to the field. The Twentieth Maine's casualties before JLC returned were 23 killed, 96 wounded, and 23 missing; some of

the wounded and missing died later (*OR* 36[1]:573, 574). The battle of the Wilderness was May 5–7, 1864, and overall Union casualties for the Army of the Potomac plus Burnside's Ninth Corps were, for those three days, 17,666 (ibid., p. 133). Using a different dating system, casualties in the Army of the Potomac were 29,410 from May 5 to May 12 (ibid., p. 195).

58. JLC, Introduction to Nash, *Forty-fourth New York*, p. xiv; JLC to Francis Fessenden, Mar. 9, 1899, LC; Nash, *Forty-fourth New York*, pp. 223–27; John Chamberlain diary, p. 45, PHS; Nevins, *Diary of Battle*, p. 325; Norton, *Army Letters*, pp. 280–81; *OR* 36(1):625. Quotations, JLC, Introduction to Nash, *Forty-fourth New York*; JLC to Francis Fessenden, Mar. 9, 1899; and *OR* 36(1):625, respectively. Rice was killed on May 10, 1864. The Laurel Hill combat was part of the battle of Spotsylvania Court House, fought May 8–21, 1864.

59. *OR* 36(1):4, 12, 13, 15–18; ibid. 33:828. First two quotations, ibid. 36(1):12, 13; April 9 order to Meade, ibid. 33:828; last, ibid. 36(1):4. Burnside's Ninth Corps was attached to the Army of the Potomac by Grant on May 24 (ibid. 33[1]:21).

60. Swinton, *Army of the Potomac*, pp. 440–41; Judson, *Eighty-third Pennsylvania*, pp. 95, 101; *OR* 36(1):20, 21.

61. JLC to Gov. Coburn, May 18, 1864, MSA; Gerrish, *Army Life*, pp. 184, 185; Humphreys, *Virginia Campaign*, p. 117; *OR* 36(1):19; JLC, *Armies*, p. 10. Quotation, ibid. General Humphreys did a careful study of troop numbers and casualties for *Virginia Campaign*. He calculates the number of killed and wounded in the Army of the Potomac plus Burnside's corps for the two battles of the Wilderness and Spotsylvania Court House at 37,335. Another tabulation enclosed in Meade's official report shows losses at 39,791 for the same period (*OR* 36[1]:195). Confederate losses are unknown, but although severe, Humphreys thought them far less than Union losses because the Southerners fought mostly on the defensive from behind entrenchments (Humphreys, *Virginia Campaign*, p. 117).

62. Powell, *Fifth Corps*, pp. 655–56; Humphreys, *Virginia Campaign*, pp. 119–23.

63. *OR* 36(1):560; *History, 118th Pennsylvania*, pp. 435, 436; "Early Memoirs," p. 61, BC; Chamberlain Association, *JLC: A Sketch*, p. 16.

64. Judson, *Eighty-third Pennsylvania*, p. 99; Pvt. George W. Carleton to the Adjutant General of Maine, Jan. 8, 1866, FPYU; *History, 118th Pennsylvania*, pp. 436–37.

65. *History, 118th Pennsylvania*, pp. 437, 438; *OR* 36(1):585, 591; three-page typewritten list, all JLC war engagements, corrections in JLC's hand, JLC Letterbook, PHS.

66. Nash, *Forty-fourth New York*, p. 193.

67. *OR* 36(1):543; Judson, *Eighty-third Pennsylvania*, p. 99; *New York Times* dispatch, May 25, 1864, in newspaper clipping, LC.

68. *New York Times* dispatch, May 25, 1864, in newspaper clipping, LC; *OR* 36(1):582, 585, 589, 612, 645; Judson, *Eighty-third Pennsylvania*, pp. 99, 100; Nevins, *Diary of Battle*, pp. 384–86; Humphreys, *Virginia Campaign*, p. 132n.

69. *OR* 36(1):77, 543, 563, 574, 577, 592; Powell, *Fifth Corps*, pp. 656, 657; Judson, *Eighty-third Pennsylvania*, p. 100; Pvt. George W. Carleton to the Adjutant General of Maine, Jan. 8, 1866, FPYU; Humphreys, *Virginia Campaign*, p. 132n. Quotation, Pvt. George Carleton to the Adjutant General of Maine, Jan. 8, 1866.

70. Humphreys, *Virginia Campaign*, pp. 129–31.

71. Ibid., pp. 131–32; Judson, *Eighty-third Pennsylvania*, p. 100.

72. Agassiz, *Meade's Headquarters*, pp. 99–100. Abatis was made of a row of large branches of trees, sharpened and laid close together, points outward, with the butts pinned to the ground (Billings, *Hardtack and Coffee*, p. 381).

73. Judson, *Eighty-third Pennsylvania*, p. 101; *OR* 36(1):78; Agassiz, *Meade's Headquarters*, p. 127; Nash, *Forty-fourth New York*, p. 195; Humphreys, *Virginia Campaign*, pp. 132, 160. Hanover Town was thirty-two to thirty-three miles, by the shortest route, below the position occupied by the Army of the Potomac at the North Anna (Humphreys, *Virginia Campaign*, p. 160).

74. Humphreys, *Virginia Campaign*, pp. 136, 158, 162, 165, 166; Swinton, *Army of the Potomac*, pp. 478–79.

75. Swinton, *Army of the Potomac*, pp. 479–81; Nash, *Forty-fourth New York*, p. 196; Humphreys, *Virginia Campaign*, pp. 162, 163, 166–78. Meade shows casualties in the Army of the Potomac from May 21 to May 31 to be 1,607 (*OR* 36[1]:195).

76. Powell, *Fifth Corps*, p. 672; *OR* 36(1):553; Pvt. George W. Carleton to the Adjutant General of Maine, Jan. 8, 1866, FPYU.

77. *OR* 36(1):21, 22, 81–88; Humphreys, *Virginia Campaign*, pp. 180–81; Swinton, *Army of the Potomac*, p. 483.

78. Swinton, *Army of the Potomac*, pp. 485–87; Humphreys, *Virginia Campaign*, pp. 182–87. Under the date June 2, 1863, Theodore Lyman commented about the Fifth Corps commander: "[Warren] is certainly the most tender-hearted of all our commanders. He said: 'For thirty days now, it has been one funeral procession, past me; and it is too much! . . . The men need rest.'" Lyman said that most officers soon grew callous with experience; they were not unfeeling but only grew accustomed to the suffering they saw (Agassiz, *Meade's Headquarters*, p. 147).

79. Grant, *Memoirs*, 2:276; *OR* 36(1):22, 195; Humphreys, *Virginia Campaign*, p. 182. Quotation, Grant, *Memoirs*. Meade's casualty figures for the Army of the Potomac for the period June 1–10 were 13,153; this did not include the Eighteenth Corps and Butler's other soldiers (*OR* 36[1]:195).

80. JLC, *Armies*, pp. 2, 3. Casualties in the Army of the Potomac from May 5 through June 10 were 54,551 (*OR* 36[1]:195). In the Fifth Corps 25,695 were present for duty, equipped, on May 4. By the time Warren's corps got to the

James River on June 16, 1864, the losses to the corps were 16,245 (JLC, *Armies*, pp. 6, 7).

CHAPTER SEVEN

1. *OR* 36(3):613–14, 652; JLC to John Chamberlain, Dec. 19, 1864, BC; Carter, *Four Brothers*, p. 428.

2. *MAGR, 1864–1865*, 1:333; Gen. Cutler to Gen. Griffin, and Griffin to JLC, penciled orders on both sides of one paper, June 6, 1864, LC; *OR* 40(3):470–71; JLC, *Armies*, p. xiv. Several weeks later, Cutler tried to have these regiments assigned back to the Fourth Division. General Warren (in *OR* 40[3]:469) thought Cutler's feelings were "personal."

3. Chamberlin, *One Hundred and Fiftieth Pennsylvania*, p. 260; Fox, *Regimental Losses*, pp. 295–304; Nicholson, *Pennsylvania at Gettysburg*, 2:654, 681, 685, 686, 726; DeLacy manuscript, p. 1, LC. JLC may not have known it, but General Warren believed that the Bucktail Brigade had not performed up to its reputation in the campaign since crossing the Rapidan, and some blamed Cutler for it. Warren had these regiments assigned to JLC, "an officer of the highest reputation," and intended to notice their performance under a new commander (*OR* 40[3]:520). At a later reorganization, all five of the old regiments went back under their old Fourth Division brigade commanders, although the Fourth Division itself was eliminated (*OR* 42[2]:800; ibid. [3]:461). JLC was always very proud to have commanded these regiments from the old First Corps. On his escutcheon (a painted, shield-shaped representation of an officer's rank and commands during the war), JLC included two First Corps brigade flags to commemorate the two brigades in which these regiments served previously. Lt. Col. Theodore Lyman thought that the troops looked less like soldiers and more like day-laborers wearing second-hand military clothes (Agassiz, *Meade's Headquarters*, p. 163).

4. Gibbs, *187th Pennsylvania*, pp. 81–83; *New York World*, Jan. 5, 1893, cited in Chamberlin, *One Hundred and Fiftieth Pennsylvania*, p. 263; Chamberlain Association, *JLC: A Sketch*, p. 12. Quotation, ibid.

5. H. N. Warren to JLC, July 7, 1888, LC.

6. Joseph J. Bartlett to Gen. S. Williams, AAG, Army of the Potomac, June 6, 1864, Charles Griffin endorsement on reverse, June 6, 1864, and G. K. Warren endorsement, also on reverse, June 6, 1864, JLC Military Personnel file, NA; *OR* 36(3):652, 709. Warren's first quotation, ibid., p. 652; second, reverse of Bartlett's promotion letter, June 6, 1864.

7. Chamberlin, *One Hundred and Fiftieth Pennsylvania*, p. 258; Nevins, *Diary of Battle*, pp. 407, 408; *OR* 36(3):651, 676, 677. Quotation, Chamberlin, *One Hundred and Fiftieth Pennsylvania*. General Griffin, JLC's division commander, had strict, no nonsense ideas about the correct and appropriate dress of his subordinates and was known for his caustic wit. A story made the rounds that during the halt at the Chickahominy, Griffin was wearing his customary

worn field uniform and sitting on the ground reading a map, when he looked up to see General Bartlett, trailed by his staff, riding up to call on him. Bartlett was dressed in a new uniform with a short jacket, embellished with braid that glittered in the sun and gold lace resplendent up the arms and down the sky blue trousers. His shirt bosom and cuffs were blindingly white. After Bartlett reined in with a flourish, Griffin eyed the gorgeous figure a moment and then asked, "Well, Bartlett, when will the rest of the circus arrive?" The Third Brigade commander's answer, if given, was not heard as he indignantly rode away. See Gerrish and Hutchinson, *Blue and Gray*, p. 405.

8. Chamberlain Association, *JLC: A Sketch*, pp. 38, 39. Libby Prison in Richmond was for Union officer prisoners of war.

9. Ibid.

10. Humphreys, *Virginia Campaign*, pp. 6, 198; Grant, *Memoirs*, 2:279–82.

11. H. N. Warren, *142d Pennsylvania*, p. 33; Swinton, *Army of the Potomac*, pp. 498–99; *History, 118th Pennsylvania*, pp. 472–73; Judson, *Eighty-third Pennsylvania*, p. 103.

12. Powell, *Fifth Corps*, p. 699; Agassiz, *Meade's Headquarters*, p. 161; *OR* 40(2):115; *History, 118th Pennsylvania*, p. 473; Grant, *Memoirs*, 2:292–93; Chamberlin, *One Hundred and Fiftieth Pennsylvania*, p. 260; Gibbs, *187th Pennsylvania*, p. 90.

13. *Brunswick Record*, Feb. 5, 1904.

14. Gibbs, *187th Pennsylvania*, p. 96; JLC, "Petersburg and Appomattox," pp. 163–64; Grant, *Memoirs*, 2:298; *OR* 40(2):654–56, 675–78; Johnson and Buel, *Battles and Leaders*, 3:540–54. The ring of defenses around Petersburg was called the "Dimmock Line" for its engineer, CSA Capt. Charles E. Dimmock (Lykes, *Petersburg*).

15. Billings, *Hardtack and Coffee*, p. 177; Gibbs, *187th Pennsylvania*, pp. 90–91; *History, 118th Pennsylvania*, pp. 474–75; H. N. Warren, *142d Pennsylvania*, p. 34.

16. Powell, *Fifth Corps*, p. 476; Swinton, *Army of the Potomac*, p. 510; Judson, *Eighty-third Pennsylvania*, p. 104; Grant, *Memoirs*, 2:297; *OR* 40(2):665, 667, 668. Gen. W. P. Hancock's Gettysburg wound had reopened, causing him to temporarily relinquish command of the Second Corps in the very early morning of June 18 (*OR* 40[2]:162, 170; Swinton, *Army of the Potomac*, p. 512).

17. *OR* 40(2):158, 159; ibid. (1):168; Chamberlin, *One Hundred and Fiftieth Pennsylvania*, p. 260.

18. *History, 118th Pennsylvania*, p. 477; Powell, *Fifth Corps*, p. 700; *OR* 40(2):172, 173, 666; Johnson and Buel, *Battles and Leaders*, 4:543. *OR* and regimental history sources variously cite the actual time of the movement as from 4:00 to 5:00 A.M. The attack was ordered for 4:00 A.M.

19. *History, 118th Pennsylvania*, p. 477; Carter, *Four Brothers*, p. 438; Parker and Carter, *Twenty-second Massachusetts*, p. 471. First quotation, *History, 118th*

Pennsylvania; second, Carter, *Four Brothers*. Several regimental histories describe the horrors of this short march.

20. Johnson and Buel, *Battles and Leaders*, 4:543–44; *OR* 40(1):757; Col. J. F. Gilmer, Col. W. H. Stevens, and Capt. Charles H. Dimmock, "Map of the Approaches to Petersburg and Their Defenses, 1863," annotated by JLC, LC; and writer's personal reconnaissance. The terrain is presently covered by houses, an interstate highway, a shopping center, and another railroad bed.

21. Baker, *Ninth Massachusetts Battery*, p. 193; U.S. War Department, *Atlas*, pl. 64, nos. 1–3. The commanding earthen fort was Fort Mahone, or Battery No. 29 of the "Dimmock Line." Taylor's Creek was also called Poo Creek or Poo Run.

22. Parker and Carter, *Twenty-second Massachusetts*, p. 471; JLC, "Petersburg and Appomattox," pp. 170–71. Quotation, ibid., p. 171.

23. Patrick DeLacy manuscript, pp. 1, 2, LC; DeLacy Military Pension records, NA. Quotation, DeLacy manuscript, p. 2. When the First Corps was reorganized into the Fifth Corps, the men were allowed to wear their old First Corps badges, which were in the shape of a circle (Nolan, *Iron Brigade*, pp. 272–73. Nolan cites *OR* 60:723 on p. 373n). DeLacy either did not avail himself of this permission or wore a combination of the two, a variation illustrated in Billings, *Hardtack and Coffee*, p. 263.

24. DeLacy manuscript, p. 1, LC; *Dedication of the Monuments, 143d Pennsylvania*, p. 53. Quotation, ibid.

25. Stine, *Army of the Potomac*, pp. 608–9; DeLacy manuscript, p. 2, LC. DeLacy later won the Medal of Honor for his Wilderness action. Singlehandedly, in full view of both of the Confederate and his own regiments, he shot the color-bearer of the opposing regiment and bore its regimental flag to his own lines (Beyer and Keydel, 1:320–21; U.S. Congress, *Medal of Honor Recipients*, p. 419). Stine thought that the Keystone Brigade would have carried the Confederate works if JLC had not been wounded.

26. Gibbs, *187th Pennsylvania*, pp. 94, 96; JLC, "Petersburg and Appomattox," p. 171; JLC to Sae, Jan. 29, 1882, UMO; H. N. Warren to JLC, July 7, 1888, LC; DeLacy manuscript, p. 3, LC; H. N. Warren, *142d Pennsylvania*, p. 34; Chamberlin, *One Hundred and Fiftieth Pennsylvania*, p. 261.

27. H. N. Warren to JLC, July 8, 1888, LC; Chamberlin, *One Hundred and Fiftieth Pennsylvania*, p. 261; H. N. Warren, *142d Pennsylvania*, p. 34. The 150th Pennsylvania may have been used as brigade skirmishers.

28. H. N. Warren, *142d Pennsylvania*, pp. 34, 35; list of war-horses in JLC's hand, JLC Letterbook, PHS; *MAGR, 1864–1865*, 1:333; Pvt. George W. Carleton to the Adjutant General of Maine, Jan. 8, 1866, FPYU; Charlemagne description, typed manuscript on Surveyor, U.S. Customs Service stationery, UMO.

29. H. N. Warren, *142d Pennsylvania*, p. 35; *Lewiston Journal*, Sept. 1–6, 1900; *Brunswick Record*, Feb. 5, 1904; JLC, "Petersburg and Appomattox," pp.

171, 173; Gibbs, *187th Pennsylvania*, pp. 198, 200; DeLacy manuscript, p. 3, LC.

30. *MAGR, 1864–1865*, 1:333; DeLacy manuscript, pp. 3, 6, LC; Lykes, *Petersburg*, p. 9; H. N. Warren, *142d Pennsylvania*, p. 35; *Brunswick Record*, Feb. 5, 1904; Gibbs, *187th Pennsylvania*, p. 96; Nesbit, *Company D, 149th Pennsylvania*, p. 34; DeLacy to JLC, Jan. 15, 1904, LC; JLC, "Petersburg and Appomattox," p. 172. Warren describes the Rebel lines as "bristling with artillery."

31. Baker, *Ninth Massachusetts Battery*, pp. 121, 123, 124, 125; *OR* 40(1):482; Nevins, *Diary of Battle*, p. 424; *MAGR, 1864–1865*, 1:333; *Lewiston Journal*, Sept. 1–6, 1900; DeLacy manuscript, p. 12, LC; Esposito, *Atlas*, pl. 138; JLC, "Petersburg and Appomattox," pp. 174, 175; Gilmer, Stevens, and Dimmock, "Map of the Approaches to Petersburg and Their Defenses, 1863," annotated by JLC, LC. Capt. (later Maj.) John Bigelow and his Ninth Massachusetts Battery had made real names for themselves on July 2, 1863, the second day of the battle of Gettysburg, fighting in three positons on the field that day and losing ten killed and mortally wounded, fifteen wounded, and two taken prisoner (Baker, *Ninth Massachusetts Battery*, pp. 63–64). In *Armies*, p. 350, and in a short notation in the JLC Letterbook, PHS, JLC erroneously concluded that Mink's, and not Barnes's, Battery had fought with him on June 18. Mink's Battery H, First New York Light, was at the edge of the railroad cut, to the right of the Taylor house, in the afternoon of that date.

32. *OR* 40(2):668; ibid. (1):761, 766; Johnson and Buel, *Battles and Leaders*, 4:543. Some regimental history references to the action of June 18 give the impression that the afternoon charge of Griffin's First and Second Brigades was much farther to the Union right and nearer the site of the well-remembered mine explosion and "Battle of the Crater" on July 30, 1864. The latter was a spectacular and futile Federal attempt to break the Confederate lines and the siege of Petersburg. In their regimental history, the men of the 187th Pennsylvania always referred to both charges they made on June 18 as "Fort Hell" or "The Ravine." The Confederate defenses opposite Chamberlain's position contained the Alabama regiments that were his adversaries at Little Round Top in 1863 (JLC, "Petersburg and Appomattox," p. 174; Johnson and Buel, *Battles and Leaders*, 4:593).

33. Agassiz, *Meade's Headquarters*, pp. 90, 91n, 167–68. Quotation, p. 91n.

34. Ibid., pp. 168–70; *OR* 40(2):155, 156, 171, 173–80, 192–96, passim; Porter, *Grant*, p. 209. Lt. Col. Theodore Lyman was detailed to Warren's headquarters, and Capt. William W. Sanders to Burnside's. Lt. Col. C. B. Comstock and Lt. Col. Horace Porter are the Grant aides known to be in Meade's front. Communications cited above in *OR* 40(2):155–65, 174–77, 191, 192, passim, show some of the confusion.

35. JLC, "Petersburg and Appomattox," pp. 171–73; DeLacy manuscript, p. 3, LC; *Brunswick Record*, Feb. 5, 1904; *Lewiston Journal*, Sept. 1–6, 1900. JLC probably never knew who the staff officer represented. It is clear that he

took him to be from Meade or Grant. An excellent candidate is Theodore Lyman, a volunteer aide-de-camp to Meade. Lyman, a young naturalist who had become friends with Meade in 1856, was touring Europe when the war started. Returning home in 1863, he joined Meade's staff in September of that year with a rank of lieutenant colonel of the Massachusetts Militia. A gentleman of humor and charm, he had no military experience, and his duties were usually not onerous. He was at Warren's headquarters all day on June 18 and telegraphed Meade at intervals. The other two lieutenant colonels known to be on the field that day from Grant's headquarters were both West Pointers and unlikely to interpret the order as making JLC's brigade a "forlorn hope." Because of JLC's illnesses and wounds, he had little, if any, opportunity to see or meet Lyman. See Agassiz, *Meade's Headquarters*, pp. viii–ix, and 167–70; Porter, *Grant*, p. 32.

36. *Brunswick Record*, Feb. 5, 1904; JLC, "Petersburg and Appomattox," p. 172; *Lewiston Journal*, Sept. 1–6, 1900. First two quotations, *Brunswick Record*, Feb. 5, 1904; JLC's reply, facsimile in *Lewiston Journal*, Sept. 1–6, 1900, copy, MHS. One soldier guessed that there were 3,000 muskets, and another guessed 5,000, in the Confederate works opposite them (DeLacy manuscript, p. 6, LC; Gibbs, *187th Pennsylvania*, p. 205).

37. *Lewiston Journal*, Sept. 1–6, 1900; *Brunswick Record*, Feb. 5, 1904. It is unclear whether JLC's reply reached any of his superiors.

38. *OR* 40(2):76–179, 183–84, 186, 187, 192, 193; ibid. (1):462; Curtis, *Twenty-fourth Michigan*, p. 262; JLC letter fragment, beginning "I spoke of having no support," n.d., MHS; Carter, *Four Brothers*, p. 440.

39. Nolan, *Iron Brigade*, pp. 15, 16, 53; *OR* 40(2):187. The *OR* reference contains a piece of correspondence sent by Cutler at 1:30 P.M. to Warren's headquarters inquiring for orders because of the receipt of the blank piece of paper. Cutler also refers to some misunderstanding with JLC in the same note. Colonel Wainwright thought Cutler a much changed man, apparently "very much broken," since the year before when he served with the First Corps (Nevins, *Diary of Battle*, p. 386n).

40. JLC letter fragment, beginning "I spoke of having no support," n.d., MHS.

41. *Lewiston Journal*, Sept. 1–6, 1900; H. N. Warren to JLC, July 7, 1888, LC; H. N. Warren, *142d Pennsylvania*, p. 35; Chamberlin, *One Hundred and Fiftieth Pennsylvania*, p. 261.

42. H. N. Warren to JLC, July 7, 1888, LC; *OR* 40(2):179, 180, 184. Quotations, ibid., p. 179.

43. DeLacy manuscript, pp. 2, 5, LC; H. N. Warren, *142d Pennsylvania*, p. 35; Gibbs, *187th Pennsylvania*, p. 93.

44. DeLacy manuscript, pp. 4, 5, LC; DeLacy to JLC, Oct. 24, 1885, LC; Ellis Spear to JLC, June 26, 1883, FPYU. First quotation, DeLacy manuscript, p. 5; last, DeLacy to JLC, Oct. 24, 1885.

45. Gibbs, *187th Pennsylvania*, pp. 204–5. Quotations, ibid., p. 205. The fort

to the far left, as JLC's men looked across the valley to the Confederate defenses across the Jerusalem Plank Road, was Fort Mahone, later called "Fort Damnation." During the siege of Petersburg, soldiers who served in the advanced rifle pits were fond of saying they were between "Hell and Damnation," referring to Forts Sedgwick and Mahone respectively. DeLacy describes charging "into a crescent-shaped position" (DeLacy manuscript, p. 7, LC). JLC describes "several strong earthworks with twelve or fifteen guns so disposed as to deliver a smashing cross-fire" (JLC, "Petersburg and Appomattox," p. 171).

46. H. N. Warren, *142d Pennsylvania*, p. 34; H. N. Warren to JLC, July 7, 1888, LC; DeLacy manuscript, p. 6, LC; Nesbit, *Company D, 149th Pennsylvania*, p. 34; Bates, *Pennsylvania Volunteers*, 4:611–76, "Bucktails."

47. DeLacy to JLC, Jan. 15, 1904, LC; DeLacy manuscript, p. 4, LC. Quotation, ibid. DeLacy stated that M. L. Blair, captain of Company E, 143d Pennsylvania, had not only written down the text of JLC's speech for him, but had reviewed DeLacy's entire manuscript and found it correct as he remembered (DeLacy to JLC, Jan. 15, 1904, LC). Of course, Blair could only paraphrase, at best, JLC's entire speech, but the phrasing and choice of words are surprisingly close to JLC's usual pattern. Commanding officers in the Civil War sometimes made short speeches to their men just before going into action, even under fire.

48. DeLacy manuscript, p. 4, LC; DeLacy to JLC, Jan. 15, 1904, LC; *Lewiston Journal*, Sept. 1–6, 1900; H. N. Warren, *142d Pennsylvania*, p. 35; Gibbs, *187th Pennsylvania*, p. 205; Carter, *Four Brothers*, p. 440; *OR* 40(1):462; ibid. (2):177.

49. W. L. Putnam to William DeWitt Hyde, Feb. 25, 1914, BC; *Lewiston Journal*, Sept. 1–6, 1900; JLC, "Petersburg and Appomattox," p. 172; Gibbs, *187th Pennsylvania*, pp. 148, 205; *Brunswick Record*, Feb. 5, 1904; H. N. Warren to JLC, July 7, 1888, LC. First quotation, W. L. Putnam to William DeWitt Hyde, Feb. 25, 1914; second, Gibbs, *187th Pennsylvania*, p. 205; third, H. N. Warren to JLC, July 7, 1888. The field return of Chamberlain's brigade for June 11, 1864, shows an aggregate of 97 officers and 2,071 men, including the brigade commander and staff. These figures did not include men in hospital or on detached duty ("Field Return of the First Brigade," LC). On June 18 the numbers must have been nearly the same. With this base for computation, two lines of battle (each line consists of a double line of men) should stretch one-fourth mile, allowing for space between regiments and companies. DeLacy estimated the brigade at a total of 2,250 (DeLacy manuscript, p. 6, LC).

50. Gibbs, *187th Pennsylvania*, pp. 95, 205–6; Nevins, *Diary of Battle*, p. 414. Lt. Ransford B. Webb was promoted to captain of his company in May 1865, was mustered out with it the following August, and lived until well past the turn of the century. Chamberlin, H. N. Warren, DeLacy, Webb, and others graphically describe the terrific fire that day.

51. DeLacy manuscript, p. 5, LC; *Lewiston Journal*, Sept., 1–6, 1900. Quotation, DeLacy manuscript. "Quaking aspen" is probably what DeLacy meant by "shaking asp."

52. *MAGR, 1864–1865*, 1:333; West Funk to the Maine Legislature, n.d. (but probably 1880), LC; DeLacy manuscript, p. 5, LC; *Brunswick Record*, Feb. 5, 1904; *Lewiston Journal*, Sept. 1–6, 1900; JLC to Sae, Jan. 29, 1882, UMO; letter from H. C. Henries, Chaplain, U.S.A., to *Bangor Whig and Courier*, dated June 28, 1864, newspaper clipping, JLC Letterbook, PHS. Quotation, *Brunswick Record*, Feb. 5, 1904. The trajectory of the bullet, described in U.S. Surgeon General's Office, *Medical and Surgical History*, 2(2):363, and interpreted for the writer by John P. Mullooly, M.D., and William H. Annesley, Jr., M.D., shows that the minié ball must have ricocheted to inflict such a wound.

53. *Lewiston Journal*, Sept. 1–6, 1900; West Funk to the Maine Legislature, n.d. (but probably 1880), LC; H. N. Warren, *142d Pennsylvania*, p. 36; *OR* 40(2):545; Gibbs, *187th Pennsylvania*, p. 98; JLC to Sae, Jan. 29, 1882, UMO. Quotation, West Funk to the Maine Legislature.

54. Nesbitt, *Company D, 149th Pennsylvania*, p. 34; Chamberlin, *One Hundred and Fiftieth Pennsylvania*, p. 254; DeLacy manuscript, p. 7, LC.

55. DeLacy manuscript, p. 7, LC; Baker, *Ninth Massachusetts Battery*, pp. 123–24.

56. H. N. Warren to JLC, July 7, 1888, LC; DeLacy manuscript, p. 7, LC. The official return of casualties for June 15–30, 1864, shows the 187th Pennsylvania as having 23 killed, 165 wounded, and 1 missing, for a total of 189 (*OR* 40[1]:223). In his official report (ibid., p. 458), Lieutenant Colonel Ramsey of the 187th states a loss of "about 200" for June 18 only. A man detailed for medical duty that day entered in his diary that by his count the regiment lost over 200 men. Since more of the wounded died of their wounds later, the number of killed is understated.

57. Carter, *Four Brothers*, p. 440; Parker and Carter, *Twenty-second Massachsetts*, p. 472; *OR* 40(2):183; *Under the Maltese Cross*, p. 294.

58. *OR* 40(1):474, 476; Curtis, *Twenty-fourth Michigan*, pp. 162, 262–63; JLC letter fragment, beginning "I spoke of having no support," n.d., MHS; Cheek and Pointon, *Sauk County Riflemen*, p. 115; DeLacy manuscript, p. 6, LC. Cutler says that he moved forward about 3:20 P.M., which seems a little late, as JLC moved at three o'clock. Watches seldom agreed at the time of the Civil War, however; there was no standard time and little synchronization. See also Nevins, *Diary of Battle*, p. 262. Bragg's brigade was still known as the Iron Brigade. Four of its regiments had been decimated in their gallant stand on the first day's battle at Gettysburg. The Second Wisconsin was gone, and the Seventh Indiana and First Battalion, New York Sharpshooters, now fought in the brigade. Many of the men lost at Gettysburg and before had been replaced by recruits, but even the latter had just survived six awful weeks of fighting and had become veteran fighters. See Nolan, *Iron Brigade*,

p. 275; *OR* 40(2):546. DeLacy stated that he saw the line break to the left and heard later that it was Cutler's division. He had earlier described the fate of the 187th Pennsylvania.

59. Nevins, *Diary of Battle*, p. 425. Wainwright had served with the First Corps Artillery.

60. Baker, *Ninth Massachusetts Battery*, pp. 121, 124. Bigelow was wounded at Gettysburg. After the war he wrote the definitive history of Chancellorsville and other treatises about the war.

61. Baker, *Ninth Massachusetts Battery*, p. 124; *Lewiston Journal*, Sept. 1–6, 1900; JLC, "Petersburg and Appomattox," p. 172; *Brunswick Record*, Feb. 5, 1904. First quotation, JLC, "Petersburg and Appomattox"; second, Baker, *Ninth Massachusetts Battery*. Bigelow humorously stated in a letter to JLC (Apr. 27, 1883, MHS) "that it is better to follow, on a battlefield, the orders of a well Captain, than those of a wounded General," an obvious reference to his men not following JLC's orders. He would have more correctly said "Colonel" instead of "General," of course. He also chided JLC for giving the impression that his Petersburg wounds caused him little trouble. Bigelow said he became "undeceived" when he saw a newspaper item that the general had had an operation because of them and was gravely ill.

62. JLC, "Petersburg and Appomattox," p. 173; *Brunswick Record*, Feb. 5, 1904; *Lewiston Journal*, Sept. 1–6, 1900; Gibbs, *187th Pennsylvania*, p. 201.

63. DeLacy to JLC, Jan. 15, 1904, LC; DeLacy manuscript, pp. 6–12, LC. After his old colonel, who had been wounded in the Wilderness, returned to the regiment and belatedly recognized his worth, Patrick DeLacy was promoted to sergeant major of the 143d Pennsylvania on October 1, 1864, and was commissioned a second lieutenant the next May, transferring to Company D. He went back to Pennsylvania with his regiment in June 1865, unscathed by shot or shell despite his daredevil ways. He was hit in the side by a piece of fence rail sent flying by a bursting shell in May 1864; his knee injury from the march to Petersburg on June 16 and 17, 1864, never did heal completely. He fathered two more children after the war and settled down, eventually becoming an alderman in Scranton, Pennsylvania. Active in veteran's organizations, DeLacy served as president of the Medal of Honor Legion of the United States and commander of the Pennsylvania department of the Grand Army of the Republic. He died of pneumonia on April 27, 1915, in Scranton, aged eighty. See Bates, *History of the Pennsylvania Volunteers*, 4:492; DeLacy Military and Pension records, NA; *Proceedings of the 43rd Encampment*, p. 6; Medal of Honor Society certificate to JLC, signed by Patrick DeLacy as President, BC.

64. Judson, *Eighty-third Pennsylvania*, p. 104; *OR* 40(2):156, 157, 180, 182, 188. Quotation, ibid., p. 157. After his experience at Fredericksburg, JLC thought poorly of putting in men piecemeal (JLC, "My Story of Fredericksburg," p. 158). Warren estimated the Fifth Corps loss for June 18 at

2,000 (*OR* 40[1]:453), which would account for most of that corps's 2,236 casualties for June 13–30. Chamberlain's brigade accounted for 314 of the First Division's 743 casualties (*OR* 40[1]:223). Many years later, JLC humorously noted "+*me*" on his brigade and division loss page in his letterbook and changed the figures to 315 and 744 respectively. The brigade command was given to Col. William S. Tilton on the evening of the eighteenth, presumably gratifying the Twenty-second Massachusetts soldier in Sweitzer's brigade. Tilton gave a vague and confusing official report of the action on June 18.

65. Nevins, *Diary of Battle*, p. 425; *OR* 40(1):474; Cheek and Pointon, *Sauk County Riflemen*, p. 116; Dawes, *6th Wisconsin*, pp. 290–91. First quotation, Nevins, *Diary of Battle*; second, Cheek and Pointon, *Sauk County Riflemen*; third, Dawes, *6th Wisconsin*.

66. Casualties in the Army of the Potomac for the period from May 4, 1864, to June 20, 1864, were 64,216 (*OR* 36[1]:195). For the Fifth Corps, from May 4, 1864, to June 19, 1864, Chamberlain used the official returns from the adjutant general's report plus the additional wounded given in the field hospital records, which would not appear in the former, to give a total of 17,190 casualties. Using the records of the medical inspector of the Fifth Corps as a basis, Chamberlain computed the casualties at 17,305, a negligible difference (JLC, *Armies*, p. 7). Confederate casualties were considerably less but are unknown.

67. JLC, *Armies*, p. 27. JLC made at least two trips to Petersburg after the war and visited the location south of Petersburg where he was wounded. The first visit was in January 1882 and the other in October 1903. During the latter he met with a group of Confederate officers, who opened up their meeting hall and had a friendly exchange of reminiscences (JLC, "Petersburg and Appomattox," p. 177).

68. *OR* 40(1):464, 465; Judson, *Eighty-third Pennsylvania*, p. 104; JLC to Gov. Coburn, Sept. 19, 1864, MSA; Chamberlain Association, *JLC: A Sketch*, pp. 12, 13; Nash, *Forty-fourth New York*, p. 201, and photograph opposite p. 217; *In Memoriam*, pp. 5, 6.

69. West Funk to Maine Legislature, n.d. (but probably 1880), LC; JLC, *Armies*, p. 352; Edward J. March to JLC, June 8, 1895, MHS; DeLacy manuscript, p. 3, LC. Quotation, West Funk to Maine Legislature. Pvt. James A. Stettler's leg was amputated later. Stettler, of Company A, 143d Pennsylvania, lived for many years after the war and never forgot the incident. March said Everett was the surgeon of the Sixteenth Michigan.

70. Chamberlain Association, *JLC: A Sketch*, p. 12; *In Memoriam*, p. 5; letter from H. C. Henries, Chaplain, U.S.A., to *Bangor Whig and Courier*, dated June 28, 1864, newspaper clipping, JLC Letterbook, PHS; U.S. Surgeon General's Office, *Medical and Surgical History*, 2(2):363; *Lewiston Journal*, Sept. 1–6, 1900; *MAGR, 1864–1865*, 1:334; Edwin J. March to JLC, June 8, 1895, MHS;

telegram, Warren to Meade, June 19, 1864, *OR* 40(2):216, 217. The promotion surely gratified Chamberlain's ambition, too. March thought the generals visited the next morning and that General Meade also came to see JLC.

The wound was described in *Medical and Surgical History*, 2(2):363: "Case 1056. Colonel Joshua L. C——, 20th Maine, was wounded at Petersburg June 17 [*sic*], 1864, and taken to the hospital of the 1st Division, Fifth Corps. Surgeon W. R. DeWitt, Jr., U.S.V., reported that 'conoidal ball penetrated both hips, and was extracted,' and that Surgeon M. W. Townsend, 44th New York, was detailed to accompany the patient to City Point, when, by direction of Surgeon E. B. Dalton, U.S.V., he was placed on the hospital ship Connecticut and conveyed to Annapolis, and promoted Brigadier General. Surgeon B. A. Vanderkieft, U.S.V., reported that he 'reached the hospital at that place very confortably on June 20, 1864, with a shot wound involving both buttocks and the urethra.' The progress and treatment do not appear on the hospital case-books, but in a letter to Surgeon J. H. Brinton, U.S.V., September 4, 1864, Dr. Vanderkieft states: 'I send you a catheter used by Brigadier J. L. C——, U.S.V. As you will perceive, it is covered by a calculous deposit. This catheter was but five days in the bladder, and was repeatedly covered in the same way. I think it a very important specimen, illustrating the necessity of often renewing catheters when they are to be used à demeure. The history you shall get when the patient is discharged. . . .' The patient was furloughed September 20, 1864, and mustered out January 15, 1866, and pensioned. The promised report of the case was not received. From Pension Examiner A. Mitchell's report, September 18, 1873, it appears that the ball entered the right hip in front of and a little below the right trochanter major, passed diagonally backward, and made exit above and posteriorly to the left great trochanter. The bladder was involved in the wound at some portion, as the subsequent history of escape of urine from the track of the wound and its extravasation testified. He very often suffers severe pain in the pelvic region. The chief disability resulting directly from the wound is the existence of a fistulous opening of the urethra, half an inch or more in length, just anterior to the scrotum; this often becomes inflamed. The greater part of the urine is voided through the fistula, the fistula itself resulting from the too long or too continuous wearing of a catheter. No change has resulted since the last examination; disability total. This invalid was paid to June 4, 1873 at $30 a month." Dr. DeWitt was the head surgeon of the First Division, Fifth Corps.

71. U.S. Surgeon General's Office, *Medical and Surgical History*, 2(2):363; Nash, *Forty-fourth New York*, p. 201; *In Memoriam*, p. 6.

72. JLC to Fannie, June 19, 1864, BC.

73. Chamberlain Association, *JLC: A Sketch*, p. 13; JLC Military Pension records, NA; letter from H. C. Henries, Chaplain, U.S.A., to *Bangor Whig and Courier*, dated June 28, 1864, newspaper clipping, JLC Letterbook, PHS; M. W. Townsend to JLC, Apr. 15, 1891, FPYU.

74. *OR* 40(2):216–17, 236; ibid. (3):421; Grant, *Memoirs*, 2:224; Grant to Secretary of War Stanton, June 20, 1864, LC. In his note to Stanton, Grant specifically pointed out that he made the promotion "in pursuance of your telegram of May 15th." The original letter from Grant to Edwin M. Stanton is in LC, with a typed copy in the NA. There are two handwritten copies of the part of Special Orders No. 39 promoting JLC, both in the same hand and both signed by U. S. Grant; one is in the NA, and the other is in LC. In a letter to JLC, Oct. 11, 1902, LC, H. L. Brinkershoff, in the adjutant general's office, War Department, offered to send JLC the originals of these papers and replace them with copies, which he apparently did. JLC's Military Personnel file, NA, has a penciled copy of the order, which must have replaced one of the two handwritten copies.

75. Chamberlin, *One Hundred and Fiftieth Pennsylvania*, p. 263, quoting a JLC interview in the *New York World*, Jan. 15, 1893; Grant, *Memoirs*, 2:297–98. Quotation, ibid., pp. 297–98. According to Bruce Catton, who examined the original handwritten manuscript of Grant's *Memoirs*, the accolade to JLC was the last item Grant added to his book. Grant died less than forty-eight hours later, on July 23, 1885; he depended on his editor to insert the paragraph in the correct place in the finished work (Catton, *U. S. Grant*, p. 179). Grant did tell JLC at one time that his was Grant's first battlefield promotion, but he recalled in his *Memoirs* that over a month before JLC's promotion, he had similarly promoted Col. Emory Upton of the 121st New York (Grant, *Memoirs*, 2:224–25). The request promoting Upton was made in the usual manner, with no special covering letter (see ibid., pp. 234–35n); however, Grant reiterates on page 235 that Upton was previously promoted specially. A variation of this story appears several times in the literature about Chamberlain, first in the letter of H. C. Henries to the *Bangor Whig and Courier* written on June 28, 1864, ten days after JLC received his debilitating wound (JLC Letterbook, PHS) and, after JLC's death, in *In Memoriam*, p. 6. Civil War participants liked to keep track of "firsts," "lasts," "youngest," "oldest," etc.

76. Letter from H. C. Henries, Chaplain, U.S.A., to *Bangor Whig and Courier*, dated June 28, 1864, newspaper clipping, JLC Letterbook, PHS; Sae to JLC, June 23, 1864, RC; *Lewiston Journal*, Sept. 1–6, 1900. Quotation, Sae to JLC, June 23, 1864.

77. Lt. Col. Charles D. Gilmore to Gen. John L. Hodsdon, Maine Adjutant General, July 5, 1864, MSA.

78. JLC's letter inferred from Gov. Cony to JLC, July 19, 1864, FPYU. It is likely that JLC's letter to the governor was dictated; he answered the governor's letter in his own hand several weeks later (JLC to Gov. Cony, Aug. 31, 1864, MSA).

79. John Chamberlain to Gen. Hodsdon, July 22, 1864, MSA.

80. JLC to Gov. Cony, Aug. 31, 1864, MSA. False rumors of Chamberlain's death continued. Captain Melcher, home recovering from his severe Wilder-

ness wound, and also spending some time recruiting for the understrength Twentieth Maine, apparently heard one of these. His reception of the news was "very painful—for as a commander I had learned to love him—and not only that but the Country will miss a brave and gallant defender . . . the army has lost a brilliant officer" (H. S. Melcher to [?], n.d. [first page or pages missing, but remaining contents of letter indicate a date of ca. August 1864], RC).

81. George E. Adams to JLC, Sept. 6, 1864, RC; JLC to Sarah D. B. Chamberlain, n.d. (from contents, probably the fall of 1864), BC. Quotation, JLC to Sarah D. B. Chamberlain.

82. U.S. Surgeon General's Office, *Medical and Surgical History*, 2(2):363; Christian Commission newspaper clipping, JLC Letterbook, PHS; Adelbert Ames to JLC, Oct. 18, 1864, LC; Little, *Genealogical History*, 1:136; "Copy of Memorandum filed with Bill before the Senate, (S. 6150), May 14th, 1906, in case of General Chamberlain," printed copy, FPYU. *OR* 42(3):663 shows JLC reporting formally to corps and division headquarters on November 19.

83. Chamberlin, *One Hundred and Fiftieth Pennsylvania*, pp. 278–79; Gibbs, *187th Pennsylvania*, p. 127; Patrick DeLacy to JLC, Dec. 17, 1910, BC; E. M. Woodward, *One Hundred and Ninety-eighth Pennsylvania*, app., pp. 70–132; JLC, *Armies*, p. 256. Quotation, Patrick DeLacy to JLC, Dec. 17, 1910.

84. Swinton, *Army of the Potomac*, pp. 511–14, 529–47; Powell, *Fifth Corps*, pp. 703–48; *History, 118th Pennsylvania*, pp. 479–530. The Fifth Corps alone lost 4,574 in three battles in August, September, and October 1864 (Powell, *Fifth Corps*, pp. 726, 735, and 747). Chamberlin, *One Hundred and Fiftieth Pennsylvania*, discusses the huge casualties of the Fifth Corps and the Army of the Potomac from May 1864 to March 1865; also see JLC, *Armies*, pp. 6–10.

85. JLC, *Armies*, pp. 21–23, 32; Buell, *Cannoneer*, p. 247; Johnson and Buel, *Battles and Leaders*, 4:708; Merideth and Merideth, *Mr. Lincoln's Military Railroads*, p. 190.

86. JLC, *Armies*, p. 12; Chamberlin, *One Hundred and Fiftieth Pennsylvania*, pp. 289–90; E. M. Woodward, *One Hundred and Ninety-eighth Pennsylvania*, p. 22; Gerrish, *Army Life*, pp. 219–20.

87. JLC, *Armies*, pp. 39–40; JLC to Fannie, July 4, 1863, LC.

88. Powell, *Fifth Corps*, pp. 748–49; *OR* 42(1):24, 443; *Under the Maltese Cross*, p. 326; Cheek and Pointon, *Sauk County Riflemen*, p. 144.

89. Gerrish, *Army Life*, p. 220; Swinton, *Army of the Potomac*, p. 549; Judson, *Eighty-third Pennsylvania*, p. 109; *Under the Maltese Cross*, p. 327.

90. *OR* 42(1):444, 612; *History, 118th Pennsylvania*, pp. 533, 534.

91. Agassiz, *Meade's Headquarters*, p. 295; JLC to Sae, [Dec. 14, 1864], BC. JLC gave his sister a detailed description of how the railroad tracks were destroyed, even including rough drawings; many regimental histories also describe the process.

92. *OR* 42(1):444; Swinton, *Army of the Potomac*, p. 550; Nevins, *Diary of Battle*, p. 489; Gerrish, *Army Life*, p. 220.

93. Judson, *Eighty-third Pennsylvania*, p. 109; Gerrish, *Army Life*, pp. 220–21; Nevins, *Diary of Battle*, pp. 488–89; *History, 118th Pennsylvania*, p. 543; *Under the Maltese Cross*, p. 328.

94. Tom Chamberlain to Sae, Dec. 13, 1864, BC; *History, 118th Pennsylvania*, p. 543; *Under the Maltese Cross*, p. 328; *OR* 42(1):445, 460.

95. *Under the Maltese Cross*, p. 329; Nevins, *Diary of Battle*, pp. 489, 490; Cheek and Pointon, *Sauk County Riflemen*, p. 147; Judson, *Eighty-third Pennsylvania*, pp. 109–10; Gerrish, *Army Life*, p. 222; *History, 118th Pennsylvania*, pp. 538, 540; Little, *Genealogical History*, 1:136; *OR* 42(1):445–46; JLC to Sae, [Dec. 14, 1864], BC. Warren apparently had some doubt about the story of the stripped Federal bodies: "Whether this is true or not, it soon became the belief of the men in the command" (see *OR* 42[1]:445–46). JLC certainly believed the story and stated it as fact in his letter to Sae and later to John Chamberlain (JLC to John Chamberlain, Dec. 19, 1864, BC).

96. JLC to Sae, [Dec. 14, 1864], BC. JLC also told his brother John that the burnings "showed war in its most disagreeable aspect, for my part, I had rather charge lines of battle" (JLC to John Chamberlain, Dec. 19, 1864, BC). JLC was able to leave guards at some houses; these were "honorably returned" later by the Confederate commanders (typed list of JLC commands and engagements, JLC Letterbook, PHS).

97. *OR* 42(1):445–47; Chamberlain Association, *JLC: A Sketch*, p. 13; Tom Chamberlain to John Chamberlain, Dec. 18, 1864, BC; Powell, *Fifth Corps*, p. 752; Swinton, *Army of the Potomac*, p. 550; JLC to John Chamberlain, Dec. 19, 1864, BC. Quotation, ibid.

98. Capt. Francis B. Jones to JLC, Jan. 15, 1865, RC; JLC to Sae, Mar. 9, 1865, BC. First quotation, Capt. Francis B. Jones to JLC, Jan. 15, 1865; second, JLC to Sae, Mar. 9, 1865. Little, *Genealogical History*, 1:136, states that JLC's corps commander ordered him north for the medical treatment. *OR* 46(2):193 gives January 13 as the date his sick leave began or was granted.

99. JLC to Joshua Chamberlain, Jr., Feb. 12, 1865, WP; Dr. Adams diary, Jan. 16, 1865, FPC.

100. JLC to Joshua Chamberlain, Jr., Feb. 12, 1865, WP; George E. Adams to JLC, Sept. 6, 1864, RC. Quotation, JLC to Joshua Chamberlain, Jr., Feb. 12, 1865.

101. JLC to Joshua Chamberlain, Jr., Feb. 12, 1865, WP; JLC to Joshua Chamberlain, Jr., Feb. 20, 1865, BC; Sarah D. B. Chamberlain to JLC, Jan. 1, [1865], RC. Quotations, Sarah D. B. Chamberlain to JLC, Jan. 1, [1865].

102. JLC to Joshua Chamberlain, Jr., Feb. 20, 1865, BC.

103. Ibid.

104. JLC to Sae, Mar. 9, 1865, BC; JLC to Joshua Chamberlain, Jr., Feb. 12, 1865, WP; JLC, *Armies*, p. 16; *OR* 46(2):741. Bartlett left for a twenty-day

leave of absence on January 6, 1865. Correspondence between Meade's headquarters and Warren and Griffin on February 3 shows that he did not return as scheduled and no one knew where he was. On February 10, in correspondence on another matter, Warren mentioned that Bartlett was absent on sick leave. He apparently returned sometime near March 14, when news of his brevet commission to major general was sent to General Meade. Meade mentioned an intention to assign him according to his brevet rank, but Bartlett returned to his old command, the Third Brigade of the First Division, which frustrated JLC's desire for that brigade's command. See *OR* 46(2):193, 362, 363, 519, 741, 965, 966.

105. Agassiz, *Meade's Headquarters*, p. 316; JLC to Sae, Mar. 9, 1865, BC; Tom Chamberlain to Sae, Dec. 13, 1864, BC; Tom Chamberlain to John Chamberlain, Dec. 18, 1864, BC. Quotation, JLC to Sae, Mar. 9, 1865.

106. JLC to Joshua Chamberlain, Jr., Feb. 12, 1865, WP.

107. JLC to Sae, Mar. 9, 1865, BC.

108. Ibid.

109. JLC, *Armies*, pp. 29–31. First quotation, p. 31; second, p. 30.

110. *OR* 46(1):253–57; Powell, *Fifth Corps*, pp. 754–66, 774–75; E. M. Woodward, *One Hundred and Ninety-eighth Pennsylvania*, pp. 29–32.

111. JLC, *Armies*, pp. 36–38; Powell, *Fifth Corps*, pp. 766–67; JLC, "White Oak Road," pp. 209–10.

112. *OR* 46(1):50–51; Powell, *Fifth Corps*, pp. 766–67; Swinton, *Army of the Potomac*, pp. 578–81. Before the preparations were complete, however, General Lee, in a surprise move, made a major attempt to split the Federal army. Early on the morning of March 25 an assaulting column of Confederates under Gen. John B. Gordon made a break through the siege lines at the Union's Fort Steadman, near the right of the Federal line below the James River. The Rebels were finally beaten back in desperate fighting (Powell, *Fifth Corps*, pp. 767–70; Swinton, *Army of the Potomac*, pp. 576–78). In the hope that the Confederates had weakened other parts of their defenses by the requirement for men in their attack at Fort Steadman, the quick-acting Federals assaulted the Rebel lines farther to their own left, attempting a breakthrough of their own. They captured some of the entrenched picket lines of the Confederates but found the main works themselves too strongly held to take. For their part in this operation, the Fifth Corps marched to the east, and after halting at several points, Chamberlain's brigade supported the Second Corps during the fighting at Watkins's Farm and took part in a minor action. After capturing one Confederate officer and several men, Chamberlain and his men marched back to camp at the end of the day, with little loss. See *OR* 46(3):112, 126; ibid. (1):267–68.

113. JLC, *Armies*, pp. 33–34; JLC to Sae, Mar. 9, 1865, BC. Quotation, JLC, *Armies*, p. 34.

114. JLC, *Armies*, p. 34.

CHAPTER EIGHT

1. *OR* 46(1):796–98, 1101; Humphreys, *Virginia Campaign*, pp. 432–33; Grant, *Memoirs*, 2:434; JLC, *Armies*, p. 42. Figures given are from the Army of the Potomac morning reports of March 31, 1865, in Humphreys, *Virginia Campaign*. The Fifth Corps force was larger on March 29. Warren gives his force apparently without officers or the artillery (*OR* 46[1]:796). Cavalry figures are for present for duty, not present for duty, equipped. Sheridan numbers his "effective force" as 9,000 (*OR* 46[1]:1101). He was using an alternate way to compute cavalry by reducing the number of troopers (exclusive of officers) by 25 percent to allow for dismounted cavalry battles where every fourth man holds his own horse and three others and does not directly participate (JLC, "White Oak Road," p. 217).

2. *OR* 46(1):799, 847.

3. Ibid., p. 799; JLC, *Armies*, p. 42; Chamberlain Assocation, *JLC: A Sketch*, p. 39. The location of Charlemagne's wound is in a list of horses in JLC's hand, JLC Letterbook, PHS. An orderly with the division, who considered the flamboyant General Bartlett, "on horseback, in full uniform, . . . the most perfect picture of an ideal officer," did not care for Chamberlain: "[Chamberlain] was a cold, unlovable man, very brave and all that, but not dashing either in appearance or manner. He always reminded me of a professor of mathematics we had in college. Still, he was a gallant officer, and had more than once been desperately wounded while leading his troops in the most deadly assaults" (Buell, *Cannoneer*, p. 322).

4. Chamberlain Association, *JLC: A Sketch*, p. 38; JLC, *Armies*, pp. 40–42. General Lee sent a dispatch to his secretary of war, received at 1:45 P.M., that Union infantry and cavalry had crossed the Rowanty and were moving toward Dinwiddie Court House (*OR* 46[3]:1362), ibid.

5. *PWCI*, Col. Theodore Lyman testimony, p. 519; ibid., JLC testimony, p. 228; Agassiz, *Meade's Headquarters*, p. 329; JLC, *Armies*, pp. 42–43; *OR* 46(1):847; JLC to Gen. Henry Merriam, Jan. 23, 1906, in *Colby Library Quarterly*, ser. 7, no. 8 (Dec. 1966): 348. JLC also testified that he directed General Gregory March 29 through April 9, 1865 (*PWCI*, p. 228).

6. *OR* 46(1):845, 847; JLC, *Armies*, p. 43; E. M. Woodward, *One Hundred and Ninety-eighth Pennsylvania*, p. 36. General Griffin, in his official report, said JLC drove the "enemy's infantry and cavalry" (*OR* 46[1]:845).

7. *OR* 46(1):847; JLC, *Armies*, p. 43; E. M. Woodward, *One Hundred and Ninety-eighth Pennsylvania*, p. 36. The location of a steam sawmill apparently was or had been not far north of the Lewis farmhouse. The 1867 Michler map in the U.S. War Department *Atlas*, pl. 77, map no. 9, shows a sawmill on the west side of the Quaker Road. Other maps, including ibid., pl. 94, no. 9, and pl. 66, no. 9, *OR* 46(1):802, and the map in JLC, *Armies*, show a sawmill on the road's east side. The latter is labeled "drawn from the official map." In his text in *Armies*, JLC does not mention a sawmill, referring only

to "a heap of sawdust where a portable mill had stood." This pile of sawdust, clearly labeled as only "Sawdust," is shown about two to three hundred yards north of the Lewis farmhouse and just east of the Quaker Road in a sketch map made on March 31, 1865, by Gilbert J. Thompson, a topographical assistant of the Army of the Potomac Corps of Engineers, and entered into evidence in *PWCI*, p. 1329. No sawmill is shown in this sketch map.

8. JLC, *Armies*, pp. 43–44.

9. *OR* 46(1):1286–87. The last returns given of the Army of Northern Virginia (dated February 25 to February 28 in the case of Johnson's division) showed "present and effective for the field" 485 officers and 6,277 men, total 6,762. Wise, former governor of Virginia, led four Virginia regiments, while Brig. Gen. W. A. Wallace had five from South Carolina, Brig. Gen. Y. M. Moody led what had been Gracie's brigade of five Alabama regiments, and Brig. Gen. M. W. Ransom had five North Carolina regiments (*OR* 46[1]:389, 1274). One of Wise's regiments, the Thirty-fourth Virginia, headed southwest on the Boydton Plank Road to operate on the Union left with Confederate cavalry and may have joined Wise later (ibid., p. 845). Although Wise later was quoted as saying that he "struck the enemy obliquely, diverging from right to left" (Wise, *Life of Henry A. Wise*, pp. 358–59), he may have been remembering the rough position of the entire Confederate line after Wallace's brigade came up, perhaps at a slight angle to Wise's right. When the Union artillery arrived near the end of the battle, the 185th New York, on JLC's left, was considerably bent back. In ibid., Wise said that his orders were to advance on the Military (Quaker) Road, and he placed two of his regiments on the right and two on the left of it. Johnson, in his official report cited above, reports that he advanced Wise's brigade in line of battle, stretching across the Quaker Road, with Wallace's, Moody's, and Ransom's brigades by the flank in rear of Wise. JLC repeatedly refers to troop movements of both sides, including charges, as up or down the Quaker Road.

10. *OR* 46(1):847; JLC, *Armies*, pp. 44–46. Some time was needed to build a bridge across Gravelly Run in JLC's rear. Griffin's pioneers built a rude one, which was difficult for artillery to use; later a pontoon bridge was built (*OR* 46[1]:800).

11. *OR* 46(1):847; ibid. (3):731; JLC, *Armies*, pp. 45–46; *Under the Maltese Cross*, p. 343. Colonel Sniper was later brevetted brigidier general for his services in the battles of the Quaker Road and the White Oak Road on March 31. A telegram was sent to the New York papers reporting JLC killed in the action (JLC, *Armies*, p. 47).

12. JLC, *Armies*, p. 46.

13. Ibid., pp. 46–48; Pvt. George W. Carleton to the Adjutant General of Maine, Jan. 8, 1866, FPYU. First quotation, ibid.; second, JLC, *Armies*, p. 48. The oversized 198th Pennsylvania evidently had two majors; Edwin Glenn was the ranking major. Maceuen was promoted from adjutant March 24,

1865, (E. M. Woodward, *One Hundred and Ninety-eighth Pennsylvania*, p. 70) and listed as major in *OR* 46(1):599, 800, 801, 848. Brevet rank was not mentioned.

14. JLC, *Armies*, p. 48.

15. Ibid., pp. 48–49. Quotations, p. 49. The wine was undoubtedly of the distilled variety.

16. Ibid., pp. 49–50; *OR* 46(1):847–48. Quotation, JLC, *Armies*, p. 50.

17. JLC, *Armies*, pp. 49, 50; *OR* 46(1):848. Quotation, JLC, *Armies*, p. 50.

18. JLC, *Armies*, pp. 50–51. Quotation, p. 51. The delay in getting up the artillery was not only due to the necessity of building a bridge over Gravelly Run, but was also caused by trees previously felled across the road by the Confederates. Infantry could negotiate such obstacles, but the timber had to be cleared before the artillery could move (Nevins, *Diary of Battle*, p. 507).

19. Buell, *Cannoneer*, pp. 339–40; *OR* 46(1):848; JLC, *Armies*, pp. 51–52. First and second quotations, ibid., p. 51; third, ibid., pp. 51–52.

20. JLC, *Armies*, p. 52; *OR* 46(1):899; Nevins, *Diary of Battle*, p. 508; newspaper clipping datelined Mar. 31, 1865, in JLC Letterbook, PHS. The newspaper article is signed by George Alfred Townsend, a well-known correspondent of the *New York World* who had previously written for the *New York Herald* (Andrews, *The North Reports*, pp. 200, 630). Townsend may have sent the earlier telegram reporting JLC dead.

21. JLC, *Armies*, p. 52; *OR* 46(1):848, 899; Nevins, *Diary of Battle*, pp. 507–8; John Mitchell to JLC, Jan. 26, 1868, LC.

22. JLC, *Armies*, p. 52; *OR* 46(1):848; Nevins, *Diary of Battle*, p. 508. Quotations, JLC, *Armies*. Gregory reported later that his troops, in line of battle, passed over "swampy and difficult grounds" and his skirmishers met some opposition. JLC accepted these as reasons for the delay (*OR* 46[1]:853; JLC, *Armies*, p. 45).

23. JLC, *Armies*, pp. 52, 53; *OR* 46(1):858. Quotation, ibid. The battle line Doolittle joined on its left consisted of the First and Sixteenth Michigan Regiments under the command of Bvt. Col. Benjamin F. Partridge (by inference from JLC, *Armies*, pp. 52–53).

24. JLC, *Armies*, p. 53; *Under the Maltese Cross*, pp. 343–44. Quotation, ibid., p. 344. Pearson later received the Medal of Honor from Congress for this action (ibid., p. 724; U.S. Congress, *Medal of Honor Recipients*, p. 537).

25. JLC, *Armies*, pp. 53, 267; *Kennebunk Journal*, Jan. 3, 1868; *OR* 46(1):899, 858, 1287; Nevins, *Diary of Battle*, p. 508. Battery B, Fourth U.S. Artillery, probably continued to shell the woods as the Confederates retreated. A tally attached to Gen. Charles S. Wainwright's official report (*OR* 46[1]:900) shows Battery B used 118 rounds of shot, shell and case, plus six rounds of canister on March 29. JLC described the Confederates as "flying up the road." In his official report (*OR* 46[1]:899) written April 21, 1865, General Wainwright stated that Mitchell fought his guns on either side of the Lewis farmhouse, which was true at the end of the battle. Wainwright did not see the fight but

only heard the sounds of Mitchell's guns; he rushed back down the Quaker Road to try to hurry up another battery and find General Warren for further orders. He was apparently delayed until the fight was over (Nevins, *Diary of Battle*, pp. 507–8). At first, at least part of the battery was placed on a rise in JLC's rear on the left and was in danger of being captured as the Confederates bent back the 185th New York (JLC, *Armies*, pp. 50, 51). Lieutenant Vose, Mitchell's subordinate, moved all of Battery B's guns up near the Lewis house as the enemy fell back at the end of the fight, and two sections of another battery were placed on either side of B (Nevins, *Diary of Battle*, p. 508).

26. JLC, *Armies*, p. 53; *OR* 46(1):801, 802, 846, 1101, 1102, and map, 802; *History, 118th Pennsylvania*, pp. 563–64. General Crawford's division was lost until after dark, when it was placed on the Boydton Plank Road facing west, from Gravelly Run to the junction with the Quaker Road. General Ayres's division was deployed across the Quaker Road in JLC's rear.

27. JLC, *Armies*, pp. 54–56; *OR* 46(1):848; ibid. (3):730. Numbers are difficult to estimate. Confederate Gen. Bushrod Johnson, in his official report written April 13, 1865, after the surrender at Appomattox, said he used Wise's and Wallace's brigades in the fight "on the Quaker [or Military] road." These brigades had a combined strength of 3,319 officers and men effective for the field at the end of February 1865. Johnson detached the Thirty-fourth Virginia from Wise and sent it down the Boydton Plank Road to operate with some cavalry (*OR* 46[1]:1287, 389). However, General Griffin reported that JLC had "met the enemy's *cavalry* and steadily drove them before him, the force *constantly increasing* until reaching a point known as the Lewis house" (ibid., p. 845, emphasis added). Johnson said that his corps commander, General Anderson, ordered the withdrawal just before Moody's brigade was ordered in. In estimating his losses, Johnson said they were "mainly" from Wallace's and Wise's brigades. The ambiguous wording of Johnson's report could be interpreted to mean that other troops were used from other brigades. JLC said in *Armies*, p. 53, that he had been fighting "Gracie's, Ransom's, Wallace's, and Wise's brigades."

28. JLC, *Armies*, p. 56. JLC was brevetted to major general for his gallantry on the Quaker Road. Although he was recommended for brevet for other actions, correspondence in NA shows that JLC wanted the Quaker Road brevet above all. Warren also called him "the brave General Chamberlain of Maine" in his official report (*OR* 46[1]:800).

29. Ibid., pp. 54, 55; *OR* 46(1):848–49. Warren states that the First Division's casualties were 5 officers and 47 men killed, 18 officers and 275 men wounded, and 22 missing, for a total of 367. Adding Battery B's casualties of 1 man killed and 1 officer and 3 men wounded gives a total of 372 (ibid., p. 803). Warren's preliminary report stated 51 killed, 318 wounded, total 369, without the missing mentioned. In his official report, JLC reported losses of 18 officers and over 400 men (ibid., p. 848). The newspaperman Townsend,

whose account of the affair is largely accurate, and who undoubtedly talked with JLC and others, said JLC's 185th New York "lost in all about 200" and, of the 198th Pennsylvania, said "222 were lost" (newspaper clipping datelined Mar. 31, 1865, in JLC Letterbook, PHS). JLC mentioned over 400 casualties in a letter to Fannie, Apr. 19, 1865, WP. Differences in counting wounded usually explains differing accounts. JLC reported burying 130 Confederate dead (*OR* 46[1]:849), and General Griffin reported 200 prisoners (ibid., p. 846). Confederate Gen. Bushrod Johnson reported only 250 casualties (ibid., p. 1287), which were clearly understated. Not all his wounded fell into Union hands, of course; some retired or were carried to the Confederate rear.

30. JLC, *Armies*, p. 55.

31. Ibid., pp. 56, 57; *Under the Maltese Cross*, p. 344; E. M. Woodward, *One Hundred and Ninety-eighth Pennsylvania*, p. 38. Quotation, JLC, *Armies*, p. 57. Dr. Maceuen was a friend of General Meade and had visited the army in late November of 1864 when his son was ill. Meade wired a family friend on March 29 to break the news of the major's death to Dr. Maceuen (Gen. George G. Meade to his wife, Nov. 27, 1864, and Mar. 29, 1865, in Meade, *George Gordon Meade*, 2:248, 268, respectively).

32. JLC, *Armies*, p. 57; E. M. Woodward, *One Hundred and Ninety-eighth Pennsylvania*, p. 38. Quotation, JLC, *Armies*.

33. JLC to Fannie, Apr. 19, 1865, WP; JLC, *Armies*, pp. 58–59; Cheek and Pointon, *Sauk County Riflemen*, p. 159; *Under the Maltese Cross*, p. 345; *History, 118th Pennsylvania*, p. 564. Quotation, JLC, *Armies*, p. 58.

34. *OR* 46(1):53, 803; JLC, "White Oak Road," p. 214; *PWCI*, H. C. Melcher testimony, p. 460; Porter, *Grant*, p. 426. Quotations, *OR* 46(1):53. Grant's headquarters were moved to Dabney's Mills on March 31 (Porter, *Grant*, p. 430). The White Oak Road war paper, the first of several JLC wrote for the Military Order of the Loyal Legion, was materially the same as a section of *Armies*. However, some clarifying information plus some notes were omitted from the *Armies* version, perhaps in the final revision, which was done by his publisher and his children (*Armies*, p. ix). Rosamond Allen remembers her mother working long hours on the *Armies* manuscript after her grandfather's death.

35. *OR* 46(1):797, 802, 803–5, 846, 849, 868; ibid. (3):308; Humphreys, *Virginia Campaign*, p. 327; *PWCI*, JLC testimony, p. 228. Griffin also issued congratulations to his division, "especially those of the First Brigade" (*OR* 46[3]:308), and Meade congratulated Warren and Griffin (ibid., p. 256).

36. Porter, *Grant*, pp. 428–29; Agazziz, *Meade's Headquarters*, p. 327. Quotations, Porter, *Grant*, p. 429. Lyman describes Sheridan as "scarce five feet high" (Agazziz, *Meade's Headquarters*, p. 327).

37. Porter, *Grant*, p. 429; *OR* 46(1):53; JLC, *Armies*, pp. 63, 68. Quotation, *OR* 46(1):53. JLC likened Sheridan to Attila the Hun (JLC, "White Oak Road," p. 247). Sheridan said in his memoirs that in his interview with

Grant, he urged Grant to continue the campaign despite the weather and said that he believed he could break in the enemy right if the Sixth Corps were assigned to him. Grant demurred, saying the condition of the roads prevented the movement of infantry and that Sheridan "would have to seize Five Forks with the cavalry alone" (Sheridan, *Sheridan*, 2:145).

38. Humphreys, *Virginia Campaign*, pp. 326–28, 330; *PWCI*, CSA Gen. Fitzhugh Lee testimony, p. 467; ibid., CSA Col. Thomas T. Munford testimony, pp. 440, 441; JLC, *Armies*, p. 41. Although Munford described himself at the Warren hearing as a brigadier general and had apparently been so appointed, Gen. Thomas L. Rosser, an enemy of Munford, said he had never been confirmed as a general (Rosser to A. S. Perham, Aug. 29, 1902, typed copy accompanying A. S. Perham to JLC, Jan. 3, 1903, LC). Warner, *Generals in Gray*, p. xix, concurs with Rosser.

39. Humphreys, *Virginia Campaign*, pp. 328–29; *PWCI*, Fitzhugh Lee testimony, p. 467; *OR* 46(3):323–24; JLC, *Armies*, pp. 63, 64. Pickett's division consisted of Stuart's, Hunton's, Corse's, and Terry's brigades, numbering 388 officers and 6,151 men on February 28, but estimated by JLC at about 5,000 (*Armies*, p. 61); Johnson's divison of Gracie's, Ransom's, and Wallace's, adding Wise's, brigades numbered 485 officers and 6,277 on February 26–28. No figures are available for McGowan's and McRae's brigades from A. P. Hill's corps, who were also in the White Oak Road entrenchments. Pickett took Ransom's and Wallace's brigades and left Hunton's when he moved to Five Forks. See Humphreys, *Virginia Campaign*, p. 328; JLC, *Armies*, p. 61; *OR* 46(1):388–89.

40. JLC, *Armies*, pp. 83–84; *OR* 46(3):325, 380. Quotation, ibid., p. 325. Sheridan had campaigned with the Sixth Corps successfully in the Shenandoah Valley and gave that as his reason for preferring the Sixth. He denied that he had any prejudice against Warren or the Fifth Corps (Sheridan, *Sheridan*, 2:168–69).

41. JLC, *Armies*, p. 65; *OR* 46(1):811–12, sketch map, p. 814; ibid. (3):284–86, 304. Fifth Corps strength on March 29, 1865 was Griffin's First Division, 6,547 men; Ayres's Second Division, 3,980; Crawford's Third Division, 5,260 (*OR* 46[1]:796).

42. *MAGR, 1864–1865*, 1:335; JLC, *Armies*, pp. 65–67; *OR* 46(3):324–25.

43. *OR* 46(3):334, 362.

44. JLC, *Armies*, pp. 68, 69, 81, 82, 110.

45. Ibid., pp. 69–71; *OR* 46(1):868–69; *PWCI*, CSA Gen. Eppa Hunton testimony, pp. 623, 625; ibid., CSA Brig. Gen. Samuel McGowan testimony, pp. 649–50. First quotation, JLC, *Armies*, p. 70; second, *PWCI*, Hunton testimony, p. 623. Ayres thought he was outnumbered "four or five to my one" (*OR* 46[1]:868). Hunton at first testified at the Warren Court of Inquiry (hereinafter cited as Warren CI) that the three Confederate brigades numbered about 7,500, but later, after talking to some friends at home, he amended the figure to 5,000 (*PWCI*, Hunton testimony, pp. 629–30).

46. *OR* 46(1):868–69; JLC, *Armies*, p. 71; *PWCI*, McGowan testimony, p. 651. Quotation, JLC, *Armies*.

47. JLC, *Armies*, p. 71; Gerrish, *Army Life*, pp. 237–38; *PWCI*, JLC testimony, p. 229; ibid., Maj. Gen. G. K. Warren testimony, p. 717; *OR* 46(1):846, 849; *History, 118th Pennsylvania*, p. 569. First quotation, ibid.; second, Gerrish, *Army Life*, p. 238.

48. *OR* 46(1):814–15; JLC, *Armies*, pp. 72–73. Quotations, ibid., p. 72.

49. JLC, *Armies*, 72–73; JLC, "Third Brigade at Appomattox," p. 339. First quotation, JLC, *Armies*, p. 72; second, "Third Brigade at Appomattox," p. 339.

50. JLC, *Armies*, p. 73.

51. Ibid., pp. 73–74; E. M. Woodward, *One Hundred and Ninety-eighth Pennsylvania*, p. 40; *OR* 46(1):849.

52. Humphreys, *Virginia Campaign*, p. 332; JLC, *Armies*, p. 74; *PWCI*, McGowan testimony, p. 650; ibid., Hunton testimony, pp. 625, 628. Hunton said that he could not see Humphreys's attack on Wise because it was too far to his left. JLC regretted that the impression later was that Humphreys attacked and drove back the troops that had attacked Ayres and Crawford, but he thought that Humphreys's subordinate, Gen. Nelson A. Miles, no doubt thought that he had done so. After explaining the positions of the two corps in *Armies*, pp. 80–81, especially in reference to General Humphreys's testimony in the Warren CI (*PWCI*, p. 1151) about being "ahead of the Fifth Corps," JLC further stated, to set the record straight: "Miles did not come in contact with a single regiment that had attacked the Fifth Corps. He struck quite to the right of us all, attacking in his own front. But it got into the reports otherwise, and 'went up.' Grant accepted it as given; and so it has got into history, and never can be gotten out" (*Armies*, pp. 80–81).

53. *OR* 46(1):849; JLC, *Armies*, pp. 74–75; E. M. Woodward, *One Hundred and Ninety-eighth Pennsylvania*, p. 40; *PWCI*, Hunton testimony, pp. 625, 629. In his official report (*OR* 46[1]:849) JLC said, "I was now ordered by Major-General Warren to halt and take the defensive," but Warren had no recollection of sending an actual order. Warren questioned JLC about it when he received JLC's official report and was preparing to write his own (Warren to JLC, Dec. 22, 1865, LC). Later JLC stated, "I received an order *purporting to be Warren's*" (*Armies*, p. 75, emphasis added). Warren thought that an order he had sent to Crawford to halt because the corps's right was advancing too fast may have gone to Chamberlain by mistake (*PWCI*, Warren testimony, p. 774).

54. *OR* 46(1):849; ibid. (3):283, 362; JLC, *Armies*, pp. 75, 109–10. First quotation, ibid., p. 110; second, ibid., pp. 109–10; third, ibid., p. 110. When Grant heard of the repulse of Ayres's and Crawford's divisions, he wired Meade, at 1:00 P.M., "If the enemy has been checked in Warren's front, what is to prevent him from pitching in with his whole corps and attacking before

giving him time to return in good order to his old intrenchments?" Just afterward, General Meade wired him that Warren would advance and "endeavor to drive the enemy back to and across the White Oak Road" (*OR* 46[3]:337). Warren did what Grant wanted almost reflexively.

55. JLC, *Armies*, pp. 75, 76; *OR* 46(1):849, 899; E. M. Woodward, *One Hundred and Ninety-eighth Pennsylvania*, pp. 40, 41; *PWCI*, JLC testimony, p. 229. First quotation, *OR* 46(1):849; second, JLC, *Armies*, p. 76. General McGowan testified that General Lee was with him on the field south of the White Oak Road personally observing the action (*PWCI*, McGowan testimony, p. 650).

56. JLC, *Armies*, pp. 76, 77; E. M. Woodward, *One Hundred and Ninety-eighth Pennsylvania*, p. 41; *PWCI*, Hunton testimony, p. 625. First quotation, JLC, *Armies*, p. 76; second, E. M. Woodward, *One Hundred and Ninety-eighth Pennsylvania*; third, *PWCI*, Hunton testimony. JLC had his men go in with an open front, not touching elbow in the usual formation, "to lessen loss from the long-range rifles" (*Armies*, p. 76). The superior effective range of the rifled musket over its unrifled predecessor had made some tactics obsolete by the time of the Civil War, with resultant heavy casualties. JLC's modification during the charge reduced casualties in his brigade.

57. JLC, *Armies*, p. 77; E. M. Woodward, *One Hundred and Ninety-eighth Pennsylvania*, pp. 41, 89; *OR* 46(1):816. Officers were more likely to keep flags and take credit themselves.

58. JLC, *Armies*, pp. 77, 78; *OR* 46(1):849, 853; *PWCI*, JLC testimony, p. 230. The Third Brigade was "somewhere to my [JLC's] rear and my left," Ayres (farther) to his left and rear, and Crawford "to the rear of my right, at a considerable distance." All of the Fifth Corps was within half a mile of the enemy works about 5:00 P.M., March 31 (ibid.). Fifth Corps casualties on March 31, 1865, were: First Division (Griffin): 23 killed, 150 wounded, 5 missing, total, 178; Second Division (Ayres): 51 killed, 274 wounded, 338 missing, total, 663; Third Division (Crawford): 51 killed, 380 wounded, 127 missing, total, 558; Artillery: 1 killed, 6 wounded, total, 7; Cavalry escort: 1 wounded; grand total, 1,407 (*OR* 46[1]:819). A military court of inquiry was convened on December 11, 1879, at the persistent request of General Warren to inquire into his conduct as major general commanding the Fifth Army Corps at the battle of Five Forks, Virginia, on April 1, 1865, and into the operations of his command on that day and March 31, as far as they related to his conduct, or to imputations or accusations against him. The court originally consisted of Maj. Gen. Winfield S. Hancock, U.S. Army; Brig. Gen. C. C. Augur, U.S. Army; and Col. Z. B. Tower, Corps of Engineers; with Maj. James McMillan, Second Artillery, recorder. Tower was later replaced by Bvt. Maj. Gen. John Newton, U.S. Army, and Bvt. Lt. Col. Loomis L. Langdon replaced McMillan. After the inquiry was well under way, in 1880 Hancock had to resign upon receiving the Democratic party nomination for president of the United States, and he was not replaced. The first accusation, called the First Imputation, is found on pp. 53 and 54 of *OR* 46(1), official report of

Lt. Gen. U. S. Grant: "On the morning of the 31st [of March 1865] General Warren reported favorably to getting possession of the White Oak Road, and was directed to do so. To accomplish this, he moved with one division instead of his whole corps, which was attacked by the enemy in superior force and driven back on the second division before it had time to form, and it in turn forced back upon the third division; when the enemy was checked. A division of the Second Corps was immediately sent to his support, the enemy driven back with heavy loss, and possession of the White Oak road gained."

Extracts from the Opinion of the Court concerning the First Imputation (*PWCI*, Opinion, pp. 1549–50): "There seems to be no evidence that General Warren, on the morning of March 31, or at any other time, reported favorably to getting possession of the White Oak road." The court then referred to a Warren proposal to Meade on March 30 to block the road but concluded that it was set aside by Grant on March 30. "General Warren's report, in his dispatch of 9:40 A.M., March 31, . . . that he had given orders to drive the enemy's pickets off the White Oak road or develop what force of the enemy held it, could not be fairly construed as being able to take possession of it." The court acknowledged General Meade's dispatch that said, in part, "Should you determine by your reconnaissance that you can get possession of & hold the White Oak road, you are to do so, notwithstanding the orders to suspend operations to-day," and then added, "And the evidence before this court shows that this order was not received by General Warren until after the fighting that resulted from the attempted reconnaissance had begun."

The court next referred to Warren's advance with two divisions, the Confederate attack upon Ayres, and the location of Griffin's division in reserve, which may have been held in compliance with Meade's earlier order for Warren to send his reserve to assist Humphreys if called upon. The court also was of the opinion that Warren should have been personally at the front directing his lead divisions, considering the circumstances and lacking Meade's express order to stay by the telegraph. (Warren had testified that he was where he could be reached by telegraph by General Meade, as he knew from experience with Meade that he required him to be there.) This opinion exonerated Warren of the First Imputation.

59. JLC, *Armies*, pp. 78, 87–88.

60. Ibid., p. 88.

61. Ibid., pp. 88–89; Humphreys, *Virginia Campaign*, p. 336; *OR* 46(1):816–17.

62. *OR* 46(1):1102–3; ibid. (3):381; JLC, *Armies*, p. 89; *PWCI*, JLC testimony, pp. 230, 232, 233; CSA Maj. Gen. Fitzhugh Lee estimated the Confederate force at 5,000 infantry, 3,200 cavalry, total, 8,200 (*PWCI*, p. 478). JLC stated 6,000 infantry and 4,000 cavalry, total, 10,000 (JLC, *Armies*, p. 111).

63. Humphreys, *Virginia Campaign*, p. 337; *OR* 46(1):817–18; JLC, *Armies*, pp. 100–102; *PWCI*, Lt. Gen. U. S. Grant testimony, p. 1046.

64. *OR* 46(1):818; Humphreys, *Virginia Campaign*, pp. 33–37; Powell, *Fifth Corps*, p. 791; JLC, *Armies*, pp. 85, 87, 100; *PWCI*, Grant testimony, p. 1046. Warren stated that his plan was for the enemy to be attacked front and rear with his whole corps, and that it should take place at daylight—the night was too dark for a successful night attack in an unknown country, in his opinion (*PWCI*, Warren testimony, pp. 777, 778, 784). Grant would perhaps have had a more realistic and favorable idea of Warren at a crucial time the next day if he had known of Warren's initiative.

65. *PWCI*, Warren testimony, pp. 729–31; ibid., Maj. W. H. H. Benyaurd testimony, p. 156; *OR* 46(1):819–21; ibid. (3):342–43. For tactical reasons, Warren had not rebuilt the bridge, found destroyed by the Confederates on March 29. Warren stated that if the bridge had been standing when he earlier received Meade's warning to be vigilant for the rear of his corps and the Second Corps, he would have been justified in destroying it then (*OR* 46[1]:820).

66. *OR* 46(1):820–21. Meade's orders, sent at 10:15 P.M. and received by Warren at 10:50 P.M., were essentially the plan Warren had advanced to Meade earlier in the evening, only now conditions had changed.

67. *OR* 46(1):825; ibid. (3):381–82; *PWCI*, Gen. Philip H. Sheridan testimony, pp. 64–68, 75–77. Quotation, *OR* 46(3):382. Meade's dispatch, showing plainly that he expected Warren to attack at *daylight*, was mistakenly dated "April 1, 1865—6 P.M." but was established before the court by the contents of the wording and the timing and wording of other dispatches on file, plus the attesting of Gen. Alexander Webb, Meade's chief of staff, to have been sent between 10:15 and 10:45 P.M., March 31.

68. *OR* 46(1):821, 822; JLC, *Armies*, pp. 89–90, 102; *PWCI*, Capt. Holman S. Melcher testimony, p. 456. Melcher, of the Twentieth Maine, was the Fifth Corps postmaster at the time. Warren's new instructions were issued at 11:00 P.M., but he did not hear of the locations of Crawford and Griffin until 1:00 A.M., April 1, and when he did, they had not moved, due to the difficulty of transmitting orders by waking each man individually; bugles or commands could not be used without alerting the enemy (*OR* 46[1]:822). Griffin told JLC to get his men ready to move only, and he remained in place (*PWCI*, JLC testimony, p. 233). Melcher said it took him over an hour to ride in the dark from Warren's headquarters, deliver the orders to Griffin, and return.

69. *OR* 46(1):823–24; *PWCI*, Grant testimony, pp. 1041–43. Quotation, *OR* 46(1):823. The distance to Dinwiddie by way of the Quaker Road was over ten miles, and troops sent this way could not arrive before 8:00 A.M. (*OR* 46[1]:824).

70. *OR* 46(1):824; JLC, *Armies*, p. 94; *PWCI*, Benyaurd testimony, pp. 155–58; ibid., JLC testimony, pp. 232–33; ibid., Warren testimony, p. 735; JLC, "White Oak Road," p. 247. Quotation, ibid.

71. *OR* 46(1):824; ibid. (3):419–20; *PWCI*, Warren testimony, p. 739; *PWCI*,

2d ser., Dispatches, pp. 1286, 1287; *PWCI*, p. 1621. Sunrise was at 5:46 A.M. on April 1 (ibid.). The original copy of the dispatch from Sheridan, noted received by Warren at 4:50 A.M., was not timed at origin, but the facsimile in Sheridan's official report gave the time of origin as 3:00 A.M. (*OR* 46[1]:1104), and he so testified at the Warren CI.

72. *OR* 46(1):824, 825; *PWCI*, Warren testimony, pp. 735–39.

73. JLC, *Armies*, p. 105; *PWCI*, Fitzhugh Lee testimony, pp. 469, 475, 481; ibid., W. H. F. Lee testimony, pp. 534–37; ibid., Gen. Romeyn B. Ayres testimony, p. 251. Quotations, JLC, *Armies*.

74. *OR* 46(1):825, 826, 1103; ibid. (3):381–82; *PWCI*, Ayres testimony, pp. 250–52. For Sheridan's reaction to some of the above, see *PWCI*, pp. 75–77, 60–63. Extracts from the Opinion of the Court concerning the Second Imputation (*PWCI*, Opinion, pp. 1550–59): "The Second Imputation is found in the following extract from General Sheridan's report of May 15, 1865 . . . [See *OR* 46(1):1103] ' . . . had General Warren moved according to the expectations of the Lieutenant-General, there would appear to have been little chance for the escape of the enemy's infantry in front of Dinwiddie Court House.'" Following a summation of the evidence and dispatches, the court gave its opinion: it supposed that "the expectations of the Lt. General" were those expressed in Grant's dispatch to Sheridan at 10:15 P.M. on March 31, where he notified Sheridan that the Fifth Corps had been sent to his support and should reach him "by 12 to-night." The court continued: "If this supposition be correct the court is of the opinion, considering the condition of the roads and surrounding country over part of which the troops had to march, the darkness of the night, the distance to be traveled, and the hour at which the order for the march reached General Warren, 10.50 P.M., that it was not practicable for the Fifth Corps to have reached General Sheridan at 12 o'clock on the night of March 31. . . .

"Notwithstanding that dispositions suitable for the contingency of Sheridan's falling back from Dinwiddie may well have perplexed General Warren's mind during the night, the court is of the opinion that he should have moved the two divisions by the Crump road in obedience to the orders and expectations of his commander, upon whom alone rested the responsibility of the consequences.

"It appears from the dispatches and General Warren's testimony, that neither Generals Mead [*sic*], Sheridan, or Warren expressed an intention of having this column attack before daylight. . . .

"The court is further of the opinion that General Warren should have started with two divisions, as directed by General Meade's dispatch . . . as early after its receipt, at 10.50 P.M., as he could be assured of the prospect of Ayres's departure down the Boydton Plank-road, and should have advanced on the Crump road as far as might be practicable or necessary to fulfill General Meade's intention; whereas the evidence shows that he did not start until between five and six o'clock on the morning of the 1st of April, and did not reach J. Boisseau's with the head of the column til about seven o'clock in the morning. The dispatches show that Generals Meade and Warren anticipated a withdrawal during the night of the enemy's forces fronting General Sheridan, which was rendered highly probable from the known position in their rear of a portion of the Fifth Corps (Bartlett's brigade) at J. Boisseau's, and the event justified the anticipation."

75. JLC, *Armies*, pp. 105, 106, 118; *OR* 46(1):54, 1102; ibid. (3):380–81; *PWCI*, Sheridan testimony, pp. 109–13; ibid., Fitzhugh Lee testimony, p. 469. At the Warren CI, Sheridan was questioned about the assertion that the Confederates had left the scene of the White Oak Road battle on March 31, marched to Five Forks, and helped push him back to Dinwiddie Court House. His answers were hostile and evasive when he was confronted with the times of the battles and the necessary logistics, and he became rattled enough to make ridiculous statements that he later formally amended. He claimed that his conclusions were based on one or two fragmentary and unconfirmed reports of prisoners' statements of their commands. Fitzhugh Lee's testimony concerning the Confederate infantry units' movements on March 30, 31, and April 1 confirmed the fact that no Confederate infantry fighting the Fifth or Second Corps on March 31 fought Sheridan that day or night. Warren's counsel in the Warren CI (*PWCI*, pp. 80–90) summed up Warren's success in following all of Meade's orders and caused Sheridan to reluctantly concede that Meade was Warren's commander until he reported to Sheridan, and that Meade's orders, not Sheridan's expectations, should have ruled Warren's actions.

76. *PWCI*, JLC testimony, pp. 233–34; JLC, *Armies*, pp. 99, 103–4; JLC, "White Oak Road," map facing p. 216. The account of the myriad dispatches and troop movements the night of March 31–April 1, 1865, near Petersburg, Virginia, is necessarily shortened in this narrative, and some details have been omitted. In writing their books, JLC, Powell, and particularly Humphreys, drew heavily on the *PWCI* testimony for their accounts of these events, and their much more detailed descriptions are recommended. JLC's account of the events of these days, together with his opinions, criticisms, and feelings, make good reading. The Warren CI testimony gives corrected copies of orders and the sequence of events, and the correspondence for volume 46 of the *OR* is sometimes corrected because of examination of original documents and comparisons at the Warren CI. The voluminous records of the Warren CI make fascinating reading for those interested and fortunate enough to have access to a copy.

CHAPTER NINE

1. *History, 118th Pennsylvania*, p. 575; JLC, *Armies*, p. 104; JLC, "Five Forks," pp. 221–22; *PWCI*, JLC testimony, pp. 233–34. Sunrise at Petersburg, Virginia, on April 1, 1865, was at 5:46 and 56 seconds A.M., mean time. Sun-

set was at 6:21 and 21 seconds P.M. (computation of Prof. P. S. Michie, USMA, in *PWCI*, pp. 1620–21).

2. *PWCI*, JLC testimony, p. 233; JLC, *Armies*, p. 104. Quotation, ibid.

3. JLC, *Armies*, pp. 117–18; *OR* 46(1):1104.

4. *OR* 46(1):1104; ibid. (3):380–81; JLC, *Armies*, p. 115. Although his official report stated that his cavalry had been forced back to Dinwiddie Court House (*OR* 46[1]:1103), Sheridan maintained later that his repulse and retreat to Dinwiddie Court House was part of a plan to lure the Confederates out in the open: "The turn of events finally brought me the Fifth [Corps], after my cavalry, under the most trying difficulties, had drawn the enemy from his works" (Powell, *Fifth Corps*, p. 819).

5. *OR* 46(3):418; *PWCI*, JLC testimony, p. 237; ibid., Col. Orville E. Babcock testimony, p. 901; ibid., Lt. Gen. U. S. Grant testimony, p. 1028; ibid., Maj. Gen. G. K. Warren testimony, pp. 786, 1234, 1235; JLC, *Armies*, pp. 118–19. Quotation, *PWCI*, Grant testimony. Although Grant denied that it was the reason for his message, a staff officer had erroneously reported at his headquarters about 9:00 A.M. that Warren and his corps were still delayed building a bridge. Overhearing, Grant sent Babcock to Sheridan immediately. Grant indicated that his knowlege of Warren's "defects" prompted him to fear that Warren would fail Sheridan (*PWCI*, Capt. E. R. Warner testimony, pp. 37, 38, and Grant testimony, p. 1030). Warren told his wife that Grant had told him that in the past he thought Warren was too self-reliant in executing his duties and did not strictly obey orders and cooperate closely enough in Grant's general plans. Meade, to whom Warren had gone after seeing Grant, frankly told him that he had complained to General Grant about the same things (Warren to his wife, Apr. 2, 1865, in E. G. Taylor, *Warren*, pp. 228–29). A final irony revealed at the Warren CI was that Sheridan said he never would have relieved Warren without Grant's unsolicited authority to do so, as he did not feel he had the authority (*PWCI*, Gen. Philip H. Sheridan testimony, p. 139).

6. Humphreys, *Virginia Campaign*, p. 344; JLC, *Armies*, pp. 120–21; Powell, *Fifth Corps*, p. 802; *PWCI*, JLC testimony, pp. 234–35; ibid., Maj. George L. Gillespie testimony, pp. 930, 932, 933. Lt. Col. H. C. Bankhead and others testified that cavalry horses in the road impeded the march of the Fifth Corps (*PWCI*, pp. 338, 339). Maj. Gen. Romeyn B. Ayres testified that the distance from the J. Boisseau house to Gravelly Run Church was 2³/₁₆ miles.

7. "*Copy*, Chamberlain's answer to questions of Genl Warren," typed manuscript, n.d., LC, repeats, then answers questions asked of JLC by Warren in a letter, Warren to JLC, Oct. 20, 1880, BC; *PWCI*, JLC testimony, pp. 1081–82; JLC, *Armies*, pp. 121–22; *OR* 46(1):1105. Quotation, ibid. The Third Imputation of Warren's conduct examined by the Warren CI was from Sheridan's official report of the action on April 1, 1865, found in *OR* 46(1):1105: "General Warren did not exert himself to get up his corps as rapidly as he might have done, and his manner gave me the impression that he wished the sun to go down before dispositions for the attack could be completed."

Opinion of the Court: "The court is of the opinion that there was no unnecessary delay in this march of the Fifth corps, and that General Warren took the usual methods of a corps commander to prevent delay. The question regarding General Warren's manner appears to be too intangible and the evidence on it too contradictory for the court to decide, separate from the context, that he appeared to wish 'the sun to go down before dispostions for the attack would be completed;' but his actions, as shown by the evidence, do not appear to have corresponded with such wish, if ever he entertained it" (*PWCI*, Opinion, p. 1559).

8. Humphreys, *Virginia Campaign*, p. 344; *PWCI*, Warren testimony, p. 744; JLC, *Armies*, p. 122; *OR* 46(1):830; map of the battlefield of Five Forks, referred to in the Warren CI as "Cotton Map No. 2," in *Argument on Behalf of Lieut. Gen. Philip H. Sheridan*.

9. JLC, *Armies*, p. 121; *PWCI*, JLC testimony, pp. 236, 1082; ibid., Warren testimony, pp. 741–42, 789, 799, 1205. Quotation, JLC, *Armies*. Warren testified that he could not place himself to actually see across the White Oak Road without risking being seen by the enemy (*PWCI*, Warren testimony, p. 789). Being seen would give away the Union attack plans. He got all his information about the Confederate position from Sheridan himself (*PWCI*, Warren testimony, p. 799). JLC's testimony describing Warren before the corps moved apparently impressed the court, from its opinion in the Third Imputation. JLC said: "I should say that those who do not know General Warren's temperament might think him to be negative when he was deeply intent. General Warren's temperament is such that he, instead of showing excitement, generally shows an intense concentration in what I call important movements, and those who do not know him might take it to be apathy when it is deep, concentrated thought and purpose. And it would not be unnatural that a stranger, looking at General Warren and not seeing indications of excitement and resolution on his face, might judge him to be apathetic, when, in fact, that conclusion might be far from the truth (*PWCI*, JLC testimony, p. 236).

10. *PWCI*, Warren testimony, pp. 746, 789, 800; ibid., Sheridan testimony, pp. 96, 97, 116; ibid., Col. James W. Forsyth testimony, pp. 1048, 1052–53; ibid., JLC testimony, pp. 237, 1082; ibid., Gen. Samuel W. Crawford testimony, pp. 572–78; Nevins, *Diary of Battle*, p. 514; JLC, *Armies*, pp. 123, 236. Several Fifth Corps officers testified they kept the sun over their left shoulders. To keep the correct angle of the lines of battle and strike the position of the enemy where it was supposed to be, Warren directed that the officers keep the sun over their left shoulders as a "guide left" when marching to the White Oak Road. In woods, the shadows cast by the trees would form a guide for the angle of the line. Characteristically observant of detail, Warren noticed that a shadow cast by the sun fell right along Crawford's formation in line of battle, and he decided to take advantage of this coincidence (*PWCI*, Warren testimony, pp. 799–800).

11. JLC, *Armies*, p. 123. JLC remembered at the Warren CI that the time it took from Ayres's arrival until the Fifth Corps moved was only about ten minutes, because his quick lunch with Winthrop had been cut short by the attack order (*PWCI*, JLC testimony, p. 1085).

12. JLC, *Armies*, p. 124; *PWCI*, Gen. Romeyn B. Ayres testimony, pp. 253, 263; ibid., Warren testimony, p. 746; ibid., JLC testimony, p. 287. *The Passing of the Armies* was published in 1915, the year after JLC's death, and was copyrighted by his children, Harold Wyllys Chamberlain and Grace Chamberlain Allen. It was prepared for publication by them and the publisher, G. H. Putnam. The map of "The Battle-Field of Five Forks, Va." included in the book is redrawn from the map prepared by Maj. G. L. Gillespie (U.S. War Department, *Atlas*, pl. 68, no. 3), which was originally drawn in New Orleans in July 1865, mostly from notes he and his staff obtained on the day of the battle (*PWCI*, Gillespie testimony, p. 938). It contains many errors as to troop movements and terrain. Had JLC chosen a map to be included with his book, it would not have been this one. The sketch map included with his war paper "Five Forks," read before the Maine Commandery of MOLLUS on May 2, 1900, is accurate as to troop formations but somewhat erroneous as to terrain. JLC was asked by the Warren court to draw the troop formations and movements as the Fifth Corps moved out from the Gravelly Run Church on one of principal maps used during the inquiry. The accuracy of JLC's placements were in "remarkable agreement" to his own, Warren said (*PWCI*, Warren testimony, p. 746), and others also agreed to their accuracy.

13. *OR* 46(1):1104, 1105; *PWCI*, JLC testimony, p. 285; JLC, *Armies*, p. 124. Quotation, ibid. Mackenzie had about 1,000 men.

14. JLC, *Armies*, pp. 124–25; *OR* 46(1):830. Quotation, ibid. Many witnesses at the Warren CI testified that the corps stepped off at 4:00 P.M. or shortly thereafter. The diagram used in this book is the one entered in evidence at the Warren CI (*PWCI*, p. 747) and is slightly, but not substantially, different from the diagram in the above-referenced *OR*. JLC used the Warren CI version of the diagram for his MOLLUS paper, "Five Forks." The order used in the Warren CI has the word "brigade" entered after "McKenzie's." McKenzie should be spelled Mackenzie.

15. JLC, *Armies*, pp. 124–26; *PWCI*, JLC testimony, p. 281. Quotation, JLC, *Armies*, p. 126. General Warren thought the diagram, used with the written directions, to be crucial to the carrying out of Sheridan's orders. Warren intended that Crawford's division strike the Confederates at the left flank of their works and expected "the heaviest battle wherever . . . their left was" (*PWCI*, Warren testimony, p. 787). "I placed the smaller division on the left of the road, which was General Ayres's, as I supposed, from the position of the enemy as given to me, that General Crawford's centre would fall right on the angle of their line, and that, if he was not able to carry it, General Griffin would be right there to sustain him, and to take advantage of any successes. General Ayres's being the weakest division, I left on the left to

engage the front and prevent the enemy there re-enforcing that angle" (ibid., p. 745). The corps would form somewhat "obliquely to the Gravelly Church road and move straight to the front so as to strike that angle" (ibid., p. 789).

The angle of obliquity of the Fifth Corps divisions was apparently deliberately exaggerated by Warren to illustrate his point in the diagram and was not to be taken literally. "The diagram says they will swing around. . . . The two go together; the diagram illustrates what kind of swing it will be; it is not a technical phrase; it is something like a wave makes; when a wave comes up to a promontory and strikes it it swings around, and that is what this line of battle would do." Warren anticipated that those who did strike the works "would be fetched up by it, and those who did not would swing around, and that is why I used such a phrase ["The line will move forward as formed till it reaches the White Oak road, when it will *swing around* (emphasis added) to the left perpendicular to the White Oak road"], which is not a military one. . . . A plan was made, on the supposition that the angle would be struck very near the junction of these roads—Gravelly Run Church road and White Oak road; we supposed it to be there" (ibid., pp. 788–89). "The position of the enemy's flank . . . on the White Oak road, that was the controlling condition. Any soldier knows that" (ibid., p. 792).

16. JLC, *Armies*, pp. 126, 159–60; *PWCI*, Col. (CSA) Thomas T. Munford testimony, pp. 439, 442–43, 453; JLC, "Five Forks," pamphlet copy, Munford annotations on p. 33 and on the accompanying map. The copy of JLC's "Five Forks" used here is a pamphlet signed by JLC to Colonel Munford and annotated with comments on several pages by Colonel Munford, found in the Bangor, Maine, Public Library. This pamphlet will subsequently be cited as "Five Forks," Munford annotated, when referring to material contained in Munford's annotations. JLC autographed and sent the pamphlet to Munford at Munford's request in the autumn of 1905 (JLC to Munford, Oct. 25, 1905, Thomas T. Munford Division, Munford-Ellis Collection, William R. Perkins Library, Duke University), and apparently Munford then returned it with his remarks to JLC. On the map, Munford altered the position identified as "Munford cavalry" at the junction of the White Oak and Gravelly Run Roads to read "Munford cavalry picket" and placed his rail barricade north of it in the woods. Confederate infantry covering the 1¾ miles of entrenchments from the Confederate left were the brigades of Brigadier Generals Matt W. Ransom, William H. Wallace, George H. Steuart, William R. Terry, and Montgomery D. Corse. Terry was wounded on March 31, and his brigade was commanded at the battle of Five Forks by Col. Joseph Mayo.

17. *PWCI*, JLC testimony, p. 273; JLC, *Armies*, p. 128.

18. *PWCI*, Ayres testimony, pp. 254, 255, 263; ibid., Joseph P. Cotton testimony, pp. 239, 243, 244; ibid., JLC testimony, p. 276; JLC, *Armies*, p. 123; JLC, "Five Forks," p. 221. The Confederate return was placed at an obtuse angle.

19. JLC, *Armies*, pp. 128–29; *PWCI*, JLC testimony, pp. 273, 274, 276, 284. Quotation, ibid., p. 274. Griffin, who had thought his division had gone too far out without striking the enemy, returned and talked with Ayres personally before Ayres carried the angle (*PWCI*, Ayres testimony, pp. 256, 269–70; ibid., Capt. R. M. Brinton testimony, p. 301).

20. *PWCI*, JLC testimony, pp. 273, 274, 289; JLC, *Armies*, p. 129.

21. JLC, *Armies*, p. 129; *PWCI*, JLC testimony, p. 274; ibid., Samuel Y. Gilliam testimony, p. 666.

22. *PWCI*, JLC testimony, pp. 274, 281, 287; ibid., CSA Lt. Col. W. W. Wood testimony, pp. 484, 485; ibid., CSA 2d Lt. J. H. Blakemore testimony, pp. 1188–89; JLC, *Armies*, p. 129. The barrier was about 3½ feet high but faded away toward one end (*PWCI*, JLC testimony, pp. 274, 287).

23. *OR* 46(1):838–39, 861, 850; *PWCI*, JLC testimony, pp. 274, 281, 264; ibid., Wood testimony, pp. 487, 488; ibid., Cotton testimony, p. 244. A low ridge ran down the Sydnor field from the White Oak Road toward the north. Its height was about ten feet at the road (*PWCI*, Warren testimony, p. 1210). Ayres testified that he saw JLC's brigade come in across the rear of the Rebel line to assist him. He did not see any other part of the First Division (ibid., Ayres testimony, p. 265). Bartlett's other regiments apparently stayed with Crawford. The 118th Pennsylvania and First Maine Sharpshooters were later assigned by Warren to guard the Ford Road crossing of Gravelly Run under the command of Bvt. Lt. Col. Ellis Spear. Spear, who had been riding on the right front of Bartlett's brigade, said he was with another "portion" of Bartlett's brigade near the Ford Road before he was asked to take these two regiments (*OR* 46[1]:862–65, 866–67; *PWCI*, Spear testimony, pp. 403–9).

24. *OR* 46(1):850, 865; *PWCI*, JLC testimony, p. 274; Gerrish, *Army Life*, pp. 241–44; *Under the Maltese Cross*, pp. 613–14. According to the official reports of Gregory and his three regiments, only Lt. Col. Isaac Doolittle's 188th New York Regiment was able to get into the fight on the Confederate left. The other two, which had been assigned as flankers and skirmishers by JLC, apparently remained on the right of that part of Bartlett's brigade that continued on with Crawford (*OR* 46[1]:854, 856–60). It seems from the evidence that only six of Griffin's regiments—three from Bartlett's brigade, Chamberlain's two regiments, and one of Gregory's—did the First Division fighting from the west side of the Sydnor field to the Ford Road.

25. *OR* 46(1):869, 1105; *PWCI*, JLC testimony, pp. 274–75; JLC, *Armies*, pp. 131–32. Quotation, ibid. This action put Gwyn ahead of Ayres's main line, which at that time was still halted in the woods east of the Sydnor field, inside the angle of the original return line, but Gwyn later joined Ayres on the march west toward Five Forks.

The "unsteadiness" in Ayres's division at the beginning of the action was the subject of the Fourth Imputation of Warren's conduct examined by the Warren CI and was from Sheridan's official report of the action on April 1,

1865, found in *OR* 46(1):1105: "During this attack I again became dissatisfied with General Warren. During the engagement portions of his line gave way when not exposed to a heavy fire, and simply from want of confidence on the part of the troops, which General Warren did not exert himself to inspire." Opinion of the Warren Court: "General Warren's attention appears to have been drawn, almost immediately after Ayres received the flank fire from the 'return' and his consequent change of front, to the probability of Crawford with Griffin diverging too much from and being separated from Ayres, and by continuous exertions of himself and staff substantially remedied matters; and the court thinks that this was for him the essential point to be attended to, which also exacted his whole efforts to accomplish" (*PWCI*, pp. 1561–62). This was the final Imputation and Opinion of the Court which exonerated Warren.

In a letter to JLC, Col. Thomas T. Munford said that during the inquiry he told General Hancock that he would like to have a copy of the court proceedings. Some time later he was sent "two *bound* Volumes." The next day he received a letter from "Hancock's staff Colonel" informing him "that they had been sent by direction of Gen'l Hancock" and adding, "I hope you have received them because an order has come recalling the entire edition." Munford remarked, "They are as scarce as Hens teeth" (T. T. Munford to JLC, Jan. 27, 1911, BC). JLC refers to the records of the court in *Armies* (p. xvii), calling them "now suppressed." Today, there are few copies extant.

26. JLC, *Armies*, pp. 134–35; *PWCI*, JLC testimony, p. 277; *OR* 46(1):840. Quotation, JLC, *Armies*, p. 134. Some of the Confederates were men of the Eleventh Virginia Infantry of Terry's (Mayo's) brigade sent earlier by Mayo to reinforce Ransom (*PWCI*, Mayo testimony, p. 499), and some were part of the Third Virginia Cavalry (dismounted) (Munford notation on p. 15 of "Five Forks," Munford annotated, Bangor Public Library). Two regiments from Steuart's brigade were also sent east to help Ransom (*PWCI*, Mayo testimony, p. 499; ibid., Blakemore testimony, p. 1188). JLC received a receipt acknowledging the capture of 2 colonels, 6 captains, 11 lieutenants, and 1,050 men by his own brigade and 470 men by Gregory's (JLC, *Armies*, p. 135 n. 2). Maj. Charles F. Gillies, Provost Marshal, Cavalry Corps, with the help of Col. F. C. Newhall, counted all the prisoners received by him on the afternoon of April 1. The number was 4,006. He sent them to the Army of the Potomac headquarters before dark that evening, and a receipt for that number was signed by Lt. C. A. Rand, ADC, on April 2. Gillies produced this actual receipt during his testimony. He said that on April 2 he turned about 2,000 more prisoners over to the Fifth Corps because he did not have the men to guard them, but he had no receipt (*PWCI*, Gillies testimony, p. 1136). In his official report, General Sheridan estimated 5,000 to 6,000 prisoners taken (*OR* 46[1]:1105). Warren reported 3,244 captures by the Fifth Corps on April 1 in his official report (*OR* 46[1]:836), but in his testimony before the court, he said that figure came from the provost marshal's report of the Fifth

Corps and was not so large as the numbers reported to him by his different commands (*PWCI,* Warren testimony, p. 1233). Documents submitted to the Warren CI from the War Department on May 25, 1880, list 2,063 prisoners captured at the battle of Five Forks on April 1, and 164 on April 2, but these figures were prepared from the military prisons records on file at the adjutant general's office (*PWCI,* pp. 1322–25).

27. JLC, *Armies,* pp. 135–36; *PWCI,* JLC testimony, p. 275; ibid., Bvt. Brig. Gen. Horace Porter testimony, pp. 911–12; ibid., Ayres testimony, pp. 253–54, 255; ibid., Sheridan testimony, pp. 101, 102; *New York World,* Apr. 4, 1865; *New York World* dispatches, JLC Letterbook, PHS. Quotation, ibid. Sheridan had instructed Warren that after the enemy's line was broken, once they "got him [the enemy] started, we were not to stop for anything" (*PWCI,* Warren testimony, p. 749). Ayres stated in his official report that he had halted by Sheridan's order (*OR* 46[1]:870).

28. *PWCI,* JLC testimony, p. 275; JLC, *Armies,* p. 130. First quotation, JLC, *Armies;* second, *PWCI,* JLC testimony, third, JLC, *Armies.*

29. JLC, *Armies,* pp. 130–31; *PWCI,* JLC testimony, p. 275. Quotations, JLC, *Armies,* p. 131.

30. JLC, *Armies,* pp. 132–33; *PWCI,* JLC testimony, pp. 275, 288; ibid., Ayres testimony, pp. 257, 266, 270. First quotation, JLC, *Armies,* p. 132; second, ibid., p. 133.

31. JLC, *Armies,* pp. 132, 133–34; *PWCI,* JLC testimony, p. 286; ibid., Ayres testimony, pp. 255, 256, 264. First quotation, JLC, *Armies,* p. 133; second, ibid., p. 134. Ayres took 2,100 prisoners and nine battle flags at the angle (*PWCI,* Ayres testimony, p. 255).

32. *PWCI,* Gen. Samuel W. Crawford testimony, pp. 573, 582; ibid., Warren testimony, p. 750.

33. Ibid., Warren testimony, pp. 750, 791; ibid., Col. John A. Kellogg testimony, pp. 219, 220, 222. Quotation, ibid., p. 219. Sheridan's staff officer was Col. George A. Forsyth. Kellogg went only a little to the south before moving due west.

34. Ibid., Bvt. Brig. Gen. Richard Coulter testimony, pp. 351–53; ibid., Kellogg testimony, p. 220.

35. Ibid., Warren testimony, pp. 750–51, 1227. Quotation, p. 750.

36. JLC, *Armies,* pp. 137, 164, 166; *PWCI,* Crawford testimony, pp. 574–76, 583; *OR* 46(1):880–81, 885. Quotation, *PWCI,* Crawford testimony, p. 583. Crawford's loss of three hundred men in the battle was the highest in the corps.

37. JLC, *Armies,* p. 137; *PWCI,* JLC testimony, pp. 277, 287; ibid., Ayres testimony, pp. 256, 1080; *OR* 46(1):850–51. Ayres testified that he had little fighting—"nothing to speak of"—after carrying the angle (*PWCI,* Ayres testimony, p. 257). JLC, however, testified that he had "continuous fighting to the Ford road" (ibid., JLC testimony, p. 277).

38. JLC, *Armies,* p. 142; *PWCI,* JLC testimony, pp. 277, 278; ibid., Capt. R.

M. Brinton testimony, pp. 303, 306, 308. Quotations, ibid., p. 303. Brinton could not remember clearly all officers who were present (ibid., p. 308). However, Warren's inspector general, Lt. Col. H. C. Bankhead, was present, and he remembered Grant's aide Horace Porter and James Forsyth, Sheridan's chief of staff (ibid., Lt. Col. H. C. Bankhead testimony, p. 340). Bankhead testified that at the time, he did not think Sheridan's action displaced Warren, but that Sheridan merely said, "General Griffin, you take command." Bankhead did not report to Griffin as corps commander until he was ordered by Sheridan that night (ibid., p. 346). Sheridan had no recollection of the incident. He testified that he notified Griffin of his promotion only after he had officially relieved Warren (ibid., Sheridan testimony, p. 103).

39. *PWCI*, Warren testimony, pp. 751, 754, 1207; ibid., Maj. West Funk testimony, p. 436; *OR* 46(1):881.

40. JLC, *Armies*, p. 141; Humphreys, *Virginia Campaign*, pp. 349n, 350; *PWCI*, CSA Col. Joseph Mayo testimony, pp. 499–500, 509–10; ibid., CSA Brig. Gen. M. D. Corse testimony, p. 428; ibid., Funk testimony, pp. 436–38. Major Generals Pickett, Fitzhugh Lee, and T. L. Rosser enjoyed a shad bake that afternoon north of Gravelly Run and for some reason did not hear the sounds of battle (Munford to JLC, Jan. 11, 1911, BC; Humphreys, *Virginia Campaign*, p. 349). Munford wrote to JLC in candid terms of his feelings: "Genl Pickett and Fitz Lee were *deep in their cups* at a Shad lunch from a little after noon until 1/2 past five P.M. and Genl R E Lee nor Genl Anderson had no official information from either of them until *their* commands *irrevocably ruined*" ("Five Forks," Munford annotated, p. 10, Bangor Public Library). "The *Shad dinner* was a *Mess of Pottage* and had justice *been done* these 3 Major Generals [he includes Gen. Thomas L. Rosser, who was also present at the affair], a *drum head* Court Martial and a file of Armed Soldiers would have been their desserts" (ibid., p. 43). Munford had sent several couriers to Pickett to no avail when he saw the Fifth Corps moving from the Gravelly Run Church; he finally saw Pickett on the Ford Road riding down toward the Five Forks junction and his shattered command (*PWCI*, Munford testimony, pp. 444–45, 447).

41. JLC, *Armies*, pp. 145–46; *PWCI*, Funk testimony, pp. 435–39; ibid., Mayo testimony, p. 500. Quotation, ibid. Col. H. N. Warren of the 142d Pennsylvania had been wounded severely the previous day at the battle of the White Oak Road. Funk saw Griffin's men marching southwest on the east side of the Ford Road and south of him. He also said he captured some prisoners, "three or four ambulances and four or five forage wagons" (ibid., Funk testimony, p. 436). Sheridan's staff officer, Col. George Forsyth, had asked Funk why he did not take the guns. Funk replied that he was waiting for orders from Coulter, and Forsyth left, but after about fifteen minutes, Funk decided to go ahead and capture them without orders. In his initial prepared statement to the Warren court, Sheridan claimed that "Crawford's

division captured some artillery . . . on the Ford road, the order for which was originally given by one of my staff officers, Colonel George A. Forsyth, to Colonel West Funk of the 121st Penn. Regiment, who was in command of two regiments. Previous to this, however, the enemy had been driven out of his entire line of works, and Colonel Funk's capture was the result and not a part of the main attack" (*PWCI*, Sheridan testimony, p. 56). In his testimony Sheridan retracted any complimentary remarks he had made about the Fifth Corps in his official report of the battle.

42. JLC, *Armies*, p. 143; *PWCI*, JLC testimony, pp. 283, 288. Quotations, JLC, *Armies*. JLC omitted this officer's name from all his accounts of the incident, presumably to save General Bartlett additional embarrassment. When directly asked to do so by the Warren court, he revealed the name.

43. *PWCI*, JLC testimony, p. 283; JLC, *Armies*, pp. 143–44. Quotations, JLC, *Armies*, p. 144. JLC's imagery of the black storm king is reminiscent of the old Indian tales of Mount Katahdin from his youth in Maine.

44. *PWCI*, Lt. F. Augustin Schermerhorn testimony, p. 693; *OR* 46(1):848, 849, 851; JLC, *Armies*, p. 138; E. M. Woodward, *One Hundred and Ninety-eighth Pennsylvania*, p. 45. First quotation, *OR* 46(1):851; second, ibid., p. 848; last two, JLC, *Armies*. In *Armies*, JLC did not specify the place and time that Major Glenn made his heroic charge, but from the evidence it must have happened at a last stand of Confederates in front of First Division troops near the Five Forks. JLC's writing contains a great deal of information, some of it learned after the events portrayed, and he rarely used footnotes. Sometimes he apparently combined events and their sequence.

45. JLC, *Armies*, pp. 138–39.

46. Ibid., pp. 139–40. First quotation, p. 139; second, p. 140.

47. Ibid., p. 140; newspaper clipping, "A Frankford Hero," *North Philadelphia World*, Aug. 31, 1901 [1907?], LC. Quotation, JLC, *Armies*. Edwin A. Glenn had joined Company E, Third Pennsylvania Reserves, as a private, served three years, and attained the rank of second lieutenant. He was then appointed major of the new 198th Pennsylvania Infantry. His promotion was a difficult matter to resolve. JLC immediately applied for brevet promotions to lieutenant colonel and colonel in recognition of Glenn's outstanding service. These were granted at once. JLC also applied for a lineal promotion within the 198th Pennsylvania structure. The colonel, Brevet Brigadier Sickel, was in hospital with his shattered arm from the Quaker Road battle. The lieutenant colonel of the regiment was on detached duty, and JLC was apparently informed by the governor of Pennsylvania that a regular promotion within the regiment could not be obtained. See JLC, *Armies*, pp. 140, 141n.

48. *PWCI*, Mayo testimony, pp. 499–501; ibid., JLC testimony, p. 288; JLC, *Armies*, pp. 144–45, 147. Colonel Munford had his own ideas about what happened at the Five Forks crossing and wrote this note to JLC: "The Cavalry of Fitzhugh and Pennington did not go over the works until after Ayres + your command had *caused* the general stampede. This is clearly shown in

the *testimony* and *especially* Gen'l Merritt's on Cross *Examination* at the Warren trial" ("Five Forks," Munford annotated, p. 23, Bangor Public Library).

49. *PWCI*, Schermerhorn testimony, p. 693; JLC, *Armies*, p. 144; list of horses in JLC's handwriting, JLC Letterbook, PHS. Most synopses of JLC's military career give five as the number of horses shot under him in battle. However, the six instances listed in JLC's letterbook seem correct, although ambiguous about the identity of specific horses. It is unclear whether Charlemagne was the horse wounded at Five Forks; it may have been another.

50. JLC, *Armies*, p. 142; *PWCI*, Col. Frederick T. Locke testimony, p. 1102; ibid., Warren testimony, pp. 793, 1207. Quotations, JLC, *Armies*. Sheridan repeatedly contended that the battle was over once Ayres captured the angle on the Confederate left (*PWCI*, Sheridan testimony, pp. 100, 101, 102). Sunset was at 6:21 P.M. mean time on April 1, 1865, but would appear to an observer to be eight minutes sooner (ibid., Warren testimony, p. 1228; ibid., Exhibit F, Michie computations, p. 1621). Warren thought Locke was mistaken about the reference to prisoners and did not think he had said anything about them; his message to Sheridan contained what he considered useful information (ibid., Warren testimony, p. 793).

51. *PWCI*, Warren testimony, pp. 793, 794; ibid., Locke testimony, p. 1102; JLC, *Armies*, p. 148.

52. JLC, *Armies*, pp. 148–49; *PWCI*, JLC testimony, pp. 277–78. Quotation, JLC, *Armies*, p. 148. Locke met Lt. Col. H. C. Bankhead immediately after taking down Sheridan's remarks and asked him, "What was the matter between Sheridan and Warren?" Although Bankhead answered that he did not know, he could have told Locke of the episode he had witnessed when Sheridan told Griffin to take command (*PWCI*, Bankhead testimony, p. 341).

53. *PWCI*, Brig. Gen. (CSA) M. D. Corse testimony, pp. 421–23; ibid., Lt. Col. Hollon Richardson testimony, p. 316; ibid., Warren testimony, p. 752; ibid., Locke testimony, pp. 1106–7; *OR* 46(1):835, 885–86. The Confederates had also built a "return" at the far right of their works that morning, perpendicular to and north of the White Oak Road (*PWCI*, Corse testimony, p. 422). Not only Kellogg's brigade of Crawford's division, but men from all three divisions of the Fifth Corps apparently were present in the Union battle line. Most, however, were Crawford's.

54. *PWCI*, JLC testimony, p. 1083; ibid., Warren testimony, pp. 752, 756; ibid., Locke testimony, p. 1103; ibid., Bankhead testimony, pp. 341, 347; Agassiz, *Meade's Headquarters*, pp. 42, 146; *OR* 46(1):835. Quotation, ibid. Warren constantly used his ears as well as his eyes to keep himself informed during a battle. JLC had followed Warren along the White Oak Road at some distance with his troops in hand. He apparently arrived at the Gilliam field too late to participate in the charge but continued west on the White Oak Road and saw the firing at the northwest corner of the Gilliam field (*PWCI*, JLC testimony, p. 1083).

55. *PWCI*, Richardson testimony, pp. 316–17; ibid., Warren testimony, pp. 752, 757, 1207, 1227; ibid., JLC testimony, p. 286; ibid., Locke testimony, p. 1103. First quotation, *PWCI*, Warren testimony, p. 757; second, ibid., p. 1227. Warren also cited a letter to him from Gen. George A. Custer of May 3, 1866 (*PWCI*, Warren testimony, p. 757). Colonel Locke, Capt. Holman Melcher, and Major Benyaurd were three of Warren's staff officers who accompanied their chief in the charge (ibid., Locke testimony, p. 1103).

56. JLC, *Armies*, pp. 150–51, 155; *PWCI*, Warren testimony, pp. 752–53; ibid., Corse testimony, p. 423; *OR* 46(1):835. Quotation, JLC, *Armies*, p. 155. Sheridan's position was placed at the northeast corner of the Gilliam field by Richardson, Bankhead, and Locke. Asa Bird Gardner, Sheridan's counsel at the inquiry, said that "General Sheridan . . . was at the time looking into the Gilliam field" (*PWCI*, p. 1539). Confederate General Corse testified that the Union infantry swept up both sides of the White Oak Road, infantry and cavalry on the south side of it. The troops he had making this last stand fired directly and obliquely into the approaching Federals; Corse then had his men cease fire, and they broke off to the Federal left, through the woods (ibid., Corse testimony, p. 423).

57. Nevins, *Diary of Battle*, p. 513; G. K. Warren to his wife, Apr. 2, 1865, in E. G. Taylor, *Warren*, p. 229; *PWCI*, Warren testimony, p. 1208; ibid., Bvt. Brig. Gen. James W. Forsyth testimony, p. 195; ibid., Melcher testimony, p. 1095; *OR* 46(3):420. Quotation, ibid.

58. JLC, *Armies*, p. 151; *PWCI*, Warren testimony, pp. 753, 757. Quotations, JLC, *Armies*. Warren worked in the Engineer Corps of the army the rest of his life; his military career was all but destroyed. In 1879 he was finally promoted to the rank of lieutenant colonel. On August 8, 1882, a little over three months before the final findings of the court of inquiry vindicating him were ordered published by the War Department, Warren died in Newport, Rhode Island. See E. G. Taylor, *Warren*, p. 248; Warner, *Generals in Blue*, p. 542; *PWCI*, p. 1551.

Crawford's failure to close on Ayres—and Warren's subsequent absence from Sheridan's presence to retrieve his Third Division commander—was one factor in Warren's removal, but not the only one. JLC thought that "Warren was deposed from his command . . . mainly, I have no doubt, under the irritation at his being slow in getting up to Sheridan the night before from the White Oak Road" (JLC, *Armies*, p. 106). However, he mentioned other reasons, including Grant's suggestion to remove Warren if he found it necessary, Sheridan's dislike of Warren's handling a corps, his "self-centered manner and temperament and habit generally, and his rather injudicious way of expressing his opinion on tender topics" (ibid., p. 176). JLC discusses the battle, Warren, Sheridan, and others in *Armies*, pp. 153–81.

59. JLC, *Armies*, p. 179. Perhaps prompting this moving observation, Warren had written to JLC expressing in poignant terms the meaning of his ordeal: "This trial—so hard upon one in my case,—I have sought, waited for,

endured. Out of it, I come a free man again before my countrymen. . . . The *facts* are now fully published. After this, I shall not fear that kindness to me may have arisen from ignorance of the facts" (Warren to JLC, June 11, 1881, LC). JLC also commented: "General Warren felt that the revelation of the facts was of the nature of vindication" (*Armies*, p. 179).

Many implied that Warren's death was, indirectly at least, attributable to what they considered his grossly unfair treatment at the hands of Sheridan: see John Haley to JLC, Dec. 20, 1902, MHS; *Baltimore American*, Jan. 29, 1902; and many others. JLC's position was clear. He could only "wonder at the courage" of such a court, inferring judgment of the propriety of the actions of the superior officer of all its members. Court members were general officers of the Regular Army, as were some witnesses (JLC, *Armies*, pp. 178–79). No one questioned the right of General Sheridan to remove Warren, of course; the hearing was held to examine the actions of General Warren. JLC felt strongly enough about the events of the last campaign of the Army of the Potomac being made known that he prepared *The Passing of the Armies* before his planned book about Gettysburg, which was never completed. Other issues than injustice to Warren, however, motivated him to tell the story of the "great scenes" he had witnessed. JLC always had a great deal of admiration for Grant, although he criticized some of his actions.

60. JLC, *Armies*, pp. 148, 151–52; *History, 118th Pennsylvania*, p. 648; Gerrish, *Army Life*, pp. 34–46; *Under the Maltese Cross*, pp. 352, 667. Quotation, JLC, *Armies*, p. 148. Sheridan sent a formal appointment to Griffin immediately after Warren was removed. Griffin was promoted above General Crawford, who was Griffin's senior in rank.

61. JLC, *Armies*, pp. 152–54. Quotations, pp. 152, 153.

62. Andrews, *The North Reports*, pp. 630–31; *New York World*, Apr. 4, 1865; *New York World* dispatches, JLC Letterbook, PHS. Quotations, ibid. The newspaperman was again George Alfred Townsend. This widely read story established his reputation as an excellent reporter. "Gravelly Run" was the name used for the battle of the White Oak Road on March 31.

63. JLC, *Armies*, p. 155; *OR* 46(1):859, 866, 879, 881, 897, 1105. JLC thought better results would have been had, and the whole pursuit of Lee to Appomattox might have been avoided, had they turned the Claiborne flank of the Confederate entrenched line and cut the South Side Railroad at Sutherland Station on March 31 (JLC, *Armies*, p. 175).

64. *New York World*, Apr. 4, 1865; *New York World* dispatches, JLC Letterbook, PHS; *History, 118th Pennsylvania*, pp. 582–83; Gerrish, *Army Life*, pp. 245–46. Quotation, *History, 118th Pennsylvania*, p. 583. Townsend added, "It is probable that the stupendous events about to occur will so overshadow all individual griefs and excellencies, that we shall never have full lists either of the suffering or the deserving of the battle of Five Forks." Warren reported that the Fifth Corps captured eleven Confederate battle flags and one four-gun battery with caissons. Fifth Corps casualties were 634 (*OR* 46[1]:836).

They were broken down by Col. Frederick Locke for the Warren CI as follows: Warren's Cavalry Escort, 1; First Division, 125; Second Division, 208; Third Division, 300 (*PWCI*, p. 1317). Fox gives total casualties for the battle as 884, which included the cavalry (Fox, *Regimental Losses*, p. 549). JLC's First Brigade took four Confederate battle flags (*OR* 46[1]:851).

65. Porter, *Grant*, pp. 442–44. On the way to Grant's headquarters, Porter's orderly shouted the news of the victory to a soldier who only thumbed his nose at them and yelled, "No, you don't—April Fool!"

66. *OR* 46(1):678, 1106; Humphreys, *Virginia Campaign*, pp. 354–55; JLC, *Armies*, pp. 184–85.

67. *OR* 46(1):679, 1106; Humphreys, *Virginia Campaign*, pp. 366, 367.

68. *OR* 46(1):679. Humphreys stated later that Miles had assured him, upon inspecting the Confederates' entrenched position, that he could defeat them. Humphreys then rejoined his other two divisions, already marching toward Petersburg (Humphreys, *Virginia Campaign*, p. 368).

69. *OR* 46(1):679–80, 1106. Quotation, p. 1106. Sheridan declared in his official report, "I afterward regretted giving up this division, as I believe the enemy could at that time have been crushed at Sutherland's Depot" (ibid., p. 1106). JLC thought that Sheridan's quest for personal glory caused him to refuse the opportunity to decisively defeat the enemy when he was no farther than two miles from the point of attack: "When he thought that Miles had been ordered to resume relations with his own corps commander, Sheridan wanted to have nothing to do with the fight" (JLC, *Armies*, p. 188). Citing Adam Badeau's *Military History of U. S. Grant*, 3:624, JLC quotes Grant's military secretary as stating, "Grant, however, intended to leave Sheridan in full control of all the operations in this quarter of the field; and supposing his views to have been carried out, it was at this juncture that he ordered Humphreys to be faced to the right and moved toward Petersburg" (JLC, *Armies*, p. 187). Grant evidently had Meade issue the actual order to Humphreys.

At the Warren CI, Sheridan said that it was Miles, under his command, who had routed the Confederates from their trenches at the Claiborne and White Oak Roads and captured eight hundred of them who could not get across the bridge at Gravelly Run and the Claiborne Road. "I was there and saw them go. . . . Then I came back as soon as I found they had gone from there. I didn't care about them anymore. . . . I saw General Humphreys' corps; and I saw General Humphreys. I told him it was not any use for me to go up there, and I went back so as to get to the railroad as quick as I could" (*PWCI*, Sheridan testimony, pp. 127, 128). In his memoirs, Sheridan's last version was that he was unwilling to cause hard feelings, so he had relinquished command of Miles and left with the Fifth Corps. After that, Sheridan continued, Miles was left to his own devices by Humphreys, who left later at an order from Grant (Sheridan, *Sheridan*, 2:172, 173). Correspondence in *OR* 46(3):468, 470, gives some additional contemporary information.

70. JLC, *Armies*, pp. 192–93; JLC, "Petersburg and Appomattox," p. 179; *OR* 46(1):851. JLC noted that the train was captured about 1:00 P.M. and had no trouble passing Sutherland Station to the east at that hour (JLC, *Armies*, p. 193).

71. *OR* 46(1):851; JLC, *Armies*, pp. 193–94.

72. Humphreys, *Virginia Campaign*, p. 368; *OR* 46(1):851; JLC, *Armies*, p. 194. JLC thought that Sheridan, by taking his infantry the roundabout way back through Five Forks and leaving Miles to take more than three assaults in three hours to defeat the Rebels alone, caused much time to be lost, and that many Confederates escaped who might not have otherwise. And, JLC noted, not only had Sheridan possibly imperiled more than Crawford did by his detour at Five Forks, where Warren was the chief victim, but here he "came perilously near . . . to being found 'not in the fight'!" (JLC, *Armies*, p. 190). To add to the injury, JLC wrote that in his *Memoirs* (2:451), Grant said of the battle at Sutherland Station that "Sheridan took the enemy . . . on the reverse side where Miles was, and the two together captured the place, with a large number of prisoners and some pieces of artillery, and put the remainder, portions of three Confederate corps, to flight" (JLC, *Armies*, pp. 190–91). Worried about Miles's division some hours later, however, Meade sent Humphreys to reinforce him, but when Humphreys reunited with his division commander, the battle was already over. Humphreys drily opined: "Probably the whole [Confederate] force would have been captured in the morning had the Second Corps continued its march toward Sutherland Station" (Humphreys, *Virginia Campaign*, pp. 368–69; quotation, p. 69).

Putting all this on record meant a great deal to JLC. Although he respected the fighting qualities of both men, he felt that better men than Sheridan were slighted or ruined by Sheridan's personal ambitions and Grant's favoritism. In his introductory to *Armies*, JLC said, "I confess some embarrassments of a personal nature in giving forth certain passages of this record. These facts, however simply stated, cannot but have some bearing on points which have been drawn into controversy on the part of persons who were dear to me as commanders and companions in arms, and who have grown still dearer in the intimacies of friendship since the war. Alas! that no one of them can answer my greeting across the bar. I feel therefore under increased responsibility in recounting these things, but assure myself that I know of no demand of personality or partisanship which should make me doubtful of my ability to tell the truth as I saw and knew it, or distrust my judgment in forming an opinion" (JLC, *Armies*, pp. xvi, xvii).

73. JLC, *Armies*, pp. 194–95.

74. Ibid., p. 195.

75. *OR* 46(1):1264–65.

76. Ibid., pp. 55–56.

77. JLC, *Armies*, pp. 194–95; *OR* 46(1):839, 1106. Quotation, JLC, *Armies*, p. 195.

78. JLC, *Armies*, pp. 197–99; *OR* 46(1):839, 1106–7.

79. *OR* 46(1):604, 840, 852, 905; JLC, *Armies*, pp. 199–201. Quotation, ibid., p. 201. Sheridan stated in his official report that he returned the Fifth Corps at General Meade's request.

80. *OR* 46(1):681–82, 840–41, 905–7, 1107–8. In JLC's opinion, it became plain at this time that Meade was no longer the real commander of the Army of the Potomac, but little more than a figurehead. Grant had joined Sheridan the night of April 5 at Sheridan's urgent summons, and after a conference, Sheridan's plans were substituted for Meade's. On April 6 the exchange of position of the Fifth and Sixth Corps was ordered, as Grant's *Memoirs* (2:473) stated, "to get the Sixth Corps . . . next to the cavalry, with which they had served so harmoniously and so efficiently" (JLC, *Armies*, pp. 205–8).

The fight at Sailor's Creek was a huge success for the Union, with the Confederates losing at least 8,000 in killed, wounded, and prisoners (Humphreys, *Virginia Campaign*, p. 304). However, friction was revealed when Sheridan complained in his official report that even though "the lieutenant-general had notified me that this [Sixth] corps would report to me," and other incidents occurred that acknowledged him as in command, Sixth Corps commander Gen. Horatio G. Wright "declined to make his report to me until directed to do so by the lieutenant-general" (*OR* 46[1]:1108).

81. JLC, *Armies*, pp. 209–15, 219–20; *OR* 46(1):852; "The Surrender of General Lee," *Kennebunk Journal*, Jan. 3, 1868. Quotation, ibid.

82. *OR* 46(1):1266.

83. Ibid.

84. Ibid., pp. 841, 852; ibid. (3):621, 622, 628, 629; JLC, *Armies*, pp. 221, 223; Powell, *Fifth Corps*, p. 849.

85. JLC, *Armies*, pp. 223–24. Quotation, p. 224.

86. *OR* 46(1):841, 1161–62; JLC, *Armies*, pp. 226–27. JLC himself must have been reprimanded for allowing his men to rest during this march. He was noted among the men of the division for paying attention to their needs on a march and allowing them to rest whenever opportunity arose; he was flexible rather than rigid in his interpretation of regulations in order to conserve their strength. Aside from humanitarian and morale questions, his methods were the most efficient use of manpower, as he lost fewer men and those remaining were in better condition to fight if called upon, a fact not lost on some of his more discerning superiors. One of the Twentieth Maine veterans stated that JLC was reprimanded many times by his superiors for "tardy marching," which was corrected, in JLC's hand, to "for too frequent rests." There was also a story recounted that on a day in which JLC had the advance in the pursuit of Lee to Appomattox, the men remained cheerful in spite of the hard marching. One said, "It's all right, Chamberlain is a head [*sic*]—he'll make it easy for us in the end" (George W. Carleton to the Adjutant General of Maine, Jan. 8, 1866, FPYU).

87. JLC, *Armies*, pp. 227–28; Gerrish, *Army Life*, p. 253; *History, 118th Pennsylvania*, p. 587. Quotations, JLC, *Armies*, p. 227.

88. JLC, *Armies*, pp. 229–30; *OR* 46(3):654; Humphreys, *Virginia Campaign*, p. 396.

89. JLC, *Armies*, p. 230. Similarly worded dispatches from Sheridan appear in *OR* 46(3):653, 654.

90. JLC, *Armies*, p. 231; JLC, "Third Brigade at Appomattox," p. 334. Quotations, JLC, *Armies*.

91. JLC, *Armies*, pp. 231–32; Gerrish, *Army Life*, p. 254; JLC, "Third Brigade at Appomattox," p. 335. Quotation, JLC, *Armies*, p. 232.

92. JLC, "Third Brigade at Appomattox," p. 335; *OR* 46(1):852; JLC, *Armies*, pp. 232–33. Quotations, ibid.

93. JLC, *Armies*, pp. 233–34; Porter, *Grant*, p. 438. Quotation, JLC, *Armies*, p. 234.

94. JLC, *Armies*, p. 234; JLC, "Third Brigade at Appomattox," p. 335; *OR* 46(1):852, 855; *MAGR, 1864–1865*, pt. 1, 1:469; *Maine at Gettysburg*, p. 284; *Under the Maltese Cross*, p. 694. The *New York Freeman's and Catholic Journal*, April 22, 1865, has the First and Second (Gregory's) Brigades of the First Division, Fifth Corps, deployed on either side of the Third Brigade.

95. JLC, *Armies*, pp. 234–37. Quotation, pp. 236–37. JLC thought, "We must believe that it was by one of those mysterious overrulings of Providence, or what some might call poetic justice, and some the irony of history, that it befell Sheridan to have with him . . . at Appomattox Court House . . . the deprecated, but inexpugnable, old Fifth Corps" (JLC, *Armies*, p. 112).

96. JLC, *Armies*, pp. 234–35. Quotation, p. 235.

97. Ibid., pp. 235–36. Quotation, p. 236.

98. Ibid., pp. 236–37.

99. Ibid., pp. 237–38; *Maine at Gettysburg*, pp. 283–84.

100. Ibid., p. 284; *New York Freeman's and Catholic Journal*, Apr. 22, 1865; JLC, *Armies*, p. 238; JLC, "Third Brigade at Appomattox," p. 336; *Under the Maltese Cross*, p. 694; JLC, "Appomattox," p. 7; JLC, "Remarks Made to the Bowdoin Club," n.p. In a letter dated April 1, 1906, and published in *Under the Maltese Cross* on pp. 693–94, JLC said that Bartlett's skirmishers did not cover his front because of Sheridan's summons breaking him from the main body of the Fifth Corps.

101. JLC, *Armies*, pp. 238, 239; JLC, "Third Brigade at Appomattox," p. 336. Quotation, JLC, *Armies*, p. 239. JLC crossed Plain Run near the Sears house.

102. JLC, "Third Brigade at Appomattox," p. 336; JLC, *Armies*, pp. 239–40; *Under the Maltese Cross*, p. 694; Schaff, *Sunset*, p. 222. First quotation, *Under the Maltese Cross*; second, JLC, *Armies*, p. 240. The right of JLC's skirmish line was at the Mrs. Wright house when the flag of truce came in, but the troops did not stop until the order to halt came. JLC stated that he was across the

Lynchburg Road when hostilities ceased (*OR* 46(1):852; JLC, "Petersburg and Appomattox," *Bangor Daily Commercial* version; JLC, "Remarks Made to the Bowdoin Club, n.p.).

103. JLC, *Armies*, pp. 240–41; *Under the Maltese Cross*, p. 694; Schaff, *Sunset*, p. 241. Quotation, JLC, *Armies*, p. 241. JLC always maintained that he was the first to receive a flag of truce. In a letter to the veterans of the 155th Pennsylvania Regiment in 1906, he stated that after hearing many stories of "the flag of truce" coming to this or that man, he had "almost begun . . . to doubt if I was there after all" (*Under the Maltese Cross*, p. 693) and that it might lead "the readers of history . . . [to suspect] that our memories were somewhat confused or possibly our habit of truth telling" (JLC, *Armies*, p. 241n). JLC identified the two Confederate officers described, one alone and one with Colonel Whitaker, as "Capt. P. M. Jones, now U.S. District Court judge in Alabama, and Capt. Brown of Georgia" (ibid.). Subsequent checking of numerous accounts has led many veterans and historians of the war to conclude that there were several flags of truce sent out and that the bearers stopped at several points along the lines.

104. JLC, *Armies*, pp. 241–42; *New York Freeman's and Catholic Journal*, Apr. 22, 1865; *OR* 46(1):852. First quotation, JLC, *Armies*, p. 241; second, ibid., p. 242. Capt. Hiram Clark was reportedly killed on the skirmish line. His death was thought by many Fifth Corps writers to be the final one in the Appomattox lines. JLC agreed but added, "The honor of this last death is not a proper subject of quarrel" (JLC, *Armies*, p. 242n).

105. JLC, *Armies*, pp. 242–43; Schaff, *Sunset*, p. 243. First quotation, JLC, *Armies*, p. 242; second, Schaff, *Sunset*.

106. JLC, *Armies*, pp. 244–45; Tom Chamberlain to Sae, Apr. 11 [12], 1865, MHS; JLC to Fannie, Apr. 19, 1865, WP; *New York Freeman's and Catholic Journal*, Apr. 22, 1865. The latter stated that the skirmish lines were moved to the edge of town for convenience.

107. JLC, *Armies*, pp. 244–45. Quotations, p. 245. Sheridan's profanity is only implied in *Armies*.

108. Ibid., p. 245.

109. Ibid., p. 246; JLC, "Petersburg and Appomattox," *Bangor Daily Commercial* version; Warner, *Generals in Gray*, p. 182. Quotation, JLC, *Armies*. JLC states in "Petersburg and Appomattox" that the bronze tablet marking the place of the last meeting of Grant and Lee on April 10, 1865, (which was in place when he visited the deserted and tumbled-down village in 1903,) was on the ground between his lines at the cessation of hostilities on April 9, 1865. He was near it when he had to turn in his saddle to see Lee pass behind him. See JLC, "Petersburg and Appomattox," *Bangor Daily Commercial* version.

110. JLC, *Armies*, pp. 246–47; JLC, "Petersburg and Appomattox," *Bangor Daily Commercial* version. Quotation, JLC, *Armies*, p. 247.

111. Porter, *Grant*, pp. 472, 475; *OR* 46(1):57, 58.

112. Porter, *Grant*, pp. 475–83; *OR* 46(1):58. Quotation, Porter, *Grant*, p. 480. In "Last Salute" (*Boston Journal*, May 1901), JLC emphatically denied rumors that he had claimed to have accepted the surrender of Lee's sword at Appomattox, or indeed, that he had ever accepted the sword. These rumors had "even gotten into the newspapers," he added. JLC's granddaughters were asked questions about the matter into the 1950s, and the writer was asked if it were true at a lecture in Maine in the mid-1980s.

113. JLC, *Armies*, p. 218.

114. Agassiz, *Meade's Headquarters*, pp. 357–58.

115. *Missouri Republican*, July 10, 1886; Norton, *Little Round Top*, p. 180; *OR* 46(2):411, 413. Quotation, *Missouri Republican*, July 10, 1886.

116. JLC, "Third Brigade at Appomattox," p. 337; E. M. Woodward, *One Hundred and Ninety-eighth Pennsylvania*, pp. 58, 59; Agassiz, *Meade's Headquarters*, p. 358; Porter, *Grant*, p. 486; Thomas Edwards to his sister, Apr. 15, 1865, in Milgram, *Abraham Lincoln Illustrated*, p. 258. Quotation, Agassiz, *Meade's Headquarters*.

117. JLC, "Third Brigade at Appomattox," p. 338; *Missouri Republican*, July 10, 1886; Schraff, *Sunset*, p. 277.

118. Tom Chamberlain to Sae, Apr. 11 [12], 1865, MHS; *Missouri Republican*, July 10, 1886. Quotation, ibid.

119. *History, 118th Pennsylvania*, p. 57.

CHAPTER TEN

1. Dr. Adams diary, Apr. 10, 1865, FPC; Stanley and Hall, *Eastern Maine*, p. 199. Quotation, ibid.

2. *OR* 46(3):666; JLC, *Armies*, pp. 248, 251; JLC, "Last Salute," p. 360; JLC to Gen. Henry Merriam, Jan. 23, 1906, in *Colby Library Quarterly*, ser. 7, no. 8 (Dec. 1966): 348. JLC said that when Grant left he told "Gibbon and Griffin (Sheridan had gone) that I was to command that phalanx. So they told me, officially." General Merritt was not present when JLC was given his orders (ibid.). General Lee appointed Lt. Gen. James Longstreet, Maj. Gen. John Gordon, and Brig. Gen. W. N. Pendleton as Confederate representatives to carry out the details of the surrender (*OR* 46[3]:666–67). Accounts vary on when JLC was told of his appointment to command the surrender parade. April 10 is most likely, although his summons may have come about midnight on the ninth (JLC, "Third Brigade at Appomattox," p. 338; JLC, *Armies*, p. 248; JLC, "Last Salute," p. 360; JLC, "Appomattox," p. 14). The junior general on the field in lineal rank, JLC wondered why he was chosen: "I never thought of claiming any special merit, nor tried to attract attention in any way, and believed myself unpopular with the 'high boys.' I had never indulged in loose talk, had minded my own business, did not curry favor with newspaper reporters, did not hang around superior headquarters." He modestly concluded that patience, a "virtue not prominent among my natu-

ral endowments," and uncomplaining willingness during his career to serve where asked, up and down in prestige, had been the deciding factors. He also thought that "General Griffin had something to do with General Grant's kind remembrance." See JLC, *Armies*, pp. 254–57.

3. JLC, *Armies*, pp. 249, 251; JLC to Sae, Apr. 13, 1865, BC; JLC to Fannie, Apr. 19, 1865, WP; *OR* 46(3):668, 691. Quotation, JLC to Fannie, Apr. 19, 1865. After Five Forks, when the ranking General Bartlett became commander of the First Division, JLC was senior in the division and could have taken command of the Third Brigade immediately. He apparently elected, however, to continue as First Brigade commander and temporary commander of General Gregory's brigade until Appomattox.

4. JLC, *Armies*, pp. 248–49; JLC, "Petersburg and Appomattox," pp. 180–81; *OR* 46(3):706. First quotation, JLC, *Armies*, p. 249; others, ibid., p. 248. Mackenzie's cavalry had earlier received the surrender of a portion of the Confederate cavalry. The plaques set out later by the government marking the left and right of his lines in the surrender ceremony read "April 11, 1865." JLC thought the error was made because of the delay from the original date of April 11 to April 12 (JLC, "Petersburg and Appomattox," pp. 180–81).

5. JLC, "The Old Flag."

6. JLC, "Last Salute," p. 361; JLC, *Armies*, p. 259; JLC, "Third Brigade at Appomattox," p. 340; *OR* 46(3):691. The regiments of the Third Brigade, from JLC's position on the right toward the west, were Thirty-second Massachusetts, First Maine Sharpshooters, Twentieth Maine, First Michigan, Sixteenth Michigan, and Eighty-third, Ninety-first, 118th, and 155th Pennsylvania. Some contained remnants of other regiments from their states. See JLC to Sae, Apr. 13, 1865, BC; JLC, "Last Salute," p. 361; *OR* 46(1):569.

7. JLC, *Armies*, pp. 258, 260; Schaff, *Sunset*, p. 298; JLC to Sae, Apr. 13, 1865, BC; JLC, "Last Salute," pp. 360–61.

8. JLC, "Third Brigade at Appomattox," p. 341; JLC, "Petersburg and Appomattox," *Bangor Daily Commercial* version; *Missouri Republican*, July 10, 1886.

9. *Missouri Republican*, July 10, 1886.

10. JLC, *Armies*, p. 261; JLC, "Third Brigade at Appomattox," p. 341; Schaff, *Sunset*, p. 215. Quotation, ibid.

11. JLC, *Armies*, pp. 260, 261; JLC, "Third Brigade at Appomattox," p. 340; JLC, "Last Salute," pp. 361, 362. JLC realized that criticism would follow his decision to mark the "momentous occasion" with the salute of arms. He added that he could say that it was to commemorate the cause of the Confederate flag going down before the flag of the Union, but his main reason was to salute "men whom neither toils and sufferings, nor the fact of death, nor disaster, nor hopelessness could bend from their resolve; standing before us now, thin, worn, and famished, but erect, and with eyes looking

level into ours, waking memories that bound us together as no other bond;—was not such manhood to be welcomed back into a Union so tested and assured?" (JLC, *Armies*, p. 260).

12. JLC, "Last Salute," p. 362; Gordon, *Reminiscences*, p. 444. Also see L. S. Merrick to JLC, Feb. 22, 1902, MHS. Quotation, Gordon, *Reminiscences*.

13. JLC, "Third Brigade at Appomattox," p. 341; JLC, *Armies*, p. 261. Quotations, ibid.

14. JLC, *Armies*, pp. 261–62; JLC, "Last Salute," pp. 362–63.

15. JLC, *Armies*, pp. 262–65; JLC to Sae, Apr. 13, 1865, BC. First quotation, ibid.; second, JLC, *Armies*, p. 265.

16. JLC, *Armies*, p. 259; "The Surrender of General Lee," *Kennebunk Journal*, Jan. 3, 1868. First quotation, JLC, *Armies*; second quotation, "The Surrender of General Lee."

17. *History, 118th Pennsylvania*, pp. 595–96; Agassiz, *Meade's Headquarters*, p. 361. Quotation, *History, 118th Pennsylvania*, p. 596.

18. *History, 118th Pennsylvania*, p. 595. Although the old soldiers who wrote the *History of the 118th Pennsylvania* tried to give the impression that their regiment stood at the McLean house, the courthouse building actually stood directly across the Lynchburg Pike, with the road circling it, and the McLean house was located west of the courthouse. It would have been extremely awkward for the lines to have extended that far. In his 1903 visit, Chamberlain noted with satisfaction the placement of a government marker near the courthouse marking the left of his command for the surrender parade. He went on to specify that his place on the right of the division was marked "300 yards further on" (JLC, "Petersburg and Appomattox," p. 180). This would place the left of the division east of the courthouse. JLC said that when he heard the Wise disturbance, he "rode down the line" to see the cause (JLC, *Armies*, p. 266).

19. "The Surrender of General Lee," *Kennebunk Journal*, Jan. 3, 1868; Dr. Adams diary, May 17, 1865, FPC. Quotation, "The Surrender of General Lee."

20. "The Surrender of General Lee," *Kennebunk Journal*, Jan. 3, 1868. Gen. Charles Griffin actually gave JLC credit for having to use only two regiments in his encounter with Wise and Wallace, although reinforcements arrived at the end: "On the Quaker road, March 29, 1865, in which with his single brigade, consisting of the One hundred and ninety-eighth Pennsylvania Volunteers and the One hundred and eighty-fifth New York Volunteers, successfully withstood and repulsed the attack of a vastly superior force of the enemy" (*OR* 46[3]:731).

21. "The Surrender of General Lee," *Kennebunk Journal*, Jan. 3, 1868; JLC, *Armies*, p. 269. Quotations, "The Surrender of General Lee." JLC did not mention General Wise's name in his book, as he did in the speech reported in 1868, but when he recounted the incident in *Armies*, he left this hint: "'The wise man foreseeth the evil and hideth himself, but the foolish pass

on and are punished, says the old proverb.' If there are no exceptions to this rule, then this gentleman was not rightly named" (*Armies*, p. 269). Wise died in 1876, without ever seeking amnesty or restoration of his civil rights (Warner, *Generals in Gray*, p. 342).

22. JLC, *Armies*, p. 269; J. W. Jones, *Personal Reminiscences*, p. 309; L. B. Eaton to JLC, July 30, 1901, WP; JLC to L. B. Eaton, Aug. 1, 1901, WP. First and last quotations, J. W. Jones, *Personal Reminiscences*; second, JLC to L. B. Eaton, Aug. 1, 1901. L. B. Eaton, an admirer and a native of North Carolina, wrote JLC, beginning with "My dear sir: Let love of chivalry be a stranger's excuse for writing." He quoted JLC's words from *Personal Reminiscences* and then, after further compliments, wished him health and comfort "in the decline of your life." JLC replied in a letter, briefly describing the scene at the surrender ceremony, commenting on the bravery of North Carolinians, and expressing a desire to meet Eaton. He ended with his characteristic optimism: "I accept with gratitude your good wishes for what you naturally consider my 'declining years.' I do not feel as if my years were declining,—except as to their numerical remainder. In all that makes their value I look upon them as mounting. 'The best is yet to be.' God grant it may so be with you." The exchange was a subject of an approving editorial in the *New Orleans Times-Democrat*, which was reprinted in the Chamberlain Association's *JLC: A Sketch*, pp. 35–36. In an unpublished manuscript ("General Chamberlain," no author [but deduced from the contents to be written by Edgar O. Achorn, Bowdoin graduate of 1881], n.d., BC), a former student of JLC's wrote about a 1901 conversation he had had with him in which he specifically asked the origin of the Confederate flag he had seen in JLC's library as a student. JLC told him the story of the tardy regiment's color-bearer and said that the flag was later given to him to keep by a superior officer, whom Achorn identified as Grant. Since Grant had left the field by that time, Achorn must have remembered incorrectly. However, the identity of the flag of the unknown regiment is borne out in an article in the *Lewiston Journal*, August [?], 1907, featuring an interview with JLC about his house and its contents, with photographs. A description of JLC's home library includes the statement, "While on one wall is the last flag surrendered by Lee on the field of Appomattox." JLC apparently did not remember to which Confederate regiment the flag belonged, if he ever knew.

23. JLC, *Armies*, p. 269. Johnson and Buel, *Battles and Leaders*, 4:753, gives the numbers of Confederates finally paroled at Appomattox as 28,231. Grant, in his *Memoirs*, p. 500, stated 28,356, plus 19,132 captured between March 29 and April 9. This does not count others killed, wounded, and missing during Lee's flight. Many of these were without arms. JLC wrote that "15000 stands of arms & 72 flags were stacked before my line" (on April 12) (JLC to Sae, Apr. 13, 1865, BC). Elsewhere he mentions seventy-three battle flags, which apparently includes the surrendered one later described in the Achorn manuscript cited above (JLC to Fannie, Apr. 19, 1865, WP). In *Ar-*

mies, JLC estimates "27,000 men paroled, 17,000 stands of arms laid down or gathered up; a hundred battleflags" (*Armies*, p. 270). His count of the arms and battle flags in the latter must have represented more than those taken at Appomattox, perhaps those of the campaign. Gen. John Gibbon reported to General Grant on April 13, 1865, that between 25,000 and 30,000 men had been paroled, with 140 pieces of artillery, 10,000 small arms, and 71 flags (*OR* 46[3]:734). Powell gives Confederates paroled as: officers, 2,862; enlisted men, 25,494; total, 28,356. Total Fifth Corps losses in the Appomattox campaign were: killed, 267; wounded, 1,743; missing, 551; total, 2,561 (Powell, *Fifth Corps*, pp. 868–69).

24. JLC, *Armies*, p. 270.

25. Ibid., pp. 271–72; *OR* 46(3):709–10.

26. Gerrish, *Army Life*, pp. 264–65; JLC, *Armies*, p. 273; *OR* 46(3):731; Spear, "The Hoecake of Appomattox," pp. 8, 9.

27 *OR* 46(3):730–731, 1011; Dr. Adams diary, May 20, 1865, FPC. First two quotations, *OR* 46(3):731; third, ibid., p. 1011. General Griffin recommended JLC for the brevet to major general on April 13, 1865, and recommended him for the rank of full major general April 29, 1865. JLC and others became distressed at the cheapening of the honor of the brevet caused by the wholesale distribution of them after hostilities ended. Some were awarded to the undeserving, while other officers did not receive them due to the differences in the policies of commanding generals. JLC finally decided to "keep up with the best" in his own brevet promotions, so that his men would not suffer injustice in comparison with other commands. In addition, Washington developed a sweeping policy of granting brevets of one grade to everyone who asked for it; some commissions were even antedated to precede the heavy fighting in the last campaign, making the recipients "rank" men who had received them for valor in battle. See JLC, *Armies*, pp. 388–89, quotation, p. 389; Warner, *Generals in Blue*, pp. xvi, xvii.

28. JLC, *Armies*, p. 272; JLC, "Third Brigade at Appomattox," p. 342. Quotation, ibid.

29. Gerrish, *Army Life*, pp. 268–70; JLC, *Armies*, pp. 273–76.

30. JLC, *Armies*, pp. 276–77. Quotations, p. 277.

31. JLC to Fannie, Apr. 19, 1865, WP.

32. JLC, *Armies*, pp. 277–79. First quotation, p. 278; second, p. 279. JLC's fears were justified. A private in the Twentieth Maine describes the dark, deep feelings within the men when they heard of Lincoln's death (Gerrish, *Army Life*, p. 271).

33. JLC, *Armies*, p. 279.

34. Ibid., pp. 280–82. JLC said later that these fears might be "smiled at" in retrospect, but with the confusion in the country at the time, both North and South, it was not unlikely that a crisis might exist, and a plot to destroy the government of the United States by assassination could be possible (ibid., pp. 281–82).

35. Ibid., pp. 282–83; JLC, "Abraham Lincoln," p. 24; *History, 118th Pennsylvania*, p. 598; Powell, *Fifth Corps*, p. 870; JLC to Fannie, Apr. 19, 1865, WP.

36. JLC, *Armies*, pp. 283–86; JLC, "Abraham Lincoln," pp. 24, 25; JLC to Fannie, Apr. 19, 1865, WP; E. M. Woodward, *One Hundred and Ninety-eighth Pennsylvania*, p. 62. First two quotations, JLC to Fannie, Apr. 19, 1865; third, JLC, *Armies*, p. 286.

37. JLC to Fannie, Apr. 19, 1865, WP.

38. *OR* 46(3):863, 922–924, 995; ibid. 51(1):1216; Ellis Spear diary, Apr. 20, 1864, in possession of Abbott Spear, Warren, Maine; JLC, *Armies*, pp. 287–90. General Bartlett probably transferred voluntarily. He seemed constantly at odds in some way with his division and corps commanders in the Fifth Corps. He was brevetted major general, apparently not through regular channels (*OR* 46[2]:193, 328, 362, 363, 519, 741, 965, 966), but was recommended for the full rank of major general by Griffin (ibid. [3]:1011). Meade recommended him for full major general in the Regular Army (ibid., p. 1259), but it was not confirmed (Warner, *Generals in Blue*, p. 24). He was called to testify at the Warren Court of Inquiry as a witness for General Sheridan, and his testimony revealed an unfriendly attitude toward Generals Warren, Griffin, and Chamberlain. JLC may have acted as division commander before the official date of April 20, though technically he was still commander of the Third Brigade.

39. JLC, *Armies*, pp. 288–90; Quotations, p. 289.

40. Ibid., pp. 289–91; Gerrish, *Army Life*, pp. 274, 277. First two quotations, JLC, *Armies*, p. 290; third, ibid., p. 291. JLC's account was somewhat sympathetic to the plight of the freed slaves, but his chiefly expressed concern was the plight of the "citizens" in his jurisdiction, "citizens of our common country we had fought to preserve. Had they been not so, humanity and honor would have commanded our aid" (JLC, *Armies*, p. 288). In civil matters, JLC generally filled the role expected of him, consistent with his opposition to disunion and slavery, with his part enlarged by his sense of humanity and fairness.

41. JLC, *Armies*, pp. 293–94, 298–99. Quotations, p. 294.

42. Ibid., pp. 299–300.

43. Ibid., pp. 300–302; *History, 118th Pennsylvania*, p. 601.

44. *OR* 46(3):562; JLC, *Armies*, pp. 302–3; E. G. Taylor, *Warren*, p. 234.

45. *Under the Maltese Cross*, pp. 378–79; JLC, *Armies*, p. 303.

46. JLC, *Armies*, pp. 304–5. Quotation, p. 304.

47. Ibid., pp. 306–7; Gerrish, *Army Life*, pp. 286–87.

48. Gerrish, *Army Life*, pp. 287–88; JLC, *Armies*, pp. 307–8.

49. JLC, *Armies*, pp. 308–10.

50. Gerrish, *Army Life*, pp. 287–89; JLC, *Armies*, pp. 311–13; Cheek and Pointon, *Sauk County Riflemen*, p. 78. Quotation, JLC, *Armies*, p. 313.

51. *Under the Maltese Cross*, p. 379; Gerrish, *Army Life*, pp. 294–95; JLC, *Armies*, pp. 315–17. Quotation, Gerrish, *Army Life*, p. 294. One officer reckoned

that the march of the Fifth Corps from the James to the Potomac Rivers was approximately 150 miles in length and took seven days to make, an average of twenty-one miles a day (E. M. Woodward, *One Hundred and Ninety-eighth Pennsylvania*, p. 63).

52. JLC, *Armies*, pp. 318–19, 328; Gerrish, *Army Life*, p. 294.

53. Dr. Adams diary, May 17, 18, 20, 26, 1865, FPC; Dr. Adams to JLC, Sept. 6, 1864, RC. Other members of JLC's staff, according to Dr. Adams's diary, included Captain Fowler, Adj. Gen., Lieutenant Walters and Lieutenant Vogel, ADC's (both JLC's aides since June 1864), Captain Bean, Captain Cane, Major Ashbrooke, Major Fitch, Captain Donnell, and Dr. DeWitt. Dr. Adams carefully wrote down many of the things that JLC and his staff told him about the last campaign, including losses to JLC's commands in different battles, which are accurate when checked against JLC's figures. Confederate officers' remarks were described.

54. Dr. Adams diary, May 20, 1865, FPC.

55. Ibid., May 21, 22, 1865, FPC; JLC Military Personnel file, NA. Quotation, Dr. Adams diary, May 22, 1865.

56. JLC, *Armies*, p. 321. Dr. Adams also spoke at the gathering, saying that he was too old to go to war but had sent "my boys" from Bowdoin and, to great applause, "my son-in-law." He was delighted when four officers pinned Fifth Corps badges on him after he expressed a desire for one. He reported that JLC's speech was "very good" and Griffin's reply "simple and appropriate" (Dr. Adams diary, May 22, 1865, FPC).

57. Letter to the *Portland Transcript* by Peter Schemthl, in JLC Letterbook, PHS; JLC, *Armies*, pp. 322–24.

58. JLC, *Armies*, p. 325.

59. Dr. Adams diary, May 23, 1865, FPC; JLC, *Armies*, pp. 329, 359; Brooks, *Washington, D.C.*, p. 273; Nevins, *Diary of Battle*, p. 526. The Sixth Corps's grand review was held in Washington on June 8, 1865.

60. JLC, *Armies*, p. 331.

61. Ibid., pp. 330, 331. First quotation, p. 330; second, p. 331.

62. Nevins, *Diary of Battle*, pp. 526–27; Brooks, *Washington, D.C.*, pp. 272–73. Quotation, Nevins, *Diary of Battle*, p. 527.

63. Nevins, *Diary of Battle*, p. 525; Brooks, *Washington, D.C.*, p. 272; JLC, *Armies*, p. 339; Dr. Adams diary, May 23, 1865, FPC; Gen. Fred Locke to JLC, May 22, 1865, MHS; Leech, *Reveille in Washington*, p. 415.

64. Leech, *Reveille in Washington*, p. 415; Brooks, *Washington, D.C.*, pp. 274, 279.

65. JLC, *Armies*, p. 327.

66. Brooks, *Washington, D.C.*, pp. 274–75, 278; Nevins, *Diary of Battle*, p. 525. According to Wainwright, Merritt and Custer were scheduled to join Sheridan immediately after the review. In his memoirs, Sheridan said that he had asked Grant for permission to delay his departure so he could ride in the review, but that Grant refused, giving the reason that his mission, to

obtain the surrender of Kirby Smith, was too important to delay. But Smith had surrendered before Sheridan arrived (Sheridan, *Sheridan*, 2:209, 211). Sheridan was made a lieutenant general when Grant became president of the United States in 1869. After Sherman retired, Sheridan became commanding general of the army in 1884. Just before his death on August 5, 1888, he was given the rank of full general. See Warner, *Generals in Blue*, p. 439.

67. JLC, *Armies*, pp. 334–36. Quotation, p. 336.

68. Ibid., pp. 336–38. Quotations, p. 338. Charles Griffin died of yellow fever at Galveston, Texas, in September 1867 at the age of forty-one (Warner, *Generals in Blue*, pp. 190–91).

69. JLC, *Armies*, pp. 328–30, 338–39; Brooks, *Washington, D.C.*, p. 270. First quotation, JLC, *Armies*, p. 339; second, ibid., p. 328.

70. JLC, *Armies*, pp. 339–40; Gerrish, *Army Life*, pp. 297–98; Charlemagne description, typed manuscript on Surveyor, U.S. Customs Service stationery, UMO.

71. JLC, *Armies*, pp. 339–40. First quotation, p. 339; others, p. 340.

72. Ibid., p. 340; Leech, *Reveille in Washington*, p. 415. Quotation, JLC, *Armies*.

73. JLC, *Armies*, pp. 330, 340–41.

74. Brooks, *Washington, D.C.*, p. 276.

75. JLC, *Armies*, pp. 330, 342. Quotation, p. 342.

76. Newspaper clipping, "The Grand Review," JLC Letterbook, PHS.

77. JLC, *Armies*, p. 342.

78. Ibid., p. 343.

79. Ibid., pp. 343–44.

80. Ibid., pp. 344, 351, 352; JLC, "Blood and Fire," p. 902; JLC from unknown soldier in Company D, Thirty-second Massachusetts Infantry, Sept. 5, 1910, MHS; Robertson, *Michigan in the War*, p. 369. Quotation, JLC, "Blood and Fire."

81. JLC, *Armies*, pp. 344–45.

82. Ibid., p. 345.

83. Ibid.; U.S. War Department, *Atlas*, pl. 175, Fifth Corps, Second Division flag; *MAGR, 1866*, pp. 480–81.

84. JLC, *Armies*, pp. 347–49; U.S. War Department, *Atlas*, pl. 175, Fifth Corps, Third Division flag.

85. JLC, *Armies*, p. 348.

86. Ibid., pp. 349–50; Nevins, *Diary of Battle*, pp. 526, 528.

87. JLC, *Armies*, pp. 351, 353–72. Quotation, p. 351. JLC first wrote an account of the grand review for a MOLLUS paper delivered in May 1906. The review lasted five hours. That day 29 regiments of cavalry, 33 batteries of artillery, and 180 regiments of infantry marched with the Army of the Potomac (Nevins, *Diary of Battle*, p. 529; Brooks, *Washington, D.C.*, p. 279). For JLC's full, moving accounts of the grand reviews, see *Armies*, pp. 326–72.

88. JLC, *Armies*, p. 376; *MAGR, 1864–1865*, 1:287, 337, 370–71, 468–69; Gerrish, *Army Life*, pp. 303, 305, 308–9; Spear diary, May 29, June 10, 1895. Gerrish gives the muster-out date as June 4. Spear was subsequently brevetted brigadier general, and Tom Chamberlain was awarded a brevet to colonel for gallantry at Five Forks (*MAGR, 1867*, pp. 15, 16; ibid., *1864–1865*, 1:337). Both were wounded, neither seriously, in 1864, Spear at the North Anna and Tom at Bethesda Church. Chamberlain's letters until he took the brigade in 1863, plus the histories of the regiment in the *MAGR* reports and Colonel Gilmore's service records in NA and sketch in *MAGR, 1864–1865*, 1:370–71, show Gilmore's absences from the regiment. Ellis Spear became a successful patent attorney after the war, with offices in Washington, St. Louis, and Boston, and for a time was U.S. Commissioner of Patents. After his first wife died in 1873, he married the widow of his Twentieth Maine friend, Capt. Samuel Keene, who was killed by a sniper at Petersburg June 21, 1864. (Information provided to the writer by Abbott Spear.) Walter G. Morrill returned to Maine and in 1876 began promoting horse races, a practice he continued for fifty-five years. Morrill died in March 1935 at Pittsfield, Maine (Vickery, "Walter G. Morrill," pp. 127, 149).

89. JLC to Sae, June 6, 1865, BC; *OR* 46(3):1011, original promotion recommendation, JLC Military Personnel file, NA.

90. JLC to Sae, June 6, 1865, BC; JLC to Col. S. F. Chalfin, Oct. 12, 1865, and JLC to Brig. Gen. L. Thomas, Nov. 1, 1865, JLC Military Personnel file, NA. Quotations, JLC to Sae, June 6, 1865.

91. *OR* 46(3):1302; JLC, *Armies*, pp. 391–92. Quotations, ibid.

92. Chamberlain Association, *JLC: A Sketch*, p. 15; *OR* 46(3):1302; JLC, "Abraham Lincoln," p. 17. Organized under the Sixth Corps commander, H. G. Wright, the Provisional Corps was formed from one division each of the Second, Fifth, and Sixth Corps. The First Division, drawn from the Fifth Corps, was commanded by R. B. Ayres and, besides JLC, had Gen. Henry Baxter and Gen. Joseph Hayes as brigade commanders.

93. *MAGR, 1864–1865*, 1:287, 337, 469; Ellis Spear to Gen. J. L. Hodsdon, Mar. 9, 1866, BC; information provided to the writer by Abbott Spear. Quotation, Ellis Spear to Gen. J. L. Hodsdon, Mar. 9, 1866. Tom Chamberlain had been retained in the army by special order of General Meade (JLC to Sae, June 6, 1865, BC). The remnants of the Sixteenth Maine and the First Battalion of Sharpshooters were consolidated into the Twentieth Maine after the original men went home. They were all mustered out July 16, arrived at Portland July 20, and were discharged and finally paid on July 25 (*MAGR, 1866*, p. 538). The Twentieth Maine had a total enrollment of 1,621 (counting replacements and recruits, and its rolls swelled by accessions from disbanded regiments after the war ended), with 9 officers and 138 men killed and mortally wounded and 1 officer and 145 men dead of disease, accidents, in prison, etc., for a total of 293 dead. An additional 381 were wounded besides those who died from their wounds (Fox, *Regimental Losses*, p. 135).

94. *MAGR, 1864–1865,* 1:336; newspaper clipping, "Gen. Grant in Maine," *Boston Journal,* found in John Chamberlain diary, PHS; Sae to JLC, July 30, 1865, RC; Tom Chamberlain to JLC, attached to ibid., RC; JLC to U. S. Grant, July 31, 1865, JLC Letterbook, PHS.

95. Furbish, *Facts about Brunswick,* p. 29; newspaper clipping, "Gen. Grant in Maine," *Boston Journal,* in John Chamberlain diary, PHS.

96. Newspaper clipping, "Commencement Dinner," JLC Letterbook, PHS; Hatch, *Bowdoin College,* p. 122; Furbish, *Facts about Brunswick,* p. 29. Quotation, ibid. One sour note was sounded in the newspaper, describing the dinner as "the meanest repast ever placed before festive mortals."

97. Newspaper clipping, "Commencement at Bowdoin," JLC Letterbook, PHS; standing photo, JLC in brigadier uniform, ca. late 1864 or early 1865, Brady Collection, NA; *carte de visite,* JLC in major general's uniform, by Alexander Campbell, ca. June 1865, WP; Dr. Adams to JLC, Sept. 6, 1864, RC; Dr. Adams diary, Aug. 14–17, 1865, FPC; typed copy, application of Maine delegation to President, Dec. 20, 1865, endorsed by U. S. Grant and Secretary of War Stanton, Jan. 16, 1866, LC; *MAGR, 1864–1865,* 1:336. The baby died August 14. The census of 1900 shows the number of children born to Fannie as five. Grace and Wyllys lived to adulthood; the others were the boy who was born and died in October 1857; Emily Stelle, born and died in 1860; and Gertrude Loraine, born and died in 1865. The names of the two baby girls are on a marker in the family plot in Pine Grove Cemetery, and Dr. Adams mentioned Emily Stelle's name in his diary when she died (Dr. Adams diary, Sept. 26, 1860, FPC). The boy's name, if he had one, is unknown. A biographical sketch written in 1880 states that the Chamberlains had had four children, the informant undoubtedly overlooking the boy who lived only a few minutes (Cleaveland, *Bowdoin College,* p. 672). Contents of a letter from a family friend seems to indicate still another Chamberlain child (Ellen A. Bacon to "My Dear Little Joshua," Oct. 26, 1872, RC). However, considering all the other evidence and the tone of the letter, it is regarded here as perhaps a game of make-believe on the friend's part with another child. JLC's muster-out date was August 24, 1865.

98. Little, *Catalogue,* p. xc; [Gov. Samuel] Cony to [Sen. Lot M.] Morrill, Sept. 5, 1865, JLC Military Personnel file, NA; typed copy, application of Maine delegation to President, Dec. 20, 1865, endorsed by U. S. Grant and Secretary of War Stanton, Jan. 16, 1866, LC; Dr. Adams diary, Dec. 7, 1865, FPC; *Lewiston Journal,* Aug. 1907, PHS; A. Bedford, Tiffany and Co., to JLC, Nov. 15, 1865, in possession of A. A. Warlam, Saddle River, N.J.; receipt for $250 from Tiffany's to JLC, dated Dec. 5, 1865, BC; Fannie to JLC, Mar. 9, 1866, RC. The bracelet consists of two oval gold bands holding twenty-four flat gold hourglass shapes, each engraved with the name of one of the twenty-four battles in which JLC participated. The hourglasses symbolized "the weary hours away from home" during the war (Eleanor Wyllys Allen to President Howell, Feb. 21, 1978, BC). On one side of the oval is a facsimile

of an officer's shoulder board, blue enameled and bordered in gold, with the two gold stars of a major general, each set with a diamond. On the opposite side is an enameled white rectangle bordered with gold, with a red Maltese cross and another centered diamond. The bracelet is now owned by Bowdoin College, the gift in 1978 of Eleanor Wyllys Allen.

99. Cony to Morrill, Sept. 5, 1865, JLC Military Personnel file, NA; typed copy, application of Maine delegation to President, Dec. 20, 1865, endorsed by U. S. Grant and Secretary of War Stanton, Jan. 16, 1866, LC; Rep. John H. Rice to JLC, Jan. 16, 1866, LC.

100. Selden Connor to JLC, Mar. 19, 1908, LC; Pullen, *Twentieth Maine*, p. 3; *MAGR, 1864–1865*, 1:336. First quotation, Selden Connor to JLC, Mar. 19, 1908; second, Pullen, *Twentieth Maine*. Connor was quoting Gen. Alexander Webb.

101. The Thirteenth Amendment to the Constitution of the United States, which abolished slavery, was declared in effect December 18, 1865. Over 600,000 men from both sides died in the conflict from wounds and disease. Many more were maimed for life. These losses devastated the country, which had a total population of about 31 million, including slaves, in 1860.

CHAPTER ELEVEN

1. JLC to Fannie, "Wednesday noon," n.d. (probably Mar. 7, 1866), MHS; Fannie to JLC, Mar. 8, 1866, RC; JLC to Fannie, Mar. 20, 1866, RC; Fannie to JLC, Mar. 19, 1866, RC; JLC to Fannie, Apr. 7, 1866, RC; Fannie to JLC, May 1, 1866, RC; printed army circular, "A History of the Fifth Army Corps . . . ," Aug. 1865, LC. "Gettysburg" and "The Surrender of General Lee" were titles of JLC's popular early talks. He never found time to write a history of the Fifth Corps, although some material for it survives in his papers. The task was ultimately completed by Lt. Col. William H. Powell, and *The Fifth Army Corps* was published in 1896. JLC read Powell's manuscript before it was published (William H. Powell to JLC, Apr. 20, 1894, MHS).

2. JLC to Fannie, Apr. 7, 1866, RC; "Governors of Maine and Their Times," *Portland Sunday Telegram*, July 9, 1911; Sarah D. B. Chamberlain to JLC, "First Day 66," RC. Quotation, ibid.

3. Little, *Catalogue*, History section, pp. lxxxiii, lxxxiv, xc; Catalogue section, p. 3; E. G. Taylor, *Warren*, pp. 237, 239; G. K. Warren to JLC, Aug. 28, 1866, LC; Chamberlain Association, *JLC: A Sketch*, p. 15.

4. "Governors of Maine and Their Times," *Portland Sunday Telegram*, July 9, 1911; Blaine, *Twenty Years of Congress*, 2:220; JLC, *Address of Governor Chamberlain, January, 1867*, p. 9.

5. R. H. Jones, *Disrupted Decades*, pp. 410–12, 420–22; Foner, *Reconstruction*, pp. 199–201.

6. R. H. Jones, *Disrupted Decades*, pp. 412–17, 427–28.

7. Ibid., pp. 428–34; Sarah D. B. Chamberlain to JLC, "First Day 66," RC. Quotation, ibid.

8. Blaine, *Twenty Years of Congress*, 2:179, 213–14; "Governors of Maine," *Portland Sunday Telegram*, July 9, 1911. Other provisions of the amendment confirmed Union war obligations, including pensions, and repudiated Confederate war debts and claims for loss or payment for emancipated slaves. See Foner, *Reconstruction*, pp. 251–61, for an extensive discussion of the Fourteenth Amendment.

9. Chamberlain Association, *JLC: A Sketch*, p. 16; Blaine, *Twenty Years of Congress*, 2:230–31; R. H. Jones, *Disrupted Decades*, p. 439; Foner, *Reconstruction*, pp. 261, 269; JLC, *Address of Governor Chamberlain, January, 1867*, p. 9. JLC's total vote was 69,637 to his opponent's 41,947. At that time, election dates varied by state, extending from September through November, instead of one national date. Before his death, Lincoln had announced a tentative reconstruction plan, which had been partially implemented in Louisiana.

10. JLC, *Address of Governor Chamberlain, January, 1867*, p. 9.

11. Ibid., pp. 5, 6, 8. First two quotations, p. 5; third, pp. 5–6; last, p. 8. When JLC's speech to the Maine legislature was made, the Southern states reconstituted under Johnson's rules had overwhelmingly rejected the Fourteenth Amendment; the speech preceded the passage of the Reconstruction Act of 1867 by Congress. The latter provided for military protection of life and property in the eleven Confederate states except Tennessee and stated the steps with which new governments could be constituted to be accepted back into the Union by Congress, including voting rules and ratification of the Fourteenth Amendment (Foner, *Reconstruction*, pp. 269, 276–77).

12. JLC, *Address of Governor Chamberlain, January, 1867*, p. 9; Foner, *Reconstruction*, p. 446; Chamberlain Association, *JLC: A Sketch*, pp. 18, 19; R. H. Jones, *Disrupted Decades*, p. 411. Quotation, JLC, *Address of Governor Chamberlain, January, 1867*. In his reference to the Fourteenth Amendment's "placing it in the power of the South to introduce into the Constitution a disability founded on race and color," JLC apparently was referring to the provision penalizing a state's representation in Congress proportionately should it deny the right to vote to eligible males. When enacted, it was thought that this provision would encourage states to allow black suffrage, but another interpretation could conclude that if a state took the opposite course, it would have constitutional sanction to withhold the right to vote because of race or color. Foner (*Reconstruction*, pp. 253, 255) reports opposition to the amendment for similar reasons by Radical Republican Senator Charles Sumner and abolitionist activist Wendell Phillips.

13. Chamberlain Association, *JLC: A Sketch*, pp. 16, 19; "Governors of Maine and Their Times," *Portland Sunday Telegram*, July 9, 1911. In 1867 JLC's vote was 57,322 to 45,990, and in 1868 it was 75,523 to 29,264. All three elections were with the same Democratic opponent, Eben F. Pillsbury (ibid.).

The other Maine senator in 1868, Lot M. Morrill, voted for Johnson's impeachment, as did all the U.S. representatives from Maine (Blaine, *Twenty Years of Congress*, 2:285, 360, 375).

14. Chamberlain Association, *JLC: A Sketch*, p. 17; newspaper clipping, "The Maine Election," n.d. (from contents, Sept. 1869), BC; JLC, *Address of Governor Chamberlain, January, 1869*, pp. 11, 14.

15. JLC, *Address of Governor Chamberlain, January, 1869*, pp. 8, 9, 11–13; JLC, *Address of Governor Chamberlain, January, 1867*, pp. 28, 29; JLC to Sarah D. B. Chamberlain, Jan. 27, 1869, BC. First quotation, JLC, *Address of Governor Chamberlain, January, 1867*, p. 29; second, JLC, *Address of Governor Chamberlain, January, 1869*, p. 11; third, JLC to Sarah D. B. Chamberlain, Jan. 27, 1869.

16. JLC to Sarah D. B. Chamberlain, Jan. 27, 1869, BC; Chamberlain Association, *JLC: A Sketch*, p. 17; newspaper clipping, "The Maine Election," BC. Quotation, JLC to Sarah D. B. Chamberlain, Jan. 27, 1869. JLC's inaugural addresses for the four years of his tenure as governor take up many issues he wanted attended to by the legislature, but he sums them up well in *Address of Governor Chamberlain to the Legislature of the State of Maine, January, 1870*.

17. Dr. Adams diary, Nov. 18, 1866, FPC; Little, *Genealogical History*, 1:133; Wilder, *Catalogue*, p. 111; Cleaveland, *Bowdoin College*, pp. 714, 735; *MAGR, 1866*, p. 306; JLC to John Chamberlain, Dec. 19, 1864, BC; JLC to Sae, June 6, 1865, RC; John Chamberlain to JLC, July 7, 1865, RC; newspaper clipping, "Correspondence of the Whig. Augusta, April 1, 1865," found in John Chamberlain diary, PHS; Chamberlain family Bible, Brewer Public Library, Brewer, Maine; Lord, "Early Church Records," #343, Brewer Public Library, Brewer, Maine; Sae to Tom Chamberlain, May 7, 1865, RC; Tom Chamberlain to JLC, Jan. 14, 1867, RC; Tom and Sae Chamberlain to JLC, Jan. 16, 1867, MHS; Sarah D. B. Chamberlain to John Chamberlain, Oct. 8, 1855, RC. Quotation, ibid. Some printed sources list John's death as August 11, but the family Bible and the church records both state August 10. The pulmonary disease was undoubtedly tuberculosis; church records state "consumption," which tuberculosis was formerly called. The family believed that John had contracted it when he served with the Christian Commission in 1863.

18. JLC, *Armies*, p. 386; JLC, *Address of Governor Chamberlain, January, 1869*, p. 8; Chamberlain Association, *JLC: A Sketch*, p. 18; JLC Military Pension records, NA; JLC to Fannie, Nov. 20, 1868, FPYU. First quotation, JLC, *Armies*; second, JLC, *Address of Governor Chamberlain, January, 1869*. JLC was made miserable throughout his life by recurring infections of his bladder, urethra, and the surrounding tissues caused by the damage from the Petersburg minié ball. These infections would spontaneously clear up, aided by a urinary fistula that allowed drainage. The latter "clearly saved his life and prevented long term obstruction or confinement of infection," according to a medical opinion by William H. Annesley, Jr., M.D., prepared in consultation with

John P. Mullooly, M.D. "The fact that the general did well to survive such injury over the ensuing years is a rather remarkable situation based on the described injuries." The writer is indebted to Dr. Mullooly for his description of JLC's Petersburg wound and its physical consequences and to Dr. Annesley for his excellent and descriptive opinion. Both physicians practice at Milwaukee, Wisconsin. Ruth Wise Shaull, R.N., M.S.N., Cincinnati, Ohio, also contributed to the writer's understanding of the injury.

19. Fannie to JLC, Mar. 8, 1866, RC; Fannie to JLC, Mar. 9, 1866, RC; JLC to Fannie, Mar. 20, 1866, RC; Fannie to JLC, Mar. 19, 1866, RC; JLC to Fannie, Apr. 7, 1866, RC; Fannie to JLC, Apr. 15, 1866, RC; JLC to Fannie, Aug. 11, 1868, MHS; newspaper clipping, "Mrs. Chamberlain's Funeral," PHS; interview with Catherine T. Smith, JLC's last secretary, *Brunswick Times-Record*, Sept. 7, 1976; JLC Military Pension records, NA. Catherine Smith was employed by JLC from about 1910 until shortly before his death.

20. JLC to Fannie, Nov. 20, 1868, FPYU; JLC Military Pension records, NA.

21. JLC, *Address of Governor Chamberlain, January, 1869*, pp. 21, 22; Daniel White to C. D. Gilmore, Jan. 12, 1869, FPYU; Johnson and Malone, *Dictionary of American Biography*, 4:197; Chamberlain Association, *JLC: A Sketch*, p. 21. U.S. senators were elected by state legislatures until the Seventeenth Amendment to the Constitution was declared in effect May 31, 1913.

22. "Governors of Maine and Their Times," *Portland Sunday Telegram*, July 9, 1911; broadside, "Republican Mass Meeting," PHS; JLC to D. L. Lane, Aug. 11, 1870, BC; H. M. Haisted [?] to JLC, Sept. 21, 1870, PHS; Blaine, *Twenty Years of Congress*, pp. 549, 695, 701; Chamberlain Association, *JLC: A Sketch*, p. 21. Quotation, JLC to D. L. Lane, Aug. 11, 1870. JLC had some opposition from the prohibition wing of the party in the Republican state convention in June 1869 but was nominated by a two-to-one majority. His vote in the general election was 54,314; his Democratic opponent, Franklin Smith, polled 39,033, and 4,736 votes were cast for a temperance candidate, N. G. Hitchborn. It is perhaps indicative of JLC's state of mind and his life in general in the summer of 1870, during his last year as governor, that he would consider writing to the king of Prussia and offering his services in the Franco-Prussian War, even if he had to resign as governor. He gave no reason for his offer, stating his qualifications and pointing out his knowledge of the language and his sympathy and admiration for the king and his people. No reply has been found in JLC's papers. See JLC to William, King of Prussia, in JLC's hand, marked "copy, translation," July 20, 1870, WP.

23. Chamberlain Association, *JLC: A Sketch*, p. 25; Hatch, *Bowdoin College*, pp. 129, 130; Little, *Catalogue*, Catalogue section, p. 5.

24. Little, *Catalogue*, History section, pp. xc, xci.

25. Ibid., p. xci. Evening chapel service lasted only a few minutes and was a real inconvenience for some men who lived in town rather than on campus; with JLC's reform, no recitation was held before morning chapel as it had been in the past (Hatch, *Bowdoin College*, pp. 290–91).

26. Hatch, *Bowdoin College*, pp. 155–57, 159; Little, *Catalogue*, History section, pp. xci, xcii; JLC's first inaugural address, "The New Education," typescript, BC. An experimental, six-week "Summer School of Science" was tried in 1877, with an enrollment of sixteen men and eleven women, the latter faculty wives and women from the town, and repeated in 1878. It was not offered again, however, with a note in the catalogue that the class was not intended to be permanent (Cross, "Joshua Lawrence Chamberlain," pp. 57, 58, BC).

27. JLC, "The New Education," typescript, BC.

28. Ibid. In 1872 Miss C. F. Low, a student at a women's college, applied to Bowdoin's medical school because she wished to be "graduated on equal terms with my brother students" in Maine, her native state (Miss C. F. Low to C. F. Brackett, M.D., Sept. 30, 1872, BC). Answering for the college, JLC replied, in part: "I perceive the reasonableness of your proposition, and regret that not having contemplated such applications we can not make such arrangements as would be fit and proper in the case. I am sure that with the high character & earnest purpose you evince, women will soon find those 'equal terms' which they so justly desire, either by building up new Colleges or by raising up the old ones" (JLC to Miss C. F. Low, Oct. 9, 1872, BC).

29. William DeWitt Hyde, Introduction to Minot and Snow, *Tales of Bowdoin*, n.p.

30. Hatch, *Bowdoin College*, pp. 127, 131. Quotations, p. 131.

31. Ibid., pp. 132, 148–53.

32. JLC, "The Old Flag."

33. Ibid.; Little, *Catalogue*, History section, p. xciii; Hatch, *Bowdoin College*, pp. 132, 146. Quotation, JLC, "The Old Flag."

34. Hatch, *Bowdoin College*, pp. 133–34; Wells, "Random Recollections," pp. 283–84. Quotation, ibid., p. 283. An example of the uniform coat, gray in color and resembling the West Point cadet uniform, is owned by the Pejepscot Historical Society, Brunswick.

35. Hatch, *Bowdoin College*, pp. 134–37.

36. Ibid., pp. 137–39. The three class statements provided that the petitions would be null and void if more than three members of each class refused to sign. All of the statements therefore met that proviso. Chamberlain acted with the approval of the faculty in the disciplinary actions. He did promise, however, in the letter to the parents, that those who complied but still objected to the drill and wished to go elsewhere to school would be given an honorable dismissal. Even some bandsmen and a few others usually exempted from the drill because of health went home in sympathy and were suspended.

37. Ibid., pp. 139–41; Little, *Catalogue*, History section, p. xciii. The boards advised the War Department to transfer its aid to the agricultural college at Orono so that the state would not lose the Federal help (Hatch, *Bowdoin College*, pp. 147–48).

38. Wells, "Random Recollections," p. 286; Hatch, *Bowdoin College*, pp. 144, 146. First quotation, Wells, "Random Recollections"; second, Hatch, *Bowdoin College*, p. 144. The Hatch quotation is from the report of the Visiting Committee to the (Bowdoin) boards.

39. JLC to Joshua Chamberlain, Jr., July 25, 1872, UMO; JLC to Grace (Daisy), Apr. 18, 1871, RC; bill of sale for sloop, Harrison Loring to JLC, May 27, 1870, WP; Fannie to Grace, June 6, 1871, RC; Grace to JLC, July 24, 1872, RC; Geo. E. Adams to Mrs. H. C. Knight, Aug. 24, 1875, FPYU; Cross, "Joshua Lawrence Chamberlain," p. 85, BC; Phineas V. Stevens, "Our Log," BC; "Estate Joshua L. Chamberlain Inventory," typescript, FPYU. A stock certificate signed by JLC as president of a Massachusetts company and another showing ownership in a steamboat company from the period are among JLC's miscellaneous papers, WP.

40. Rand, "Chamberlain House," pp. 4, 5, PHS; JLC to Fannie, Apr. 7, 1866, RC; Fannie to JLC, Apr. 15, 1866, RC. The house still stands at 226 Maine Street, on the corner of Maine and Potter Streets, Brunswick. Throughout their married life JLC and Fannie followed the custom of the husband making the decisions and providing the home for the family, and the wife choosing the decorations and furnishings. Each usually asked the other about personal preferences.

41. Hatch, *Bowdoin College*, p. 214; JLC to Grace, Apr. 18, 1871, RC; Rand, "Chamberlain House," p. 6, PHS; photograph of hall, glass photographic plate, PHS; Sae Chamberlain to JLC, May 8, 1859, RC; newspaper clipping, *Lewiston Journal*, Aug. 1907, PHS; Alice M. Farrington to Rosamond Allen, Oct. 26, 1954, WP. Chamberlain's initial salary as president was $2,600, plus the housing allowance. From 1874 to 1880 he waived the latter when the college could not afford to pay it. The portrait of JLC's mother is now in the Brewer Public Library, along with one of his father. The latter was done by the artist Willard of Sturbridge, Massachusetts, who probably painted another portrait of JLC's mother now owned by the Brewer Historical Society. Mrs. Chamberlain wore the same costume in both paintings. The portraits were probably done in the early 1870s (JLC to Sarah D. B. Chamberlain, Sept. 8, 1871, BC). Fannie naturally required a domestic staff to help with the maintenance of so large a home, and census and letters mention various servants and helpers. The 1870 census showed an Andrew Tozier and his wife living in the house as domestics along with their young son. Tozier was without doubt the former color sergeant of the Twentieth Maine.

42. Newspaper clipping, *Lewiston Journal*, Aug. 1907, PHS; interview with Catherine Smith, *Brunswick Times-Record*, Sept. 7, 1976; photograph of drawing room from photographic plate, PHS; Eleanor Allen genealogy notation on Palmer House, Chicago, notepaper, RC; information provided by Rosamond Allen; writer's personal observations. Amelia Dyer Trumbull Wyllys was the widow of Joseph Trumbull, brother of the artist, when she married Fannie's maternal grandfather, Col. Hezekiah Wyllys. The portrait, now in

the Connecticut Historical Society, a gift from Rosamond Allen, was painted about 1777 and was altered several years later by artist Robert Earl (Thompson R. Harlow to Rosamond Allen, Sept. 20, 1954, WP). Fannie's ancestors "for 150 years were high officers of government in Connecticut. She was a lineal descendant on her mother's side of Mabel Harlakenden, conspicuous in early colonial history as 'the Princess of New England,' being of royal lineage in the line to which nearly all the monarchs of Europe are related" (Chamberlain Association, *JLC: A Sketch*, p. 27). There is some evidence that Fannie also was a descendant of Miles Standish (Charlotte Adams to Fannie, Apr. 10, 1846, WP).

43. Little, *Genealogical History*, 1:139; JLC to Joshua Chamberlain, Jr., May 16, 1873, WP; JLC to Fannie, Mar. 6, 1878, RC; Grace Chamberlain to H. G. Allen, postcard, June 18, 1880, WP; Rand, "Chamberlain House," photo 4 (1876), PHS. Quotation, JLC to Joshua Chamberlain, Jr., May 16, 1873. The 1871 house colors were determined by modern analysis by restoration experts. The "greenhouse" JLC spoke of may have been the glassed-in porch on the south side of the first floor—Grace spoke of a conservatory in her postcard. The Chamberlains entertained many famous individuals in their home, both on Potter Street and in the enlarged mansion on Maine. Those mentioned most often besides Longfellow are Union generals Grant, Sherman, McClellan, Warren, O. O. Howard, Griffin, Ayres, and Sheridan and U.S. senators Carl Schurz (also a former Union general), William P. Fessenden, Lot Morrill, William P. Frye, Eugene Hale, and James G. Blaine (Little, *Genealogical History*, 1:139).

44. Little, *Genealogical History*, 1:139, 140; *Portland Evening Express and Daily Advertiser*, Feb. 24, 1914; two photographs of the library from different views, photographic glass plates, PHS. General Griffin had requested that the bugle, flag, sword, and his cap be sent to JLC after his death; JLC received them through the War Department. The flag of the First Division, Fifth Corps, was also sent to JLC by the War Department after Griffin's death. The library wallpaper has been duplicated by the Pejepscot Historical Society and restored. The library and study now form part of the Joshua L. Chamberlain Civil War Museum.

45. Newspaper clipping, *Lewiston Journal*, Aug. 1907, PHS; Little, *Genealogical History*, 1:139; notation in Grace Chamberlain Allen's hand on back of family photograph of the library and study beyond, WP.

46. Ashby, *First Parish Church*, pp. 157, 260–64, 367, 368; Wheeler and Wheeler, *History of Brunswick*, p. 711; E. P. Pennell to JLC, Jan. 20, 1883, MHS. Quotation, Wheeler and Wheeler, *History of Brunswick*. Dr. Adams left Brunswick in August 1870 to become pastor of the new Trinity Congregational Church, which he helped found in East Orange.

47. JLC, *Maine: Her Place in History*, pp. iii, v; Foner, *Reconstruction*, pp. 575–82. Originally delivered on November 4, 1876, JLC's centennial speech was repeated to the Maine legislature the next year on February 6. The state

afterward published it under the same title with the report of the commissioners of the (Maine) Centennial Commission appended (JLC, *Maine: Her Place in History*, title page).

48. Foner, *Reconstruction*, pp. 276, 277; R. H. Jones, *Disrupted Decades*, pp. 454–55, 457, 460–61, 464.

49. R. H. Jones, *Disrupted Decades*, pp. 452–53, 457–60; Foner, *Reconstruction*, pp. 581–83.

50. JLC, "The Old Flag."

51. Ibid.; JLC to President Hayes, Mar. 8, 1877, Hayes Papers, RBHC. In 1876 the Supreme Court had virtually struck down the Enforcement Act of 1870, finding that under the Fourteenth and Fifteenth Amendments, states were restrained from passing laws contrary to those amendments, but crimes against blacks by individuals could only be punished in state and local courts (R. H. Jones, *Disrupted Decades*, pp. 463–67; Foner, *Reconstruction*, pp. 530, 531). In his letter to the president, JLC congratulated Hayes on his inaugural speech and praised his choice of cabinet, especially William M. Evarts as secretary of state and U.S. senator and Union general Carl Schurz as interior secretary. The appointments of Evarts and Schurz to his cabinet signaled strongly that Hayes "planned to put Reconstruction behind him and identify his administration with the party's 'reform' wing" (Foner, *Reconstruction*, pp. 581–82). Evarts had been President Johnson's counsel at the latter's impeachment trial.

A part of the Republican party led by Schurz had favored civil service reform, free trade, and a more liberal policy toward the South. In the spring of 1872 Schurz and his followers broke with Grant and, under the name of Liberal Republicans, nominated Horace Greeley for president at a Cincinnati convention. JLC's name appeared in a New York paper on a list of candidates for vice president recommended to that convention (Selden Conner to JLC, Apr. 25, 1872, LC). The Republicans nominated Grant. Desperate to defeat Grant for a second term and hoping to gain needed additional support, the Democrats soon after also nominated Greeley and his Cincinnati-chosen running mate, B. Glatz Brown, but lost the election to the still-popular Grant. A garbled, later account of JLC's part in the election states that JLC was distrusted by the Republican party leadership because of his stands on Johnson's impeachment and the Fifteenth Amendment and that Greeley actually asked JLC to run with him, implying that it was as a Democrat. It also had JLC declining Greeley's offer, because to accept would "misrepresent his position on the main questions at issue before the country" (Chamberlain Association, *JLC: A Sketch*, p. 19). Chamberlain would hardly oppose Grant openly, in any case.

52. JLC, "The Old Flag." Adelbert Ames, when carpetbagger governor of Mississippi, had other, firsthand views. He wrote to JLC that the "old rebel here" hated the Union and was "devoting [himself] to misrepresenting those of different politics. The whole question south is that of the liberty

and security of the negro. He has them not in the democratic states. . . . You can have no idea of the true state of the case here. Every word Phil Sheridan has uttered is the gospel truth. We do hope the north will stand true to the rights of the colored men. Let the democracy prevail and the negro will rue the day he was made free" (Ames to JLC, Jan. 22, 1875, LC). Grant had sent Sheridan into Louisiana with troops to protect blacks but demurred when Ames later asked for troops in Mississippi for the same reason and to keep the 1875 elections unobstructed. Ames was later forced to resign the governorship on trumped-up charges after those elections put the state legislature in the hands of the Democrats (or "the democracy," as Ames and others called the party).

53. JLC, "The Old Flag." The slow working out of the design of Providence by man was a strong and recurring theme for JLC. Speaking of the men of both armies, he wrote, "We were all of us factors of that high will which, working often through illusions of the human, and following ideals that lead through storms, evolves the enfranchisement of man" (JLC, *Armies*, p. 271).

54. JLC, *Armies*, pp. 279, 232. JLC delivered his war paper, "Appomattox," where the last quotation first appeared, to the New York commandery of MOLLUS on October 7, 1903.

55. JLC, "Don't Judge Hastily," p. 78. A Maine newspaper, criticizing JLC for an 1879 Memorial Day speech containing the story, thundered, "Does not God always fight for the right, and make it triumphant?" Conceding JLC's "noble service" in the war, it still contended that in the story and other parts of the speech, he was questioning the integrity of the Union cause. The newspaper further declared that JLC had intimated that opposition to the South's coming back into power legislatively was caused by jealousy; it stated its own opinion that "the South, in coming back, brings with it the same disorganizing influences and sentiments which she held and carried before the year 1865" (*Oxford Democrat*, Paris, Maine, June 10, 1879).

56. JLC, "Don't Judge Hastily," p. 78.

57. S. M. Allen to JLC, Apr. 26, 1876, LC; S. M. Allen to JLC, Apr. 29, 1876, LC; N. P. Banks to Stephen M. Allen, May 8, 1876, LC; JLC to A. H. Rice, Apr. 28, 1877, Hayes Papers, RBHC; JLC to President Hayes, marked "Private, to the President," Jan. 26, 1878, Hayes Papers, RBHC; JLC to Peleg Chandler, Mar. 7, 1878, Peleg Chandler Collection, RBHC; JLC to his parents, June 14, 1878, BC; Little, *Genealogical History*, 1:138. JLC wrote the governor of Massachusetts that he meant to stand by the president as the "battle lines" were being drawn in Maine: "I believe his policy, as I understand it, is all that is going to save the country or the party." He apparently wanted the prestige of this recognition by the president, so that he would have some excuse to speak out in support of Hayes more easily, in spite of his position at the college. See JLC to A. W. Rice, Apr. 28, 1877, Hayes Papers, RBHC.

58. JLC to his parents, June 14, 1878, BC; Grace to Horace [G. Allen], Sept. 28, 1878, FPYU; JLC to Fannie, Mar. 6, 1878, RC. Quotation, Grace to Horace, Sept. 28, 1878. A total of $2,400 was to be paid to JLC for his services as commissioner (F. W. Seward, Acting Secretary of State, to JLC, May 2, 1878, LC, cited in Wallace, *Soul of the Lion*, p. 334). JLC, however, thought the trip would cost him at least $5,000 (JLC to Fannie, Mar. 6, 1878, RC).

59. Little, *Genealogical History*, 1:138; Thayer and Ames, *History and Families*, pp. 77, 78; information provided by Rosamond Allen.

60. Chamberlain Association, *JLC, [A Sketch], Supplement*, pp. 3, 6; Little, *Genealogical History*, 1:138. Quotation, Chamberlain Association, *JLC, [A Sketch], Supplement*, p. 6. In this writer's opinion, most of the supplement to the sketch of JLC's life concerning the state government election crisis in 1880 was written in the third person by JLC himself, unlike the original *Sketch*. The supplement apparently was published a little later than the *Sketch*, which was a report of the Chamberlain Association of America, a genealogical organization. Both were later bound together into one paperbound edition, labeled "Joshua Lawrence Chamberlain" on the cover.

61. Blaine, *Twenty Years of Congress*, 2:709; Cross, "Joshua Lawrence Chamberlain," p. 72, BC.

62. Cross, "Joshua Lawrence Chamberlain," pp. 72, 73, BC; Chamberlain Association, *JLC, [A Sketch], Supplement*, pp. 4, 5, 17; James G. Blaine to JLC, Dec. 24, 1879, WP.

63. Chamberlain Association, *JLC, [A Sketch], Supplement*, pp. 6, 7, 8, 18.

64. Ibid., pp. 6, 7, 14, 23.

65. JLC to Fannie, Jan. 9, 1880, RC; Chamberlain Association, *JLC, [A Sketch], Supplement*, pp. 8, 9, 24.

66. Chamberlain Association, *JLC, [A Sketch], Supplement*, pp. 5, 7, 18; JLC to Fannie, Jan. 7, 1880, RC; F. B. Ward to JLC, Jan. 15, 1880, LC. Ward served in Company F of the Twentieth Maine. Other letters of support for JLC during the crisis are found in the major JLC collections.

67. JLC to Fannie, Jan. 15, [1880], BC; Chamberlain Assocation, *JLC, [A Sketch], Supplement*, pp. 12, 15, 19, 26. Quotation, JLC to Fannie, Jan. 15, [1880].

68. Chamberlain Association, *JLC, [A Sketch], Supplement*, pp. 24–25.

69. Ibid., p. 25.

70. Ibid., pp. 13, 14, 16; James G. Blaine to JLC, Jan. 14, 1880, WP; James G. Blaine to JLC, "14 Jany 1879" [*sic*], WP; JLC to James G. Blaine, Jan. 16, 1880, WP; James G. Blaine to JLC, Jan. 16, 1880, WP; Cross, "Joshua Lawrence Chamberlain," p. 74, BC; "General Orders No. 4," Augusta, Jan. 17, 1880, MHS. First quotation, JLC to James G. Blaine, Jan. 16, 1880; second, "General Orders No. 4." A plot to assassinate Blaine and destroy his house was foiled and the ringleaders arrested by JLC. Blaine was the undisputed boss of the Republican party in Maine for many years and came close to being named that party's presidential candidate in 1876 and 1880. In 1884 he

won the Republican nomination but lost a narrow election to Grover Cleveland.

71. JLC to Fannie, Jan. 15, [1880], BC.

72. JLC to J. W. Spaulding, Oct. 4, 1880, MHS; JLC to G. C. Dodd, Oct. 4, 1880, MHS; Johnson and Malone, *Dictionary of American Biography*, 1:325, 4:51, 52, 103–4; Chamberlain Association, *JLC, [A Sketch], Supplement*, pp. 16, 26; Chamberlain Association, *JLC: A Sketch*, p. 21. Much later, in an unrelated matter, JLC thought that Frye and Hale might dislike his "conservative political ideas" (JLC to Gen. [Henry C.] Merriam, Mar. 11, 1906, in *Colby Library Quarterly*, ser. 7, no. 8 [Dec. 1966]: 350), but there is no question that his political views were usually conservative. The Republicans lost the governorship by 164 votes in the 1880 fall elections, although the Republican presidential candidate Garfield carried the state by 6,000 votes (Blaine, *Twenty Years of Congress*, p. 669). At the end of 1880, in an obvious attempt to discredit JLC, Republicans publicly questioned his party loyalty by referring to a letter he had written to Chief Justice Appleton the previous January 12, during the crisis, urging that Lamson, the president of the state senate, whom the Democrats wanted recognized as governor, be "recognized." JLC made the letter public and explained that its ambiguous wording only referred to asking the court to recognize Lamson's right, as president of the senate, to put a series of questions to the court. This would have been clear had Lamson's questions, which JLC had seen, been submitted by Lamson to the judge. Apparently only JLC's letter and not Lamson's questions had reached the judge. It was JLC's opinion that his position as a military officer made it improper to put questions formally to the court, and he thought that he would know how to proceed and that a way out of the mess could be found if the court answered Lamson's questions, or refused to do so. Nevertheless, JLC's political hopes were virtually ended by his unselfish service to the state in the crisis of 1880. See Cross, "Joshua Lawrence Chamberlain," p. 74, BC; Chamberlain Association, *JLC, [A Sketch], Supplement*, pp. 3, 25; draft of JLC to Judge Appleton, Jan. 1, 1881, MHS; Charles E. Nash to JLC, Jan. 3, 1881, MHS; statement of J. W. Spaulding, Dec. 31, 1880, WP. Much correspondence and copies of official documents of the "Count-out" or "Twelve Days" crisis are in FPYU, LC, and MHS.

73. JLC to Fannie, May 11, 1880, RC; *In Memoriam*, p. 10.

74. *In Memoriam*, pp. 10, 11; Eisenschiml, *Fitz-John Porter*, p. 274; newspaper clipping, "Army of the Potomac Reunion," LC; newspaper clipping, "Army of the Potomac, The Address of General Chamberlain," LC. First quotations, ibid.; last quotation, *In Memoriam*, p. 11.

75. JLC to Fannie, May 11, 1880, RC. JLC's "Military Operations on the White Oak Road" and "Five Forks" were read to the Maine commandery of MOLLUS on December 6, 1893, and May 2, 1900, respectively, and the book was, of course, his *The Passing of the Armies*.

76. Little, *Genealogical History*, 1:133; Thayer and Ames, *History and Families*, pp. 249, cxliii, cxliv; *Farrington Memorial*, p. 43.

77. JLC to Sae, June 6, 1865, BC; JLC to Sarah D. B. Chamberlain, Nov. 27, 1877, UMO. First quotation, JLC to Sae, June 6, 1865; second, JLC to Sarah D. B. Chamberlain, Nov. 27, 1877. Joshua Chamberlain, Jr., died August 10, 1880, and Sarah Dupee Brastow Chamberlain died November 5, 1888. Sae's children who grew to adulthood were Alice M. Farrington (1869–1960) and Dana C. Farrington (1878–1925). They had no known descendants. Three little Farrington boys did not survive infancy; one was named Lawrence Joshua.

Few of JLC's birthday letters to his mother survive, but one of the last ones bears repeating in full: "My dear Mother: This is my birthday and I must write you my letter, as I always do to bless and thank you for my life; for all your suffering for me & tender care, and faithful guidance & good instruction. I trust I have made the life of some good to the world, and a joy to you. Perhaps I have not made all that was possible of my life, but I trust that God has still use for me, and has spared me through so many perils and so many years, for a blessing somewhere yet to be given and received. I pray that you may be kept in health and peace & that God's peace may rest in your soul. I thank Him & I thank you, for the happy little meeting we had a few days ago. I trust I can be of some comfort and use to you still in these sweet evenings of the years. Your prayers for me are always in my heart. God has answered them for my good, and will do so still. It is a day full of gratitude to you & to God for my spirit, & I am happy and ready for anything to which I may be called. May God bless & keep you. Your loving son, Lawrence" (JLC to Sarah D. B. Chamberlain, Sept. 8, 1887, LC).

78. Grace to JLC, July 24, 1872, RC; JLC to Grace, Apr. 18, 1871, RC; JLC to Grace, May 27, 1876, MHS; JLC to Grace, Apr. 27, 1870, FPYU. First quotation, Grace to JLC, July 24, 1872; second, JLC to Grace, Apr. 18, 1871; third, JLC to Grace, May 27, 1876.

79. Engraved invitation to Grace's wedding, WP; Grace to "My Dearest Horace," Sept. 28, 1878, FPYU; JLC to Grace, Dec. 12, 1886, BC; JLC to [Grace], "on train, Richmond Va., 1/4 to 12 Monday morning," n.d., BC; Horace Allen to JLC, Feb. 4, 1887, FPYU; JLC to Grace, Oct. 20, 1887, BC; information provided by Rosamond Allen. Horace Allen's father, Stephen M. Allen, became a Chamberlain family friend and later a business associate of JLC. It was he who tried to have JLC appointed to the diplomatic post in England. Through the years a great deal of visiting in Boston was done by all the Chamberlains, Wyllys and Fannie sometimes staying weeks and months at a time, JLC stopping for short visits whenever he could. JLC's devotion to Grace is clear in all of his letters to her. Although her father approved of the higher education of women, Grace did not choose it. A clue to this decision, perhaps, is Fannie's remark to her that "I should be afraid

you were studying too hard . . . if I did not know you were not of that kind. You never did study hard, you know" (Fannie to Grace, "Home, April," n.d. [but ca. 1871], RC).

80. Wilder, *Catalogue*, p. 152; Little, *Genealogical History*, 1:140; H. Wyllys Chamberlain to JLC, May 7, 1888, FPYU; Wyllys to JLC, Mar. 22, 1889, FPYU; Wyllys to JLC, "Aboard the Pinafore, May 25," [no year], MHS; Wyllys to JLC, Nov. 2, 1892, FPYU; Wyllys to "My Dear Little Ma," "May," [ca. 1892], MHS; JLC to Wyllys, Dec. 26, 1901, MHS; JLC to Wyllys, Oct. 18, 1913, MHS; Cross, "Joshua Lawrence Chamberlain," p. 78, BC; information provided by Rosamond Allen.

81. Little, *Catalogue*, History section, p. xcv; Cross, "Joshua Lawrence Chamberlain," p. 77, BC; JLC to Sae, Jan. 29, 1882, UMO. Quotation, ibid.

82. Chamberlain Association, *JLC: A Sketch*, p. 22; J. H. Warren, M.D., to JLC, Mar. 2, 1883, FPYU; JLC to Fannie, Apr. 19, 1883, BC; Grace to Fannie, Apr. 19, 1883, BC; newspaper clipping labeled "N.Y. Times, July 27," in Fitz John Porter to JLC, July 27, [1883], FPYU; statement of the Bowdoin College Boards, July 11, 1883, in the *Brunswick Telegraph*, July 27, 1883; JLC to the Trustees and Overseers of Bowdoin College, July 8, 1873, MHS; Hatch, *Bowdoin College*, pp. 158–60, 163, 178, 179; Cleaveland, *Bowdoin College*, pp. xciv, 124. Letters in the collections show that in the 1870s JLC wrote many of his friends and acquaintances, from Adelbert Ames to J. G. Blaine, for donations to the college and traveled as far as Illinois on fund-raising trips. One celebrated graduate of Bowdoin's scientific department was Adm. Robert E. Peary, credited with finding the North Pole. Chamberlain congratulated Peary and expressed his pride in him when he returned in triumph in 1909 (JLC to Admiral Peary, Oct. 5, 1909, BC).

83. Chamberlain Association, *JLC: A Sketch*, pp. 19–20; William DeWitt Hyde, eulogy to JLC, *Lewiston Journal*, Feb. 27, 1914; newspaper clipping, "Every Honor Accorded Maine's Dead Soldier, Statesman, Scholar," BC. First quotation, Chamberlain Association, *JLC: A Sketch*; others, Hyde eulogy.

84. Little, *Catalogue*, History section, p. xcv; Chamberlain Association, *JLC: A Sketch*, pp. 21, 22; statement of the Bowdoin College Boards, July 11, 1883, in the *Brunswick Telegraph*, July 27, 1883; Wilder, *Catalogue*, p. 98; Hatch, *Bowdoin College*, pp. 179–80. In the spring of 1884 a friend recommended JLC to President Chester A. Arthur as minister to Russia, and upon request of the same friend, JLC wrote the president a very reserved letter endorsing the idea (Dexter Hawkins to JLC, Mar. 1, 1884, FPYU; Hawkins to Pres. Arthur, Mar. 4, 1884, FPYU; JLC to Pres. Arthur, Mar. 4, 1884, FPYU). JLC was a member of the Board of Trustees at Bowdoin for forty-seven years, from 1867 to 1914.

85. JLC to Sae, Jan. 29, 1882, UMO; JLC to [Grace], "on train, Richmond Va., 1/4 to 12 Monday morning," n.d., BC. First quotations, JLC to Sae, Jan. 29, 1882; last, JLC to [Grace], n.d. JLC picked up several bullets at Petersburg to keep with the one he already had, "that made so straight a way

through me" (JLC to Sae, Jan. 29, 1882, UMO). In his war paper "Reminiscences of Petersburg and Appomattox: October, 1903," in which, with skillful wording, he apparently combined incidents of a 1903 trip he made to the old Virginia battlefields and the 1882 journey, JLC recounted that he picked up a small vest button from near the same place and was given a piece of shrapnel with two lead bullets held by an iron band, in addition to finding five minié balls and a pistol bullet (JLC, "Petersburg and Appomattox," p. 175).

86. JLC, "Petersburg and Appomattox," p. 177; *In Memoriam*, p. 10; Chamberlain Association, *JLC: A Sketch*, pp. 23, 24, 26; JLC to Grace, July 13, 1888, BC; *Brunswick Record*, Feb. 5, 1904. First quotation, JLC, "Petersburg and Appomattox"; second, JLC to Grace, July 13, 1888. Letters from veterans to JLC mentioning seeing or talking with him at Memorial Day services, plus many invitations to speak and newspaper clippings of his speeches, are in the JLC collections at BC, MHS, and LC. The widow of a New York officer who had died in the Georgetown hospital when JLC was a patient there in the winter of early 1864 sought him out at a Memorial Day speech at Syracuse to thank him for all the kindnesses he had shown her when she had nursed her husband at the hospital and to introduce him to her daughter, whom her husband had never seen (Mrs. J. F. Robinson to JLC, May 30, 1888, FPYU). JLC also dedicated several Civil War monuments at towns in Maine and a war orphans' home in Bath. His consistent thoughtfulness, kindnesses, and favors are remarked upon throughout letters in the manuscript collections.

87. *Maine at Gettysburg*, pp. 249–50, 545–59; *Dedication of the Twentieth Maine Monuments*, pp. 4–7, 26–31; Chamberlain Association, *JLC: A Sketch*, p. 23. Quotations, *Maine at Gettysburg*, pp. 548, 550. The Little Round Top monument was placed in 1886 and paid for by the regiment; the one on Great Round Top was erected by the State of Maine. Right and left flank markers of the regiment were placed on Little Round Top, as well as a marker at the stone wall where Company B stood before the charge. Several paragraphs of JLC's speeches that day have been quoted elsewhere in the text of this book.

88. *In Memoriam*, pp. 10, 11, 12; JLC, "Appomattox," p. 260; Grace Chamberlain Allen to George T. Little, Apr. 23, 1914, BC. Quotation, *In Memoriam*, p. 12. JLC delivered "Abraham Lincoln" again for the Maine MOLLUS on March 3, 1909, and it is published in that commandery's *War Papers*, vol. 4. JLC was an original companion of the initial MOLLUS organization founded in Philadelphia and became a charter member of the Maine commandery when it was formed. JLC gave "Loyalty" again to the Maine commandery in 1912 (JLC to Henry S. Burrage, Jan. 22, 1912, MHS).

89. Tucker, *Hancock*, p. 308; *New York Times*, Aug. 9, 1885; JLC to Fannie, Aug. 8, 1885, Maine State Museum, Augusta, Maine.

90. JLC to Fannie, Aug. 8, 1885, Maine State Museum, Augusta, Maine.

91. Ibid.

92. Chamberlain Association, *JLC: A Sketch*, p. 22; JLC to Grace, Dec. 13, 1886, BC; Claudius B. Jewell to JLC, Apr. 23, 1886, RBHC; Wyllys to JLC, May 7, 1888, FPYU; JLC to Grace, Jan. 18, 1889, BC; Wyllys to JLC, Mar. 22, 1889, FPYU; JLC to Grace, July 13, 1889, BC; Mr. Willard to JLC, July 18, 1889, FPYU; John H. Jarvis to JLC, Sept. 9, 1889, FPYU; Sae to JLC, Jan. 3, 1886, RC; letterhead, JLC to J. E. Rankin, n.d., MHS; letterheads, passim, Box 7, FPYU; Wallace, *Soul of the Lion*, pp. 274–75. JLC's apartment address in New York was 101 West Seventy-fifth Street. The offices of his companies were on Wall Street and various locations in southern Manhattan Island.

93. Fitz John Porter statement of JLC disability, JLC Military Pension records, NA; JLC to Mrs. [Bvt. Brig. Gen. Richard T.] Locke, Feb. 7, 1893, MHS; U.S. Congress, *Medal of Honor Recipients*, p. 401; Col. F. C. Ainsworth to JLC, Aug. 17, 1893, FPYU; Mitchell, *Badge of Gallantry*, pp. 127–31; James Otis to JLC, Mar. 3, 1896, MHS. Quotation, ibid. Otis died before publishing his book, but some of the material that he collected for it formed the basis for *Badge of Gallantry* (Mitchell, *Badge of Gallantry*, Introduction, p. xv). Formal application for JLC's medal was made by Bvt. Brig. Gen. Thomas H. Hubbard, Bowdoin class of 1857 and a veteran of the Twenty-fifth and Thirtieth Maine Infantry Regiments. He was one of the most generous alumni to Bowdoin and remarked in his application for the medal for his old professor, "In Maine we have always thought General Chamberlain's military service deserved any reward the Government could bestow." See *MAGR, 1864–65*, 1:506. Quotation, Thomas H. Hubbard to War Dept., Mar. 1, 1893, JLC Military Personnel file, NA.

94. Hatch, *Bowdoin College*, p. 180; Sen. John B. Gordon to JLC, Feb. 26, 1892, RBHC; Wyllys to "My dear Little Ma," "May," [ca. 1892], MHS. Quotation, ibid. Much JLC correspondence in MHS from the period 1892–94 concerns land sales in Brunswick. Senator Gordon was the Confederate general who saluted JLC at the Appomattox surrender ceremony.

95. Thomas D. Chamberlain Military Pension records, NA; JLC to Joshua Chamberlain, Jr., Feb. 12, 1865, WP. Quotation, ibid. JLC invested in part ownership of at least one ship and also used his own connections to help his younger brother get business outfitting vessels, at the request of their father (JLC to Joshua Chamberlain, Jr., May 16, 1873, WP).

96. Sae to JLC, Jan. 3, 1886, RC; Fannie to Grace, Jan. 8, 1888, RC; Mr. Willard to JLC, July 18, 1889, FPYU; John H. Jarvis to JLC, Sept. 9, 1889, FPYU. Quotations, Mr. Willard to JLC, July 18, 1889, and John H. Jarvis to JLC, Sept. 9, 1889.

97. Thomas D. Chamberlain Military Pension records, NA; JLC to Fannie, June 30, 1896, BC; Sae to JLC, July 23, 1896, FPYU; Sae to JLC, July 30, 1896, FPYU; JLC, *Armies*, p. 339. First quotation, Sae to JLC, July 30, 1896; second, JLC, *Armies*. Delia Chamberlain lived until 1923 and left $200 to the Brewer, Maine, library in memory of Tom (*Bangor Evening Commercial*, Aug. 1, 1923).

98. Chamberlain Association, *JLC: A Sketch*, pp. 23–26; JLC to Searles,

Nov. 13, 1893, MHS; Alexander S. "Andy" Webb to Seward [Webb], May 2, 1893, LC; Selden Connor to JLC, Mar. 19, 1908, LC; Warner, *Generals in Blue*, p. 545; JLC, *Universities and Their Sons*, 1:25–42; JLC to the Secretary of War, Apr. 22, 1898, JLC Military Personnel file, NA; JLC to Sen. William P. Frye, Apr. 22, 1898, JLC Military Personnel file, NA; Secretary of War to JLC, Apr. 30, 1898, JLC Military Personnel file, NA; Ames, *Adelbert Ames*, p. 516; William C. Oates to Elihu Root, June 2, 1903, GNMP; Krick, *Lee's Colonels*, p. 268. Oates was governor of Alabama and served in the U.S. House of Representatives for years after the war (ibid.). JLC was also recommended to the president for the position of governor of the Philippines (George O. Cutler to John D. Long, Secretary of the Navy, May 6, 1898, and John D. Long to Mr. President, May 11, 1898, JLC Military Personnel File, NA).

The Artist-Artisans school taught crafts, interior decorating in textiles, and metalwork as well as painting and sculpture. JLC's other organizational affiliations were vice-president, American Huguenot Society; president, Alpha Delta Phi fraternity; president, Webster Historical Society, Boston; American Political Science Association; Egyptian Exploration Society; vice president, American Bible Society; vice president, Humane Education Society; a director of the Maine Institute for the Blind and American National Institute, Paris; Maine Historical Society; Colonial Society of Massachusetts; Military Historical Society of Massachusetts; American Historical Association; American Geographical Society; the Egyptian Research; National Red Cross; life member, American Board of Commissioners for Foreign Missions; and associate of the Philosophical Society of Great Britain (Chamberlain Association, *JLC: A Sketch*, pp. 25, 26).

99. JLC to Gen. John T. Richards, Dec. 26, 1899, MHS; J. A. Porter, Secretary to President McKinley, to Alexander S. Webb, Nov. 28, 1899, RBHC; William P. Whitehouse to [Amos L. Allen], Nov. 20, 1899, BC; Ellis Spear to the Hon. Amos Allen, Dec. 4, 1899, BC; A. O. Shaw to JLC, Dec. 5, 1899, MHS; The Hon. Amos L. Allen to G. M. Elliott, Dec. 12, 1899, RBHC; The Hon. Amos L. Allen to JLC, Feb. 12, 1900, RBHC; Office of Secretary of the Treasury to JLC, Mar. 27, 1900, FPYU. Quotation, JLC to Gen. John T. Richards, Dec. 26, 1899. The surveyor was paid $4,500 annually, an excellent salary for the time (Raymond, "Joshua Chamberlain's Retirement Bill," p. 342). Amos Allen was a member of the House of Representatives who evidently had the (patronage) power of final recommendation to the president for the surveyor and collector posts. The political pressure put on him in JLC's behalf finally forced him to do something for JLC (Amos Allen to G. M, Elliott, Dec. 12, 1899, RBHC). Spear especially emphasized JLC's fine character and high standing among the old soldiers and also pleaded that JLC was very poor, but proud, and the appointment would save the old general from penury in his old age. There is no doubt that JLC badly needed the job, but he apparently still owned his properties in Brewer and others in Brunswick. At the request of Allen, JLC delayed taking up his du-

ties as surveyor until April 1 to oblige the current occupant of the office, a Democrat, who was in need of the salary (The Hon. Amos L. Allen to JLC, Feb. 12, 1900, RBHC).

A 1906 bill (S. 6150, Fifty-ninth Congress) to pension JLC as a brigadier general in the Regular Army, at $4,125 per year, failed in the U.S. Congress like many other pension bills for Union volunteer officers (Raymond, "Joshua Chamberlain's Retirement Bill," pp. 342, 343, 353, 354). According to a Portland newspaper at the time of JLC's death, the failure of these bills was largely due to the opposition of "Southern Members of Congress" (newspaper clipping, "Notable Gathering," MOLLUS War Museum, Philadelphia). However, the expense of such pensions seemed to be the major factor against them. Raymond's article contains an interesting series of JLC letters (owned by Colby College) about his bill and others.

100. JLC to Gen. John T. Richards, Dec. 26, 1899, MHS; Myra Porter to JLC, Sept. 8, 1905, MHS; JLC [to Grace], Aug. 28, 1909, RC; [Achorn], "General Chamberlain," n.d., typescript, pp. 2, 4, BC; Stevens, "Our Log," BC. Quotation, JLC to Gen. John T. Richards, Dec. 26, 1899.

101. Grace to Fannie, Apr. 19, 1883, BC; JLC to Grace, Dec. 13, 1886, BC; Wyllys to "My Dear Little Ma," "May," [ca. 1892], MHS; JLC to Grace, July 13, 1888, BC; JLC to Fannie, "Friday eve.," n.d., n.p. (but from contents, New York in early 1890s), MHS; JLC to Grace, Feb. 14, 1892, BC; Wyllys to JLC, Nov. 2, 1892, FPYU; JLC to Fannie, Oct. 23, 1894, MHS; JLC to Fannie, June 30, 1896, BC; JLC to Grace, Dec. 4, 1898, MHS; JLC to Grace, Jan. 29, 1899, RC; Ellis Spear to Hon. Amos Allen, Dec. 4, 1899, BC; JLC to Fannie, July 10, 1902, BC; JLC to Fannie, Feb. 11, 1903, BC; JLC to Grace, Aug. 3, 1903, RC.

102. JLC to the Secretary of the Treasury, Oct. 22, 1900, MHS; JLC to the Secretary of State, Oct. 25, 1900, FPYU; another letter, JLC to the Secretary of State, Oct. 25, 1900, FPYU; JLC to Fannie, Nov. 6, 1900, BC; JLC to Arthur L. Farnsworth, Jan. 7, 1901, in newspaper clipping, "Letter Received from Gen. Chamberlain Who Is in Egypt," PHS. Quotations, JLC to Fannie, Nov. 6, 1900. JLC sailed up the Nile sight-seeing and received courtesies and privileges because of his government credentials and personal and military reputation (Chamberlain Association, *JLC: A Sketch*, p. 22).

103. JLC to Grace, Aug. 3, 1903, RC. Miss Lillian Edmunds, Fannie's housekeeper and companion during the last years of her life, was a distant relative of the family who stayed on as JLC's housekeeper after Fannie's death. JLC's numerous love letters to his wife appear throughout the major manuscript collections. It is apparent from many varied letters in the collections that JLC was very attractive to women and that his attitude toward them was thoughtful, gallant, and admiring. In early life, his young cousin Annie was obviously in love with him, and others reflected affection and sometimes love for him (Annie [Chamberlain] letters, RC; Sarah Sampson letters, MHS; Mary Clark letters, MHS; Elizabeth K. Upham letters, MHS

and FPYU). One correspondent, when JLC had at last joined the ranks of the "superannuated," combined romantic fantasy with religious metaphor in her letters (Myra Porter letters, MHS). In *Armies*, JLC's references to the "witching Washington belles," his incidents with the "belle of Dinwiddie," and the girl at the last review of the Army of the Potomac directly show his keen appreciation of feminine charm and beauty (JLC, *Armies*, pp. 311, 293–96, 339–40).

104. Newspaper clipping, "Mrs. Chamberlain's Funeral," PHS. Quotation, from pastor's eulogy, ibid.

105. Myra E. Porter to JLC, Aug. 9, 1905, MHS; JLC to Fannie, Aug. 12, 1905, RC; Little, *Genealogical History*, 1:140; newspaper clipping, "Mrs. Chamberlain's Funeral," PHS; newspaper clipping, "Death of Mrs. Chamberlain," BC. Quotation, JLC to Fannie, Aug. 12, 1905.

106. Helen R. Adams to JLC, Nov. 26, 1905, BC; *Lewiston Journal*, Aug. 1907, PHS; Dr. Adams diary, May 8, 1865, FPC; JLC, "Last Review of the Army of the Potomac, May 23, 1865," p. 317. Quotation, ibid.; quotation also appears in JLC, *Armies*, p. 342.

107. Newspaper clipping, "Dashing Civil War Leader/Hero of Little Round Top," MOLLUS War Museum, Philadelphia; *Lewiston Journal*, Sunday Supplement, Sept. 1–6, 1900; JLC to Grace, Oct. 13, 1910, RC; JLC to Grace, May 6, 1911, RC; Copeland, Mrs. Catherine Smith interview, PHS; recollections of Catherine T. Smith, *Brunswick Times-Record*, Sept. 7, 1975. First quotations, newspaper headlines; last, Copeland, Mrs. Catherine Smith interview. Mrs. Smith called Portland's Back Cove "Back Bay." After the turn of the century, many newspaper articles referred to JLC as "the hero of Little Round Top."

108. Recollections of Catherine T. Smith, *Brunswick Times-Record*, Sept. 7, 1975; *Portland Evening Express and Daily Advertiser*, Feb. 24, 1913; Copeland, Mrs. Catherine Smith interview, PHS; information provided by Emery W. Booker to the writer in May 1982. Quotation, *Portland Evening Express and Daily Advertiser*, Feb. 24, 1913. Dr. George T. Little, longtime Bowdoin librarian, was quoted in the Portland newspaper. Booker, whose father's store was adjacent to JLC's Brunswick home, remembered JLC clearly from when he was a boy and said JLC was always courteous and would introduce him to others. Years later Booker bought the Brunswick home from Rosamond Allen. JLC's Portland house still stands at 499 Ocean Avenue, Portland (it was numbered 211 when he first lived in it). Comparing the Portland city directories of 1911 and 1912 shows the homes on the street were renumbered between those dates. The old Customs House also still stands.

109. Little, *Genealogical History*, 1:140; JLC to Rosamond Allen, Dec. 27, 1909, WP; JLC to Grace, May 24, 1909, RC; JLC to Grace, May 11, 1911, RC; JLC to L. B. Eaton, Aug. 1, 1901, WP; information provided by Rosamond Allen. First quotations, Rosamond Allen; last, JLC to Rosamond Allen, Dec. 27, 1909. Grace was crippled for life in an automobile accident in 1910. JLC took great interest in his granddaughters and urged that Eleanor Wyllys Al-

len (1893–1980), the eldest, attend the college of her choice (JLC to Grace, Dec. 9, 1911, RC). Eleanor afterward earned a law degree and served with the U.S. State Department in the foreign service, and Rosamond Allen (1898–) attained a graduate degree in social work, specializing in children's welfare. Beatrice Lawrence Allen (1896–1943), whom Rosamond thought strikingly resembled their maternal grandfather when he was young, did not seek higher education and married David Kennedy Patten in 1918. There are no other descendants. (Information provided by Rosamond Allen.) Rosamond Allen also strikingly resembles JLC, both in old age and photographs when younger.

110. Roland Phillips to JLC, Nov. 1, 1912, MHS; W. F. Bigelow to Gen. Morris Schaff, Nov. 2, 1912, MHS; Morris Schaff to JLC, Nov. 4, 1912, written on back of ibid., MHS; W. F. Bigelow to JLC, Nov. 2, 1912, MHS; Roland Phillips to JLC, Nov. 12, 1912, MHS; Ferris Greens to JLC, Dec. 23, 1912, MHS; Roland Phillips to JLC, Feb. 15, 1913, MHS; Roland Phillips to JLC, Feb. 27, 1913, MHS; Perriton Maxwell to JLC, Apr. 10, 1913, MHS; Perriton Maxwell to JLC, May 12, 1913, MHS; JLC to Fannie Hardy Eckstorm, Aug. 28, 1913, Fannie Hardy Eckstorm Papers, UMO; JLC to Grace, Feb. 28, 1913, RC; JLC, *Armies*, Introductory, p. xii. Morris Schaff's *The Sunset of the Confederacy* was first serialized in the *Atlantic Monthly* magazine before its publication in 1912. The complimentary passages to JLC are on pp. 296–99 in the book. Both articles by JLC were written in a florid, highly descriptive style favored by the Hearst magazines. Houghton Mifflin of Boston offered to publish in book form any material JLC cared to write, but G. P. Putnam's Sons published *Armies*.

The publication of "My Story of Fredericksburg" in December 1912 seemed to set off an unexpected and sad series of events. In the March 20, 1913, issue of the *National Tribune*, the newspaper of the Grand Army of the Republic, a letter by JLC's old friend Ellis Spear gave his recollections of the Appomattox surrender ceremony, an account materially different from JLC's description of it in his various, well-known accounts. In May 1913, while giving a war paper about Appomattox to the District of Columbia commandery of MOLLUS, Spear completely digressed to Fredericksburg with a sarcastic reference refuting a personal incident described by JLC in his magazine article (Spear, "The Hoecake of Appomattox," p. 10). Sometime later, Spear wrote a long calumny against JLC, systematically refuting and many times ridiculing every assertion JLC had made in the article (Abbott Spear, *The 20th Maine at Fredericksburg*). He sent a copy to Adelbert Ames, whose answer, if any, is not known (Spear to O. W. Norton, Jan. 18, 1916, Oliver W. Norton Papers, Clarke Historical Library, Central Michigan University, Mount Pleasant, Michigan).

Modern independent research finds that many of Spear's allegations are false, others obviously a product of a poor memory, and still others unprovable, for Spear counts events he did not personally witness as false. Spear had sent an affectionate Christmas letter to JLC in December 1910 (Ellis Spear to JLC, Dec. 24, 1910, BC); the cause for his later hatred for JLC is unknown. It probably had its origin in Spear's faulty memory and its culmination, perhaps, in a poor physical condition. Spear letters to Oliver W. Norton and Strong Vincent's brother vilifying JLC with distortions and falsehoods are in Clarke Historical Library, Central Michigan University, and date from July 5, 1913, to February 1, 1916. They also seem to reveal a deep envy of his former friend. Spear died April 3, 1917, in St. Petersburg, Florida.

111. JLC to Perriton Maxwell, May 22, 1914, unsigned typed letter, corrected in JLC's hand, MHS; Grace Chamberlain Allen to Eleanor Allen, Jan. 15, [1914], RC; *Fiftieth Anniversary of the Battle of Gettysburg*, pp. 27, 28, 32–37, formal portrait of JLC between pp. 6 and 7, and photographs opposite pages 34 (figs. 9 and 45), 36 (fig. 14), and 37 (fig. 15).

112. *Fiftieth Anniversary of the Battle of Gettysburg*, pp. 36, 37, 171, 172; newspaper clipping, "Dashing Civil War Leader/Hero of Little Round Top," MOLLUS War Museum, Philadelphia; newspaper clipping, "Twentieth Maine Reunion," *Piscataquis Observer*, July 24, [1913], BC. Both newspaper accounts state that JLC did not attend the fiftieth anniversary Gettysburg reunion. The *Observer* also mentions the absence of Ellis Spear and lists Twentieth Maine survivors who did attend. Less than three weeks before the reunion, a lengthy article signed by "Ellis Spear, Colonel, 20th Maine," in the June 12, 1913, issue of the *National Tribune*, gave all the credit for the charge to a spontaneous action of the men, praised Ames, who had trained them, made a pointed reference to Vincent as the "*real* Hero of Little Round Top" (emphasis added), and did not even mention JLC's name. JLC's reaction to Spear's public remarks against him are unknown.

JLC was also one of the fourteen Grand Army of the Republic Standing Committee members for the reunion. Regardless of his poor health, his bearing is as straight and commanding as ever in the photograph opposite page 34 in *Fiftieth Anniversary of the Battle of Gettysburg*. The preliminary meeting was held May 15–16, 1913, with photographs taken May 17.

113. Rosamond Allen diary, Aug. 11, 13, and Dec. 13, 26, 1913, in possession of Rosamond Allen, St. Petersburg, Fla.; JLC to Fannie Hardy Eckstorm, Aug. 28, 1913, Fannie Hardy Eckstorm Papers, UMO; JLC to Wyllys, Oct. 18, 1913, MHS; newspaper clipping, "Dashing Civil War Leader/Hero of Little Round Top," MOLLUS War Museum, Philadelphia; recollections of Catherine T. Smith, *Brunswick Times-Record*, Sept. 7, 1975; Grace Chamberlain Allen to Eleanor Allen, Jan. 15, [1914], RC.

114. Grace Chamberlain Allen to Eleanor Allen, Jan. 15, [1914], RC; JLC to Sae, Jan. 20, [1914], UMO. Quotations, ibid. One newspaper friend recounted that JLC always refused opiates to ease his pain and continued this rule through his last illness ("Tribute by Max," *Portland Daily Press*, Feb. 25, 1914).

115. *Portland Daily Eastern Argus*, Feb. 25, 1914; newspaper clipping, "Dashing Civil War Leader/Hero of Little Round Top," MOLLUS War Muse-

um, Philadelphia; newspaper clipping beginning, "In 1855 Gen. Chamberlain was married," PHS; Helen Root Adams diary, Feb. 24, 1914, FPC. Historian Bruce Catton thought that JLC was probably the last Civil War soldier to die of his wounds (Catton, "Survivor," under "Postscripts" in *American Heritage* 30, no. 1 [Dec. 1978]: 111). JLC left a comparatively modest but substantial estate to his children. An inventory listed his Brewer, Brunswick, Portland, and South Portland real properties and personal property including the contents of his Portland and Domhegan houses, boats, etc., as worth a total of $33,608.11, but it inexplicably excluded the Brunswick home and its contents ("Estate Joshua L. Chamberlain Inventory," typescript, FPYU).

116. "Tribute by Max," *Portland Daily Press*, Feb. 25, 1914; *Portland Evening Express and Daily Advertiser*, Feb. 24, 1914; Helen Root Adams diary, Feb. 25–27, 1914, FPC; Lord, "Early Church Records," #351, Brewer Public Library, Brewer, Maine; *Portland Daily Eastern Argus*, Feb. 28, 1914. Quotation, "Tribute by Max." Sae died May 19, 1921. Helen Adams lived until 1922.

117. Newspaper clipping, "Funeral Gen. Chamberlain," BC; *Portland Daily Eastern Argus*, Feb. 28, 1914; newspaper clipping, "Every Honor Accorded Maine's Dead Soldier, Statesman, Scholar," BC; newspaper clipping, "Notable Gathering," MOLLUS War Museum, Philadelphia; Helen Root Adams diary, Feb. 27, 1914, FPC; *In Memoriam*, p. 12. Quotations, "Funeral Gen. Chamberlain" and "Every Honor Accorded Maine's Dead Soldier, Statesman, Scholar," respectively. One newspaper estimated 5,000 mourners in City Hall.

118. *Portland Daily Eastern Argus*, Feb. 28, 1914; newspaper clipping, "Notable Gathering," MOLLUS War Museum, Philadelphia. Quotations, ibid.

119. *In Memoriam*, p. 13; newspaper clipping, "Notable Gathering," MOLLUS War Museum, Philadelphia; recollections of Catherine T. Smith, *Brunswick Times-Record*, Sept. 7, 1975.

120. Newspaper clipping, "Every Honor Accorded Maine's Dead Soldier, Statesman, Scholar," BC; recollections of Catherine T. Smith, *Brunswick Times-Record*, Sept. 7, 1975; *Portland Daily Eastern Argus*, Feb. 28, 1914.

121. Ashby, *First Parish Church*, p. 206; newspaper clipping, "Every Honor Accorded Maine's Dead Soldier, Statesman, Scholar," BC. Quotation, Ashby, *First Parish Church*.

122. Recollections of Catherine T. Smith, *Brunswick Times-Record*, Sept. 7, 1975; *Portland Daily Eastern Argus*, Feb. 28, 1914; information provided by Rosamond Allen. After Horace Allen's death in 1919, Harold Wyllys Chamberlain continued with his inventions and made his home with his sister and her family until his death in 1928. Grace Chamberlain Allen died in 1937. Horace Allen is buried at Marshfield, Massachusetts. (Information provided by Rosamond Allen.)

123. JLC, "Early Memoirs," p. 52, BC; recollections of Catherine T. Smith, *Brunswick Times-Record*, Sept. 7, 1975; writer's observations at Pine Grove Cemetery, Brunswick, Maine.

EPILOGUE

1. Quotations, JLC, "Through Blood and Fire at Gettysburg," p. 909.

APPENDIX

1. Joined corps June 28. The Second Brigade left in the Department of Washington.
2. Includes organizational and command changes of JLC (only) effective May 18, 1864, June 6, 1864, and June 18, 1864.
3. Became First Brigade, Second Division, June 6.
4. Ayres assigned Second Division command June 6; Col. Edgar M. Gregory assigned First Brigade (Second Division) command June 6.
5. Was Third Brigade, Fourth Division, up to June 6, except 187th Pennsylvania added June 6.
6. Assigned First Brigade (First Division) command June 6.
7. Returned to command May 18.
8. In command from evening of April 1.
9. Ibid.
10. Wounded March 29.
11. Mortally wounded April 1.
12. In command from evening of April 1.
13. Brady's and Jardine's companies, Michigan Sharpshooters, attached.
14. Mortally wounded April 1.
15. In command from April 3.
16. In command from evening of April 1.
17. Wounded April 1.
18. Wounded March 31.
19. Wounded April 1.
20. Wounded March 31.
21. Killed April 1.
22. Mortally wounded March 31.
23. Wounded March 31.
24. Wounded April 1.
25. Wounded March 31.
26. Mortally wounded March 31.
27. Wounded March 31 and killed April 1.
28. In command from April 3.
29. Wounded March 31.
30. Consolidated April 1 and commanded by Major Funk.
31. Ibid.
32. Wounded March 31.
33. Wounded March 29.

SELECTED BIBLIOGRAPHY

UNPUBLISHED MANUSCRIPTS

Augusta, Maine
  Maine State Archives
    Miscellaneous correspondence
Bangor, Maine
  Bangor Public Library
    Thomas T. Munford. Annotated copy of Joshua L. Chamberlain, "Five Forks" (Read May 2, 1900). Pamphlet.
  Bangor Theological Seminary Library
    Bangor Theological Seminary Historical Catalogue inquiry form filled out in Joshua L. Chamberlain's hand.
Brewer, Maine
  Brewer Public Library
    Chamberlain Family Bible.
    Ethel Kenny Lord, comp. "Early Church Records, First Congregational Church of Brewer, Maine, Organized Sept. 9, 1800, and 100 years of Church Membership, 1813–1931." Typed manuscript, compiled from the original records, 1942.
Brunswick, Maine
  First Parish Church
    Dr. George E. Adams Diaries.
    Helen Root Adams Diaries.
  Hawthorne Longfellow Library, Special Collections Room, Bowdoin College
    Bowdoin College Archives
    Joshua L. Chamberlain Collection
    Elisha S. Coan Papers
    Robert M. Cross. "Joshua Lawrence Chamberlain." Unpublished senior essay, 1945.
    Oliver O. Howard Papers
  Pejepscot Historical Society
    John C. Chamberlain. Diary or Journal, June 1, 1863–July 16, 1863.
    Joshua L. Chamberlain Collection
    Joshua L. Chamberlain Letterbook.
    Elizabeth D. Copeland. Interview with Mrs. Catherine Smith. Audiotape, 1977.
    Pejepscot Historic Survey

Pvt. John Lenfest. Letters.
Sally W. Rand. "The Chamberlain House."
Cambridge, Massachusetts
Arthur and Elizabeth Schlesinger Library, Radcliffe College, Harvard University
Chamberlain-Adams Family Correspondence
Carlisle Barracks, Pennsylvania
U.S. Army Military History Institute
Photographic Collection
Concord, New Hampshire
New Hampshire Historical Society
John B. Bachelder Papers
Durham, North Carolina
William R. Perkins Library, Duke University
Munford-Ellis Collection, Thomas T. Munford Division
Fremont, Ohio
Rutherford B. Hayes Presidental Center
Joshua L. Chamberlain Papers
Peleg Chandler Papers
Rutherford B. Hayes Papers
Gettysburg, Pennsylvania
Gettysburg National Military Park
Gettysburg Battlefield Commission Map, Blueprint, 1893.
William C. Oates Correspondence Scrapbook.
Twentieth Maine Volunteer Infantry File
Indianapolis, Indiana
Miscellaneous Chamberlain letters and photographs in possession of Alice Rains Trulock and James A. Trulock.
Mount Pleasant, Michigan
Clarke Historical Library, Central Michigan University
Oliver W. Norton Papers
New Haven, Connecticut
Manuscripts and Archives, Yale University Library
Frost Family Papers
New York, New York
New-York Historical Society
Gen. James Barnes Papers
Orono, Maine
Raymond H. Fogler Library, Special Collections Department, University of Maine
Joshua L. Chamberlain Papers
Fannie Hardy Eckstorm Papers
Philadelphia, Pennsylvania

Military Order of the Loyal Legion of the United States War Museum
Joshua L. Chamberlain File
Portland, Maine
Maine Historical Society
Joshua L. Chamberlain Papers, Collection 10
Saddle River, New Jersey
Miscellaneous Chamberlain papers in possession of A. A. Warlam.
St. Petersburg, Florida
Rosamond Allen. Diaries, 1911–13. In possession of Rosamond Allen.
San Marino, California
Huntington Library, Art Gallery, and Botanical Gardens
John P. Nicholson Papers
Warren, Maine
Ellis Spear. Letters and Diaries, 1863, 1864, 1865. Originals in possession of Abbott Spear.
Washington, D.C.
Library of Congress
Joshua L. Chamberlain Papers
National Archives
Mathew B. Brady Collection
Joshua L. Chamberlain Military Pension Records, Military Personnel File, and Military Service Records
Thomas D. Chamberlain Military Pension Records
Patrick DeLacy Military Pension Records
Charles D. Gilmore Military Service and Pension Records
Twentieth Maine Regimental Records

NEWSPAPERS AND PERIODICALS

American Heritage
Bangor Daily Commercial
Bangor Daily News
Bangor Evening Commercial
Bangor Historical Magazine
Bangor Whig and Courier
Boston Herald
Boston Journal
Brunswick Record
Brunswick Telegraph
Brunswick Times-Record
Colby Library Quarterly
Congregationalist and Boston Recorder
Cosmopolitan Magazine

Daily Eastern Argus (Portland, Maine)
Gettysburg, Historical Articles of Lasting Interest
Hearst's Magazine
Kennebunk Journal (Augusta, Maine)
Lewiston Journal
Lincoln County News (Waldoboro, Maine)
Missouri Republican (St. Louis)
Morningside Notes
National Tribune (Washington, D.C.)
New York Freeman's and Catholic Journal
New York Herald
New York Times
New York World
North Philadelphia World
Oxford Democrat (Paris, Maine)
Pennsylvania Magazine of History and Biography
Philadelphia Public Ledger
Piscataquis Observer
Portland Daily Press
Portland Daily Telegram
Portland Evening Express and Daily Advertiser
Portland Press Herald
Portland Sunday Telegram
Quarterly Journal of the New York State Historical Association
Somerville (Mass.) *Journal*
Southern Historical Society Papers

BOOKS AND PAMPHLETS

Agassiz, George R., ed. *Meade's Headquarters, 1863–1865: Letters of Colonel Theodore Lyman from the Wilderness to Appomattox*. Boston, 1922.

The American Heritage Pictorial History of the Presidents of the United States. Foreword by Bruce Catton. 2 vols. New York, 1968.

Ames, Blanche Ames. *Adelbert Ames: General, Senator, Governor, 1835–1933.* New York, 1964.

Ames, Blanche Butler, comp. *Chronicles of the Nineteenth Century: Family Letters of Blanche Butler and Adelbert Ames*. 2 vols. Clinton, Mass., 1957.

Andrews, J. Cutler. *The North Reports the Civil War*. Pittsburgh, 1955.

Argument on Behalf of Lieut. Gen. Philip H. Sheridan, U.S.A., Respondent, by Asa Bird Gardner, LL.D., Judge-Advocate, U.S.A., of Counsel before the Court of Inquiry Convened by the President of the United States, (S. O. 277, Ex. 6, Army Hd. Qrs., A. G. O., 9 Dec. 1879,) in the Case of Lieut. Col. and Bvt. Major-General Gouverneur K. Warren, Corps of Engineers, Formerly Major-General

Commanding the 5th Army Corps, Applicant. Delivered July 27th, 28th, and 30th, 1881. Chicago, 1881.

Ashby, Thompson Eldridge. *A History of First Parish Church of Brunswick, Maine*. Brunswick, 1969.

Baker, Levi W. *History of the Ninth Mass. Battery: Recruited July, 1862; Mustered in Aug. 10, 1862; Mustered out June 9, 1865, at the Close of the War of the Rebellion*. South Framingham, Mass., 1888.

Bandy, Ken, and Florence Freeland, eds. *The Gettysburg Papers*. 2 vols. Dayton, 1978.

Bates, Samuel P. *History of the Pennsylvania Volunteers*. 5 vols. Harrisburg, 1870.

Beyer, W. F., and O. F. Keydel, eds. *Deeds of Valor*. 2 vols. Detroit, 1905.

Billings, John D. *Hardtack and Coffee; or, The Unwritten Story of Army Life, Including Chapters on Enlisting, Life in Tents and Log Huts, Jonahs and Beats, Offences and Punishments, Raw Recruits, Foraging, Corps and Corps Badges, the Wagon Trains, the Army Mule, the Engineer Corps, the Signal Corps, Etc*. Boston, 1887. Reprint. Williamstown, Mass., 1973.

Blaine, James G. *Twenty Years of Congress: From Lincoln to Garfield, with a Review of the Events Which Led to the Political Revolution of 1860*. 2 vols. Norwich, Conn., 1884–86.

Boatner, Mark M., III. *The Civil War Dictionary*. New York, 1959.

Buell, Augustus. *The Cannoneer: Recollections of Service in the Army of the Potomac*. Washington, D.C., 1890.

Brooks, Noah, *Washington, D.C., in Lincoln's Time*. Edited by Herbert Mitgang. Chicago, 1971.

Carter, Capt. Robert Goldthwaite. *Four Brothers in Blue, or Sunshine and Shadows of the War of the Rebellion: A Story of the Great Civil War from Bull Run to Appomattox*. Washington, D.C., 1913. Reprint, with foreword by Frank Vandiver. Austin, 1978.

Catalogue of the Theological Seminary, Bangor, 1853–55. Bangor, 1853–55.

Catton, Bruce. *Bruce Catton's America*. Edited by Oliver Jensen. New York, 1979.

———. *Glory Road*. Garden City, N.Y., 1952.

———. *Mr. Lincoln's Army*. Garden City, N.Y., 1951.

———. *A Stillness at Appomattox*. Garden City, N.Y., 1953.

———. *Terrible Swift Sword*. Garden City, N.Y., 1963.

———. *U. S. Grant and the American Military Tradition*. Edited by Oscar Handlin. Boston, 1954.

Chamberlain, Joshua Lawrence. *Address of Governor Chamberlain to the Legislature of the State of Maine, January, 1867*. Augusta, 1867.

———. *Address of Governor Chamberlain to the Legislature of the State of Maine, January, 1869*. Augusta, 1869.

———. *Address of Governor Chamberlain to the Legislature of the State of Maine, January, 1870*. Augusta, 1870.

———. *Maine: Her Place in History*. Augusta, 1877.
———. *The Passing of the Armies: An Account of the Final Campaign of the Army of the Potomac Based upon Personal Reminiscences of the Fifth Army Corps*. New York, 1915.
———, ed. *Universities and Their Sons: History, Influence, and Characteristics of American Universities with Biographical Sketches and Portraits of Alumni and Recipients of Honorary Degrees*. 6 vols. Boston, 1898–1923.
Chamberlain Association of America. *JLC, [A Sketch], Supplement*. N.p., [1906].
———. *Joshua Lawrence Chamberlain: A Sketch*. N.p., [1906].
Chamberlin, Thomas. *History of the One Hundred and Fiftieth Regiment, Pennsylvania Volunteers, Second Regiment, Bucktail Brigade*. Philadelphia, 1905.
Cheek, Philip, and Mair Pointon. *History of the Sauk County Riflemen, Co. A, Sixth Wisconsin Veteran Volunteer Infantry, 1861–1865*. Madison, Wis., 1909. Reprint, with introduction by Alan T. Nolan. Gaithersburg, Md., 1984.
Cleaveland, Nehemiah. *History of Bowdoin College with Biographical Sketches of Its Graduates from 1806 to 1879, Inclusive*. Edited and completed by Alpheus Spring Packard. Boston, 1882.
Coddington, Edwin B. *The Gettysburg Campaign: A Study in Command*. New York, 1968.
Coggins, Jack. *Arms and Equipment of the Civil War*. New York, 1962.
Crawford, Richard, ed. *The Civil War Songbook*. New York, 1977.
Curtis, O. B. *History of the Twenty-fourth Michigan of the Iron Brigade, Known as the Detroit and Wayne County Regiment*. Detroit, 1891. Reprint, with introduction by Alan T. Nolan. Gaithersburg, Md., 1984.
Dawes, Rufus R. *Service with the 6th Wisconsin Volunteers*. Marietta, Ohio, 1890. Reprint, edited by Alan T. Nolan. Madison, Wis., 1962.
Dedication of the Monuments and Reunion at Gettysburg, Sept. 11 and 12, 1889. Association of the 143d Regiment, Pennsylvania Volunteers. Scranton, n.d.
Dedication of the Twentieth Maine Monuments at Gettysburg, October 3, 1889, with Report of Annual Reunion, Oct. 2, 1889. Waldoboro, Maine, 1891.
Eisenschiml, Otto. *The Celebrated Case of Fitz John Porter: An American Dreyfus Affair*. Indianapolis, 1950.
Esposito, Col. Vincent J., ed. *Atlas to Accompany Steele's American Campaigns*. United States Military Academy, 1956.
Farrington Memorial: A Sketch of the Ancestors and Descendants of Dea. John Farrington. N.p., 1899.
Fiftieth Anniversary of the Battle of Gettysburg: Report of the Pennsylvania Commission, Presented to His Excellency, John K. Tener, Governor of Pennsylvania, for Transmittal to the General Assembly. Harrisburg, December 31, 1913.
The First Parish and the First Parish Church (United Church of Christ), Brunswick, Maine, 1717–1983. N.p., 1983.

Foner, Eric. *Reconstruction: America's Unfinished Revolution, 1863–1877*. New York, 1988.
Fox, William F. *Regimental Losses in the American Civil War, 1861–1865*. Albany, 1903.
———, ed. *New York at Gettysburg*. 3 vols. Albany, 1903.
Frassanito, William A. *Antietam: The Photographic Legacy of America's Bloodiest Day*. New York, 1978.
———. *Grant and Lee: The Virginia Campaigns*. New York, 1983.
Freeman, Douglas Southall. *Lee's Lieutenants*. 3 vols. New York, 1946.
Fremantle, Sir Arthur J. L., and Frank A. Haskell. *Two Views of Gettysburg*. Edited by Richard Harwell. Chicago, 1964.
Furbish, John. *Facts about Brunswick, Maine*. Brunswick, 1976.
Gerrish, Theodore. *Army Life: A Private's Reminiscences of the War*. Introduction by Hon. Josiah H. Drummond. Portland, 1882.
Gerrish, Theodore, and John S. Hutchinson. *The Blue and the Gray: A Graphic History of the Army of the Potomac and That of Northern Virginia Including the Brilliant Engagements of These Forces from 1861 to 1865*. Bangor, 1884.
Gibbs, James M., comp. *History of the First Battalion, Pennsylvania Six Months Volunteers, and 187th Regiment, Pennsylvania Volunteer Infantry: Six Months and Three Years Service, 1863–1865*. Harrisburg, 1905.
Gordon, John B. *Reminiscences of the Civil War*. New York, 1903.
Grant, U. S. *Personal Memoirs of U. S. Grant*. 2 vols. New York, 1885.
Hamlin, Augustus C., comp. *Nineteenth National Encampment of the Grand Army of the Republic Held at Portland, Maine*. Augusta, 1886.
Hardee, W. J. *Hardee's Rifle and Light Infantry Tactics*. New York, 1862.
Hatch, Louis C. *The History of Bowdoin College*. Portland, 1927.
Haythornwaite, Philip. *Uniforms of the Civil War*. New York, 1976.
History of the 118th Pennsylvania Volunteers, Corn Exchange Regiment, from Their First Engagement at Antietam to Appomattox, to Which Is Added a Record of Its Organization and a Complete Roster. The Survivors' Association. Philadelphia, 1905.
History of the 121st Regiment, Pennsylvania Volunteers. Survivors' Association. Philadelphia, 1893.
Houston, Henry E. *The Thirty-second Regiment of Maine Volunteers: An Historical Sketch*. Portland, 1903.
Howe, Daniel Walker, ed. *Victorian America*. Philadelphia, 1976.
Humphreys, Andrew A. *The Virginia Campaign of '64 and '65: The Army of the Potomac and the Army of the James*. New York, 1883.
In Memoriam: Joshua Lawrence Chamberlain, Late Major General, U.S.V. Circular no. 5, series of 1914, whole number 328. Military Order of the Loyal Legion of the United States, Commandery of Maine. Portland, 1914.
Johnson, Allen, and Dumas Malone, eds. *Dictionary of American Biography*. 20 vols. New York, 1928–37. Reprint. New York, 1957.

Johnson, Robert U., and Clarence C. Buel, eds. *Battles and Leaders of the Civil War*. 4 vols. New York, 1884–87.

Jones, J. W. *Personal Reminiscences, Anecdotes, and Letters of General Robert E. Lee*. New York, 1875.

Jones, Robert H. *Disrupted Decades: The Civil War and Reconstruction Years*. New York, 1973.

Judson, Amos M. *A History of the Eighty-third Regiment, Pennsylvania Volunteers*. Erie, Pa., [1865]. Reprint, with introduction by James A. Trulock and Alice Rains Trulock. Alexandria, Va., 1985.

Kaufman, Martin. *Homeopathy in America: The Rise and Fall of a Medical Heresy*. Baltimore, 1971.

King, W. C., and W. P. Derby, comps. *Camp-fire Sketches and Battlefield Echoes of the Rebellion*. Springfield, Mass., 1887.

Krick, Robert K. *Lee's Colonels: A Biographical Register of the Field Officers (Colonels, Lieutenant Colonels, and Majors,) of the Army of Northern Virginia*. Dayton, 1979.

Leech, Margaret. *Reveille in Washington*. New York, 1941.

Little, George Thomas. *General Catalogue of Bowdoin College and the Medical School of Maine, 1794–1894*. Brunswick, 1894.

———, ed. *Genealogical and Family History of the State of Maine*. 4 vols. New York, 1909.

Livermore, Thomas L. *Numbers and Losses in the Civil War*. Introduction by Edward E. Barthell, Jr. Bloomington, 1957.

Lykes, Richard Wayne. *Campaign for Petersburg*. National Park Service History Series. Washington, D.C., 1970.

McPherson, James M. *Battle Cry of Freedom*. New York, 1988.

Maine Adjutant General. *Annual Reports of the Adjutant General of the State of Maine*, 1861–67. Augusta, 1862–68.

Maine at Gettysburg: Report of the Maine Commissioners, Prepared by the Executive Committee. Portland, 1898.

Maine Commandery, Military Order of the Loyal Legion of the United States. *War Papers*. 4 vols. Portland, 1897–1915.

Maine State Archives. *Special List No. 1: Records Relating to the Civil War Career of Joshua Lawrence Chamberlain*. Augusta, n.d.

Meade, George. *The Life and Letters of George Gordon Meade*. 2 vols. New York, 1913.

Merideth, Ray, and Arthur Merideth. *Mr. Lincoln's Military Railroads*. New York, 1979.

Meyer, D. H. *The Instructed Conscience: The Shaping of the American National Ethic*. Philadelphia, 1972.

Milgram, James M. *Abraham Lincoln Illustrated*. Northbrook, Ill., 1984.

Minnesota Commandery, Military Order of the Loyal Legion of the United States. *Glimpses of the Nation's Struggle*. 6 vols. St. Paul, 1887–1909.

Minot, John Clair, and Donald Francis Snow. *Tales of Bowdoin*. Augusta, 1901.
Mitchell, Joseph B. *The Badge of Gallantry*. New York, 1968.
Munson, Gorham. *Penobscot: Down East Paradise*. Philadelphia, 1959.
Nash, Eugene Arus. *A History of the Forty-fourth Regiment, New York Volunteer Infantry, in the Civil War, 1861–1865*. Chicago, 1911.
Nelson's Biographical Dictionary and Historical Reference Book of Erie County. Erie, Pa., 1896.
Nesbit, John W., comp. *General History of Company D, 149th Pennsylvania Volunteers, and Personal Sketches of the Members*. Rev. ed. Oakdale, 1908.
Nevins, Allan, ed. *A Diary of Battle: The Personal Journals of Colonel Charles S. Wainwright, 1861–1865*. New York, 1962.
New York Commandery, Military Order of the Loyal Legion of the United States. *Personal Recollections of the War of the Rebellion: Addresses Delivered before the Commandery of the State of New York, Military Order of the Loyal Legion of the United States*. 4 vols. New York, 1891–1912.
Nicholson, John P., ed. *Pennsylvania at Gettysburg*. 2 vols. Harrisburg, 1893.
Nolan, Alan T. *The Iron Brigade*. New York, 1961.
Norton, Oliver Willcox. *Army Letters, 1861–1865*. Chicago, 1903.
———. *The Attack and Defense of Little Round Top, July 2, 1863*. New York, 1913.
———. *Strong Vincent and His Brigade at Gettysburg, July 2, 1863*. Chicago, 1909.
"Not a Sound of Trumpet." Pamphlet. Brunswick, 1982.
Oates, William C. *The War between the Union and the Confederacy and Its Lost Opportunities*. New York, 1905. Reprint, with introduction by Robert K. Krick. Dayton, 1974.
Parker, Barrett, and Sylvia J. Sherman, comps. and eds. *In Commemoration of Joshua Lawrence Chamberlain: A Guide—Bibliography*. Augusta, Maine, [1978].
Parker, John L., assisted by Robert G. Carter. *History of the Twenty-second Massachusetts Infantry*. Boston, 1887.
Pennsylvania Commandery, Military Order of the Loyal Legion of the United States. *Ceremonies in Commemoration of the One Hundredth Anniversary of the Birth of Abraham Lincoln, Philadelphia, February 12, 1909*. Philadelphia, 1909.
Phisterer, Frederick, comp. *New York in the War of the Rebellion, 1861–1865*. 5 vols. Albany, 1912.
Porter, Horace. *Campaigning with Grant*. New York, 1897. Reprint. New York, 1981.
Powell, William H. *History of the Fifth Army Corps (Army of the Potomac): A Record of Operations during the Civil War in the United States of America, 1861–1865*. New York, 1896.
Proceedings of the 43rd Encampment of the Dept. of Pennsylvania, Grand Army of the Republic, June 9 and 10, 1909. Harrisburg, 1909.

Proceedings of the Third Brigade Association, First Division, Fifth Army Corps, Army of the Potomac, Held at the Time of the National Encampment, Grand Army of the Republic, Washington, D.C., 21 December 1892. New York, [1893].

Proceedings of the Third Brigade Association, First Division, Fifth Army Corps, Army of the Potomac, Held at the Time of the National Encampment, Grand Army of the Republic, Indianapolis, Indiana, 6 September 1893. New York, [1894].

Pullen, John J. *The Twentieth Maine: A Volunteer Regiment in the Civil War*. Philadelphia, 1957.

Robertson, John, Adjutant General of Michigan, comp. *Michigan in the War*. Lansing, 1882.

Schaff, Morris. *The Sunset of the Confederacy*. Boston, 1912.

Sears, Stephen W. *Landscape Turned Red: The Battle of Antietam*. New Haven, 1983.

Sheridan, Philip H. *Personal Memoirs of Philip Henry Sheridan: New and Enlarged Edition, with an Account of His Life from 1871 to His Death in 1888 by Brig. Gen. Michael V. Sheridan*. 2 vols. New York, 1902.

Smith, Donald. *The Twenty-fourth Michigan of the Iron Brigade*. Harrisburg, 1962.

Sobel, Robert, and John Raimo, eds. *Biographical Directory of the Governors of the United States, 1789–1978*. Westport, Conn., 1978.

Sommers, Richard J. *Richmond Redeemed: The Siege at Petersburg*. Foreword by Frank E. Vandiver. Garden City, N.Y., 1981.

Spear, Abbott. *The 20th Maine at Fredericksburg: The 1913 Accounts of Generals Chamberlain and Spear*. Warren, Maine, 1987.

Sprague, Richard S., ed. *A Handful of Spice: A Miscellany of Maine Literature and History*. University of Maine Studies, 2d ser., no. 88. Orono, 1968.

Stampp, Kenneth M. *The Era of Reconstruction, 1865–1877*. New York, 1966.

Stanley, R. H., and George O. Hall, eds. *Eastern Maine and the Rebellion*. Bangor, 1887.

Stine, J. H. *History of the Army of the Potomac*. 2d ed. Washington, D.C., 1893.

Stowe, Charles Edward. *Life of Harriet Beecher Stowe, Compiled from Her Letters and Journals*. Boston, 1889.

Swinton, William. *Campaigns of the Army of the Potomac: A Critical History of Operations in Virginia, Maryland, and Pennsylvania from the Commencement to the Close of the War, 1861–1865*. New York, 1882.

Taylor, Deems, William Sharp, John Tasker Howard, Ray Levi, and Dorothy Berliner Commins. *A Treasury of Stephen Foster*. New York, 1946.

Taylor, Emerson Gifford. *Gouverneur Kemble Warren: The Life and Letters of an American Soldier, 1830–1882*. Boston, 1932.

Thayer, Mildred N., and Mrs. Edward M. Ames. *Brewer, Orrington, Holden, Eddington: History and Families*. Brewer, Maine, 1962.

Townsend, George Alfred. *Campaigns of a Non-combatant*. New York, 1886.

Reprinted as *Rustics in Rebellion: A Yankee Reporter on the Road to Richmond*, with introduction by Lida Mayo. Chapel Hill, 1950.

Tucker, Glenn. *Hancock the Superb*. Indianapolis, 1960. Reprint. Dayton, 1980.

Under the Maltese Cross, Antietam to Appomattox, the Loyal Uprising in Western Pennsylvania: Campaigns of the 155th Pennsylvania Regiment, Narrated by the Rank and File. Pittsburgh, 1910.

U.S. Army. Adjutant General's Office. *Proceedings, Findings, and Opinions of the Court of Inquiry in the Case of Gouverneur K. Warren*. 3 pts. Washington, D.C., 1883.

U.S. Congress. Senate. Committee on Labor and Public Welfare. Subcommittee on Veterans' Affairs. *Medal of Honor Recipients, 1863–1963*. Washington, D.C., 1964.

U.S. Secretary of War. *Revised Regulations for the Army of the United States, 1861*. Philadelphia, 1861.

———. *U.S. Infantry Tactics, May 1, 1861*. Philadelphia, 1862.

U.S. Surgeon General's Office. *Medical and Surgical History of the War of the Rebellion (1861–65)*. 3 vols. in 6 pts. Washington, D.C., 1870–88.

U.S. War Department. *Atlas to Accompany the Official Records of the Union and Confederate Armies*. Washington, D.C., 1891–95. Reprint, with introduction by Richard J. Sommers. New York, 1983.

———. *The War of the Rebellion: A Compilation of the Official Records of the Union and Confederate Armies*. 70 vols. in 128 pts. Washington, D.C., 1880–1901.

Wallace, Willard M. *Soul of the Lion: A Biography of General Joshua L. Chamberlain*. New York, 1960.

Warner, Ezra J. *Generals in Blue*. Baton Rouge, 1977.

———. *Generals in Gray*. Baton Rouge, 1959.

Warren, H. N. *Two Reunions of the 142d Regiment, Pennsylvania Volunteers; A History of the Regiment; Dedication of the Monument; A Description of the Battle of Gettysburg; also a Complete Roster of the Regiment*. Buffalo, 1890.

Wheeler, George Augustus, and Henry Warren Wheeler. *History of Brunswick, Topsham, and Harpswell, Maine*. Boston, 1878. Reprint. Somersworth, N.H., 1974.

Whitman, William E. S., and Charles H. True. *Maine in the War for the Union*. Lewiston, 1865.

Wilder, Philip S., ed. *General Catalogue of Bowdoin College and the Medical School of Maine: A Biographical Record of Alumni and Officers, 1794–1950*. Brunswick, 1950.

Wise, Barton H. *The Life of Henry A. Wise of Virginia*. New York, 1899.

Woodward, C. Vann. *Reunion and Reaction: The Compromise of 1877 and the End of Reconstruction*. Boston, 1966.

Woodward, E. M. *History of the One Hundred and Ninety-eighth Pennsylvania Volunteers: Being a Complete Record of the Regiment, with Its Camps, Marches and Battles; Together with the Personal Record of Every Officer and Man during His Term of Service*. Trenton, 1884.

ARTICLES, ESSAYS, LECTURES, AND PAPERS

Catton, Bruce. "Survivor." *American Heritage* 30, no. 1 (December 1978): 111.

Chamberlain, Joshua L. "Abraham Lincoln." (Read March 3, 1909.) In Commandery of the State of Pennsylvania, Military Order of the Loyal Legion of the United States, *Ceremonies in Commemoration of the One Hundredth Anniversary of the Birth of Abraham Lincoln, Philadelphia, February 9, 1909*, pp. 9–27. Philadelphia, 1909. Also in Maine Commandery, Military Order of the Loyal Legion of the United States, *War Papers*, 4:53–72. Portland, 1915.

———. "Appomattox." (Read October 7, 1903.) In *Personal Recollections of the War of the Rebellion: Addresses Delivered before the Commandery of the State of New York, Military Order of the Loyal Legion of the United States*, 3d ser., edited by A. Noel Blakeman, pp. 260–80. New York, 1907.

———. "The Army of the Potomac." Speech given at the first reunion of the Army of the Potomac and the organization of the Society of the Army of the Potomac, New York, July 4, 1869.

———. "Dedication of the Maine Monuments on the Battlefield of Gettysburg, October 3, 1893." Apparently given in the U.S. Cemetery at Gettysburg. Pamphlet. Augusta, 1895. Variation of "The State, the Nation, and the People," address at the dedication of the Maine Monuments at Gettysburg, October 3, 1889.

———. "Don't Judge Hastily." In *Camp-fire Sketches and Battlefield Echoes of the Rebellion*, compiled by W. C. King and W. P. Derby, p. 78. Springfield, Mass., 1887.

———. "Five Forks." (Read May 2, 1900.) In Maine Commandery, Military Order of the Loyal Legion of the United States, *War Papers*, 2:220–67. Portland, 1902.

———. "The Last Night at Fredericksburg." In *Camp-fire Sketches and Battlefield Echoes of the Rebellion*, compiled by W. C. King and W. P. Derby, pp. 131–35. Springfield, Mass., 1887.

———. "The Last Review of the Army of the Potomac, May 23, 1865." (Read May 2, 1906.) In Maine Commandery, Military Order of the Loyal Legion of the United States, *War Papers*, 3:306–33. Portland, 1908.

———. "The Last Salute of the Army of Northern Virginia," *Boston Journal*, May 1901. In *Southern Historical Society Papers* 32 (1904): 355–63. Reprint. Millwood, N.Y., 1977.

———. "Loyalty." Initial address at the original meeting of the Military Order of the Loyal Legion of the United States at Philadelphia, February 22, 1866. Two typescripts, both corrected in Chamberlain's hand, are known to exist, one at the MOLLUS War Museum in Philadelphia and the other at the Hawthorne-Longfellow Library, Bowdoin College.

———. "The Military Operations on the White Oak Road." (Read December 6, 1893.) In Maine Commandery, Military Order of the Loyal Legion of the United States, *War Papers*, 1:207–53. Portland, 1897.

———. "My Story of Fredericksburg." *Cosmopolitan Magazine* 54 (December 1912): 148–59.

———. "Night on the Field at Fredericksburg." In *Camp-fire Sketches and Battlefield Echoes of the Rebellion*, compiled by W. C. King and W. P. Derby, pp. 127–30. Springfield, Mass., 1887.

———. "The Old Flag—What Was Surrendered? And What Was Won?" *Boston Journal*, January 4, 1878.

———. "Remarks Made to the Bowdoin Club of Boston, Massachusetts, May 3, 1901." In "Not a Sound of Trumpet." Pamphlet. Brunswick, 1982.

———. "Reminiscences of Petersburg and Appomattox: October, 1903." (Read March 2, 1904.) Full text, as delivered, in the *Bangor Daily Commercial*, March 3, 1904. Also in Maine Commandery, Military Order of the Loyal Legion of the United States, *War Papers*, 3:161–82. Portland, 1908.

———. "The State, the Nation, and the People." Address at the dedication of the Maine Monuments at Gettysburg, October 3, 1889. In *Maine at Gettysburg*, pp. 546–59. Portland, 1898.

———. "The Third Brigade at Appomattox." War Paper. First printed in *Proceedings of the Third Brigade Association, First Division, Fifth Army Corps, Army of the Potomac, Held at the Time of the National Encampment, Grand Army of the Republic, Indianapolis, Indiana, 6 September 1893*, pp. 134–42. New York, [1894]. Edited form appended to *The Attack and Defense of Little Round Top*, by Oliver Willcox Norton, pp. 333–43, New York, 1913; *Army Letters*, by Oliver Willcox Norton, Chicago, 1903; and *A History of the Forty-fourth New York Volunteer Infantry in the Civil War, 1861–1865*, by Eugene Arus Nash, pp. 243–49, Chicago, 1911.

———. "Through Blood and Fire at Gettysburg." *Hearst's Magazine* 23 (June 1913): 894–909.

Curtis, Charles A. "Bowdoin under Fire." In *Tales of Bowdoin*, by Richard Clair Minot and Donald Francis Snow, pp. 261–72. Augusta, 1901.

Georg, Kathleen R. "Our Principal Loss Was in This Place." *Morningside Notes*, June 1984, pp. 1–10.

Hamilton, Milton W. "Augustus Buell: Fraudulent Historian." *Pennsylvania Magazine of History and Biography* 80, no. 4 (October 1956): 478–92.

Hill, Edward. "The Last Charge at Fredericksburg." War Paper read December 21, 1892, before the Third Brigade Association. In *Proceedings of the Third Brigade Association, First Division, Fifth Army Corps, Army of the Potomac, Held at the Time of the National Encampment, Grand Army of the Republic, Washington, D.C., 21 December 1892*, pp. 30–35. New York, [1893].

Oates, William C. "Gettysburg—The Battle on the Right." *Southern Historical Society Papers* 6 (1878): 172–82. Reprint. Millwood, N.Y., 1977.

Perham, Aurestus S. "Major General Gouverneur K. Warren in the Battle of Five Forks." *New York State Historical Association Quarterly Journal* 4, no. 3 (July 1923): 148–70.

Rand, Edwin H. "Chums at Bowdoin." In *Tales of Bowdoin*, by Richard Clair Minot and Donald Francis Snow, pp. 1–16. Augusta, 1901.

Raymond, Harold B. "Joshua Chamberlain's Retirement Bill." *Colby Library Quarterly*, ser. 7, no. 8 (December 1966): 341–54.

Rittenhouse, Benjamin F. "The Battle of Gettysburg as Seen from Little Round Top." War Paper no. 3 read before the Military Order of the Loyal Legion of the United States, Washington, D.C., Commandery, May 4, 1887. In *The Gettysburg Papers*, edited by Ken Bandy and Florence Freeland, 2:517–29. Dayton, 1978.

Simonton, Edward. "Recollections of the Battle of Fredericksburg." War Paper read October 3, 1888. In Minnesota Commandery, Military Order of the Loyal Legion of the United States, *Glimpses of the Nation's Struggle*, 2d ser., pp. 245–66. St. Paul, 1890.

Spear, Ellis. "The Hoecake of Appomattox." War Paper no. 93 read before the Military Order of the Loyal Legion of the United States, Washington, D.C., Commandery, May 7, 1913.

———. "The Raising of the Regiment." War Paper no. 46 read before the Military Order of the Loyal Legion of the United States, Washington, D.C., Commandery, March 4, 1903.

Vickery, James R. "Walter G. Morrill: The Fighting Colonel of the Twentieth Maine." In *A Handful of Spice: A Miscellany of Maine Literature and History*, edited by Richard S. Sprague, pp. 127–51. University of Maine Studies, 2d ser., no. 88. Orono, 1968.

Wells, Christopher H. "Random Recollections of 1871–1875." In *Tales of Bowdoin*, by Richard Clair Minot and Donald Francis Snow, pp. 81–93. Augusta, 1901.

Wilder, Philip S. "Stars on Their Shoulders." Lecture delivered January 11, 1963, for the Town and College Club, Brunswick, Maine. Edited version in *Bowdoin Alumnus*, March 1963.

INDEX